APPETITE FOR LIFE

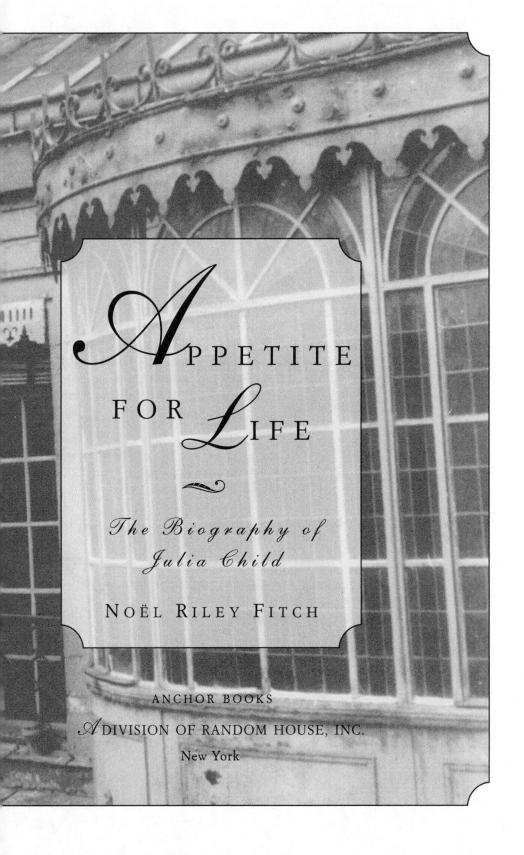

Appetite
FOR Life

The Biography of
Julia Child

NOËL RILEY FITCH

ANCHOR BOOKS
A DIVISION OF RANDOM HOUSE, INC.
New York

FIRST ANCHOR BOOKS EDITION, MAY 1999

Copyright © 1997 by Noël Riley Fitch

All rights reserved under International and Pan-American Copyright Conventions. Published in the United States by Anchor Books, a division of Random House, Inc., New York, and simultaneously in Canada by Random House of Canada Limited, Toronto. Originally published in hardcover in the United States by Doubleday in 1997. The Anchor Books edition is published by arrangement with Doubleday, a division of Random House, Inc.

Anchor Books and colophon are registered trademarks of Random House, Inc.

The Library of Congress has cataloged the Doubleday hardcover edition
of this book as follows:
Fitch, Noël Riley.
    Appetite for life : the biography of Julia Child / Noël Riley
Fitch. — 1st ed.
        p.   cm.
    Includes bibliographical references and index.
    1. Child, Julia. 2. Cooks—United States—Biography. I. Title.
TX649.C47F57   1997
641.5′092—dc21
[B]   97-11061
                                           CIP

ISBN 0-385-49383-5

Book design by Maria Carella

www.anchorbooks.com

Printed in the United States of America

10 9 8 7 6 5

For my sisters

Lynn and Gail

and

for my husband

Albert Sonnenfeld

with whom I share the joys of the table

"*I too am an Epicurean.*"

THOMAS JEFFERSON

CONTENTS

CONTENTS

An American in Paris (Marseilles, Bonn, and Oslo)

Our Lady of the Ladle

Empress of Cuisine

Appendices

Appetite for Life

WESTERN PIONEERS AND BLUE BLOOD

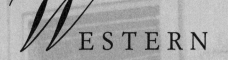

$\mathscr{B}$EGINNINGS

(1945, 1848 – 1912)

"How like autumn's warmth is Julia's face"
        PAUL CHILD, *August 15, 1945*
        〜

PERCHED ON THE railing of a veranda in Kunming, China, Julia McWilliams was aware only of the uniformed man beside her, reading the poem he wrote for her thirty-third birthday. She stretched her very long legs out in front of her, crossing them at her ankles, so Paul Child could see what he would later call "my beloved Julia's magnificent gams." She barely noticed the formal gardens beyond the porch or the miles of rice paddies stretching toward Kunming Lake. Nor did her gaze settle on the mist-shrouded Shangri-La of temples carved into the rock of West Mountain. It was his voice that captured her, each word he read a note weaving a melody through her heart: "The summer's heat of your embrace . . . melts my frozen earth."

The cotton dress clung to her slim, six-feet-two-inch body. Here she was in China, a privileged girl, seeking adventure, even danger, in the civilian opportunities of World War II, and she had found it, not in the Registry of the Office of Strategic Services, nor in the backwoods refugee city of Kunming at the end of the Burma Road, but in the urbane, sophisticated, multilingual presence of forty-three-year-old Paul Child. They talked all evening, his intellect challenging her, his experienced touch awakening her. In the last China outpost of Lord Mountbatten's command, surrounded at sea by Japanese forces, warplanes droning in the distance, Julia McWilliams felt alive.

How like autumn's warmth is Julia's face,
So filled with nature's bounty, nature's world. . . .

The cadence of his voice, reciting his sonnet "To Julia," intensified the
air of anticipation between them, dimming for the first time the news they had
received that week of the dropping of the atomic bomb on Hiroshima and
Nagasaki. Russia was invading Manchuria to the north. Just hours earlier they
had heard of Japan's surrender and knew the world was changing for everyone, not just themselves.

I cast this heaped abundance at your feet:
An offering to summer and her heat.

———

PAUL DROVE Julia by jeep to a mountain retreat for a weekend, where
they talked of meeting each other's families: he had a twin brother, whose
family lived in Pennsylvania, she two siblings and a father in California. The
differences in their height (he was a mere five feet ten and three-quarters
inches), age, education, cultural and political backgrounds, and values seemed
less severe in this foreign territory where the future was so uncertain. He
called theirs a "sweet friendship" in his sonnet, but she wanted much more
from this wartime embrace in a strange land. When he read aloud "the awakening fields abound / With newly green effulgence," he could have been
talking about her.

They had met just the year before in a tea planter's veranda in Ceylon,
when he was courting several women and seemed far beyond her reach in
knowledge and experience. He had the worldly-wise caution of a man who
had supported himself since he was a child, sailing the high seas, working at
physically demanding jobs, and educating himself in the classics, art, and
music. Despite her degree from Smith College, the gangly girl from the West
seemed to have little in common with this cosmopolitan ladies' man. "I was a
hungry hayseed from California," she would declare half a century later:

There were a lot of women around and he was ten years older than I.
Very sophisticated. He had lived in France and I'd only been to Tijuana!
So I found him very impressive, you see. And he was also an intellectual.
I was a kind of Southern California butterfly, a golf player and tennis
person who acted in Junior League plays.

She was indeed a party girl, a child of well-to-do parents, who had never had to work. Though she occasionally held jobs in New York City and Los Angeles, marriage was the usual goal of her generation. Had the war not come, she said, she "might have become an alcoholic" amid the society life of Pasadena. Julia stood out in any crowd, not just because of her height, but because she was strikingly beautiful in a wholesome way. She was also like a magnum of champagne, the effusive life of the party, even, as far as Paul was concerned, occasionally "hysterical." But as he learned more of this woman, he saw the depth of her character, and her joy lifted him from his isolation and reserve. Thirty-five years after their wedding, he told a Boston newspaper, "Without Julia, I think I'd be a sour old bastard living off in a cave."

Chinese food brought them together, at least talk of food did. He thought she could cook, but in fact she had a keen interest in food largely because she was always hungry. They loved the Peking-cuisine restaurants in this refugee city where the first cookbook was written around 3000 B.C. and the "earliest restaurant" opened during the T'ang Dynasty. They drove out with OSS friends whose parents were missionaries here and who knew the language and food, and they feasted on the many regional Chinese cuisines. Paul also spoke to Julia about the food of France, which he had enjoyed in the 1920s. Fluent in French, he talked with such a distinct inflection he seemed British to Julia. He would have been seen as effete in her native Pasadena.

Paul was unlike the Western boys she hung around with in her large circle of friends in Southern California, unlike any of the men her friends married. In hearing about his life, she soon realized he had no religion, few family connections, and held the business world in disdain. He was an artist and raconteur, a black belt in jujitsu, who could mesmerize colleagues with his stories. He represented a world she ached to know, an intellectual and European world, typical of the OSS personnel (such as anthropologists Gregory Bateson and Cora DuBois) whom she had come to admire during the past year in India and China. When she described her Presbyterian-raised father, a man of business and prominent in the civic affairs of Pasadena, Paul realized how dissimilar she was to any woman he had ever loved, for they all, including a woman he had lived with for many years, were petite, dark, and sophisticated in dress and manner. In contrast, Paul found Julia youthful, but "tough-fibered" and "natural."

"It wasn't like lightning striking the barn on fire," Paul said of their meeting in India. "I just began to think, my God, this is a hell of a nice woman, sturdy, and funny withal. And responsible! I was filled with admiration for this classy dame." If love grew slowly with him, for her it was the *coup de foudre,* and she made immediate plans to learn to cook for him. Like her paternal grandfather, John McWilliams, who left all he knew to follow the Gold Rush in 1849, she was ready to consider a break with her past.

CALIFORNIA GOLD:
MIDWESTERN GRANDPARENTS

"Pick your grandparents"
JULIA CHILD

John McWilliams first dreamed of going to California in 1848 when he read Richard Henry Dana's *Two Years Before the Mast* (1840) and when news came of the discovery of gold at Sutter's Mill. While John was obsessed with going to the New Eldorado, his father, James (who served in the Illinois legislature), dismissed the idea, worried about his son's bouts with chills and the dangers from uncertain weather and Indians. But John had what he called the "going fever": "Father, I am going to California, if I have to run away. I am going, or die."

Despite his father's wishes, sixteen-year-old John, one of his cousins, and two friends outfitted themselves for the trip with guns, ammunition, bacon and flour. John took one book with him, a copy of Plutarch's *Lives.* On April 9, 1849, with a wagon and four oxen, they left Griggsville, in Pike County, Illinois, for the California territory. Eight days out, John, only 121 pounds on his six-foot-one-and-a-half-inch frame, turned seventeen years old. On the ninth day he found a shroud in the bottom of his trunk and realized that his family feared he would die on the trail.

During the three years he panned for gold in the Sacramento Valley of California, he gained nearly thirty pounds and a wealth of survival experience. With a gold nugget in his pocket, he took a steamer out of San Francisco to Panama and, via railroad and steamship, reached New Orleans and eventually St. Louis. He had been gone from Illinois nearly four years. The spirit of adventure and the beckoning call of California would never leave him.

Drawn West by reading Richard Henry Dana's work, her grandfather would marry not one but two Dana girls. At the death of his wife, Mary Dana, John McWilliams married her sister, Clara Maria Dana, by whom he had three children, including one son, John McWilliams, Jr., whose oldest daughter, Julia, inherited her grandfather's tall, lean frame (though not his Dana coloring), his healthy physique, and his egalitarianism, curiosity about life, eagerness for adventure and travel, and intrepidity.

When Julia was growing up, her grandfather was an elderly gentleman who had chosen to return to the New Eldorado to spend his final years. He could spin great stories at the head of the table and continued to watch over his rice fields in Arkansas and land investments in Kern County, California. (He learned to thresh rice when he ran a mill near Savannah after his march to the sea with General Sherman, and as a panner for gold in '49, he knew the value of the earth's minerals.) As Julia listened to his stories, her imagination wove pictures in which she would blaze new trails and dine with heroes, then serve the public interest with discipline and leadership. She would have him in mind when she was asked in the 1990s for her best advice on a healthy life: "Pick your grandparents." But if Julia was influenced by the pioneering spirit of her paternal grandfather, she was even more imprinted by her dynamic, redheaded mother, Julia Carolyn Weston, who married young John McWilliams, Jr., in 1911.

THE WESTON TWINKLE:
NEW ENGLAND GRANDPARENTS

Tall, redheaded "Caro" Weston was born into a family of old money, Massachusetts colonial lines, and Congregational habits. Both her parents died before her daughter Julia's birth, but the Weston family influence could not have been stronger had they lived. Captain Byron Curtis Weston and Julia Clark Mitchell, twelve years his junior, married just after the Civil War (1865) and had ten children over the next twenty-six years. They lived in Dalton, Massachusetts, not far from Pittsfield, in a gabled, towered, and turreted mansion called Westonholme, which looked like a French château made of wood. The vast home, which no longer exists, was maintained by servants, nurses, a governess, a coachman, and cooks, and was supported by the Weston Paper Company, which Byron founded in 1863. Byron Weston traced his family back to the eleventh century in England; the first Weston in the New World was Edmund of Plymouth Colony. With lineage and money, Byron was a leading citizen of Berkshire County. He gave the Grace Episcopal Church to Dalton and the athletic field ("Weston Field") to Williams College. His paper won a Gold Medal at the Paris Exhibition in the summer of 1878. He served three terms (with Governor John D. Long) as lieutenant governor of Massachusetts.

Julia Clark Mitchell, his wife, was a direct descendant of Governor William Bradford and Elder Brewster of the Plymouth Colony and also Priscilla Alden and Experience Mitchell, who came to Plymouth in 1623. With five ancestors in the Revolutionary War, Julia Mitchell was a proud member of the

DAR, a charter member of the Peace Party Chapter of the Colonial Dames, and a New England Congregationalist. Because she was the favorite niece of poet William Cullen Bryant, whom she visited at the *Evening Post* in New York City on her honeymoon, she gave the middle name Bryant to two of her children, as she gave two others the middle name Mitchell. By the time her seventh child was born (three babies were already dead of diphtheria), she named the girl after herself and her husband's mother (Carolyn Curtis): Julia Carolyn Weston, the future mother of Julia [Carolyn McWilliams] Child.

These Weston grandparents of Julia McWilliams were reared amid the influence of the Reverend Sylvester Graham (1794–1851), who lived in the neighboring town of Northampton. Graham's influence reached far beyond western Massachusetts. A former Presbyterian preacher and temperance lecturer, Graham was a self-styled doctor of medicine, specifically a dietetic expert, who bathed daily in the Miller River and preached against meat and white flour. The central staple of his diet was slightly stale bread made from coarse, unbolted flour and oats. This inventor of Granola, graham crackers, Grape-Nuts, and Kellogg's, had influential followers: the founder of Oberlin Institute, revivalist Charles Finney, Bronson Alcott, and, for a while, Joseph Smith, Horace Greeley, and Thomas A. Edison. Such revivals/rituals, whether they be spiritual or nutritional, do not outlast the generation or overcome family habits, so the later Westons were meat eaters, for Byron loved to hunt, and the family frequently had pigeon, goose, duck, partridge, or rabbit on the table.

In addition to family wealth and household servants, Julia Carolyn (Caro) Weston grew up surrounded by family, gifted with the freedom that filled the space left by busy, inattentive parents. Caro's mother was either traveling with her father, socially engaged, or giving birth (Philip Bryant, Dorothy Dean, and Donald Mitchell were born after Caro). When Caro is mentioned in her mother's diary, she is always in trouble for climbing or falling or reading adult books. She was "the more adventurous one," according to niece Dana Parker. She loved her dog Gaston, playing tennis and basketball, and driving her motorcar about town—the first woman in the county to have a driver's license.

At Smith College, Caro was the outstanding athlete, basketball captain, and winner of first place in running, high jump, and sprinting. She had hair more pink than carrot, and a prominent nose, features that led some people to believe she was Jewish. Full-lipped, eyes riding high on her face, she wore her luxurious and wild hair in a mass atop her long oval face. "Slender" and "graceful" were the words her classmates used in their Smith yearbook to describe her striking appearance. The only ungraceful note was her voice, which wavered in the high ranges, never seeming to emanate from her chest. Her strong presence and authority was balanced by her tiny feminine waist, cinched in by a fashionable corset and accentuated by huge puffy sleeves from elbow to shoulder. Her friends noted in their yearbook her "striking individuality," a New England inheritance nurtured by childhood freedom and money, a legacy she would give her two daughters, Julia and Dorothy.

When she was a sophomore at Smith, her father had a stroke; when she was a junior, he died and her thirty-two-year-old brother, Frank, took over the Weston Paper Company. Two years after her Smith graduation in 1900, Caro's mother died at fifty-eight of Bright's disease, an event that would alter Caro's life by leaving her the oldest Weston daughter at home. "Momma died at ten minutes to two. We are all orphans. We need her so," she wrote in her diary. She would care for Donald (eleven years), Dorothy Dean (fifteen), and Philip (twenty-one). When Dorothy came down with consumption (tuberculosis), Caro took her to California and Colorado in hopes of a cure.

If her daughter Julia McWilliams Child inherited the McWilliams intelligence, organization, and stubbornness, these were moderated by the charm and *joie de vivre* of what was called the "Weston twinkle." It was a strong dose of the natural, sometimes naughty, child's delight in nature and the company of others, exuding a warm, uncritical acceptance of life and other people. It came not from old Byron Weston, the patriarchal gentleman who founded the Weston paper mill, but from Grandmother Julia Weston, who, as a Brewster, descended from William Cullen Bryant and Oliver Wendell Holmes.

Julia McWilliams Child never met her maternal grandmother, Julia Mitchell Weston, but grandmother passed her "twinkle," her name, Celtic complexion, independent attitude, and joyful heart to daughter and granddaughter. Though Caro was tall (for that day) at five feet seven inches, her daughter Julia would grow seven inches taller than that and her daughter Dorothy eight.

Caro, displaying an early feminist attitude, claimed not to like her father, Byron Weston, because he "wore out" her mother by giving her ten children. Of these ten children born over a twenty-five-year period from 1866 to 1891, three died before they were three years of age and only one lived past sixty. It was the Weston curse: high blood pressure and strokes, despite Caro's parents frequently taking the waters, from California to the Continent. Caro, who would have her first stroke when her youngest, Dorothy, was thirteen, was sixty when she died; fortunately her children inherited the McWilliams longevity. Which is why Caro chose John McWilliams in the first place: she was determined to bring "new blood" into her deep but narrow New England gene pool. She brought in his strength and intelligence and Scotch Presbyterianism as well, while passing to her children her independence and joy.

$\mathscr{P}$ASADENA PARADISE: POP AND CARO

Julia's father, John Jr., was a second-generation pioneer, born into the comfortable home of a man who once crossed the country by wagon and panned for Eureka gold, before building a family estate of farm and mining lands. This father's legacy was a heavy enough burden for young John, but he also had the father himself at his elbow each day until the old man died at ninety-three years of age in 1924. Such a mixed blessing could have broken a man less quietly determined and controlled.

Born in Odell, Illinois, on October 26, 1880, young John inherited his father's height and his mother Dana's coloring (an olive complexion, so the story goes, from family roots in Sicily). John was sent to prestigious Lake Forest Academy for the last two years of his high school education before enrolling at Princeton University one month before his seventeenth birthday. He graduated in history in the Class of '01.

After college, patriarchal destiny drew him immediately back to and through the doors of his father's Bank of Odell (Illinois), where he began as an assistant cashier and helped his father manage their rice farmland in Arkansas. Only when the elder McWilliams sold his interest in the bank and established the State Bank of Odell (to take over their business interests) did young John become president. It was 1909 and his father moved to California to manage his land near Bakersfield. Young John joined the University Club in Chicago and began his courtship of Caro Weston. The family tells the story—whenever they want to illustrate his stubbornness—of one visit on horseback to his future bride. When his horse would not cross the stream, John forded the stream himself to see his Caro; returning later, he forced the horse to wade the stream.

Caro Weston met John McWilliams, Jr., in 1903 in Chicago through mutual friends. Thus began what Caro's brothers called "the eight-year war of their courtship." Both the war and the courtship continued as John followed Caro and her sister Dorothy Dean from one spa to another in search of a remedy for the tuberculosis with which Dorothy had suffered since youth. Caro would not leave her sister to marry. They went to Santa Barbara and Colorado Springs, where John stayed with his Princeton classmate H. Alexander Smith, then an attorney with Judge Lunt (and later a U.S. senator from

New Jersey, 1944–59). The Weston girls were part of Smith's social clique in Colorado society. Once Dorothy Dean met and married Wilber Hemming, son of the president of the El Paso National Bank, Caro was finally free to announce her engagement to John McWilliams.

John and Caro, with Alexander Smith as their best man and Dorothy Hemming as the matron of honor, married on January 21, 1911, in Colorado Springs. John and Caro went by train to Pasadena, honeymooned at the Coronado Hotel in San Diego, then moved in with his parents in Pasadena (the old forty-niner had recently moved from Bakersfield to this community of Midwesterners just east of Los Angeles).

Caro remained a free spirit even as a married woman. "See the world before settling down," she would tell her daughters. By the time she married John, she was thirty-three years old and her independence a practiced virtue. She was always considered daring, living on her own for several years; now she seemed locked into her husband's life and the lives of his parents, who expected Caro and John to share their time and Sunday meals. She adapted to the confines of a traditional marriage in the manner women have used through the centuries: by doing exactly what she pleased within the context of propriety. When her thrifty husband was out of town on business, she redecorated the downstairs and bought new china. "I do what I want," she told her children.

Her free spirit dictated that since she was in California, she would adapt to the place and drop the traditions of her childhood. "She probably threw all that New England tradition away when she came to the West," says her oldest child, Julia, who would behave in like manner as she moved about the world. Her father had expressed the same attitude when he wrote to the Princeton class's tenth reunion committee that he intended to remain in the "Golden West" and "grow up with the country." He, like his father, became a pioneer, now of modern Pasadena, and what his elder daughter called a civic "do-gooder" in this paradise.

First Indians, then Spanish explorers and missionaries (including Father Junípero Serra), and finally Mexican ranchers occupied the rich, fan-shaped land beneath Mount Wilson. The shape of the land was formed by alluvial deposits from the streams that flowed from the San Gabriel Mountains. The transcontinental railroad brought the next wave of settlers from Indiana, Iowa, and Illinois, who planted vast orange groves. The land was called the Indiana Colony in 1874. Escaping the industrial revolution, these Midwestern pioneers determined to make every home a garden and to resist modernity, even a post office. But the 1880s brought a rail line in from Los Angeles, about ten miles away, and then a connection to the Santa Fe Railroad to Chicago and the East.

Mr. Walter Raymond of Boston built the first grand hotel, the Royal Raymond, which cleverly offered free rooms for writers (who soon spread the word to readers in the East). Pasadena was a city built by sunshine and the promise of good health.

The city, incorporated in 1886, became famous as a winter resort for George Pullman, Andrew Carnegie, and John D. Rockefeller. By the 1890s, Armenians fleeing the Turks brought ambition and industry to the city. When the first McWilliams arrived—actually it was a twentieth-century return—this was a paradise inhabited by visionary and ambitious men. By the time Julia McWilliams was born in 1912, 34,000 people lived in Pasadena, the city tripling its population in a decade.

Pasadena was an entrepreneurial paradise, a fertile time and place for the birth of Caro and John's first child, Julia.

Chapter 2

A Place in the Sun
(1912 – 1921)

"She was wild, really wild."

DOROTHY MCWILLIAMS COUSINS

JULIA CAROLYN MCWILLIAMS was born in Pasadena, California, on August 15, 1912, when the orange groves were fragrant beneath the snowcapped San Gabriel Mountains and the Tournament of the Roses was already planning its twenty-fourth local parade. It was an era when telephone lines were shared by several families, and horse-drawn wagons delivered ice, vegetables, milk, and eggs daily to the house. "These were the days of 'the iceman cometh,'" Julia likes to remember.

She was born in Paradise. Across America, Pasadena represented the utopia for those who could afford the transcontinental train ride to spend their winters settled into one of the palatial hotels in this sunny haven. Woodrow Wilson, Theodore Roosevelt, and William Howard Taft each had visited the year before Julia was born. Members of the Valley Hunt Club, including the McWilliams family, drove flower-adorned carriages in a rose parade from hotel to hotel (where the Easterners were staying), passed family homes bearing the names of Wrigley, Busch, Steinway, Huntington, Gamble, Libby, and Armour. Pasadena was an entitled world, feeding on the fruits of American capitalism in a balmy climate where children and oranges grew well.

John and Caro took their firstborn home from Pasadena Hospital to 225

State Street, just a few blocks from Adolphus Busch's famed gardens, a major tourist attraction that summer. The August heat had ripened the orange trees and the McWilliamses (parents and grandparents) were planning to move to a larger house farther west at 627 South Euclid Avenue. Grandfather McWilliams's three-story Euclid house, which remained in the family until 1957, was built four years earlier to re-create the nostalgic Midwestern farmhouse, with large verandas trimmed with balustrades. Now a protected monument, its Victorian and Edwardian features include protruding porches, a two-story bay window, and high narrow windows with pillared trim. When asked for her first memories, Julia replied:

> Earliest memories are always of traumatic things. I locked myself in the bathroom and they got the fire department to get me out. Another memory is of a train trip with my grandfather to Santa Barbara where my Aunt Bessie, my father's sister, lived. We were sitting in the parlor car when I realized that I was leaving my mother. I began to scream. They finally had to come get me and take me back. A third traumatic memory involved driving up to Santa Barbara when I was about three years old to the Miramar Hotel, where there were wooden steps going down to the ocean. I refused to go down, thinking that the ocean would swallow us up, and I sat there screaming.

One of her happiest early memories occurred at Christmas, when she, her brother, and her sister would awaken early:

> First we'd do the stockings, which were filled with candy canes and apples and a lot of small presents. Then we'd have a big breakfast with eggs and bacon and fruit, but we'd all be panting for gifts. One year Santa Claus left his pipe on the mantel. It was a meerschaum filled with tobacco and had been smoked. We children marveled over it for years.

When Julia was two years old, her brother, John McWilliams III, was born. It was August 27, 1914, following what for Caro and John was a night in Natty's Tavern and a bumpy ride in the hills above Santa Barbara. After her confinement and their summer holiday ended in Santa Barbara, Caro and John Jr. sold the State Street house to the Stevens family and moved their growing family to their own home at 625 Magnolia Avenue, a block away from his parents. Fortunately for Julia, Mrs. Davies's Montessori school was located just around the corner and eight houses from her grandparents.

Mrs. Davies's School

From birth until the third year of age a child has an absorbent mind, believed Dr. Maria Montessori. According to the Italian doctor's influential theories, the following three years of the child's psychological development are a "sensitive period" of adapting to her surroundings. Thus the child should begin the Montessori program before she is four and a half. The McWilliamses enrolled four-year-old Julia in the school of May and Augustus Davies, who had studied with Dr. Montessori.

Their ungraded, open-space school was located in a former stable or carriage house behind their home at 693 South Euclid. "Juke" (variously Jukie, JuJu, or Jukes), as Julia was called by the children, learned to use her fingers with skill. "I started doing hand work when I was three," she told two journalists in 1981, crediting the Montessori hand work of ringing little bells and buttoning buttons for the coordination so important in her profession. Always the tallest, she was reed thin and freckled, with curly reddish-blond hair. She learned coordination of movement and posture (eighty years later she still remembered the exercise "Walkie, walkie, walkie on the line"). She learned grace and courtesy and the early foundations of language and mathematics. "We rang bells, learned the scale, put buttons on button frames . . . and once when we were having tea we threw the cups out the window in some kind of mass hysteria. I do not remember why we did that." Her brother, John, who enrolled two years later, remembers learning penmanship without being allowed to touch the paper with his fingers.

During her first year at Mrs. Davies's school, Juke had her tonsils removed; the second year she learned to sing "It's a Long Way to Tipperary," "I'm Forever Blowing Bubbles," and "Over There." The country entered a world war in the same month (April 1917) that her baby sister, Dorothy Dean, was born, named after her mother's deceased sister. The third year, in 1918, when Juke turned six and the family moved for the last time, she led the schoolchildren in single file around the block while they beat on pans in celebration of the end of the war.

> *Kaiser Bill went up the hill to take a look at France*
> *Kaiser Bill came down the hill with bullets in his pants*

Juke felt personally involved because since the end of August her father had been stationed in the Field Artillery in Kentucky. He was honorably discharged on December 11, commissioned in the reserve corps, and continued his service by becoming business manager of the Pasadena Red Cross.

The election of President Wilson and the ratification of prohibition would not affect Julia until later years, nor would the oil gush at Huntington Beach that brought a decade of oil boom and scandal to the Los Angeles basin. What directly influenced her was the family's final move to a large tract of land near their original Pasadena neighborhood.

Place is important in any childhood, and the McWilliamses' warm wooden house at 1207 South Pasadena Avenue had a sleeping porch across the back of the second floor, a laundry room behind the garage for the children to wash their Airedale dog, and a playhouse, tennis court, shed, rose garden, large lawn, and small orchard of citrus and avocado trees. Here the children built memories out of acting plays in the attic, rearing rats in the playhouse, entertaining tennis matches and school dances.

Julia's room was the top room in the left-hand corner of the house, which she used for her clothes and toys and as a place to sleep when she was ill. She had her own bathroom. Her strongest memories were of sleeping on the outside porch, which was partitioned into areas for each family member in the manner of the day.

When Julia was born, the Arts and Craft Movement of California, which had its roots in Victorian Britain, was coming to a close after twenty years. Pasadena had been fertile ground for this aesthetic that shunned the machine age, emphasizing a building's harmony with its environment and "the good life" of simple living and high thinking—a philosophy reflecting the progressive beliefs of people who came to the city at the turn of the century, who supported public gardens and national parks, woman suffrage, progressive education, and healthful living. Their buildings had upper-floor wraparound sleeping porches, low-slung roofs, cool rooms of polished wood full of handcrafted Mission furniture. Chief architects of these homes were Greene & Greene (whose bungalows had massive timbers), Louis B. Easton (redwood shingles), Ernest Batchelder (tile maker and friend of Igor Stravinsky)—all of whom designed their homes down to the doorknobs.

"Our house was right out of *Upstairs, Downstairs,*" Julia said years later. "We had help, Irish or German immigrants." As did most families at that time, the McWilliamses had an upstairs maid, who kept the house; a little Scottish nurse named Annie Hignett, who cared for baby Dorothy and whom the children did not like; an Irish cook; and a gardener named Clearwater, who kept up the acre of land, the orchard and garden, tended the chickens, and groomed the tennis court. Eventually Miss Williams (Willy) came to care for Dorothy and to help Caro with the household management. She was a part of the family, eating at the table with them. Willy was from the South and was a good friend of Mrs. Fairfax Proudfitt Walkup, the teacher at the Pasadena Playhouse. "Willy was a lady," remembers Dorothy.

As a typical older sister, Julia could be bossy and controlling, and a tormentor of her siblings. Dorothy was enough younger (five years), and under the supervision of Willy, to avoid her sister's influence until later in life, when Julia became her mother figure. As a child, Dort was volatile and cranky, given to tantrums and anger, feeling neglected, always passed off on nurses. Julia did not help when she gave Dort's favorite doll to a neighbor.

$\mathscr{P}$OP'S GIRL

Julia was reared by two socially active and athletic parents who loved the outdoors and belonged to several country clubs, including the Valley Hunt Club for swimming and horseback riding, the Midwick Country Club for polo and golf, and the Annandale Country Club for golf. They and their friends, the Myerses, Cliffords, Carpenters, and Stevens, provided community leadership. Today one of their neighbors remembers that the McWilliams clan was considered "wealthy" and "aristocratic (in the best sense)."

"Pop" had his office with his father at 42 North Raymond Street, intersecting Colorado Avenue, along which the commercial section of the city had grown up. Today this area, after long disrepair, is called Old Town and has the most active nightlife in the region. Together father and son managed their four thousand acres of Arkansas rice land (owned from 1905 to 1935) and mineral rights in Kern County lands as well as their investments. For the first thirty years of her life, Julia harbored a godlike idealization of her father. He was building his place in the community, serving as president of the Pasadena Chamber of Commerce, regional trustee of Princeton University, and a member of numerous boards. His example of community service and leadership became a motivational force in Julia's later creative compulsions. She learned what she *should be* from him, what she *was* from her mother. Like the snow-capped San Gabriel Mountains that loomed over the town, her father was a steady and reassuring presence. His opinions were firm, his attitudes conservative. In 1953, his older daughter would describe him in more objective terms, but still with a reverence for his leadership capabilities:

> My Pop [and I are] on such different beams. Can't mention politics or philosophy [to him, but] he is a darling fellow, a most generous father, a real "do-gooder" in the community (how he would hate that term) as he

is on the Community Chest, the Chamber of Commerce, the Republican
Committee, the School and Hospital Board[s]. He just has everything it
takes to be a fine citizen and a responsible member of his community;
except he is violently emotional over politics (so am I, but I am trying to
be intellectual about them . . . but they roll around in my stomach
rather than coming out in a quietly poignant yet devastatingly unanswer-
able thought-piece). He could really be a world-beater if he had had
more intellectual training, which would have opened his mind and
would have made him more tolerant and inquiring. He is an example of
how not to be, and how one must continually struggle for understanding
and experience and wisdom.

His presence each evening called for quiet, implying deference for his
work and responsibility outside the home. His children thought him reserved.
He was stern because *his* father was stern, and he was of the generation that
had feelings but kept them to themselves, thereby "enriching" them. Julia's
best friend, Orian (Babe) Hall, remembers that "you always wanted to do
things the right way around him." His friends thought that this handsome Ivy
League man was sociable; women found him charming in his bowler hat, wire-
rimmed glasses, and deep-set eyes; a man's man who enjoyed playing golf and
hunting with men. Today, several family members observe that Julia is most
like her father, particularly in her strong will, her reserve in private matters,
and her public service. She too would become practical and organized, sociable and charming, athletic and outdoorsy.

MOTHER CARO

To the community she was Mrs. John McWilliams, Jr.—surrounded by tight
corsets, antiques, and antimacassars. But to her friends, and later her adult
children, she was Caro, who loved petting her dogs, playing tennis, and chat-
ting with friends. She was no Victorian fussy-dusty who occupied her time in
domestic concerns. She never taught her daughters to sew or manicure their
nails. But she surrounded them with her approval, showing them how to love
sports, laughter, and friends and follow one's own whims.

Julia and her sister Dort were eager learners. While Julia was growing up
her mother was a "dynamo," to use her son's word. "She was wonderful, full
of fun and spontaneous sayings, keeping all of us (father, specifically) from
being too stuffy." Julia wrote in her diary about a "funny little wiggling [of]
the top of her tongue the way only she could do it—faster than anyone I ever

saw." With vitality and humor she ran a large household, planned the meals, and entertained friends and business associates of her husband.

Yet, as a result of her early independence, Caro kept a life of her own and had her own dog, a bull terrier named Flicker. Caro sat at the head of the table to keep control of the dinner conversation, played tennis almost daily with her friends, and loved the theater. "She had an amusing petulance," Julia remembered, "but it was more playful than serious." Letters to her daughters when they were away at school suggest that she never missed a new theatrical production. Mrs. McWilliams had "afternoons" to receive her friends, hosted a book club (though her husband's sister Bessie exclaimed, "Carolyn McWilliams, you read more books and know less than any woman I know!"), and helped to found the Little Town Club, where her friends could have lunch (the men never came home for lunch) and one night a week—the cooks' night off—take their reluctant husbands to eat.

Caro was a laissez-faire mother, encouraging her children to "have fun." When her daughter Dort dropped Latin in high school, Caro responded by saying, "Why didn't you tell us you were overworked. There is always time to get educated." One younger family member now observes that "Caro was an upper-class mother who did not *really* spend a lot of time rearing her children." Yet Julia remembers:

> We loved her and we did lots of things with her; she was usually there when we came home from school; she was more like a friend than a mother; I can remember as kiddies we would all lie on the couch and Mother would read to us. I remember she was reading us something like *Bob, Son of Battle* and we three were sobbing. She was very emotional. She was also very outspoken, right up front. She would be sitting at the table and would say, "Oh, hot flash, hot flash, open the window." She was open about life and the body—plainspoken, an unpretentious New Englander. Neither style nor the latest fashion was important to her.

"Julia had the most fabulous mother," thought Julia's friend Gay Bradley, the daughter of a Pasadena lawyer. "I liked best that she would sit and talk to us. . . . We would sit on the couch when we came home in the afternoon. She had beautiful red hair, and she was so receptive to us. She always made us feel great. She was one of those women you love to know."

THE FAMILY TABLE

Food meant weekly Sunday dinners *en famille,* the arrival of the milk-and-egg wagon, and learning to make fudge from Fannie Farmer's *Boston Cooking School Cook Book,* published in 1896. Yet the kitchen, Julia would later tell Lewis Lapham, was a "dismal place" she stayed away from. Hired cooks presided there. She remembers little of what she ate, which, according to family memories, was the traditional European meat-and-potatoes diet of the day, but with the addition of citrus, avocado, and vegetables from their garden. Oriental and Mexican food was bountiful in the Los Angeles area, but at that time remained confined to the homes of its native cooks. Few restaurants existed (prohibition held serious dining at bay for more than a decade) apart from the grand hotels where social events took place.

The only cooking news that appeared in the newspapers was coverage of a food faddist's lecture in town: Horace Fletcher, the fasting-and-bowel-regulation crank, was turning family dining into marathon slow-chewing sessions (thirty-two chews a bite!) called "Fletcherizing." Culinary historians bemoan the trends of that period, when home economists in white were incorporating frozen foods and bad attitudes (eating was science, not pleasure) into their recipes. But most lecturers in Pasadena, by contrast, were healthful and sane from today's perspective. Soon after Julia's birth, her mother's Shakespeare club hosted a talk by Dr. Margaret C. Goettler, who urged that children be given simple fruits and vegetables and be allowed one and a half hours for lunch. Meat is not necessary, she exhorted the three hundred women, and "Don't eat fried food unless you can digest carpet tacks." Julia's mother listened, but trusted her own tradition when she served fried mush or, more frequently, deep-fried codfish balls on special Sunday mornings. After all, had not Yankee Senator George Frisbie Hoar risen on the U.S. Senate floor to declare that the dish belonged to those "whose theology is sound, and who believe in the five points of Calvinism"?

"All my mother knew how to cook was baking powder biscuits, codfish balls, and Welsh rarebit," Julia would say years later. The food Julia remembers most vividly from her childhood came from her mother's New England family: codfish balls, the kind of domesticated, ladylike white and creamed dish that was part of the New England cooking tradition during this century's first decades. Made from dried, salted cod soaked overnight, then poached and whipped with mashed potato and egg, molded into a ball, and deep-fried, they were served with white sauce containing chopped hard-boiled egg.

Codfish Balls
One package of dried, salted cod
Cooked or leftover mashed potatoes
Two fresh eggs
Fat for deep frying
White sauce with two chopped hard-boiled eggs

Little wonder that Ogden Nash declared this New England staple "such an utter loss / That people eat it with egg sauce." Julia remembers it as delicious.

Even though her mother was not a good cook, Julia remembers that on the cooks' night out (Thursday), if they did not go to the dining club, her mother would make baking powder biscuits. Decades later, when a newspaper asked Julia to recall her mother's cooking, she gave them the recipe.

Buttermilk Herb Baking Powder Biscuits
3 cups all-purpose flour
2 teaspoons salt
4 teaspoons double-acting baking powder
1 teaspoon baking soda
4 ounces or 8 tablespoons chilled vegetable shortening
4 tablespoons fresh minced chives
4 tablespoons fresh minced parsley
2 eggs
1½ cups buttermilk

Into a mixture of the dry ingredients, Mrs. McWilliams cut the shortening until it was in small pieces, at which time she stirred in the herbs and then briefly blended in the wet ingredients, which had already been whipped together. (Many Yankee homes did not use the eggs.) The molded mixture was then turned onto a floured board, kneaded, and patted flat to half an inch or more and cut into rounds with a glass, its rim dipped in flour. After the biscuits came out of the 450 degree oven in ten to fifteen minutes, "they smelled so good," said Julia, ". . . and I liked to put butter, real butter, on them and watch it run down the sides."

Julia learned very young how a tomato tastes and smells. One of her favorite memories is "the vegetable wagon driven by the Chinaman who brought litchi nuts." The Pasadena Grocery at the time advertised that their rock cod sold for fifteen cents a pound, twenty-five cents for two pounds.

Nash's department store would deliver food. Had they not had their own gardens and the year-round vegetable wagons, Pasadena women would have been more dependent on the brand-name products from the American Cereal Company, Pillsbury, Campbell's, Heinz, and Kraft that filled the women's magazines of Julia's childhood. (By 1913, according to one report, "Jell-O was distributing fifteen million recipe books a year" and Heinz had increased its canned goods production fifteenfold since 1900.) Most cooks in the United States did not always have fresh fruits and vegetables, and refrigeration consisted of a small icebox, which was cooled by a block of ice delivered each week by a man in a brown leather apron carrying oversized metal tongs.

Neighbor children all thought that Mrs. McWilliams was a strong advocate of rest and nutritious food. Babe Hall, who lived across the street, remembers that they were not allowed to snack after school and sometimes they would buy food at the local market or take fruit from someone's tree. If Julia or John ate across the street with the Halls on Saturday night, they had New England baked beans and brown bread, for the Halls were New Englanders who also served fried cod cakes on Sunday mornings.

Julia grew up during rapid changes in eating and cooking habits. During the first twenty years of the century, "scientific" eating prevailed, dominated by the U.S. Food Administration and the home economists, who talked of chemistry, calories, protein, fat, and carbohydrates. The war stimulated food production and the discovery of vitamins, as well as the growth of food growers' associations such as the Sun Maid Raisins in the San Joaquin Valley. Despite many food historians' laments about the eating habits of Americans during these early decades, the Pasadena newspapers reflected a continuing emphasis on natural produce, simple cooking, and outdoor living. For years, special speakers in town urged an active outdoor life and sunshine (an easy pitch in Pasadena). A man named J. C. Elliot called for his audience to "cut down your food supply, throw open your windows, sleep in the open screen porch, take your morning cold bath, avoid anger, hatred and fear, get out in the sunshine and breathe fresh, pure oxygen, if you wish to avoid a cold." Arthur Taylor, the chef de cuisine at the Raymond Hotel, told the *Pasadena Star-News* in 1916 that his clients wanted the best of fresh produce and shunned highly seasoned dishes that "disarrange digestion." This was the year that the paper began printing menu suggestions and recipes.

Caro had little trouble in feeding her children, though young John was thin and she urged him to take naps to grow stronger. The mantra in Pasadena may have been "remember the starving Armenians," but she never worried or used guilt on her children, who were always hungry. Caro was too busy conducting the conversation from the head of the table, where she was always served first. "We did not talk about food." Julia remembers, "and we ate as much as we could at every meal." They drank water in gold-rimmed, long-stemmed glasses, not because of prohibition, but because there was no tradition of wine-drinking. Her father had cocktails, including one called an "orange lady." When he tried to make wine in the basement, the children blew into the curved glass and the experiment did not work.

Sunday dinners could swell to tremendous proportions of noise and dishes when McWilliams relatives or friends of her grandfather visited. The Pasadena sun was an attraction for the McWilliams clan, especially Grandfather's nephew Charles, who came every year from Dwight, Illinois, and provided Julia with her only male cousins—Alex, John, and Charlie McWilliams, who were two to six years older than Julia and attended the Thatcher Academy in Ojai while their parents lived at the Raymond Hotel in Pasadena.

Julia learned the secret of life at an early age: appetite. "I was always hungry, I had the appetite of a wolf," she would say after living in Norway. The best cook in the family was her father's mother, according to Julia, "a modest and retiring little woman with gray hair in a bun at the back of her neck." Though Grandmother was always occupied caring for her older husband, Julia remembered the foods she prepared: "Grandmother McWilliams was a great cook who made wonderful donuts and some of the best broiled chicken I ever ate. . . . She grew up in the farming country of Illinois and her family had a French cook in the 1880s."

McHALL GANG OF FOUR

The McWilliams children were more attuned to their Airedale dog, Eric the Red, and their neighborhood friends than to their cousins. By the time Julia began attending elementary school, she and John formed a gang with the Hall kids across the street: Charlie and Babe (her name was really Orian, but she was the baby of the family). Sometimes George Hall, who was older, would join in on the plays in the vast McWilliams attic. Julia wrote the plays, which she remembers as "terrible," and they dressed in Caro McWilliams's old clothes. John ran the curtain. Charlie remembers working the lights in the attic, which often blew the house circuits, and Mrs. McWilliams's casual acceptance of this major inconvenience. When Babe and Julia tried to raise white rats in their half of the playhouse, they called it the McHall Rodent Farm.

Babe Hall was a short, wiry girl with as much daring and courage as her friend Julia, who was one year older—the same age as Babe's brother Charlie.

They did not like the other girls whom their parents invited over. Juke and Babe loved to "take things"—everything from the fruit on the trees at the Raymond Hotel, where Babe's grandmother spent each winter, to nails at a construction site. They were accomplished liars, but were spanked when they were caught.

Julia early on showed a preference for group play. The McHall gang (or Delta Club) roamed the neighborhood on their bicycles, followed by Eric the Red, as far as the rolling foothills and the boulder-strewn, oak-shaded ravine—the Arroyo Seco (dry wash)—that bordered the western edge of the city. Above them loomed the new Colorado Street Bridge, completed the year Julia was born. One could still go trout fishing in the river below and the Arroyo Park had a fishing pool, archery, and golf. In addition to the Arroyo Seco, their landscape was characterized, except for bedrock outcroppings such as Monk Hill, Raymond Hill, and Devil's Gate, by a long gradual incline toward the Los Angeles basin.

No child's neighborhood would be complete without a Mrs. Greble, whose very name could evoke their collective screams. "Mrs. Greble was the witch of the neighborhood," Julia remembers. "She had two haunted houses that were vacant. We managed to get into one and took down the chandelier; it had long glass things and was triangular; we buried them; she was not nice; everyone hated her."

Mrs. Mary D. Greble lived on Columbia and owned the land between the McWilliamses and Orange Grove Boulevard. There was a thick oak tree on her land that Julia remembers well: "We took Father's cigars up into the oak tree and smoked. It must have been funny to see the smoke puffing up." Babe Hall, her accomplice, remembers that they chose that spot in order to glimpse any approaching adults, for they were smoking "for the sake of getting away with it." Charlie Hall said that his sister and Juke "smoked everything in pipes, which they kept in cigar boxes mounted in the tops of trees or buried in some remote area. In addition to purloined tobacco, they smoked prunes, corn silk, etc. I don't believe there was anything they didn't try to smoke!"

Julia, who would always test the boundaries of authority, experimented at length with smoking before her father eventually called his three children together and offered a thousand-dollar bond to each if they would not smoke until they reached twenty-one years of age. "We did not smoke after that," claimed Julia. "I kept my bargain. At one minute after midnight on my twenty-first birthday I began smoking and smoked for thirty years, at least one to two packs of cigarettes every day."

In reality, Babe and Julia feared little, even from Mrs. Greble. They discovered a way to slide a piece of paper under the lid of Mr. McWilliams's musical cigarette box and press it down just right so that they could lift the lid in silence and steal a cigarette. It was a more difficult procedure than lifting one of Mr. Hall's cigars, so they smoked more cigars. One day when the mud was oozy and malleable they molded mud pies on a garage roof on Freemont Street, where the road was narrow, and threw them at passing cars, then ducked. One victim of their prank suddenly appeared at the back of the roof. The girls jumped and ran, with the man close behind them. He caught Julia's leg as she got to the top of the next fence. "I am taking you to the police. Come down!" he demanded. She cried and pleaded to be released so she could come down. When his hand relaxed, said Babe, Julia leapt over the fence and they ran like hell over lawns and fences until they could hide in safety. "Julia made the most of every opportunity," says Gay Bradley. "She was always the leader, the center of things, the instigator. All activities centered around Julia, who was a lively prankster."

When Julia found a piece of tar (left from a new roof), she and Charlie decided the gang would melt it in a pan on the stove of the laundry room. "This is not a good idea!" protested John. Nothing deterred her until the hot tar took the bottom off the pan and flowed over the top of the stove. Charlie now believes the McWilliamses, whom he considered his second parents, were "long-suffering" saints.

The two girls one day noticed that one of the windows was open in a vacant house belonging to Mrs. Greble. They climbed onto the roof and hand by hand inched along a trellis to the window and went inside. On the way back Julia got her finger caught on a wire nail and could not free it. In desperation, she jumped to the ground below, leaving an inch of skin behind. The following day they returned and Babe retrieved the skin as a memento of their daring adventure. Their mischief was physical and sometimes downright dangerous. Julia and Babe sent for a mail-order blank cartridge gun under the name of Babe's older brother. When their parents were away, they fired the gun from the roof, or dropped rocks on the Santa Fe passenger train from Columbia Street, sneaked rides on streetcars, milk wagons, and trucks, played telephone tricks, and hung around with the tramps at the railroad tracks. Julia got caught in the chimney of a house under construction and they had to break parts of the chimney to free her, according to Babe. She climbed too high into a cave in the Arroyo Seco and had to be rescued. When she cut off the long braids of Beatrice Freeman, the pastor's daughter, Beatrice's family temporarily forbade them to play together. They collected broken polo mallets at Midwick and played polo on their bicycles (they were adept at replacing the spokes in their bikes). Her brother John remembers Julia placing a bag inside a Robinson department store package, placing it in the middle of the street, and running a string from the package to the other side of the hedge between the McWilliams property and the street. The streets were paved, but the cars, slow-moving, were few. Cars would stop to examine the package and just as they reached for it, Julia would yank the string.

Twelve months a year Julia and Babe played outside. Bicycles and roller skates (key always worn on a string around the neck) were their mobility and freedom from parental supervision. Every Christmas brought a new pair of skates and the wheels of the old were promptly attached to a coaster and box; if you were really daring you went down the hill on Arbor Street. Pasadena had long been hospitable to the bicycle, having planned at the turn of the century to build an elevated bike road into Los Angeles (only 1.4 miles of it was completed). And every New Year's Day they hung around the preparations for the Tournament of Roses on Orange Grove Boulevard just a block away.

The physicality of Julia's childhood centered on her hands, on action, tactile contact, physical results, and sensual pleasures. She was a physical and social being. She grew up into a mighty oak, like the one in Mrs. Greble's yard, but also grew deep into the earth. She was what is called an "extrovert . . . fond of movement, recreation, change," a girl "marked by activity, vivacity, quickness, and opportuneness rather than by persistence and consistency."

Summer Travel

The McWilliamses, as their parents before them, enjoyed travel and passed this adventurousness on to Julia. "They took us on some wonderful trips," said John, nearby to Mount Lowe, Squirrel Inn at Lake Arrowhead, Palm Springs, La Jolla, and Mount Whitney in the High Sierra.

The more extensive trips sometimes involved business travel back to Arkansas, when their father often took one of the children with him for his annual inspection of the rice land. Julia ate delicious squirrel on one of these trips, she said. The land lay east of De Witt, where the Arkansas and White rivers came together, their father calling it "the Old Home Place." They visited his childhood home in Odell (it had become a gasoline station), and visited relatives in Dwight, Illinois, as well as Dalton, Massachusetts. One summer Caro took her family to a dude ranch in Wyoming for a reunion with members of the Weston family from all over the country. Her mother organized horseback riding, setting up Indian tents, and canoeing, and, according to Julia, wore a riding jacket and handsome laced-up boots. It was a memorable trip for Julia, who was impressed more by their Weston connections than by the McWilliams tribe, who were familiar.

City women took their children away to the sea for the summer, with husbands joining them each weekend when possible. Thus California beaches, along with well-patched inner tubes, weekend fathers, and sunburns, were a large part of every child's summer. After one summer in Santa Monica, Caro settled on the Santa Barbara area, where she and John had courted in 1905 (according to her diary) and where so many Pasadena families lived. The McWilliamses drove in their touring car from Pasadena to Montecito Park, adjacent to Santa Barbara, where Julia learned to swim in the city swimming pool ("I can still remember the wet swimming pool smell").

They rented an old gray-shingled house in a circle of homes built around a green lawn and surrounded by bamboo groves (in 1927 the homes would be moved to make way for the Biltmore Hotel). They took the maid, the nurse, and Eric the Red: "When we went out to eat there on Sunday noon, we ate at the Miramar Hotel in a big circular dining room. I was fascinated by the fact that they served sherbet in the middle of the meal. We used to go swimming there; Mother wore a black swimming costume and black stockings. She was well covered up."

There was "quite a nice beach there until they built the marina in Santa Barbara. It changed the entire coastline." Eric the Red would romp on the beach with the children. As far as Julia was concerned, she wrote in a letter to Babe, "just about all the people in this park are sissys." It was not long before Julia discovered she could make a pipe with the local bamboo and smoke corn silk. While the mothers chatted on the beach, the children ran about, inventing fantasies of smugglers arriving on the shore at night; when a ship wrecked at Point Magu and they saw a Chinaman washed up onshore, it confirmed their sea and piracy fantasies.

Julia attended Camp Asoleado the summer of 1921 before entering the Polytechnic School. Because it was at Hope Ranch (where her mother took her first fully straddled horseback ride in 1905) on the mesa just north of downtown Santa Barbara, her parents were not far away. She was certain "they were glad to be rid of me." The camp was run by "Aunt Sally" Leadbetter, to whom Julia ran for help one day when an older girl told a younger group of them about this "terrible thing" that happened when you got blood in your pants. The girls were horrified to hear about "the curse," but eventually during the following summer camp it came to them all. "My mother may have told me, but it did not make any sense until I heard it at camp. I don't know when I learned everything else. I guess I gradually learned the rest."

Calling menstruation a "curse" had as much to do with the physical trauma of bleeding as it did with the pre-Kotex ritual of belt, pins, and cloth-wrapped cotton, which had to be unwrapped and hand-washed.

At Camp Asoleado, the girls wore knee socks and elastic-bottomed pants above the knee. For three years Julia attended this camp with her cousin Dana, the daughter of her father's sister Annie McWilliams Gans, from Hagerstown, Maryland. Also at the camp was "sweet and pretty" little ten-year-old Barbara Hutton, who had to do KP duty, according to Mary Stuart and Dana Parker. Later Julia would reminisce: "The camp was owned by two women who were very good cooks. Every Sunday there was a pancake race to see how many we could eat. That was before the days when everything was restricted."

Julia had other cousins who lived in Santa Barbara, for her father had a second sister, Elizabeth McWilliams Patterson. Aunt Bessie's two daughters, Harriet (who had the Dana dark skin and would marry Noble Cathcart) and Patsy (with blond hair and Celtic skin), were around Julia's age. She adored her older cousin Harriet, who taught her to sew: "Harriet taught me how to fix my nails. That was very important." Harriet was an older, well-dressed role model for Julia. Aunt Bessie, who terrified Julia when she was very young ("she was not a loving person"), would spend the last years of her life in the El Encanto Hotel, in the hills of Santa Barbara.

During the school year, Grandfather McWilliams presided at the head of the long table every Sunday afternoon. He usually finished saying grace at about one o'clock. His eyes looked up from behind his wire-rimmed glasses. Despite his ninety years, he sat erect, his gray beard riding high above the suit and vest he wore to the Presbyterian church that morning. As if by magic, his butler, Richard Thompson, appeared, invisibly summoned by the small button John McWilliams, Sr., pressed under the table, carrying the primary dish of the meal, a large leg of lamb, roasted to the color of a gray headstone. Mint jelly glistened in an elegant cut-glass bowl nearby. Other Heinz condiments, offered in family crystal, were symbols of the wealth, progress, and modernity of the McWilliams family. Though the avocados and oranges were ripening on the trees outside the window, there was little smell of the earth on their plates.

The three grandchildren, who until a certain age ate their evening meals with the cook and butler, always attended Sunday midday dinner, which alternated weekly between their parents' house and their grandparents' house. One Sunday at the senior family home, the clan was expanded by McWilliams relatives from Illinois. The talk over dinner began with the coming Jack Dempsey fight and President Harding's signing of the formal peace with Germany. But the presence of William McCarty, the bugler in Grandfather's Civil War company, ignited the old man's memories of the war and Sherman's march to the sea. Young Julia had just finished the third grade and could not wait to conclude the lengthy ceremonial meal. Nearly nine years old and already a head taller than her playmates, she ate rapidly, paying scant heed to the gray lamb, white potatoes, turnips, and carrots; she could hardly wait until she was playing with her best friend, Babe, and planning their summer camp. She preferred her company to that of her cousins, and the warm outdoors to the dining room or kitchen.

Restless though she was, Julia and her sister and brother continued to observe the family customs of saying grace, learning kinship obligations, and listening to her grandfather's stories of courage and adventure. As in most families, the McWilliams's culture was transmitted largely around the table, and her patriarchal grandparent was omnipresent. He would die in the fall of 1924 at his office, with his boots on, so to speak, leaving what the local newspapers called a "frontier legacy."

Chapter 3

$\mathcal{E}$DUCATION OF AN EXTROVERT
(1921 – 1930)

"Why languish as a giantess when it is
so much fun to be a myth?"

JULIA CHILD

JULIA JUMPED on her bicycle and came to the back door of the Halls' house, as she would every school day morning for six years to pick up Charlie. The two nine-year-olds rode up the street and turned right onto Glenarm Street, which took them across Fair Oaks and Los Robles to Oak Knoll Circle and Arden Road to "Poly."

$\mathcal{P}_{OLY}$

The Polytechnic School, which Julia attended from the fourth through the ninth grade, was on the south side of California Boulevard, opposite the California Institute of Technology (Caltech). There were no streetlights and few stops signs then. Once they "hooked" a ride home on the back of the bus that ran down Los Robles to Glenarm, says Charlie Hall, then west to South Orange Grove and South Pasadena avenues. Suddenly a loud explosion of the engine and a cloud of black smoke frightened them silly. The bus driver had cured their hooking by dangerously backfiring the bus. John remembers that they then hooked trucks, which moved slower. After school they would ride horses, play kick the can, croquet, or tennis. The Halls' Welsh terrier, Gyp, retrieved their tennis balls. There were so many dogs on their street that there was a major dogfight at least once a week. On rainy days, they would set up the curtains and footlights in the big attic.

Poly, which eventually expanded to ten acres, was a typical California school with numerous accesses and covered outdoor corridors in its single-level, H-shaped frame. It was atypical in the beauty of its campus: large oak trees lay beyond the tennis court, and there were acres of green grass. Julia would remember few of her teachers except for one in English, "one of those inspiring teachers; we loved her." There was a young, slender brunet French teacher, and Miss Grace Henley was the headmistress from 1915 to 1946 of this private school, which eventually added grades through twelve.

After school the children rode their bikes down to a sandy, desolate area of the Arroyo Seco to watch the construction of a stadium out of what was once a dump. The big scooping machine dug out a "bowl" (actually a horse-shoe-shaped hole) and loaded tons of dirt onto horse-drawn wagons. By October 28, 1922, the first unofficial football game of this "Rose Bowl" stadium was played by the University of Southern California Trojans and the University of California (Berkeley) Golden Bears.

That summer the McWilliamses were again at 9 Montecito Park when Julia wrote letters to Babe, whose family visited relatives in Maine every other summer. The McWilliamses also traveled this year to the East Coast for a lengthy trip that included the Yale-Harvard boat race (in her letters to Babe, she was more impressed by the drunken fans) and a visit with Aunt Annie's family in Hagerstown, Maryland. Letters to Babe were signed "Yours till Ivory soap sinks."

Not only a creative prankster, Julia was considered a great athlete—more because of her height and strength than her dexterity, it turns out, as one classmate remembers Julia tripping over things. She was a gifted scene stealer, acting in plays through grade school, high school, and college, always playing the emperor or the lion, never the princess. As a popular member of the class, she participated in everything, including entering their dog Eric the Red every year in the pet show. "He never won anything," she claims.

Julia later confessed to her diary that she believed she was "like no one else," the possessor of "unique spiritual gifts" and "meant for something" special. Her sense of being "unique" stemmed in part from being the first-born, in part from her height, and to a large measure from her mother's approval. She had the firstborn's presumed dominant position, but rather than be her parents' lieutenant, as are most firstborn children, she was the instigator of mischief. The firstborn's conscientiousness (expressed in responsibility, organization, and drive for achievement) would kick in later in life. She was assertive and verbal; she looked down physically as well on her two siblings and her classmates: "I was always one size bigger than you could ever buy. And why languish as a giantess when it is so much fun to be a myth?"

The neighborhood gang remained strong, enjoying weekends up at the Halls' two cabins (one for boys, one for girls) two and a half miles above Sierra Madre in Santa Anita Canyon. They had no running water, and took their food and supplies up the hill on a donkey from Sierra Madre station. After unloading it, they turned the donkey loose and it returned to the station. They embraced the adventure.

The mountains also offered a popular resort in those days: both families took the funicular railway up to the train to Mount Lowe, next to Mount Wilson. The Halls pooled their Christmas money for a stay in the hotel up there. Although Julia does not remember their mother pouring maple sugar on the snow to share one of her New England experiences with them, her siblings do.

Julia paid little attention to religion until it started to become an irritation, particularly long sermons. Caro and John McWilliams were "churched out" and attended infrequently and then at the nondenominational Neighborhood Church, which no longer exists. This lack of interest in religion was probably strongest on the Weston side, for a reading of Caro's mother's diary at the turn of the century reveals that her illnesses usually coincided with the all-day church services in Pittsfield, Massachusetts. Grandfather McWilliams, on the other hand, was a serious churchgoer who took his grandchildren to the Pasadena Presbyterian Church. The Reverend Dr. Robert Freeman, the city's most prominent minister, who served on the board of directors of nearby Occidental College (which the three Hall children would attend), ran the most child-friendly church in town (though the children complained about the length of his prayers). The skating rink, the dinners at the community center at the church, and playing with the Freeman children, especially after the McWilliamses moved to a home at 625 Magnolia, near her grandparents, were treasured activities in Julia's life. Later, when the children walked to church on their own, they took the dime for the offering and often never made it as far as the church, according to sister Dort.

It was in November 1924, when she was in the seventh grade at Poly, that twelve-year-old Julia experienced her first family grief. Her grandfather, driven every morning to the office by his chauffeur, died at his desk. Her parents had taken Grandmother McWilliams to Hawaii (with their Aunt Annie), so the chauffeur drove to the house to tell the McWilliams children of their grandfather's death. The children would long miss this imperious grand-parent, remembering his false teeth and Smith Bros. cough drops, which he always kept on the top of his grandfather's clock.

After grieving at his father's death, John experienced a sense of freedom in making his own professional decisions. He moved to a new office at Union Street and Fair Oaks Avenue, expanding his business connections into down-town Los Angeles. Caro McWilliams also traveled more to Los Angeles, taking the streetcar (there was no Pasadena Freeway until 1930) down Orange Grove, past the ostrich farm on Huntington Drive to the city, where she bought her clothes from East Coast clothing representatives (De Pinna and Brooks) who set up their exhibits in the hotels there. Julia loved to accompany her mother into Los Angeles, especially to the Biltmore Hotel: "My mother would take us to lunch. We loved the Biltmore because it had revolving doors. Los Angeles was so exciting in the twenties." If her mother was indulgent and unquestioningly affirming, their father was a stern disciplinarian. He emulated his own father's strict demeanor. According to Dorothy: "My father was too hard on Julia because she was the oldest. He could be very intimidating!"

When Julia was thirteen and in the eighth grade in 1925, the Pasadena Community Playhouse was built on Fair Oaks Avenue and became an integral part of city life. Charlie Hall was involved in running the lights, and Julia was captivated by the new theater. The Halls and the McWilliamses also listened to the radio on Sunday nights to hear the charismatic preacher Aimee Semple McPherson. "Mother needs a new coat, everybody be generous . . . I do not want to hear the sound of money [coins]," she declared from her Angelus Temple in nearby Echo Park. Anna Pavlova gave a dance performance in a local auditorium, and musicals were popular—*Desert Song, Hit the Deck, Indian Love Call,* and *The Student Prince.* Julia shared her mother's interest in films (called "photoplays" in the newspapers) starring Fatty Arbuckle, Charlie Chaplin, and Mary Pickford, and showing at the Strand. There were lectures at the Shakespeare Club, where Julia's and Babe's mothers sent the girls to the Little Artist Series each Saturday morning for lectures on painters, artists, and musicians.

Julia's height and her voice kept everyone from suggesting that she fol-low a theatrical career, though in fact she eventually became a star. She spoke in a standard youthful California manner, but she had an expressive voice like her mother and sister, resonating less from her chest than her head. A high-pitched, breathy sound drew Julia's vowels up and down a musical scale in such a way that her sentences turned into arias. When she was excited, her voice sounded like a honking falsetto. When she was ecstatic, her voice might chortle, guffaw, crack, or half yodel.

For two summers Julia went camping at Lake Tahoe in the High Sierra, at a summer camp for girls. It was on the north shore near Kings Beach (the boys' camp was near Ponderosa) and had horses, which the girls learned to take care of, boats on the lake, and tents with wooden floors. The two women who ran the camp strove to give the girls self-confidence and survival skills; they were "strong," said Eleanor Roberts; Babe believed their name, Bosse, was appropriate. Julia thrived. She packed in with mules, fished, rode, and swam several times a day (they learned the Red Cross swimming program). Babe, who attended one summer, wrote home to her mother: "Juke went up to Watson Lake and went in swimming in her B.V.D's. Miss Fuller asked Miss Cherry what she considered swimming and Cherry said 'up to the neck' and seeing Juke had only been in up to her waist she wasn't punished." The second summer, Eleanor Roberts (who would later serve as West Coast representative of *Vogue* magazine) told Julia that she looked like a taller, skinnier version of the leading movie star, Mae Murray *(To Have and to Have Not,* 1919), a flapper with short, curly hair: "Jukie had a slender nose and beautiful silhouette. She was not a big, gawky girl, but a real beauty."

One of the big events in Julia's life in 1925 was the earthquake in Santa Barbara, which registered 6.3, damaging buildings in Pasadena and taking her father away to numerous meetings of the hospital board. Eventually a new hospital was built with money from the family of Mr. Henry E. Huntington and the following year, in January, Pasadena had a new city hall. It was the same year that the McWilliams family listened to the first radio broadcast of the Los Angeles Symphony. Julia was more excited about the flooding of the Arroyo Seco gorge on Easter Sunday. She and the gang rode their bicycles past the Craftsman homes and down into the gorge to check on the damage to their favorite cave.

Sports strengthened Julia's body and helped her overcome some of the awkwardness of her ungainly height. One boy in her class said that she once walked into a classroom with a tiny rise at the door and fell flat on her face. She was lovely, but not "pretty," which then as now meant petite and feminine. Mary Kay Burnam was the "pretty" girl in the class and Bill Lisle was smitten. The boys were reading *Penrod and Sam* by Booth Tarkington and beginning to notice the girls. Betty Parker was becoming more of what she called a "society girl" and interested in boys, while Julia remained the gamine. Her appetite for food and physical exercise was larger than life.

Dancing class was one of those stomach-churning social necessities in Julia's youthful circle. Beginning in the fourth grade, the children took dancing lessons from Mrs. Travis, who conducted them in the Vista del Arroyo Hotel and then at the Shakespeare Clubhouse: "As I recall, neither Julia nor I was very good," wrote Joseph Sloane, an art history professor whose father had graduated from Princeton with Mr. McWilliams. Robert P. Hastings, who would found a distinguished international law firm in Los Angeles, remembers hiding from the dancing classes and the girls in the men's room. Charlie Hall, who said they started in the third grade and went through high school, claims the classes were really about manners, not dancing. The boys had to wear white gloves, and everyone had to wear patent-leather shoes. Bill Lisle, the class president, believed that if his grandmother bought him black patent-leather shoes he would automatically know how to dance. Short for his age then, he still shrinks at the thought of the McWilliamses hosting the eighth-grade dance in their home and his mistake of catching Julia's eye and having to dance with her: "She blocked out the light. I came to her bosom. She was a fine girl."

Julia was a tomboy who loved the rough-and-tumble life and competing with the boys in sports. There were only two drawbacks to this active life: she was not considered feminine (a fact that did not seem to bother her) and she tore the lunar cartilage of her knee, which would bother her occasionally the remainder of her life. "Julia McWilliams and Peggy Winter could throw our softball overhand as hard as the boys did," said classmate Betty Parker (now Mrs. Elizabeth Kase). "Peggy's mother ran the tearoom at the Pasadena Play-house, and Julia and Peggy were tomboys, more boy than girl," she added, reflecting the gender distinctions of her era. Indeed, Julia devoted much of the first three decades of her life to hiking, hunting, swimming, playing golf and tennis. Not surprising then that when Julia was twelve years old, a study by Professor Horace Gray in the *Journal of the American Medical Association* showed that the daughters of the graduates of Vassar, Wellesley, and Mount Holyoke were found to be one inch taller than their mothers; young Julia was four years away from college and already moving well beyond her mother's height.

Because her mother did not herself perform domestic chores, Julia was not drawn to the kitchen or sewing room. Interestingly enough, though her mother subscribed to popular women's magazines with articles and advertise-ments focusing on domestic preoccupations, one of the major story formulas (or subgenres) of the fiction in these magazines (*The Ladies' Home Journal, McCall's, Woman's Home Companion*) was the "New Women success story." According to Maureen Honey's *Breaking the Ties That Bind: Popular Stories of the New Woman, 1915–1930,* the women portrayed in these stories published during the first fifteen years of Julia McWilliams's life were sporty, outspoken, and independent ("Give up my job? My job? Oh, my dear man! Go chase yourself"). The dialogue was quaint and the stories were resolved by the man's coming around, but the heroines were closer to the life that Julia would find for herself. Both Julia and the region in which she lived had greater promise than anyone foresaw.

The 1920s in Los Angeles would be characterized by historians as a decade that idealized business and bred speculation, corruption (in the booming petroleum development), absence of government regulation, and a building boom in a city growing to over a million inhabitants. It was a city of boosters, and John McWilliams was one of them. The speculators built a harbor in San Pedro, took water from the Owens Valley, built grand city halls (in both Pasadena and Los Angeles), and nourished a new industry that would define the city called Hollywood.

Prohibition made lawbreakers of the best citizens and Tijuana into a flourishing restaurant and drinking destination. "One of my earliest remembrances of restaurant life was going to Tijuana in 1925 or 1926 with my parents, who were wildly excited that they should finally lunch at Caesar's restaurant," wrote Julia. Caesar Cardini had invented the Caesar salad in a day before refrigerated trains, when "salads were considered rather exotic," she adds. "I can see him break two eggs over that romaine and roll them in, the greens going all creamy as the eggs flowed over them. . . . It was a sensation of a salad from coast to coast." Fifty years later in *From Julia Child's Kitchen,* she would tell this story and give the recipe, including the fresh Parmesan and oil-basted croutons, after a long talk with Caesar's daughter, Rosa.

In June 1927, fourteen-year-old Julia graduated from Poly's ninth grade with six boys and twelve girls. Her brother, John, who should have been two years behind her, was held back, according to the family, because he had dyslexia (then an undiagnosed reading disorder), though his letters do not demonstrate this. Julia's mother, who was helping Julia plan a move to a private girls' school to complete her high school years, was increasingly suffering from high blood pressure and related illnesses. Though she had trouble sleeping and some nights slept in three different beds, according to her son, she "was always cheerful in the morning." Her children did not realize that her health was failing her.

Julia was poised for new adventure. She had physical daring, mental curiosity, and a need to push boundaries. Though her mental outlook lacked depth, she was intelligent and adaptable. She had no deep personal convictions, but cried easily, was friendly, approachable, positive, and related directly to others and to outward experience. She seemed to feel more than she thought.

THE KATHARINE BRANSON SCHOOL: AN ENCLOSED GARDEN

The white ferryboat rolled across the blue of San Francisco Bay in the September sun. With no bridge from San Francisco to the upper peninsula, the water leg of Julia's trip to boarding school took her to the city of Ross in Marin County. From the boat the bare hills looked like the backs of gray elephants in sharp contrast to the water of the bay. The brief trip inland was over land where once the bay lapped up, close to the College of Marin. Ross was a 60 percent Republican town nestled against the wooded foothills of Mount Tamalpais State Park. Julia and her cousin Dana rode past stables and elegant homes; when they turned from Shady Lane onto Fernhill Road, they looked up and saw 2,600-foot Mount Tamalpais to the south.

Passing under the high Spanish gates of the Katharine Branson School for Girls, they felt the cool, damp feeling of woods. Ahead rose the natural feature of the campus, a giant cedar tree. Beside it was the original house of the Martin estate—a building housing the residence, dining hall, and library. It set the architectural style of campus with its Mission style: cream and red colors, stucco, red tile, and wide veranda.

Here, on a woodsy hillside in Northern California, in a school even smaller than Poly, Julia would spend three years in a class of sixteen, the largest to date, which included ten boarders and six day girls. She would develop leadership skills to be used throughout her life. "She took responsibility, but not solemnly," said classmate Mary Zook, the daughter of a superior court justice and founder of the school. In a prefiguring of her role in the cooking world, Julia would become "head girl," the leader of the pack and instigator of activity. "She is much beloved," recorded Miss Branson two years later. But it was her commanding physical presence, her verbal openness, and her physical pranks and adventure that made her "head girl."

The Katharine Branson School was a private, rural preparatory girls' school named since 1920 for its headmistress. It was located on the former estate and dairy farm of John Martin, acquired in 1922. The lower grades were slowly being eliminated, and the only boarders were at the high school level. It cost John McWilliams $1,500 a year to send his oldest child here, but some of her Poly classmates had been sent to far more expensive private schools around the country. The cost guaranteed a quality education and, inevitably, a certain homogeneity. Julia moved into one of the two houses—called Circle Cottage—used as a spillover from the main residence, with her cousin Dana and a roommate. The cottage was characterized by a front gable that rose to what looked like a witch's hat.

Julia's course of study was simple and basic: yearlong courses in English, French, Latin, and mathematics. This was a preparatory school for college, not a "finishing" school stressing "character and poise." At graduation she would have three years of English, three years of French, three years of Latin (one year devoted to Virgil), and three years of algebra, plane geometry, and physics. The only other courses she took were in ancient and American history. The program could not have been more traditional, for it reflected Miss Branson's Bryn Mawr degree and her close association with the Seven Sisters colleges. Miss Branson scorned vocational training, which had swept the country since 1917, when the Smith-Hughes Act was passed. No cooking or sewing classes at KBS.

All the teachers were women, with Miss Branson as the formidable and intimidating headmistress, who taught Latin. Her ancestry was English, Welsh, and Scot. She was called a "patrician with humor and gentle wit," whose Keatsian motto was "Beauty is truth, truth beauty." The girls never felt they measured up to her high idealism—until they took national tests. She was severe-looking and high-minded. Julia remembers her "enormous blue eyes," probably because they were often trained on her. Miss Branson "enjoyed a good laugh," explained Clara Rideout, who remembers that Miss Branson's "favorite" girls were "very naughty and prankish, and rather quirkish girls, but bright." Another student, Roxane Ruhl, Julia's classmate from Oregon, said, "I remember her often smiling with amusement at Julia."

Julia herself was attracted to strong and independent girls, as she had been to Babe. One girl, Berry Baldwin, was a classmate who lived almost across the street from the school in her grandfather's house, where her uncle served as her guardian. "Berry was a wonderful crazy individual," said her classmate Aileen Johnson. Some days, after school, Julia would visit Berry and they would make themselves martinis from her uncle's liquor supply.

In addition to Miss Branson, Miss Martha Howe, the English teacher, was an influential adult in Julia's high school education, as she was for most of the students. When Howie, as Julia called her behind her back, repeated yesterday's lesson, the girls did not once giggle, out of respect and fear. Howie was small and strict and "very forceful . . . she was a terrier nipping at your heels," said Clara Rideout. The material that appeared in *The Blue Print,* the literary annual (there was no school paper or yearbook), is testimony to her high standards.

Julia's essay in *The Blue Print* her senior year is a model of essay form, complex sentence structure, and articulate expression. In "A True Confession," she admits "I am like a cloud." With a passing reference to William Wordsworth, she attributes her childhood tearfulness to "weak tear glands," and thus "mechanical" tears: "So think of me, if you must, as a pregnant rain-cloud, a weak-glanded maiden with hot tears laden; but bear in mind always that an X-ray would show my heart to be no softer than a rock!"

Her junior short story the year before appeared in *The Blue Print* and was entitled "A Woman of Affairs." In it she captures her sense of unease riding on a public train by herself and her desire to appear sophisticated and a woman of the world in the train's dining car. "The idea of going down [to the dining car] alone was not at all unpleasant to me, it gave me a sense of proprietorship over my soul." Economizing by ordering only a salad, she politely takes a small helping from a bowl "as big as a bathtub." Suddenly the waiter sweeps the bowl away and she is left with an inadequate meal and only a few cents for a tip. A series of other stumbles ensues, yet she forges ahead. The story is based on her train trips from Pasadena to San Francisco, where the chaperone always met the KBS girls and took them to the ferry.

She would call on these writing techniques in her future career. Fortuitously, she studied French; surprisingly, she did not do very well. This was not French taught in the language as much as the study of verb forms (explained in English), vocabulary tests, and reciting French sentences. The first year Mademoiselle Begue recorded that Julia's pronunciation was "not as true" as it should be: "explosive consonants attributed to Scotch ancestry!" The second year Mademoiselle Liardet recorded an "inability to detect shades of sound in French." And Miss van Vliet later said that her "grammatical and inflectional vagaries are constant and alarming!" The final record says she was musical but had no ear for French: "Oral is insurmountable." One day she would correct these French "vagaries" on site.

In another example of failed prophecy, Julia's science teacher recorded that with her "considerable energy, the study of medicine would be a good outlet. She wants to be a doctor or chemist." Not surprisingly, her teachers noted that she "reads detective and adventure stories; likes poetry if it tells a story; loves outdoor activities . . . has a good sense of humor; shows initiative and shows auto-criticism; practical; wholesome type of girl with superior intelligence."

Standing on the wide veranda of the central building, Julia could look through the portals and down the green hillside, past the archery tree, to see the playing fields of KBS. Here the learning that occurred outside the basic core courses—learning that years later would become institutional credits for athletics and arts—filled their spare time. A barnlike gymnasium was built her first year there, a soccer field lay beside Blue Tam Creek, and the two tennis courts, outdoor basketball court, and small baseball field were surrounded by the noisy stream and shady oak trees. Beyond the swimming pool on the right, nestled in a curve of the stream, were two classroom buildings: Oaks, devoted to languages and history, and Stairways, housing English and science. Barbara Ord, another daughter of a founding family, liked the "noisy" and "outgoing" Juke and once saved her from drowning in the swimming pool, she claims.

Though it seems ironic that Miss Branson was an avid follower of John Dewey—considering the elitist approach of her school—she was a pragmatic administrator, even in her enforced religious ceremonies. Julia's parents' casual attitude toward church attendance helped to prejudice Julia's views of religion at KBS, where boarders said grace before meals and had Vespers with group singing every Sunday night. Each girl was required to bring a Bible to school with her. Because "courtesy, Christianity, and college" were treasured goals at KBS, every boarder was expected to attend church on Sunday morning. "The school was a bastion of racial and religious purity," says the school's historian. Except for a rare Catholic girl (the only minority allowed in the school) who walked to Mass, all the girls lined up in two rows and walked to the end of the street to St. John's Episcopal Church. "I hated having to go to church," says Julia. "One time we revolted by wearing our cloche hats backward; we thought it was terribly funny, but no one noticed." This required attendance and the long sermons turned her against all religious sects. However, she would still, even in 1953, cling to what she called "the nut of Christianity (Love the Lord thy God, with all thy heart, and with all thy soul, and with all thy mind . . . [and] thy neighbor as thyself)."

Branson was also influenced by the Child Study Movement, which began in the late nineteenth century and emphasized the teaching power of nature. Its patriarch, Stanley Hall, believed that adolescence was its own separate world, and guardians "should strive . . . to keep out of nature's way." The beautiful garden that was KBS, says its historian Mark Baur, was "ideal" for this romantic naturalism, for it was "enclosed, sprayed, and weeded . . . [but] at the same time healthy and natural."

Beyond the classrooms were sports for every season, required athletic training (only riding, tennis, and dancing lessons were optional), an annual drama staged on the lawn, and afternoon international current events lectures (on days when there were no organized athletics). On one of their trips to San Francisco by ferry from Sausalito, the girls heard ten-year-old violinist prodigy Yehudi Menuhin play with the symphony. Art and music appreciation (noncredit) classes supplemented the recitals, concerts, and crafts. It was a verdant, nurturing world that one girl described years later as a protective ivory tower and the school's historian called "a Garden Enclosed." Yet, coming back from a San Francisco trip, the girls were grousing together when one of the chaperones said, "These are the happiest years of your lives!" The girls looked at her in stunned silence.

————

MURDER IN PASADENA'S Stevens family brought a loss of innocence for Julia and her friends at the end of her first semester at KBS. The incident occurred in early December when one of John McWilliams's best friends killed his two sons and then committed suicide. It rocked the community and shook the children, who were playmates and classmates of the Stevens children. Their daughter, Julia's close friend and a senior at Westridge with Babe, survived, along with her mother.

The murders and suicide made the front pages of the Pasadena papers because fifty-one-year-old Francis Everett Stevens was a lawyer, founder of the North American Life Insurance Company, and vice president of the First National Bank and the First Trust and Savings Bank. He left the bank one morning and picked up his thirteen-year-old son, George (whom the papers called "subnormal"), at his elementary school, shot him in the head, and placed him under a blanket on the floor of the back of his sedan; at the Los Encinas sanitarium, he locked the car, threw sand on the gas tank where blood was beginning to drip, and asked for his twenty-year-old son, Francis, who was being treated in long-term care after a head injury suffered in a car accident at the University of Michigan. The father placed a packet of papers on the desk at the sanitarium and went for a walk with his son to the tennis court, where he shot young Francis in the temple, then put the gun in his own mouth. Two hours later, after breaking the car window, the police found the body of George.

Among the papers in the packet of stocks, bonds, and a will was a letter to John McWilliams, his close friend. The Stevenses had bought the McWilliamses' home on State Street and the children had grown up together. Betty Stevens called Caro to come over. The McWilliamses were prostrate with grief; the entire community was stunned. The two newspapers treated the deaths, with front-page analysis, as a story of "Father Love: Tragic Fate Overtakes Three." They portrayed "the love of a father who gave his own life to prevent his only two sons from becoming a helpless burden upon society, a curse for themselves," or as "high moral conviction that his duty lay in saving his sons from impending insanity." After the private funeral, one newspaper invoked Stevens's strong will and called the murder story "pitiable, but almost sublime."

Dinner conversations at the McWilliams table included talk about inherited family mental illness, bank problems, heart troubles. Franker conversations went on across the street about the mental problems of both boys (George had once been in Charlie's class), and the Halls told their children that it was a sex-linked mental deficiency in the family. Jim Bishop, who attended the Webb School with George, declared that George was expelled for homosexuality. Betty Parker believed he was just "weird and retarded." Had the word "homosexuality" been mentioned in the home of most of the children, they would not have known what it meant. Though the McWilliams children were protected from some of the lurid details, they nevertheless struggled with the tragedy that befell their friends. Julia would later write a play about it for her college playwriting class.

Since the death of Julia's grandfather in 1924, her father was free to be his own businessman (when his own son came of age, he would compensate by keeping his hands off his son's career to the point, his sisters felt, of neglect). When Julia graduated from Poly, her father joined the prestigious California Club in downtown Los Angeles, where he often lunched. For a week each summer he would romp in the woods of Northern California with the Bohemian Club. By the end of the 1930s, John McWilliams was often in downtown Los Angeles in his capacity as vice president of the J. G. Boswell Company, which owned 20,000 acres of farmland in Kings County, where it raised stock, grain, and cotton. He knew the central regions of California like the back of his hand and was a natural consultant for the giant company. He was instrumental in their developing the Buena Vista Lake property.

Julia's father had long been a friend of the Boswell brothers in Pasadena, especially Jim Boswell, because they both had land in Kern County. When their father began working for Jim Boswell about 1940, all the McWilliams children knew was that their father was some kind of consultant for Boswell, a shrewd businessman with a strong Southern accent. How much this work contributed to their sizable family inheritance they are uncertain. Colonel James G. Boswell was the largest cotton grower in the world. He was driven out of Georgia by the boll weevil and settled in California to become one of the most powerful farmers in the state and marry Ruth Chandler, the daughter of land baron and *Los Angeles Times* publisher Harry Chandler. The Boswell empire, run from its downtown Los Angeles headquarters, extended northward and centered in the San Joaquin Valley, the state's most fertile region, where Boswell grew cotton, wheat, and seed alfalfa. Through the end of the century, his company would supply the cotton for Jockey underwear, L. L. Bean shirts, and Fieldcrest towels.

Los Angeles's development was symbolized by the new LA city hall, a twenty-eight-floor building towering over downtown. Construction, which began when Julia was away at school, cost $4.8 million. Her father knew the movers and shakers of America's fastest-growing area. During her holidays at home, Julia continued to visit downtown with her mother and to share Sunday dinner now with Aunt Annie McWilliams Gans, who moved her family from Hagerstown, Maryland, into a home on Euclid in order to care for Julia's grandmother Clara Dana McWilliams. Cousins Alice and Dana became a steady presence in Julia's life.

The summer before Julia's senior year, Caro suffered a stroke in Santa Barbara, after which one side of her face permanently sagged. She took to bed increasingly with the Weston curse: high blood pressure. Dorothy, five years younger than Julia and not yet a teenager, felt forsaken by her mother. Caro, as her own mother before her, would inevitably abandon her chicks, a painful reality for a woman who, in Julia's words, "loved being a mother. She was a great deal of fun . . . [and] so devoted a mother."

———

FROM THE FIRST to the last day at KBS, Jukie was immensely popular. She was never interested in domesticity or food, except when hungry, and she was often hungry. Despite her "love of jelly donuts," she remained as lean and tall as an adolescent boy. From today's perspective, she looked like a fashion model.

The school uniform was becoming on her, especially the blue-and-white-plaid winter skirt (with white blouse). She was hipless, so the skirts gave her a certain fullness. No one looked particularly fetching in the blue-and-white-checked gingham summer dresses (dresses whose length rose and fell according to the current style of each decade over fifty years). The blue crepe de chine dresses with Peter Pan collars that the boarders wore for dinner were no more appealing. French blue was Miss Branson's (and Julia's) favorite color. Only through scarves, belts, and socks could the girls express any individuality. Julia had an advantage: her height. Her friend Roxane gives the best description of Julia at this time:

> She was . . . gangly, a little awkward, standing tall but stooping slightly to look benignly down on the rest of us. She was serious about life, but had a unique way of seeing the humor in incidents, and expressing it in her deep, rather thick manner of speaking. She wasn't trying to be funny. In fact she was very modest and unassuming, totally lacking in exhibitionism. She was just reacting naturally to a situation. . . . What she

was thinking, she said, and it was usually very apt. And often very funny. . . . She wasn't attention-seeking, nor aggressive, nor competitive, nor ambitious. . . . She is just herself. . . . But as I think back, I suppose her complete lack of self-consciousness, her modest natural responsiveness, feeling at home and at ease anywhere, was true of her then and is now, and is the secret to her charm and appeal.

This lack of competitiveness and ambition that her friend observed was evident especially in her classwork. On national intelligence tests her scores were considerably above average. Yet her limited attention span, her undeveloped study skills, and her willingness to settle for merely passing grades led to an average school record. Why she was happy to settle for average grades could be explained in terms of her parents' leniency in expecting high performance or Julia's desire not to stand out (other than physically) in the crowd, but to be liked and accepted as one of the group. One teacher recorded that she earned "good to excellent grades"; another noted that she earned "100 points perfect in school spirit."

During these three high school years, Julia experienced a rigid society for the first time. She was awakened in the morning and sent off to sleep each night by the sound of a bell, and moved through the structure of each day. She rejected the religious aspects, but seemed to enjoy some of the traditions of KBS. She was assigned to the Blue Bonnet team and wore a blue cardigan sweater and beret with her uniform; half the girls were Tam o'Shanters and wore red. These two teams, chosen at registration, played against each other in every sport. When the school basketball team left campus to play in San Francisco or East Bay, they dreaded appearing in their hated "bloomers." The KBS athletic uniform consisted of "dreadful" black satin bloomers bound in by elastic at the knee, white middy blouses, which some girls would starch until the neck bled, a black silk tie, and black cotton stockings inside high white laced sneakers. When they walked onto the court and saw the "cute little uniforms" of the opposing team, said Mary Zook, they felt humiliated. But with Julia as the "jumping center" (the court was divided into three parts), KBS beat Miss Burke's School 58 to 12. Outdressed, but victorious. Viola Tuckerman, who lived in Circle Cottage with Julia, said that Julia, the captain of the team, was one of the most popular girls in the school, with her "great sense of humor and [so] easy going." For Julia, the games were play, not competition (another member of the team remembers Julia never being angry when another girl made a mistake). In fact, she was not a great player, just unbeatable in the jumping circle.

Her personal progress consisted of adapting to the KBS world. "The peculiar nature of the extrovert," says Jung, "is to expand and propagate himself in every way . . . If [one] thinks, feels, acts, and actually lives in a way that is directly correlated with the objective conditions and their demands, [s]he is extroverted." She believed in her group, and they trusted her. At KBS, as in her later life, she would find in community her work and her happiness. Had she done better in French, she would have known that the role she played was as a *boute-en-train*—one who promotes gaiety and joy in others, the life and soul of the party.

The KBS "traditions" that Miss Branson carefully cultivated meant less to Julia as sentimental occurrences than as occasions of frolic. She endured the morning march into assembly for prayer, song, and announcements, but threw herself into other communal activities. She became president of the Vagabonds, a hiking group that once a year, accompanied by Miss Branson, climbed Mount Tam's 2,600-foot peak. There were fall and spring outings to the beaches (Bolinas, Stinson, Newhall) for swimming, marshmallow roasts, and beach parties, a Halloween party, and Field Day at Seminary Field for competing on Mr. Youngman's horses. Before Christmas each girl carried her lighted candle through the orchard and up the hill to carol under the lights of the giant central cedar tree. There was the Senior Dance (canceled her senior year because of a mumps outbreak), for which Miss Branson had to approve each gown, and Play Week, and May Revels, with strings of flowers and a maypole.

Play Week brought all classes to a halt for a week of creative expression and hard work. The play was chosen in early spring, complete with tryouts for the roles, and lines memorized, and a professional drama coach brought in. Everyone served on at least one committee that built sets or wrote programs and invitations, acted or prompted. Because of her height, Julia always played the man or the fish, she remembered, and when as "John Sayle" she had to embrace the leading lady in *Pomander Walk*, everyone got the giggles, until the final performance for trustees and parents. She also starred in *Michael, the Sword Eater* and in *The Piper*. The final plays for the spring of 1930 were *Dickon Goes to the Fair* and *The Admirable Crichton*.

During her senior year, after mumps canceled both the Senior Dance and the spring holiday, Julia took a memorable trip to San Francisco with Roxane Ruhl. When the ferry landed at Fisherman's Wharf, they had artichokes with hollandaise sauce and cinnamon toast oozing in butter. At the City of Paris shop they bought lipstick and Prince Matchabelli perfume ("We thought we were so elegant," she remembers). On Market Street at the army-navy store they bought white sailor pants, a daring adventure in an era when neither girls nor women wore slacks. "We wore them with great glee during vacations," said Roxane. "I suspect the other Branson girls our age were more interested in attracting boys than being like boys."

At her graduation under the cedar tree, Julia garnered all the awards: captain of the Blue Bonnets, captain of the basketball team, Vagabond Chief, member of the track and swimming teams, jumping center, and president of the student council. Not surprisingly she was voted unanimously for the White Beret—the highest honor that can fall to a resident girl. When at graduation they brought out the School Cup for presentation to the "School's First Citizen," no one was surprised when she was called forward. Miss Branson had the last words on record: with her standard of perfection, she thought Julia's academic work was "moderately good," but her "genuineness" was "excellent." Then she listed Julia's assets: "integrity of mind and heart, joyousness of spirit, kindliness, refreshing naiveté, understanding, generosity—a thoroughly lovable and perfectly delightful girl."

Though Babe Hall was convinced that she and Julia were sent to girls' schools so that they would become more feminine, Julia had attended a private liberal arts school because it was a tradition in the Weston family to be sent to boarding schools. She gained self-confidence, learned leadership skills, and was not distracted by the presence of boys. A recent Mount Holyoke College study shows that girls are overlooked and undervalued in most coeducational classes, especially in math and science. Years later, as if to justify her private high school, Julia noted that "girls' academic achievement at fourteen or fifteen drops drastically when they discover boys."

It was not surprising either, in the tradition of her family and the girls of KBS, therefore, that she would plan to attend Smith College, where both her mother and her father's sister Annie were alumnae. Nearly all the KBS girls went to college, either directly or after another year of study or European travel. Julia would go to Smith, Mary Zook would go to Vassar, and Berry Baldwin to Bryn Mawr. Her educational track (two private schools) continued what her future husband would call her smooth move through life under "the protection of her money and position." She was well educated and connected, a young woman confident and comfortable with herself. Julia seemed to know that she could do the work, she just did not value academic achievement. After all, her mother had been center on the Smith College basketball team, and she *was* still Caro's daughter.

$\mathcal{S}$MITH COLLEGE:

IVY WALLS AND JELLY DONUTS

(1930 – 1934)

"The day I was born I was enrolled at Smith College. . . .
If I hadn't gone, it would have broken her heart."

JULIA CHILD

CAROLYN WESTON and Helen Janney were graduates of the class of "naughty-aught" (1900) and determined that their daughters should also go to Smith College and become friends and roommates. "Our mothers arranged our 'marriage,'" said daughter Mary. It was September 1930 when the mothers proudly made the match in a very old house in Northampton.

> In the door came Julia, this tall, very slender, very happy person smiling at me, saying, "I'm Julia McWilliams." I have never had a roommate who was so utterly fun to be with; she was almost too much fun. . . . She was very tall and I was about five feet five inches, and she was very thin, and I was very plump—about 160 pounds, for I had eaten too many hot fudge sundaes.

Despite their differences in academic aspirations and physical appearance, Mary and Julia became fast friends. Mary Case, a serious and idealistic student who would make Phi Beta Kappa, was soon christened "Fatty." Julia, who would minor in academics and major in socializing, was called "Skinny."

Julia made two immediate discoveries: the cot she tried to sleep on the first night was several inches too short and, horror of horrors, her clothes did not conform to the grooming habits of the Northeastern female of Ivy League lineage. The first problem was solved by a telephone call from her mother, says Connie Thayer, one of the other freshman girls on her floor. The new longer bed that the college immediately provided would be hers for the next four years. The second problem took longer to resolve:

> I was a Western girl at Smith and dressed in the Western way; when I got to Smith *everything* was wrong; in those days you had Brooks Brothers crew neck sweaters; pale, pastel tweed skirts from Best & Co. and a camel's hair polo coat fastened up to the neck; brown and white Spaulding saddle shoes; and a strand of five-and-dime pearls. I was miserable until Mother came at Thanksgiving and we went to New York City and bought all these things. Then I fit in. I was in.

What impressed Julia, as it did the other girls who came from small preparatory schools, was the size and freedom of Smith. Founded in 1871 by Sophia Smith to offer to young women a higher education equal to that offered to young men, this Seven Sisters college was opened in Northampton in the Connecticut River valley of western Massachusetts in 1875. Though it was within a twelve-mile radius of Amherst and Mount Holyoke colleges and the future University of Massachusetts, and although it was only eighty miles to Yale, ninety-three miles to Harvard, and 156 miles to Princeton and Columbia—all crucial to the dating practices of the daughters of Smith—it was three thousand miles from Pasadena. And in terms of the life of an eighteen-year-old girl, it might as well have been a million miles from home.

What eased Julia's way into this alien climate was her mother's experience and membership in the club. Julia immediately belonged to the "Granddaughters Club," those whose mothers had attended Smith, and was initiated into her mother's secret society, the Orangemen; Mary was initiated into *her* mother's secret society, the AOH (Ancient Order of Hibernians).

$\mathcal{T}$HE CAMPUS

Julia and her mother had approached the campus from the little town center of Northampton. Driving up the hill, with the ornate campus gate and college administration building ahead of them, they forked left into West Street and immediately entered Green Street, turning right into the campus. Hubbard Hall, built in 1878, was on the left, a three-and-a-half-story brick house with ivy climbing up the side and two chimneys rising high above the attic dormer windows. The house was named after Sophia Smith's lawyer, the college's first treasurer and trustee, but more important to Julia was that Hubbard House was strategically located close to the downtown shopping and the hundred-year-old Rahar House (then a speakeasy) on South Street. Directly across the street from Hubbard was a drugstore and soda fountain, where Mary bought her hot fudge sundaes from Mr. Curly. There, Julia quickly found the best jelly donuts in town.

Hubbard Hall would be Julia's home for four years. In the tradition of Smith, there were no sororities and girls lived and ate in their respective houses, which contained students from each class level. Not surprisingly, the five freshmen in Hubbard soon formed an alliance that they would call the Gang of Five: Mary Case, Julia McWilliams, Hester Adams, Peggy Clark, and Connie Thayer. Three of the five were at Smith because their mothers had attended, though Peggy's mother attended only two years (this generation would all graduate). Peggy was a slender and shapely girl who had had polio and thus needed assistance to walk. She wore a heavy brace on her left leg, and during the winter months Julia would put Peggy, whom she adored, on a sled for the forays down the hill into town.

What united them in part was their "Mother Hubbard," Mrs. Holly Phillips Gilchrist. Gilley, as they called her, was the housemother who held the social fabric together, or tried to. Every afternoon she had tea, to which any girl was welcome. Motherly advice was dispensed when asked for, but many of the girls found her too old-fashioned and simpleminded for words. Julia called her "nice, but not too bright." Connie Thayer said they also called her "Pouter Pigeon" because she was stout, shaped like a pigeon, somber, and lacking a sense of humor. "Girls, girls, you're using just too much toilet paper!" was a lament of hers they would remember for sixty years. Gifted at imitating, Julia would mimic the lament to peals of laughter.

Julia and Mary (also often called Casey) lived at the top of the first flight of carved wooden stairs in a spacious corner room with two windows. Unfortunately, Dr. Abbie Mabel O'Keefe, the faculty resident and the college's

Director of Medical Services, lived immediately below them. Dr. O'Keefe had flaming red cheeks, white hair, and a quick temper, "very Irish," the girls thought. One afternoon when she was having a tea for other doctors and professors, Julia and Mary played a typical freshman prank: "Why don't we lower our rug down over Dr. O'Keefe's window and block out the light during the tea." They were roaring with laughter, according to Mary, when the doctor burst in and "exploded." Swiftly, they received their demerits from the Judicial Board. Forty years later, the roommates offered their "official" version to the alumni organization: they hung the rug out on the fire rope and, to their horror, "it slipped" down to cover the window below.

On another occasion, Mary locked Julia in their room with a girl whom Julia disliked ("She's like a wet dog!"). Mary slid the key out when she saw the girl in their room, and eventually Julia crawled out through the transom with some difficulty, looking like a wreck. "How could you do that to me, Fatty? Lock me in with the 'wet dog'?"

"When I came to college I was an adolescent nut," Julia Child told the official college oral history project years later: "Someone like me should not have been accepted at a serious institution. I spent my time growing up and doing enough work to get by." The confidential file of Mrs. Gilchrist revealed that though Julia may have grown up, she never lost her rebellious and independent nature: "A grand person generally but she does go berserk every once in a while and is *down* on all 'Suggestions and Regulations.' " And "inclined to let her opinions overrule her good judgment; this spells youth mostly. I believe she will outgrow her impulsiveness somewhat—but I believe there will always be things she will balk at." If Gilley did not think Julia was always "emotionally stable," she at least noted that she was "charming," "cooperative," and "an excellent organizer and manager."

Though her college environment resembled a sorority of largely privileged girls, Smith in 1930 was more diverse than KBS. There were a few African-Americans and a scattering of Jewish students. Of the 654 freshman students, Julia McWilliams was the tallest. "For this reason she was known by nearly everyone!" said Connie Thayer, one of her freshman dorm mates. Another classmate, Anita Hinckley, who came from Rhode Island, said, "I came from the smallest state of the Union. When I saw Julia, a great big California girl, I thought that everyone in California must be that tall." The pictures of Julia in the 1933 and 1934 yearbooks show her standing in the back row, serious, as was the custom in photographs of the day, though both her clothes and her stance were casual. While Gilley noted in her final evaluation that Julia "managed her height well" and was "well dressed," one of Julia's classmates declared, "She was never very stylish," and a professor's evaluation offered the irrelevant opinion that she "needs to give more attention to personal appearance." But the same friend who remarked that her skirts were not stylish and that she seemed to be all arms and legs, added that "later she became beautiful and graceful." Julia, when asked sixty years later about experiencing any conflict between being pretty and being successful in college, said that this conflict was lessened in a college without boys: "Being very, very tall, I had difficulties from that point of view [attracting boys]. So I did not go through some of those things that a short, pretty girl does. I was always struggling to be a pretty person, but it was difficult because you could not get the proper shoes or clothes." She confided in her diary that she felt "big and unsophisticated."

Because her mother was a Smith basketball star at five feet seven inches, Julia was expected to continue her mother's starring role as "jumping center" in three-sectioned girls' basketball. But Smith changed the rules of the game and did away with the jump ball in favor of throwing the ball into the court. Julia retired: "I was not good at the rest of the game."

Once again Julia found herself in a purportedly Christian environment, with most mornings beginning with chapel. Smith called itself a Christian college, though "entirely nonsectarian in religion." It expected all students "to affiliate themselves with the churches of their own denomination in the city." Julia, it appears, did not. (By her senior year she wrote "not a church member" on the religious preference questionnaire.) No more walking to the same church in two rows as they had done at KBS. Although attendance was not taken, chapel was indeed required and "we did what we were supposed to do," explained Charlotte (Chuss) Snyder, another of her classmates. "We certainly lived by the rules." The convocation was held in John M. Greene Hall and consisted of a hymn, a prayer, and an address. Named for the pastor who had advised Sophia Smith on the founding of the college, Greene Hall is a magnificent brick building with mighty Greek columns.

Usually President William Allan Neilson, who also taught Shakespeare, spoke to the women about current events or issues on campus that pleased or displeased him. He was forthright, witty, and personable. The women were united in their love for this Scotsman who never forgot a student's name, even years later. Julia's classmate Charlotte Snyder Turgeon still has his photograph hanging in her study. According to Julia, Neilson was a little man (she would point to her waist) who smoked a "twisted kind of stogie," and he was "adorable":

He had a pink face, twinkling eyes, a white goatee, and a white mustache . . . he was so cute! [In 1972 she recalled him as] a charming, charming man: [President] Neilson was just so cute you wanted to hug him, you had tremendous respect for him and he was wonderfully witty. I can't keep from crying thinking of him because he was such a charming man. Everybody felt the same way.

One day in chapel he addressed the issue of smoking on campus: "Now I have to talk to you girls about smoking. This is a custom which is unhealthy, which is not ladylike. But it is a custom that I adore."

Julia and her classmates were exposed to several major cultural figures during their Smith days. Julia remembered that Paderewski played the piano and Amelia Earhart spoke to them. When a woman from the Metropolitan Opera gave a concert, Julia went backstage. "She was a big fat soprano with a bosom so big and protruding that I went backstage to get my program autographed to see for myself." Julia also attended two days of eleven Beethoven quartets played by the London String Quartet on campus ("It was quite a trial, but I went to all of them," she wrote her mother), and she attended Gertrude Stein's *Four Saints in Three Acts* in Hartford, Connecticut, not only because it was avant-garde and a class project; she adored the theater.

Julia took her courses seriously enough, but only as a necessary part of her college experience and to be passed successfully. "We were a big class and by the midterm about half of us were on probation," said Connie Thayer, who thought both Mary and Julia were "brilliant." (Mary studied and earned A's; Julia studied little and was a B or B– student, except her sophomore year, when she earned C's.) "I never was afraid of getting a low grade," remembers Julia, "though I was not a very good student."

Connie, who was considered the naive and innocent member of the Gang of Five ("I thought that storks brought babies"), was from Worcester. On a couple of vacation periods, Julia went home with Connie to visit her parents, and she went to Providence some weekends with her friend Anita Hinckley and to Washington, DC, one spring with Roxane Ruhl, her Oregon friend from KBS, who had gone to Vassar.

ℋOLIDAYS AND FAMILIES

The major destination for family holidays, however, was west of Northampton in Dalton, her mother Caro's hometown. Westonholme, built by her grandparents, echoed of the richness of her mother's New England heritage. In the Queen Anne style, built with one round tower and two octagonal towers and a lookout on the rooftop, Westonholme was an adventure to visit. Uncle Philip and Aunt Theodora presided over what Julia called "this monstrosity" full of cozy corners and towers. Christmas was crowded with cousins. These warm family memories would be spoiled years later in a bitter quarrel over the Weston Paper Company.

In fact, the family waters had already been muddied by Aunt Theodora, who, upon the death of the eldest Weston (Frank, who ran the paper mill), put their Uncle Philip, her husband, "in a primogeniture position" to run the family business. Julia and her sister Dort thought this "grande dame duchess" a manipulating and subtly denigrating "monster." "I was always careful to tell Aunt Theodora when I felt she was boasting about her illustrious antecedents that John Alden and Priscilla were indentured *servants!*" Though Julia spent many holidays in Dalton, the memory of this aunt never dimmed. As late as 1986, after visiting the Napa Valley, she wrote to M. F. K. Fisher about the "Mafia Mothers" of the winemakers, comparing them in detail to her Aunt Theodora.

When Julia did not visit Dalton and nearby Pittsfield during the holidays, she took the train home to Pasadena. When the train stopped in Chicago she always visited her Aunt Nell—Ellen (Nelly) Weston, who was married to Hale Holden and lived in Winnetka, Illinois. Aunt Nell had a lovely older daughter Julia's height, who became her stylish role model. "Eleanor was tall and beautiful, a wonderful character, a wonderful dresser who wore Empress Eugénie hats and great clothes. That is why I stopped in Chicago so frequently." According to her letters to her mother (usually addressed to "Dear Coco," "Mamy Dear," "Dear Cocacola," or "Dear Mother Caro"), she visited the Art Institute in Chicago and attended concerts with her cousins. She would sign off her letters: "be good . . . sweetie apple" and "love to big J."

In the summers Julia returned to her California paradise, made more idyllic with the addition of a summer home for the McWilliams family in San Malo, California, near Oceanside, more than an hour's drive down the coast from Los Angeles. Mrs. McWilliams built the house with a walled patio to keep out the ever-present white sand. Friends of Julia remember the tall doors and handles, built especially for this tall family. Julia had all her friends down for parties, and was sweet (one friend says) on a boy named Charley Crane one summer. Relatives occasionally visited, including her cousin Dana, who had attended KBS with her one year and was now enrolled, along with her sister Alice, at Scripps College for Women in Claremont, California.

Julia knew little about what had happened in her hometown during the years she had been away. Like most college students, she did not read the newspapers. Los Angeles was going through a decade-long building boom (the county population more than doubled, to two million). Yet the Depression was now exposing corruption, and many of the men who built Los Angeles—both businessmen and public officials—were going to San Quentin. The news was full of scandals and receiverships (three hundred businesses, "representing more than half a billion dollars in assets," according to one historian, would be placed in receivership during the early 1930s).

Though John McWilliams was disgruntled about the scandals and the political climate—Roosevelt's Democrats swept the country in the fall of 1932—no scandal touched him or the company he worked for, the J. G. Boswell Company. And he continued to support Julia's Ivy League education. Her brother Johnny graduated from Poly and was going on to Lake Forest Academy, a hope eventually undermined, according to his sisters, by his dyslexia.

When Julia returned for her sophomore year, she arrived with a drum she bought when the train stopped in Albuquerque. When others were trying to study, she pretended to be a Navajo chief and beat out her rhythm on the tom-tom. Mary Case had already suggested that they live separately this year so that she could study better ("I couldn't play all night and laugh with Julia and stay in college. . . . Julia did not really worry much about anything"). The previous year, when Mary had hung a green rug on the fire rope between their two beds to protect her study time, Julia tossed a jelly donut over to her roommate. She also fed her ravenous hunger on brownies with chocolate sauce, toasted cheese sandwiches, and chocolate ice cream sodas from across the street.

ACADEMICS AND DORMITORY FOOD

Julia's grades dropped during her sophomore year in part because she no longer shared a room with the studious Mary and in part because she became very active in campus activities. She served on the elite Grass Cops (they blew whistles when someone walked on the lawns) with her former roommate Mary Case, with Marj Spiegel, the pretty daughter of the Chicago retail merchant, and with Dickie Fosdick, the daughter of Harry Emerson Fosdick, New York City's famous minister and member of Smith's Board of Trustees. Fosdick "was our class star," said Mary, "class valedictorian who lived on a complete schedule and could do all sports." Julia also was chosen to be on the Sophomore Push Committee, another great honor, with Charlotte Snyder, Madeleine Evans, and Dorothy Fosdick—all three campus leaders. The Push Committee helped people get through commencement, even if it meant picking all the thorns off the roses. As one class member pointed out, among the aggressive girls there were those who partied with their dates at the Dartmouth carnival and those who were the campus leaders.

Julia was a leader but a casual student and had not even taken her college boards or aptitude tests seriously. Though she ranked in the high eighties percentile in intelligence in her class, her aptitude tests were only above average (highest in plane geometry, 82; in physics, 78). She assumed that as the daughter of a graduate she would be safe if she just passed her courses. Years later, in an interview with the Smith College *Sophian,* she offered the following suggestion: "My father was a conservative antediluvian Republican who thought that Phi Beta Kappas were up to no good." In the college's oral history she expressed it in stronger words: "For my father, intellectuality and communism went hand in hand. So you were better off not being intellectual. And if you were Phi Beta Kappa you were certainly a pinko." What he valued was friendship and good citizenship, and she excelled in each. Moreover, girls her age were not ambitious and few graduated from college. Even in 1940, only "five percent of the female population" had a college education. It is remarkable that she persisted to graduation, for of those who did go to college, only a third graduated. The statistics were considerably better at Smith, where only one-third of her Smith class of 654 dropped out before graduating (perhaps in part because of the Depression). "I never thought of leaving Smith; it would have killed my mother," said Julia. In her self-deprecating way, she added, "I was always one of the crowd. I had a good time and, in spite of myself, I learned something."

As a sophomore, Julia began the fifth of her six years of studying French grammar and literature. For her and her parents' generation, reared to be Anglophile, the study of Western and Northern Europe was the civilized pursuit. They studied European languages, museums, and cathedrals—but not the sensuous elements of daily French life. Cold climate, hard currency, Northern respectability, and hearty food—these were the keys to virtue. At the time, Julia did not question these values, nor was she as yet aware of her hedonistic nature. Several of Julia's acquaintances were planning to spend their junior year in France, including Charlotte Snyder of Boston and Catherine Atwater, who later in life would be closer to Julia when she married John Kenneth Galbraith and the Childs became their neighbors. Julia did not have the proficiency or interest to consider a junior year abroad. She took one more year of French after completing two years of Italian (Smith required two languages), never knowing how valuable the learning would become.

If Julia picked up bad eating habits in college, she did so in a positive way, associating her dining experience with the fellowship of friends. Hubbard Hall had a kitchen and a cook and the girls had to show up promptly for their meals, over which Gilley presided. The fare was all-American, which meant "real New England food, meat and potatoes and traditional food," said Charlotte Snyder. It also meant, in the trend of the day, shelves of products from General Foods, a company that already owned Jell-O, Postum, Baker's Chocolate, Minute Tapioca, Post cereals, Log Cabin syrup, and Maxwell House Coffee (and soon Birds Eye frozen foods). The disastrous effects of the Depression on small retailers and farmers had only encouraged these national companies and the large supermarkets.

Charlotte Snyder was the only classmate of Julia's who remembered the food, beyond a general comment about its fat and sauce content. Charlotte's father owned Batchelder and Snyder, a large meat distributor/wholesale food business in Boston (much later bought by Birds Eye), and when he visited the college he was mightily impressed when he was served sweetbreads. Though Charlotte would eventually go on to the Cordon Bleu (before Julia did) and make a career in the food world as an editor of the *Larousse Gastronomique* (1961), she claimed that "none of us was into food then."

While Julia and Charlotte were eating tasty junk food, Americans were being sold foodstuff for its purity, uniformity and "scientific" goodness. Crisco advertised its product as "used wherever a housewife takes pride in a clean, sweet kitchen." Baker's cocoa was "scientifically blended" and "corrects the action of the digestive organs." Nothing in the official advertising about freshness, taste, aroma, or pleasure. Little wonder these students did not care about food preparation or careful dining. They had a kitchenette on the second floor of Hubbard Hall, but no one remembers any cooking: they stored ice cream in the refrigerator; Julia had a reputation for never doing the dishes.

Nevertheless, during Julia's freshman year, an event occurred in St. Louis that would eventually make a major impression on her life. Irma Rombauer, a German-American widow, and her friends put together a collection of recipes that they self-published: *The Joy of Cooking*. Five years later, after many rejections, it was printed by Bobbs-Merrill, and its sales, thanks to its accessibility and practical approach, increased steadily to more than a million a decade later. It would become Julia's first cookbook after she herself discovered the joy of cooking.

Rombauer's book, emphasizing the pleasure of cooking and eating, went against a trend dominating American cooking for two generations: domestic science, which tried to marry science and cooking. It was a trend stoked by the food-processing companies and factory farms, which emphasized sanitation, uniformity, and "health." Perhaps the Depression Dust Bowl helped undermine an agrarian society and fresh produce, but it was greed and the hair-netted "scientists" in the lab (no cooks need apply) that destroyed American eating habits. Their crowning achievement, suggests Laura Shapiro in *Perfection Salad,* was the invention of Crisco, advertised as an "Absolutely New Product" of scientific cookery. Crisco ads pointed out its "pure cream white" appearance and the fact that it never spoils (but not that it never leaves the arteries). This "model food of the twentieth century" is probably what Julia's jelly donuts were cooked in.

Ironically, it was the work of the grandfather of her classmate Catherine Atwater that laid the foundation of the domestic science movement. Catherine Galbraith would discover decades later that Wilbur Olin Atwater, who had studied in Germany and was professor of chemistry at Wesleyan before he became the head of the Office of Experiment Stations in Washington, DC, was the pioneer of nutrition, the popularizer of the word "calorie," and the developer of food composition tables. His numerous books, published between 1887 and 1898, made him the first to investigate food and digestion; he became the "mentor of scientific cooks." (Atwater's father was a Methodist preacher who founded a temperance newspaper near Burlington, Vermont.)

TRADITIONS

When the chapel bell rang, as it did unannounced every October, Julia jumped for joy. It was Mountain Day, and by tradition everyone left the campus to go out into the New England foliage. Julia's gang grabbed their sandwiches and went to the Mount Tom recreational area to hike. Smith's traditions were much older than those at KBS, and even more effective. Rally Day was a day of skits, mostly ridiculous, put on by each class, along with singing on the steps of Hubbard Hall. Julia was always in the skits and was by nature a ham, said one of her classmates.

Although she had "retired" from the basketball team, Julia remained physically active. The gymnasium was across Green Street, and the playing fields with tennis courts and riding stables were up Green Street and across the bridge. She engaged in hockey, tennis, archery, and baseball as well as swimming and riding. "I did not do as much in [organized] sports at Smith. I played hockey, which I had never played before; lacrosse I did not like because there were no boundaries and you ran your legs off." She did play in a junior/senior game her last year and told her mother, "They were awfully mad at me for being so big."

The spring of her sophomore year the Lindbergh baby was kidnapped and the girls rallied around Connie Morrow, the baby's aunt. Constance was a

Smith freshman and friend of Anita Hinckley when they both attended Milton Academy. When the baby's body was discovered about eleven days later, the campus was devastated. Reality had intruded into the idyllic world of Smith.

The Olympic Games were held in Los Angeles in the summer of 1932 and Julia's friends were caught up in the excitement. When a group of them gathered in San Malo, they staged their own Olympics and played to the point of exhaustion day after day. To her brother, who was dating lovely Southern California girls, Julia's physical play and short hair and girl's school manner indicated that she did not want to be a girl. She was interested in boys, he thought, but her associations were more like being "one of the boys."

Before returning to school, Babe Hall came over to lunch with Julia and her mother. "Julia seemed much older than I, much more sophisticated," said Babe, who was attending Occidental College. But Mrs. McWilliams had not changed a bit. She was just as lenient and whimsical as ever: When Julia told her mother and Babe about staying out all night with a group that included boys, her mother's only comment was: "Did you have any breakfast? Don't do that again, dear, until you have gained ten pounds." Babe was amazed that Mrs. McWilliams was not warning her daughter against sneaking in, but against failing to eat out.

While protecting the intelligence and virtue of America's finest young flowers, Smith nurtured their leadership abilities and experience. Eleven years before, the Board of Trustees established a student government association that gave the women some power in establishing the rules and regulations of their social life: Student Council, the Judicial Board, the House of Representatives, and the House Councils. In her junior year, Julia was elected Junior Class Representative to the Student Council. Madeleine Evans, a prominent campus debater, served as president; Connie Thayer was vice president, and Mary Case was treasurer of their class. Julia was again appointed to the Grass Cops along with Marjorie Spiegel, Dorothy Fosdick, and Mary Case, and was refreshments chair for the prom committee, headed by Marjorie Spiegel. During this year she became friendly with a senior named Elizabeth (Betsy) Scofield Bushnell from New Haven, who more than a decade later would become her best friend when Julia married into the Bushnell-Bissell-Kubler-Child-Prudhomme tribe of friends.

JUNIOR YEAR

"I certainly hated to leave our Sunkist paradise," she wrote her mother from the train headed back to Northampton, "But I do think it is much better for you not to have all of us around to worry about." She was traveling with Gay Bradley, her childhood friend who after flunking out of Smith her freshman year was attending (and would graduate from) Radcliffe. They played bridge most of the way. During this junior year the Gang of Five was joined by Happy Gaillard, who, like Hester Adams, with whom she roomed, was from New York City. Happy had gone to Vassar, hated it, and transferred into Hubbard House and Smith. As a transfer student, Happy would not match the campus leadership roles of the other girls, but she would enjoy the fun. Charlotte Snyder, who lived in Ellen Emerson Hall on the other side of Paradise Pond, said, "That group had a great sense of humor. I was in awe of them. I was terribly serious [and pious] at the time."

Another change in the gang was the distraction of young men who came to call. Connie remembers that Hester, a freckled girl with an old-fashioned face and wide smile, would come home at the last minute and just as the bell was ringing and her friends were looking out the window, Henry, her future husband, would kiss her good night. That summer Connie also met her future husband, a senior at Yale, and drifted away from the weekend activities of the gang.

One of the most important events of the junior year was the declaration of a major. Though Julia took more classes in music (a passion she shared with Mary), she chose history: "It had more options." Yet a majority of her friends—Peggy, Connie, and Mary—chose the same major. Perhaps they used the same reasoning, though Julia remembered, "In those days there were not many options: secretary or teacher or nurse seemed the only [ones]," but marriage was the priority. Maybe they were influenced by politically liberal teachers, one of whom took his students to a walkout at the textile mill in Northampton (much to the dismay of Anita Hinckley's father, who believed she was becoming a "flaming communist"). The history teachers were popular, as was Roosevelt, who won in a landslide in November 1932. Julia, who still thought like her father, wanted Hoover to defeat FDR and was still largely unaware of union leader Harry Bridges and the crippling strikes on the West Coast.

Julia took Dr. Leona Gabel's Renaissance and Reformation course (History 351) and earned B+ both semesters. She thought that Gabel was "a real brain." Gabel wrote in Julia's academic record that she admired Julia's "qualities of leadership," her "droll, humorous, likable personality," and her ability to take "criticism not only kindly but responsively." Julia's paper on one of the promiscuous Renaissance popes caused quite a sensation in the class, remembers Mary Ford (Cairns), one of two sisters from Pasadena who were ahead of Julia at Smith.

Because of the popularity of English professor Mary Ellen Chase, a famous "lady novelist" or "authoress" as they called her in those days, many students thought about writing careers. Chase gave a very good course on the novel to crowded classrooms. Though she did not take Chase's course, Julia decided to become a "woman novelist": "My plan was to be a woman novelist . . . there were some famous women novelists in those days." During an interview decades later for the oral history of Smith, Julia could only explain her failing to take a course with Chase as pure romanticism, thinking "I had to live first and then I'd write. I was . . . an utter adolescent. The idea was to get everything else so that you can get the writing later. I was a very adolescent person all the time up till I was about thirty."

Later she partially justified ignoring the novel-writing class by saying that when she went to hear Chase give a lecture in Washington, DC, in the 1950s, she was disappointed, calling her a "semi-charlatan" and a "show-off . . . it was like watching a piece of theater. You were there to see her, not to learn anything." Julia told an interviewer in 1980 that she was "inspired" to be a writer by reading the stories of Somerset Maugham. Instead she became something of a Maugham character, meeting her husband-to-be in a Ceylonese teahouse and following him all over the world.

She was particularly impressed with Marjorie Hope Nicolson, then the Dean, who later became the first woman full professor in graduate studies at Columbia University. Her admiration began when Nicolson took over a chapel talk in which the students expected to hear their beloved President Neilson. "I am Banquo's ghost," she said at the beginning of a witty talk that would make her career with the students. She was a Renaissance scholar, and Julia took a course in Milton with her. Julia remembered little about her classes, except breeding drosophila fruit flies in her biology class.

Julia had originally asked Alex McWilliams (their grandfathers were brothers) to the junior prom, but he was busy pole-vaulting for Princeton, and she settled on another young man with a connection to her family. Julia was a junior usher for the 1933 commencement, an honor accorded to those contributing the most to college life. Hester Adams, another member of the gang, was head of the junior ushers. The experience of participating in the final ceremonies was the best motivation for a successful senior year ahead.

*S*ENIOR REWARDS

A second motivation was a car. Seniors with high enough grades could have a car on campus, and that was inspiration enough for Julia to improve her grades and for her mother to buy her an open 1929 Ford, which she named Eulalie, the first model with gear shifts. It was black with two seats and the top folded back. "I am reveling in my automobile and haven't walked a step since I got it here," she wrote her mother on April 25, 1934.

During the campaign for the repeal of prohibition, the Smith girls, particularly the Gang of Five (which included Happy but not innocent Connie), partied more than ever. Julia had certainly drunk alcohol before, but never in these amounts: "I remember it well. During prohibition a group of us drove in the Ford to a speakeasy in Holyoke that was on the top of a warehouse; we all had one of everything. Luckily we had an open car, because we were all quite sick. That was very terribly exciting."

On December 5, 1933, at 5:32 P.M., the repeal of prohibition was ratified. Now they could openly and legally drink at the Hotel Northampton. But one happy night they created such a commotion that Gilley asked Mary to come down and demanded that as house president she had to restore order. Mary went back upstairs and discovered Julia on her hands and knees in the hall.

Drinking had always gone on during Christmas vacation, especially on the train to and from Pasadena. One of the Pasadena girls who was a year ahead of Julia at Smith remembers that during her senior year she traveled home on the Twentieth Century to Chicago and the Santa Fe to Pasadena. Julia also remembers that trip: "We had some rather wild times on the train. . . . Everyone came back for Christmas and there was a lot of drinking going on. Those were the days!" Gay Bradley adds, "Those were wonderful trips in which nearly fifty of us would party for four or five days."

With all the celebrating and student activities, it is not surprising that Julia let her English and music grades slide a bit in her final semester. She chaired the Community Chest, which put her on the Activities Board, was a Grass Cop and assistant editor of the *Tatler,* the school paper, which was headed by Margaret Hamilton. Hester Adams, one of the Gang of Five, was the editor of the yearbook and Catherine Atwater her associate editor. Julia learned a Latin carioca dance for the Rally Day show, and acted in the musical variety show jointly presented by Smith and Amherst.

Julia took three memorable courses her senior year and did well in all of them. From Merle Eugene Curti, professor of American history, she took

modern American history (after 1870) and earned B's. He was the professor
who had assigned the study of propaganda and its effect on the strikers in
Northampton. When asked for the "most interesting and profitable class" of
her college career, Julia named the one taught by Curti, who earned a national
reputation for his textbooks after he left Smith to teach at the University of
Wisconsin. He won the 1944 Pulitzer in history for *The Growth of American
Thought.*

She took a course in writing one-act plays from Samuel Atkins Eliot, Jr.,
which tapped into the fun she had had writing plays for the McHall acting
troupe in her mother's attic and would lead to her writing several short plays
for the Junior League. Eliot had a severe stutter, but he inspired her to write
about the traumatic event of her first year at KBS, the Stevens triple murder-
suicide. She told an interviewer from Smith years later that her play was
"terribly dramatic" and had "wonderful potentialities": "About a friend of my
family's who found he had heart trouble. And unfortunately he had two boys,
one of whom was a moron from birth and the other one who developed
dementia praecox and he was horrified about dying and leaving his wife with
these two idiot boys." Julia followed the murder and suicide as closely as one
can tell from the newspaper accounts, but included a scene in which her own
mother, Caro, went to the tennis court with the mother of the murdered boy
and offered to drive the car home. That is when they found the second murdered son. "So it made a wonderful play, you can imagine. It was never
performed, of course."

She also took international relations (Government 39) from Dr. Alice M.
Holder, who gave Julia her only two A's. Miss Holder, who believed that Julia
had "the reputation of being very humorous," commended her "good intelligence and keen interest in what she does" as well as her "general enthusiasm
. . . considerable personal attractions and plenty of *savoir faire.*"

Her final semester was, as all commencement speakers point out, a looking backward and a beginning. In January her mother arrived for the funeral
in Dalton of Julia's uncle Philip Weston. Julia bought a copy of James Joyce's
Ulysses because Noble Cathcart, married to her cousin, had published an essay
on the novel in his *Saturday Review of Literature.* She did not have time to
brush up on her Homer, as she told her mother, and read only part of the
novel. But she was stimulated by the courses she was taking from Professor
Curti and Associate Professor Holder. And she was distracted by a boy named
Luther, on whom she was sweet. Since February she and her classmates had
been wearing their graduation gowns to chapel, sometimes over their pajamas.
But behind the daily distractions and plans for commencement was the ever-
lingering question of vocation.

When Julia enrolled at Smith, she listed her vocational choices as "No occupation decided; Marriage preferable." She was typical of her class. When Mrs. Gilchrist wrote her reference evaluation of Julia she said that her family was "wealthy" and thus she "will not need 'a job' I do not believe. She would do well in some organized charity or social service work." Such were the expectations to be lived up to. Five years later President Neilson told them that they were "not the brightest class that ever graduated from Smith, but you were the marryingest class." However, Charlotte Snyder Turgeon claims that 80 percent of her Smith house went into the foreign service. The lack of a sense of direction was something Julia shared with most of the women of her class. Because Julia could not anticipate the marriage track, she abandoned her "lady novelist" fantasy and was looking at journalism. "I only wish to god I were gifted in one line instead of having mediocre splashings in several directions," Julia wrote her mother on November 26 of her senior year.

Julia invited a boy named Fred Allen to the senior prom, but he could not get away from Harvard because of his grades. Then she tried Win Crane, who worked at the Weston paper mill and whom she had met at her relatives'. If the latter had not accepted, she was going to send the entire sex to Hades, she told her mother. Accustomed to being chosen first for any team of girls, she did not have the same score with boys.

In addition to the prom was Ivy Day, when she walked in her white dress and red sash between the two sophomore lines carrying ivy chains, and she and Mary were joint toastmasters at their senior dinner—a gig they would repeat for reunions. She would stay close to her buddies, though they immediately moved on to marriage and children. Mary, who would name her first baby Julia, emphasized that the greatest characteristic of her roommate was "compassion . . . human kindness." This opinion of Hubbard House's "head girl" was echoed by the rest of the gang.

When she graduated, Julia became an active Smith alumna for the remainder of her life, returning to class reunions, opening her home to them, joining the "club" that would eventually include Nancy Reagan, Sylvia Plath, and Gloria Steinem. She wears this association proudly, defending the school against what she saw as "charges" of homosexuality when by the 1990s Northampton had become synonymous in some minds with lesbians. Smith would give her a New England association that never failed to surprise some people when they learned she was born and reared in Pasadena.

Her mother, sister, and brother came for the elaborate Smith College graduation ceremonies on Monday, June 18, 1934. Dean Christian Gauss of Princeton was the commencement speaker. The three siblings drove Eulalie back across the country. "Now this car is very old and we will drive no faster than between forty and forty-five miles an hour," Dorothy remembers her brother John declaring. Indeed, Eulalie had over 50,000 miles on her, and forty miles an hour was as fast as the car would go. "It took us almost two weeks to get across the country."

John Dillinger was loose that summer, and every time they saw a black limousine, they were certain they were going to encounter the famous bank robber and murderer. He was shot dead by the FBI in Chicago that July, but until that time the police search was exciting and took their minds off the grueling trip. They were driving through the Dust Bowl in heat that reached 110 in Oklahoma. Dorothy remembers: "This enormous tan cloud was coming toward us and it was dusk and it blew over us and Julia's hat blew off, and the dust blew past and then it rained and then it got to be 100 degrees again. We stayed in Tourist Courts—auto courts. When it got too hot, the water fell out. John taped the water radiator and we continued. Once when we stopped a million flies surrounded us." They arrived home dirty and exhausted and headed for the beach.

The lovely photograph of Julia in the Pasadena newspaper announced her graduation from Smith College with a major in history: "She will return here after graduation and will pass the summer with her family at the McWilliams beach home at San Malo."

Chapter 5

CAREER SEARCH
(1934 – 1943)

"I am quite content to be the way I am—and
feel quite superior to many a wedded mouse."
Julia McWilliams's diary

"MIDDLE-CLASS women did not have careers," explained Julia McWilliams, who spent one year at home after Smith College. "You were to marry and have children and be a nice mother. You didn't go out and do anything," she told Andy Warhol's *Interview* magazine in 1989. Without serious marriage prospects, she spent the summer of 1934 in San Malo and then lived at 1207 South Pasadena Avenue helping her mother, whose high blood pressure was not improving. She spent her time playing piano (as well as accordion and bugle), socializing with her friends (particularly Gay Bradley), and still occasionally dating a young man named Luther, whom she could not even recall fifty years later. She gave a "whirl of parties," according to her mother's letters to Dorothy (now a senior at Katharine Branson School): fourteen friends for a weekend at St. Malo, sixteen for a buffet lunch, a black-and-white ball for forty at their Pasadena house. When she was not giving her own parties, she attended some of Babe Hall's Sunday soirees across the street. On one occasion, according to Babe's brother, Julia put a bottle of brandy in the punch, considerably enlivening the party.

She became increasingly restless living at home without purpose. The Smith alumnae news reported that "Miss McWilliams has been taking up German and music this winter and also supervising youngsters at a clinic." But she told the vocational guidance office at her alma mater that she wanted a "literary" career on a "newspaper, magazine, critical, etc." in the Los Angeles area.

The Junior League was the civic expression for all young middle-class women her age in Pasadena. She and Gay Bradley studied for the Junior League "as if we were working for a Ph.D.," said the latter:

> Of course, no one ever studied, so we got 100 percent. Julia was the center of attention and activity; when we were all together she was always the focus, always the funny one, always the clown (of course, she had her serious side); when she was little she was always the first one throwing butter at the ceiling, the ringleader . . . always the kind of person people follow because she had great magnetism.

Not long after attending Dorothy's graduation at the Katharine Branson School, where Dort followed her sister's example in winning the School Cup as outstanding student, Julia went east to Providence, Rhode Island, for more than a week. She was one of eighteen bridesmaids at her classmate Anita Hinckley's wedding to Charley Hovey. Julia helped write thank-you notes as the gifts arrived at the Hinckley house. She was the life of the party, said the bride, who claimed, "All the ushers were absolutely crazy about Julia, especially Stacey Holmes and Eugene Record. Whether at the clambake at their Narragansett summer home or the dinner parties and wedding reception, Julia was adored in every way but romantically. After all the reception toasts had droned on, Julia arose with dramatic flair, lifted her glass, and said only "Hinckley, Hovey, Lovey Dovey." Anita would never forget Julia's toast. The effect of this grand society wedding was to pull Julia back to her East Coast friends and emphasize her need for a purpose in life. Anita was the example of traditional "success," both in her choice of marriage and in her husband— Harvard varsity crew and law school graduate.

New York City Career Girl

Julia, Dort, and their mother, Caro, drove East in September 1935 to take Dort to Bennington College, where she would study drama, and Julia to western Massachusetts, where she would stay with her Aunt Theodora and study secretarial skills at the Packard Commercial School. Aunt Theodora was a woman who could take everyone's measure and everyone came up short. Julia quit the stenography program in a month or two when, after applying and persisting, a job appeared (which did not need shorthand). She was hired in October by the prestigious home-furnishing firm of W. & J. Sloane in New York City.

New York drew Julia and a number of other 1934 graduates of Smith, certainly those who did not marry. She rented an apartment at 400 East Fifty-ninth Street with Julie Chapman and Lib Payson. "Julie [Chapman] has been promoted to the position of personal shopper at Best & Company, and Libby seems to be doing very well at Lord & Taylor. The Maguires are still at Bonwit Teller, and Libby has also been promoted to personal shopper. Georgia Williams has just come into Sloane's," she proudly informed Smith's vocational office. "The salaries of all are comparatively small, but we are all happy." Later she would say, "I loved it. I started out at eighteen dollars a week. . . . I remember lunch across the street from Sloane's was fifty cents." Living was cheap because of deflated Depression prices, the subway (five cents) was clean and safe, and with her long legs she could stride down the streets at any hour, her head thrown back confidently. She lived frugally, though her parents sent her (as they would for years) a $100-a-month allowance. Advertising, she reasoned, would be an avenue into the publishing world.

In a large brownstone building at the corner of Fifty-ninth Street and First Avenue, the women shared a small apartment costing $80 a month, and Julia could park her Ford (her second car) across the street and under the Queensboro Bridge, which loomed above them. On stormy days they could hear the waves breaking against the rocks on the riverbank. In the middle of the East River was Welfare Island (now Roosevelt Island), a cigar-shaped piece of land housing welfare institutions, a hospital, home for old people, and the New York Cancer Institute. The bridge to Queens, built in 1909, passed high over Roosevelt Island, necessitating an elevator so that people, ambulances, and fire trucks could service the island.

Julia ate chiefly at the apartment, which meant she did not eat well. But food prices were low and Birds Eye frozen foods were booming (250 million pounds of frozen fruit, vegetables, and meat by 1938). There was Delmonico's and the Café des Artistes, but Julia was not interested. Indeed, she ate only to defeat her hunger. However, she said, "I used to go to Grand Central Station Oyster Bar and watch them make the oyster stew." She patronized the chains: Schrafft's had thirty-eight outlets in Manhattan, Childs had forty-four, and Huyler's had eleven, all with soda fountains.

The city burst upon her with its million electric lights and mountains of steel buildings. The fast-paced life (1.5 million people on 22.2 square miles) and its mixed colors of the fashion world set against the impoverished street life stimulated her. This ratatouille of races, still struggling to come out of the Depression, challenged her McWilliams social assumptions about success and forced her to look at stark poverty. She would later claim that this civic lesson eventually led her to become a Roosevelt Democrat.

Sloane's was located at 575 Fifth Avenue, only a fifty-cent cab ride or a brisk six-and-a-half-block walk west on Fifty-ninth and south for twelve blocks on Fifth Avenue. Sloane's sold furniture and all the beautiful lamps, tables, antiques, and accessories for the home. They specialized in displaying artwork from other countries and filling special orders for well-to-do clients. Julia proudly shipped an elegant coffee table to her roommate Mary Case when she wed Leon Warner in Minnesota.

Her boss was A. W. Forester, advertising manager for W. & J. Sloane, who admired her writing and her ability to get along with people. She was tactful and conscientious, he would later record. She worked for him from October 1935 to May 1937, performing secretarial chores, contacting the press for publicity, arranging photography, and writing press releases. She loved the variety of her experiences and the challenge of learning. "I am learning quite a bit about store management and interior decoration. In fact, I couldn't be more pleased," she informed her alumni vocational office.

In addition to her roommates, Julia saw several of her Smith classmates who lived in the city, including Peggy Clark, with whom she went to Wagner's opera *Die Meistersinger.* She also attended plays, seeing *Reflected Glory,* starring Tallulah Bankhead, whose similarly unmistakable voice was as low and steady as Julia's was high and swinging. Briefly Gay Bradley, transferred to New York by the J. Walter Thompson agency, roomed with Julia and her two roommates until she married Gabriel Wright in 1937 and moved to San Francisco.

Julia was dating a young man named Tom Johnston, her first serious boyfriend. "I am delighted she is seeing more men and finding out how to manage the sweet creatures," her mother wrote Dorothy. Tom was a literature major ("full of Melville," she told her diary) but was trying to get a job in New York. She had met him at Smith, but now she thought she was madly in love ("I had never been profoundly in love before"). By midsummer of 1936 she sensed that the freshness had gone out of their relationship, that he was under financial stress, and that she was both tired and sexually frustrated ("in heat," as she put it picturesquely). Self-control is civilized, she believed, but she had a strange feeling that being in love with someone and not able to consummate was destructive of the relationship, for love is both physical and psychological.

She also had a strong attraction to her cousin's husband. "They were my family when I lived in New York," she said of her cousin Harriet Patterson (Aunt Bessie's daughter, who had taught her to do her nails in Santa Barbara) and Harriet's husband, Noble Cathcart. They lived almost around the corner, on Fifty-seventh Street. Cathcart was editor of the *Saturday Review of Literature,* and he gave her, as well as his daughters, a lot of attention. Julia playfully claimed later to have been "madly in love with Noble, though curbed my passion because I was so fond of my cousin Harriet." In her continuing desire to write for a living, Julia secured one assignment for the *Saturday Review of Literature,* to write a short blurb about Sherwood Anderson, whose latest book *(Puzzled America,* 1935) was being published. It was a small assignment, but she failed to complete it—blaming overwork and laziness. But she continued to send in short human-interest pieces to *The New Yorker,* to no avail. "I intended to be a great woman novelist, but for some reason *The New Yorker* didn't ask me to be on its staff, and I ended up in the advertisement department of W. & J. Sloane (just to gain experience)," Julia told me many years later.

Her most successful work was writing advance copy for Sloane's. The unpublished writing she was doing during this period of her life reveals maturity, an admirable vocabulary, but mixed results. Her least successful writing attempts were book reviews, which she obviously wished to have published in *The New Yorker.* Three survive and they reveal fairly shallow analysis and lack of polish. Two short humorous pieces submitted to *The New Yorker* show a more natural style and wit: a piece about Sloane's flying the national flag with the Boy Scout flag on November 11 reveals playful puns ("flaggish sensitivity" and "Boys had been scouting"). The essays she wrote about Sloane's art exhibits (textile design, painted French screens, British antiques), which had to be rewritten for release to the major New York newspapers, are her most polished and sophisticated work. Her boss believed that she had a "flair for writing." But try as she might, she would never become a "lady novelist."

THE JILTING OF JULIA

On September 6, 1936, Tom wrote a "Dear Julia" letter, in which he said he did not love her, and immediately left town. Two weeks later she bought a gold-leafed, lockable ledger to confide her heartbreak. She called it jilting—she sobbed when he told her before fleeing to Detroit—and she called it "excruciating." It hurt her stomach. When a friend told her this was not unusual, she concluded it was merely a biological fact.

She lost him to a Smith College acquaintance a few years ahead of her: Isabel (Izzy) Holmes McMullen (Smith '32), and she felt betrayed when she found out he had been seeing her all along. But she gave her emotional "blight" one year. Her roommates comforted her, as did Dort during a visit to the city, and Gay Bradley, who was living there at the time. One called him "a jerk . . . he did not tell her he was going with another girl, typical male behavior if they can get away with it." Julia also found comfort in poetry, copying Elinor Wylie's "My heart's delight, I must for love forget you" into her diary (the next December she wrote "pooh!" beside the poem).

Julia converted her heartache into action for her younger sister, Dort, who was studying at Bennington College and had come to visit Julia during the Bennington weekend dance. Julia gave her a good talking-to about accepting her height. Julia understood the feeling of being "big and unsophisticated"—wrote her a "fighting" letter about learning to be at ease socially. Perhaps because Dorothy was even taller than her six-foot-two-inch sister and without Julia's status as the eldest child in the family, she cultivated her distinction by joining others who were outside the traditional gang. She sought out the artists and misfits, with whom she identified. They were also more interesting. Julia, in part because she was the "responsible" older sibling with self-esteem, and in part because she truly wanted to be accepted, chose the role of class clown and best friend.

In talking about the social and financial advantages of being tall, John Kenneth Galbraith, Julia future's neighbor, says:

> General De Gaulle once said to me at a big gathering in Washington, "Professor, what is your philosophy of your vast height?" So I said what I've said before, "We tall men are taller than anybody else, therefore we're visible, therefore we're more closely watched, therefore our behavior is better, and the world instinctively trusts tall men." And De Gaulle said, *"Magnifique."* And then in a wonderful rolling voice added, "There's one thing you have forgotten. The small man must be treated without mercy."

The advantages of height for adult men may be evident, but the price that is paid for taking up space and power as an adolescent girl is a high psychological one, despite the future advantages.

Julia spent the next several months analyzing her emotions and what men want in women. She made a list of what she wanted from marriage, beginning with intellectual stimulation and ending with "FUN and complete mutual understanding and respect." She concluded that she had little sense emotionally and later regretted that she had written Tom that she still loved him. She called on discipline and daily heroism after reading Aldous Huxley's *Eyeless in Gaza.* Her turn to books helped her get over her heartbreak, especially reading Huxley, for she admired his life of discipline and "greed for achievement." Having discipline must be ecstasy, she declared, before deciding that her diary "is a catharsis of the emotions!" An immature catharsis. She was also reading Gertrude Stein, finding that her work may sound pretty clever, but lacked discipline, "like playing the piano and missing the tempo." And she read Bernard DeVoto on James Joyce's *Ulysses,* the novel she had tried to read at Smith ("the last chapter is . . . the holy devil to read until you get in the mood"). Punctuation and order were assurances she needed at this time in her life, she said in a brief essay on the subject in the back of her diary.

During a cocktail party she was giving in January 1937 to introduce Gay Bradley to friends, she was told privately that Tom and Izzy were married on New Year's Day. She broke down in tears again. When his letter came informing her of his marriage, she wrote several bitter and childish drafts of a return letter into her diary, expressing anger at his deception, then mailed a breezy and affectionate congratulations to the newly married couple. She determined she disliked writing publicity stories, because she hated "pushing" and "selling" things. Finally, she found herself "bored with nightclubs" and champagne. "Julia of the almost spring," she wrote self-mockingly toward the end of her diary keeping. It was April, and when she would go home for Gay's wedding in May, she would stay.

Though later Julia believed she left New York in the spring of 1937 because her mother was ill, family letters reveal that no one knew how ill her mother was at that point. Though her diary declared she was leaving the city because "I do not want to be a business woman!" her job at Sloane's had never been better. She received a raise to $30 a week and her boss had great confidence in her. When she informed him she was leaving in May, he insisted, "In two years, I can make you the biggest advertising woman in New York City!" She joked in her diary that she already *was the biggest!* Perhaps the compelling reason for her flight, other than emotional immaturity, was depression over the failure of her first passionate love. This girl of boundless energy had lost her confidence. She started missing deadlines in the office.

New York offered a post-baccalaureate education without specialization, though she honed her writing and management skills and acquired a bit more sophistication (Babe certainly considered her more worldly-wise; Caro called her "more methodical and business like" and "less nervous.") In fact, Julia's face—to echo a Graham Greene line—bore no experience beyond the school.

Years later, when a friend complimented her on her "wonderfully worldly expression" in a photograph, Julia replied, "It is the face I always try to wear when I am in New York, with no success." She was also slowly changing her social and political views, voted for Roosevelt in 1936, and was reading more socially engaged literature. One of the book reviews she tried writing was of *Give Us This Day,* Louis Java's story of a struggling baker whose daily one hundred hand-kneaded loaves cannot compete with the machines of big business. Beneath a brief and sympathetic review of this mediocre novel, someone typed a tough statement that could have been written by her father saying that the novel was "communist" and "full of dull defeated people."

She herself was not ready to compete in this tough city, especially not emotionally. She shared the belief of John Steinbeck, who fled the city (from her neighborhood) in defeat several years earlier, that the "climate is a scandal . . . traffic is madness . . . competition is murderous"—but if you can succeed, it has "everything." After returning with success behind him in 1943 and making the city his home, Steinbeck added, "All of everything is concentrated here . . . and its air is charged with energy." Julia also would embrace the city after her own success, but it would take her more than a decade.

CARO'S ILLNESS

When Julia arrived home in Pasadena, her mother was ill with what they thought was the "indigestion." In fact years of (then) uncontrollable high blood pressure had affected all her mother's organs. But the family was not fully aware of the extent of her deterioration. A touch of "the flu" was really kidney damage—uremic poisoning. She had already been regularly to Scripps Memorial Hospital in La Jolla for "successful" blood pressure and kidney treatments. When her complexion became yellow and her nausea and dizziness increased, she was taken by ambulance to San Diego again. On July 10, Julia wrote Dort that their mother was "100% better." She died at sixty years of age on July 21, 1937, two months after Julia's return. Julia was the only child at her side because John was in Massachusetts working for the Weston Paper Company and Dort was doing summer theater stock in Peterborough, New Hampshire.

The loss of her mother—a loss that grew more devastating for Julia each month—drove her back to the diary she began in New York City at the loss of her first great love: "I had a feeling, I guess I really knew before I came out here that she would die. I knew it, I knew she'd be dead by this fall, but I didn't realize it. I could have been much nicer to her. I could have been with her more. . . ."

After Dort and John returned from the East Coast together, Julia Carolyn Weston McWilliams was cremated and a minister conducted a simple funeral in the family home. Unknown to the children, their mother's ashes were kept in an urn in their father's office.

Julia would remember staying home to help supervise the house staff and offer support for her father; but her siblings remember that Willy took over the management of the house. Instead of breaking with her father's conservatism, Julia was brought back into his world, playing golf with him at the Midwick Country Club. Filial love softened the edges of the distance she always experienced with this reserved man.

> He is a strange but wonderful man [she wrote in her diary], and doesn't have much of the light touch or the abandon that would make this easier. He has wit and humor of course. I can see something else, he does not have an abandon for life. He sees it well-planned and sober, and, I think, pretty unexciting. . . . that McW family is pretty sober and serious, and he, being his Father's only son, had a great deal of resp[onsibility] drummed into him from the beginning.

Julia's brother remembered that during these years when he and his sisters were older and brought strong opinions of their own to the table, Mr. McWilliams sometimes stormed out of the dining room. His children could no longer "be seen but not heard."

Julia loved the sprawling, sunny openness of Southern California, which demanded an assertion of will against its broad spaciousness. Her will, however, was not strong just then. She did not stay home just to support her father. During this fall there were two job opportunities sent to her from Smith College: assistant to the advertising manager at Harcourt, Brace & Company in New York City and secretary at Reid Hall in Paris (a residence hall for the International Association of University Women). Though Julia had long wanted a job in the publishing world, she did not respond to either opportunity. Grief-stricken and still under the influence of her father, who wanted her to stay home, she felt as though her wings were clipped. She also had a job writing a monthly column on Southern California fashion for a new magazine to be published by family friends in San Francisco.

Coast, which she described as a *New Yorker* type of magazine, would publish in 1938 and go bankrupt in mid-1939. Julia spent the fall of 1937 contacting the major department stores in Los Angeles for information about their clothes and accessories. Before she left to spend a family Christmas with Aunt Theodora in Dalton, she sent in an article on fall suits, coats, hats, and accessories at Los Angeles stores and informed the magazine that she was stopping in New York City to contact the major department stores about getting fashion information early, as did *Vogue* and other publications. Though it was not a full-time job, her work at *Coast* had promise (even if they were late in sending her the $25-a-column fee).

The pieces she researched and wrote each month demonstrate a growing sophistication. Her style moves from a respectable "with matching accessories" style to her own jaunty voice ("On this matter of ski wear, I should like to say with sepulchral firmness: Don't dress yourself up like a bloody Alpine Christmas tree"). The essays gave the inside tips on society and clothes, with price and location, revealing that Julia got around and talked to many people (always at Bullocks-Wilshire, Robinsons, Saks Fifth Avenue, and several other stores from Beverly Hills to Palm Springs). An essay describing a group of stores entitled "Fifth Avenue on Wilshire" (June 1938) covered the opening of Saks Fifth Avenue and included photographs of Mrs. Gary Cooper, Dolores del Rio, and Sophie Tucker. Other essays focused on ski equipment and clothes (January 1938), travel clothes (July 1938), Paris fashions available in Southern California (October 1938), and the clothing styles of UCLA, USC, and Scripps College students (September 1938). For each essay Julia arranged photographs and quoted prices. The energy and ingenuity of her administrative and artistic skills as Southern California fashion editor went largely unrewarded when the magazine went bankrupt. But they show, even in a restricted and cliché-ridden medium, that Julia's writing skills were strengthening.

SOCIAL BUTTERFLY

By January, Julia told her diary: "Have decided I am really only a butterfly. All I want to do is play golf, piano, and simmer, and see people, and summer and live right here." She would later call the five years after her mother's death her "social butterfly" years. Sometimes when she sat for interviews about her life, she would leave out this period altogether. There were moments when she was bored, restless, hopeless, impotent, and depressed that everyone else was married. "I shall be interested to see if I am ever a happy success."

She assessed herself in her diary in 1940 and decided to have energy and enthusiasm: "Charm—get it!" she wrote. She was following her mother's dictates: "personality is everything." Caro had written in a letter to Dort on

January 17, 1934: "You two girls certainly are following my old motto 'person-ality is everything.' " Two months before she had written: "Get up and do more things and be much more—don't be a nobody." Thus, Julia kept active. Her albums are full of photographs of her hunting, golfing at Pebble Beach, skiing in Idaho, playing tennis. Her favorite sport was golf. She cut back on skiing after she again damaged the lunar cartilage in her knee. By May 1941 she had to have cartilage removed from one of her knees, exacerbating her early injuries. As with many people taller than average, her knees would be her weak spot all her life, yet she traveled from Tijuana, Mexico, to San Francisco, where she conferred with the editors of *Coast* and frequently visited with her friend Gay Bradley Wright. Julia was full of energy and curiosity about the world around her. Reading (Ortega y Gasset) and music absorbed her also, and she went to the Los Angeles Symphony, where Marian Anderson ap-peared in March 1938. In the back of her diary, she listed texts that had inspired her, and she continued to study music and language in this era of self-improvement and Dale Carnegie.

In June 1939 she attended both Dort's graduation from Bennington and her own fifth reunion of the Smith class of 1934. Connie Thayer (now Cory) planned the reunion, which saw them dressed in Scots kilts, sash, and hat in honor of President Neilson. The day of the parade, they marched at dawn to the president's home and sang to him and his wife, in bathrobes: "Oh, Presi-dent Neilson, to you we sing / Whatever may happen, what'er time may bring . . ." A lot of giggling and fun, it seemed to Julia, who also observed that everyone, including Connie, was pregnant and talked a lot about babies. When her girlfriends went home to babies, living out the dream of the "social-ized" young woman of that time, Julia returned to Pasadena alone.

Julia became more involved with the Junior League, which turned out to be an outlet for her playwriting and dramatic talents as well as a commitment to her civic responsibilities, following in the footsteps of her good-citizen father. The league, which met at the Huntington Hotel, gave plays for children in the civic auditorium to raise money for charities and family services. Julia played Abu, the faithful servant of an inventor in *Arabian Nights,* on February 10 and 11, 1939. Mary Frances Russell and other friends saw in these perfor-mances the star quality, drama, presence, stature, and commanding voice of would-be famous Julia Child. As she had done for the attic productions of the McWilliams and Hall gang, Julia wrote several of the plays for the Junior League, including "Bean Boy," a two-act musical set in Monterey in 1820, "The Bells of Brittany," a two-act fantasy, and "The Mississippi Belle," set in 1875. In each, she placed young people in period clothes either on the water or in caves, escaping an evil figure. Among these scripts in her private collection is a tight and cynical black radio drama set in New York City, "A Helping Hand," which is certainly not intended for children.

Julia also wrote essays for the *Pasadena Junior League News,* a professional publication, including an essay, "The Intelligent Woman Voter," which encouraged involvement in the League of Women Voters. She continued to write book reviews, as she had in New York, which reveal a growing depth of analysis and sophisticated writing style, though the choice of books was sometimes questionable. Even a two-page witty verse encouraging Junior Leaguers to sell tickets to the annual dog show at the Santa Anita Kennel shows a writer in development.

Apart from civic involvement, Julia now had an active social life: "I want lots of people around who are stimulating and with whom I feel intoxicated and clever and charming and a part," she told her diary. Now that Gay Bradley was in San Francisco, her closest friend was Katy Gates, who in November 1939 had married Julia's friend Freeman (Tule) Gates. The Gates family had long been friends of the McWilliamses, and Tule, like her male cousins, was a graduate of the Thatcher School in Ojai. He was a strapping guy like so many of her California friends. Their parties centered on San Malo, where the Meyers twins lived next door, and on the ranch of Tule's cousin Florence Baldwin in Ojai, near Santa Barbara. Julia remembers the "wild weekends" at San Malo, where her father had built a large dormered, Ye-Olde-English house on a cliff above the beach, a home with brick walls surrounding the house.

Then there were the games in Ojai, at Rancho Matiliji, "a sort of Tibetan monastery made of weathered wood." Robert Hastings, who graduated from the Thatcher School as well as Yale (after Harvard Law School he would found a great law firm in Los Angeles), characterizes their weekends at the ranch by the play they all wrote and dramatized, "The Legend of the Screeching Cliff." After some serious drinking, the group pretended a shoot-out, throwing a dummy over the cliff, with Harrison Chandler (of the *Los Angeles Times* family) filming it all. Julia was probably paired with Chandler, a thirty-seven-year-old graduate of Stanford, that weekend; though Hastings remembers that they were all just friends, Gay Bradley Wright remembers that "he was crazy about Julia." Except for Katy, who was five years her junior, most of these friends were older. "I took to Julia absolutely," says Katy, "loved her straight off because she is so outgoing and so much herself."

Despite the mores of her time that expected her not to have a career, Julia had enough Scots and Puritan heritage in her to believe that she should be doing something "useful." In the fall of 1939 she weighed a job offer to be advertising manager of the Beverly Hills branch of W. & J. Sloane. She balanced the loss of freedom against the opportunity to meet new faces, especially male ones, and a sense of doing something valuable.

By the time Julia began her job at Sloane's she had come into her mother's inheritance and was feeling confident about herself. She was in charge of public relations and advertising and had one secretary. She confided in her diary, which she had taken up again briefly, that at sixteen she had been hurt when people looked at her with curiosity and that her earlier lovesick ramblings about Tom in her diary displayed "callow adolescence." Every year "brings more peace of mind, adjustment, and pleasure," she assured herself. The security of her own money and the responsibility of her job, which paid $200 a month, even lessened her worry about her unmarried state.

"And thank heaven I am getting over that fear and contempt of single maidenhood (or should I say maiden head—guess not)," she wrote in her diary. "I am quite content to be the way I am—and feel quite superior to many a wedded mouse. By god—I can do what I want! Though I do hate to have to scurry around for extra men every time I give a party—and of course—sex is nice. But it is a mighty difficult subject—and a mighty self-indulgent one too." Julia made it very clear in later years that "I had had several affairs before meeting my husband, but we did not go all the way. . . . One did not in those days."

In the back of her diary, in an undated entry, Julia copied the following verse:

Oh why do you walk though the fields in gloves,
Missing so much, so much?
Oh fat, white woman whom nobody loves,
When the grass is as soft as the breasts of doves
And shivering sweet to touch
Why do you walk through the fields in gloves—
Missing so much and so much?

From the first of March 1940 until the summer months, Julia arose early and drove down the hills to Los Angeles and Sunset Boulevard, which took her through Hollywood to Beverly Hills. There was no freeway yet, though the county was building one, much to the distress of John McWilliams, who lobbied against it. Julia loved progress and change. She detailed the basis of her confident and happy life in her diary: a grand house, plenty of money, "each with independent incomes," good social position and heritage, the freedom to do what she wanted, and a "pleasant perfect relationship" with her father.

As inspiring and as much fun as her job was, Julia was in a position beyond her training. With a budget of $100,000 a year, she had to hire newspaper artists, typographers, and printers, plan advertising campaigns and write copy. She believed she was doing well after four months until an incident when she forgot to clear the copy for a policy statement with national headquarters before sending it to the printmaker and the newspapers (actually she forgot to call in the changes when they arrived because they seemed minor). The New York office was deeply and rightfully angered, and Julia was fired for rank insubordination. She apparently took it well, because four years later she recorded on a government job description an explanation why she left W. & J. Sloane: "Fired, and I don't wonder. One needs a much more detailed knowledge of business, buying, markets, and more experience in advertising than I had had for so much responsibility. But I learned a great deal, and did pretty well in establishing the mechanics of the office and the business personnel."

During one of Julia's big cocktail parties when brother John was home for the holidays, he took one look at Josephine Smith, who had been brought by one of the Meyers twins, and it was love. Jo was fair and handsome, a classic California girl. Following their marriage in June 1940, the young John McWilliams moved to Massachusetts and the Weston Paper Company. Though he continued to manage the investments of his sisters—their inheritances had been equal—Julia would never again spend a sustained length of time with him. Indeed, especially during the war years to come, they did not even remain in correspondence for periods of time.

Dorothy, on the other hand, finally returned home to Pasadena after a year of work at the Cambridge School in Waltham, Massachusetts, and some theatrical stage-managing for Menotti's operas *The Medium* and *The Telephone* in New York City. Her presence eventually allowed Julia to take a job in the East. Dort had probably been closer to Willy than to her sister ("I do not think I was a particularly good sister because I did not know Dorothy very well. She was young and a nuisance," admits Julia). Now, as adults, the sisters became close friends. Indeed, as they aged, people often confused their voices and figures.

After nearly four years at home, Julia had matured emotionally. Certainly the equanimity with which she took any possible shame in her firing from Sloane's, which she blamed on herself, illustrates this. The return to Pasadena had been a step backward when it was taken, yet by 1940–41 Julia herself began to notice, upon rereading her diary, her burgeoning maturity. Without tearing out the childish pages, she added dated notes in the margins: beside a lovesick poem, she wrote "trash"; beside her emotional reaction to her jilting, "history of delayed (or prolonged) adolescence. May 7, 1941." She had now even forgotten the boy's name, she claimed. Perhaps this "delayed adolescence" was a gift from her emotional mother, set down in Julia's loving diary at her mother's death: "She was really run by emotions . . . child-like . . . fresh and spontaneous. . . . she would give of herself and her energies actively and aggressively, with her whole heart and interest. I should like to be like Mother in all that."

At the same time, Julia's diary shows her growing skepticism about religion, politics, and herself. "I think it is particularly interesting how the years dissolve nobility of spirit. When I was in school and later, I felt I had particular and unique spiritual gifts. That I was meant for something, and was like no one else. It hadn't come out yet, but it was there, warm and latent. . . . It still lingered in N.Y., and here at B.H. Today, it has gone out and I am sadly an ordinary person . . . with talents which I do not use." In another passage in which she declares, "Lord, how I hate the good," she deplores such self-conscious goodness in favor of "an unconscious wicked devilish goodness." Using her only reference to food, she writes: "I like [the] 'good' but it must be with salt and pepper, a small onion and a bay leaf. August 3, 1940."

She thought through her religious beliefs and values during the painful recovery from knee surgery in March 1941. The highest value, she concluded as the rain fell outside her hospital window, was in relations with others; introversion and self-analysis were fine for creative geniuses, but for a "happy full life," human relationships are paramount. Her religious beliefs were moving far away from those of her Presbyterian ancestors: the human spirit, a part of God that returns to God (the "God Stream"), is trying to make "his kingdom come on earth." Rejecting resurrection and miracles, she writes that while Jesus was the perfect living example for human behavior, all earthly events could be explained by natural causes.

POLITICS AND A PROPOSAL

When Julia decided to leave home to enter government service and the international arena in 1942, it was not a sudden move. With Japan's invasion of China in the fall of 1937 she began her first political commentary in her diary. When Hitler demanded the right of self-determination for Germans in Austria and Czechoslovakia the following February, she began reading political articles. Still, in the autumn of 1939 she felt the war was "remote" and not "our war." By June 1941, even while she was continuing those weekend parties for twelve in San Malo (followed by pages of limericks in her diary—probably written under the martini influence: "Residue of W[illiam] C[ullen] Bryant, arise!"), she wrote not of dating Harrison Chandler but of the crisis in world affairs. For her, Roosevelt's speeches signaled approaching war.

As her father's daughter, Julia was always involved in civic concerns. She had discussed the building of Union Station in Los Angeles, argued with her father over the building of the Pasadena Freeway (opened on New Year's Day 1941) and the merits of FDR's social programs, and had done local precinct work during elections, as well as raise scholarship funds for Smith College. She had two favorite columnists—Walter Lippmann and Dorothy Thompson—and used their arguments in her conversation, clipping the best articles for her diary. When she decided to do precinct work and vote for Wendell Willkie instead of FDR ("I voted for Roosie in 36"), it was less her father's influence than her own belief that FDR's reform had gone far enough. She wanted more individual freedom and responsibility, for she had just read Huxley's *Brave New World* and Dorothy Thompson's article about the WPA, which argued that Roosevelt's WPA, by paying according to a man's needs, was conditioning him to "increase his needs and decrease his abilities." Julia pasted the article into her diary. She admired Thompson's style and was provoked by her ideas. Pages of analysis in the diary reveal Julia's lively intelligence and a well-read mind. This keen interest in politics and world affairs would never leave her.

Her first proposal of marriage capped the summer of 1941. Harrison Chandler, who had been part of their San Malo and Ojai ranch crowd for years, asked her to marry him. She always thought that when this flattering moment arrived she would "handle that situation with enormous elegance and *Saturday Evening Post* finesse—but I found I was just as embarrassed as he was and didn't know at all what to say." Harrison was a good friend, handsome, well dressed, and good company. Gay thought he was not exciting enough for her. Actually, he was shy and would not marry until he was fifty-five years old (to a fifty-one-year-old divorcée in 1958). Harrison Gray Otis Chandler, one of six children and the middle son of Harry Chandler and Marian Otis Chandler, became, when the dynasty was inherited, the head of the Times Mirror printing operations. How different life would have been for Julia and the cooking world had she taken the easy choice and married into this Los Angeles establishment.

Julia did not know if she liked Harrison enough to marry him. She asked him that late August day if he wanted to live in Pasadena and have three or four children (there is no record of what he said). "I have an idea I may succumb," she told her diary, waiting to see what Dort thought of him. Julia was flattered and continued to date him, testing her feelings toward him. "I took him seriously for about a month," she admitted in 1996. "He was very nice in a somewhat stiff way. I don't remember what happened to him."

While Julia was making up her mind (and dating him for seven more months), she began volunteer work with the American Red Cross of Pasadena in September 1941, serving as head of the Department of Stenographic Services, typing and mimeographing. Following the Japanese bombing of Pearl Harbor on December 7, 1941, she was caught up in the need to have her country join the war: "I am definitely anti-isolationist. What kind of world would it be if we were alone surrounded by enemies." Her reasoning was not ideological, but based on her recently articulated philosophy of the primacy of human relationships.

Because of the world war, the Tournament of Roses was canceled New Year's Day 1942. The next month, as Japan took Singapore, Rangoon, and Burma, Julia added the Aircraft Warning Service to her Red Cross work. A short undated clipping from the local newspaper reveals how well she worked with this group: "Everybody called everybody either 'Mr.' or 'Mrs.' at the Fourth Interceptor Command with the exception of Julia McWilliams whom everybody addresses as Julia."

The only relationship she could not seem to find charming was the one with Harrison Chandler. In the second week of April she declined his marriage proposal. "4/10/42—NO. A cooling from both parties. And—I hope I shall maintain this position—it is a SIN to marry without LOVE. And marriage while utterly desirable, from my point of view, must be the right one. I know what I want, and it is 'sympatico'—companionship, interests, great respect, and fun. Otherwise and always—NO."

Continuing her double volunteer work, she added the occasional line of poetry at the back of her diary, such as Edna St. Vincent Millay's "Now that love has perished" stanza that begins by addressing her "erstwhile dear" who is "no longer cherished" and has a line about love having "come and gone." But the times called for action, not poetry. Her friends, including Bob Hastings and Tule Gates, were joining the Navy. Janie McBain, a San Francisco friend whose husband was stationed in Italy, urged Julia to come and stay with her in Washington.

Pragmatism—an efficacious activism—ran through Julia's body like a current. She was a doer. After asking herself several times in her diary what she should do about her strong political beliefs, she took the Civil Service exam, stopped keeping a diary, essentially ceased her writing practice, resigned her Red Cross and aircraft warning work, and applied to the WAVES and WACS. She wanted to be in the Navy and knew that Dorothy would stay home with their father. In midsummer she packed her bags and typewriter and boarded the train for what would prove to be her most life-changing journey. Katy Gates, who was already in Washington with her Navy husband, said, "Washington was where the action was. New York was passé. Julia always wanted to be where something was going on. She wanted to keep up with the times." Julia added: "The war was the change in my life."

$\mathcal{M}$ISS McWILLIAMS
GOES TO WASHINGTON

As Julia left the magnificent Union Station with her suitcases, Washington, DC's white monuments seemed to intensify the summer heat. The spirit of action in the city was contagious, young civil servants caught up in the midst of world events. The arena fit her size. The sight of the Capitol brought tears to her patriotic eyes. Volunteering for the Aircraft Warning Service and the Red Cross in Pasadena had not been enough.

After a brief stay with Janie McBain, whose father was an influential San Francisco lawyer who knew many leading figures in the political world, Julia settled in the Brighton Hotel on California Street and waited for news about her application to the WAVES. The Naval Reserve returned her letter with an "automatic disqualification." The form was checked as a "physical" disqualification, though the category listed only "under five feet," with no mention of the other extreme. But someone had circled the phrase in her letter mentioning she was six feet one inch, an understatement at that. "I was too long," she would explain later. Thereafter, she would list her height as six feet—a shaving-off of two inches.

With adventure on the high seas beyond her reach, Julia took a job the end of August 1942 as Senior Typist for the Research Unit of the Office of War Information, Department of State. In short, "Mellot's Madhouse," after the Director and the frenetic environment. The Assistant Director was Noble Cathcart, husband of her cousin Harriet. She worked in a building opposite the Willard Hotel, madly typing white file cards for every government official mentioned in the newspapers and official documents, listing full title and agency. In two months she had typed herself through 10,000 cards and to the door of madness. She applied for a job with the Office of Strategic Services, where she had friends. "I worked so hard they replaced me with two people," she said of her stint at Mellot's Madhouse.

Still a social animal, Julia, when she was not typing and enlivening the office madness, partied with her growing number of friends in Washington from Pasadena and Northampton. The dinner parties and martinis of Smith College and San Malo beach continued in Washington, but the nights were not as late.

In December, wearing a new leopard fur coat to the work, Julia began her career in the Office of Strategic Services (OSS) as Junior Research Assistant in the office of the Director, William Donovan, on E Street. She was now in the Secret Intelligence (SI) branch of government. Her immediate supervisor was Marian O'Connell, an old friend of the Director and in charge of the Registry, which processed all records and correspondence. Edwin J. (Ned) Putzell, Jr., the Executive Officer and Assistant Director of the OSS, remembers Julia as "the life of the group. Julia was energetic, light of spirit, always of good humor—and willing to jump into any assignment." Aline Griffith, who later became a countess and authored *The Spy Wore Red* (1987), also worked with Julia before going to work in Spain. *The Spy* captured the cloak-and-dagger atmosphere quite dramatically.

Occasionally they were visited by the Director himself, who flew in from world hot spots. William (Wild Bill) Donovan was a corpulent, rather dumpy-looking man who was anything but wild. He had intense personal magnetism, but spoke with a restrained voice when he was in the office or in the field. Unemotional, but a risk taker. Julia's personal memory of him was that she only said "yes, sir" and "no, sir" to him: "He was rather small and rumpled [with] piercing blue eyes; and it was said that he could read a document just by turning the pages, he was so fast at it, and he was . . . somehow fascinating [to people]. He gave you his complete attention and you were just fascinated by him."

Donovan had been a Wall Street lawyer and Republican when Franklin Delano Roosevelt and he planned what would be called the OSS, America's first espionage unit. FDR was impressed with Donovan's prophecy that Britain would withstand the Nazi blitz and wanted an intelligence organization equal to that of the "Brits." Nothing like it had existed in any previous American war.

Donovan reported only to FDR, a status that, together with his loose administrative style (he was in fact a terrible organizer), provoked much jealousy and criticism from other government people, particularly in the military. Donovan (a lawyer) was not of the military establishment, nor were his Ivy League employees. Just as the British Secret Intelligence Service seemed to be staffed from *Burke's Peerage,* so the Office of Strategic Services was composed of blue bloods or, as some called them, "a bunch of college professors" or "Donovan's amateur playboys." Like Julia, they came from wealthy families and did not need the money; hence Donovan reasoned they were not bribable.

Political views were irrelevant to the Director—indeed a number of communists were recruited. He valued creative intelligence, a love of adventure, and a willingness to fight the enemy. And he left them alone to plan their capers. At the time this was positively un-American—shrouded in secrecy and outside any military or governmental system. And it was exhilarating—not only for Julia and the file keepers in Washington—but for those abroad. Thus Donovan gathered around him the best and the brightest, from James B. Conant to Moe Berg of Red Sox fame; from filmmaker John Ford to David Bruce, Allen Dulles, and Junius S. Morgan. One cynic said that Donovan staffed the OSS with "potential postwar clients."

Julia was promoted to Clerk within the Director's office in the spring of 1943, and at the beginning of the summer she became Senior Clerk, reaching the salary of $1,800 a year, all of which was transferred to the First Trust and Savings Bank of Pasadena.

When a new section concerning air-sea rescue opened in midsummer, Julia was transferred out of Donovan's office. Several branches of government were involved, but the OSS paid for the office personnel, equipment, and space. The Information Exchange of the Emergency Rescue Equipment (ERE), started by Harold Coolidge and Henry Steel to aid fliers downed at sea, was located in Temporary A Building at the corner of Second and T streets. Julia dubbed it the "fish-squeezing unit" because one of their experiments was to see if survivors in life rafts could squeeze a fish and drink the water from the fish's body. Julia and her colleague Alice Carson carpooled to the market and bought the fish for their test. Naive, perhaps, but certainly in keeping with the experiments of America's first espionage organization. ERE's most important work was developing exposure suits, and their pioneering work, according to one of Julia's colleagues, became "the founding of the Coast Guard's air-sea rescue service."

The OSS budget was "largely unvouchered," claimed one historian, who documented that Donovan bought ships, houses, printing plants, and planes. "Every eccentric schemer with a harebrained plan for secret operations (from phosphorescent foxes to incendiary bats) would find a sympathetic ear in Donovan's office."

Histories of the OSS are filled with stories of the early attempts at black espionage against the Germans and the Japanese. Because the OSS was filled with Ivy Leaguers and professors, and Donovan did not want to stifle action and creativity, there were some inventive plans to sabotage the enemy's reputation in occupied lands, including the manufacture of a substance that smelled like dung, to embarrass the Japanese in China.

Only Donovan's closeness to Roosevelt kept him safe from his detractors. The military believed that the OSS was a "fly-by-night" organization; West Pointers called it "Donovan's dragoons"; the isolationist Charles Lindbergh said the organization was "full of politics, ballyhoo, and contro- versy"; J. Edgar Hoover was a bitter rival; and Herr Goebbels called it a "staff of Jewish scribblers." By the end of the decade, it was clear to everyone that "Donovan's Dreamers" were idealistic and "helter-skelter but brilliant," a far cry from the view that today demonizes its successor, the Central Intelligence Agency.

Long before Julia was promoted from Senior Clerk to Administrative Assistant, she was supervising an office of forty people (directly overseeing eight), securing office furnishings, hiring clerical help, and initiating proce- dures related to financing, office security, and supplies. When Julia wanted to talk to Lieutenant Commander Earl F. Hiscock (Coast Guard Reserve, which eventually took over the unit) about the many sinkings of merchant vessels carrying supplies to Europe (this bureau was gathering all the information on sinkings, survivors, and possible new equipment), she turned over the waste- basket to sit on and talk to him at eye level, according to her friend Alice Carson, who later married Hiscock.

While Julia was working six days a week in a domestic branch of Amer- ica's Secret Intelligence, she lived in her cramped apartment in the Brighton Hotel with a two-burner hot plate on top of a refrigerator in her living room. She did what she later called "some minor cooking" and had "nice crowded parties." Alice Carson, who graduated from Smith the year Julia enrolled, remembered eating a fried chicken dinner at Julia's apartment. Julia remem- bered, "I got chicken fat all over the wallpaper," in her awkward attempt at cooking.

Another friend whom she met in the "fish-squeezing unit" was Jack Moore, art school graduate and Army private who worked for a civilian named Paul Child in the Presentation Division (photography, graphics, maps). Jack and Julia met in the Naval Yard because the ERE needed some graphics. His boss had just been shipped out to New Delhi to work for Supreme Com- mander Mountbatten, and Moore would soon follow. Moore, who would be the initial illustrator for her first cookbook, thought of Julia "as a woman of extraordinary personality. She was just not any kind of an American stereo- type. By virtue of necessity—I mean, here is this six-foot-two-inch-tall Ameri- can woman looking down on all the males she ever meets—she had to evolve a sense of herself that was different from the person who is a physically standard specimen."

Her promotion at the end of 1943 placed Julia closer to her dream of more active service, even if it meant returning to files again. She became

Administrative Assistant in the Registry of the OSS, returning to Donovan's office. There was a $600 raise for the new year and a feeling of being part of America's first espionage organization. Donovan had decided he could not collect intelligence by having all his people in Washington, DC, and began establishing bases around the world. Julia wanted to serve overseas (her brother John was in German-occupied France, though they had no news of his whereabouts). When she heard the organization wanted volunteers for work in India, she applied. She was free, white, and thirty-one.

Spying

and

Romance

Chapter 6

*I*NDIA INTRIGUE

(1944 – 1945)

"A cook should possess generous worldly experience."
NORMAN DOUGLAS, *South Wind*

THE THREE WOMEN had their orders to leave Newport News, Virginia, by troop train on February 26 for Wilmington, California. Julia McWilliams, Eleanor (Ellie) Thiry, and Dr. Cora DuBois (a well-known anthropologist) had been sworn to secrecy, a vow that precluded keeping a diary. "If people ask you why you are here, tell 'em you are file clerks," they were instructed. "We were a very bedraggled-looking bunch," said Julia. The civilian women were a source of curiosity and amazement to the soldiers on the train, wrote Ellie Thiry, who (against orders and with several others) kept a diary of her experience. Ellie had dark, curly hair and was practical (she would always decorate the women's living quarters).

*S*LOW BOAT TO INDIA

After a week by train, there were seven more days in California being "orientated" in a barracks, attending movies and lectures, being issued fatigues and gas masks and told to practice ship evacuation by rope over the side. Rewarded with a couple of days of free time, the women went to the McWilliams home in Pasadena, where they met Julia's handsome father, now the object of several widows' attentions. Until they headed for Wilmington, their port of embarkation, the women filled the house on South Pasadena Avenue with laughter.

With bedroll, canteen, gas mask, and pith helmet on her back, Julia and nine other women boarded the SS *Mariposa,* a cruise ship serving as a troopship. They were greeted that March 8 by band music, wolf calls, and whistles, the only women on board with more than 3,000 men. This raucous reception stoked the flames of adventure in some, fear in others. In addition to Julia, Cora, and Ellie, there were Rosamund Frame, Virginia (known as Peachy) Durand, Mary Nelson Lee (of the Virginia Lee family), and two other women. "An utterly strange experience," wrote Julia, who had started a short-lived diary (entitled "Oh So Private") two days out to sea. Naturally, the captain set aside a portion of the deck "exclusively for the gals," said Peachy. "We were called girls," insists Julia (who was called Julie). The next morning Julia organized the women to spread the word they were traveling missionaries. The ploy never worked.

Among the civilians on board was Gregory Bateson, an eminent British anthropologist (married to Margaret Mead) who spoke Malay. He was six feet five inches tall and looked "like a sardonic horse," Paul Child later described. He "had a veritable genius for making the obvious obscure," wrote one OSS colleague, but another called him a "dazzling conversationalist." Julia liked him, and not just because he was her height: "He always looked like his pants were falling off because they hung low on his hips. He and I took Chinese lessons on the deck of the ship. He was very interesting because he was asking about relatives and relationships." These conversations with Bateson, DuBois, and some of the other well-educated civilians (such as Rosie Frame, who was giving the Chinese lessons) made Julia feel she had been "vegetating" mentally, physically, and spiritually.

Julia longed to talk to someone to help "crystallize" her ideas about this voyage. Hence the origin of a new diary. "What kind of mind do I have?" she asked herself after being in the presence of "anthropologists, world thinkers, and missionaries" on board. She questioned her religious beliefs, her lack of permanence, the war, even the designs that one woman seemed to have on her (probably Cora DuBois, a lesbian who was to head the Research and Analysis Division in Ceylon). Julia's initial revulsion, based on inexperience and fear, was soon replaced by what would become a lifelong friendship. Years later Julia would say that "the OSS was my first encounter with the academic mind."

There was not a chair on board except at the dinner table, so the women sat on their life vests or on their bunks. Because Julia typed the ship's newspaper, she got below deck and learned about the sailors' attitude toward the war, which fell far short of her patriotic idealism. She wrote sketches of each woman for the newspaper: Ellie joined the ship's band, which practiced each day; the petite and dark-haired Rosie Frame was breaking all the hearts on board—even Bateson thought her "a little minx"—but she was romancing a man named Thibaut de Saint Phalle.

In cabin 237, the nine women slept on three triple-decker bunks, using one tub for cold saltwater baths, one toilet, one sink, and one drawer each for their personal items. Two cups of water in their helmets washed their panties. When they docked on March 28 in Australia and took on fresh water, the women soon had their bunks strung with lines of drying clothes. Naked bodies moved about, looking for missing socks. Julia remembered with discomfort the "mass living" at the Katharine Branson School and Smith College. Compensating for the lack of privacy was the beauty of the sunsets, the star-studded nights, and ahead India and China, the greatest adventure of her life.

Because of the possible presence of Japanese submarines, they had a military escort during the first week in April before reaching Bombay (they were originally assigned to land in Calcutta). On the thirty-first day, Julia later said on several occasions, "the ship drew up to the coast and I could see and smell the haze. Oh, my God, what have I gotten myself into? After that, I never had any fright." Despite a bad cold, Julia could smell the leafy cigarettes, incense, and ancient dirt of India when she and Peachy disembarked on Easter Sunday.

India housed many war-weary British and American military. The CBI (China, Burma, India) personnel called themselves Confused Bastards in India. Julia did not share the cynicism of those Americans who had been there a few months and picked up the British colonial hatred of the Indians; they called her an "eager beaver." "Have met practically no one who likes India. I do," she wrote in her diary. She described the lazy clip-clop of gharries, squeaky shoes, the white-jacketed, skirt-panted men with black crooked-stick umbrellas, and baskets of fruit and vegetables with live chickens softly lying in the middle. The children would swarm around her, curious and laughing: "You desire to sit?" they said to the tall American woman.

She accompanied a few of the men, including Joseph R. Coolidge (another OSS colleague, a cartographer, who kept a diary of the train and boat trip), to dinner and then on a merry motor tour of the red-light district. She liked John Bolton-Carter, a South African, who invited her and Mary Nelson up for drinks. She later went golfing and dancing with him. Rosie Frame, fluent in Mandarin as the daughter of missionaries in Peking, wanted to go to

China, but was first sent to New Delhi. The women remaining shared a comfortable house for a week, shopping and sightseeing freely until there were severe explosions at the docks. Soon they were told they would not go to New Delhi but to Ceylon, where Mountbatten had moved his headquarters. The confusing orders were snafu (situation normal, all fucked up).

There was "a killing train ride across India, four in a compartment with a tremendous lot of luggage," Julia wrote (though fifty years later she described the trip as "beautiful" and "fascinating"). Ellie Thiry and another woman slept on top, Julia and another woman on the bottom. The dust rushed into the train's every crack from the vast and relentlessly flat terrain. When they stopped, Julia was struck by the yelling of "incomprehensible languages." One Singhalese police officer talked to her at length about Buddhism and the 150-year oppression of Ceylon (a pear-shaped island near the southern tip of India) by the English. The heat bothered everyone except rail-thin Julia. From Madras they ferried to the island. At every stop there were groups of officers to escort them around town ("pursued by the U.S. Navy," is the way she expressed it), men about whom she speaks disparagingly in her diary.

LAND OF THE LOTUS EATERS

On April 25 they arrived in Colombo, Ceylon (later to be called Sri Lanka), and were met by S. Dillon Ripley ("I always liked his looks"), head of the Secret Intelligence Division there. A year younger than Julia and typical of the OSS brass, Ripley, a Yale and Harvard biologist and ornithologist, was an authority on the birds of the Far East and had lived in the region. He would later spend two decades of his life administering the Smithsonian Institution in Washington, DC.

"I want to fish and shoot, and meet some active sports! But this is Wah." She settled for swimming in the Indian Ocean. Colombo was a hot and steamy port city, ten degrees from the equator. Gnats hovered in the air above her head as if buzzing in a thick soup. At 8 A.M. the next day they boarded what the Americans called the Toonerville Trolley (Julia called it the Mountbatten Special, for it was run by the British). They traveled through lush tropical hills to reach Kandy, a safe headquarters 1,200 feet above sea level.

Two months to the day after they had left Washington together, Julia and Peachy were sharing a large room in the Queens Hotel in Kandy. She liked Mary Nelson and Cora DuBois and Peggy Wheeler (daughter of General Raymond Wheeler, a Deputy Supreme Allied Commander), but "Peachy and I see eye to eye," she told her diary. "Peachy was like our kid sister, a woman with dark hair, innocence, and enthusiasm," she remembered years later. They slept in canopy beds (four-posters with mosquito netting) and contended with clogged drains and occasional water.

> Life is pastoral and easy-going [she wrote]. We are wakened at 7:15 by our room boy who knocks heavily at the door, murmurs "Morning, Missie," and paddles into the room in his bare feet carrying morning tea and fruit. We leisurely dress, leaving 5 minutes for breakfast, and at 8:05 our 2-ton truck is at the door of the Queens Hotel and we are off, at the fast clip of 19 to 24 miles an hour to our office, 7 miles away.

Headquarters was a tea plantation—a colonial estate called Nandana—where they worked in basha (palm-thatched) huts connected by cement walks and surrounded by barbed wire. Primitive, airy, and comfortable is the way Julia described it. Her basha was just beyond Mountbatten's botanical garden. Supreme Commander Lord Louis Mountbatten (who oversaw the OSS) had arrived April 15 to live in the King's Pavilion; "Kandy is probably the most beautiful spot in the world," he declared, settling into the miniature white palace. Everyone ate lunch together in a thatched mess hall on a hill about three-hundred yards from the offices, which closed about 5 P.M. The civilians then had two hours of sunlight for tennis and golf ("It was nice to have a transportable hobby").

A Shangri-La setting with a sinister purpose: guerrilla warfare against the Japanese. The move to Kandy, according to historian Barbara Tuchman, signaled a "direction [to] the sea . . . providing a fleet base in the Indian Ocean" to attack Japan, for General Stilwell believed "the future of Asia was at stake." The headquarters camp looked over the lake to the surrounding mountains and the flowering trees and terraced rice paddies below. Eighty degree temperatures (Julia described it as "skin-warm"), banyan trees, and monkeys. "Land of the Lotus Eaters," one woman called it. The wide porch of the main bungalow had deep summer chairs. Palm-straw padding covered the walls and roof, and the appearance was rustic but neat. Colonial.

Kandy was inhabited by gentle Singhalese, who were Hinayana Buddhists (as opposed to the Hinu Tamil or the fierce-looking black Muslim Moors in the north). Their gongs and fire crackers punctuated the days. The women wore saris; the OSS women wore cotton dresses. Heavy work was done by small elephants, who would bathe in the lake at the end of each day. Coolidge remembers the day that Julia climbed on one of the elephants, straddling its neck, and the animal produced an erection of at least three feet.

"When she dismounted, the thing was still evident, and she crowed with laughter."

Though she knew more about golf clubs than international cables and espionage, Julia, with a high security clearance, was head of the Registry, which processed all classified papers for the invasion of the Malay Peninsula. After spending the second day filing treatises, she wondered in her diary, "Why did I come over as Registry. I hate this work." Yet she soon discovered she was good at organizing the central headquarters for dispatches, sensitive orders, and espionage/sabotage for the South East Asia Command (SEAC), headed by forty-four-year-old Mountbatten (Supremo, in British shorthand).

General Douglas MacArthur, according to several OSS historians, did not cooperate with Donovan's OSS or Britain's MI6, whose work in Southeast Asia was under Mountbatten and was directed from this island off the east coast of India. The word was that MacArthur, who had his own Army Intelligence, hated Donovan (a civilian) and threatened to arrest any OSS caught in *his* territory. The intellectuals disdained the Regular Army, and the attitude was mutual.

The warm tropical climate and palm trees reminded her of home, until she discovered scorpions in the drawers. There were also tarantulas, tiny noiseless mosquitoes, leeches, ravenous termites, and four-inch cockroaches. The vegetation was tropical and the rain arrived about four each afternoon. "Penicillin" grew on folded clothes. Yet Julia awakened each morning thrilled with the adventure, if not with the routine of her office. She was eager to be a part of the civilian intellectual world of Cora DuBois, Gregory Bateson, and Dillon Ripley, opening her mind to stimulating ideas and sophistication.

One afternoon when Julia and Gregory Bateson were having drinks on the hotel porch, she again met Betty MacDonald, who thought that Julia had, when she knew her in Washington, "a highly developed security sixth sense." Betty was a journalist with Scripps-Howard when she was recruited by the OSS because she had lived with a Japanese family in Hawaii and had learned the language in order to go to Japan. "Pearl Harbor ended this goal," she wrote. Her husband, a lieutenant commander and journalist who would later found the *Bangkok Times,* was stationed in Kandy, and Betty was on temporary duty (from New Delhi) in Ceylon with MO (Morale Operations, otherwise known as black propaganda). Betty was tanned from tennis, was outgoing, and loved puns. She liked Julia immediately, she says, especially the fact that "bureaucracy did not faze her at all. She was always making fun of the bureaucrats." Betty would later become the historian for the women of the OSS (*Sisterhood of Spies,* 1997).

Colonel Richard P. (Dick) Heppner (on leave from Donovan's law firm) arrived to be their CO. He was a handsome graduate of Princeton and Columbia Law School. Ellie worked for him in one room off a large basha hut housing the War Room, maintained by Paul Child and Jack Moore. The third room of the basha hut was occupied by Heppner's deputy (Lieutenant Colonel Paul Helliwell) and secretary. The Registry occupied its own basha hut. The MO lived on what they called "Fleet Street," with field photography laboratories (John Ford's branch) on "Hollywood Boulevard."

The civilians, including Julia McWilliams, socialized with the officers. The youngest officer, Byron Martin ("He was pert, bright, and lots of fun," writes MacDonald), was a decade younger than Julia and also a former Pasadenan who was impressed with both officers and civilians of the 404th Division. "They were sophisticates, and I often thought Julia was the most sophisticated of all. She was witty, fun, extremely well-informed, and always the most personable. I adored her and generally regarded her as my peer, despite the actual age difference, thanks to her warm personality."

While Ivy League men and women of the OSS China Command were privileged and educated, they were in search of more worldly knowledge. Years later, Julia, gazing heavenward with her hand on her chest, would say, "I was a playgirl looking for the light." The OSS was called "Oh So Secret" or "Oh So Social," or even "Oh Such Snobs" (probably the military view). They may have suffered from GI food and dysentery, but the distance from familial boundaries, the threat of danger, the excitement of service and adventure, and the anesthetic of gin created a compelling camaraderie, leading to many affairs, several marriages, and, ultimately, quite a few divorces.

PAUL CUSHING CHILD

By May 1 (when she first mentions his name in her diary), Julia McWilliams met Paul Child on the tea planter's veranda that was now the main headquarter's building. Paul was an older man, a friend of Bateson's who was an urbane and multilingual OSS officer and artist working with Generals Donovan, Wedemeyer, and Chennault to create the maps and graphs for the War Room of the OSS China Command, first in New Delhi (fondly called "Per Diem Hill") and then in Kandy. By the end of the month she placed a long description of him in her diary:

> I have a nice time with the office men—not *Whee,* but pleasant. There is Paul Child, an artist who, when I first saw him, I thought as not at all nice looking. He is about 40 [he was forty-two, she almost thirty-two],

has light hair which is *not* on top, an unbecoming blond mustache and a long unbecoming nose. But he is very composed. I find him both pleasant, comfortable and very mentally get-at-able. We have dinner frequently and go to the movies.

Initially, their meeting was tainted by her love of practical jokes. One day at lunch, according to Louis Hector (a great piano player from Miami, Florida), she announced she was "really terribly tired because she had spent so much time the evening before censoring all the outgoing mail." Paul, sitting at the same table, blanched, "grew very agitated, got up from the table, [and] ran to the commanding officer . . . to demand why he had not known that his letters were being censored and particularly who was censoring them." Heppner calmed him down, recognized Julia's sense of humor, and suggested that her jokes thereafter not disturb "the morale of the operations."

Paul's first mention of Julia McWilliams by name in his letter-diary to his twin brother, Charlie, was on July 9, 1944, when he wrote she "has a somewhat ragged, but pleasantly crazy sense of humor." On July 19 he sent a photograph (as he did of other friends) to his brother, referring to "the 6'2" *bien-jambée* [leggy] from Pasadena." The picture, in which she is seductively bending one leg for the camera, showed her lying on an Army cot. Paul sent the picture of her and the interior of his hut, to show his brother their living quarters: "a typical 10/11 feet [hut] with coir matting, woven cadjan walls, wooden shutters and army bed with folded-up mosquito net above." Paul's letters, which he considered an art form, drew vivid verbal pictures of the country, people, and women.

Though Paul and Julia (and Jack Moore) would take trips together to mountain communities, Paul was writing to his brother about all the women on the post, eager to find a lover to replace the great love of his life, Edith Kennedy, who had died just months before he joined the OSS. He was still half in love with Nancy Toyne, wife of a British officer and part-time mistress of Tommy Davis, the husband of his longtime Boston friend Nancy Davis. (Paul had earlier spent time with Tommy in New Delhi, but his letters to his brother Charlie call Nancy "Zorina—a sexy dame.") Though Nancy and Tommy would eventually divorce, Paul changed her name to "Ellen" when he typed his diary letters.

Julia was as inexperienced with sexual skills as she was at kitchen skills, both essential talents admired by Paul. He had dated several women in the Command and thought Julia a bit "hysterical." She seemed "slightly afraid of sex," he wrote his brother, "but *extremely* likable and pleasant to be around." He had always chosen women who were unafraid of their own sexuality, and he appeared to have little in common with this gangly girl from California. He was a ladies' man, worldly, a decade older than she and several inches shorter. To Julia, he seemed inaccessible. One could gather from the letters Paul was writing to his twin brother in Washington that he had settled on the seduction of Jeanne Taylor, who was coming to assist him and Jack Moore in the War Room. Jeanne, according to Jack Moore, was very genteel and intellectual, a good painter and art school graduate, good-looking but with bad skin. She was Julia's age, but more sophisticated (later, Jeanne and Cora DuBois became lovers when they returned to Washington).

Moore, whom Julia met in Washington, was a GI (draftee) and the former art student assigned to Paul Child the year before. He lived on the compound and would watch the civilians leaving for the town every afternoon. The OSS, he said, comparing it with the later CIA, was about "heroics" and idealism. They were "tremendously educated and interesting people" who did "wild and dangerous things." The new technology allowed them to make a bicycle that folded into a parachute and a camera that looked like a matchbook. Not surprisingly, William Colby (later head of the CIA) would call the OSS "an exercise in improvisation."

One day Mountbatten came in to find Child and Moore crawling around on the floor with a three-dimensional map for the British/American invasion of Burma (their two-dimensional maps had already been sent to Churchill). "It's a waste!" the Supremo declared. Of course, the men had already discovered that the topography of the central Irrawaddy Valley was virtually flat: there was no terrain.

Moore, who knew Julia first but Paul best, described Paul's perfectionism, his intellectual rigor and precise, almost effete, speech of an aesthete. Paul, he added, was a masculine black belt in jujitsu and had fine taste in women. There was "nothing ever ambiguous about his interest in women."

Mountbatten was the "one hero in my life," said Paul Child in 1979 when an IRA terrorist bomb blew up Mountbatten's yacht. "He was charming, witty, handsome, intelligent. We need such noble, splendid people in this world! To think that anyone would kill him!" He told another journalist at that time that he "wanted to go into a corner and bawl."

Though there were numerous cocktail parties and dances off the base, Julia complained in her diary about the few dates she had in what one man claimed was a paradise for unmarried women. "There aren't any attractive Americans at all—I did meet 3 English I liked—and have a date Tuesday— that is all." She threw herself into golf, which several of the men played, and devoted diary space to men, particularly Paul Child and Dillon Ripley. She mentions Guy Martin, "a cute fellow and a live wire," who was Byron's brother and a fellow Pasadenan. Julia liked the younger man enormously, but not in a romantic way.

Guy Martin was a Navy officer (his brother was Air Force) on leave from Donovan's law firm, who was stationed in Kandy for nearly a year, though he worked also at the Navy base in Trincomalee. He compared the climate in Kandy to that of Lake Arrowhead. He remembers long talks with Paul and his interest in seeking out good places to eat when they had to travel: "He was an intellectual, curious, observant, with a lively mind about everything." If Paul was "tense" and "not an easy man," Guy found Julia to be a "wonderfully normal human being without hang-ups." One time they were fooling around the pool and she picked Guy up and threw him in the water. She was "exuberant and extraordinarily outgoing socially—if you put her with a hundred people, by the end of the afternoon she would know fifty by name."

By July 1, Julia was assuring herself that she enjoyed the emotion of anguish. She was bored dancing with drunken correspondents. But she cheered up herself and the office with an official-looking order for the Fourth of July: "It has been reliably reported that OSS/SEAC is planning some kind of a blow-out in celebration of the American 4th of July (date commemorates a British-American controversy in the late 18th century)." The recipients recognized the McWilliams humor.

A study of OSS documents she sent back to Washington reveals an occasional refreshing break with the numbers and espionage codes: at the bottom of an official document stamped "Confidential" is her typed message: "If you don't send this Registry some kind of a report or something, I shall fill the pouches with itching powder and virulent bacteriological diseases, and change all the numbers, as well as translate all the material into Singhalese, and destroy the English version" (May 25, 1944). On another occasion she asked, "Would it be possible for you to send us by Air Pouch one of those books you have giving people numbers and funny names, like 'fruitcake' #385. Frequently we find references to them here and no one knows who on earth is being referred to. . . . This document will be kept very securely in a fire-proof Mosler safe, and will be available to no one except Col. Heppner."

Following a concert of Beethoven ("The master was murdered," she declared), which she attended with Gregory Bateson and two other men, Julia had a "lovely Sunday" taking photographs of an elephant with Paul Child, Jack Moore, and a couple of others. "Sunday, I decided I thought Paul was really very attractive. Now, I think I am rather jealous because he suddenly thinks Peachy is wonderful, and I thought he liked me." She rightly concludes that "he likes a more worldly Bohemian type than me. . . . Wish I were in love, and that what I considered *really attractive* was in love with me." While she was considering a guy named Gunner (Lieutenant Commander, OSS, Michelson), who seemed to like her, neither Dillon Ripley ("quite attractive in a scholarly rather aesthetic carefully cultured, nice way," she told her diary) nor Fisher Howe ("attractive in a warm big gay way") seemed interested in her. Howe, who would later serve in Oslo with Paul, knew Julia briefly in Washington and came to Ceylon to inspect camps with Ripley (he eventually headed the maritime unit in Trincomalee). He says Julia had a "highly sensitive" role at the "nerve center" of the region.

THE BRAIN BANK

Julia would later disparage her work as "file clerk" and wish that she could have been more "academic (I could be studying things)," yet all the sensitive documents of spying (which is gathering information) came through her hands and she organized the system for numbering and cross-referencing them. She described her work as "leading a mythical piece of poisoned fruitcake dropped in a manila envelope project through an imaginary system and every time I got it started somebody has something else." Yet Byron Martin, formerly a bomber navigator and in Air Force Intelligence before being assigned to the OSS, where he worked in the basha next to Julia, asserts that her work, "in which she was privy to virtually every top secret," was vital: "It required a person of unquestioned loyalty, of rock-solid integrity, of unblemished life style, of keen intelligence. It required a person of deep-set seriousness far removed from the outgoing, gay, warm Julie we always hear of at first." She had "a truly awesome responsibility." Betty MacDonald wrote, "Morale in her section could not have been higher."

According to Louis J. Hector, head of the Secretariat, Julia insisted that all security documents had to be located in one place. When she was in China the following year, senior officers, especially Colonel Paul Helliwell, resisted, complaining that they had to have each paper taken down a flight of stairs and across a courtyard. She "held her ground" with the "support of the commanding officer . . . and the Registry in Washington," says Hector. Julia broke the tug-of-war with Helliwell by moving the SI files to the office beneath the colonel, cutting a hole in the floor, and installing a dumbwaiter right beside his desk, demonstrating her stubbornness and creative imagination.

Initially, Julia did not have much time to date because, until help arrived, she worked late nights and four hours on Sunday that summer. There was no time to "scintillate" (one of her favorite words). She had become boring socially, and bored with being a "file clerk"—even though Betty MacDonald called the Registry the "OSS brain bank." By mid-September, her assistant, Patty Norbury, arrived, just as Julia "reached the saturation point." The reports and letters in OSS files reveal the volume and complexity, cross-indexing, and endless code numbers clogging her office. Patty, a soft-spoken Ohio woman, asked for the transfer because she was looking for her husband, who had been shot down and captured by the Japanese. He would indeed be recovered.

Since the Allies had begun overwhelming the German airpower and retaken Western Europe, military attention focused on beating back the Japanese in eastern Asia. Most of the espionage work centered on the Burmese peninsula, which the Japanese held. Their two Japanese-Americans could not speak or write Japanese well, but the missionaries' children, such as Howard Palmer, whose parents were missionaries in Thailand, were fluent in their respective languages. Headquarters worried about the three M's: morale, monsoons, and malaria. They were cutting Japanese supply lines and depots and engaging in underwater sabotage, while the British and Americans were pushing through the Burma Road to China. Julia learned to keep confidences from several branches of government (there was talk of mutual spying between the British and the Americans). Good training for her work in the food world fifty years later.

The ever-curious Bateson, according to Julia, "went out on an exploring trip from Ceylon with several military fellows because he was interested in studying the people, especially their nose-picking habits and other anthropological things." Guy Martin remembers him wearing a tennis outfit to travel the countryside with a guide. Because he knew the Burmese superstition about the color yellow, he suggested that they drop yellow dye into the Irrawaddy River and have the MO branch spread rumors that when the Irrawaddy runs yellow, Japan will be kicked out. He won permission, according to Betty MacDonald, but the dye, which turns yellow in ocean salt water, just sank in the fresh water. Southeast Asia seemed an anthropologists' or linguists' workshop for American academics hired by the OSS, just as all the European towns counted only as art for the Oxford scholars recruited by British intelligence.

> Ceylon was an Elysium far removed from reality [Jane Foster wrote to Betty MacDonald] where everyone had an academic interest in the war but found life far too pleasant to do anything too drastic about it. To the red-blooded Americans . . . Ceylon [was either] another form of British tyranny—frustration without representation [or] . . . a palm-fringed haven of the bureaucrat, the isle of panel discussions and deferred decisions.

Jane Foster was one of the most important persons that Julia Child met in Ceylon, important because of the devastating effect she would have on the lives of Julia McWilliams, Paul Child, and others in the years to come. Born in San Francisco the same year as Julia, Foster joined the Communist Party in California in 1938, though she later dropped her membership—more a "Cadillac communist" than a serious one, writes MacDonald. Foster applied to work in counterintelligence because she was antifascist and had lived in Java (her California master's thesis was on the Batu Islands). She was short with blond hair and freckles and "the jolliest party girl on land or sea; the only communist who had a sense of humor," according to Guy Martin. Everyone enjoyed Jane's sense of humor, including Paul Child. She and Julia, who she thought had a "phenomenal memory," enjoyed laughing together.

Humor continued to be Julia's way of dealing with the tedium of her paperwork—for she would have preferred to be out in the field with Bateson, trudging through jungles and talking to native people. One day she addressed a memorandum to Louis Hector and Dick Heppner saying that henceforth all documents would be classified by the color of the ink, using a super-sensitive, color-determining apparatus. She explained this new panchromatic classification so convincingly, says Hector, that "the commanding officer took the bait, stormed out of his office [and] into the Registry" to berate Julia. She broke into laughter. "He joined [in] and announced that Julie was one of the things that made life tolerable in the far reaches" of the world.

By September, Julia and Paul had learned a great deal about each other. She learned he had lived in Paris during the 1920s and was a gourmet. Serious and introspective, he could be loquacious with friends. He worked on freighters, traveled the world, and taught French and art at Avon Old Farms School in Connecticut in the 1930s (where Paul wrote the school song, "Men of Avon," in 1941 and one of his students was future folksinger Pete Seeger). Though he suffered from a weak stomach since a bout with dysentery in Mexico, and from migraines since a near-fatal accident in 1941, he was a black belt who taught jujitsu. He was a great admirer of women with beauty and brains (Julia would eventually learn about Edith Kennedy, the "flirtatious, witty, naughty, dynamic and intelligent" woman, in Paul's words, with whom he had lived for more than a decade).

Before joining Mountbatten's office in New Delhi, Paul worked in Washington in the Visual Presentation Division (graphics and photography department) with Budd Schulberg, Garson Kanin, Ruth Gordon, John Ford, Bob Vance, Cora DuBois, and Eero Saarinen. Before that he had done professional portrait photography while he taught at Avon. His letters to his brother revealed that one day, out of curiosity, he took apart an old movie camera made in Dresden in 1909, went to Spanish class after work, and that night dined with a couple with whom he took turns reading James Joyce's *Dubliners*. Such versatility could not have been immediately evident to Julia McWilliams.

THE CURRY BELT

What Paul learned about Julia was somewhat misleading. "She is a gourmet and likes to cook," he innocently informed his brother Charlie. "She is trying to be brave about being an old maid!" He added, "I believe she would marry me (but isn't the 'right' woman from *my* standpoint!)." In this three-page description (September 7, 1944) to Charlie, Paul called her a "warm and witty girl," devoted to music, who gasps when she talks, gets overstressed in conversations ("her slight atmosphere of hysteria gets on my nerves"), and lacks savoir faire. He concluded that she is "in love with her father, in an unconscious and pleasant way . . . [for he] sets the key for much of her thinking and acting." She has a good mind but is a sloppy [unchallenged] thinker and given to "wild emotionalism," which he blamed on the fact that she has "moved safely within the confines of her class and station and consequently had almost no challenge." He feels sympathy for her "fear" of but "fascination" with sex because he "knows what the cure is," but it "would be too much for Dr. Paulski to risk attempting." The "working-out implies training and molding and informing," which would take more time and effort than he wanted to devote. He sought a companion "who has been hammered *already* on life's anvil and attained a definite shape."

Julia saw Paul on almost a daily basis. When he received a jar of geranium jelly from his brother, Julia, Peachy, and Jane Foster helped him eat it at one breakfast sitting. When Tommy Davis and his other friends visited Kandy, they all expressed pleasure in her company. With Cora and Tommy she had Australian gin and canned orange juice in Paul's room before dining at a local Chinese restaurant. Paul was attentive, but beyond her reach.

They shared an interest in food in this region associated with the Indonesian "rijsttafel" curry belt, where a curry lunch is an all-day affair:

There are three curries [according to Louis Hector]: one meat, usually lamb; one fish, usually shrimp; and one fowl, usually chicken. One first lays down a good bed of rice all over a plate, takes generous helpings of each of the three curries, and then covers this all over with as many condiments as the human imagination can devise: chopped coconut flavored with curry powder, paprika, pepper, cardamom, crumbled bacon, crumbled fried bananas, and chutneys of every hue and flavor. The whole is washed down with much beer and the event ends with everyone taking a lovely Sunday afternoon nap. It was Julia who organized these in Kandy.

Julia remembers that the food cooked on the base was a "sort of Singhalese-Western . . . mixture . . . that was very nice," but it was cooked in unsanitary conditions, which led to "Delhi Belly." She also remembers that Dillon Ripley collected "durian fruit that stunk to high heaven." Ripley undoubtedly loved the fruit, but Julia described it as smelling like "dead babies mixed with strawberries and Camembert. They served it to us several times in our mess. Then they banned it!"

Just after a visit by General Donovan and a great cocktail party and dinner with Chinese and American generals, Heppner was promoted to full colonel at the same time the October monsoon rains drenched the compound, occasionally dampening Julia's papers. Weights held the pages down against the wind gusts. Several times a week the electricity went out in the hotel. Mists shrouded the peaks. A walk in the underbrush was a brush with leeches. When rats invaded one major's office, a native exclaimed in the usual participle manner, "Burning much coconut—putting on mouse machine. Master catching much rats." It was not unusual to see either a four-foot lizard or a saffron-dressed monk from the monastery up the hill. A welcome respite from the rains came with the appearance of Noël Coward, who stayed for a week at the request of his friend Mountbatten.

One day in late October, after yet another "flying circus"—much coming and going of Generals Stilwell, Wedemeyer, Merrill, Stratemeyer, Donovan, Mountbatten, and others—Julia heard the news: Stilwell was removed from China and the brass was moving. Her boss, Dick Heppner, took over in Kunming, and Wedemeyer took over China from Stilwell. Paul Child wrote to his brother in December that his "wonder woman" had not yet appeared, but he received Christmas greetings from "my three Jays": Julia, Jane, and Jeanne. Paul was soon transferred to China during the last days of 1944. It would not be too many weeks before Julia was transferred too.

The effect of the OSS presence in Ceylon is best explained by Guy Martin, who after attending an OSS reunion with Betty MacDonald in Bangkok in 1991, returned to what is now Sri Lanka. Among the group of Siamese he helped to train in Trincomalee—men who went into Thailand on missions for the OSS—sixteen were at the reunion: they were all MIT graduates and all engineers, one a foreign secretary, one the head of the Army, another the head of a large bank, another the head of the university. After 1948, when the

British granted independence to Ceylon, the OSS-trained people were leading their country.

Julia's experience in Ceylon was formative in teaching her survival skills, organization, and responsibility. Paul told a Smith College interviewer decades later that the pressure of wartime work brought out her "innate capacities." This land of tea and elephants proved to be rich soil for a developing friendship with Paul Child. She still lacked much of the "worldly knowledge" he had sought in vain in his lengthy analysis of her. But he had added in the letter to his brother that "she responds to companionship and love and is *extremely* likable and pleasant to have around."

Chapter 7

To China with Love
(1945)

"Julie is tough and full of character,
a real friend."

PAUL CHILD, *letter, September 3, 1945*

AFTER TEN MONTHS in Mountbatten's headquarters in Kandy, Julia Mc-
Williams left the lush jungle foliage of Ceylon at 7 A.M. on March 8, 1945. Her
plane, rising with the sunrise, headed north from the equator toward the
teeming delta city of Calcutta.

Julia had a week in this city where American OSS personnel often experienced their first culture shock at the uglier manifestations of British imperial-
ism. (SEAC meant Save England's Asiatic Colonies, the cynics believed.)
Julia's reaction to the fleshpots of Calcutta was a moral one:

> I remember I was horrified and disgusted and disturbed when I was
> going to China and I came up to Calcutta . . . horrified by the group of
> people in headquarters; they were into dirty sex; nurses necking in the
> living room . . . it all seemed so degenerate. I talked to Colonel
> Heppner [later in China] about it because it looked like a brothel. You
> have to have someone running things. . . .

FLYING THE HUMP

On March 15 she flew "the Hump" from Calcutta, India, to Kunming, China, to set up and run the OSS Registry in China, now the focus of the war. This flight over the Himalayas with their 15,000-foot peaks was the most dangerous route of the war, for planes had to fly at twice their normal altitude. Some on board prayed while most of the thirty passengers made it a white-knuckled 500-mile trip. On the plane, an unpressurized and freezing rickety C-54, they wore parkas and parachutes and carried oxygen masks. The Himalayan peaks were veiled by rain clouds, and the wind currents, sometimes clocked at 250 miles per hour, could flip, toss, and suck down a plane in seconds. As many as 468 Allied aircraft ultimately went down on that route, leaving what historian Barbara Tuchman called an "aluminum trail" from India to China, from Mandalay to Kunming. Because the Japanese occupied Burma in the spring of 1942, it became a vital but costly lifeline: 1,000 persons would be lost.

On board, Julia chatted with Louis Hector and Betty MacDonald regaled them with the story of OSS officer Lieutenant Colonel Duncan Lee (an Oxford-educated missionaries' son) and newsman Eric Sevareid parachuting from a disabled plane only months before, with time to grab a bottle of Carew's gin before jumping.

After nearly three hours, Julia's plane suddenly began to plummet, the lights went out, pieces of ice ticked against the window, and one of the men got quietly sick into his handkerchief. According to Betty MacDonald, who would give the best description of flying the Hump, "the C-54 shuddered, leveled off with a roar," found a hole in the clouds, and eventually headed for the red clay runway just south of the city of Kunming. Julia sat confidently reading a book. Betty, who thought Julia was "so cool," still clutched Chester, her gremlin lucky charm (a pilot at a dance in Calcutta once asked to borrow Chester to make his first Hump flight).

The plane landed at Roger Queen Airport, just north of blue Kunming Lake, and taxied beside a long row of shark-faced Flying Tiger planes. Two minutes later another plane landed. Blue-jacketed coolies were grading the edge of the field, MacDonald remembers:

> Julia, climbing down first, looked over the low, red hills and the curling rooftop of a small temple near the field, received a cheerful "Ting hao" greeting from some red-cheeked children, and turned back to her fellow passengers. "It looks *just* like China," she told us.

Betty's first reaction was how natural and free the people were, even after seven years of Japanese occupation of their coastal lands. She had never seen any Indian children happily romping. Yet here in China there was a greater sense of the war and imminent danger. Paul Child, who flew in earlier, said Kunming "looks like California, feels like Denver."

Dick Heppner and Paul Helliwell met the plane, three hours overdue, nervous about the OSS personnel on board. Their OSS jeep took them past millet fields, rice paddies, and a flock of ducks and into the walled city of Kunming. The "OSS girls" (who were outnumbered by the men twenty to one) lived in a red-tile-roofed building with circling balconies in a large garden of a new suburb. The next morning she and Betty took a truck trip to the Detachment 202 compound over muddy roads crowded with rickshaws and wagons and with fetid sewers flowing down the middle of the road. Julia met with Colonel Richard P. Heppner. Many of her OSS associates—together with OSS officers freed after various victories in Europe—were assembling in China: Ellie, Peachy, Rosie, and Paul.

The OSS moved into China at this late date in the war under the leadership of Captain Milton "Mary" Miles of the Navy, who disliked the OSS and was an ally of General Tai Li, the head of Chiang Kai-shek's secret service (the Gestapo, Stilwell called it). It was what one historian called a "forced [and] unhappy alliance with Miles and Tai Li." The previous fall, Chiang Kai-shek demanded and won the ouster of Stilwell, an intellectual Yankee (Paul Child called him "the Sunday School Teacher" because of his wire-rimmed glasses) who spoke Mandarin and Cantonese and hated the warlords, especially Chiang, whom he called "a peanut" because he would not attack the Japanese. (One of Stilwell's assistants in the Imperial Hotel was Dean Rusk, who later served as Secretary of State for Presidents Kennedy and Johnson.) The OSS was now openly in China, the center of its focus after MacArthur went into the Philippines and the Marines took Iwo Jima and Okinawa.

General Albert Wedemeyer, Mountbatten's Chief of Staff, was appointed to take Stilwell's place. "He was a tall, blond, blue-eyed, upper-class man with a German temperament," says Guy Martin, who was quartered for a while at Wedemeyer's house while he supervised demolition agents. Wedemeyer, whom Paul Child affectionately called Uncle Al (to get past the censors), brought in his good friend Heppner from Kandy to be OSS commander in SEAC. Heppner in turn asked Paul Child to join him. That January, Paul met with Donovan, Wedemeyer, Chennault, and Hurley to plan the design for Wedemeyer's China War Room. Paul reluctantly left his well-organized and well-equipped Kandy War Room to begin again, first in Chungking, the free

China capital and the location of the American Embassy. By spring the War Room was moved south to the mountain city of Kunming (headquarters for the OSS and Chennault's Flying Tigers, now under Chiang Kai-shek). Journalist Theodore White earlier called the city a "medieval cesspool" with filthy alleyways, an opium stronghold. Kunming, once home of the refugee university fighting the Chiang dictatorship, was now a wealthy black-market center.

Julia, always excited by new adventure, this time China, and by her proximity to the war itself, was not excited by the minutiae or the volume of the paperwork. Her office primarily served intelligence branches, opening, numbering, and directing all mail and order forms. She had to devise a simpler system for code names and keeping track of the secret papers; she and Lieutenant Colonel Helliwell used pouch labels to speed up and secure the information. Her "Confidential" letters to other agents were riddled with number and letter codes as well as detailed instructions that reveal the tediousness of her job.

It is evident from her letters that she took care of promotions for her staff and lifted their spirits when needed. She had a staff of nearly ten assistants. Her task was daunting at this critical point in the war when the United States was planning an attack on central Japan. Years later, when she disparaged her work as "a clerk," Paul declared: "She was privy to all messages, both incoming from the field, or Washington, etc., and outgoing to our agents and operatives all over China-Burma-India."

Louis Hector remembers the day she turned over "a small, heavy steel footlocker which contained a large cache of tan, tallowy bits about the size and shape of Hershey's chocolate kisses, each wrapped in a greasy bit of paper." She handled this secret currency with tact and secrecy. It was their "operational opium" to pay spies.

No matter how valuable the documents she handled, Julia hated the work she did. Though she scrapped her original card-indexing system from Kandy because of lack of time, she despised the daily routine and longed for real spy work. But the daughter of John McWilliams was hired to do this job and set her jaw to tough it out, a personal characteristic of honor combined with stubbornness that would carry through her personal and professional life. The McWilliams backbone was as firm as it was tall.

Early spring winds brought brick-colored dust that coated her teeth and eyes and covered the rice fields and the old walls in Kunming. The "dust was deep and omnipresent," said Paul Child, who had arrived in China before Julia. His presence made the temporary assignment far more appealing, for she enjoyed his company and hoped a romance with him would begin.

Paul was struggling with the difficulty of beginning yet another War

Room, securing equipment, and waiting for a team of seven, which would include Jack Moore and (by June) Jeanne Taylor. He came to China, as he had to India, "at General Wedemeyer's request" and immediately loved this "unquenchable and gutsy country," its mountains, its food, and its "beautiful" people. Yet he confided to a friend that he felt like a man from Mars, out of place in the military environment: "These military humans are no soil for my roots. Warfare, with which I am intimately connected, never was my work of art, and though I help shape the clay I detest the statue." Paul asked for carte blanche in his work, and Heppner and Wedemeyer gave it to him. As he wrote in his diary: "Whatever happens in my life I'm going to be Stage Manager, take in the money at the Box Office, write the play, act in it and have a box seat for the performance."

Yet Paul was indescribably lonely, still looking for the woman of his dreams. Julia was apparently not considered for this role, but their friendship was deepening. He reported to his brother Charlie that "Julie, who is here on temporary duty, is a great solace." She listened to his complaints about lack of office equipment and supplies and his battle with his stomach and the Yangtze Rapids (equivalent to the Kandy Kanters and Delhi Belly and also known by some as the Chiang Kai Shits).

CHUNGKING AND KUNMING

The plane to Chungking in April brought Julia to Chiang Kai-shek's capital on the Yangtze River. It was a city that seemed to be built on one hundred hills and cliffs, a cosmopolitan, intense, overpopulated place that Paul Child, who had been there at the beginning of the year, called a "busted and ragged city" but "wildly stimulating." A painting of Chungking he would create, from a photograph, hung on their dining room wall in Cambridge, Massachusetts, for years.

The Chinese, whom she loved to look at, stared at her light brown hair and towering presence. Children were aggressively friendly. The weather in Chungking was more extreme, and the water and clothes were always brown. Though the plum trees were in blossom, Julia had little time for touring. She was sent to reduce and organize the files (the staff was "dull, slow, dense") in keeping with the system set up in Kunming, which would now be the central headquarters. Chungking, "a mail room run by a girl with a mind like a withered rose," Julia wrote to a friend, made Ceylon look "civilized, beautiful, green, and comfortable." With the usual woman shortage, there were plenty of dinner parties following gin after the hard workday. News that Franklin Delano Roosevelt had died arrived as Julia was leaving, and she was uneasy about getting back to Kandy.

Returning to Kunming, she became increasingly aware that she would not be going back to Kandy. "China was more formal; Ceylon had been like a big family." Yet three months later Julia concluded that China "is so much alive." Betty MacDonald remembers being in the mountains of western China with the Japanese all around, "so it was a different feeling. You felt behind enemy lines. That made for camaraderie—several marriages and the breakup of others." She became openly involved with Heppner.

Julia did indeed like Kunming, for it reminded her of California with blue mountains beyond the eucalyptus trees. This city in the hills of southern China was in the backcountry, so it had what one historian calls "the atmosphere of a frontier town." It was not only the end of the supply line to China, it was now the base of Detachment 202, from which all field projects were organized, where Chinese troops were trained, and where sabotage teams were sent into the field. The plateau was over 6,000 feet above sea level—west of Burma and north of Hanoi and French Indochina. The soil was the red soil of Burma and the surrounding hills were bare; but beyond the city lay Kunming Lake and high above it a cloudy Camelot of temples carved in the rocks of the mountains.

The Chinese wore padded blue coats, tucking their hands into opposite sleeves; the shopkeepers wore embroidered slippers; and herds of black pigs roamed the countryside. It was all very colorful, but, as her friend Ellie said, an environment that was "ominous and austere." The Chinese were either eking out a living or serving with the ragtag group of peasant soldiers exploited by greedy merchants (who sat out the war) and corrupt politicians. The scorn of ignorant GIs did not help, though the presence of so many missionaries' children in China may have diminished some of the racism inherent in the war in Asia.

Paul wrote to his brother:

Julia and I managed to borrow a jeep from a friend last Sunday afternoon and, after buying a bottle of mulberry wine, struck off into the great unknown, for about 40 miles. The weather was incredibly inspiring: hot sun and cool air, sparkling sky, breeze enough, scattered clouds. The great mountains lay around us like back-broken dragons. God what beautiful country—the mud villages with their green-tiled towers, the herds of black swine, the blue clad people, the cedar smoke, the cinnamon dust, were all eternally Chinese, and connected us with the deep layers of past time. We saw a beautiful red sandstone (avon color) bridge set in the midst of a paddy-field. The stones were all wind-worn, like the tourelles at Château Neiric, so they looked like soft loaves of bread. We sat on it and drank our wine, and got sunburned, and looked at the mules going over it, and relaxed, and life came right for a spell.

Paul smoked a new pipe given him by Charlie, who regularly sent cigars and film. After taking pictures of each other and wandering through a graveyard, Julia and Paul returned from "a good afternoon," Paul concluded on April 17, 1945. Such tranquil moments were few.

CHIANG VS. MAO

The records Julia McWilliams kept in Kunming were more vital and her trustworthiness more important than ever before. The files bulged with data of the OSS training of Chinese infiltrators, of the internal political strife, and the bumbling of the Chinese, who had little heart for bravery or risk after years of fighting and internal corruption. Not only was the OSS caught in the crosshairs of Chinese political factions; it also instigated some of the conflicts. Julia, like the others, heard fascinating firsthand stories from the interior, stories they were not allowed to set down in words.

The major internal conflict for years was between Chiang Kai-shek and Mao Tse-tung, especially since the Japanese split free China in two. Chiang in the south was a powerful warlord with shaved head who ruled official China in Chungking. He knew one English word, "darling," for he was married to a Wellesley graduate. He "converted" to Christianity for her, but only by the widest stretch of the imagination could he even be regarded, in Theodore White's words, as "an Old Testament Christian." The OSS considered him and his loyal henchman and spymaster General Tai Li to be corrupt, ruthless, and more interested in fighting for power against the communists in the north than against the Japanese. In White's view, Chiang ran a "corrupt political clique that combines some of the worst features of Tammany Hall and the Spanish Inquisition." Stilwell, before he left, had called it "this rotten regime."

Julia shared the view of the old China hands that Chiang was a cruel despot. Many of her friends and colleagues were born in China, the children of missionaries, and loved the people. The missionaries' children believed that the Allies would do better to back the communists in the north, who could fight with greater heart. Their views would, in the McCarthy era of the 1950s, cost many their careers and reputations. By the time Julia came to China, the U.S. ambassador, Patrick Hurley, nicknamed "the Albatross" by the OSS group (he once called Chiang "Mr. Shek"), was completely in the pocket of Chiang, and Wedemeyer had to apologize for courting the communists' help in the war against the Japanese. Julia would confide in a friend eight years later, "We never ran into anybody who did not distrust and dislike the Chiang regime (possible exception of that fool, Pat Hurley)." Paul told his brother that "the war of back alleys, back rooms, big parties, magnificent whores, and equally magnificent blackmails . . . almost becomes the 'real' war and the news-war is only the surface expression."

Mao Tse-tung led the Yenan communists in the mountains of northern China. It was generally considered by those with experience in China that Mao and Chou En-lai (Paul Child was very impressed that he spoke excellent, though accented, English) would make effective allies against the Japanese. Overt diplomatic missions, long urged by Stilwell, to get the joint cooperation of these warring Chinese factions together to fight the Japanese were thwarted by Chiang. (His political clout was reinforced by a number of Americans who were paid for writing pro-Chinese propaganda.) Covert operations in both regions continued.

THE OSS WOMEN

Rosamond (Rosie) Frame, who spoke fluent Chinese and worked in covert espionage, exposed some Chinese nationals' collaboration with Japan in the south. Her partner was later severely injured in retaliation for their mission. Rosie was enterprising. (She told the childhood story of being given $2,000 by her missionary parents for schooling in Switzerland and finding her way to the school by herself.) Later she went on to Heidelberg and the University of Chicago.

According to historian Harris Smith, Julia's intelligence files "bulged with reports about the incompetence of the Chinese [Chiang] military command." He adds that "OSS officers were sickened by the treatment [that] the Chiang government afforded its troops." They recorded attacks against OSS convoys by Chinese government troops posing as bandits and murdering Chinese agents who worked for the OSS. Despite these revelations and the shifting alliances, Chiang kept the public relations ear of the Allies.

Rosie Frame, who had broken all the hearts on the ship from California to India with Julia and exposed the Chinese collaborationists, was compiling target studies for the Chinese in Chungking, where she was romanced by Paul in January. He told his brother that it was a "passionate friendship though not *profoundly* passionate." Soon he realized she was not his ideal woman. After he left for Kunming and Julia arrived in Chungking, Rosie helped Julia organize the intelligence files there. The daughter of a Christian college dean in China, she spoke Mandarin and Cantonese as well as French. Paul described her woman hockey player's figure, yet praised her attractiveness, brilliance, and energy. Betty MacDonald called her "one of the most alert, brilliant women the OSS sent into the field, a modern Mata Hari." She also called her "Sub Rosy" and described her romantically clad in fur-lined flying jacket, boots, and slacks, with a carbine strapped over her shoulder. After the war Rosie would marry Thibaut de Saint Phalle, whom Betty described as the "scion of a famous French family," who was with the OSS on the China coast.

Other friends from Washington and Ceylon lived with Julia in the women's house: Ellie Thiry, Marjorie Severyns, and Peachy Durand, who was transferred from Chungking. Ellie, while working in Chungking the previous month, had fallen in love with a British major named Basil Summers (whom she would eventually marry).

In the women's house, white parachute silk draped the common room and deep blue coolie cloth covered the beds. The women were crowded five or six in a room, until Julia took over an addition to the women's house, where she bunked with Mary Livingston Eddy, who had arrived (considerably later than expected, from Cairo) to take over the Registry. Because Julia had the office under control and Heppner wanted her to stay, she and Mary decided to divide the work between them.

In a letter to a former colleague in Kandy, Julia confided that the OSS originally intended to send her to Calcutta when Mary arrived, and that she indeed received "propositions" to enter Secret Intelligence. But "by the time I learned anything about China the war would be over." She was now convinced, she told her father, that China was the important place, "a life or death issue," and "S.E.A. is now all British, and this is really US, and the OSS has a big contribution to make." No one did her job better than she. She had an unflappable nature and daring enough to make a great spy.

Mary Livingston joined the OSS to escape a failed marriage to a man named Eddy (she would marry Dillon Ripley after the war) and served in Algeria and Italy before China. She was five feet eight inches tall and elegant. Despite her New York 400 background she was adventurous and roughed it with aplomb. Unflappable as Julia, she enjoyed walking through the rice paddies to work with Paul, who remembered stumbling over a corpse there one day. Of her roommate, Julia wrote: "We had our sleeping bags and rolled them up on a cot made of ropes for a mattress across the bars of the cot. I would have loved to have Clorox because the plumbing, even when it worked, smelled so bad." Mary: "I was in awe of Julia because she was older and so much in possession there; we knew what was going on and the people were fascinating. We had a big house and a cook who prepared American food, but Kunming had a lot of good restaurants and it was a treat to go out to eat."

They were accustomed to mechanical breakdowns (occasionally Julia would get all lathered up in the shower and the water would stop running), so when the projector stopped in the middle of a movie, everyone waited patiently. When the lights came up, they knew it was not an electrical failure, but a proclamation by radio: Churchill announced that Germany had surrendered that day, May 9, 1945. According to Ellie's diary: "We listened to the announcement, and nobody said a word, except 'that's that,' and we returned to the show. Soon it will end here as well, they all thought."

$\mathcal{E}$ATING CHINESE

Julia was dining at a local Szechwan restaurant one hot summer night several weeks later with Jeanne Taylor and three men, including Paul Child and Al Ravenholt, a correspondent who spoke Chinese and knew the restaurant scene. On the other side of the pink silk screen was a Chinese general and his party of friends. After much noisy drinking the general became sick. "It was fortunate 2 gals were tough and worldly," Paul wrote, "because there's something about a Chinese general vomiting loudly a few feet away that might otherwise have taken the fine edge off the bowl of eels and garlic we were eating."

Julia was always hungry; in fact, Paul would later say, "she's a wolf by nature." But China awakened her discriminating taste: "[American] food in China was terrible; we thought it was cooked by grease monkeys. The Chinese food was wonderful and we ate out as often as we could. That is when I became interested in food. There were sophisticated people there who knew a lot about food. . . . I just loved Chinese food." She was just as impressed that her sophisticated colleagues "talked so much about" the food they ate.

In 1995, she recalled a visit to a family restaurant—probably Ho-Teh-Foo—in a building several stories high surrounding a courtyard where the kitchen was located. The waiter would "yell down the order and when ready they would pull the trays up by rope. The entire family was in the kitchen, mother and grandmother and children—just like the French family—everyone had a good time." She relished the pleasure the Chinese took in dining, "making these great swooping, slurping noises as they ate." She also preferred small portions of a great variety of food: "nuggets of chicken in soy sauce, deep-fried or in paper; always rice, pork, sweet-and-sour soup. The duck was always good, and everyone had a good time." Manners dictated that when reaching for a bowl in the middle of the table, they had to keep "one foot on the floor, where we placed the tea when it was cold and the bowls when they were empty."

Though some praised the Army mess, the bland American food cooked by the Chinese in the barracks, Julia did not; she told *Parade* magazine in 1994 about "the terrible Army food: rice, potatoes, canned tomatoes and water buffalo [sic]. We would sit around and talk about the wonderful meals we remembered." Betty remembers "mostly potatoes and stuff from cans" but not buffalo meat in the Army chow. This official cooking was presumably more sanitary, but Betty remembers that "we would get dysentery easily." At one time or another, everyone (particularly Paul Child) suffered from some form of diarrhea or dysentery. One day one of the local chefs, who had been cooking over hot charcoal, was found dead on the floor. Dinner was served anyway.

Those with educated mouths demanded taste and authenticity. Spending time with Paul meant more adventurous hunting for food, which was secured by OSS personnel who had been born in China and knew the language well. Louis Hector, who remembered the "beautiful Yunnan hams and the purple potatoes," said Paul and Julia "organized the splendid feasts," but Paul would remember that Theodore White first introduced him to the best eating places. Of course, in dining out they risked infection (the Chinese fertilized with "night soil [human waste]"), but the risk was worthwhile. Julia learned about Peking, Szechwan, Cantonese, Annamite, and Fukien techniques. As she noted in 1945, Chinese cuisine emphasized diversity, elegance (small portions), and health. "I am very, very fond of northern, Peking-style Chinese cooking. That's my second favorite [cuisine]. It's more related to French; it's more structured," she wrote.

The restaurant as such originated in China (though its flowering in the West was due to French traditions) in the T'ang Dynasty (618–907 A.D.). According to anthropologists Peter Farb and George Armelagos, during the ancient Chou Dynasty twenty different methods of cooking were practiced in this oldest and most developed cuisine, where "a knowledge of food and drink marked one as educated."

Paul's five years in France, beginning in 1925, led to talk of French cuisine and the dishes he looked forward to eating. He and Julia talked endlessly about food; as Gertrude Stein said about the French in general, they talk about talking about food. Paul met Stein and many other artists in Paris, including sculptor Jo Davidson and newspaperman Paul Mowrer, now married to Hadley Hemingway (Ernest's first wife). He spoke lovingly of the preparation of quenelles and soufflés. For a girl who grew up thinking of the kitchen as "a dismal place," Julia found revelations in the local Chinese cuisine and Paul's food talk.

THE CHILD TWINS

Julia was learning a great deal about Paul and his identical twin brother, Charles (Charlie or Charleski), who was married with children and working for the State Department, first in Washington and for a while in San Francisco. The father of Paul and Charlie died when they were six months old, and their mother, Bertha May Cushing (of the famous Boston Cushings), supported them and an older sister, Mary (or Meeda), by singing in Boston and Paris and through the kindness of strangers. His mother, an utterly impractical, pre-Raphaelite creature who died in 1937, taught her boys that (in Julia's words) "artists are sacred." Paul, whose only real family was Charlie's family, returned from China with paintings and hundreds of photographs of the country and its people.

Paul's letters to his brother reveal his romantic consideration of several women in the compound. It had been Rosie Frame first in New Delhi, then in Chungking. Now it was Marjorie Severyns, who was bright, quick, and "my kind of woman." The competition was "ferocious," said Paul: "even the snaggle-toothed, the neurotic, the treacherous and the dim-witted among the women are hovered over by men, as jars of jam are hovered over by wasps." But for Marjorie "the humming turns to an angry roar." Guy Martin agreed: "She was sort of the ladylove, everybody thought of her as being very sexy; she had that kind of appeal. Marjorie and Rosamond were the best-looking ones." Marjorie, the child of missionaries and a graduate of the University of Washington, had several affairs. However, Paul's worldly charm (and devotion to women) could not defeat his chief rival, news correspondent Al Ravenholt, whom she would wed after the war. "None of the women seem to be the answer to my loneliness," he wrote Charlie, after mentioning Rosie Frame and Nancy Davis, whom he still claimed to love deeply but who was writing only once a month. And he always came back to Edith Kennedy:

> You will never know what it is to feel profoundly lonely, to have y[ou]r
> vitals twisted by the need for companionship . . . but when you have

sown the seed of love, weeded and watered its field, reaped its harvest and stored the golden grains, and: Then! The barn burns down, and the fields are flooded—well you become empty, unbased, and bereft. . . . since Edith's death I am rootless, or soil-less.

He was able eventually to tell Julia about the woman he had loved for seventeen years, who died painfully of cancer just months before he joined the OSS. He would tell her about their house on Shepard Street in Cambridge and the earlier apartment in the rue d'Assas in Paris. Edith was an intellectual, a friend of May Sarton and Helene Deutsch, and the mother of three boys before she became involved with Paul, nearly twenty years her junior.

What Julia did not know yet was that Paul and Charlie had had their stars "read" by an astrologer named Jane Bartleman and that Charlie sent periodic updates. Paul, since April 1945, had waited for his foretold "intelligent, dramatic, beautiful" woman to come, bringing "some complication inherent" in their relationship. He referred to this reading as his "cave-of-emeralds future." In the margin of a May 13 letter to Charlie, which recalled the prediction and in which Paul confessed his loneliness ("More than all else—more than security, more than art, more than music—I need love), Paul wrote years later: "Julie, you Idiot! Wake up!"

At the time, Paul did not yet see Julia as a serious love interest, though she took it more seriously. Fifty years later she would remember that their romance began in Ceylon and continued in Kunming: "It was a gradual getting together; by the time we went to China we were in love. There were a lot of attractive women around. He loved women." As the years went by, they would invest their love in China with a commitment beyond any evidence suggested by his letters. Indeed, he spoke of other women, one with whom he wished to "rise with the sea-tides, put the pungent flavor of wild sage on her tongue, and comb her hair with the wind." He did write of Julia: "Tommy and Julie and I together last night at his quarters. I read them all your letters since 25th of April—Julia knows you by now" (June 2). "I am really *starved* for a certain kind of companionship" (June 10). "I am aching from the rudeness and savagery of life . . . I have lost the sense of savor, the feeling and creativity, the expansion that comes through love given and returned." On June 19, he wrote: "I cannot seem to rid myself of the touchstone of Edith, against which I try the others. Nobody begins to measure up to that standard." He threw himself into his work: "I shall bend my energies in large measure to this incredibly shocking, stupid and futile war." On Edith's birthday, June 27: "I miss her terribly." He thanks Charlie for photos: "Julia and I have decided they look like some Fairy's version of the real thing. Jeanne says they look as though you've 'gone Hollywood.'" Paul wanted to be "released from the prison of this time and place," but "where would I go?"

ℒIQUOR IS QUICKER

The end of the European war brought more visits from friends, who carried in the liquor for what Julia called "the five o'clock refreshment period." "A glass of pure water is as remote as Châteauneuf du Pape," declared Paul, but finding spirits was somewhat easier. According to Betty MacDonald, it was difficult but necessary to get liquor: "We had parties at the big house. Because it was hard to get liquor in China, the pilots would come in with Carew's gin. Then the Navy began to take alcohol out of the steering wheel box that lubricated the steering wheel. Anything for a drink. There was [also] some alcohol available through the French, who came out of Indochina."

The music at the parties was the same as it had been in Ceylon, but without the British note, such as "There's a Troopship Just Leaving Bombay" or "Waltzing Matilda" (the latter from Australia). The songs on the few phonographs in the camp included "You Are My Sunshine," a favorite of 1942, "Pistol-Packin' Mama," and "Blues in the Night." If the McWilliams backbone said do your job well, the Weston imp drove her to dance. For one party, planned by Paul, a jazz band of black soldiers played until 5:30 A.M. for the boogie-woogie dancers.

Among the friends who were in and out of Kunming and Chungking were John Ford, the film director and now naval officer, who with his crew of cameramen seemed to be shooting another movie. Jane Foster, the party girl and leftist expert on Java, Bali, and Malaya, came briefly from Kandy, according to Paul's letters. Ned Putzell, as he had in Ceylon, accompanied General Donovan on a Kunming visit. According to Mary Livingston Eddy, Donovan remembered most of the names of his OSS personnel. When Byron Martin was touring with another general, Julia ran to greet him: "She . . . grabbed me under the arms and lifted me to my toe tips (I was rather slight of build at the time) and planted a kiss. I felt as honored as I ever have been," he wrote. Paul greeted Joe Alsop, who (he informed Charlie) was thinner, balder, and sporting an even "strong[er] atmosphere of Cafe Society, with quite a sound fake British accent." They preferred his two brothers, Stewart and John, who were in the OSS in Europe.

Theodore H. White was a favorite of both Julia and Paul. He had been in China since 1939, when, as a twenty-eight-year-old with a Harvard fellowship, he continued his study of Chinese and worked as a translator in Chung-king. John Hersey of *Time* found him, and White reported on the war for *Time, Life,* and *Fortune.* Years before Julia arrived in China, White was cover-ing the war and explaining China and the Chinese to his American readers in a more comprehensive way than any other reporter. He believed that the real power of the Orient resided in the Chinese, not the Japanese. Julia found him affable, and Paul enjoyed his visits to Kunming.

While the Chinese transplanted the rice in the paddies and harvested the wheat, Julia joined Jeanne, Paul, Jack Moore, and another man for an over-night holiday. "We left Sunday afternoon at 4:30 packed in a jeep," wrote Paul. There was a monsoon in progress and they all got soaked in spite of ponchos, "but nobody cared because it was lovely, lovely, *Freedom!*" They drove out past Paul's favorite red bridge for another hour before turning off the main road to a lush valley surrounded by purple mountains. Here they checked into a tiny resort hotel at a hot spring. The next day in the rain they went walking along rice paddies, watching local peasantry transplanting rice, looking at the big waterwheels, swollen river, and deep mist on mountains. There were "startling patches of emerald green when the sun broke through and red brick soil where eroded," wrote Paul. They sat on a high plateau and chewed pine needles, smoking and talking and taking pictures of each other.

Mary, Julia's roommate, says that when Dillon Ripley came to visit and look at birds, Julia took him to the hot springs, about an hour's drive away. Julia adored soaking in the hot water. According to Jeanne Taylor, she de-clared: "Do you realize that if everyone in the damned war had a Sani Hot Springs bath every day, it would be over by now?" Jack Moore, who worked with Paul, remembered trips with Julia and Paul to visit the springs, temples, journeys over "spine-crushing dirt roads" that were a sharp contrast to the British-built country roads of India, and to commercial restaurants for "real meals. . . . They had obviously done a lot of exploration with Chinese food."

That summer Paul went to the hot springs with others, including Jeanne. It is not surprising, therefore, that Mary Livingston Eddy said, "I was not aware that Julia and Paul were romantically involved in China. I saw them together, but we all were together."

By August both the war and the partying quickened. "There have been quite a few visitations of the big WD/IBT [General Donovan]," Julia wrote in a communiqué to Ceylon. Clearly the focus was on concluding the war in Asia. Personal life went on as usual, with Paul's longing for "The Big Affair," and Julia involved in busy social life, longing for him. She acted the role of Miss Preen in a production of George S. Kaufman and Moss Hart's *The Man Who Came to Dinner* with a cast of two dozen, calling themselves the Area Entertainment Guide. Lieutenant Colonel Birch E. Bayh, the Theater Special Services Officer (a future U.S. senator from Indiana), pronounced the production a "splendid success."

The women were renovating their house during July for even greater parties. After hiring a new number one boy, redoing the floors, repainting the walls, and recovering the furniture (much damaged by the five resident dogs), they hosted the visiting generals and OSS personnel—seventy-five in all, says Ellie's diary. The rains began that night and did not stop until three inches covered the new living room, while holes were drilled in the ceiling to keep it from collapsing. Somehow, by hiring help and working diligently, they cleaned the house up and hosted three hundred people (including General Donovan) for cocktails that August evening, with guests spilling out onto the large veranda circling the house. "The rain stopped, the party was a huge success, and the visiting general was very pleased!" Before the week was over, the compound was under three feet of water and Julia was frantically rescuing top-secret documents.

Within hours of the party, the United States dropped an atomic bomb on Hiroshima (August 6). Two days later Russia invaded Manchuria, and the following day another bomb obliterated Nagasaki. General Douglas MacArthur told Teddy White, "There will be no more wars, White, no more wars."

If the war was ending, romance was heating up. Betty MacDonald remembers Paul coming over to spend time with Julia: "He would read to her a lot. One of the books was about sex. Dick [Heppner, said MacDonald] made fun of them and asked, 'What's Paul doing with this book about sex?' Perhaps he was catching her up." Betty was not the only one to notice that Paul was "blossoming around Julia." For Julia's thirty-third birthday he wrote her a poem about her "melt[ing]" his "frozen earth."

An Uncertain Romance at War's End

The poem is dated August 15, 1945, the same day the news arrived of the final surrender of the Japanese. In Kandy, Jane Foster won a case of scotch for correctly guessing the date of the surrender. She was sitting at a desk opposite Gregory Bateson when the loudspeaker announced the news that "an atomic device" exploded over Hiroshima. In Kunming, Ellie wrote to her parents: "It seemed unbelievable that it is over, and there was very little hilarity or celebration here—everyone was too busy I guess."

The next day Paul wrote to Charlie that he was fond of Julia and hoped that Charlie and his wife would meet her someday, for "even in a USA context she will show up very well":

> Over the 18 months or more that I have known Julia I have become extremely fond of her. She is really a good friend, and though limited in relation to my concept of la femme intégrale, she still is understanding, warm, funny, and darling. . . . [S]he is a woman with whom I take much comfort, and she has helped me over many a rough spot by just simple love and niceness.

Everyone stayed up late at night talking about the coming peace accord and what it meant to their futures. The big excitement in the OSS was organizing commando groups to be sent to Japanese prison camps around Asia. It was the OSS's last important operation, and historians agree on the valor of the OSS in rescuing POWs, among whom was General Jonathan Wainwright, captured by the Japanese on Corregidor early in the war.

Uncertainty about the future of China gripped everyone. America's policy for a postwar China was a "model of ambiguity," notes one historian. Indeed, there was no policy. With the Japanese defeated, Chiang now resumed his civil war against the Chinese communists, and OSS agents were left inside communist territory. Theodore White said that with their victory over Japan the United States had lanced a boil in China, and the killing would continue until it became the "greatest revolution in the history of mankind." Both sides lied and killed, but Mao had the people on his side (White makes it clear that the United States chose the wrong side to support).

Continued flooding killed refugees, whose bloated bodies floated by in the river. Rats started to eat shoes, belts, soap, and pistol holsters. Local restaurants were now off-limits, but Julia would remember the effect years later when she told *Parade* magazine that she learned to love food in China: "We always talked a great deal about food, particularly . . . because there was a plague going on, and we couldn't eat the Chinese food." During this time women were required to have two men escort them, according to Mary Livingston Eddy. "Julia was upset because she wanted to stay in China; I wanted to go home, but was ambivalent because I had put my family through enough worry."

For Julia, the awareness of her unsecured future ripened with the news of the war's end and Paul's birthday poem to her. She loved Paul, but there seemed so many obstacles. He was unsure, though his poem spoke of the "scattered seed" of their "Sweet friendship" growing "to final ripened grain." He was ten years older, introvert to her extrovert, experienced to her inexperience. She had a strong father; he had none. She had the privilege of an Ivy League education; he had none. Though he attended Boston Latin and took some extension courses at Columbia University, he was self-taught and had supported himself since youth. Everyone from this period of his life remembers him as highly intelligent and, in Jack Moore's words, "interesting, complex and very articulate (an untutored American might have thought he was a Brit)." His grasp of poetry, music, painting, languages, and the sciences put her education to shame. She had no intellectual rigor, was highly emotional, and given to spontaneous merriment.

She certainly did not match his ideal of women, especially in contrast to his Edith, who was petite, dark, chic, sophisticated. Nor did he conform to her image of Western manliness: Paul was a cosmopolitan man who loved the company of women, for, as he told his brother, "the friendly association of beautiful women is a panacea for almost anything." Yet his hard body revealed the years of physical labor aboard oil tankers and at a munitions factory in Lowell. When he looked at one of his hands, he wrote in 1943, he saw his experience:

> Thousands of hours of engraving which now make a burin fit with such comfort, the manila ropes that have raised blisters there hoisting sail on the Nova Scotia schooners, the judo jackets that have broken its fingers, the sheets of stained glass that almost severed its thumb, the ax handles that have glazed it, the breasts it has caressed, the paint brush handles that have numbed its fingers, the wine glasses it has lifted in delight, the photographic solutions it has stirred, the violin bows it has guided through the intricacies of Bach, the dogs it has scratched behind the ears, or its knowledge of Venice water, egg-beaters, ski-wax and hand clasps.

The touch of this hand taught Julia how dough feels when it is plunged into boiling oil. She was in love. But the contrasts were so great that Paul did not foresee his love for Julia, except as one of many girls with whom to romance. Years later he would castigate himself in the margins of his diary at every casual mention of "Julie." ("What stupidity that Julia was *right there,* and I never realized it was *she!!* It was Julia, of course! I never guessed it!")

To some of his correspondents, Paul sounded like a man in love. Professor George Kubler, an old friend of Paul's who taught art history at Yale, received a lengthy letter about a long-legged California girl. As he read the letter to his wife, Betty, she realized it was her classmate at Smith, Julia McWilliams. To Charlie, he pointed out Julia's strengths: "A constant, steady and driving worker—quite self-disciplined and a wonderful 'good scout' in the sense of being able to take physical discomfort, such as mud, leeches, tropic rains, or lousy food." Though he still questioned her ability "to sustain ideas for long," he thought she was "tough and full of character, a real friend," he wrote Charlie. "I am very fond of her," he adds, informing Charlie he had invited her for Thanksgiving dinner.

In early September it was not settled between them. The Japanese signed the peace accord aboard the USS *Missouri* in Tokyo Bay, but Julia did not want to leave China. There were farewell parties for those who were leaving. "Life is chaotic here," Ellie wrote to her parents. Peachy was sent home early; Marjorie became a war correspondent for *Fortune* in Chungking; Betty was flown home after helping to write the history of OSS/China and began working on her memoir *Undercover Girl* (1947) while rooming in New York City with Jane Foster. "People are departing right and left and the airport has been busier than usual getting them over the hump." And "so many close relationships that have been built up over a period of months and months" make "everyone so uncertain," Ellie added. "We find ourselves hanging in mid-air." Betty MacDonald described it as "a sudden vacuum which peace had brought."

When Gregory Bateson arrived to visit Kunming, Paul accompanied him to his university lecture and Julia went with him and a young Chinese sociologist to visit temples in the western region and listened to their tales of Chinese social customs. She was sorry she had seen so little of China.

Julia was recommended in September for the Oak-Leaf Cluster award by Colonel Richard Heppner for her "meritorious service as head of the Registry sections of the Secretariat of the Office of Strategic Services, China Theater." (In May she received an Emblem for Civilian Service.) But awards did little to dispel the weeks of waiting and boredom and frustration with her housemates.

Julia resumed a diary, as she had during other critical moments of her life. The irritation that she felt toward her roommates (even their morning throat clearings drove her to distraction) was probably displaced sexual frustration. She concluded one page with an example of the practicality and perseverance she learned in China: the mental tack to take, she told herself, is "genuine love and understanding of individuals as part of the human fabric of life." Still the upbeat girl from Pasadena, but a more experienced one.

At the end of September, Julia and Paul took more trips to the lovely hot springs, this time alone. Halfway up the mountain above the springs, in the cool air under a hot sun, Paul wrote to his brother: "Julia is here beside me and we have been reading aloud to each other from a collection of Hemingway's short stories." On a second visit he described her sitting beside him on the hilltop above the springs, she in pale blue slacks and dark blue sweater. The rains had stopped and the deep soil erosions were the color of cinnamon. Far beneath them were the yellowing rice paddies and the collapsing world they had known for two years: Donovan returned to his law practice when Truman announced the dissolution of the OSS, scheduled for October 1; Paul's Presentation Unit was transferred to the State Department, but he had no assignment; Julia was arranging for the transfer of all papers to the OSS Archives in Washington; most of the OSS branches were to become a part of the War Department; and everyone was turning in their guns and buying jade. Julia and Paul both feared they would soon be out of a job. They talked about meeting each other's families when they returned.

With the cholera epidemic dissipating, Julia and Paul decided to go on "a terrific binge of spring rolls with garlic (jaodze) [steamed dumplings], duck (yaadze), mixed green vegetables with hat on, sweet-sour big fish, pig meat, green beans [and] pudding, not to mention duck-wind-pipe hot soup." Paul described the roasting chestnuts now in season and the orgy of eating he enjoyed with Julia.

She was sitting on her string bed in her "moldy room," writing in her diary, regretting her departure from China, where she had found the intellectual stimulation that would feed her natural curiosity for the remainder of her life, and wondering if she would win Paul Child (who had asked to be sent to Peking). Her "affair of friendly passion and companionship" with Paul had no clear future:

> I am not the woman for him as I am not intellectual. He is probably not the man for me as he is not constant nor essentially vigorous enough— which is hard to explain. Perhaps it is his artisticness [sic] that makes him seem to lack a male drive. But his sensitiveness and the fact that we can talk about anything and there are no conventional barriers in thought communication make him a warm and lovable friend.

What she interprets as the lack of "male drive," is (as is clear in lengthy letters to his brother) complete exhaustion ("I couldn't even get an erection") and lack of physical passion for her. Tucked inside her diary is a page on which she wrote the lyrics of a popular song beginning: "A Man without a woman / Is like a ship without a sail."

Julia spent her last month briefly confined to quarters during a Chinese uprising (Chiang was solidifying his power) and saying goodbye to friends. The few women who were left gave a party for about sixty people in the house, with punch that packed a punch, and a phonograph for dancing. "We tried sunning on the balcony . . . [but] the bullets would fly overhead," wrote Ellie. During one encounter in Yunnan province, an arrogant young red-headed Air Force intelligence captain who could speak Chinese because he was the son of a fundamentalist Baptist missionary stupidly stood up against a group of Chinese communists and was shot. His fellow OSS intelligence colleagues considered John Birch's act stupid, an overreaction at a roadblock. For the political far right, his death would become a martyrdom, the first of the Cold War, the seed of the John Birch Society.

Bradley F. Smith argues that the OSS played a "marginal part" in China, but historian R. Harris Smith thinks otherwise. Although historians do not agree on the importance of the impact of the OSS on the war, it is clear that America's first attempt at international espionage was to give birth to the CIA in the months to come. The latter organization would not be characterized by the "free-wheeling, intellectually stimulating, and politically liberal" environment of the OSS (indeed, Ralph Bunche would be amazed at the rigidity, conservatism, and prejudiced environment of the organization that took the place of the OSS). One of the best historians of the OSS, Harris Smith, charges that the initial hamstringing of the OSS in China led the United States to overestimate Chiang and Russia, which in turn led FDR to make his deal with Russia at Yalta. Theodore White agrees that the United States forced Mao to throw in with Russia. Both assert that the OSS should have backed Mao and kept the Russian influence out of China. The OSS performed one clear service, argues Stanley Lovell: Donovan's OSS "amassed an incredible amount of information about practically every nation in the world," data that would be used for years to come in every branch of the military. In this process, Julia McWilliams played a key role.

Just before Paul flew to Peking and Julia to Calcutta, they had their last meal together in their favorite restaurant in town, Ho-Teh-Foo, which specialized in Peking cuisine. Paul described the meal to his brother:

We had spring rolls (a mixture of vegetables, meat and garlic rolled into a sort of lady-finger and fried in boiling sesame oil); long leaf cabbage and Yunnan ham; winter mushrooms with beet tops; Peking duck (broiled and de-boned into little half-dollar-size pieces). The bones were mixed with transparent noodles and spinach and an egg, and made into soup. The duck-pieces were brought sizzling-hot with a stack of thin, freshly-cooked, limp, unleavened wheat cakes, into which [they] rolled the duck and leeks, brown fermented-applesaucy soybeans, and any odds and ends left from other dishes. [We] finish[ed] off the meal with the soup. [October 8, 1945.]

At one of their final parties the few women remaining were dancing every dance, but Julia's thoughts were on Paul in Peking. "Beloved Julie," he wrote October 15, where the reception for the Americans was like a hundred Mardi Gras, "at the risk of sounding trite, *I wish you were here.* I need you to enjoy these marvels with, and I miss your companionship something awful. Dearest Julie, why aren't you here, holding my hand and making plans for food and fun! Love, Paulski." She would not receive the letter until she was in Washington the following month, but she clung to his promise that they would meet each other's families and see what each looked like in civilian clothes and surroundings. All those years of hunting through others' recipes for an adult life had led her to Paul.

$\mathscr{E}$ASTWARD HO

(1945 – 1946)

"Life without you is like unsalted food."
PAUL CHILD

AFTER A MONTH on board the troopship *General Stewart* with 3,500 people, the three women were starving for a taste of America. Julia McWilliams, Ellie Thiry, and Rosamund Frame, knowing that their bags would not be found for hours, carried out the plan they agreed upon on board ship. After Thibaut swept away Rosie, his new fiancée, to Elizabeth Arden's, Julia and Ellie found a cab near Pier 88 and asked for New York City's famous "21" Club, the former speakeasy for "Ivy League clientele," now turned restaurant. There they ordered their celebratory martinis and oysters, the best food and drink of home. The journey had been long and uncomfortable.

$\mathscr{H}$OMEWARD BOUND

More than a month before the troopship's arrival in America, Julia flew back over the Hump to Calcutta, where she was stuck for ten days living in a ten-foot-square room with five other women and a dog. All the planes had been commissioned to deploy troops from North Africa to the Pacific. She wrote of her dilemma to Paul, who was in Peking before traveling home via Hawaii.

Finally she was put on a troopship for a spartan and difficult journey, nothing like the original journey to India on the SS *Mariposa,* a converted cruise ship.

The *General Stewart* moved down the thick Hooghly River from Calcutta and into the Bay of Bengal on October 27, 1945, with the last three women of the original group. Julia, Rosie, and Ellie had been out the longest, feeling dirty and exhausted. "We did look like we had come off a cattle boat," said Julia. "We had been in China with few clothes and no makeup." Eighteen women from several countries shared a single stateroom. Deafening Navy loudspeakers just outside their stateroom carried reveille at 5 A.M., awakening the thousands of people on board ship, including 400 in the ship's hospital. Taps sounded at 9 P.M.

When they pulled into the tree-lined bay at Colombo, Ceylon, for refueling, the harbor was crowded with warships and freighters. Julia felt years older than the young woman who first sailed into this harbor. After stopping at Port Said in the Suez Canal for water, the transport sailed for New York Harbor, as Julia and Rosie and Ellie made plans for a festive arrival.

The "21" Club was followed by shopping and a "perm" for Julia. Unlike Rosie, Julia had no fiancé, but Paul, who had left Shanghai for Pearl Harbor, then San Francisco, made plans for her to meet his family in Washington, DC. "We were not engaged then," Julia said later. "We wanted to see our families before anything was decided."

For the second time Julia passed through the cavernous dome of Union Station and checked into the Brighton Hotel in Washington. The station, hotel, and Q Building carried such a feeling of normalcy that her two years in Asia seemed a dream. The bustle and urgency were gone; Q Building felt like the morgue for a dying OSS. Discharge forms were in triplicate as usual, and when Julia had her final physical examination before being discharged, she was told she had a slightly rapid pulse, but no sign of hypertension.

Her heart quickened further with Paul's arrival and her brief meeting with his double, Charles. Chafred, Paul's name for his identical twin brother and his wife, Fredericka (Freddie or Fred for short), lived at 1311 Thirty-fifth Street in Georgetown. Charlie Child was still working for the Department of State (chiefly on UNESCO), while his wife worked as a nurse's aide at Georgetown University Hospital. Their daughters, thirteen-year-old Erica and eleven-year-old Rachel (little Jonathan was only three), do not remember meeting Julia at this time, but they would have seen her only as one of Uncle Paul's many friends. On his return trip from China, during which he tanned his body nut brown on the deck of the ship, Paul wrote to Charlie of his continuing grief for Edith Kennedy, but his references to "Julie" were increasingly positive: "You will appreciate her warmth, and you can quickly learn, as

I have, to discount the slightly hysterical overtones of her manner of talking." Her warmth and naturalness were indeed what they first admired. Paul and Charlie were now forty-four years old and, though Charlie was to celebrate his twentieth wedding anniversary that April, Paul had never married.

Before she left for California, Julia applied for another job in government, as Paul would also do. Her form (December 12) asserted that she was willing to locate "anywhere." The work she preferred was "public relations"; she did "not want to do any more" office administration, "particularly anything to do with *files.*" Though she fudges on her height, saying she is only six feet tall, she honestly explains that she was fired from Sloane's for "insubordination, actually for general immaturity." Within seven months she would change her mind about wanting to work for the government again.

Julia was increasingly aware of the changes in herself, especially when on the way home to Pasadena she visited Pittsfield, where she no longer cared about the approval of Aunt Theodora. Paul, reflecting on the past year, also thought she had changed since he met her. In his Christmas letters from Charlie's permanent home in Bucks County, Pennsylvania, then under eighteen inches of snow, Paul tells her that he finds comfort in writing to her:

> I have been warmly and deeply aware myself, since I first met you on the porch of the tea-planter's bungalow . . . , how you have been emerging from the mists, indecisions and attitudes of your past into a fuller and more balanced life. I am curious to know if your family will have noticed that you are indeed a newer and better Julie, a more emotionally stable Julie, a more thoughtful Julie, a darlinger sweeter and lovelier Julie—or are these perhaps qualities which you always had and which it took my old eyes two years to see—finally? I would be unworthy of my semantic salt if I did not allow the possibility that it was I who had changed—not you—I who had become more perceptive, I who had finally been able to see the reality. But there is another possibility which we must both take into consideration. That we have changed each other for the better, because I believe that a relationship based on appreciation, understanding and love can work that sort of double-miracle—and whether we do or do not manage to live a large part of our future lives together, I have no regrets for the past, no recriminations, and no unresolved areas of conflict. It was lovely, warming, fulfilling, and solid—and one of the best things that ever happened to me.
>
> *Affectionately, Paulski*

$\mathcal{T}$HE EDUCATION
AND SEDUCTION OF JULIA

For the first six months of 1946, Julia was in Pasadena, preparing herself in several ways for the arrival of Paul, who was concluding his work for the Department of State. With Jack Moore, he was preparing a map showing the locations of the State Department's employees around the world for the Senate Appropriations Committee, and in March he was decorated with the Medal of Merit. His letters, at first signed "affectionately," then "love," convey the healing environment of his family, as well as his worrisome burden with the "frightening world"—both extremes he wanted to share with her. As one wag said a long time ago, the two most dependable aphrodisiacs are the presence of a desirable woman and her absence.

By contrast, Julia was taking music and cooking lessons. It was no accident that both art forms were close to Paul's heart. "Paul's mother was a good cook and he had lived in France. If I was going to catch him, I would have to learn to cook." She experimented with cooking for weeks, sharing her triumphs and failures in letters to Paul, until she finally decided she needed formal training. Her best friend, Katy Gates, remembers that "Julia was smitten with Paul and said, 'We must go to cooking school, Katy.' I said, 'All right, we'll go to cooking school.'"

In the spring, Julia and Katy Gates drove three times a week to Beverly Hills for cooking classes at the Hillcliff School of Cookery, taught by Mary Hill and Irene Radcliffe. Julia called them "two old English ladies" who featured "waffles, pancakes, and omelets." According to Katy, Julia wanted to learn to make soufflés. "Mrs. Hill had never seen anything quite like Julia," whose ambition and enthusiasm matched her physical strength. Katy recalled their practice dinner parties, especially their "Béarnaise Connection" dinner, for which they substituted lard for the unavailable butter and discovered to their dismay that at the buffet table, beside the steak and vegetable, the "béarnaise" sauce had turned to solid lard. Neighbors Douglas Gregg and Ed Valentine loved to tell about the time she forgot to puncture a duck—they had all gone hunting together—and it exploded in the oven. Old KBS pal Berry Baldwin recalled being served oxtail stew, to the wonder of the guests.

Every triumph and disaster of their cooking school experience was reported in Julia's letters to Paul. After a pancake disaster (she had not yet learned how to cook with eggs), Paul wrote a letter assuring her she would eventually be a "wonderful cook because you are so interested in food." He likes "sensual folk," he added, "in the sense of those who use and enjoy their senses on all fronts."

Probably at the suggestion of the government doctors in Washington, DC, Julia consulted her Pasadena doctor, who discovered that Julia had a goiter wrapped firmly around her vocal cords and removed it surgically. For years she had thought she had a "fat neck." "I noticed immediately, after I threw up my dinner the first evening it was out, that my voice had cleared. It was getting more gruff and hoarse daily. Now it is a clear, compelling bell-like coo," she wrote Paul as if to assure him that her voice was maturing.

Because in his letters Paul mentioned titles of his major interest, general semantics, she took S. I. Hayakawa's *Language in Action* with her to the hospital. Paul called himself a Korzybskian semanticist, and for years credited this scholar's work for disciplining his mind and writing style. To discipline her own mind, Julia subscribed to the daily *Washington Post* and the Sunday *New York Times* to become more informed and (she told Paul) to distinguish the missing and discolored stories presented by the Chandler family in the *Los Angeles Times.* (Paul would later call this newspaper "a Tory-angled, extreme-rightist, Republican die-hard paper.") He suggested other book titles and wondered if she had friends with whom she could discuss world affairs. He also suggested she meet the Beaches (and makes a point to say that Beach was bisexual), whose two boys Paul tutored in Asolo, Italy, in 1925. These friends near Pasadena would be an "opening wedge for you in a different world," he wrote her on February 11, 1946.

The letters between Julia and Paul proved an important instrument in the growth of their love. They exchanged gifts (engraved silver cigarette box from Julia, poetry from Paul), ideas, opinions on current political events (such as Paul's enthusiasm for the newly created UNESCO, for which he seemed "ideally shaped and created"), and words of endearment. "I adore you," he wrote January 10; "I long and languish for you," she wrote five days later. The next month her letters began: "Dearest one." The following month he wrote: "You play a leading role in my fantasy life," and later: "I have kissed no one since I kissed you." His letters were lengthy, articulate, and artful; hers briefer and initially quite simple. Most evident in Paul's letters were his continuing guidance, especially in expanding her knowledge about sex.

He encouraged her to read Henry Miller and, when she announced her sixty-five-year-old father might remarry, made frank references to body parts in a dissertation on the penis of the elderly male. He also sent a witty detailed description of graffiti in the men's room of the State Department auditorium. After Jane Bartleman, the astrologer upon whom Paul and Charlie depended for astrological guidance, made a detailed prediction about Julia's future—a prediction that had Paul and Julia falling in love with other people—Julia responded that Bartleman was probably in love with Paul herself. "Then,

Saturn will not be sitting on your sun sign; it will be Venus, with limbs askew, upon your Capricorn," she wrote. In response to Paul's detailed analysis of Henry Miller's *Tropic of Cancer,* a "forest of stiff pricks through which one wanders amazed, delighted, and revolted," Julia agreed with his assessment of Miller, liking the "surrealistic 'stream' sequences which seemed amazingly Daliesque." A clever, eager-to-learn woman signed her letters: "Much loving and more so—." Henry Miller was an earthy teacher in Paul's absence. "You seem to be expanding on all fronts—semantics, cookery, Henry Miller. How's your bosom?" he wrote, pleased by her frank and natural response.

It was Julia who then took the initiative in love. She first wrote "I love you" and spoke of her "warm love lust." And she was the first to suggest a concrete plan of action: "Why don't you fly out about in August and drive across the continent with me? We could say we were meeting some friends in Needles." Paul responded immediately: "I want to see you, touch you, kiss you, talk with you, eat with you . . . eat you, maybe. I have a Julie-need. Come on back and sit in my lap and let me bite off your earrings again. I have never *tasted* such delicious pearls!—let other gourmets eat their oysters. I will take pearls (on your earlobes) and be more tantalizingly and magnificently fed than they. So to bed, pearl-hungry." The food references were the key metaphor of longing in part because Julia was regaling him with her cooking feats. "Why don't you come to Washington and be my cook—we can eat each other," he again suggested. "If I buy a Buckminster Fuller house will you come and cook for me and play the pianola?"

Julia told her father that she intended to look for another job "because life in Pasadena is comfortable and lovely but not for me." Her sister Dorothy, who ran the McWilliams household and worked in an Army hospital all during the war, wanted to go to New York City to work in the theater (she would later do stage-managing for Gian Carlo Menotti's operas). She believed Julia should stay with their father. Paul warned Julia about the delayed adolescence resulting from living with parents. John McWilliams, Sr., settled the question when, after two years of keeping company with Phila O'Melveny, he decided to marry the fifty-year-old widow, much to Julia's relief.

Philadelphia Miller O'Melveny was from the families of Gail Borden and Roger Williams; she was named not for the city but for the daughter of Williams, founder of Rhode Island. A friend of several in Julia's Pasadena group, "she became part of my father's generation when she married him." Julia adored her. Phila was the widow of Donald O'Melveny, youngest son of the founder of Los Angeles's oldest law firm, O'Melveny and Meyers. Fifteen years younger than John McWilliams, who had been widowed for nine years, she was a Roman Catholic with several children of her own. Soon she became (in John McWilliams, Jr.'s words) "mother to all three of us and all our children just as though we were hers." Dorothy went to school with Phila's children, echoed her brother's praise, and would name her only daughter after her stepmother (younger Phila would inherit the older woman's wedding ring at her death). "Phila's father was a fierce Republican," said Julia, which so reinforced John McWilliams's views that "we ended up not being able to agree on the weather."

Julia's father continued to be active in California politics, particularly in financially supporting a "fine, upstanding young Navy lieutenant" (in his words) from nearby Whittier named Richard Nixon, who in 1946 ran against and easily defeated Democrat Jerry Voorhis, a five-term incumbent in the House of Representatives. Nixon smeared him as a communist sympathizer, and the easy win encouraged him to run against "that woman" (as McWilliams, who did not approve of women in politics, called Helen Gahagan Douglas). Interestingly, it was Julia's noisy communal cooking orgies, as well as her disagreement over politics, which drove her father more frequently to dinners at the home of widow O'Melveny.

For the May 8 wedding of her father and Phila, Julia's brother John came from Massachusetts with his wife, Josephine. He had been in the war earlier than Julia and was severely wounded in the field artillery when he was blown off a bridge in France. Since 1940 he and Jo lived in Pittsfield, where he worked in the family business, the Weston Paper Company. He shared his father's good looks and his politics.

Julia's loyalties were already with the Democratic Party and her artistic, liberal Paul. After he suffered a recurrence of dysentery and a sense that he was "deeply tired way down inside," she suggested he come West for a month and live with her. They would eat well, relax, and turn slowly in the sun "like chickens on a spit." Yet he made no immediate plans to visit California because he was still working at the State Department, looking for a career for himself, and keenly aware that he had little savings, no house, and no car. He was also waiting for the government to sort out how much leave time he had accumulated.

In the six months of their correspondence, Julia and Paul became increasingly intimate with each other as they shared their deepest secrets. In the sharing, Julia's insights into herself matured:

> Until I was about 25, I was usually so self-conscious that I actually hurt if I thought people were looking at me, then I somehow realized that so many people were so busy with themselves that they were not looking at me at all. And I am continually trying to keep "ME" out of as much of

my relations with people as possible, and transfer a full interest to you/ them, which automatically, and actually, makes me a more lovable person to them. . . .

Julia and Paul were also building a base of mutual friends and acquaintances. Paul spoke in detail about his discussions with old Paris and Washington friends such as Paul Nitze (later an arms-control adviser to Presidents), Jo Davidson ("Like you, [Julia,]" Paul wrote, Davidson is "interested in life as a whole instead of in parts"), Dick and Annie Bissell (he moved from the OSS to the CIA), Richard and Alice Lee Myers, Professor George Kubler, Archibald MacLeish, and Julian Huxley. (Paul knew Davidson well in Paris; Huxley he met at the home of Edith Kennedy in Cambridge.)

Paul kept Julia abreast of the movements of their OSS friends, including Guy Martin (who went back to Donovan's law firm), Marjorie Severyns, General Wedemeyer, and Mary Livingston Eddy. Paul and Charlie invited Jack Moore and later General Wedemeyer for dinner at the Child household. Tommy and Nancy Davis left for San Francisco in March. Ellie was to marry Basil Summers in November, and Gregory Bateson would divorce Margaret Mead. Numerous OSS personnel (Arthur Schlesinger, Stewart Alsop, Allen Dulles, David Bruce, Arthur Goldberg, Richard Holmes, William Colby, C. Douglas Dillon, Clark McGregor) were now part of the new CIA. Teddy White published a book about China, predicting that Chiang would "inevitably" collapse. Henry Luce fired him.

ℐEEING DOUBLE

Most important, Julia learned more about Freddie and Charlie, with whom Paul was living. She learned about their warm supportive family life in their home (called Coppernose) in Lumberville, Pennsylvania, where the family spent weekends cultivating and planting the gardens.

Through his letters, Julia learned more about Paul as well, when he described the differences between himself and his brother: Paul was precise and formal in his speech and writing, Charlie a rapid and emotional talker; Paul was right-handed, Charlie left-handed; Paul liked the "architectonic boys like Mozart and Stravinsky," Charlie responded to Wagner and Sibelius; Paul's painting was controlled and designed, Charlie's suggestive and dynamic. Strangely, it was Paul who lived the wilder and more adventurous life: "broke my hip, 7 ribs, a shoulder, 3 fingers, a wrist, a collar bone, etc. I got the needle in the eye [it was Charlie's doing]. I joined the Canadian Army at 16, I worked on schooners and tankers and arms and at stained glass while Charlie was being a Harvard man. I went to Europe first, and made fake furniture while he followed, married and settled down. I had a mistress. . . ." Paul was, in Child language, a "finnie"—that is, a "finished product," one who had "an innate sense of form." He thought that his young niece Erica had his artistic sense and spent hours teaching her about form and color in art and music. She and her brother and sister would always look upon Paul as their second father.

Paul was a natural teacher, a quality that Julia would later discover in herself. And his organized approach to life would draw out the McWilliams Presbyterian order in her. His discipline, which would have a profound effect on her later career, had a source in family but more specifically in his own will. As he told his brother in 1968, their chaotic and unstable childhood led him into "a major struggle . . . toward clarity and toward formality, simply to hold down the cover of my personal Pandora's box." While Charlie seemed to "opt for chaos" and "hug blinding Mystery and Chaos to [his] bosom," Paul, "always [aware] of earthquake, nightmare, discord and vertigo trying to sweep me into their world," chose "the realm of discipline" as the only means of action, creation, or usefulness. Not surprisingly, fifty years later, his favorite niece, Erica, would suggest that Julia embodied the extremes of the Child twins: "Julia is very emotional and sentimental (you cannot go to a movie without Julia crying). . . . But she is one of the most disciplined people I know."

Paul's discipline was reinforced by his study of semantics and jujitsu practice. When young boys, the twins had seen a photograph of two Japanese men "all tied in knots" in the office of Edward Filene's Boston store. When "Uncle Ed," their mother's paramour, explained jujitsu to them, they tried it on the floor, went home to practice on a mattress on the floor, and after taking formal classes in later years Paul became a black belt. He maintained his physical conditioning, despite blindness in one eye, car accidents, exotic diseases caught in foreign lands, and occasional severe headaches and double vision.

Paul's insistence on physical toughness began, Julia later learned, when the twins, dressed in their Little Lord Fauntleroy suits for a musical performance with their mother, were taunted by other boys in Boston Common. Paul's violin and Charlie's cello did not survive the melee.

"I would rather have my head resting on your breasts than throbbing up here on my shoulders," Paul wrote on May 22, 1946, during one of the four-day headaches he had suffered with since a severe concussion several years earlier. In their correspondence now, they were "aching" for each other. Julia took a two-week holiday to the San Francisco area to visit her friends Gay (Bradley) and Jack Wright and Paul's friends Tommy and Nancy Davis, who were expecting a baby. Paul accidentally ran into Phoebe Brown, just returned by air from Shanghai with the news that Julia and Paul were seen romancing in Washington. Meanwhile, Paul was struggling with the bureaucracy to get a five-week leave to come West for Julia.

"I can't think of anything nicer than a month with you, all over the country," wrote Julia in May. She was "ready to roll" out of Pasadena anytime after July 4. The plan was to have him visit her family, then they would drive up to see the Davises, and cross the country to Lopaus Point, Maine, where they would holiday in a cabin built by the Child family.

Paul left Washington July 4 on a new coast-to-coast train, arriving in Los Angeles July 7. Between introducing Paul to her friends and visiting his acquaintances in the area, she prepared special meals for him: she and Katy made brains in red wine sauce and naively stirred them as they cooked, leaving a mushy mess of white lumps. Julia was dismayed: "It was awful. Paul said he married me in spite of my cooking," she would later say on many occasions. This disaster caused her to wipe the Hillcliff School of Cooking from her résumé memory. In a Cooking Club Chat on America On-Line in 1996, she said, "I had really never done any cooking until France."

According to her friend Gay Bradley Wright, who came down from San Francisco for the event, Julia's father gave a party to introduce Paul to her friends. "When I met him we talked all evening; I just adored Paul." When he was comfortable with someone, "Paul was a raconteur who could mesmerize associates with his stories," said later friend William Truslow. "He was an artist and could put in detail, creating an atmosphere. Though inner-looking, he cared what others thought of him. Julia, by contrast, always wanted to know what *you* thought." Julia's stepmother, Phila, also liked Paul immediately, as she would all of the spouses of her husband's children. Julia believed that her mother, Caro, would also "have loved them all."

Father John was a different matter, not just because Julia was his first daughter but because Paul was an artist with a European aesthetic and appearance. He wore scarves in his open-necked dress shirts and cultivated the sensual. "My father was very difficult," explained Julia in 1988. "He was a very conservative Republican, and he thought all artists [and intellectuals] were communistic. Paul was an artist *and* a Democrat." A traditional father, he wanted his daughter to marry a man like himself.

Having lost his own father when he was a baby, Paul was probably anticipating a fatherly relationship with Julia's parent—at least this was Julia's wish. But the differences between the two men were immediately evident and never bridged. Paul talked with precision and daily tested "operational truth" with a detached rationality. John was settled comfortably in his political and religious beliefs, not accustomed to evaluating these beliefs or himself. It became clear to Julia that there would be no harmony and the choice of loyalty must be made.

LEAVING POP

When Julia and Paul drove out of Pasadena in her Buick, she made her final move away from home. She would visit briefly in the years to come, but this trip signified the break she had to make, not just physically but psychologically. Her choice separated her from the life in which she was born and reared, a life insulated by privilege and intellectual provincialism. She would move into a life perhaps just as insular, but a life of art, sensuality, and intellectual discipline.

After a weekend in Ojai with Julia's friends, they drove north to San Francisco to see the Davises and their new daughter, then to Crescent City, and, in a large northern sweep from Bend, Oregon, to Spokane, Washington, and Coeur d'Alene, Idaho, to Billings, Montana, and Flint, Michigan, then into Canada and down through Rochester, New York, to Maine by the first of August. They took turns driving every hour and tried to cover at least three hundred miles a day. Their guides were the AAA and Duncan Hines.

Paul had seen some of this country before, both during the time he worked in California in 1924 (painting sets in Hollywood) and during a trip across the country seven years before with Edith Kennedy, Charlie, and his wife, Freddie. In Paul's current letters to his brother, he made occasional comparisons with these earlier trips. In the Ojai Valley, where they spent their first weekend with Julia's old friends, including the Gateses (Freeman's cousin owned the 3,500-acre ranch), Paul discovered he could ride well after his eleven years of polo riding while teaching at Avon Old Farms School in Connecticut, a very English school founded by Theodora Riddle. Paul dreamed of having a house there someday. (Thirty-five years later, he and Julia would buy a home nearby on the coast at Santa Barbara.)

If Paul made his own comparisons with earlier trips, it was Julia's trail that was the more historically interesting. Her journey eastward made a revealing if not ironic reversal of the journey her grandfather McWilliams took westward to California in 1849. Indeed, she crossed his path in the Sacramento River valley, at the Columbia River, and on the Lewis and Clark trail, where he "had to decline [Chief Alikit's] liberal offer" to marry his daughter.

While her seventeen-year-old grandfather and his wagon train companions were refreshed and thrilled by the mighty Columbia River gorge, Julia and Paul, nearly one hundred years later, found the rugged, 115-degree journey from Briggs to Spokane hellish. Where McWilliams found dense forests and Indians, Julia and Paul saw endless "dry tortured canyons" and the "naked horror" of a mighty river. In contrast to her grandfather, who carried the Bible and Plutarch's *Lives* in his wagon, Julia brought along in her Buick eight bottles of good whiskey, one of gin, and a bottle of mixed martinis. Julia's reversal of her grandfather's pioneering voyage was modern and illicit. She and Paul spent each night together in a $2.50 to $5.00 trailer park or motel. Yet, as was her grandfather, Julia was a pioneer in leaving her family and blazing a trail, not westward, but eastward, and eventually back toward Europe.

As much as they delighted in the enormous redwoods wrapped in fog, the dramatic Crater Lake, and the snowcapped mountains of Idaho and Montana, they delighted most in the discovery of each other. They talked and read to each other from newspapers or *Time* and *Life.* Paul's physical prowess and ingenuity were tested by a tire blowout in the sage-and-lava-strewn wilderness of Oregon. Her strength and sportsmanship were demonstrated daily. "She is a splendid traveling companion," wrote Paul from Crescent City, California, on July 19, "loves to look at everything, likes small places with local color flavor better than big ones, for both eating and sleeping—is jolly, objective and considerate." Five days later, in Billings, Montana, he wrote:

> Julie is a splendid companion, uncomplaining and flexible—really tough-fibered, a quality which I first saw in her in Ceylon and later in China. She has great charm and ease with all levels of people without in any way talking down to anybody. She's got a much tougher stomach than I have, and in the 3 years I've known her in War and Peace, in tropics and in USA, has never been sick from anything. She also washes my shirts! Quite a dame.

She used that "great charm" on the border guard when they crossed into Canada for a day (he allowed them to take in more than one bottle of liquor). In a rugged little town in Montana, she got out of the car in her bare feet with red-painted toenails and, without concern, walked into a lumbermen's restaurant with Paul, sat down, and drank a beer. It was July 22, 1946. Everyone was "goggle-eyed" reported Paul, "but no cracks."

$\mathscr{A}$ CABIN IN MAINE

After leaving Highway 102 and passing through the tiny town of Bernard, Maine, Paul drove to the end of the peninsula, Lopaus Point, crossing what he now called "Burma Road," a gnarled and dippy lane he warned Charlie not to cement over. Here on the rugged coast of New England, southeast of Bangor on Mount Desert Island, Julia and Paul spent an exhilarating ten days, during which Julia became a member of the Child family. She was the first woman since Edith whom Paul brought "home." They were rechristened JuPaulski. Paul holidayed here in the years before the war and used a Lopaus stone as a paperweight on his desk in India. This family and this land were his stone.

Julia and Freddie were instant friends, and the photographs of them reveal their freckled sisterhood, though Freddie was half a foot shorter with flaming red hair. The only criticism Julia would ever make of her was that she was very protective and defensive of her family and household. She was a marvelous and inventive cook, and Julia relished the fresh lobsters during this first visit. Because the quarters were still partly tented and without running water and electricity, their intimacy and compatibility were immediately tested.

Julia closely observed her lover and his double as they dragged in the logs for a new section of the house, working without need of verbal communication. Both were physically strong, both jujitsu experts and artists, and now employees of the Department of State. Their long devotion as well as their prickly relationship became evident to her. In part this was a result of their different temperaments and in part, Julia thought, because of Charlie's guilt over Paul's blind eye. As a child, Paul had turned to look over his shoulder and the needle Charlie was holding went into his eye. Charlie's children, years later, described the twins: "Paul was pessimistic, introverted, and didactic. Charlie was optimistic, extroverted, and spontaneous. They gave each other these roles and played them to the hilt!"

Charlie was smitten with Julia's "tall willowy" figure and "blue, blue eyes, as jolly and gay as Paul was serious." Thus he would describe her in his memoir of Maine and their cabin building: "She possessed more than a touch of the unexpected: she was a tough relentless worker."

The children loved Julie (or Aunt JuJu), as everyone called her, especially Rachel, who was the most like her. "When Paul brought her to Maine, it was a significant event," says Rachel Child, who fifty years later still remembers the color of Julia's dress and her long, beautiful legs. "They talked about war stories, and she was so funny. We kids were mesmerized. I was infatuated with her. For one thing, she was the kind of person who would drop things, and so was I. She was a wonderful addition to our family; she arrived like a breath of fresh air. She was a great mentor for me, being so positive and optimistic, and taught me that life does not have to be so considered; you can just DO IT. It was like having our own Auntie Mame."

The entire family observed Julia's qualities, qualities that Paul listed in his last letter crossing the country. This first analysis of Julia remains the best we have. Though her balance and logic, which Paul praises, are McWilliams qualities she seriously cultivated to please him, the strong and natural woman he adored is the California girl she always was:

> She *never* "puts on an act," or creates a scene. She's direct and simple about natural functions such as defecation, urination and belching, and has no measly Mrs. Grundyisms concerning sex. She frankly likes to eat and use her senses and has an unusually keen nose. She appreciates the special local overtones of both places and people and never gravitates toward the stuffy and safe. She is unusually strong physically and marvelously healthy. She has a firm and tried character in seeing a job through and is naturally very clean and sweet at all times. She has a cheerful, gay humor with considerable gusto as well as subtlety, and appears not to be frightened easily and is therefore emotionally steady rather than hysterical when things get tough. She has a frank and warm liking for men, and no apparent bitchiness about other dames. She loves life and all its phenomena, a quality which shows to great advantage in traveling. . . . She has deep-seated charm and human warmth which I have been fascinated to see at work on people of all sorts, from the sophisticates of San Francisco to the mining and cattle folk of the Northwest. She would be poised and at ease anywhere, I should say; she tells the truth, and for the most part uses balanced rather than extravagant language. In this connection I believe that her thinking has become much more careful, logical and objective in the last two years, and I find her interesting and fun to talk to at any time. And I love her dearly.

In turn, Julia loved this close and devoted Child family. According to Rachel Child: "She bought the Child family and what it stood for and it stood for good eating and good wine and talk—preparation for the table, rituals." Most important, Julia was deeply in love with Paul. She always admired and respected him: she fell in love with him in China, but now she trusted him.

She knew that if she gave Paul her life, he would not drop it. The rest seemed "inevitable."

"We are going to get married, and right away," Paul announced to his family.

"Well!" said Freddie and Charlie with one voice. "We thought you'd never come out with it!"

$\mathscr{F}$LAVORS OF MARRIAGE
(1946 – 1948)

"No matter what happens in the kitchen,
never apologize."

JULIA CHILD

～

THE APPROACHING truck lost its brakes; Julia saw it heading straight for them. Paul could not swerve the car out of the way in time. He and Julia had left Lumberville on this three-lane road that almost became the end rather than the beginning of their life together. "It was nip and tuck," reports Jack Moore (Paul's colleague at State). "If the truck had been just six inches closer, they would have both been dead. I remember being heartbroken."

Paul bruised his ribs on the steering wheel, hit the windshield, and was thrown out the car door. Julia remembers that she "hit the windshield and was thrown out the door and my shoes came off. I was knocked out and covered with blood from a head wound." The car was totaled. "A woman and her husband who were passing by took us to the nearest hospital emergency room somewhere in New Jersey. After they patched us up, we called my father." Before the accident Julia and Paul left Charlie and Freddie's Pennsylvania home to meet her family, who had gathered for a McWilliams engagement party at the River Club in New York City the day before the wedding.

A BANDAGED BRIDE

Julia insisted on going ahead with the ceremony. "We were married in stitches," Paul said, "me on a cane and Julia full of glass." The civil ceremony was held at noon on September 1, 1946, at the home of prominent lawyer Whitney North Seymour (a friend of Charlie's) in Stockton, New Jersey, where the legal waiting time was brief. Charlie stood up with his brother, Dorothy with her sister.

Across the Delaware River in beautiful Bucks County, Pennsylvania, their families and closest friends gathered to celebrate the union of Julia Carolyn McWilliams (thirty-four) and Paul Cushing Child (forty-four) with a garden party in the backyard of the Childs' home. It was a country wedding lunch, very casual, with big dishes of food lining groaning tables. The men shed their jackets and rolled up their white shirtsleeves under the late summer heat. Food, like mashed sweet potatoes stuffed into oranges, and wine were plentiful.

The bride "had the most beautiful, bean-thin figure I've ever seen . . . slender but curves in all the right places," declared Fanny Brennan, a longtime friend of the Childs'. Julia's nieces reported, "Julia was exuberant and warm and gorgeous and had beautiful legs." She wore a slender, short-sleeved, belted dress that looked like a summer suit with high heels that made no attempt to disguise the fact that she was taller than Paul.

Coppernose, Charlie and Freddie's house in Lumberville (seven miles from the popular New Hope village), was as polished and decorated as possible on such short notice. Only a month before, Paul and Julia had arrived in Maine with no definite plans to marry. Now the wedding, appropriately and symbolically, was on the Child family property; Freddie Child, who came from a wealthy family, had inherited a nearby house in 1927 and bought Coppernose when the owner died. Paul, who had his own room here, had helped Charlie lay the large brick terrace with Charlie's diamond pattern. There was a brook and a small waterfall, and a swimming pool. The wedding guests ate their lunch on the terrace and lawn. This grand home, with its gardens and brook, was Paul's only home since the death of Edith in Cambridge early in the war.

When Julia and Paul cut their wedding cake, they shared a bit of it together—a tradition dating from the Middle Ages that bonds a couple at the moment of their first shared food. Julia's family gathered around. Stepmother Phila came with Julia's father from Pasadena; Dort from New York City where she was working in the theater; brother John and his wife, Jo, drove down from Pittsfield, Massachusetts. Present also was Aunt Bessie's daughter, Patsy Morgan, from New Canaan.

John McWilliams, as a traditional father, wanted to give the wedding. But it was a Child event, which "got Julia and Paul off on the wrong foot with Pop," admits Dorothy, who is even today reluctant to acknowledge that Julia was "rejecting" her family. Indeed, the break for Julia was a necessary and significant one. Paul's nieces believe that he was not "disapproving of the McWilliamses, he was bored by them." His attitude had its basis in his unstable childhood and his prejudice against business, particularly money made in land speculation. "It was a kind of fear of money," they add, pointing out that both twins married women with money who took over their finances. The political antagonism between the two men in Julia's life was unambivalent and mutual.

The wedding guest list was as meaningful as was the reception site for Julia's future, for included with the two immediate families were the people who comprised Paul's larger family: the Myerses, the Kublers, and the Bissells—all part of Paul's Paris and Connecticut life before the war, a group that continued a gourmet "orgy" of food and drink at the Mayflower Inn each New Year's Day. These people would become Julia's new family.

Tall and stately Richard Myers in his crocheted St.-Tropez beanie came from New York City with his daughter and son-in-law, Fanny and Hank Brennan (his wife, Alice Lee, could not attend). Daddy Myers was Paul's connection to the world of food, wine, and music in Paris, where the Myerses lived for nearly thirty years. He was part of the F. Scott Fitzgerald and Gerald Murphy group of wealthy expatriates who lived in Paris and on the Riviera. Myers then worked for American Express and served as head of *The Ladies' Home Journal* in Europe (where Charlie painted his portrait), before serving with the OSS in London during the war. Fanny, who was younger than Julia, thought Paul was "very, very masculine." Everyone, she adds, "was very happy for Paul because Julia was so ebullient."

George Kubler met Paul when the latter taught at the Avon Old Farms School and George taught art history at Yale. The two men traveled together in Mexico in 1938, where Kubler met his wife, Elizabeth (Betty) Scofield Bushnell, a Smith '33 classmate of Julia. Because of this double connection they would henceforth be among the closest friends of the newlyweds.

Completing the Avon-Yale circle of Paul's friends, his extended family, were the Bissells, its social center and probably the family that unofficially adopted him. Paul's artistic blossoming occurred at the salon of Marie Bissell, a wealthy patron of the arts in Farmington, Connecticut (near the Avon Old

Farms School). In fact, Paul helped design some of her charity balls. Marie and Richard Bissell had three children. Son Dick (Richard Jr.), who was of Paul's generation, had been in the OSS and was now headed to MIT as an economics professor. Later he would become the top planner in the CIA and meet his Waterloo with the Cuban Bay of Pigs debacle. He was married to Ann Bushnell, Betty Kubler's sister.

Thus the reception included the extended family to which Julia would become sister and daughter for the remainder of her life. As they enthusiastically touched wineglasses, Paul called out *le carillon de l'amitié*—the bell of friendship! Though Julia and Paul were an integral part of this expansive clan, they remained a tight unit of two, "emotionally dependent upon each other" (as one family member says). "They each needed someone who would never leave. . . . They were devoted to each other." He never had parents upon whom he could depend; she left her family for him.

Because they had had their honeymoon on the cross-country journey and Paul needed to return to work, they moved immediately to Washington.

WASHINGTON HOUSEWIFE

The nation's capital, once a port on the Potomac River, was a sleepy Southern town in the late 1940s, colored by postwar drama—a dozen Nazi war criminals were hanged at Nuremberg that October—and visions of European peace and recovery, bolstered by the United Nations and the Marshall Plan. Columnist Drew Pearson set the tone of political gossip in this one-industry city. Black servants worked in the homes of government officials. And every weekday morning, Dean Acheson walked to the State Department with Felix Frankfurter, having agreed never to talk of Palestine or Zionism. Georgetown's cobblestone streets and neighborhood grocery stores were the ideal setting for a new bride.

Julia set about becoming the consummate housewife so typical of this period later defined by Betty Friedan in *The Feminine Mystique*. Paul left for his office at the Department of State, and Julia planned the evening meal and social appointments. Because the city was full of their friends, there were frequent cocktail and dinner parties with Dick Bissell, Guy Martin, Dick Heppner and Betty MacDonald, Joe Coolidge, and others from their OSS years, as well as Charlie and Freddie, who lived nearby.

They settled in a small house at 1677 Wisconsin Avenue, where they plastered, papered, rewired, and painted to make it home. Julia had twenty-five cookbooks on a shelf above her stove, and Paul hung six of his favorite OSS photographs on the wall of the stairs. As soon as the curtains were hung, they began inviting friends over for cocktails.

Though Paul's Washington ties went back as far as 1943, both had a wide network of associations there. Paul's 1943 diary, written the year after the death of his beloved Edith, contains the names of many people he worked with who later went on to politics (Paul Nitze, Bob Vance, Dick Bissell, Sherman Kent) and to the arts (Budd Schulberg, Garson Kanin, Ruth Gordon, John Ford, Sol Kaplan, Eero Saarinen) as well as OSS friends Cora DuBois and Jeanne Taylor. He records two funerals this year, for Dickie Myers, who was shot down while flying for the RAF, and Steve Benét, who had read drafts of his "John Brown's Body" to Paul in Paris (his friends staged a rereading after the funeral). The introspective, lonely, illness-plagued Paul who wrote the 1943 letter-diary seems in sharp contrast to the contented married man of 1947 and 1948.

One Christmas Eve, Julia met Paul's Cambridge, Massachusetts, "family" after a drive to Boston: Robert, Fitzroy, and Edmond Kennedy, sons of Edith. Bob and Gerta Kennedy—he was a professor of architecture at MIT—welcomed Paul and his bride to their home and family, which included two children. Paul had been closest to Bob, who was fourteen when Paul became surrogate father to Edith's sons in Paris and Cambridge. Also there were Joan and George Brewster, he an architect and she a poet and longtime friend of Paul who attended Edith Kennedy's salon and short story course in 1936 or 1937. "Paul's wife is a big tall girl with an open, friendly face; not good-looking but immensely attractive. I liked her at once and was delighted he had married 'a golden girl' and not some rarefied creature," Joan Brewster wrote in her diary that evening. Today she adds: "Julia was loved by all the Kennedy family, and why not?! She was ebullient . . . [and] uncomplicated Paul's life a bit."

It was just a month after a wonderful holiday season, including the New Year's Day reunion at the Mayflower Inn, when Paul and Julia were awakened by the smell of smoke at four o'clock one February morning. When they opened their upstairs bedroom door, a wave of vinegar-smelling smoke poured into the room and they could hear the crackling flames downstairs. The lights and phone were dead. "We spent an explosive three minutes pitching into the street below whatever clothes we could lay our hands on in darkness," Paul later told the Kublers. Julia pitched out her shoes, always the most difficult apparel to acquire in her size. They managed to crawl through the hot smoke, unlock the window in the next room, and jump out on a lower roof and to the ground. They had nothing on under thin robes and the weather was twelve degrees in a stiff wind. While Paul went to warn the woman next door, "Julia stood in the middle of Wisconsin Avenue and, fingers-in-mouth, whistled a night cab to a stop."

The fire, which started in an unoccupied house next door, blackened everything; the firemen knocked holes in all the walls and scattered their belongings everywhere. Julia and Paul retreated to the home of Charlie and Freddie, where they remained until their house was renovated. During the nearly two months it took to restore lights, heat, water, gas, and walls, their little house was burglarized twice. At the same time Charlie and Paul learned that they would be "let go" from the Department of State on March 15. Many people were dropped from State because of budgetary and political troubles (the Republicans had seized power from the Democrats).

For one year, Paul would remain self-employed. The loss of his government job left him in a "pool of confusion," as he described it, and convinced that Life is not regulated by an Omnipotent Intelligence. The two Child families were not destitute, however, because Paul had his OSS savings account and both Julia and Freddie had annual incomes from their inheritance. John McWilliams bought his daughter and son-in-law a 1947 Buick, "a steel-blue wonder-chariot presented to us as a consolation prize by my father-in-law. The possession of this thunderbolt has ironic overtones, however, in a context of joblessness," he told the Kublers. He and Charlie spent a lot of time painting and applying for jobs at organizations such as UNESCO, the Atomic Energy Commission, and the United Nations. By spring Julia and Paul were back in their little house, and Charlie was making plans to move his family permanently back to Lumberville, where he would continue his portrait painting.

Paul was able to cope with this double blow of firings because he had always lived with some degree of insecurity during a dozen careers. His mother imbued in her boys the sense that artists were special and gifted, and that attitude, together with her monetary irresponsibility, resulted in both insecurity and the habit of adjusting to that insecurity in her children. She had survived on her talents; they would too. Not surprisingly, Freddie and Julia always kept the family checkbooks and accounts.

Julia was always aware that Paul painted, but until she visited Lumberville for the first time she did not see much of his work. She knew he was happiest when he was working on a new painting, and many of his letters to Charlie through the decades, especially from Paris, talk of his work and his theories of painting. Paul's work is "very accomplished," according to Professor Colin Eisler of the Institute of Fine Arts at New York University. Had he wanted to be a professional artist, he had the talent to do so. Eisler places Paul's painting in the Precisionism of the 1920s and 1930s, which is hard-edged and studied.

Paul himself analyzed the difference between his and his brother's painting: he was stirred by "formal relationships" (shapes) in nature, while Charlie was stirred by "energy expressions" (movement). Indeed, Paul's paintings are so completely detailed that they do not seem to have any air in them. Unlike James Thurber, his acquaintance in 1920s Paris who drew in minimalist pencil strokes like a blind man, Paul completed every detail of a scene like a photographer. Both Paul and Thurber were marked for life when a brother accidentally blinded them in one eye during play, and yet both became skilled draftsmen (Thurber for *The New Yorker*).

THE JOY OF COOKING

Commerce and psychology were reinforcing the image of a "wholly compliant femininity," says writer Laura Shapiro of the 1950s woman. *The Ladies' Home Journal,* which had shown women defending the home front in uniform, now reproduced smiling wives and mothers hanging up the wash or transporting children. As these roles of femininity grew more powerful, Shapiro points out, "cooking went into retreat." Campbell's Soup and women's magazines portrayed cooking as a nuisance, in a trend for convenience that would culminate in the first frozen TV dinner in 1953.

Going against this trend, Julia focused on learning to cook the food that Paul valued and enjoyed. Contrary to the feminine image of the day, she had an appetite and labored over recipes calling for fresh ingredients, taste, and texture. Reinforcing her labors was Paul's view of the centrality of good food and drink and the artistry of the toiler in these vineyards. In France *cuisine des mères* was venerated, and all professional chefs were men. While Julia labored for hours, *The Ladies' Home Journal* advertised: "Learn to Cook in five meals!"—meaning learn to open tins, pudding boxes, and frozen vegetables ("cut two boxes of frozen cod fillets in halves"). Julia was learning to cook with the 1943 edition of Mrs. Irma Rombauer's *The Joy of Cooking:* published seven years earlier, it became the best-selling edition.

The Joy of Cooking was the first real attempt to move away from the antiseptic, diet-reform boredom of the domestic-science home economists. The daughter of German immigrants, Rombauer wanted to find a balance between French béarnaise sauce and American pancakes. Historian Robert Clark claims her book represents a movement away from the domestic science of Fannie Farmer "toward flavor." Her directions were accessible and her style ebullient, even blithe. There was a vivid sense of personality in the writing that appealed to Julia. Indeed, Rombauer's biographer describes the style as "charming, civilized, irreverent, original, [and] irrepressible"—adjectives that could describe Julia's own speech. *Joy* was American, not because it focused on indigenous produce, but because it was egalitarian and middlebrow, avoiding both the gourmet and the cooking school marm. It was American because it focused on meat and potatoes, or, specifically, hamburgers, casseroles, and cakes.

Though the book was a huge compendium of recipes and sold nearly 1.1 million copies by the end of the decade, it changed little about the average American diet. Contrary to James Beard's later assertion that the GIs returned from World War II with a taste for "the real thing," Americans, whether GIs or civilians, preferred instant coffee, Jell-O products, and gloppy casseroles.

Julia, apparently not a natural or instinctive cook, struggled with recipes. Her first broiled chicken: "I put it in the oven for twenty minutes, went out, came back, and it was burned; I needed better directions." Sometimes Paul had to wait until late in the evening for the dishes to be ready for eating, but they enjoyed entertaining their friends for meals:

> I was not much of a cook when we first married. I was using magazines and *The Joy of Cooking*. We would not eat dinner until around ten because it took me so long to cook. I was doing fancy things. Paul would help. He would do anything. He was a wonderful companion; he was never, ever boring.

Julia and Paul set a pattern as ideal hosts. Her spontaneous merriment matched his tight order and structure. While she busily banged away with pots and pans, he set a perfect table, coordinating the colors and placing the silver precisely. With their guests, she showed instant rapport and cozy friendship, while he poured the wine and directed the dinner conversation to weighty and stimulating topics. "Paul was somewhat more of a recluse," says later friend Mary Dorra, "but Julia was a vacuum cleaner: She picked up everybody." Paul agreed that Julia was his "magic catalytic agent for friendships."

Julia continued her education, reading, in addition to *Time, Harper's* (Paul was fond of Bernard DeVoto's "Easy Chair" column), *The New Yorker,* and the Paris *Herald Tribune.* She also subscribed to a magazine founded in December 1941 called *Gourmet.* Within the next few years she became aware of several people who were writing about food—Lucius Beebe, Clementine Paddleford, M. F. K. Fisher, and, by the summer of 1948, James Beard, who contributed a two-part series on outdoor cooking. Because the Childs had no television, she did not see Dione Lucas's or Beard's cooking programs from New York City.

After living in close proximity to Charlie again, Paul occasionally suffered what he called "anxiety neuroses or phenomena of generalized fear," for which he would seek professional help early in 1948. He carefully analyzed the intense love-hate relationship with his twin brother and his long tendency to define himself in opposition to Charlie. He now determined to live as a separate entity, to control his own attitudes and shape events and his own future. He also reprimanded himself for his pessimism. Though he did not say as much, he certainly married Julia in part for her optimism. He later claimed to have been "trained as I am in the Pollyanna attitude" by her.

THE CHILD-BICKNELL COMMUNE

After a year on Wisconsin Avenue, Julia and Paul moved into the very large house that Chafred still owned at 1311 Thirty-fifth Street in Georgetown. It was Paul's home after his return from China, and he used the studio in back of the garden for his painting. Beginning in October 1947, they shared the house with Sally and Nigel Bicknell, neighbor friends who were looking for larger quarters. The Bicknells vacationed in August in Maine with all of the Childs before moving into the Thirty-fifth Street house. Nigel was a "golden boy" of the Royal Air Force and stationed in Washington. Julia thought he was "difficult," and he did not get along well with Paul. (Their opinions of him were reinforced later when he left Sally for his mistress of eight years.) But they both adored Sally ("Paul loved intelligent women," Julia explained), who was pregnant. Their first son, Julian Bicknell, was four years old and had a Scottish nanny, who also lived with them.

Sally remembered that the day she went into the hospital to give birth to Marcus, Julia babysat Julian, Paul drove her to the hospital, then Julia prepared a beef heart for company that night: "She had begun to be adventurous and go to the meat and the fish markets. She had a healthy appetite always. When I returned, Julia told me that she had thrown away the beef heart because 'it did not work out.'" Sally added, "Julia at that time was not a great cook, but she wanted to know how food worked. She wanted to know about everything." Mary Case Warner, Julia's Smith College roommate, remembers visiting the "commune in DC" and being served kidney pie, "which I couldn't eat. And we had cocktails with avocados in them. Avocado cocktails! We sat on orange crates, but Julia was always herself."

The Childs and Bicknells ate every meal together, and the women loved cooking together. Because of Julia's adventurous cooking and because Nigel's diplomatic work as a civil air attaché demanded entertaining, they had many cocktail parties and dinners, their guests including Rosamond and Thibaut de Saint Phalle, Dick Heppner and Betty MacDonald, Cora DuBois and Jeanne Taylor, as well as General Wedemeyer and columnist Joe Alsop. When Julia sat down at the piano to play something silly, Paul was not pleased, Sally Bicknell observed. She and her husband noted Paul's serious and restrained demeanor, but Nigel responded to it with humor, if not a mean spirit. He deliberately placed Paul's tools on the wrong hook in the garage. In his careful manner, Paul would always outline the tool or the pot or pan on the wall of his workroom and in Julia's kitchen.

Julia and Paul bought a house at 2706 Olive Street in Georgetown. The title cleared on May 17, just a couple of days before the farewell party for the Bicknells, who were transferred back to their Foreign Office in London. Julia was thrilled with their first home. Despite their car accident, the destruction of some of their possessions in the fire, and Paul's job loss, she was optimistic. She lacked only a child or a career. Though Paul always admired bright and accomplished women, Julia refused to work again for the government as a file clerk.

Three days after the title to the house cleared, they drove to Boston with Chafred for the wedding of Paul's nephew, Paul Sheeline, to Harriet Moffat. Sheeline was the first son of Charlie and Paul's sister, Meeda, of whom they disapproved and about whom they rarely spoke. She had several marriages (Sheeline counts a total of nine marriages between his parents) and wrote for *Town & Country* in Paris before her death in 1941. Sheeline grew up in Paris, attended boarding school with Jack Hemingway near Versailles, and served with the OSS in France during the war (the schoolboys Paul and Jack met again at OSS headquarters in Avignon). He was attending Harvard when he met his wife-to-be, and he would go on to become a corporate lawyer on Wall Street. Sheeline had not seen his uncles in many years, nor had he met his Aunt Julia, whom he liked immediately.

Following a month on Lopaus Point in Maine, where they ate lobsters cooked in every manner and celebrated the birthday of young Rachel Child, Paul returned to Washington to rejoin the State Department with the promise of work overseas. As if to say farewell to family, they also paused on the way up to see John and Jo McWilliams in Pittsfield and on the way back stopped at Avon and Lumberville. Paul wrote to the Kublers in late September that "the FBI has finally declared us Kosher, so we're back—sucking at the govt. tit— and we'll be leaving for Paris around the end of October. . . ." They rented their new house, got all their medical shots, bought spare parts for the Buick, which they called the Blue Flash, and three cases of whiskey, gave away their cat, and made plans to spend Christmas with the Bicknells in London.

They boarded the SS *America* in New York City on October 27, 1948, with fourteen pieces of luggage and six or seven trunks along with their car. The following day the ship's photographer caught the Charlie Child family waving from Pier 61 at Twenty-first Street as Paul and Julia sailed toward France. In yet another reversal of her McWilliams family migratory history, Julia was crossing the path of her grandfather's Scottish grandfather, who was born on board a ship to America.

After five days of a bone-bruising, stomach-heaving gale and then wet fog—cheered only by the showing of *Unfaithfully Yours,* a movie by Paul's pal Preston Sturges—Julia and Paul docked at Le Havre, claimed the big blue Buick, and headed toward his new appointment as "Exhibits Officer" for the United States Information Service in Paris. More important, they were heading toward a career for Julia.

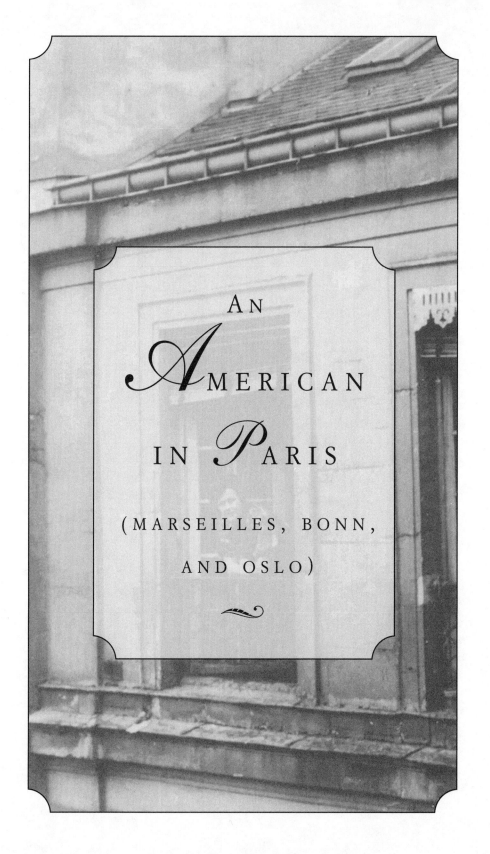

AN
American
IN *Paris*

(MARSEILLES, BONN,
AND OSLO)

Chapter 10

A PARIS
(1948 – 1949)

"There are so many kinds of hunger . . .
memory is hunger."

ERNEST HEMINGWAY

HER EPIPHANY occurred in Rouen, in a restaurant called La Couronne. Julia and Paul stopped for lunch on November 3 on their journey to Paris, the back seat and trunk filled with suitcases. They had been up since 5:45 A.M., before the ship landed, then sat around yawning and smoking for two hours before the car was off-loaded to the dock. Their stomachs were shriveled after five days of the tasteless food on board ship.

TASTING FRANCE

Briny oysters *portugaises* on the half shell and a bottle of chilled Pouilly-Fuissé awakened their palates and hearts. The ritual of an expectant welcome, white tablecloth, formal wine presentation, and incredible tastes brought time to a worshipful standstill. *Sole meunière,* sputtering hot and browned by "golden Normandy butter," followed. Then a green salad, crème fraîche, and finally *café filtre.* All at a reverential pace. Julia savored each dish as if it were the first food she had ever tasted. In a way, it was.

When they left the medieval, quarter-timbered house of La Couronne to walk through the streets of Rouen past the mighty cathedral, still damaged from the war, past the merry-go-round of the festival of St.-Romain, Julia was full of a warm, winy awareness that the world of pleasure lay before her. She later described the meal, and by implication herself, as "quietly joyful." Thus began the second romance of her lifetime. "The whole experience was an opening up of the soul and spirit for me. . . . I was hooked, and for life, as it has turned out."

At Ambassador Caffery's crowded cocktail party for General Marshall the next night, "Julie with green-feathered hat" looked "divinely tall and svelte," according to Paul. It was "like a Washington clambake," he wrote Charlie, "and there were Avis and Chip Bohlen." (Bohlen would become U.S. ambassador to Russia in 1953.) According to Theodore White, their journalist friend from the China years, America's "finest group of American civilians in government since Roosevelt gathered his war cabinet in 1940–42" was working on the Marshall Plan: W. Averell Harriman, Paul Gray Hoffman, David Bruce, Richard Bissell, to name just a few of those who were in Paris during the coming months. All had a common purpose: the Cold War.

Julia and Paul took their morning *café complet* at the Café aux Deux Magots, a sentimental place for Paul, who, during a bone-chilling day in China, recalled for Charlie the days the two brothers had huddled with Edith and Freddie by the charcoal braziers of this literary café in St.-Germain-des-Prés. That first week when Julia and Paul were sitting outside facing the church and watching a mob of actors with reflectors and cameras making a movie with Franchot Tone, Paul talked to Buzz Meredith, an actor friend from Hollywood, dressed in bohemian clothes and smeared with greasepaint. Julia and Paul immediately began a month of whirlwind diplomatic social life and paperwork, apartment hunting, and dining out with friends. They preferred, according to Julia's datebook, the Michaud restaurant, just around the corner from their hotel.

Michaud, an Old World place at the corner of the rue des Saints-Péres and the rue Jacob, was where the James Joyce family ate regularly when they lived in the neighborhood in 1922 and where Hemingway and Fitzgerald had a famous lunch. Julia and Paul's first Paris lunch cost a total of $3.00 (there were 310 francs to the dollar in 1948). Julia had to have sole again, this time with spinach, and Paul had *rognons sautés au beurre* (kidneys) with fried potatoes; and finally Brie for them both. "Julia wants to spend the rest of her life right here, eating sole, rognons, drinking wine and looking at Paris," Paul wrote in his diary to Charlie.

The Childs lived a month at the Hôtel du Pont Royal on the corner of the rue Montalembert and the rue du Bac, halfway between the Seine and the Boulevard St.-Germain on the Left Bank. They could see the Seine and the old pewter buildings and green mansard roofs of Paris. The embassy lay on the Right Bank, with its elegant shops, commerce, and banks; the Childs always chose to live on the Left Bank, with the artists, publishers, and university people. Their hotel was steps from Gallimard, France's most prestigious publishing house, and its editors and writers hung out in the hotel bar beneath the lobby.

While Paul made his first visit to the embassy office that Friday, Julia took the car and, map in hand, found the ambassador's residence, where she left their card. Employees were expected to leave a total of two hundred cards at the residences of all persons of their own rank and higher. An anachronistic practice, Paul thought. He showed Julia the Paris he had not visited for eighteen years: they walked along the Seine, past medieval churches, the Louvre, and theaters (the first week alone they saw a French farce, a film of *Hamlet,* and Sartre's *Les Mains Sales (Dirty Hands),* Versailles the first Saturday and Fontainebleau the second. Their most important walk was by his 1920s haunts: the Childs' favorite restaurant and the building where Charlie and Freddie had lived on the rue de Vaugirard were gone, as was Foyot's restaurant, now a little garden. He took her to the Cluny Museum, where in the 1920s he studied and copied the furniture on exhibit there. Paul detailed all the changes in letters to Charlie and Freddie. They walked by the American Church, where Paul had helped to install the stained-glass windows made by Charles Connick, Jr., of Boston. Paul worked for the stained-glass maker in 1920–21, and when he was in Hollywood in 1923 he also worked in stained glass (and painting sets).

There was still gasoline rationing, but food rationing was over; French governments would come and go during the coming years, but there were hot loaves of bread at least three times every day. There was still rubble, the weather was bitter cold (some evenings they huddled in bed to read their books), and the electricity occasionally went out. Whole chunks of the 4th Arrondissement were "ripped out," Paul reported to Charlie. There were plaques commemorating those who fell in particular streets during the war, but he was too happy with Julia to mourn long the missing or bombed sites: he loved showing Paris on a cold autumn day to "a beloved and sensitive person who's always wanted to see it, and who wasn't the least bit disappointed."

Julia was in a constant state of excitement for months and could not get enough of Paris. "I was practically in hysterics from the time we landed," she explained. "I was a late bloomer who was still growing up. I didn't get started on life until I was about thirty-two, which was good because I was old enough to appreciate it. I had it all ahead of me." She ordered sole three times the first week, and spent an entire day speaking only French while she got the car repaired, filled it with gasoline, negotiated for French classes at Berlitz, rode buses, ate out by herself, and contacted an apartment rental agency. She was a great sport and filled with enthusiasm, which in turn intoxicated Paul: "I love that woman," he wrote in mid-December, ". . . only pleasure and growing satisfaction, never once a harsh word, or a bitterness, or a sense of disappointment."

Almost immediately she began French lessons at Berlitz three times a week from ten o'clock to noon. Even Paul originally had trouble with the French colloquialisms and slang in the Sartre play, but Julia, even after years of schoolroom French, was in need of formal help. Twenty years before, her various French teachers at the Katharine Branson School for Girls described her "explosive consonants" (Mademoiselle Liardet), her "grammatical and inflectional vagaries" (Miss van Vliet), and her "insurmountable" oral French. Little did they know her present motivation.

In their effort to become a part of French life, they called on Madame Hélène Baltrusaitis, who was recommended by George Kubler. Her husband, Jurgis (a Lithuanian art historian), was concluding a semester of teaching at Yale and would return at the new year. They loved her immediately. "Hélène Baltrusaitis is charming, brainy, sophisticated, and quiet," Paul wrote two decades later. Her sparkly dark eyes telegraphed her mischievous wit. Just five years younger than Julia, she shared her sense of humor. "It was an emotional time for me right after the war and life had been so awful and I had lost so many people and suddenly this was such happiness to have Julia."

If Paul's artistic friends were literary in the 1920s, they would be art historians now. On December 1 they joined the Focillon group, which met each Wednesday night at the Baltrusaitis home to hear papers about art history by former students of Henri Focillon, Hélène's deceased stepfather and Kubler's substitute father at Yale, when the elder French art historian taught there. (A similar Cercle Focillon met in New Haven.) When Paul taught at Avon, he met Focillon. Hélène would hereafter be Julia's best friend in Paris. During these weekly wine-filled, intellectual discussions, Julia would miss about every fifth word—"like oyster stew," she characterized it—but she loved the company.

Julia was like a big tree [said Hélène Baltrusaitis]. Everything she did was enormous. Never something small or dainty. Whenever she was cooking something, it was grand. She was always taller than everyone, but this never bothered her at all. She was intensely curious about the

world around her. She had a great sense of friendship. I seldom in my
long life saw anyone like her. We were more than sisters, we were great
friends.

Julia and Hélène met in the Closerie des Lilas, one of Paris's oldest cafés,
which lay between their two apartments. "Julia spoke very poor French when
we first began meeting. She wanted to read Baudelaire, and I wanted to read
The New Yorker, and we exchanged magazines and books once a week. Julia
later claimed, during an oral history for Smith College, that though she went
to Berlitz, it was "Hélène who really, I think, taught me French as much as
anyone." Julia was reading the nineteenth-century novels of Honoré de Balzac,
which she borrowed from Adrienne Monnier's bookshop. "That's my man!"
she would say about Balzac. "I was a Balzacian because you learn so much
about French life from his novels." Later she added, "I did not consider
Balzac fiction . . . it is life!" and in 1980 linked him with Beethoven as
"meat and potatoes [artists]—very out-front, essential-type people."

Julia found in Hélène a charming French woman. Aside from the few
Frenchmen she met in China, Julia's expectations were formed first by the
gray and foreign French classes of Smith, then by the glamour of *Vogue* magazine, and finally by the movies: exquisite, dainty women and Adolphe Menjou
dandies. The first Frenchman she encountered on the dock in Le Havre as the
crane swung their Buick from the hold to the dock was a burly blue-coated
dockworker, Gauloise cigarette hanging from the corner of his lips. "There
were actual blood-and-guts people in this country!" she exclaimed decades
later. "I was immensely relieved." She gushed to her *Smith Alumnae Quarterly,* "I never dreamed I would find the French so *sympathique,* so warm, so
polite, so tender, so utterly pleasurable to be with."

Paul was keenly aware of what he described as the occasional "bitchy
and difficult" French temperament, as "uncooperative and shoulder-shrug-
ging as ever (though with a certain sardonic charm. Damn them!)." But Julia
adored the French. Though Paul noticed a distinct improvement, even ac-
knowledging that he himself was now "less sour than I used to be," he believed, that one reason was Julia. "With her warmth and charm and directness
she would bring out the best even in a polecat. So she naturally thinks the
French are just the most charming and wonderful people in the world and she
wants to stay here forever," he told the Kublers when thanking them for
introducing Hélène to their lives.

Julia loved the chestnut vendors, the white poodles and white chimneys,
the fishermen on Ile St.-Louis, the gentle garlic belches after eating escargots,
and the lengthy walks around Paris with Paul. They thought nothing of leaving

the apartment at ten on Saturday morning and exploring numerous quarters of Paris until nearly six in the evening. She wanted to live in the Place des Vosges; she saw her first whores parading their wares in the rue Quincampoix (no *poules de luxe* they); admired the gargoyles on Notre Dame and the tottering sides of old buildings shored up with long poles. Paul never missed a detail during their walks. "Lipstick on my belly button and music in the air—that's Paris!" he believed.

THE LEFT BANK

After December 4, Julia and Paul lived near the Seine River, almost nestled between the National Assembly (Palais Bourbon, which faced the Place de la Concorde across the Concorde Bridge) and the Ministry of Defense. They were at 81, rue de l'Université (Roo de Loo, for short), in the most elegant district of the Left Bank and within a fifteen-minute walk of the American Embassy on the Right Bank.

They rented the third floor of an elegant town house owned by Madame Perrier and her family, including Monsieur and Madame du Couëdic. (In 1997 Madame du Couëdic, recently widowed, still resided there.) The Couëdic-Perrier family also had a château in Normandy, to which Julia and Paul would eventually be invited. As Americans, the Childs rented for $80.00 a month (the French would have paid $20). From their rooms they could see into the garden of the Ministry of Defense and, beyond, the twin spires of the church of St.-Clotilde. It was a location for an artist, and Paul painted the Paris rooflines and chimneys from his windows.

They could park directly out front or drive their car through the double doors, under the front of the building, past the entrance to the building to the open stone courtyard, and park next to the high wall that guarded the ministry. Parking was a factor in their location, and for a month Paul had searched every night in the dark (only parking lights were allowed) for a place to leave their Buick. Once inside the courtyard, they could look up and see the full length of their L-shaped apartment with its curved, glass-faced hallway that joined the two wings. This angle allowed him to take loving photographs of Julia looking out at the urban landscape. In their part of town, the city looked green: the lush ministry garden and the square in front of the church were typical of a quarter of vast gardens hidden behind stone walls that fronted the narrow streets.

From the courtyard they could see a small room built out from the back of the fourth-floor roof (formerly servants' rooms) to accommodate a large kitchen. A narrow stairway and dumbwaiter connected this kitchen to their five-room apartment. One room was given over to the furniture and bric-a-brac they took out of a dark and crowded, overdecorated and "very French" apartment. Julia described to the Kublers the Louis XVI salon with tapestries, gilt chairs, moldings and mirrors, the leather-walled dining room, and the bedroom that had been General Perrier's study. Little wonder that their visitors remember the apartment as dark with labyrinthine hallways. Initially the apartment was "as cold as Lazarus's tomb" and the potbellied stove made a feeble attempt to dry out and warm the place.

The week they moved in was during the worst fog on record across Northern Europe. The Berlin airlift was halted. Paris had the acrid smell of smoke, and Paul got tired of "blowing black sludge" into his handkerchief. Low air pressure and the burning of cheap coal occasionally cut visibility to zero. On what they called a "clear day" that winter, they could see five blocks. "We had enormous bouts of fog and had to have galoshes," said Julia, "and I remember on one trip in our car it was so foggy I had to walk in front of the car to lead the way." Later in 1949 Paul would pay to garage his car, away from the wildly undisciplined drivers in Paris's increasingly chaotic traffic.

France was still emerging from the war and struggling to return to the program for rural electrification that had started before the war. In many ways, it was still a nineteenth-century country. Few households had refrigerators, washers, or dryers, and the electricity in Paris frequently went out for hours. With few phones, people used *pneumatiques,* which were letters on blue paper sent through underground tubes from one post office to another and hand-delivered immediately. Bicycles outnumbered cars.

The facades of Paris were "grimier," historian Herbert Lottman points out, "and they had to wait more than a decade for a scrubbing," but the postwar celebration continued in intellectual cabarets and cellar jazz clubs and cafés. Various irreverent intellectual factions debated conflicting affiliations, and the communists were strong. Julia and Paul lived in the neighborhood of André Gide, who had won the Nobel Prize for Literature the previous November. Gide would die in three years at the age of eighty-one, and the new generation, which hung out in the St.-Germain-des-Prés area nearby, now ruled. There were Jean-Paul Sartre, Simone de Beauvoir, Albert Camus (*The Plague* was published the previous year), Louis Aragon, the surrealist turned communist, and Alain Robbe-Grillet, the novelist. To compensate for what Beauvoir called its "having become a second-class power," France glorified and exported its chief products: fashion, literature (existentialism), and (later) cuisine. Waverley Root, Alice B. Toklas, and Julia Child would figure in this effort.

The Childs were living near St.-Germain-des-Prés, which intellectual historian Lionel Abel (who arrived a month after they), called "the heart of Paris in 1948. You were always on the stage, always in front of the footlights." A major stage was the Deux Magots, their neighborhood café. Years later, Julia's friend M. F. K. Fisher said that journalist Janet Flanner remembered the Childs as "Apollonesque"—in other words, not part of the Dionysian crowd. Julia's curiosity took her alone to the spectacle of Bébé Bérard's funeral in St.-Sulpice the next year. Christian Bérard had been a painter and the set designer for Jean Cocteau and Louis Jouvet. Julia told Fisher it was her "first Parisian event" and she "marveled at the greats of the era [including Colette] tottering about in formal black and mink capes."

There were new expatriates in Paris as well, American novelist Richard Wright (who arrived in 1947), Chilean poet Pablo Neruda, and British novelist and biographer Nancy Mitford, who fled drab England for the "daylight" of Paris after the war. The Childs frequently spotted the Russian novelist Vladimir Nabokov. Three American journalists lived at 44, rue du Boccador on the Right Bank: Theodore (and Nancy) White, who (as he put it) lived like a bourgeois on the strong dollar; Ann and Art Buchwald, a twenty-four-year-old ex-marine who wrote the "Paris After Dark" column for the *Herald Tribune;* and Irwin (and Marian) Shaw, who also worked for the *Herald* at 21, rue de Berri (where it is still located) and wrote novels. "Everyone came to Paris in the fifties," wrote Buchwald, who took a course at the Cordon Bleu, better to write his restaurant reviews. He enjoyed Julia's company: "Julia Child was the only one in Paris who had a sense of humor about food."

There were remnants of the expatriate 1920s crowd that Paul had known: Alice B. Toklas (Gertrude Stein's companion for forty years until the latter's death), Waverley Root (a newspaperman who spent the war in Vermont), Hadley and Paul Mowrer, and Janet Flanner (Paris correspondent for *The New Yorker).* Others just turned up for visits, such as the Bissells and Dick and Alice Lee Myers (she had gone to school with Janet Flanner). Charlie had painted many of their portraits and sold his paneled screens for radiators in Mrs. Myers's boutique in the 1920s, a boutique founded to employ White Russians. Now it was chiefly the next generation, such as pals Honoria Murphy and Fanny Myers Brennan, who visited Paris, and looked up the Childs.

The Mowrers became their family in France. Although they were more than a decade older than Paul, Julia immediately loved the natural and earthy Hadley, the mother of Jack Hemingway. Paul Child met Hadley when she was still married to Hemingway in the mid-1920s in Paris, and Julia heard stories of his neglect and humiliation of Hadley. "The Mowrers were our foster parents; we were like their children. We saw them all the time and went out to dinner and traveled with them." To one of Hemingway's biographers, she said, "They became rather like an aunt and uncle to us." Paul Mowrer was now foreign editor of the *New York Post,* a lesser assignment, and Paul Child thought that the Mowrers had lost some of their "essential vigor." Julia and Paul spent Thanksgiving at the Mowrer apartment on the same street as theirs but across the expansive fields of the Hôtel des Invalides.

Before Christmas, the art historians gathered to light their Christmas plum pudding. Julia would later use the incident when asked in 1996 for a "holiday cooking disaster": not knowing that the brandy had to be hot before it flamed, "they poured practically a whole bottle of brandy over it while trying to light it. It never did flame, but it was nicely soaked."

They would also spend their first Christmas at the country home of the Mowrers in Crécy-en-Brie (Paul's pressing office work kept them from visiting the Bicknells in England). To save money, the Mowrers had just bought a house in New Hampshire and planned to move there when he retired. Julia and Paul would spend at least one weekend a month at the Mowrers' country home until they left Paris.

Working the Cold War

The political climate during the Childs' tenure in Paris was pivotal: they learned of Truman's election the day they arrived in France, the United Nations met at the Place du Trocadéro that fall, and then came the Prague uprising and the revelation of the atom blast in Russia the following September. The world was in transition, while De Gaulle was in Colombey writing his memoirs, and General Marshall resigned from the American delegation to the United Nations the following January to retire to his farm.

Theodore White called the Marshall Plan (1948–50), with its more than $13 billion investment, "an adventure in the exercise of American Power." Buchwald put it in more personal terms: "We arrived at the Golden Age for Americans in France. The dollar was the strongest currency in the world, and the franc was one of the weakest."

Paul was in charge of exhibits and photography for the U.S. Information Service, founded along with the Central Intelligence Agency when the war ended. It was America's propaganda agency, replacing the wartime Office of War Information and now directed against communism. Again Paul had to organize an office and staff with little money, yet meet demands for immediate photographs and exhibits. He had photo archives of everything from Hoover

Dam to an American high school classroom. Housed in the American Embassy (the old Rothschild mansion) at 41, rue du Faubourg St.-Honoré, he often had dealings with the Marshall Plan office, located in the rue de Rivoli in the Talleyrand mansion.

Though personally frustrated with his office, Paul realized that to be in Paris during this period of history was to be blessed. Teddy White described this era as having a "wedding party" atmosphere. It was the story of money and romance. America was rebuilding France, and the Marshall Plan goodies were plentiful, for the Americans were determined to reverse Russia's plans to move across Western Europe. American money even financed the tobacco that the French smoked every morning in the cafés.

A turning point in the political climate and for Paul Child came when a senator from Wisconsin (elected in 1947) gave a speech in February 1950. Joseph McCarthy's denunciation of communists in the highest government offices brought him national attention and growing power. The tentacles of his paranoia would reach into the diplomatic service and eventually shake Paul and ruin several of their friends.

The Marshall Plan, not the USIS, received the generous budget from Washington, and though Al Friendly and his other Marshall Plan friends promised help with USIS funding, Paul squeezed very little from them. In an interview about their diplomatic service in France, Julia later said, "The USIS was kind of a stepchild, and we were not really considered part of the brotherhood. We were always down around rank four, so we didn't have to do any embassy things. We were free to live a normal life." Sylvie Pouly, who was Paul's "smart and stable" assistant from 1949 to 1951, remembers that Julia did not do any official entertaining (the embassy did that), but she did invite Paul's colleagues to dinner. The young French woman was impressed with the numerous copper pots and the refrigerator in Julia's kitchen. She also noted that Julia was "always in a good mood" and had a "marriage of love." Several in Paul's office remember him talking about Julia's desire for a career, including a young woman named Janou, the reference librarian for the USIS.

To EAT LIKE A GOD IN FRANCE

Julia and Paul explored a different quarter of Paris each weekend, including its bistros and restaurants. Though the *Guide Michelin* was their bible, they did some independent testing, placing the names and addresses of their favorite places inside Julia's datebook. In the back she listed the wines and their good years. They noticed that most restaurants, like the ones they visited in

China, had potbellied stoves with stovepipes going across the ceiling and out the window.

They enjoyed *poulet gratiné* at Au Gourmet in the rue des Canettes and tripe at Pharamond near Les Halles, took Dick Bissell to Au Cochon de Lait, returned frequently to La Truite, located off the rue Boissy-d'Anglas near the American Embassy, owned by the same family who owned La Couronne in Rouen. Michaud remained a favorite, as did Escargot d'Or, where the first week they lunched on a dozen escargots with a half bottle of Sancerre, followed by *rognons Bercy* in wine and mushroom sauce with a half bottle of Clos de Vougeot, followed by *escarole salade,* and finished with *café filtre.* They thought they had discovered Le Grand Véfour and its chef, Raymond Oliver, and its sommelier, Monsieur Hennoq, until they caught a glimpse of Colette there. "I remember the *estouffade* at Le Grand Véfour. It is a dish made by hollowing out a loaf of bread and rubbing it with creamy butter, then baking it to a golden brown and filling it with *crevettes* [shrimp] in cream and butter." They had "truly elegant" gratins of shellfish at Lapérouse, beer and sandwiches at La Closerie des Lilas, and oysters and wine at the Brasserie Lipp after a cold day prowling Montmartre. And it was almost always to the Deux Magots for drinks or after-dinner coffee.

Although Michaud's has since disappeared, a number of the restaurants that Julia listed in her datebooks of this period are still serving meals under the same name fifty years later: Chez George, Marius (rue de Bourgogne, just steps from the Childs' flat), Pierre, Prunier, Pharamond, and Lapérouse. Paul frequently expressed gratitude that "Julie loves Paris so much." She is a "darling, sensitive, outgoing, appreciative, characterful and interesting woman!" he wrote Charlie and Freddie early in 1949. "Well, let's face it: I'm a lucky bastard."

Though restaurants may have originated in China, they flourished in modern times in France after the French Revolution, when chefs who had worked for the aristocracy went into business for themselves. The word "restaurant" originated both from "to restore" and from the French term for fortifying soup. French taste dictated the scale and suitability of the proportions, the sculpture, and the presentation of the food, the ritual of the tablecloth and wineglasses—every detail of the selection, preparation, flavoring, and timing of meals. The amount of bread crumbs on the tablecloth spelled out the crisp quality of the bread. Gastronomy in France is reserved for the fine arts and sciences, and the art of the table is accorded a reverence akin to religion.

The city surrounded and embraced the river, Paul pointed out to her, unlike Boston, where the great homes turned their backs on the basin. These elements of French taste at table and in architecture were discussed and evaluated with Paul. Julia's response was ecstatic, both in appetite and in the way she dressed. She now wore a suit and hat and regularly had her brown hair permed. "The artistic integrity of the French," Edith Wharton pointed out, "led them to feel from the beginning that there is no difference in kind between the curve of a woman's hat-brim and the curve of a Rodin marble."

"What I remember most is the elegant but genuine cordiality of the restaurants," said Julia. And the subtlety of tastes. If food is linked to human behavior, so the reasoning of cultural anthropologists goes, then French "subtlety of thought and manner is related to the subtlety of its cuisine," just as the reserve of the British is attributed to their "unimaginative diet" and the German stolidness to heavy food. As the German expression for pleasure goes, "happy as God in France."

With her continuing studies at Berlitz, her market shopping, and her menu reading, Julia was amassing a large vocabulary of French food. Because the French had codified cheeses (325 varieties!), wines, foods, and cooking techniques, many of their words were already a part of her vocabulary: *menu, sauce, fruit, salade, mayonnaise, céleri, bifteck, meringue, raisins, paprika, hors d'oeuvre, dessert.* She discovered a language saturated with food imagery: *crème de la crème* (top of society), *gâte-sauce* (beginner).

Although Julia would later say they had little money and ate out only once a week, according to her datebooks their first months in Paris were filled with restaurants. They set aside the $100 from her family income and used it to dine out. They could eat in a good French bistro for a dollar. Fifty years later she would exclaim, "I was so fortunate! This was before the nutrition police had reared their ugly heads; it was still the old French cooking with butter and cream." And: "There were no nutritionists in Paris then, thank God!"

Markets in Paris were a sensuous delight. Julia stared at pig's heads, sniffed sausages, poked fish, salivated over baskets of mushrooms, and practiced her French with the fat market people in wooden shoes, black aprons, and red faces who yelled at each other over the cacophony of market sounds. The carts and tables were piled high with mussels, squash, leeks, and chrysanthemums when she first arrived in Paris. The cabbages were as green as those in China. The spring brought endives and mandarins, and the summer provided strawberries, green beans, and tomatoes. Because each growing season was limited, the arrival of the first tomato or the first strawberry was celebrated. Little could be preserved anyway, for most people had only an icebox. No wonder she remembered that she was "in hysterics for months." France's national passion became hers.

She bought staples such as cigarettes, chocolate, and soap at the American PX and Normandy cream, butter, and cheese from the *crémerie* and *fromagère* in the rue de Bourgogne. The cheese shop, Julia remembered, "was run by a buxom blonde who could tell me whether the cheese should be eaten tonight or for lunch tomorrow." There were small individual shops for meat and bread, and wine, but in these days before supermarkets, there were only open-air markets for a variety of fresh produce. She walked up the Boulevard St.-Germain to the market in the rue de Buci or, "if I had enough energy to walk, I would cross the Champs de Mars to the largest market on the Left Bank." She quickly learned she had to establish a relationship with the vendors to get the best produce: "I learned human relations in France," she would say.

Paul joined a men's gastronomic club. Through Pierre Andrieu, its adviser, they went to choose some good wines at the Foire de Paris, where they sipped Armagnac, brandy, champagne, and Sancerre, Bordeaux, and Alsatian wines. "It was an expensive excursion . . . and we were feeling very jovial indeed," Julia wrote a friend. "About two weeks later cases upon cases of wine arrived at our apartment, so much that we had to buy two wine racks for the cellar; we had quite forgotten what we had ordered."

Across the river was Les Halles, the belly of Paris, a living organism of fruits, vegetables, animals, and fowl, where every restaurant in Paris bought its produce. And Les Halles aux Vins, the vast hall of wines at the east end of the Left Bank's Boulevard St.-Germain, was a collection of vendors whose wine stained the streets and filled the air of this quarter of the 5th Arrondissement. The sheer magnitude overwhelmed her, but she studied the names of the foods and wines.

Though she still had not mastered *The Joy of Cooking*'s recipes, Julia continued to cook and entertain. She prepared toast and two fried eggs each morning, a simple lunch (she would greet Paul's return "with a whoop," he said), and a more elaborate dinner if they were entertaining. They had a maid for a month but hated her cooking, disliked the time regime, and decided to economize. Thereafter, twice a week they had a *femme de ménage* named Jeanne "la Folle" (the crazy woman), who urged them to buy a cat to get rid of the mice. Julia adored Minette, who ate the mice and one day brought a bird in from the roof and ate it on the Persian rug. Thereafter they would be devoted cat lovers.

Spring brought green fuzz to the chestnuts on Paris's trees and peach blossoms to the Mowrers' country home in Crécy. Paul and Julia enjoyed picnics, visiting friends, and trips with Hélène Baltrusaitis. "We would walk along the banks of the river on the quais," recalled Julia. "We were great picnickers, even picnicking on the first floor of the Eiffel Tower (before there was a restaurant there). It was lovely." Her datebook reveals she had lunch or tea or drinks or dinner with friends nearly every day. Among her guests their first year in Paris, including the Mowrers and Baltrusaitises, were May Sarton (poet and longtime friend of Paul visiting from New England), the Bicknells (visiting from London), Dick Bissell, *Life* reporter and photographer Helen Morgan, painter Buffie Johnson, French art critics Roger Caillois and Philippe Verdier, as well as nephew Paul Sheeline and his wife, and her good friends the Chamberlains. Sam Chamberlain was a great cook, writer, and photographer, and was accompanied by his wife, Narcissa, with whom he would soon publish *Bouquet de France: An Epicurean Tour of the French Provinces.*

The first trip in France with Hélène was a five-day February excursion (what Paul called Julia's "first crack at France-as-a-whole") to Nice, where they visited the vacationing Mowrers. In the spring they took day trips ("picnics") and during school vacations Hélène had to take her young teenage son, which made her uneasy because she believed that Paul hated children. But she learned when to keep silent with him and sensed that he appreciated her wit ("our friendship was special"). She was honored when one day he told her the full story of his "very difficult" early life. She remembers often stopping for long periods while Paul waited for just the right light for a photograph:

> At first we took day picnics, but eventually we traveled all over France together [said Mrs. Baltrusaitis]. We visited every region but Brittany (because it was too far). Julia could never resist asking questions. She is really intelligent and very curious and loved to meet people. Because she was so tall, people were curious about her and made remarks. It was courage and love for Paul to marry Julia, whom everyone noticed. He never wanted to be noticed. It was not just that he was shy, but he loved Julia and wanted the light on her.

For a three-day trip to Normandy in May, the three of them took art critic Philippe Verdier, a member of their Wednesday group, whom Paul found too talkative. That summer they returned to Normandy, visited Chartres, and the Champagne region, where Hélène's family had a house in Maranville, a tiny village bordering Champagne and Burgundy. When they stepped on a rusted German helmet in the forest beyond Lunéville on the way to Strasbourg, the war seemed not so distant.

Paul took hundreds of photographs and spent weeks and months working on a single painting. While he painted a stained-glass medallion of and for the Focillon group, Julia worked out a classification system for his private and professional photograph files. He designed the first of many annual Valentine's cards to send in lieu of Christmas cards to their family and friends. This spring he completed a painting of a street of Paris and in the summer an aqueduct.

The only time Julia ever thought she might be pregnant was about this time in Paris. "I was delighted," Julia reported fifty years later, remembering that the "feeling" lasted for "about a month." Not until Paul mentioned it in a letter to his brother did Julia realize it was only stomach fatigue, "I was bilious . . . too much cream and butter." Though decades later she would claim she was not heartbroken about her failure to conceive a child, her family and friends are sure she was disappointed. Several family members believed Paul did not want children. He was a loving father figure to two nieces and a nephew and to Edith Kennedy's three boys. But years of teaching boys in France, Italy, and then Connecticut gave him his fill of squirming boys. "I don't think Paul was mad to have children," said Julia, "but it would have been very different if it had been his own." In 1988 in *McCall's,* Julia remarked, "I would have been the complete mother," and the reporter added: this was her "one regret." A decade later, as if in justification, she exclaimed, "If I had had a child, I would not have had a career. . . . because I was freelance."

Julia's sister Dorothy arrived April 8, just about a week before her thirty-second birthday and at the peak of spring green, for an extended visit. Julia had written to tell her to leave the family home, buy a diaphragm, and come to Paris to complete her education. She was "wildly enthusiastic," according to Paul, when they settled her into their guest room and then took her on the "JuPaulski standard tourist walk" around the St.-Germain quarter, ending with drinks at Deux Magots. After a Sunday with the Baltrusaitises and Mowrers at the latter's country home, they took her on Monday to the Foire aux Jambons, where Julia and Dorothy (at six feet four inches) collected a crowd. In the months to come she traveled about Europe with friends and became involved with an English-speaking theater group in Paris.

Paul's photographs and letters capture their April trip to Lyons for an exhibit that showed the results of the Marshall Plan, an exhibit (it would go to Lille in July) that Paul had worked on since his arrival in Paris. From there they took a ten-day trip in the Blue Flash (Buick) to England to see Nigel and Sally Bicknell, their former housemates in Georgetown. It was the first visit to London for both Julia and Paul, and they delighted in the bowler hats and umbrellas, were struck by the absence of handshaking, and found the English pace vigorous and bustling, but the people ponderous.

They traveled on to Cambridge to meet the other Bicknells, Nigel's brother Peter and his wife, Mari, a graduate of the Cordon Bleu cooking school in Paris. Peter and Mari, with whom they were perfectly compatible, would remain lifelong friends. Despite the affection for their friends, Julia preferred what she called "little old France," with its "sweet naturalness and healthy pleasures of the flesh and spirit." Later she declared that England "seemed more foreign than France" to them.

"Americans are flooding into the city like the tide at Mont St.-Michel," Paul wrote to Charlie. The terraces of the Deux Magots and the Café Flore were crowded with people watchers, "the national pastime in France." More old friends were in town, including the Brennans, who were there for a month (Hank, working for Henry Luce and writing an article for *Fortune* magazine on the recovery of France, had been to the Lyons exhibit). "Julie cooked a goose" for eight people, Paul added, "and very well too." The meal ended with strawberries and *crème d'Isigny.* His letters to Charlie were sprinkled with newly invented mixed drinks for the cocktail hour.

ℋEMINGWAY WEDDING

Hadley asked Julia if she would serve as maid of honor for the wedding of her son Jack, "Bumby," and Julia made her dress and hat (she had been taking hat lessons with a friend) for the occasion. John (Jack) Hemingway and his bride, Byra (Puck) Whitlock, whose first husband had died in the war, wished to be married with a church wedding in the old-fashioned manner. Because Puck was still in Idaho and Jack was stationed in Berlin with Army Intelligence, it fell to Hadley and Paul Mowrer to make all the arrangements and take care of the complicated legal papers. Once Julia agreed to serve as maid of honor (Puck was a tall girl also), Paul agreed to stand by as best man if Jack could not get a friend released to come with him, and the Childs offered to put up Jack when he arrived in Paris on June 20, 1949 (Hadley planned to keep the couple separated until the church wedding).

Jack, Julia informed a biographer of his father, was "an attractive, blond, good-looking American boy, who wed an attractive, unsophisticated and ex-tremely nice young woman." Paul thought that Puck was "a lovely tall dark girl with a face full of character" and described the groom as "a vigorous, extroverted, attractive, thick young man. He's a U.S. army captain with lots of medal-ribbons and paratrooper's wings. He was in OSS and was dropped behind the German lines to form agent-teams. He's bi-lingual, was captured and escaped no less than four times. Like his Poppa he is nuts about fishing, and thinks of Ernest's estancia outside of Havana as home." Papa, however, did not attend the wedding.

On Thursday, the night before the civil wedding, Julia and Paul hosted a cocktail party for the Hemingway wedding party and Mowrer friends, a "big good party," Julia described it (Paul normally preferred a maximum of eight guests at a time). Many old-time American expatriates were there; Julia was particularly thrilled to meet Alice B. Toklas, whom Paul had met through Daddy Myers in the 1920s. Toklas and Stein had witnessed for Jack's christening.

Jack's friend Lieutenant Bob Shankman, who was six feet six inches tall, squired Dort around Paris that weekend, attracting attention wherever they went. "When the two of them got out of her little MG TC and stood up," remembered Hemingway, "crowds would gather and stare in awe at the wonderful mismatch." The wedding party, Dort's friends at the American theater where she was working on staging, and various colleagues in UNESCO and USIS wandered in and out of the Child apartment. Julia seemed to thrive on the chaos and numbers of people. Staying in their apartment were not only Jack Hemingway and Dorothy, but Peter Bicknell, who was on his way back to London. Paul complained that "a steady tunnel of liquor flows from our bar down all these throats."

According to French law, Jack and Puck were married in a civil ceremony first at 4:45 P.M. on Friday, June 24, at the *mairie* (town hall) of the 7th Arrondissement, with a rehearsal for the church wedding following. Alice Lee Myers gave a cocktail reception before the Mowrers' bridal dinner.

On Saturday, the wedding—Julia calls it the "Mowrer wedding" in her datebook—took place at 11:30 A.M., with Julia and Lieutenant Jack Kelly as witnesses in the American Church on the Quai d'Orsay. U.S. ambassador to France, David Bruce (formerly head of OSS in Europe), Richard (Daddy) and Alice Lee Myers, and Fanny and Hank Brennan were in the congregation. Hélène Baltrusaitis believed this was "the only time I ever saw Paul Child," whom she describes as "an aggressive atheist," inside a church. He should have been at home in this particular church, however, because in the 1920s he had spent hours putting in the stained-glass windows. Tarzan of the Apse, Charlie named him.

The reception was held a few blocks from the church in the Mowrers' apartment, and thanks to Dick Myers, who represented the distributor Sherry-Lehmann, champagne flowed freely. Close friends, including Julia and Paul, then drove to Crécy for a dinner at the Mowrers' country home. Paul took the wedding photographs by the garden wall, Jack remembered.

Dort, who was closer to Jack and Puck, visited the newlyweds in Berlin in early August after the theater season ended and again in 1950 after the birth of their first daughter, Joan (Muffet), in Paris. Paul, who thought the final production of three one-act plays amateurish, was pleased that she was visiting the Hemingways, for he thought Dort's theater crowd was "rather emotional."

August 15, 1949, was Julia's thirty-seventh birthday, and Paul wrote to Chafred in Maine that it was an auspicious day: it was the fourth anniversary of "Japanese acceptance of Allied surrender terms. It's the first anniversary of the proclamation of the Republic of Korea. It's the second anniversary of the proclamation of independence of India and Pakistan. It was the day when the cease-fire in Indonesia officially came into force, it's the 70th birthday of Ethel Barrymore and it's Julie's birthday. A great and glorious day."

More important, it was a passage for Julia. She and Paul may have been nostalgic for the smell of balsam wood in Lopaus Point, Maine, but they were making plans for Julia's future that would tie them forever to France. She was planning to enroll in the fall at the Cordon Bleu cooking school. Several people have taken credit for suggesting that she enroll: Janou, the librarian at USIS, suggested to Paul that Julia's enthusiasm for French food should lead her to the famous school; Jean Friendly, the wife of Paul's associate in the Marshall Plan, says "my husband suggested she study at the Cordon Bleu"; certainly the influence of Mari Bicknell in Cambridge, who graduated there and with whom Julia cooked, must have been significant. Julia visited the school on June 2.

She eagerly wrote to ask Freddie to come over and "be a Cordon Bleu too," but by the time of her birthday she gave up on the hope that her sister-in-law would join her. Paul joked about them opening a restaurant together. His birthday gift was *Larousse Gastronomique* ("1,087 pages of sheer cookery and foodery, 1,850 gravures, 16 color plates, definitions, recipes, information, stories and know-how—a wonder book," Paul told Freddie).

In preparation for her new career, she took a long trip to Marseilles with Paul after saying a tearful farewell to Hadley and Paul Mowrer, who were retiring to New Hampshire. Their final meal together was a four-hour lunch. The fish course was the best lobster Julia had eaten in France, accompanied by a fine white Burgundy.

On a grand gastronomic tour introducing Julia to some of the variety of France's cheeses, wines, and produce, and to celebrate their third anniversary, Julia and Paul left Paris on September 3, drove south through the heat and burning land in the most serious drought since 1909 and through the hills and cooler gorges of the Auvergne. Hélène Baltrusaitis and the French art histo-rian Philippe Verdier (who agreed not to talk too much) accompanied them for half the journey. A few days out, happy with lunchtime wine and blinded by the sun, Julia drove over a high curbstone and the gas tank fell to the ground. "Paul was upset but not condemning. He never scolded Julia," remembered Hélène.

Marseilles is "a wonderful vibrant, colorful bouillabaisse," declared Paul when he arrived to complete arrangements for his exhibit and hold a press conference. They arrived with a case of Pouilly wine in their trunk and stayed with Abe Manell (who had worked with Paul) and his wife, Rosemary, for whom Julia had an immediate liking. Rosie had been in the WAVES during the war, and Paul described her as "a big, blond, Earth-mother, young, California sculptress wife." In Rosie, Julia found a friend for life and her future food designer. Rosie remembered having heard so much about Julia before meeting her: "I thought they must be exaggerating because no one can be this interesting, this funny, and I couldn't believe it—she was better even than I thought." On the drive to Marseilles and back (alone) through the Dordogne, Julia and Paul visited layers of time: Roman aqueducts, medieval castles, an eleventh-century abbey, and Renaissance fountains. Julia was especially thrilled with the gastronomic discoveries of the present: bass with fennel, grilled lamb flambé with fennel branches, wild duck, truffles, confit, and a visit to the Roquefort caves. She was ready to learn more about this fertile and complex country.

Chapter 11

Cordon Bleu
(1949 – 1952)

"I've got the Cordon Blues."
Country-western song,
1970

JULIA WALKED past the American Embassy to the corner building at 129, rue du Faubourg St.-Honoré, where for fifty-four years the Cordon Bleu cooking school had been housed. She carried her white apron, cap, kitchen towel, knives, and notebook as she paused to look in the window at the display of brandy. It was 7:30 A.M. on Thursday, October 6, 1949. After two frustrating mornings in a class of amateurs, she was finally transferred to a class she wanted.

Le Cordon Bleu

In Chef Max Bugnard's class for ex-GIs who intended to become professionals, Julia was the only woman. (The morning classes, on the other hand, were six-week courses attended mostly by women.) Julia and eleven veterans, whose tuition of 4,100 francs a week was paid by the U.S. government, were taking a ten-month course of twenty-five hours a week, with their days taken up by hands-on cooking from 7:30 to 9:30 in the morning, then three-hour afternoon demonstration classes. The GIs had a friendly irreverence, one observer noted, and renamed the traditional white sauce originally named after Marquis de Béchamel as "Bechassmell."

Devoid of the shiny appliances and painted walls of modern cooking schools, the Cordon Bleu was crowded into seven rooms on the ground floor and basement. (Decades later Julia would remember sixteen students and "very roomy quarters.") Only the office of Madame Elisabeth Brassart, the owner-director, was not crowded (one disillusioned student noted). Julia began dressing pigeons that morning in one of the two kitchens in the basement next to a storeroom. When they finished, they cleaned the wood tables with salt and vinegar, and Julia rushed home to prepare lunch for Paul.

That afternoon she took her place upstairs in a rising row of chairs that faced a demonstration kitchen where she watched Monsieur Max Bugnard. She was awed by the seriousness and passion with which the chefs worked, but was a little overwhelmed by the number of new French words she was having to learn at once. "My French was very sketchy at first, but the Cordon Bleu was a lesson in language as well as cookery."

On Thursday, Julia wrote in her datebook *pigeons rôtis délicieux* and then prepared the same dish for Paul and Dorothy: "If you could see Julie stuffing pepper and lard up the asshole of a dead pigeon you'd realize how profoundly affected she's been already by the Cordon Bleu," Paul wrote to Charlie and Freddie. Dorothy remembers Julia walking down the steps from the kitchen with "meadowlarks" on sticks, "their little feet through the eyeballs," and the cat Minette on Julia's shoulder crying for a bite.

On Friday the class cooked "veal and beans," and she prepared the same dish at home that night. By the next Monday, Dorothy had *une crise de foie,* the familiar French stomach fatigue, and on Tuesday Paul was stricken as well. Fortunately, on Wednesday the group, who were presumably going into the restaurant business, visited Les Halles with Bugnard. It was a glorious week for Julia.

With her usual enthusiasm and concentration, Julia poured her time and effort into learning to cook. Paul referred to himself as "practically a Cordon Bleu Widower. I can't pry Julia loose from the kitchen day or night—not even with an oyster-knife." By October 15, he confided to his family, "Julie's cookery is actually improving! I didn't quite believe it would, just between us girls, but it really *is*. In a sense it's simpler, more classical (in the French tradition of bringing out the natural flavor rather than adding spices and herbs). I envy her this chance. It would be such *fun* to be doing it at the same time with her."

Soon they were planning eight-person dinner parties for Julia to practice her new skills. Her datebook is filled with names, from the leading French and American art historians (Jean Ache from the Foçillon group was Paul's favorite), to visiting Bicknells and Hemingways, to Paul's colleagues, including Ed Taylor (former OSS pal, now correspondent for several large publications), and Bill and Betsy Tyler (he also a former OSS buddy, now Public Affairs Officer for France). One of their most frequent and respected guests was Helen Kirkpatrick, a senior at Smith when Julia was a freshman ("Who could forget that tall figure?" said the six-feet-two-inch Kirkpatrick) and now information officer for the Marshall Plan (official title Public Liaison Director of French ECA). Occasionally Kirkpatrick, who was also a great friend of the Mowrers, brought Cornelia Otis Skinner.

It took brawn to get to the brine, and Julia's stamina was more than a match for most of her male fellow students. Unlike Sabrina, the delicate Cordon Bleu apprentice played by Audrey Hepburn in the 1954 movie of the same name, Julia was strong and determined. Madame Brassart, Simone Beck, and Louisette Bertholle (she would not meet her co-authors until the next year) all have commented on the value of her physical strength in hefting iron pots and pans in the kitchen. "When I first saw her stature and enthusiasm," declared Bertholle, "I knew she would be a great success." The great chef Escoffier, by way of contrast, had to wear elevated shoes to reach the stove.

But as important as physical strength was the strength of her commitment. "I just became passionate. I had been looking for a career all my life," she informed an OSS interviewer. "Julia's strongest personal trait is dogged determination," said Helen Kirkpatrick. Hélène Baltrusaitis credited both her intelligence and her seriousness: "Julia was sharp, quick, and perceptive. Her mind was always working, but sometimes she could look naive. She had these two wonderful faces: she cooked with all her heart and seriousness, but could dissolve into laughter and silliness the next minute." Paul declared she had a "quality of raucous humor" even in her most chic creations, and he later described for Chafred one of her cold fish dishes, decorated with five-point stars cut from leek leaves for the eyes, and strips of anchovies to suggest the skeletal structure.

Instead of struggling to express herself with words, as she had first envisioned her career before joining the OSS, Julia was finding expression in cutting, molding, and cooking the elements of nature that on the table bring friends together for conversation and good wine. This was not American "home economics," with its undercurrent of nineteenth-century melioristic scientism, but a century-old tradition at the center of French life. Julia observed the French need for formulating and tabulating nature and art, and she

Grandfather John McWilliams (1832–1924) followed the Gold Rush to California from Illinois when he was seventeen years old. In the twentieth century he moved his family from the Midwest to Pasadena, from where he managed his Arkansas rice farmland and Kern County, California, mineral rights.

Westonholme: Grandfather Byron Curtis Weston's home in Dalton, Massachusetts, taken in the winter of 1899. Julia's mother, Julia Carolyn, was born here, the seventh of ten children of Byron (1832–1898), founder of the Weston Paper Company, and Julia Clark Mitchell (1844–1902).

*J*ulia Carolyn McWilliams, born August 15, 1912, with her parents, John and Caro, on the veranda of their first house, at 625 Magnolia Avenue in Pasadena, one block west of her McWilliams grandparents.

*J*ulia Carolyn (Caro) Weston (thirty-three) and John McWilliams, Jr. (thirty), on their honeymoon at the Coronado Hotel in San Diego, California, in January 1911. A happy ending to what her brothers called "the eight-year war of their courtship."

*E*ulalie, Julia's 1929 black Ford, which she was given in her senior year at Smith in 1933–1934. She drove her gang to the speakeasies in Holyoke during the campaign to repeal prohibition.

*C*aro (in her tennis clothes) and her three children, John III, Julia, and Dorothy, about 1923 or 1924, in Montecito, on the shore next to Santa Barbara, where the family rented a home each summer until the mid-1920s.

*T*he Gang of Five from Hubbard House, Smith College (1930–1934), Northampton, Massachusetts: Constance Thayer, Peggy Clark, Julia McWilliams, Mary Case (her roommate), and Hester Adams. Julia's animal is the only one that is not stuffed.

*J*ulia McWilliams on the steps of the family's summer home in San Malo, near Oceanside, California, 1936. This was her "social butterfly period," when the weekend parties included a house full of friends and plenty to drink.

*D*ort, John, and Julia, sitting on the brick wall that held off the sand around their summer home in San Malo, in the late 1930s, about the time that Dort was going to Bennington College and John into the family business (the Weston Paper Company).

*J*ulia in a Pasadena Junior League play, probably *The Emperor* (1938). Her acting and playwriting began in the family attic. Fifty years later she told Charlie Rose, "I'm on TV for the same reason you are, I'm a ham!"

$\mathcal{P}$aul Child (forty-one) at Kapurtala House, New Delhi, India, in early 1944. Paul built the War Room for Mountbatten in New Delhi, then in Ceylon, where he met Julia. The photograph reflects both the heat of India and the de rigueur after-five behavior of the Office of Strategic Services (OSS, the United States' first espionage organization).

$\mathcal{J}$ulia (almost thirty-two) on an Army cot (with folded mosquito net above) in Kandy, Ceylon (Sri Lanka), July 19, 1944. The photograph was taken by Paul Child, whom she had met during the last days of April.

$\mathcal{T}$he wedding reception of Julia and Paul, September 1, 1946, at the home of Charlie and Freddie Child in Lumberville, Pennsylvania. They had been in a serious car accident the day before: "We were married in stitches," said Paul, "me on a cane and Julia full of glass."

$\mathcal{A}$ few of the China OSS gang, including Julia McWilliams and Paul Child on the far right, in Kunming, the mountain headquarters for Chennault's Flying Tigers and the OSS in southern China at the end of the Burma Road.

*J*ulia and Paul with his twin brother, Charlie, and his family: Fredericka, Erica, Jonathan, Charlie, Julia, Paul, and Rachel in the late 1940s. When they were not living near each other, the twins wrote to each other daily.

*T*wins Charles and Paul Child, born January 15, 1902, six months before their father's death, were reared in Boston by their artistic mother, Bertha May Cushing Child. "Mrs. Child and Her Children" performed together (Paul on violin, Charlie on cello). (*Right*) Child twins at work in Maine, clearing the land for Charlie's cabin at Lopaus Point on Mount Desert Island, where the family holidayed for years. "Paul and I were like two old horses," Charlie wrote in his memoirs, *Roots in the Rock* (1964).

*J*ulia Child working on the cabin in Maine. Paul had written Charlie from China that Julia was "a wonderful 'good scout' in the sense of being able to take physical discomfort, such as mud, leeches, tropic rains, or lousy food."
(Paul Child)

*J*ulia in the Childs' apartment in Paris, where Paul worked for the U.S. Information Service (he was in charge of exhibits). She is wearing a suit made from tweed purchased in London and holding their first of many cats, January 1950.

Julia looking out of their bedroom window toward the gardens of the French Ministry of Defense. The Childs rented the top apartment at 81, rue de l'Université, in the 7th Arrondissement, not far from the Concorde Bridge across the Seine.
(PAUL CHILD)

Paul with Hélène Baltrusaitis, Julia's best friend in France, during one of their many picnics from 1948 to 1953. The women would study English and French together by meeting at the Closerie des Lilas each week.

was well aware that she needed to learn to codify food and cooking. There were, after all, a hundred ways to cook a potato, and every variation in a sauce gave it a different name (she learned the first week that adding grated cheese to a béchamel made it a Mornay).

One month later—in fact, it was a year ago to the day that she landed on French soil—Julia went alone to Les Halles with chef Max Bugnard, a distinguished man with fine mustaches. Trained as a boy with Escoffier at the Carlton Hotel in London and a former restaurateur in prewar Brussels, he was a classicist of French cuisine, specializing in sauces, meats, and fish (which would be Julia's specialties). He was, she told Simone Beck four years later, *"mon maître* chef Max Bugnard . . . with impeccable standards." With him she studied the produce in the market that Saturday. With him she prepared, during the first six weeks, the following dishes: *terrine de lapin de garenne, quiche lorraine, galantine de volaille, gnocchi à la florentine, vol-au-vent financière, choucroute garnie à l'alsacienne, crème Chantilly, pets-de-nonne, charlotte de pommes, soufflé Grand Marnier, risotto aux fruits de mer, coquille St.-Jacques, merlan à lorgnettes, rouget au safran, poulet sauté Marengo, canard à l'orange* and *turbot farci braisé au champagne.*

The list of dishes was compiled by Paul. His respect for French cuisine and for her future career would be an essential element in her success. French women of Julia's class hired cooks, and their American friends thought she was "a nut" to shop, cook, and serve her own food. Americans disdained (and some argue they still do) home cooking, which was being pushed aside by economic growth and time-saving shortcuts (Pillsbury and General Mills had just introduced the first cake mixes). Food historians agree that the post-World War II period was the nadir of American cooking. But Julia did not know this; she could only revel in crowded street markets, drama in the kitchen, and a nation obsessed with eating well.

Paul shopped with her when he could, joined a gym, immersed himself in photography during her hours in the kitchen ("If I don't sit in the kitchen and watch I never see Julia"), and eagerly awaited each meal. He also helped her critique her dishes. It was clear to their friends that she adored and respected him. The only real tension in their marriage was Julia's love of big dinners and cocktail parties. He preferred small groups and occasional solitude: "It's inconceivable to Julie that I don't really enjoy what she called 'getting out in the world and seeing a few *people* now and then'!" he complained to Charlie in January 1950.

Paul gives us this first description of Julia the chef, in December 1949. Though the word "stove" is called "piano" in French, Paul chooses another musical instrument:

The sight of Julia in front of her stove-full of boiling, frying & simmering foods has the same fascination for me as watching a kettle drummer at the symphony. Imagine this in y[ou]r mind's eye: Julie, with a blue-denim apron on, a dish towel stuck under her belt, a spoon in each hand, stirring 2 pots at the same time. Warning bells are sounding-off like signals from the podium, and a garlic-flavored steam fills the air with an odoriferous leit-motif. The oven door opens and shuts so fast you hardly notice the deft thrust of a spoon as she dips into a casserole and up to her mouth for a taste-check like a perfectly timed double-beat on the drums. She stands there surrounded by a battery of instruments with an air of authority and confidence. Now & again a flash of the non-cooking Julie lights up the scene briefly, as it did the day before yesterday when with her bare fingers, she snatched a set of cannelloni out of the pot of boiling water with the cry, "Wow! These damn things are as hot as a stiff cock."

An affectionate portrait of a lusty, loving wife in their private kitchen, reported by her sophisticated husband to his brother. Paul marveled at her ability to remove all the guts of a chicken out through a small hole in the neck and then loosen the skin for the insertion of truffles. She could remove the bones of a duck without tearing the skin: "And you ought to see that Old Girl skin a wild hare—you'd swear she'd just be Comin' round the Mountain with Her Bowie Knife in Hand."

He described their kitchen as an "alchemist's eyrie," full of the instruments of her craft. She bought tart rings, zester, a tortoiseshell to scrape a tamis, copper pans, maplewood stirring paddles, a conical sieve, whisks (the French had eight kinds), long needles for larding roasts, scales, and rolling pins at E. Dehillerin, her favorite food-equipment store in the main street of Les Halles. "The store owner was a friend of Max Bugnard and they let us buy on credit," she remembered. Buying pots, pans, and gadgets "became an obsession I've never been able to break." She hung her pots around the stove, somewhat as in her great-grandfather's pre-Civil War wood cabin in Griggsville, Illinois, where cookery pots hung around the clay fireplace and where corn bread was the staple meal and migrating pigeons were so thick they bent the tree limbs outside.

The Cordon Bleu, however, had only the basic equipment in 1950. It had only one sink, did not have electrical equipment other than stoves (and some of them did not work). The English word "Frigidaire" was adopted by the French to refer to their iceboxes: "zinc-lined block-ice dripper-coolers," to use Paul Child's description. There were certainly no blenders. On the day they made a ham mousse, Julia and the nine men present had to pound the ham by hand: "We pounded it in this great big mortar, and they had one of those big drum sieves, and they rubbed it through the sieve and scraped it off the bottom. And it was absolutely delicious, but it took about an hour and a half to make. That would be two minutes or less in the food processor," she said recently. When it came time to make quenelles (which Paul had so lovingly described for her in China), they pounded the pike for thirty minutes ("a horrifying chore"), then forced it through a tamis for the day's demonstration. The dish was a divine morsel, in sharp contrast to the fried codfish cakes of her childhood.

When she wanted to make *quenelles de brochet* at home, Paul accompanied her to the Marché aux Puces (flea market) to buy just the right instrument. Paul said that as if "by some special chien-de-cuisine instinct Julia ran to earth at the end of an obscure alley of packing-box houses on the remoter fringes of the market a marble mortar as big as a baptismal font and a pestle." With muscles honed by pulling logs in Maine, Paul was able to carry the instruments on his back through the market to their car. He judged the slave labor worth the effort when he tasted the quenelle, though he described it "as a sort of white, suspiciously suggestive thing, disguised by a multiform yellowish sauce for which, if you saw it on the rug, you'd promptly spank the cat."

In order to puree any food, Julia recently explained to *Food & Wine* magazine, "you would have to pass it through a hair sieve—meaning that you first pounded the cooked rice and onions in a mortar, then pushed them through a fine mesh stretched over a drum-shaped form with a wooden pestle, and finally scraped the puree off the other side with a tortoiseshell scoop. That took some doing, and I know since it's how we pureed in my Paris school days in 1949."

A controversy about the hygiene at Cordon Bleu arose in 1951 when an American woman wrote a satiric exposé of the school ("First, Peel an Eel"), describing the dirty drawers, endless dipping of fingers into pots, the reuse of unwashed pots and pans, and food dropped on the floor, "delicately known as a *coup de ballet parisien* and forthwith returned to the mixing bowl [instead of being kicked under the table, as the expression suggests]." The school "stands firmly aloof from almost all equipment invented since the beginning of the school. . . . In my six weeks at the Cordon Bleu I never spied a thermometer, mechanical mixer or pressure cooker." The author described the peeling of live fish and the drowning of little rabbits in white wine. She added that with the absence of green vegetables, salads, and fruit, and the excessive sauc-

ing and cream, it was little wonder that "every Frenchman complains perpetu-
ally about his liver and why the larger eaters go to Vichy for periodic cures."

Julia blamed the dirty facilities and lack of modern appliances on the
stinginess of Madame Brassart, who had bought the school in 1945, when it
was clear that the charity (for orphans) which had inherited it at the death in
1934 of the founder, Marthe Distel, could not manage it. The Cordon Bleu
began as a sixteenth-century chivalric order of a hundred gastronome aristo-
crats who wore a Maltese cross on a blue ribbon *(cordon bleu)* and gathered
for "first-class feasting," according to Catharine Reynolds. The weekly magazine *Cordon Bleu* was started in 1895 by Marthe Distel, who gathered the
subscribers and household chefs for demonstrations by great chefs. Brassart,
who studied with Henri-Paul Pellaprat (one of France's greatest professor-
cooks), bought both the magazine and the school. She introduced the first
hands-on classes and saw to it that only *cuisine classique* was taught.

There was no love lost between Madame Brassart and Julia Child. Brassart, after reading harsh criticisms from Child, said as late as 1994 that "Mrs.
Child was not marked by any special talent for cooking but for her hard
work." She repeated the judgment that Mrs. Child did "not have any great
natural talent for cooking," but added that she was a *bonne exécutrice* who
understood French cuisine and what was important about it for Americans.
Certainly Mrs. Child lacked "taste memory," an expression coined by James
Beard, whose mother had brought him up amid the gathering, preparing, and
serving of food in Portland, Oregon. To make up for lost time, Julia studied
and researched recipes and food and practiced long, hard hours. During the
winter while other Parisians leisurely watched from the Deux Magots the
renovation of the church of St.-Germain, Julia stayed in the kitchen or
haunted the markets, cooking shops, and specialty shops, such as Androuet,
the famous cheese emporium behind the Gare St.-Lazare.

Brassart also said, however, that "Julia was a woman of character, a good
communicator. She was courageous. She worked very hard." After her American student achieved fame, Brassart would say that she was the only student
allowed to conclude her studies after just four months [she studied six].
Bugnard praised her work, according to Louisette Bertholle: "Max Bugnard
and Claude Thillmont said that you were the most gifted of us all. They were
not only talented chefs, they were also good predictors." Julia's eagerness to
learn offset the French suspicion of foreigners. She was a spy in the house of
food, in the temple of gastronomy, and would reveal its secrets. One day she
would make them clear and apparently simple to her compatriots.

Despite what she thought of Madame Brassart, she valued her lessons at

Bugnard's stove and enjoyed the teaching of chef Pierre Mangelotte, a "young, sad-eyed" magician with dramatic skills, who was chef at the Restaurant des Artistes in Montmartre. He always held his audience's attention. Holding his knife high in the air, he announced in a loud voice, *"Voici!* A potato!" His enthusiasm over his creations was loving. Raymond Desmeillers was also one of her demonstration cooks (it was he who peeled the live eel for the woman who wrote the exposé on a dirty Cordon Bleu). She also studied with Claude Thillmont, the pastry chef at the Café de Paris, who was once associated with Madame Saint-Ange. Paul called him "a fine, honest, salty technician with a ripe and rapid accent, and a wonderful way with a pie-crust." He gave her individual classes in cake making the next year (she remembered beating eggs for a cake for twenty minutes).

Maurice-Edmond Saillant, known by his pen name Curnonsky, also came to teach at the Cordon Bleu. A key figure in gourmet circles, he wrote a thirty-two-volume encyclopedia of France's regional foods and in 1928 founded the Académie des Gastronomes. The author of *Cuisine et Vins de France* had just turned seventy-seven.

By March 24, 1950, Julia decided she had completed the course and learned what she could from the Cordon Bleu. The recipes were getting repetitive, and she preferred to study independently with Bugnard, attend afternoon demonstrations, and practice for her exam. She spent six months, except for the Christmas holiday when she cooked with Mari Bicknell in Cambridge, England, preparing food in the early morning for two hours, cooking lunch for Paul, attending three-hour demonstrations in the afternoon, and then preparing the same dishes that night for Paul, Dorothy, and friends. (She did essentially nothing else, except, she told one interviewer, "I would go to school in the morning, then for lunch time, I would go home and make love to my husband, and then . . .") Probably no one at the school worked that thoroughly. The halfhearted GIs would continue three more months, but Julia wanted no more of the six-thirty wake-ups. Later when she asked Madame Brassart when she could take the final examination, Julia heard nothing from her.

It would take more than a year, the written testimony of Max Bugnard, and finally a blunt but professional letter to Madame Brassart before she received a signed diploma. Julia's letter a year later (March 28, 1951) detailed her work and the failure of Brassart to set an exam date, and insisted she must take the test before leaving on a trip in mid-April: *Il est surprenant de vous voir prendre si peu d'intérêt à vos élèves* (It is surprising to me to see you take so little interest in your students). Everyone at the American Embassy, including the ambassador, she added threateningly, knows that she has been studying at the Cordon Bleu. In a postscript she offered her own well-equipped kitchen if there was no room at the school for her exam.

Results were immediate, her exam completed, and the diploma sent with a date that preceded her letter by thirteen days. Julia thought that the written portion of the exam was far too simple for her training, and she was self-critical about her cooking techniques and failure to memorize several basics for the final meal prepared for Bugnard (though Helen Kirkpatrick, who was a guest, remembered that "Bugnard ate everything at the dinner with gusto"). Both Bugnard and Julia were pleased that the paperwork was complete. In his Christmas letter to her, he expressed admiration for her and asked for her help in answering the exposé article in *Life International*. Not surprisingly, when Julia publicly responded to the article, she charged the school only with "poor administration." And two years later, she would write to a friend, "I hate only a very few people, one being Mme. Brassart, head of the Cordon Bleu, who is a nasty, mean woman, [Senator] McCarthy, whom I don't know, and Old Guard Republicans, whom I see as little as possible."

While Julia was giving herself up to Cordon Bleu recipes, "that bastard from Wisconsin!"—as Paul called Red-baiting Senator Joe McCarthy—was making life miserable for several of their friends, as well as for Secretary of State Dean Acheson. They took a keen interest in the "trial-by-McCarthy," France's war in Indochina, and the crippling strikes during the spring of 1950. Julia, whose appliances were gas-generated, had to cook her food on the stoves of the Cordon Bleu and put a block of ice in her refrigerator for a large dinner party she gave during the gas strike. She thrived in adversity, and Paul reported the party's success: he poured Chablis '37 with the oysters, a Corton '32 with the beef, and a Volnay '45 with the Brie.

They always maintained, beyond their cooking and photography, a rich French intellectual life, attending plays (they saw Louis Jouvet in Molière's *Tartuffe* that spring), documentary films and discussions at their *ciné* club, the Wednesday medieval art history nights at the Baltrusaitises (they found Jurgis egotistical and difficult, but adored Hélène), and their Sunday mornings' in-depth exploration of another quarter of Paris (marking each section off on a map of Paris they kept on the wall). One day in May, as she listened to Weber's "Overture to Oberon" on the radio and could smell the soup gently simmering on the stove, she wrote that the "gentle soft night was lovely, Brie cheese is at its peak right now, strawberries are just coming in, and cream is thick and butter yellow." She reveled in these sensuous pleasures.

An American in Paris with Gene Kelly and Leslie Caron was the movie of 1951 and an impetus for travel (the Childs would reluctantly see the movie the following year and enjoy it). The beginning of the spring influx of visitors, including Julia's cousins, both their families, and an assortment of friends made it impossible for Julia to continue her early morning Cordon Bleu classes. The arrival of family and even the most distant of friends made great demands on their time and entertaining capacity.

FAMILY MATTERS:
DIVORCE FROM POP

Easter brought the McWilliamses, father John and stepmother Phila, otherwise known as Philapop, for a three-week holiday with Julia (and, for a while, Dort) in Italy. Because Julia and Paul forged a secret pledge to make Pop happy (which meant no political discussions) and because he was on their turf, the days in Paris were pleasant, and Paul was pleased. Pop was generous, and they stayed at the Ritz. They all dined at the best restaurants, including Lapérouse, Pré Catalan, Tour d'Argent (for the McWilliamses' anniversary), and in the Palais Royal, Le Grand Véfour—the latter, according to Paul, was their "favorite ritzy eating place" costing "a million dollars," but "because Julie is both unusually tall and unusually nice, everyone always remembers her, and we get the royal-carpet treatment."

Julia and Paul had never been apart more than two days since their wedding, and it was difficult for both of them when she left to travel with her father and Phila to Naples and back through Lucerne. Difficult for Julia because her father's back hurt him (they spent only a half an hour in the Uffizi, she noted in her datebook), and she knew after two weeks he wanted to be back in California. He was indeed Old Republican Guard and Scotch Presbyterian, so she did not disagree with him when he contrasted clean Switzerland with dirty France. But she spoke positively: "Pop is an old darling, who has mellowed mightily in every respect but that old Tory hard-core of politics." She wrote Charlie and Freddie her response to the trip: "What surprised and interested me is how far away I am from their life and interests. We have just about nothing in common any more, no reactions, likes, life, anything." Paul, who felt that life without her was "like unsalted food" ("You are the smell to my flower, the butter to my bread, the breath to my life"), was pleased to observe that "Julie finally got her divorce" from her father.

Dorothy returned early from Italy to work at the American Club Theater and keep Puck Hemingway company until the birth of her daughter at the American Hospital (Jack stayed at his job in Berlin). Dort still had her own room in their apartment and preferred the company of outsiders, misfits, and bohemians. Paul was urging her to leave the theater group (she was demoted from her nonpaying job) and the company of Ivan Cousins, whom he did not like. Paul complained twice in letters to Julia about the theater company "fairies," with their speech patterns and walk, who hung around Dort's room.

Ivan was a former Navy man (captain of a PT boat in World War II) from Greenfield, Massachusetts, who worked for the Marshall Plan (Office of Small Business) and occasionally acted in the theater company. Because he had studied in New York at the Neighborhood Playhouse with classmates Gregory Peck and Efrem Zimbalist, Jr., he played the father in Thornton Wilder's *Happy Journey*. He had come to Paris at the urging of poet Lawrence Ferlinghetti, a Navy buddy with whom he roomed in Paris for two years. When Ivan's mother arrived for two months, including travel with Ivan, Paul urged Dort to make the break ("he's a dreary, emasculated youth"). Instead she found her own apartment in July and by the end of the year went to Washington to be with Ivan.

Ivan was Irish, "witty, fun, and social," says his daughter, "he played the piano by ear and had many talents and had the joie de vivre that Julia does." Julia thought him "jolly and huggable." Louise Vincent, who acted with Ivan, remembered he "had much of an overgrown child in him" and "Dorothy was a protective figure for Ivan." For Dorothy, she added, "Ivan was the traveler, the adventurer, the artist, the troubadour, and far removed from her father." They completed and accepted each other. Clearly Ivan saw in her the McWilliams (or rather Weston) love of life. "One of the reasons I married her is that she makes me laugh so much," he later told a journalist.

The most joyous reunion came in July when Charlie, Freddie, and their three children arrived in St.-Malo, Brittany, where Julia and Paul drove to meet them. By Bastille Day on July 14 the Child clan was cooking a big dinner together in Paris, including the Bicknells, who had come from Cambridge, and some of the Focillon group. Julia served a huge stuffed breast of veal poached in wine with, as she told me, one of the best stocks she would ever make. In helping to clean up, Charlie mistakenly threw out the pan of stock (Julia would remember it forty-five years later). Nevertheless, she whooped it up, taking them to a demonstration at the Cordon Bleu and to the Dehillerin kitchen shop, to picnics and Paris sites. Paris was where Charlie and Freddie had fallen in love after college and where they lived together before marrying and rearing a family.

After two weeks the Chafred family went to Cassis in Provence near Marseilles, where Julia and Paul joined them at the end of July for three weeks. They stayed in the Marseilles home of Rosie and Abe Manell and visited with Richard E. (Daddy) Myers before returning, on Julia's thirty-eighth birthday, through Geneva. After the family left by boat train for Cherbourg and the *Queen Mary,* Julia and Paul celebrated a late joint birthday for Julia and Hélène with her Foçillon family at Maranville. They had foie gras, *poulet de Bresse,* and Meursault.

"J. feeling middle-aged," she wrote several times in her datebook that fall. The autumn rains, the ebb tide of tourists, falling horse chestnuts, the war in Korea, and Paul's hospitalization all brought on a fall melancholy. Doctors finally diagnosed Paul's amoebic dysentery (which had plagued him since India and China) and prescribed months of treatment, including a rigid diet that curtailed Julia's cooking and entertainment. Even the Foçillon group, which launched them into French intellectual life, suspended meetings. (They resumed in December.) While he was housebound, Paul painted one of his best works, the rooftops of Ile St.-Louis, and Julia read Stefan Zweig's biography of Balzac and the latter's *Le Lys dans la Vallée* (and she resumed the French-English sessions with Hélène at Closerie des Lilas). Soon she was diagnosed with a milder case of amoebic dysentery (left over from China), and they took medicines together. Nevertheless, they went to Marseilles for Thanksgiving with the Manells, who were to be transferred to Paris in December, because they wanted to "say farewell" to that lovely house and city.

December at last brought better health, the arrival of the Manells, Paul's USIS Grandma Moses exhibit (with more than a thousand visitors the first week), and a visit from their OSS and Washington, DC, friends, Fisher and Debby Howe and the Walter Lippmanns. A celebration lunch with the Howes included *soufflé Grand Marnier* with Château d'Yquem. The exhibits and parties seemed trivial to Paul, who was distracted by the French fifth column and the communist threat in Europe. While Paul predicted war for many months, Julia did not. ("Julie's different, thank god. She prolly [sic] truly represents the Hope That Springs Eternal in the Human Breast . . . I prefer her attitude.")

Paul was a discreet and sensitive man with an aesthetic sense of appreciation for both wines and his wife. He wrote poetry about the smell of her cooking and the curve of her ankle. As he was storing a new order of wine in his well-stocked cellar, he observed, "It's like a Harem full of beautiful and eager women—waiting to be ravished." He later described for Charlie his coming home with Julia after dinner one night: "Going up w/Julie in our little elevator, smelling those fresh lilies-of-the-valley, buzzing gently from Chambertin '28, and stroking the lovely bottom of a lovely woman—all at the same moment—I thinks to myself, 'Thaaat's Paris, Son—That's Paris.' "

Several grand meals at the end of 1950 reveal Paul's growing expertise in wines as well as Julia's culinary skills. As she cooked dinner, he read to her, first Faulkner's short stories and later Boswell's London *Journal.* For a dinner party of art historians, they served oysters with Pouilly-Fumé '49, and *noix de veau à la Prince Orloff* with Château la Mission Haut-Brion '45. For a three-hour dinner at the Restaurant des Artistes in the rue Lepic, where Mangelotte (one of Julia's teachers at the Cordon Bleu) was chef, Paul chose to drink with the *loup de mer* (Mediterranean sea bass stuffed with fennel leaves, broiled over charcoal, and served with lemon-butter sauce) a 1947 white wine from the Jura called Château-Chalon, made from dried grapes so the wine had a deep topaz color. With Paul's venison cutlets with *purée de marrons* and Julia's roasted *alouettes* (larks) and puffed-up potatoes they had a St.-Emilion '37. After coffee, Mangelotte talked to them of his academy of professional chefs and projected cookbook (both to rescue the art of French cuisine) as well as his belief that the Cordon Bleu was badly organized and doing a disservice to the métier.

The finale was a series of meals they all cooked—"in our happy British family bosom"—at the home of English architect Peter Bicknell and his wife, Mari, a ballet teacher, and, in Julia's words, "one of the best cooks I know." As they did the year before and would do for the next several Christmases, Julia and Paul took the boat train from the Gare du Nord to Victoria Station and, except for a final few days in London with the Nigel Bicknells (their former Washington housemates), they spent the holiday cooking, ice skating, and attending a children's ballet performance in Cambridge. Minutes after arriving this year, Mari and Julia were preparing potted shrimps on toast, to be accompanied by Alsatian wine, and two Scottish pheasants, by a young Burgundy. Their dessert was *soufflé Grand Marnier* with a Château d'Yquem '29 they had brought from Paris. Another meal was *sole bonne femme* (Mari made the best, Julia still claimed forty years later) with Hermitage '29. All four of them would cook in the kitchen of Finella, one of the university's grand old homes.

Dorothy left with Ivan Cousins for the boat train and New York City on January 12, 1951. In the months before, when Dorothy rented her own apartment and moved into Ivan's life, Paul accepted the inevitable. Before Dorothy left Paris, Julia threw what she proudly called "a large, wildly successful party," with Hélène and Rosie helping her create platters of food centering on an "art-galantine made out of boned chicken and farce-fine, decorated with flower design and covered with a layer of madeira-flavored jelly," the whole platter in turn decorated with geometrical designs using hard-boiled egg whites, red pimentos, leaves, and truffles. When they heard three months later that Dort and Ivan were engaged, they arranged for their leave to coincide with the wedding so they could give her the moral support she needed, for, as

Paul told Charlie, her "Papa [is] not wildly enthusiastic about this husband either." Another incident coincided with their plans to return to the United States: the Blue Flash broke down on the Concorde Bridge, and they decided to sell the Buick her father had given them in Washington, DC.

Julia and Paul took their home leave six months late, sailing on May 4 and returning to Paris on August 5. First they made a large circle by train from Lumberville (where they twice saw Budd Schulberg, Charlie's friend and a former colleague of Paul in the OSS in Washington, and attended Rachel's high school graduation) to Pasadena (where they spent a long weekend with her old friends the Hastings, Wrights, and Nivens), to San Francisco (Gay Bradley, Janie McBain, the Davises), and back to New York City and Lumberville. They attended her father's fiftieth reunion at Princeton, then visited for six days with friends in Washington, DC, checking their house, before moving on to New York City to attend Dort's wedding on June 23. All the McWilliams family gathered at St. John the Divine (Episcopal) Church for the simple ceremony and a hotel reception nearby. Julia and Paul drove (in a new Chevrolet) to see the Mowrers in New Hampshire before moving on to Lopaus Point, Maine, for the Childs' annual lobster-filled holiday for two weeks. Soon Paul found himself recoiling when Charlie turned braggart and loquacious. While driving south through Avon and New Haven, Connecticut, they analyzed the Charlie-Paul relationship—an anguish that Paul always suffered through after visiting his sometimes beloved twin.

They sailed on the *Nieuw Amsterdam* (the sea calm and Julia was bored), docked in Le Havre, off-loaded their car, and drove for a second time to have lunch at La Couronne, ordering the same meal that excited Julia two and a half years earlier. This time, she renewed her commitment to making cooking her career.

*M*EETING SIMCA

Since January 30, 1951, Julia had been attending the Cercle des Gourmettes, a club of French women dedicated to French gastronomy. She was privately cooking with Freddie Child, Mari Bicknell, and Rosie Manell, but now she wanted the French connection. A woman named Simone Beck Fischbacher, whom she met at a party at the home of George Artamonoff (a Russian-born American, first president of Sears International and now with the Marshall Plan), told her about this French cooking club. Julia resumed her informal French lessons with Hélène and returned to the Cordon Bleu in January to attend pastry demonstrations by Claude Thillmont. After dining at the Restaurant des Artistes one night (she loved the chef's chicken cooked in tarragon), and learning that Mangelotte was teaching another class, she attended his course at the Cordon Bleu for several weeks. When she invited Max Bugnard to lunch on February 20, they discussed her frustration with the failure of Madame Brassart to give her an exam. She also put a notice in the *Embassy News* announcing that Bugnard, now retired from the Cordon Bleu, was available as chef for private dinners and lessons.

The Gourmettes dined together bimonthly, either at one of their homes or at a restaurant such as Maxim's. Occasionally their husbands would dine together elsewhere. When they dined at the Chambre des Députés, their husbands accompanied them. Despite the strikes that nearly crippled the city that spring, Julia did not miss a meeting. By April 2, when she was formally accepted into the club, her closest friend in the group was Simone Beck, whom she took a liking to at their first meeting—"one of the great encounters in culinary history," says one of Beck's students.

Simone Beck was nicknamed "Simca" (the name of a French car, and the name she preferred) by her husband, Jean Fischbacher. She was a Norman who liked Americans, and Julia especially. Her father was an Anglophile. Julia described her as "a tall blonde with a remarkably vivid pink-and-white complexion; she was good-looking and dashing in a most attractive and debonair way, full of vigor, humor, and warmth." Simca, in turn, admired the joy that Julia brought to every location, calling it "la Juliafication de la vie." In a videotape made by Peter Kump in 1990, Simca says:

> Julia told me she got her Cordon Bleu certificate because she could skin an eel. She was always a very funny person. A very, very good actor. She is a very clever person . . . [with] a fantastic palate. She was the first person to really excite me. She impressed me in many ways.

Simca's friend Louisette Bertholle (both were about seven years older than Julia) had had an English governess when a child, traveled extensively in the United States, and wrote, with Simca, a little French cookbook for Americans. Each had a household cook in residence, unlike their American friend. They both saw in this tall and food-obsessed American a potential partner in their plan to write a larger book. Perhaps they were convinced by a meal Julia served at her apartment.

Julia asked Bugnard to help her prepare a lunch for her favorite Gourmettes, Simca and Louisette, and their husbands, on Friday, April 13. On the twelfth he helped her pound the crab and on Friday morning he assisted again. In her datebook she mentions only the crab, but says their lunch was "great fun." On April 27 they dined chez Bertholle, as they would frequently during the coming months.

In her heavy schedule of lunches and dinners this fall and winter, Julia records only one detailed menu in her datebook and letters. This one she prepared before a 1951 Thanksgiving week in Bruges, Belgium, and the left-overs fed the Bicknells when they arrived for a visit:

> Terrine de Canard (boned duck, meat farce, truffle, etc., duck and veal strips, all wrapped in duck skin after marinating in cognac) baked, cooked, then sliced and decorated with jelly; Roast leg of venison (mari-nated for 3 days in red wine, cognac and spices) served with purée de céleri rave, and prunes stewed in white wine and meat stock. It was a superb dinner, if I do say so.

She entertained nephew Paul Sheeline, Alice Lee Myers, Robert Penn Warren, the Fischbachers, chefs Bugnard and Mangelotte, the Teddy Whites, and Narcissa Chamberlain; picnicked with the Manells and Baltrusaitises; and so-cialized with Judge and Mrs. Learned Hand and, in a lunch for embassy wives, with Evangeline Bruce and Mrs. Dean Acheson.

The collaboration with Simca and Louisette was building. Julia soon learned that Simca's specialty was desserts and pastries. In early December the three women lunched with Mangelotte at the Artistes one week and the next he joined them for *pâte feuilletée* at Julia's apartment. By December 17 they met at the Bertholles' apartment to discuss the idea of a cooking school and Louisette's plans to renovate her kitchen, which they would use for classes.

After Julia and Paul's Cambridge Christmas and a big dinner to cele-brate Paul's fiftieth birthday—a dinner for which Bugnard cooked (freeing Julia to be with the guests)—the three women got down to business over a dinner for them and their husbands at the George Sand restaurant. L'Ecole des Trois Gourmandes they would call their cooking school, and each would credit the other for pushing through the idea: Louisette said it was Julia's idea, Julia said it was Simca who hurried it along, when she herself claimed she was not ready to teach.

On Wednesday, January 23, 1952, they gave their first cooking class for three women in Julia's kitchen. They had not planned to begin so soon (Louisette's kitchen was not ready), but Mrs. Martha Gibson, a wealthy widow from Pasadena, insisted upon having a class and recruited two friends, a Mrs. Mary Ward (also a widow) and Miss Gertrude Allison, who owned an inn in Arlington, Virginia, and was studying at the Cordon Bleu with Bugnard (she was not happy with the Cordon Bleu, or with Dione Lucas in New York City, whom she found not very scientific). For the next five days, Julia, Simca, and Louisette met nearly every day to plan the physical arrangements and do food preparations. This time Julia typed up seven detailed pages, including menu, steps in preparation, and detailed ingredients and techniques for poached fish, beef knuckle, salad, and banana tart (the menu for January 29). Their class commenced at 10 A.M. with lunch at 1 P.M. every Tuesday and Wednesday from January 29 through May 7, 1952.

Julia hardly noticed the muddy water boiling around tree trunks along the quai. The workload and enthusiasm of the gourmandes rose in February, along with the floodwaters of the Seine. They were gourmandes in the sense of being connoisseurs of good things (not in the recent sense of being heavy eaters). Julia described the purpose and dynamic of the school to Fredericka, her first sister-in-cooking:

> L'Ecole . . . is to be mostly technique, as we feel that once one has one's tools one can adapt them to [other cuisines]. . . . I have just been lucky having so much time with two professional chefs [Bugnard and Mangelotte], which has taught me good methods of cutting things up, handling the knife, cleaning and carving and saucery. And my colleagues, with a lifetime in France, and having spent three years over writing a cookbook . . . it's a good combo. I can also bring the practical side of being an American, and cooking with no servants anywhere . . . The atmosphere is . . . homey and fun and informal, and passionate pleasure from both pupils and professors.

Jeanne la Folle, her housekeeper, got into the spirit by coming in at one o'clock to wash everything up. Dehillerin gave them a 10 percent discount on purchases by their students. And, she added, "my shopping quarter is fascinated with our project. My darling chicken man on the rue Cler is giving us a special price and is most anxious to give a demonstration to us and our pupils on how to pick out a fine chicken; the butcher ditto."

Initially, each class cost the student 600 francs ($2.00). The school was not affected by the 23.5 percent rise in the cost of living in France during the previous year. Food was up 21 percent and heat and light up 42 percent. But the students were Americans who could afford the expense. Paul, who gave an occasional lecture on wine (the Americans were used to drinking only white wine), worked out the finances so that there was a profit for the school. In April, he designed the logo for Trois Gourmandes, which Julia would use for more than forty years.

A new class began on March 12, after Julia put a notice in the embassy newsletter. The five women—Paul called it a "floating population"—included Anita Littell, whose husband, Bob, headed the European office of *Reader's Digest,* and Jennifer (Mrs. Samuel) Goldwyn of Beverly Hills. Short-term student-guests for classes and/or lunch included friends of Julia such as Gay Bradley Wright (who with her husband, Jack, was spending a month in Paris) and Harriet Healy (who ran a Florida cooking school and store, for which she was buying goods in Europe's flea markets). Occasionally Julia invited guests for the class lunch (Bugnard and Rosie Manell) and gave individual lessons. After one such lesson, Julia wrote to Freddie: "I have just given my first solo lesson today, to a French woman in *pâte feuilletée.* . . . I learned a great deal, and would have gladly paid my pupil . . . it's such fun. Really, the more I cook, the more I like to cook. To think that it has taken me 40 yrs. to find my true creative hobby and passion (cat and husb. excepted)."

Scholars of French cuisine, such as John and Karen Hess, have criticized Julia for becoming an "instant chef." Indeed, none of the three was a "chef," meaning an administrator with years of training in all areas of cooking. In terms of training, it may have been presumptuous for them to begin a school. Yet they viewed themselves as "home cooks." Both Simca and Louisette had taken some women's morning classes at the Cordon Bleu (Simca with Henri-Paul Pellaprat), and when Simca thought about completing her diploma five years later, Julia called it "useless" for someone with her knowledge, assuring her that she did not intend to make any use of her diploma.

Julia's class time was indeed brief but intense, and she was still studying with Bugnard and using him as her tutor for the school. "We won't feel good about it until we've given at least 100 lessons," she told Freddie, "and have thoroughly tested everything out. Getting recipes into scientific workability is very interesting." Metrics could not be automatically translated into teaspoons and ounces, as she learned in making béchamel sauce. Paul described it as the "practical use of General Semantics" or "subjecting theories to operational proof," and admired his wife for not trusting any recipe, no matter what the source, without testing it. She had found her home with the French, who see themselves as a people who appreciate method and logic, symbolized in René Descartes, their emblem of rational thought.

The working relationship of Julia, Simca, and Louisette was best expressed by Paul: "Louisette appears to have a Romantic approach to cooking, while Simka [sic] and Julie are more 'scientific' [they measure quantities]. . . . Simka and Julie are both hard workers and good organizers." In private letters they shared the belief that Louisette did not know enough about cooking. Hélène believed that "Simca was somewhat pedantic and a perfectionist and Julia was not." But they both practiced "operational proof" in testing—

for example, the different results from making pie crust with French and American flour (American flour needed one-third more fat) and with butter, Crisco, and margarine. They also, Paul noted during a trip to the Normandy home of Simca's mother in March, were "relentless sightseers." Temperamentally, they were driven women with boundless energy. Neither, unlike Louisette, was inhibited by domestic responsibility, which in part triggered a compulsive urge to create. Each called the other *une force de la nature.* Julia also called Simca *la Super-Française.*

Louisette, it seems clear now from the beginning, did not have the drive for professional success that her partners did. She had children—indeed, two of her daughters (from her first marriage) got married that year—and homes in Passy and Chinon. But it was she who had the initial idea to teach Americans how to cook French food, and it was she who had the best social contacts. The three couples enjoyed each other's company, though Paul believed the "fat and charming" Paul Bertholle was a "preening egocentric." Jean Fischbacher, on the other hand, had "sensitivity wedded to physical vigor and generosity." He was a forty-six-year-old Protestant, a chemical engineer (*parfumeur*), "vigorous and intelligent," who had spent five years in German prison camps.

When Brentano's windows began filling with maps of Paris and displaying banned books such as Henry Miller's *Tropic of Cancer* and D. H. Lawrence's *Lady Chatterley's Lover,* they knew it was spring and tourist season. Though Paul declared they "dove for the bomb-shelters," in fact they did not; Paul's USIS window exhibits increased to fourteen in one month and Julia hosted lunches and dinner almost daily. A rising tide of visitors came from Pasadena and Pittsfield, from Smith College, from the OSS days (Rosie and Thibaut de Saint Phalle, Jack and Hedi Moore, Joseph Sloane). Smith classmate Kitty Smith remembers Julia driving them to Chartres and stopping at a poultry shop to choose a chicken to be killed for lunch on their return trip. After their eighth trip to Versailles in six weeks, Paul revolted.

The best arrival of spring was baby Phila, Dorothy's baby, named after their stepmother, Philadelphia McWilliams. Phila would become, in many ways, the daughter that her Aunt Julia never had: tall, freckled, and Celtic. Ivan, who had his Navy pension, began working with the government, then started a job with Garfinckel's Department Store in Washington, DC.

Knowing that his four years in Paris would be over this fall, and with it the government funding for his position, Julia and Paul traveled extensively when the Gourmandes' classes were not meeting. Except for a train trip to Lucerne (where a few of Paul's photographs were on exhibit) and Venice

(Paul's "beloved city"), they drove the Chevy, which they called the Black Tulip or La Tulipe Noire. Julia knew, as Balzac did, that one dines best in the provinces. They made friends with chefs, innkeepers, and vintners (helping the son of one go to dental school in Iowa) as they traveled west to the Atlantic, east to Alsace, and south to the Loire. When they visited Julia's Smith chum Mary Belin in her Château Andelot in the Jura, Paul designed a wine label for her cellar.

Another session of the cooking classes was announced in the *Embassy News* on June 20, emphasizing the informality and the "cook-hostess" angle [that is, no hired cook]. The fee was now 2,000 francs, including lunch, "which is prepared and served by" the five students and three teachers. According to Louisette, Ann Buchwald was in their class. They taught "basic recipes, cuisine bourgeoise or haute cuisine." By contrast, women in the United States were learning to cook chicken pot pies, corned beef hash, confetti Jell-O, carrot-raisin slaw, and macaroni and cheese.

Paul had mixed feelings about his own job: "I love living in Paris w/ Julia. My job makes it possible. I believe it is useful work." Other times Kafka-like frustrations at the embassy reminded him of Menotti's *The Consul,* an opera that gripped him. Yet the work gave him an opportunity to meet leaders in the art and political world: Man Ray, Cartier-Bresson, Jackson Pollock, Nadia Boulanger, and Edward Steichen (head of photography at the Museum of Modern Art in New York City). With Darthea Speyer, who was in charge of exhibits, Paul helped plan numerous photography and art exhibits. But he was no workaholic; he was always a balanced person. People like Abe Manell worked weekends, but Paul always went home by seven and had time to paint, photograph, and write carefully crafted letters to Charlie, Daddy Myers, or George Kubler. He finished a couple of paintings this year (one for the Bicknells and one for the Littells) and bought a Foujita painting of a girl in a French kitchen for Julia's kitchen.

For nearly five years now, Julia had been tasting the artistic life of postwar Paris, a period which saw a new generation of Americans, many of them black, come to Paris. Though New York City was to take Paris's place as the center of art, the residual fame of the great School of Paris was still luring young artists to the Seine. Julia and Paul always seemed to be going to one embassy or French vernissage or another: Raymond Duncan came to the Frank Lloyd Wright exhibit in his dirty toga and sandals. At a New York City ballet performance in Paris, they chatted with Janet Flanner and Glenway Westcott. After Steichen judged the American photo exhibit and acquired five of Paul's photographs for MOMA, Julia and Paul drove him to Luxembourg, where he had been born seventy-two years before. Among their friends who painted seriously were Rosie Manell and Jane Foster (newly discovered), with whom Paul exchanged paintings.

"We have finally tracked down Jane Foster (Mrs. George Zlatovsky)," Julia wrote on their next Valentine's card to Ellie and Basil Summers and other OSS colleagues. They found her through an advertisement for an exhibition of her paintings. "She is still just as much fun as ever, and doing wonderfully good paintings. They've been here three years, but everyone thought she was lost." Jane had worked for the USIS in Austria, was now married to a Russian, and (according to Betty McIntosh) was reporting the names of all CIA people, as well as Paul's name, to the communists. Eventually Jane Foster would disrupt their lives.

Julia was forty years old on August 15, the calmest Parisian day of the year, when everyone who had not already left the city was doing so. They tried a dozen restaurants, which were all closed, and settled on the Ritz Hotel with the Manells. Afterward they sat on the balcony of the Manells' Ile St.-Louis apartment, and, while Paul sketched yet another scene of Paris rooftops, Julia went to the movies with Abe. The next day Julia and Paul alone ate at Lapérouse: sole in a cream sauce with truffles and a half bottle of Chablis, followed by roast duck and Chambertin '26. As the famous American diner Julian Street (*Where Paris Dines* was Paul's first guide to Parisian restaurants) said about the place: "I had there one of the finest dinners I have ever eaten." Lapérouse, not Le Grand Véfour (where Paul had recently gotten ptomaine poisoning), was now their luxury restaurant of choice. For the best bistros this year, they chose the Restaurant des Artistes, La Grille, Au Grand Comptoir, Chez Anna (the old lady had seven cats), Chez Marius, and La Truite.

Julia was reading the *Herald Tribune* carefully one day because their autumn was filled with worries about the elections (they preferred Adlai Stevenson to Dwight Eisenhower), McCarthyism, and Nixon's Red-baiting. Suddenly she burst out laughing when she read the front-page story of the Nixon Fund, which listed the businessmen who had contributed to his secret slush fund. There it was: "John McWilliams, Pasadena Rancher."

Soon her stepmother and brother wrote to ask that Julia not write anything more in defense of Charlie Chaplin and against Nixon. Her father canceled his subscription to *The New Yorker* when they ran a profile of Mrs. Roosevelt. Julia was just as uneasy with her father's politics as she was with the anti-Semitism of some of their upper-class friends. The Childs' enlightened liberalism extended to lesbians (such as Cora DuBois), but Paul shared his generation's scorn of male homosexuals ("fairies," he called them). Paul seemed to be comfortable with what Joseph Alsop called the "Wasp Ascendancy" in U.S. foreign policy following the war, for some of his dynamic friends (Dick Bissell and Charles Bohlen) were helping to run the world. Ambassador Bruce, who came to France to head the Marshall Plan and then serve as ambassador, left Paris (for Washington, then Bonn and London), and was replaced by, in Paul words, "careful and colorless Jimmie Dunn."

When the end of Paul's USIS assignment came, he was appointed to the regular foreign service in order to keep him on the job. There was much talk about him being assigned as Public Affairs Officer in Marseilles or Bordeaux ("both Julia and I are good at public relations") or Exhibit Director in Vienna. They preferred to stay in France.

$\mathscr{A}$ COOKBOOK FOR AMERICANS

Though she was studying with two chefs (the Cordon Bleu distributed no recipes), Julia was very aware (as well as skeptical) of cookbooks. On July 4, Louisette introduced Julia to Irma Rombauer, the author of Julia's first cookbook as a bride: *The Joy of Cooking.* Rombauer was in France for a ten-day visit on her way to Germany, dining at the Bertholle home, and very interested in Les Trois Gourmandes. Her book—the latest editions revised with her daughter—she told them, was written for the middle class and avoided anything too fancy. "We all have copies of Mrs. Joy," Julia wrote a friend the next year. "Somehow, old Mrs. Joy's personality shines through her recipes. . . . She is terribly nice, but pretty old, now, about 70 or so; and just a good simple midwestern housewife. She said she'd been in some way weaseled out of something like royalties for 50,000 copies of her book, and was furious." Julia claimed also to have a copy of Fannie Farmer's cookbook, though she did not use it, and a 1909 edition of Mrs. Beeton (as a collector's item). Such were the offerings in the United States.

Julia was much more interested in French cookbooks, and owned the encyclopedic *Larousse Gastronomique,* the Chamberlains' *Bouquet de France* (she found a number of "unprofessional" mistakes), and *Le Livre de Cuisine,* by "Madame Saint-Ange"—"sort of *The Joy of Cooking* for France," Julia said about what she called "one of my bibles then." Marie Ebrard (her husband's first name was Saint-Ange) had, according to her granddaughter, rewritten the recipes in her (and her husband's) *Le Pot-au-Feu: Journal de Cuisine Pratique et d'Economie Domestique,* founded in 1893 as a monthly.

But Julia's greatest reverence was for Georges-Auguste Escoffier (1846–1935), the world-famous chef who cooked for royalty and high society during the Belle Epoque. Escoffier invented assembly-line cooking, stock reductions for sauces, and food endorsements ("foodiebiz"), as well as further codifying conduct and recipes (*Guide Culinaire,* 1903, and *Ma Cuisine,* 1934). Fifty years later she would call him her greatest hero, the man under whom her chef Max Bugnard studied. She now added two great French chefs—Carême and Escoffier—to Balzac and Beethoven as her supreme heroes. Her choices reveal her traditional approach: her moment in French culinary history fell at the end of the classical approach (Thillmont and Bugnard were both in their seventies).

The current god of the food world in Paris was Curnonsky. For the Great Gastronomic Banquet celebrating Curnonsky's eightieth birthday, all eighteen French gastronomic societies were invited, including Julia's Gourmettes and Paul's Le Club Gastronomique Prosper Montagné. Nearly four hundred people who, in Paul's words, "whirl around the French food-flame" attended, many bedecked in decorations, and each with nine glasses in front of his plate. During one of the final speeches, about quarter to one in the morning, Paul and Julia drifted out.

Ten days later, Julia and Simca called on Curnonsky at 14, Place Henri Bergson. He greeted them in his pajamas and bathrobe at four in the afternoon. He was a spirited and charming old man, Julia discovered. As a gesture of admiration and friendliness, Julia gave him a carton of Chesterfields. He had written an introduction to the forty-eight-page, spiral-bound book that Simca and Louisette self-published (Editions Fischbacher) in April. It was written in French and translated into English. *What's Cuisine in France,* consisting of fifty recipes for Americans, sold about 2,000 copies. Louisette took it and a larger manuscript to New York, and Sumner Putnam of Ives Washburn bought it for $75.

The same booklet in its blue, white, and red cover, was published in New York City by Ives Washburn. But this sixty-three-page edition was entitled *What's Cooking in France* and had three authors' names: Louisette Remion Bertholle, Simone Beck, and Helmut Ripperger, identified as the author of many books on cookery. Ripperger, the "food adviser," chose the recipes and wrote the bridge passages from the recipes by Simca and Louisette, who were identified as "Parisian hostesses and expert amateur cooks." The book was dedicated to Dorothy Canfield Fisher, who "loves France," and stated that the three authors were "preparing a larger volume." Even at $1.25 the booklet did not do well.

When Ripperger gave up on editing their volume in the summer of 1952, Simca and Louisette had already prepared six hundred typed pages of recipes entitled *French Cooking for All.* "I am the one who had the idea . . . after one of my trips to America," says Louisette Bertholle. Putnam informed them that they would have to get an American collaborator and adapt their French recipes to the American method. Naturally, Julia would become their co-author. "Julia is exceptional," Bertholle said in 1992. "You will never find another Julia for maybe half a century." Putnam agreed with their proposal and wanted to deal directly with Julia, but sent no contract.

Meanwhile, Julia, who thought the recipes were "not very professional," began testing, organizing and typing the sauce recipes for *French Cooking.* To a confidant she said it was "just a big collection of recipes" and "not one of the recipes will stand as they were written." It was her job to rewrite the original technical instructions and get everything into readable English. Because none of the recipes stood up, she confided to her friend Avis DeVoto, they were going to write an entirely different book: a book for American home cooks that would present cuisine bourgeoise using the techniques of haute cuisine—that is, the techniques their chef teachers had taught them. "Julie is girding up her loins and spitting on her Underwood," Paul reported.

La Julification des gens, Paul called her "special system of hypnotizing people so they open up like flowers in the sun." She went to Chez la Mère Michel, which specialized in *beurre blanc nantais,* in order to learn how the woman herself made the *beurre blanc.* Indeed, Julia talked her way into the kitchen and watched them make the foaming white butter sauce. Disappointed that *Larousse Gastronomique,* Flammarion, Curnonsky, and others were vague on the subject, she went to the source and then perfected the method in order to write it up for their book.

Julia typed for weeks and experimented with sauces, during the winter cold and fog. They now called the book *French Home Cooking* (a title chosen by Putnam). When the publisher wrote on November 20 to say they were returning the Simca-Louisette manuscript by embassy pouch, Julia wrote a joint letter informing them the book was entirely changed and the sauce chapter was being sent.

Before their annual Christmas in Cambridge with the Bicknells, Julia finished the chapter on sauces "as a sample of style and method," then sent it to Paul Sheeline, Paul's French-born nephew, and their lawyer, who gave it to Putnam. She also sent copies of her sauce chapter to Avis DeVoto (her Boston "pen pal"), Freddie, Katy Gates and Susy Hastings (the latter two old Pasadena pals), and others "for critical and helpful comments." She kept out three "top secret" recipes and warned these friends to keep the recipes and format secret, for "the cooking business is as bad as Georgetown real-estate or La Haute Couture . . . it's cutthroat."

Immediately Julia began on soups, which she thought would make a better first chapter (sauces being too Frenchy). Her approach was to prepare one soup each day, beginning with *soupe aux choux* (cabbage), and spread out for comparison Montagné's *Larousse,* Ali-Bab's *Gastronomie Pratique,* Curnonsky, and several regional cookbooks (probably the monthly *La France à Table).* She made two traditional recipes and one experimental, preparing the latter in a pressure cooker. ("Stinking, nasty bloody pressure cooker, I hate them! I can spot and taste a pressure cooker dish anywhere," she said.)

Though Louisette was discouraged by Putnam's failure to respond to the sauces chapter, Julia and Simca were not. They were hoping that Julia's "pen pal" would interest Houghton Mifflin, with whom she had connections, to take the book. At the end of December 1952, Mrs. DeVoto responded enthusiastically to their professional recipes and asked their permission to show the manuscript to her husband's publisher.

Avis DeVoto was an invaluable link in the career of Julia Child as well as a precious friend. They had corresponded since Julia sent a French knife to Bernard DeVoto. Julia read DeVoto's "Easy Chair" column in *Harper's* in which he asserted (at his wife's behest) that stainless-steel knives were no good because, though they did not rust, they could not be sharpened. Julia heartily agreed, sent a fan letter with a French carbon-steel paring knife, and the correspondence about food began. Avis, a very good cook, received and tested Julia's recipes for months.

Julia's long letters to Avis reveal their growing friendship as "heart-to-heart" correspondents. In addition to sending photographs of themselves and their husbands, Julia included on February 23 a written description of herself:

> Julia, 6 ft. plus, weight 150 to 160. Bosom not as copious as she would wish, but has noticed the Botcelli [sic] bosoms are not big either. Legs OK, according to husband. Freckles.

By the end of January, encouraged by Avis's confidence and connections, they broke with Putnam, who rejected the book as too unconventional. Julia received a contract and $200 advance from Houghton Mifflin in February. She was to draw up a separate contract between herself and the other two women. Avis assured her, "I am in a state of stupefaction. . . . it is going to be a classic."

The transfer to Marseilles came suddenly that month. Julia and Paul left Paris with reluctance, he recorded. "Our hearts have been infected and will always skip a beat at the mention of our city." Julia said, "How lucky we have been to live here this long, and I shall never get over it."

Chapter 12

MARSEILLES: FISHING FOR REDS (1953 – 1954)

"What a meaty, down-to-earth, vicious, highly sensual old city this is."

PAUL CHILD, May 30, 1970

~

THOUGH MARSEILLES, France's first seaport, has always suffered from a lack of respect in the rest of France, Julia found it exciting, wonderful, and noisy (three words she would repeat in her many letters). The level of noise, pungent fish smells, and seedy streets excited her. She told Katy Gates she liked the "meridional" temperament and the warmth of the people, "always talking, gesticulating, eating, laughing." The climate, roof tiles, and eucalyptus trees reminded them of California, the sound of the seagulls evoked Lopaus Point, Maine.

OLD PORT HOME

Paul was appointed Cultural Affairs Officer for the southern coast of France, located in the American Consulate at 5, Place de Rome. Moving to Marseilles meant being pulled from the orbit of her Paris partners and her new career.

But Julia and Paul understood the system and were good troupers, even eager for new frontiers. They had previously visited this southern port city on the Mediterranean for a week of reconnoitering in mid-February 1953—it was their first glimpse of sunshine in many months and they loved it. As usual, they made a study of their new base and read history books about the twenty-five centuries of Marseilles.

When Julia did not have to accompany Paul on his diplomatic survey of the region (they visited mayors, newspapermen, and academicians from Perpignan to Nice), she roamed Marseilles looking for the markets and for a neighborhood home. They would choose the rectangular Old Port (Vieux Port), where the fishermen first unloaded their catch. Here in the fertile south were abundant markets, especially the one behind Noailles in the Place du Marché des Capucins, where the first ripe fruit and vegetables appeared each season. Women of various shades of olive skin joked loudly among themselves and called out the price of their eel—hence the term *criée aux poissons.*

Before settling in, they returned to Paris for Paul to take photographs of Julia, Simca, and Louisette preparing food in their kitchen before it was dismantled. Paul and Julia went "weeping through the old streets" of Paris, she confided to Avis DeVoto, distressed at leaving and dismayed by "oriental tummy trouble" just when they planned to glut themselves with Parisian food and then "descend slowly to the south from one great restaurant to another, arriving bilious but filled with glory. What a thing, to have this trouble for someone in my profession!"

Julia had felt bilious since a farewell dinner party for twelve that Louisette and Simca gave her in Paris. Unbeknownst to Julia or Paul, who was urged to bring his camera, Curnonsky surprised her when she arrived. With cries of pleasure, they fell into each other's arms like old pals. Indeed Julia had been visiting him, Paul noted, "like a public affairs officer keeping in touch with a *préfet.*" Paul added a description of this "Prince Elu des Gastronomes": "short, fat, eagle-beaked, triple-chinned, pale-blue-eyed, witty, egocentric, spoiled and knowledgeable." Curnonsky posed for pictures with the three Gourmandes, and the night before Julia left town, she paid a visit to give him the photographs. Privately she confided to Avis that at their party he acted like "a dogmatic meatball who considers himself a gourmet but is just a big bag of wind."

In Marseilles, Julia threw herself into the constructing and testing of recipes, official entertaining, and shopping the markets, where she struggled to adjust her ear to the local dialects and accent (which added a *g* to many words: *ving blong* for white wine). Paul, meanwhile, was trying to adjust to an unhappy consulate, led by Consul General Hayward G. Hill, known as "Hill the

Pill." The staff was demoralized by what they saw as a fastidious "mother's boy," a stickler for protocol, afraid of germs, and always dressed, as if he were in Paris, in a gray suit and homburg hat. Paul described him as careful, mediocre, and twitchy, "nervous as a virgin in a whorehouse." Furthermore, Julia added in a letter to a friend, he seems "uninterested in eating."

From the windows and balcony of Apartment A at 28, Quai de Rive Neuve, the street that ran along the south side of the old port, Julia looked out on the vertical masts of the fishing boats and the seagulls circling against the blue sky. They were subletting from a Swedish consul home on leave for six months. Her view was "heavenly" as she typed, she told Simca. Looking seaward, she saw Fort St.-Nicolas to the left and Fort St.-Jean to the right, their stone breakwaters guarding the wide outer bay. Every vista was intersected by the vertical masts of the colorful boats. When she wrote to her sister Dorothy, who was expecting another baby and was now living in Sausalito near San Francisco, she would think of San Francisco Bay as well as their summers in Santa Barbara—both waters so different from this teeming gateway to Africa and the centuries-old quais at her feet.

"Sometimes at night we'd hear hearty shouting, and slapping of wet fish on the pavement at the edge of the water . . . where the boats were unloading their tuna under our window," Julia wrote M. F. K. Fisher twenty years later. La Criée aux Poissons, the wholesale fish market, was on their quai, just steps from the front door.

Happily nestled in a new building in the row of tight old houses ringing the port, she could hear the seagulls. Some mornings she and Paul were awakened by arriving fishing boats beneath their windows. They could also hear the construction behind their building. A decade before, the Germans, under the pretext of public health, forced 40,000 inhabitants from the old quarter and razed the densely populated buildings and narrow streets, leaving only the houses along the quais. Ill-famed, this district was picturesque. Even in 1953, the consulate staff remarked about the danger of the Childs' neighborhood. Though the year before Le Corbusier was making a name for himself in Marseilles with modern buildings known for their audacious and original designs, time would judge them ugly intrusions on the landscape.

The summer of 1953 brought with it the smell of wild lavender. After parsley (the only winter herb), thyme, and bay, Julia was enjoying the season of tarragon, chervil, and chives. In Provence, she learned, they added fennel and basil to their dishes. The French do not use many herbs, she informed one friend, and they never use wooden salad bowls! Such fine distinctions were irrelevant on the Fourth of July when she had to help turn inferior Navy canned food (sardines, salmon, liverwurst) into something edible for five hundred cocktail party guests of the consulate. After visitors from three U.S. Navy destroyers one week and an aircraft carrier the next, Julia and Paul relaxed on their balcony with friends on July 14, watching their adopted homeland celebrate its independence day with fireworks and "The Marseillaise."

Of course, Julia and Paul frequently ate out, savoring the best restaurants in Marseilles and along the coast (their disappointment at La Baumanière in Les Baux was duly reported to Simca). They both loved the smell of fish and garlic in the restaurants along the waterfront, Julia always observing the presentations of the dishes and varieties of ingredients. "I loved the sea scallops in wine sauce baked in a seashell." After one such meal she exclaimed, "I would happily die with a bottle of white Burgundy in my mouth."

She soon struck up an important friendship with Monsieur Guido, whose restaurant by that name was located nearby on the rue de la Paix. It had been open eight months, and Julia believed it was the best fish restaurant in the city. Unrated when she discovered it, it received its second Michelin star by 1956 ("excellent cuisine, worth a detour"). Not surprisingly, the Michelin lists Guido's first specialty as *bouillabaisse des pêcheurs à la rouille.* Occasionally during the coming months, Julia would ask him about the ingredients and techniques that he used, and he would recommend wine sources to Paul. His name came up frequently in their letters—even to Charlie, who bought holsters, a belt, and two "six-shooters" for Guido's son, who was crazy about American cowboys. Guido was "a Mangelotte type," Julia told Simca, "absolute perfection and care in everything he does." "Thank god I can talk French," she wrote to Avis. She did not care about her accent as long as she could "talk and talk and talk."

"IS THERE A RED UNDER YOUR BED?": McCARTHY WITCH HUNTS

The major topic of conversation among the U.S. Information Agency personnel was Senator Joseph McCarthy of Wisconsin. They heard from friends at the embassy in Paris that Roy Cohn and David Shine, McCarthy's assistants, came through the capital city to check the library and the correctness of the staff. Theodore White would say that they "moved through Europe examining the books and shelves of the USI[S]." They were apparently dismayed that they could not find the *American Legion Weekly.* When Larry Morris, head of the Paris cultural section of the USIS, came into his office and found two young men with their feet on his desk, he demanded that they remove themselves and give their names. McCarthy's two henchmen immediately complied, but called a staff meeting for Easter Sunday. Afraid for their careers, everyone showed up and waited at length until someone checked Cohn and Shine's hotel at four-thirty and learned that they had slept in after a late night. "Most people were scared to do anything," Julia later explained. News of the harassment spread through the American diplomatic community. When Cohn and Shine got to Berlin they found White's *Thunder Out of China* in the USIS library, burned it, and reported the purge to the *New York Times.*

Theodore White, located not far away on the Riviera in the fishing village of Le Lavandou since 1952, was writing books, fearing the blacklist, and hoping to redeem himself. White's brother Robert (removed from his security clearance at MIT) and others from the China theater were threatened. On a number of occasions, Julia and Paul visited with Theodore and Nancy White in Les Mandariniers, their huge old whitewashed villa with its orange tiled roof. They had bouillabaisse and talked of the great Chinese food they had shared in Kunming. Nancy White later said that Julia "devoured every morsel" that her excellent cook Marie produced. Talk always turned to McCarthy and the general distrust they all had of Chiang in China. "Since when was China ours to lose?" asked Julia. "Chiang and [Tai Li] did the trick, helped on by the China lobby and Henry Luce." Political tides ended White's comfortable French life when, on June 17, workers rose in East Berlin and Russian tanks mowed them down. White and anyone who had appeared sympathetic to Mao or the communists were soon out of work. Later, in his book *In Search of History,* White recalled this period, saying there were many as yet unknown Americans in the south of France—he included Julia's name here—who were "all there *doing* things."

The growing power of Senator McCarthy was reported in the newspapers and magazines. His denunciations of communist sympathizers and traitors in every branch of government made his name symbolic of an era in American history that would see Julius and Ethel Rosenberg put to death for treason and anti-American demonstrations in Paris. Allen Dulles (formerly of the OSS, then the head of the CIA) stood up to McCarthy, Julia noted, but "[Secretary of State John] Foster Dulles did not stand up to anyone."

Julia held strong opinions about the rise of political intimidation in her homeland and shared White's views of China and the botched American policy there. Their friend Dick Heppner was now Deputy Assistant Secretary of Defense for International Security Affairs under Eisenhower, but several other OSS friends lost their jobs, including John Carter Vincent and John Stewart Service. (The latter was reinstated after six years of litigation, directed by Heppner when he was still in Donovan's law firm.) Duncan Lee (China-born Assistant General Counsel of the OSS) was accused but not charged. Charles

E. (Chip) Bohlen was smeared by McCarthy, who questioned his sexual per-suasion. Not surprisingly, Julia and Paul considered the possibility that the paranoia could touch them. Paul remembered signing a petition in the 1930s; Julia recalled putting one of her own books on China (written by a woman later identified as communist) in the USIS library. But neither thought seri-ously about their friendship with former OSS colleague Jane Foster. "She was lots of fun, and every time we went to Paris we would see her," Julia informed her OSS correspondents.

"I'm terribly worried about McCarthyism," Julia confided to Avis DeVoto on February 28: "What can I do as an individual? It is frightening. I am ready to bare my breasts (small size though they be), stick out my neck, won't turn my back on anybody, will sacrifice cat, cookbook, husband and finally self . . . please advise. I'm serious." Avis warned her to be careful because of Paul's job. The DeVotos (in Cambridge, Massachusetts) could have told her stories of faculty opening student mail at Harvard for the FBI the year before and Princeton professors taping their lectures to avoid being misquoted by student moles. Bernard DeVoto had stood up to the House Un-American Activities Committee in September 1949.

By March 1954, Julia was so worked up over McCarthyism in America (and Foster Dulles's capitulation) that she was determined to prove she and Paul would not be intimidated. The event triggering this decision was news that an anonymous "Committee for Discrimination in Giving" fingered five faculty members as "communists" at Smith College and wrote to the alumnae. Julia's March 14 letter is a classic of reason and fortitude, saying, in part:

> According to proper democratic methods, charges of this grave nature should first be brought to the attention of the President and the Trust-ees. You have assumed a responsibility for which you were not ap-pointed. It is clear that you do not trust your elected officers, and that you do not have confidence in democratic procedures. . . . In Russia today, as a method for getting rid of opposition, an unsubstantiated implication of treason, such as yours, is often used. But it should never be used in the United States.

With a check doubling her annual contribution to the Alumnae Fund, she adds, "In the blood-heat of pursuing the enemy, many people are forgetting what we are fighting for." Unwisely, she sent a copy to her father (only later understanding that it was directed in part at him), who informed Julia and Paul that they were playing into the hands of the communists.

Paul was hurt and depressed by his father-in-law's letter and took to his bed. He reported to his brother that "since the USIS has been under attack by Sen. McCarthy, the monthly book-buying has been cut from 20,000 to 1,592." That summer Paul was asked to compile a list of every book in order that they be cleared, destroyed, or refiled. Though Paul continued to be worried about the growth of communism in Europe, he believed McCarthy made the situation worse. McCarthy, he added, "is a dirty and astute demagogue, advancing himself, like a surf board rider, on a wave of fear." The French may have a "deep-seated national neurosis" that toppled each new government, but "we have McCarthy."

Julia's professional work provided an outlet for dealing with the tension and connected her both to her homeland, through her interpretation to Simca of American tastes and products, and to her new French home, with its hundreds of varieties of fish and fresh produce. She would explain which beans or fish were not available in the United States or that Americans had an aversion to too much butter, and she could clarify the language for their readers. Occasionally she sent Simca copies from American cookbooks, but she was reading *Gourmet* more skeptically since Narcissa Chamberlain had warned her about its unreliability. Though she left the final judgment of French recipe titles to Simca and Louisette, who were continuing their school in Louisette's big blue kitchen, she did not hesitate to say that something was not "Frenchy" enough or that the French cooking authorities she consulted said this or that. Julia missed their cooking classes and the appearances of Thillmont and Bugnard at the blue kitchen at 171, avenue Victor Hugo.

Entertaining combined her professional work and Paul's diplomatic responsibilities. It was immediately evident to the consulate that a meal at the Childs' apartment was both a personal pleasure and a diplomatic advantage in entertaining guests. Three months after their arrival, Julia had the British consul general and the head of the French Chamber of Commerce to dinner.

Whether she served fish in wine sauce or a shoulder of lamb, each dish was an experiment reported to Simca. Officer Roland Jacobs (number two man in the U.S. Consulate), and his wife, Janine, remember a superb *boeuf bourguignon* and the Childs' "neat sense of humor." Howard B. Crotinger, in the Department of State foreign service, remembers that he and his bride, Annelie, were treated to "delicious" meals. Lee Crotinger was impressed by Julia's height and her command of the French language. Crotinger, who was a Signal Corps photographer during the war, admired Paul's photographs hanging in the foyer. American diplomats, most of whom were not fluent in French, were in awe of the Childs' command of French, their popularity with the French, their sense of humor, and their "courage" in living in this "dangerous neighborhood," where no other foreigners rented. Their avant-garde reputation was confirmed when Julia showed the Crotingers a jar of absinthe, wormwood included, that she was preserving in the back of her dark closet. She found an old recipe for this lethal, now outlawed, drink and shared a taste of her brew with adventurous friends.

Despite the demoralizing effects of McCarthyism, Paul maintained the Cultural Center and its library, exhibited the work of American artists, and entertained lecturers and visitors. During this first year in Marseilles, the USIS became the USIA, an independent agency of the government, and Paul was put in charge. He organized fifteen French departments along the Mediterranean between the Italian and Spanish borders and supervised one assistant and eight staff members. In addition to publicity and visiting celebrities, he oversaw sections on management and administration, an information center, press and radio services, motion pictures (including the Cannes film festival), and exchange of persons. Paul's staff "adored the Childs," Crotinger remembers.

Julia was learning to balance her demanding professional standards with her role as wife to Paul, who wanted her to travel with him when she could. She confided to Simca in early December that if she were able to give as much time as she wanted to her work, "we would soon be having a divorce, I fear. Luckily, however, now that he has his studio, [Paul] is well-occupied during the weekends!"

Their marriage seemed to be happier than ever, perhaps in part because the demands of the book kept Julia's social life less frantic than in Paris. "We just love living together," Paul told Charlie, and when apart missed each other "terrifically [for] we clearly have developed a sort of emotional interdependence." In December he told Charlie, "Julie . . . is now and then . . . an unconscious therapeutic agent for me." She calmed his nerves. Twice this year Paul commented on their like-mindedness: "Julia and I are such twinnies in our reactions and tastes," and "We are pretty twinnyfied that way, reflecting each other's atmospheres like two mirrors."

Paul was keenly aware of the charm that Julia had both on him ("I hate to think what a sour old reprobate I might have been without that face to look at") and on the French ("I watched with fascination [one] night at Lipp's as she turned a fat, tired, old waiter into a responsive, gay, flirtatious, pleasure-filled man. [She is an] electric-energizer and responder. . . . I am continuously conscious of my good fortune in living with her."

He specifically credited her sensitivity to "emotional atmospheres." When she was excited, "Julia's eyes begin to glow like emeralds":

Her eyes are as sensitive to emotional atmospheres as a coal-mine canary is to fire-damp. If there's the slightest wonder or sentiment or excite-

ment in the air those curious green orbs develop a phosphorescent sparkle; and that mobile mug takes on a look of pleasurable anticipation—
and the first thing you know she's imbued the atmosphere with her own
aurora-borealis.

MASTERING THE ART

Julia's horizon was the future publication of their book. She was convinced
that they were writing a precedent-setting work: "What a book this will be, if
we ever finish it." And she was convinced that they must keep their work
secret, especially their experimentation with high technology. The letters were
often labeled "Top Secret" or "never seen in print before." Simca must never
show the blender to Bugnard, because he had many American students. She
was especially concerned that they be the first to incorporate the use of the
Waring blender in cooking classic French recipes. "Love that Waring Mixer,"
she told Avis. Simca went to a demonstration at a kitchen fair in Paris, and
Julia wrote to the American companies who manufactured blenders, just as
she had written to the Wine Advisory Board of California the previous year.

A second innovation they hoped to pioneer was directions for cooking
some dishes ahead of time (a dimension never introduced by their teachers,
who were *chefs de cuisine).* The women would inform their readers where in
the recipe they could stop and how they could reheat. These ahead-of-time
tips were uniquely Julia's contribution, for she did not have a live-in maid or
cook and understood the pressure of being both cook and hostess.

Julia was working on soups and then testing Simca's recipes for sauces.
She consulted the authorities (remembering Bugnard's method or Thillmont's
method or looking up Escoffier); experimented with the ingredients (butter
versus oil), with procedures (mixing at the table, cooking a dish ahead of time,
cutting down on the milk in Simca's recipe for *sauce à l'ail);* fine-tuned the
language, what Louisette called the "blah-blah" ("holding pan of boiling butter in left hand, wire whip in right hand, *pour . . .");* and tested equipment
(the pressure cooker did not prove satisfactory for soups). "What minute
checking we must do!" she informed Simca. "We must always remember that
we are writing for an audience that knows nothing about French cooking."

Julia's peculiar responsibility was to translate the book into the American language—a challenge because in the United States there was no culinary
vocabulary as there was in France. The name of recipes were in French, but
the directions had to be in English. Julia would explain to Simca that "stale"
meant leftover; "broken eggs" meant something other than to break an egg;

"into" meant closed up inside. Yet when it came to recipe decisions, she insisted (October 25, 1953) that the book "is most definitely a joint book" on which "we all three must absolutely agree on all points. . . . It is rather like Existentialism, I suppose, in that we alone are responsible for how this book turns out." She also suggested, and DeVoto agreed, that the ingredients be printed on the left, the method on the right.

"Julia is woodpeckering the Royal Portable right next to me, jiggling the table like a tumbrel on cobbles," Paul complained to his brother. When she was not shopping and laboring over the stove, she was typing single-spaced letters of several pages (she was their official typist) and five or six carbon copies of each recipe. "The most difficult part of the cookbook was writing all those letters," she said later. "Then correcting those six copies. It was terrible, just awful." (Yet their transfer to Marseilles, which necessitated voluminous correspondence, provides the culinary historian a unique opportunity to study the development of a classic cookbook collaboration.) She used up boxes of onionskin and carbon paper, for she often (but not always) sent copies of letters to Louisette as well. The recipes called for multiple copies because she was having Avis DeVoto in Cambridge, Katy Gates in Pasadena, Freddie (and niece Rachel) in Lumberville—her "guinea pigs"—cook the recipes and report every detail of success and failure. The typewriter and the stove were her daily instruments. But neither were built to her height, perhaps contributing to her stooped back in years to come.

In all things, Julia was a consummate professional. She informed her partners that they must not put their names on any recipe (these were French classics). She consulted them on every matter of business ("We are a team!"). She was the go-between with DeVoto (their unpaid agent) and the Houghton Mifflin editor, Mrs. Dorothy de Santillana, who was happily "overcome" (according to Avis) when she first saw their manuscript. Julia distributed to Simca and Louisette the contracts and composed biographies for their approval. (Houghton Mifflin insisted on dealing only with Julia.) It was Paul's nephew, Paul Sheeline, who would iron out the contract with Houghton Mifflin. Julia arranged with Waring Blender to get a discount and free cookbooks for their blenders. Because she had a small income of her own, she became the cooking trio's banker and paid for expenses that seemed necessary (they were to reimburse her from future royalties), including their membership in the order of Tastevins, a famous old wine-tasting society in Burgundy (they traveled to Dijon for the annual Tastevin dinner in November). She called the bank account the "Child French Cookbook Banking Fund."

She insisted that they be as accomplished as possible, using *Gourmet,* certain self-proclaimed "experts," and some of the French chefs' cookbooks

("La Fumisterie" [fakery]) as contrasts: "In other words, we must be Descartesian, and never accept anything unless it comes from an extremely professional [French] source, and even then, to see how we personally like how it is done," she wrote Simca on November 5, 1953. To be absolutely accurate on ingredients, she persuaded Paul to give her *Larousse Agricole* for her birthday. "If we depart from the French tradition to cater to American tastes, or to our personal tastes," she told Simca, "we must always so indicate."

Julia had the classic French cookbooks, such as Escoffier, on hand for constant reference. But from a simple regional recipe book such as *La Bonne Cuisine du Périgord* to the works of Escoffier, recipes were too brief and general for her ("place casserole on a moderate fire" or "add a soupspoon of shallots"). She quickly noted that they "all copy from one another." She kept up with current reading, noting in her letters that a new review, *Gastronomie le Neuvième Art,* quoted "those two boys," Brillat-Savarin and Grimod de La Reynière, on every other page. She half agreed with Baudelaire that Brillat-Savarin was "a kind of old brioche whose sole use is to furnish windbags with stupid quotations [tell me what you eat and I'll tell you what you are]."

Because they were virtual newcomers to Marseilles, visits from dear friends were important. The Nigel Bicknells, now living in Istanbul, came by with their two children. The Childs visited Dick and Alice Lee Myers several times in nearby Cassis, once just a day after Ernest Hemingway had stopped by on his way to Africa. On a trip to Monte Carlo with the Peter Bicknells, they watched Colette being wheeled to her table near them at the Hôtel de Paris. France's famous novelist, who would be dead within months, had "an imperial look in her eye," remembered Julia, and her "gray-white hair [was] moplike and flying in its unmistakable way." Julia does not remember what Colette ate, but she herself began with consommé because she was working on that recipe at the time.

In early summer (before strikes stopped telephones, mail, newspapers, and garbage pickup), George and Betty Kubler came from their Portugal sabbatical to Marseilles to visit their old friends. Julia and Paul then joined them on a two-week trip to Spain and Portugal. Paul's photographs later accompanied Kubler's "A Yale Professor Goes to Spain and Portugal," published in the Yale alumni magazine. Paul was also taking photographs of Julia cutting up chicken and preparing vegetables. It was her idea, he told Charlie, that they be taken over her shoulder, a whole new way of documenting food preparation.

When Paul's fellow OSS photographer John Moore visited from Zurich with his wife, Hedi, Julia talked to him about illustrating their cookbook (a friend named Pierre Comte earlier tried some drawings, which did not please Julia or Paul). The line drawings were to be made from the photographs Paul had so painstakingly taken. John agreed and began working from Paul's photographs, even after they returned to Washington later that year. Less frequently than the visits of their beloved friends were the routine arrival of U.S. destroyers and aircraft carriers with their thousands of sailors and what Paul called the "protocol, stripes, basketball games, religious services," and hosting of officers—all part of Paul's duties. Less frequently came the relentless mistral winds that rattled their windows and outdoors could turn Paul's hair white with salt and trip the hem of Julia's skirt.

When Julia announced the completion of the first draft of the soups chapter, Paul noted sardonically, "That really means every part of it has been gone over twenty times." Though she did all the shopping and housework and entertained business associates, French dignitaries, and friends, she reserved part of six days a week for her work: "The Wifelet sticks to her 5-hours-a-day schedule of Cook-Book-Work," Paul frequently reported.

During a spring weekend in Paris for the semiannual Public Affairs Officers (PAO) conference, the grand banquet with Ambassador Dillon ("a highly charged ulcer-type," Paul thought) coincided with general strikes that crippled the city's transportation system. Julia walked (with her shoes in her hand) to the American National Ballet performance at the Palais de Chaillot and then all the way to the Dillons' ambassadorial residence. We are no longer Parisians, Julia informed Simca upon their return to Marseilles. Clearly she missed cooking in the kitchen with Simca, a regret that echoes in her letters.

When the original owner of the Childs' Old Port apartment returned that winter, Julia and Paul had to find another home. They moved up the hill above their first apartment to a broad, tree-lined street. Number 113, Boulevard de la Corderie offered them north and south balconies and a spectacular seventh-floor view of the harbor and Fort St.-Nicolas. They could see, a few miles off the coast, the infamous Château d'If, where Alexandre Dumas's Count of Monte Cristo was falsely imprisoned on spy charges. The extra rooms and space allowed them to get the other half of their possessions out of storage. Julia used the dining room as her workroom. The kitchen workroom, as usual, was not made to accommodate Julia's height. As was her custom, she "hung everything in sight." "If we ever get into the money," she told Avis, "I am going to have a kitchen where everything is my height, and none of this pigmy stuff, and maybe 4 ovens, and 12 burners all in a line, and 3 broilers . . ." Though the building was poorly built with noise echoing from neighboring apartments, she informed friends that it was "a nifty little apartment with balconies and a view of the sea"; repairs went on for months.

Their first winter in Marseilles, Hill the Pill left the consulate, and morale changed overnight. Clifton Wharton, who was to become the first American Negro career ambassador, was accessible and enthusiastic about his work and interested in other people. Paul thought he was a "wonderful guy." Julia and Paul immediately became friends with Clifford and Leonie Wharton, who frequently dined at their apartment and lived not far away at 335 Promenade de la Corniche. ("Hope Big John doesn't ever meet him!" she confided in Dorothy, referring to their father.) Later, Julia and Simca, who was visiting for the week, prepared *boeuf bourguignon* for a beautiful birthday party for twelve in honor of Cliff Wharton.

Inspired in part by Henry Miller's *The Colossus of Maroussi,* as well as by the opportunity to travel with Peter and Mari Bicknell, Julia and Paul spent Christmas and New Year's in Greece. They stopped in Venice on the way and Paul took photographs for a painting of canals he would create.

For another year Julia typed the results of her recipe experiments and the cross-testing of Simca's recipes on pounds of onionskin paper. She finished her egg chapter early in 1954. When Avis DeVoto received a copy of the egg chapter, she was "absolutely overwhelmed" by the amount of work, found that it read "like a novel," and claimed "famous professionals like Dione Lucas would be green with envy."

While Simca tested meat recipes, Julia began testing Simca's chicken recipes and researching the raising and cooking of chickens (consulting, among others, Madame Saint-Ange's method for *poulet en cocotte*—cooking the potatoes before putting them in the hot fat). "There is a fine old girl," Julia said to Simca two years later about her growing appreciation of Madame Saint-Ange. With the research and typing and housekeeping (she missed Jeanne, her Paris *femme de ménage),* Julia had little time for reading the remaining Balzac volumes. Certainly Proust would have to "wait for some long prison term" or illness ("I have never gotten beyond the church steeple and the cup of tea in *Swann's Way,"* she confessed). When she read a biography of Florence Nightingale, she thought her speed and stamina for work paralleled Simca's. Julia did keep up with *Gourmet,* for her research; finding errors there reassured her of the need for accuracy in their own recipes and testing.

When each chapter was ready to be shown to Dorothy de Santillana, Julia mailed it and awaited the response. Their editor wanted less cross-referencing and more discussion of the use of frozen and canned produce—disheartening news, but they tried to comply. Simca experimented with canned consommé and clams. Julia cautioned against using a lot of truffles and foie gras because "Americans are not used to spending as much money on food as the French are, as food is not as important."

Julia's contribution to what was now being called *French Cooking in the American Kitchen* is clearly revealed in the massive correspondence with Simca. One sees the endless testing, arguing over techniques, hammering out of language, and thousands of hours of typing that went into this masterpiece. Julia's observations and opinions vacillated between two occasionally contradictory goals: making the recipes practical for the American cook and representing the true and historic recipes and techniques of classic French cooking.

On the practical side, Julia informed Simca that a recipe was "too rich for Americans," that certain food products or utensils were not available in the United States (no conical *chinois* (sieve); the lack of mortar and pestle necessitated a blender for quenelles). She had Avis send her shallots to compare with the French onion and bottled herbs to test in recipes. When *Time* magazine talked about a new tenderizer, she sent for some. She insisted that the readers be able to "adapt the recipe" to their available produce, "or they will find our recipes useless." Occasionally she reminded the three of them not to become too encyclopedic: this is "a cookbook for the average cook." Yet it was she who always asked the detailed questions: why indeed should one hang birds by the head and animals by the feet? Why clean some and not others? They did not want to frighten the reading cooks with lengthy recipes, yet they wanted their recipes to be foolproof. She omitted the *oeufs filés* (an egg drop consommé), complicated and not pretty, concluding, "Just because Escoffier and the other boys include it, is no reason why we have to!"

On the side of idealism and the integrity of French cooking, Julia insisted, "We must be French!" (July 6, 1953). "But that is not French, is it!" she exclaimed the following October. "This must always be Frenchy French, though practical for US." After insisting that they incorporate a candy thermometer "because it is standard equipment in the USA," she adds that the "Thillmont method must also be included." She told Simca, "Thank heaven we both agree on the effort to reach perfection, by the road of 'scientific method.'"

When the Pasadena testers complained about the pedantic tone of her typewritten instructions, Julia insisted on keeping to the "classical tradition" of French cooking, suggesting that the United States might be the final preserve. She did admit, "I find it is very difficult to shorten up an explanation, yet give every step that is necessary for its successful making." The effect on Paul of all this experimenting was what he called "Julie's Law," which meant "my critical faculties concerned with food are becoming elevated to the point where other people's meals often seem banal."

One theme in Julia's letters to Simca that is interesting in light of her future fame on television was her insistence that they perfect their knife filleting skills so they could demonstrate their savoir faire. "Always pretend we are cooking in front of an audience," she wrote Simca on May 7, 1954, "that will help us to discipline ourselves. I don't expect we will ever appear on television, but possibly we will give demonstrations if we are successful."

*I*N SEARCH OF
THE PERFECT BOUILLABAISSE

From her first week in Marseilles, Julia was interested in experimenting on the great fish soup called bouillabaisse and with the Provençal sauces based on oil, tomatoes, onions, garlic, and herbs, so unlike Paris's butter, flour, and cream. "To choose bouillabaisse as a theme," said Raymond Oliver in his great history of gastronomy, in which he gives it an entire chapter, "is to select the most vibrant and passionate . . . dish which in itself represents a whole region and its deepest motivations and symbols."

Specifically, Julia was interested in *bouillabaisse à la Marseillaise,* made with mullet, gurnard, sea eel, rascasse, and bream, all laced with olive oil and garlic-heavy rouille. She began research (which she delighted in doing) to find similar American fish ("California Rock Cod or Rockfish looks just like Rascasse," she insisted confidentially to Simca). She sent her bisque recipes to her niece Rachel Child, who was cooking in Maine, and Rachel sent them back with comments. At the fish market Julia frequently inquired about *"la vraie bouillabaisse,"* receiving dogmatic but conflicting advice as to the true ingredients: one said absolutely no tomatoes, one said saffron, another no saffron. Julia, who had read every French food history and classic recipe book, became "irked" at their dogmatism and occasional ignorance. "Balls," she replied in private. But she confided in Avis: "I don't say anything, as, being a foreigner, I don't know anything anyway."

She began her own "bouilla-ing" in July 1953 by making *bouillabaisse borgno* (with saffron flowers, fennel, bay, and thyme) for lunch and decided not to strain it because she liked to see the vegetables (onion, leek, potatoes) floating; another time she put it through the food mill to thicken it; tried it with and without potatoes; insisted that though it was a main dish, it should be placed in their book with the soups; in September 1953 she cut lobsters and crabs into pieces before cooking them so they would take up less room and make final serving easier. Each variation was reported to Simca and, occasionally, Louisette.

Julia's relationship to Louisette was always cordial and loyal, but Louisette did not share the intense professional commitment Julia had with Simca ("We have both worked like dogs"). Louisette contributed the extra touches (adding fresh peas or strips of fresh tomato pulp to a soup), novelties in *"l'esprit américain."* "You and I," Julia informed Simca, "are more straight chef-type cooks, I think." Louisette's letters are always loving, concerned about Paul's happiness. The correspondence among the three women reveals that Louisette's contribution was comparatively negligible and that they did not believe she knew as much about cooking as they. Julia suggested to Simca that they write a contract among the three of them because "you and I do not want to be allied always to L, I don't think."

Paul confided to Charlie that "for the sake of good working relations everyone must maintain the fiction that there are three authors, sharing equally in the work, the knowledge and the drudgery." By the next year, Julia wrote to Simca, "I have a strong feeling that this book we are doing is not at all the kind of book that is her [Louisette's] meat. I think she is temperamentally suited to a gay little book, like *What's Cooking,* with chic little recipes and *tours de main,* and a bit of poesy, and romanticism. The kind of recipes in *Vogue, Harper's Bazaar,* and the smart magazines." However, she believed that Louisette would be "wonderful, the cute, darling little Frenchwoman" who looks like "everyone's dream of the perfect Frenchwoman" and sees her on the American cooking circuit, "even going on television." When Simca agreed with her about "our dear Louisette," Julia shrewdly pointed out that "she has all those women's club connections," which "will be very useful" to their book. The women's clubs do indeed "represent the mass market."

When Louisette expressed her regret that she was not contributing as much work as her partners, Julia wrote an understanding letter in March about Louisette's family and social demands and suggested that her contribution would be a careful review of the manuscript, some suggestions for nice touches, and connections to women's clubs, their potential mass market ("Get hold of a mailing list from them"). When Julia and Simca finished the chicken recipes, Julia suggested that Louisette could write the list of suggestions for accompanying vegetables, which she did.

The new year brought numerous upheavals. The most dramatic was the birth of Julia's nephew. After a critical period in which the doctors believed that the baby would be lost, Sam was born two months early at three pounds—"No bigger than a fine roasting chicken? Ye gods," gasped Julia.

Then came the news that Paul and Julia would have to leave France because the government decreed that diplomats could stay no more than four years in one country; they had been in France for more than five. Julia and Paul learned late in March that they would be transferred later in the year, though they were not told where. Soon they suspected Bonn, which did not please them. After living on the Mediterranean, Julia and Paul's compass turned southward. Thus, when asked on their annual government form to express their future interests, they said they wanted to learn Spanish and go to Spain.

The good news this spring was the arrival, after much delay, of their contract with Houghton Mifflin. The contract was dated June 1, 1954; they would receive $750 as an advance against royalties, to be paid in three installments of $250. Paul's nephew Paul Sheeline, acting as agent, declined the legal fee, suggesting that his aunt and uncle could buy something for his house worth $50. "If you become famous and on TV and another Dione Lucas and need a lawyer," he added, "my firm, Sullivan and Cromwell, will be glad to represent you," he wrote in March.

Riding high with her contract, Julia accompanied Paul to a five-day PAO conference at the American Embassy in Paris. During her stay she cooked with Simca, dined with chefs Bugnard and Thillmont at Louisette's home, and visited other friends. The chestnut buds were ripe and ready to burst on the trees lining the Seine in Paris. While in Paris they learned they would be transferred to Bonn, a place "terribly GI," Julia reported to Dort: "I had enough of that meat-ballery during the war to last me a lifetime." She added a note of fear to her sister: "After the events of the last few years, I have entirely lost that nobility and esprit de corps. I feel, actually, that at any moment we may be accused of being Communists and traitors." Every month there was news of a China associate losing his job.

Paul hated to think of leaving Marseilles: "This is hard on Julie's Bookery. Just *Hellishly* hard. Every time she just gets settled-in, establishes a time-schedule, gets her pots and knives and spoons hanging, Wham!" Paul wrote her a "Nostalgic Folk Song" a decade later that began—

Carry us, Bach, to old Parigi,
Là où le Métro et Les
Halles sont toujours beaux!

Leaving France was also "painful" for Paul, who had spent eleven years of his life in that country. During April and May, before they began their packing, Julia experimented with rabbit, *pâte brisée, gratin dauphinois,* pork, and quenelles.

Before they were to report to Bonn, Julia and Paul were required to return to the United States for a sabbatical. They had a farewell dinner with Guido, and the Whartons gave them a grand final party. Months before, Julia confided to Freddie that she had "a terrible wave of homesickness for real and life-long friends, and the USA." She blamed it on the fact that they had not made many intimate friends in Marseilles.

They saw their most intimate friends during a week's stopover in Paris, having their last bouillabaisse, dining with Simca and Jean Fischbacher one evening and at the Baltrusaitis apartment the last night before the boat train. They sailed on June 18, 1954, and arrived in New York Harbor on the seventeenth. Charlie and Freddie Child met them at the dock.

Julia's request was for a lunch of "US steak first thing" (it was the only dish the French could not match). According to her datebook, she found New York City "loud, fast, hot, mechanical." Julia and Paul picked up their new Chevy and reported to Washington for a week. For their official holiday they visited the Sheelines in New York City as well as other friends and family before driving to Boston. When they finally drove up to 8 Berkeley Street in Cambridge to meet face to face with Avis and Bernard DeVoto, their book's godmother and *Harper's* "Easy Chair" columnist already seemed like "old friends." When Julia said that she wanted "one of those martinis I've been reading about" (his famous *Harper's* article on the dry martini was collected in *The Hour,* 1951), Bernard was smitten. Like Julia, he was a Westerner (Utah) and a "Populist . . . an honorable word," wrote his friend and neighbor Arthur Schlesinger, Jr. Julia and Paul also had fish and Chablis at Locke-Ober and visited with May Sarton, Edith Kennedy's longtime friend, and Edith's sons. Julia concluded that Boston was "civilized," with an "English feeling of old houses and tradition."

It was a long train ride to San Francisco, where they stayed with Dorothy and Ivan and met baby Sam and his sister Phila. Julia visited the new, large supermarkets with Dort, impressed with the changes in American consumer products, television, and chlorophyll toothpaste. And finally, after much dreading by Paul since John McWilliams's letter accusing them of aiding the "communist" agenda, they spent eight days with Julia's father and Phila in Pasadena. Dorothy warned them that their father believed "McCarthy was a victim of an international Jewish plot in which Cohn and Shine are the bad ones." Julia believed her father was "horrid" to Paul, avoiding whenever possible even addressing him by name. "It was a Westbrook Pegler atmosphere," she confided in Dort.

They returned to the East Coast and the Child family vacation house in Maine. On the cool cliff over the ocean, they celebrated Julia's forty-second

birthday and then enjoyed two and a half weeks of continuous lobster prepared in every form, hot and cold. There were many visits from old friends
and picnics with the Walter Lippmanns (who owned a nearby home). And, as
usual after his visits with Charlie, Paul fretted about the twin bond during a
final stop in Cambridge, where Julia and Avis finally met with Dorothy de
Santillana, the editor who had signed them up with Houghton Mifflin.

During this visit to the United States, Julia investigated everything from
cream and butter to meat thermometers, constantly noting changes in lifestyle.
Americans were now more informal, people were eating more frozen food,
wine was still not a national drink, and chickens differed, even between Massachusetts and Maine. Though she told Simca she would avoid "cooking experts" in New York City until their book was done ("They are a close and
gossipy and jealous little group"), she did visit the kitchen of the A&P's
Woman's Day.

In mid-September, they returned to Washington for less than a month of
German study. In her datebook, under a list of people to see in Washington,
she noted one couple and beside their names wrote "Democrats, Secretariat,
good taste, intelligence. Eat and Talk." All values she and Paul cherished.
Then, on October 15 they sailed for Paris, crossing the Belgian border to
Germany on the twenty-third. The following month, unbeknownst to them,
Jane Foster would have her passport confiscated, beginning a chain of events
that would shake their world.

Chapter 13

A LITTLE TOWN IN GERMANY (1954 – 1956)

"It is such fun, this work of ours."
JULIA CHILD *to Simone Beck,*
December 3, 1954

~

"WOE—HOW DID WE get here!" Julia wrote in her datebook for October 24, 1954, the day they arrived in Bad Godesberg, Germany. They would spend two years here, learning the rudiments of the language, searching (in vain) for good restaurants, and going to Paris as frequently as possible for Julia to work with her collaborator. Though this was Paul's most important government assignment, far surpassing his job in Marseilles (he was now in charge of exhibits for all of Germany), it would be their unhappiest assignment.

GOLDEN GHETTO ON THE RHINE

Upon arrival Julia called their home in Plittersdorf on the Rhine "a housing project." A year later she called it a "dump." There was no denying that Apartment 5 at 3 Steubenring was modern, sterile, and efficient—without any of the charm or character of the German country itself. The inhabitants called it the "Golden Ghetto on the Rhine," according to Lyne Few (a colleague in Düsseldorf), or "Westchester-on-the-Rhine," according to Lee Fairley, who served here, as he had in Paris, as Assistant Cultural Officer.

Despite the military living environment, Julia immediately learned to love walking along the western bank of the mighty Rhine River. Still, Paul was ill at ease in an environment emphasizing weekly car washings, football scores, and drunkenness. Postwar Germany, not surprisingly, had the largest concentration of American military in Europe. There were 250,000 soldiers in this country alone, without counting support staff. Thus, the role of the USIA was the most vital one in Europe. But Julia and Paul valued quality of life above job status:

> It was a terrible place because we did not like living in the military housing. The town housed mostly the military who really did not want to be there anyway and did not take any interest in the language or the people. We resented living in that kind of environment. We wanted to live with the Germans. If we had lived in the city and on the economy I would have been very happy.

"I feel we are on the moon," she told Simca, and immediately threw herself into the poultry chapter of her book, testing the meat recipes Simca sent, and learning the language.

She began classes in German at the local university, telling Simca that "to function at all properly as a cuisinière, I must absolutely learn the language. Without it, one is too cut off." Later she said, "I went to the university, but it takes more than two years to learn a language." As she and Paul shopped, patronized restaurants, and visited the sights, they used their dictionaries as much as possible. Few Americans tried to learn any German or take part in the community, but the Childs were different. Within a year Julia was understanding the language and communicating, but Paul did not have her marketing practice or her sense of freedom to make mistakes and thus never learned the language well enough: "Paul just doesn't like Germany, really, and he gets furious because he can't speak German," she confided to Simca the following July.

Plittersdorf was the riverside suburb of Bad Godesberg, a town just south of Bonn (now a suburb of Bonn). Julia soon realized that this province of North Rhine-Westphalia was a vital region of what was now the strongest country in Europe. Germany was broken in 1945, its cities in rubble and its bridges blasted, but now with massive Marshall Plan dollars it was booming, exporting resources and goods worth four and a half billion dollars a year. The occupation of Allied forces (under High Commissioner James B. Conant) would soon be dismantled. All this industry was thriving north in Cologne and in the Ruhr Valley or southeast in Frankfurt.

Bonn itself, though now the capital city, was relatively untouched by the bombing and had been the least Nazified. Yellow trolley cars rolled along cobblestone streets lined with trees. Famous as the birthplace of Beethoven, Bonn was once a sleepy university town "snuggled along the curve of the Rhine," said Theodore White, "just across the river from the murky hills where Siegfried slew his dragon." White compares the city to the university town of Cambridge, Massachusetts, fifty years before, a city where Paul and Julia would eventually settle. The gold, red, and black flag of the German Republic snapped in the wind above the government building where Chancellor Konrad Adenauer presided (White in 1949 had called him "a wrinkled mummy breaking into voice"). Compared with Berlin, this city was tranquil and placid, which is why Julia and Paul would have preferred to live there rather than in Plittersdorf had they the choice.

Among the hard-drinking Americans and what White called the "dull, dreary, plodding men of Germany," Paul found few kindred spirits. One of Paul's assistants, a German national named Freifrau Dorothea von Stetten, remembers Paul's "gentle personality, his fairness and his quest for excellence." He was "very sincere and totally unbureaucratic," she adds, and when events at the office became difficult, he would take her home for Julia's dinner and a dose of "the sincerity and warmth which surrounded me in their home." She eagerly read each copy of *The New Yorker* when they finished it (they continued a subscription in her name when they left the country).

*T*HANK HEAVENS FOR THE BOOK

"Thank heavens for the book," Julia would say later about their years in Germany. At the end of the second week in Plittersdorf, they returned to Paris to see about their furniture and to work with Julia's collaborators. On their way to Bonn, they had stopped in Paris and dined with the Fischbachers and Bertholles. This time they began with breakfast at Deux Magots, lunch at Le Grand Véfour, cocktails with the Walter Lippmanns, and dinner at La Grille. Just like old times. Julia attended one of their school's cooking classes, conducted by Thillmont, and spent the entire next day with Simca in Neuilly, working on the organization of the book and discussing the letter to Louisette that Julia drafted and Simca approved. "We must be cold-blooded," Julia told Simca, ". . . I shall love her more once we get this settled."

"Dear Louisette," Julia wrote, explaining that after months of working together and seeing "how we actually do function," and after hearing from her that she "cannot put in the 40-hours a week that Simca and I can," they wished to reassign duties and designations. Because the book would take another year and a half at least, and the "major responsibility for the book rests on Simca and me," they wished to be known hereafter as "Co-Authors." For her editorial criticism, ideas, and public relations, Louisette would be called "Consultant." These titles, they said, in fact described how they were collaborating. Louisette's responsibilities were clearly listed and amounted to three hours in the cooking school and six hours on research and kitchen work a week. The letter, postmarked November 19, 1954, praised Louisette's gifts and her contribution.

Julia and Simca listed their own responsibilities, suggesting that the book be entitled *"French Cooking in the American Kitchen* by Simone Beck and Julia Child with Louisette Bertholle," and stating a "fair split" of 10 percent for Louisette and 45 percent each for Simca and Julia. They long knew that Louisette had, in Julia's words, "gotten mixed up in a type of Magnum Opus" that was not to her taste. By mid-December, Julia informed her lawyer and nephew Paul Sheeline that they were probably stuck with the three authors' names as listed in the Houghton Mifflin contract, but confided to Simca that "it is bad for the book for her to present herself as Author, as she really does not cook well enough, or know enough, and it is not good publicity." The final arrangement on the cookbook came sometime later, and was a distribution of royalties with Louisette receiving 18 percent and Simca and Julia each 41 percent. This agreement was clear and mutually agreed to years before the publication of the book, which carried all three of their names in alphabetical order. As far as the world knew, they were equal authors. Their private royalty agreement reflected the reality.

Snow-covered blocks of ice were floating down the Rhine in early spring when Julia moved into high gear on the poultry chapter (including some recipes that Simca had done two years before). It was a chapter Julia would work on all year. The chapters on soups, sauces, and eggs were finished. They thought they were almost done with the fish chapter, but would still be working on it in 1956. Simca was writing up the meats and sending them to Julia. Because Avis asked about *pommes de terre duchesse,* Julia spent one week cooking a different recipe each day (this pureed and molded potato dish would not appear until their second book). In January, Julia made chicken casserole several ways and *poulet farci au gros sel* (they finally chose a chicken stuffed with mushrooms); in February *poulet grillé à la diabolique* (broiled chicken with mustard, herbs, and bread crumbs); and in March several others of the more than two hundred possible chicken recipes *Larousse Gastronomique* listed.

They chose recipes for several reasons, primarily because a recipe was a traditional French dish. But they also considered its usability in the United States (where some ingredients were not available, and no one had a duck press), and its flexibility, meaning its potential for using several other ingredients to make another dish. In other words, they attempted to have a recipe for each method. For example, for sautéed chicken they included crisp, simmered, and fricasséed.

Julia and Simca took nothing for granted, checking every detail themselves. They consulted Carême, Larousse, Ali-Bab, Madame Saint-Ange, and lesser known great French cookbook authors—all of whom present their classical dishes in more or less summary fashion. "Mme Saint-Ange," Julia said, "is an inspiration." She thought *Good Housekeeping* "dull" whenever she looked at it, and *Gourmet* inaccurate: "I prefer Mrs. Joy *[The Joy of Cooking]* . . . and I love Saint-Ange. Ours must be the best of all!" For the availability and measurement of produce in the United States, Julia wrote to organizations such as the National Turkey Foundation and the U.S. Department of Agriculture.

For this cooking Julia had to use electric burners, which she loathed because the heat was so hard to control ("but I am learning its problems"). Each chicken dish and several meat dishes appeared at the dinners Julia and Paul held for new friends. Julia and Simca wrote each other about every detail of ingredient and language. They already knew each other's quirks, such as Julia's dislike of tomato sauce, especially with beef or chicken, and Simca's hatred of turnips, which Julia loved.

She and Simca now expected to spend two more years completing their book. They appear not to have taken notice of the appearance of *The Alice B. Toklas Cookbook,* published in 1954 in London. A collection of memoirs and largely untested recipes by the charming seventy-seven-year-old companion of Gertrude Stein, it was not in their league. Alice was a Sunday and holiday cook, and her book had celebrity appeal (custard Josephine Baker) and recipes that called for canned soup. She was scandalized when she discovered one recipe submitted by a friend included hashish in the cookie dough and succeeded in having it eliminated from the American edition of her book.

They took more seriously Sadie Summers's *American Cooking dans la Cuisine* (1954), a book in two languages for the overseas American and her French cook, because it contained an equivalents chart; but they needn't have worried, for its focus audience was narrow. Julia was concerned briefly the following March with a new series of *grande cuisine* dishes by Diat in *Gourmet* magazine. Another American who was working on a food book was Waverley Root, then living in The Hague and editing Fodor travel guides. His *The Food of France,* a regional history, would appear in 1958.

Food for the American enclave in Plittersdorf was provided by a modern American grocery store, full of all the most recent canned and frozen food. Julia missed the regional markets, but consoled herself with the idea that she needed to know all these products to be aware of what American women were buying in supermarkets. Their cookbook would have to accommodate itself to the food available in the United States, just as Julia was cooking Simca's recipes with frozen chicken from the commissary on her American electric stove. For this reason, Julia constructed a table of American poultry names and their French equivalent to open their chapter (a stewing chicken is a *poule de l'année*).

Julia learned about meats while in Germany. When she later mentioned the food of Germany, she said, "We had venison and lots of potatoes." Another time she said the food was "interesting, with wonderful lamb and pork and sausages." She told Simca she was safest in ordering well-known dishes such as sauerkraut, sausage, smoked pork, and beer. And she delighted in buying the large, heavy mixers and grinders sold in Germany (for a cooking performance with Jacques Pépin in 1996, she brought out a huge potato ricer from Germany that was a hit with the audience). When May arrived it was asparagus time, thick white juicy asparagus. She was also taken with the mushrooms, and told Simca and Louisette about the girolles, cèpes, and morels growing in the German forests. What should they do about such mushrooms in the book, when Americans cannot find them in their markets?

The Childs' holiday celebrations this first winter were hardly worth mentioning, except for the frozen turkey from the PX, which Julia called a Turkey Fiasco Dinner for six people. There was a Wassail party on Christmas night, and a dull New Year's Eve. "So many US army [are] depressing," Julia wrote in her datebook for January 2. "But I got quite a bit of working and cooking in, so it was not wasted!" she told Simca. Julia planned weekend trips to distract Paul, including a brief one to Nuremberg on the first weekend of the year. Six months later, after many more German lessons, Julia informed Louisette:

Although I continue to dislike Les Tristes Lieux de Plittersdorf, every time I get out of it to market, or something, I am quite happy. Paul just doesn't like it here at all, and has a blockage against the language . . . *il est trop français!* I, as seems to be my habit, am "adapting" quite well, and can get around fairly decently with the language. But I wish we were in Munich or Berlin, where there was a bit of civilization. . . . I am not a country girl!

As if to revolt against the German austerity and repression, Paul designed their Valentine's card for 1955 with a naked man and woman (her nipples carefully dotted) pulling on each end of an arrow threaded through a heart with their names on it. It was a saucy and sophisticated scene amid floating hearts encircled by a continuous scroll of the word *liebenswürdig* (lovable). Many of their friends framed Paul's annual work of art.

They spent weeks painting the hearts red, as they did every year to add a splash of color, and the individual messages were upbeat. "We are struggling to learn the language, which just bristles with grammar," Julia told her old Smith friend Ellie (and Basil Summers). To Hadley and Paul Mowrer she wrote, "We shall never be so comfortably housed. Everything works, all is clean and utterly convenient. Only thing we lack is Germans! But we are not glued here by any means and have already made quite a few trips."

Indeed, Paul and Julia explored the country, and "what a vigorous bustling country this is—we'd better keep it on our side!" Julia told Hadley. During their two years there they visited the cities along the castle-lined gorge of the Rhine: Düsseldorf and Cologne to the north of Bonn; Mainz to the south; and beyond Mainz, Heidelberg, Frankfurt (a two-and-a-half-hour drive), and Nuremberg. They also visited the large cities in the north of Germany: Bremen, Hamburg, and, on numerous occasions, Berlin (they found a good Chinese restaurant there). They went as far east as Dresden (in 1956) and as far south as Munich in Bavaria. Because they were in West Germany, which bordered the Netherlands, Belgium, Luxembourg, France, and Switzerland, they visited the major cities in each, most frequently Amsterdam, Antwerp ("fried potatoes everywhere—smell," Julia wrote in her datebook), Brussels (once with Lee Fairley and his wife and several times to see Abe and Rosemary Manell), Strasbourg, Basel, and Geneva. Fairley remembered that Paul "kept meticulous notes on the wine." The last city visit was for Paul's exhibit on the peacetime uses of atomic energy, which President Eisenhower attended.

Part of their explorations included studying German wine. They visited the winemaker of Niersteiner Domtal, one of Paul's favorites. In 1976, Paul would proudly show off his collection of Rhine and Mosel wines to *New York Times* wine critic Frank J. Prial.

Their tour of duty coincided with their desire to travel and explore. Paul, as Exhibits Officer of Germany, was visiting each of the Amerika Häuser, the U.S. cultural centers. Julia found most of the diplomatic dinners "boring," but she loved walking through the cities with Paul, always checking out the local produce and cuisine. In her datebooks during these years, she listed restaurants, particularly in Brussels, Berlin, Düsseldorf, and Frankfurt, and wrote Ollie Noall, an early friend of Paul, "We spent the entire two years looking for a good French restaurant."

Julia's favorite trip was back to Paris and work with Simca. "Simca [is] an incarnate French driver," Julia wrote in her datebook during a second visit to Paris. They were visiting Curnonsky, shopping at Dehillerin for pots and pans, and cooking together. While Julia was there, Louisette signed their new agreement.

KAFKA MEETS McCARTHY

When Paul was suddenly called back to Washington, DC, he and Julia assumed that after years of working at foreign service rank four (sometimes without diplomatic status), he was being promoted at last. Paul did not like the people he was working with in Germany, in part because of the military environment (the diplomatic corps always looked down on the military) and in part because one of the heads of the outfit and his wife were alcoholics. "It is terrible to be with people who are uninspired," Julia later explained. "We did not admire them." There were exceptions, of course, but morale was not high and Paul's immediate boss was called "Woodenhead," with his assistant known as "Woodenhead the Second."

Paul was informed on Thursday, April 7, 1955, to report to Washington the next Monday. Julia and the Manells, who had come from Brussels for a visit, drove Paul to the airport in Düsseldorf on Sunday. Julia was full of anticipation: "I was sure he was going to be made head of the department." Next day she attended the reception for High Commissioner Conant with a sense of pride in her husband.

"Situation confused," Paul telegraphed from Washington, DC, his first day there. As if in a modern reenactment of Kafka's novel *The Trial,* Paul sat outside one office after another waiting for various people to return. No one he talked to knew anything of why he was there. Each person with whom he discussed his situation (and he had friends in high places) suggested several possible reasons for his return, most of which involved new assignments or promotions (he eventually compiled a list of ten possibilities). He wrote to Julia suggesting she put off her trip to Paris because she might need to come home. When a man named Parker May told him he was "not allowed to" say anything, but the wait "was in [Paul's] own interest," he telegraphed Julia: "situation here like Kafka story I believe I am to [be] in same situation as [Rennie] Leonard." Suddenly, Julia understood. "Paul is being *investigated!*" she wrote in her datebook on April 13, terrified of everything from Paul's being fired to his being arrested. Immediately she consulted their trusted friends, talking that very night to foreign service officer James McDonald until four in the morning.

Paul was called into the Office of Security for the USIA and relentlessly interrogated the rest of the day and evening by Special Agents Sullivan and Sanders, "McLeod's Boys," he called them. R. W. (Scott) McLeod, whose mentor was J. Edgar Hoover, was a former FBI official whom Hoover had placed in the Department of State when Eisenhower became President in 1953. McLeod headed the Bureau of Security and Consular Affairs and essentially took over Personnel through his appointment of Ruth Shipley as head of Passports. Neither Eisenhower nor his Secretary of State, John Foster Dulles, could or would curtail the reign of terror that ensued. Shipley proudly confiscated or denied passports to any left-winger who criticized the government, from Howard Fast (novelist and biographer of Thomas Jefferson) and Paul Robeson to Dulles's sister Eleanor. In one year more than three hundred passports were taken or denied.

Sitting before McLeod's Boys that day was a foot-high dossier on Paul Child. First they grilled him for hours as to what he knew about Jane Foster, then they asked about Morris Llewelyn Cooks, an old-time liberal whose name Paul once gave as a reference. Guilt by association. They asked him "a type of question particularly embarrassing to them." In his dossier was a charge he was homosexual: "How about it?" Paul burst out laughing. "Drop your pants," they insisted. Paul got angry and refused. "Homosexuals often have wives and children," they explained. "As I have a wife but *no* children perhaps that gets me off the hook," Paul responded. Except for the bitterness of his humor, he kept cool and rational. They soon veered off to Jane Foster again, apparently judging by his response that he was not a homosexual. Because the records were "routinely destroyed" in 1986, there is no way of knowing if an informant interpreted Paul's European refinement as fey, but during McCarthy's reign, communists were frequently linked with homosexuals and aliens. McLeod was fond of saying, "I hate drunks, perverts, and commies!" But Paul called their bluff with his rhetorical logic. Eventually he charged his tormentors with handling the entire business "in an amateurish and preposterous fashion," and left believing he was cleared, "a monument of innocence."

"Investigation concluded successfully for me," he telegraphed Julia, writing her to give copies of his detailed letters to two friends and colleagues, including Joe Phillips, the Director of Public Affairs for Germany. When he demanded a written clearance, they mentioned a thirty-day period of investigation. Paul went directly to the top security official in the USIA and demanded clearance, which he received, telegraphing the news to Julia. Staying in Washington, he threw himself into securing Edward Steichen's "Family of Man" exhibit for Berlin, going to the Museum of Modern Art in New York City (where Steichen took him on a two-hour private tour). The exhibit (and the universally popular book that would follow) included five hundred photographs of faces from twenty-six countries. Paul's calm and professionalism were betrayed by a series of physical ailments and insomnia that plagued him all month. The only solace and balance he had were the letters from the woman he called "my beloved wifelet," and the knowledge that she was driving to Paris, their city, where he would eventually join her. "I can't get over how *good* I feel about your being in Paris! And I love to think of you and Bugnard working together. And you and Simca."

It was ironic that during the time Paul was suffering under accusations of treason, he was being entertained with a party honoring him in Washington by Marie Bissell, the mother of Richard Bissell, his friend and a leader in the CIA. Of course, Bissell was considered "a liberal." Hoover's witch hunt always focused on the Department of State, and recent history has uncovered the antagonism that Hoover and the FBI had for the OSS/CIA, a "secret war" that claimed a number of former OSS people as its victims. "The FBI happily assisted in the purge of CIA officers," says historian Harris Smith.

Julia, who thought the "investigation inexplicably weird," sent special delivery letters and telegrams to Paul and called on the telephone. "You are finer, better, more lovable, more attractive, deeper, nicer, nobler, cleverer, stronger and more wonderful [than other men] . . . and I am so damned lucky even to know you, much less (or more) to be married to you," she assured him. "Your lovely long letter came in this morning," he wrote back April 26, 1955, "in which you made a two-line list of superlative adjectives about your husband, which he lapped up like a cat lapping up cream, shame on the old bastard." Not only his wife was smiling on him: Paul finally received clearance for the "Family of Man" exhibit for Germany (its first European showing) and was asked by the government to go to Brussels on his way home to negotiate with the Commissioner-General for a noncommercial American exhibit in a World's Fair planned for 1958.

Though Julia and Paul would never forget the injustice of the charges leveled against Paul, the Jane Foster affair was not over. In August, when they were again in Paris sunning themselves at the Deux Magots, they encountered Jane's husband, George Zlatovsky, who told them that when Jane went to see her dying mother in San Francisco she was caught there, her passport confiscated by Ruth Shipley. Julia and Paul decided to write a letter defending their friend: "We cannot with decency turn our back on a former colleague," Julia wrote in a letter to warn her father that they might be thrown out of the government. They did not send the letter to Pop, but did write to Jane in New York City: "We really don't know anything about your political affiliations . . . but consider you our friend. And we are terribly sorry you are in this predicament." Two years before, Julia had written to Avis DeVoto wondering what she could do to fight McCarthyism: this letter was her stand. She wrote it believing they would pay the consequences. (Some of their friends, for example Budd Schulberg, who named fifteen people, did not stand by their friends and appeared as friendly witnesses before House Un-American Activities Committee.)

Jane, who suffered an emotional breakdown and was hospitalized, eventually found a good lawyer and regained her passport. She immediately sent a telegram on August 27 to the Childs saying she was safely in Paris with her husband. She followed through with a lengthy letter to "Julie and Paul" thanking them for their support and detailing her travails. Jane and George were safely in Paris in 1957 when they were indicted on five counts of spying. The United States and France did not have an extradition treaty related to espionage, so Jane held off the press behind locked doors in Paris until the charges were dropped. Julia and Paul stood by a friend they believed innocent (while holding doubts about her husband); Julia was surprised and disappointed when Jane gave up her citizenship for a French passport.

Finally, on October 25, 1955, six months after his interrogation, Paul received a letter from the Chief of the Office of Security at the USIA (Charles M. Noone) informing him that his "case had been considered . . . and a favorable decision reached." His "case" was over, but the hysteria lingered on, ensnaring other former OSS personal friends, including Duncan Lee, George Jenson, and John Paton Davies, Jr. Davies, born in China of American missionaries, was transferred to an obscure post in Peru the same month as Paul's investigation. Indeed, in his 1995 memoir, Robert McNamara charges that the "ignorance" about Southeast Asia that led up to the war in Vietnam "existed largely because the top East Asian and China experts in the State Department—John Paton Davies Jr., John Stewart Service, and John Carter Vincent—had been purged during the McCarthy hysteria of the 1950s. Without men like these to provide sophisticated, nuanced insights, we—certainly I— badly misread China's objectives and mistook its bellicose rhetoric to imply a drive for regional hegemony. We also totally underestimated the nationalist aspect of Ho Chi Minh's movement. We saw him first as a Communist and only second as a Vietnamese nationalist."

Despite Paul's exoneration, he was to witness the continuing threat of McCarthyism when exhibits were suddenly canceled because some U.S. senator objected to something trivial such as "the brother of one of the artists who once subscribed to the *New Masses*" journal. He was angry that Eisenhower did not stand up to McCarthy and was dismayed the following year when Ike, after a heart attack, announced he would run for a second term. He and Julia preferred, as they had four years before, Adlai Stevenson.

Escaping to Paris and Poultry

Loading their car with her files and a food-stained manuscript, Julia drove to Paris for a three-week working session as soon as she realized that Paul would be in Washington for a while. Their best friends were in Paris, and they supported her, as Paul's friends (including Charlie and Freddie) supported him through his ordeal in Washington. Julia expressed her anger, talking over *l'affaire* and McCarthyism with Paul's former colleague Bob Littell. She also attended the Gourmettes luncheon and the Trois Gourmandes cooking classes, cooked twice with Bugnard, and dined with the Bertholles and Fischbachers, and worked diligently with Simca in choosing, cooking, and composing the introductions and recipes for their book. Paul urged that they keep their introductions lighthearted.

Julia returned to Bonn, German lessons, and further chicken recipes. By summer she completed the section on sautéing and gave a few private cooking classes. Louisette sent her comments on the poaching and stewing sections (thirty-two pages), and Simca and Jean visited in time for the brief asparagus season. Julia and Paul celebrated Julia's forty-third birthday with a brief weekend in Paris. They had breakfast once again at the Deux Magots, visited Dehillerin's (for some knives for Avis), saw an exhibit of Picasso's work, and dined for her birthday lunch at Lapérouse, just down the street from Picasso's former studio on the rue des Grands-Augustins. Julia was disappointed in the meal of *tourte gelée* (crab) and *ris de veau braisés* (sweetbreads). Her improved recipe for the latter dish would appear in the book in progress.

With each return to Germany, she threw herself into another poultry dish each day: fricassée, sauté, and *canard à l'orange* with a disappointing sauce. "Our tenure in Cologne was all poultry," said James McDonald, who frequently dined with his wife at the Childs' home. Each of these recipes would be perfected for the book. And each one was tried by Avis DeVoto in Cambridge, as well as by Julia's other "guinea pigs." With hundreds of traditional and precisely named French recipes for chicken, duck, and goose, they would choose the recipes Julia thought most Americans could and would prepare. They already had hundreds of pages of recipes to date, far more than would eventually be included.

When she got discouraged and "beset by doubts, wishing we had been working with Escoffier for twenty years before ever undertaking such an enterprise!" she reminded herself and Simca that "then, of course, we would not have a housewife's point of view at all." "We" must do exacting experiments "to be absolutely sure of our conclusions," she told Simca in May 1954 as she tested their *pâte feuilletée* with the flour she bought in Bonn. Julia continued to experiment with her duck in orange sauce, which would be one of only three duck recipes included, each with variations. For example, *canard à l'orange* had two variations (cherries and peaches: *caneton aux cerises,* also called *caneton Montmorency,* and *caneton aux pêches).* Accompanying these recipe groups were clear and simple descriptions of how to choose, wash, disjoint, truss, or stuff poultry, how to tell when it is done, and suggestions for vegetable, sauce, and wine with each.

Julia took her manuscript and files with her during the Steichen exhibit in Berlin in September (where 30,000 people saw "The Family of Man") and in Frankfurt and Munich in November, as well as on their two-week gastronomic vacation in France in October. They drove through Colmar, Bourg-en-Bresse, and Les Baux to Marseilles, where they stayed with the Whartons, then through the wine country, where the air was filled with the work of wine presses, to a foggy Paris, for a full day of work with Simca.

While nursing Paul through nearly two months of infectious hepatitis, with his high fever and jaundice, Julia finished and sent to Simca (and Houghton Mifflin) the section on cut-up chickens, asked Louisette for vegetable suggestions, and worked up the section of recipes for *suprêmes de volaille* (skinless, boneless chicken breasts). Not surprisingly, these recipes with little fat *(pot-au-feu, poule-au-pot)* came at a time when Paul was restricted to a no-fat regime. "I find to my surprise that I can grill meats and chicken with no fat . . . I usually put in a bit of salt and lemon juice." She also learned to vary her recipes by using shallots, lemon juice, and vegetable stock. By the time Paul was able to return to work for half days in January 1956, she had completed this work. Unfortunately, they missed their second Christmas in Cambridge with the Bicknells. The day after Paul's doctor told him to go south for two weeks, he bought train tickets to Rome and Julia began her first research on cooking a goose. In Rome she had the best baby peas of her life and for the first time had the fennel bulb thinly sliced in a salad.

"Have you seen Dione Lucas's new book?" Julia asked Louisette in January. "I find it very poor in many respects . . . and it is certainly not French cooking." She told Simca *("ma plus que chère et adorable amie")* three months before that Lucas's *Meat and Poultry* was a little "sloppy" and not as detailed as theirs, but "with our snail's pace we have a chance to study our competitors." None of the Trois Gourmandes personally knew Dione Lucas, the most prominent cooking figure in New York City in the 1950s, but since 1948 she had both a cooking school and a local television cooking program. Lucas was a severe and dry English woman, but her cooking programs (her name was synonymous with omelets) hold up even today. Several people in the New York food world, including cookbook writer James Beard, questioned the validity of Lucas's claim to Cordon Bleu training, a question echoed in Julia's judgment. But her book first gave Julia and Simca the idea that they might publish their work in several volumes.

"Your old prince is but an unhappy octogenarian," Curnonsky replied to a Christmas card from the Julia. The great man had taken a terrible fall and broken several ribs. The doctors put him on a *un régime terrible* that excluded wine, salt, sauces, and cream. He had "been around too long" and was awaiting death, he said, but "with no regrets," for he had tasted the wonderful joys of life. He asked her to visit again on her next trip to Paris, for her presence would bring great joy.

Julia and Paul's most daring Valentine card was sent in 1956. Instead of an original artwork prepared months in advance and colored with a spot of red by Julia and Paul, they sent a photograph of themselves in a bubble bath with a red stamp above their heads that read: "WISH YOU WERE HERE." Their bare shoulders and upper chests showed above the bubbles. Stamped on the bubbles: "Happy Valentine's day from the heart of old downtown Plittersdorf on the Rhine." In retrospect the photograph seems an implicit retort to the special agents' earlier charges against Paul. Julia inscribed one card to an OSS friend: "Your old CBI companions in one of their more formal diplomatic moments."

Good health was very much on their minds this spring, both because of Paul's lengthy recovery from hepatitis and because Julia, at the age of forty-three, was having to deal with weight gain for the first time. Since the long and successful treatment of their amoebic dysentery in Paris, Julia had added some weight (she weighed 155 pounds, Paul 165). "My stomach keeps getting fatter and fatter . . . which is probably only the onslaught of *un certain âge*," she confided to Simca. The previous May she had five polyps removed and this April they returned, so she had a curettage (*"les malheurs d'un certain âge"*), but not without taking her duck manuscript to the hospital. "Back on the old regime," she would say about dieting at the end of a trip. After a series of articles about cancer and smoking in the *International Herald Tribune,* Julia and Paul gave up smoking. "I have always smoked too much anyway," she wrote Louisette, "but I did enjoy it so much." What began as rebellious play in a Pasadena treetop, was now to be regarded, she said with her typical strong will, "as a poison, pure and simple, not a pleasure." Their resolve would be short-lived.

During her last five months in Germany, from February to May, Julia focused on duck. While she had frequently served *caneton à l'orange* to guests, now she experimented with various techniques: boned stuffed duck, braised duck in a crust (which they eventually put with a terrine section in a cold buffet chapter), *salmis* (partially cooked duck, cut up and cooked again in sauce), and *civet* (stewed in a sauce thickened by duck blood), which did not make the cut. Her experimentation even extended to dehydrated potatoes. After turning away when she first spotted them on the commissary shelf, she bought two packages of instant potatoes and after adding butter and cream served them to Paul, who noticed nothing. Though there was no question of ever including them in their cookbook, she sent a package to Simca to get her reaction.

Articles and advertisements reinforced what Julia had noticed on her last visit to the United States: the country was in the middle of what social historian Harvey Levenstein would label "the golden age of food processing," referring specifically to frozen food, even frozen meals in restaurants. She wondered in a letter to Simca as early as March 2, 1954, if in fifty years cooking would be only a handicraft hobby such as bookbinding and hand weaving. "Too bad for our cook-book [if we] face such 'progress.'"

She was almost done with the duck portion of the poultry chapter (and was looking ahead to goose and vegetables) when they joined Avis DeVoto, whose husband, Bernard, had died the previous November, for a trip that Paul had planned to cheer her. From London, they took her to meet Peter and Mari Bicknell in Cambridge, and together they made the traditional *soufflé Grand Marnier,* drunk with Château d'Yquem '29. They then took her to Paris for a series of classes at L'Ecole des Trois Gourmandes taught by chefs Bugnard and Thillmont and a luncheon with the Gourmettes with Julia's two partners. Simca carefully planned the Paris visit to impress Avis, the "godmother" of their book. Julia made a special visit to see the ailing Curnonsky, who would die this July. When Julia and Paul took Avis to Bonn for three days, she read the manuscript (one hundred pages on poultry alone) and was slightly overwhelmed. They talked about publishing sequential volumes.

Julia, always curious about German cuisine and history, decided she would learn more about its literature by taking a course on Goethe, the national poet. She took a three-week course at the University of Bonn, wrote a paper (though "it is a bit over my head"), and passed the examination. She also had the entire university class over for a party. Paul, off planning seven international exhibits (on police work, therapy, peaceful uses of atomic energy, American painting, architecture, social work, and the Berlin industrial fair), returned to find, he wrote Charlie, "Cat's away—mice get out of hand (they begin to go intellectual)." Home in time to take her to her birthday dinner, he told her of the rumors that Washington would be asking him to return for a new assignment.

Julia and Paul entertained often, but the only lasting friendships they made in Bonn were with Lyne and Ellen Few, who were stationed in Düsseldorf ("very nice people," Julia called them at the time, "our type of people"). They were also fond of Elizabeth and James McDonald, she a sculptor and he director of the U.S. Information Center in Nuremberg and then Cologne, nearer Bonn. Julia had come to McDonald's rescue by mobilizing a half dozen women to help prepare the food for the Cologne Amerika Haus inauguration.

Not long after Julia and Paul celebrated their tenth wedding anniversary in Berlin (ten hours' drive away), where Paul was supervising three exhibits (Conant, now ambassador to West Germany, singled him out for praise), they received the order to return to the United States for home leave and transfer by November. "Won't it be fun to have friends again! What effect will this removal have on THE BOOK?" he wrote Charlie. Julia informed Simca that the return to the United States "would be useful indeed for the final going over of our finished chapters." In a sort of grand finale for them both, Paul had a one-man exhibition of his photographs in Cologne in October 20 (the packers had already come and gone), and Julia concluded the poultry chapter with several recipes (from Simca) for goose. Only two goose recipes would be included in the book, one with prune and foie gras stuffing (*oie rôtie aux pruneaux*) and one with chestnut and sausage stuffing (*oie braisée aux marrons*).

"We really enjoy working together very much and make an excellent team," Paul reported during their move. Though they had expected to spend another two years in Germany, they were glad to be leaving and to be stopping in Paris before going home. "My, how we long for Paris and our friends . . . in this desert!" she wrote to Louisette. As they drove toward Paris, Paul reported, "our European impressions are heightened, magnified and made potent." They tried, "almost desperately," to absorb and fix every sight and taste and sound of France. Their last ten days in Europe were spent in the Hôtel du Pont Royal, where they had lived almost eight years earlier when they began this great European adventure.

Chapter 14

Back Home (and Cooking) on the Range (1956 – 1958)

"We lived in an age . . . of the decline and pall
of the American palate."

JAMES BEARD, New York Times, *1959*

BEFORE JULIA and Paul settled into Eisenhower's Washington, more specifically into the Georgetown of Stewart and Joe Alsop, they reacquainted themselves with their country. Itinerants in their own land for the last two months of 1956, Julia and Paul moved from rural Pennsylvania to Boston, from Chicago to Southern California, from Northern California to Boston, and back through Pennsylvania to the District of Columbia, reuniting with family and friends. But they began and ended their travels with Charlie and Freddie at their house in rural Pennsylvania, where they had wed ten years earlier. Finally, their Georgetown house, rented out while they were in Bonn, was available, and their goods and furniture arrived from Germany.

One of Julia's initial observations was that the country had become partial to flaming food, either in pretentious restaurants or on the backyard barbecue (three million dollars were spent the following year on barbecue equipment alone). On top of that, James Beard, now the dean of American cooking, had published *The Complete Book of Outdoor Cookery* two years before. Had Julia stayed longer at her father's Pasadena home, she would have learned of

Joseph Broulard, a native of the Jura in France, then the reigning chef in Los Angeles, a city whose top restaurants were French. Broulard, she later discovered, spawned several Los Angeles restaurants and chefs from his Au Petit Jean.

They also discovered the boom in population and building in Los Angeles, along with the quality of the wine at the Charles Krug vineyard in the Napa Valley. Though it took many years before Paul would acknowledge domestic wines in the same sentence with French, he found the bottles they sampled surprisingly good and bought a case.

Julia was astonished to realize how many Americans were letting Swanson do their cooking and eating on tin trays in front of the television. Twice in their wanderings, families turned on their television sets after a meal, much to Julia's amazement. At the Childs' in Pennsylvania they enjoyed *The $64,000 Question,* but found the TV game show "a waste of time." The country had turned to prepackaged quiz shows and prepackaged food.

VILLAGE LIFE IN GEORGETOWN

Julia bought a new range, an enormous black restaurant range, on which she would cook the remainder of her life, during two months of major renovations on their house at 2706 Olive Street, the last house on Olive before it curved into Twenty-seventh Street at the little green parkway. They were on the outskirts, in an area of smaller houses, of the most elegant place to live in the city. Georgetown had a village atmosphere in the middle of a city of monuments, and everyone knew each other because they went to the same market, post office, and barbershop.

They exchanged the third floor of a modern housing development in Plittersdorf on the Rhine for a 150-year-old three-story wooden house. Julia finally got her gas range, and instead of the cold, wet winters, they enjoyed the comfort of an air-conditioning machine on each floor. Though there would be snow this winter, Washington, DC, summers were unbearably hot and humid. With the rent money Paul had wisely collected and banked for eight years, they had enough to redo bathrooms and ceilings to stop the leaking, take out a partition to make the kitchen larger, replace the wiring to avoid any possible fire, and repaint the house. Even the walkway above the ground-floor kitchen, which connected the street to the sitting- and living-room floor, had to be rebuilt. But the first room Julia finished was her bedroom/office (on the top floor with Paul's tiny studio and the guest room), where her typewriter and books awaited her.

If the rent money financed the renovations, the estate of Julia's mother underwrote her career, including the gas range and the cooking equipment from Dehillerin. She bought a new dishwasher (to save on a maid, she told Simca) and a sink with a grinder to dispose of the waste. She informed Simca that her mother's inheritance "allowed me to carry on extensive cookery work. My, I hope we don't have to move out of here in 2 years . . . I couldn't stand it! . . . I shall . . . cut my throat." Caro Weston McWilliams, who cared little about high cuisine or cooking, would have been thrilled with her daughter's enthusiasm and sense of fulfillment.

Julia and Paul would have preferred to be living in Paris. Yet, in retrospect, it was fortuitous for her book that they were home again, where she could cook each recipe with the food available to the people who would buy their book. They were also enjoying being homeowners, especially since they could afford to fix it up with style; both took pride in their little nest. Paul's aesthetic sense turned each room into variations on a different color, and he became a "madly enthusiastic gardener," Julia confided to Simca:

> It is great fun being back here to live. I never could get the feel of it when we just passed through on vacations. One thing I do adore is to be shopping in these great serve-yourself markets, where . . . you pick up a wire push cart as you come in and just trundle about looking and fingering everything there is. . . . It is fine to be able to pick out each separate mushroom yourself. . . . Seems to me there is everything here that is necessary to allow a good French cook to operate.

The new supermarket around the corner on M Street (which curved into Pennsylvania Avenue) was not the only discovery: there was now scouring powder for copper pots, which she sent to Simca, and an electric skillet with a thermostat and timer, ready-mixed pie crust, and Uncle Ben's rice (she had no use for ready-made pie crust or soup). Each new invention was tested and reported to Simca, who promised to visit early in 1958. Julia's curiosity and enthusiasm were infectious.

Paul shared Julia's professional passion, but no longer had much enthusiasm for his own career. He liked the art work and the perspective it gave him on the international political scene, but he mainly worked for the income and the occasional pride he could still take in his work. In December, while he was in California, he had finally been promoted to foreign service rank three (FSS-3), where he made a modest $9,660 a year.

"Julia thinks I should be President," Paul once told his brother. His efficiency reports (one acknowledged he was "underrated") gave him the highest rankings for character and ability, dependability and thoroughness, organization, and his wife: "Mr. Child has an intelligent and charming wife who is an asset to him professionally as well as representationally." Other evaluation phrases explain why he remained at rank four so many years: "interests primarily cultural" and "impatient with certain administrative details . . . and tendency to be self-effacing." That he ranked low in "knowledge of administrative practices" and was thought "to doubt his ability as an executive" reflect his disdain for office politics and the bureaucracy. Thus he lacked ambition for promotion (though his letters to Charlie through the years reveal that he expected promotion). In 1959 he was promoted, nevertheless, to Acting Chief of the Exhibit Division.

Because Washington was a hub through which many passed, Paul and Julia entertained a number of people they knew earlier in Washington and in India, China, Paris, Marseilles, and Bonn. There were also, of course, Julia's friends from California and Smith (Mary Belin lived in nearby Evermay mansion) and Paul's Connecticut connections. As always, Julia was interested in political and social issues. With Nancy Davis, who had worked for Adlai Stevenson, Julia went to hear Dean Acheson address Congress, attended *Inherit the Wind* starring Melvyn Douglas, and sat in the front row to watch Eisenhower's inaugural parade. ("I find I am a mad parade watcher," she wrote Simca the following October when Queen Elizabeth came to town, "and besides I have never seen a queen.") She awakened early to try (unsuccessfully) to see Sputnik circle the globe and watched the squabbles on Capitol Hill with keen interest.

They missed the Washington of Dean Acheson, believing the government was now run by lesser men. Secretary of State John Foster Dulles, Acheson's "despised" and "untrustworthy" successor, seemed to have a callous absence of loyalty to the professionals of the State Department, firing many, and supporting the rule of Chiang Kai-shek. The closest Julia came personally to the government was on February 14, 1957, when the FBI interviewed her about Jane Foster, though all she remembers telling them was that she did not "think someone that funny and that scattered could be a spy." In her datebook she pronounced the visit "very pleasant," which reflected both relief and the influence of her proximity to the seat of government.

All Washington loved to dine out, though few took to cooking as a serious profession. For several months after Julia's kitchen was finished, they entertained "like mad": dinner or cocktails for Cartier-Bresson (the French photojournalist); Walter and Helen Lippmann; Nancy Davis, who was marrying Wing Pepper of Philadelphia; Helen Kirkpatrick, former Information Officer for the Marshall Plan in Paris and recently Assistant to the President at

Smith College, who was marrying Robbins Milbank; Sherman and Nancy Kent, whom they had last seen in Marseilles; Avis DeVoto from Cambridge. Several OSS buddies, including Guy Martin, were living nearby.

During their wanderings, they had seen all of Julia's family, but now they looked forward to their frequent weekends at Coppernose in Pennsylvania, where Julia and Freddie cooked seriously, most often a large turkey (poultry not readily available in France, thus requiring careful changes in timing and cooking temperature). At the wedding the following spring of Erica, the eldest of the Child children, Julia arranged the flowers, Charlie decorated the cake, the Kublers provided the music, and Paul took the photographs. Her wedding to Hector Prud'homme (Rachel Child married Anthony Prud'homme several years later) was indeed a family matter, for now the Childs were connected by marriage to the Bissells (Marie and Richard Bissell's daughter Anne Caroline was married to Hector Prud'homme, Sr.) and to the Kublers (the elder Bissells' son Dick Bissell was married to Betty Kubler's sister). This tight band of people (Julia called it an "ingrown," happy family) remained their emotional support as well as the best company for holidays, including the traditional August in Maine.

Julia and Paul's new red Ford pounced out onto a rocky point of land which stuck out into the sea on Mount Desert Island. They were surrounded on three sides by ocean, rocks, and lobster pots. With the excitement of being "home," they drank in the sea smells and familiar surroundings of Lopaus Point, examining every improvement, the new addition, and Freddie's herb garden. This was the first real herb garden Julia had seen; "I found it just heavenly," she wrote Simca. They picked blueberries and raspberries and reminisced. They waded out into the surf and sea spray to take the lobsters out of their anchored cages.

They hardly had their fill of lobsters when it was time to drive down to Cambridge for book and cook work, taking ten lobsters along with them to Avis.

IN NOTHING ELSE SO HAPPY OR SAD

Julia's greatest joy was in the kitchen, testing recipes, discussing tastes and results with Avis or Freddie—if she was in their kitchens—or taking notes for Simca—if she was home. She had less success cooking with Freddie ("It must be something psychological," she said about working with her sister-in-law).

She shared everything with Simca: variations in cooking techniques, ways to bring down Simca's high blood pressure, America's feelings about the racial tensions in Little Rock, Simca's servant problems (with her prickly temperament, she had trouble keeping a maid), and the wisdom of Simca publishing some articles and recipes in French periodicals (Julia frequently encouraged her to assert her professional authority).

The Houghton Mifflin people and Avis (who was working as a scout for the publishing house of Alfred A. Knopf) encouraged Julia to place recipes in *The Ladies' Home Journal* (the food editor said the recipes were "too involved"), *House & Garden,* and *Town & Country.* Julia sent several recipes to *Woman's Day,* a publication of the A&P grocery store chain, but never heard a word back from them. The *Washington Post* called because they heard of her kitchen, but when the article appeared she was disappointed they had not used any of her recipes or made any mention of Simca. By the fall of 1957 the manuscript was so dog-eared, they had to get it retyped.

Simca's correspondence was equally loving and encouraging. She was testing Julia's poultry recipes, as Julia was testing her vegetable recipes. Simca reported on "Chef Oliver," Raymond Oliver, who cooked on French television. They used yellow and rose onionskin paper for their carbon copies to keep track of their chapters and responses to their responses, which they kept carefully filed. Theirs was truly a collaborative work, and one they believed would be seminal. Aware of James Beard's new American recipes and each American cookbook (*Betty Crocker's Picture Cook Book* had sold more than three million copies since 1950), they took seriously the few attempts to present genuine French recipes, such as in *Gourmet Cookbook II,* which they considered "poor." *"Ach, la concurrence!"* Julia sputtered when a new book or recipe appeared. "Ours will have to be better!" They worked as hard as they could and would not compromise quality; the only compromise would be a multivolume publication.

Several issues were emerging that affected the development of their masterpiece. Most immediately, Julia noticed changes in the produce, equipment, and cooking habits of her native country. In Bonn, she had noticed at the commissary that America was enthusiastic about what culinary historians Karen and John Hess called "precooked frozen gourmet glop." The Hesses criticized Craig Claiborne, the new food editor of the *New York Times,* who graduated from a Swiss hotel school, for hailing fifty-five new items from General Foods' "Gourmet Foods" line and calling others "exciting products" of 1958: Seabrook's "inspired beef à la bourguignonne," Pepperidge Farm's frozen puff pastries, Betty Crocker's "glamorous" new instant meringue, Carnation's "excellent and quickly made" Golden Fudge, Fluffo margarine, and Campbell's frozen fruit pies. Very discouraging for two women who had spent the better part of five or six years preparing a book to teach French recipes.

Moreover, there were several issues related to the cookbook itself. On her first visit to Cambridge the month they arrived, Julia tried to convince her Houghton Mifflin editor, who was also testing their recipes, to publish what they had so far (soups, sauces, poultry, vegetables), then work on other volumes. They would need four or five more years to complete the fish and meat chapters, Julia argued, in order to make her appeal more convincing. (Privately to Simca, Julia acknowledged that a multivolume plan complicated their relations with Louisette.) At first the editor agreed, saying they would publish this first volume at Christmas 1958, calling it *French Cooking, Vol. 1: Sauces and Poultry.* Then Lovell Thompson, the general manager, said they wanted only one book, but Julia would not make a decision until Simca arrived in January 1958.

Cooking problems also delayed completion, from the oversized turkeys that had to be cooked differently from the French poultry to the difficulty of finding crème fraîche (Julia informed Simca that adding buttermilk or yogurt to cream and keeping it at room temperature for a day produced the same results). American veal was not as pale and tender as the French; U.S. butchers offered different meat cuts; except for parsley, few fresh herbs were available; Americans ate a lot of broccoli, which was rare in France—and so the discoveries went. Occasionally a recipe, when retried, did not produce the same results it had in Paris, Marseilles, or Bonn. "HELL AND DAMNATION, is all I can say," Julia wrote Simca on July 14, 1958, in a rare expression of frustration: "WHY DID WE EVER DECIDE TO DO THIS ANYWAY? But I can't think of doing anything else, can you?"

Two other, more personal factors, prolonged the completion of the book, though eventually ensuring its validity and longevity. First was the lack of experience on Julia's part. Never having cooked seriously before going to Paris, she approached her work as a novice studying an established tradition instead of acting on a creative or instinctive level to discover recipes or taste combinations. She approached foods and recipes deliberately, asking basic questions of *why* and *how,* thus enabling her to write the clearest and simplest explanations for readers. Second was the influence of Paul Child's rhetorical analysis (they were now taking memory classes together), which subjected everything to logic and thorough testing, sometimes six different ways. "Paul pushed her to a certain standard," say his nieces and nephew. This influence from Paul cannot be underestimated in evaluating the quality of the manuscript Julia and Simca were preparing.

Julia was overjoyed when Simca and Jean Fischbacher (his stay was briefer) at last arrived from Paris in January, for she had done little else the final months of 1957 but revise the chapters and have them retyped. Simca stayed three months and would visit friends or former students in New York City, Chicago and California. But the great event was the trip to Boston, buried then in a blizzard. Because the trains were not running, Julia and Simca took the long bus ride from New York City and arrived on Avis's doorstep at one o'clock in the morning. Avis recorded her memory thirty years later:

> I waited up for them, and it was snowing fiercely. They went in to see Houghton Mifflin with this huge box of manuscript. [They] presented over seven hundred pages on poultry and sauces *alone,* which is when HM said they weren't about to publish an encyclopedia. Although Dorothy [de Santillana] was extremely anxious to publish the book, because she had cooked with a lot of the recipes and knew they worked, all the men said, "Oh, Americans don't want to cook like that, they want something quick, made with a mix." They were pushing a cookbook, a Texas cookbook, by Helen Corbett—there seemed to be marshmallows in everything, and that's where their advertising money was going. Houghton Mifflin has regretted it ever since.

When Julia heard them say, "We are not going to publish an encyclopedia. . . . Americans wouldn't cook that way," she said to Avis and Simca with her usual dogged determination, "We'll just have to do it over."

That is just what they did, said Avis, spending "the next two years completing a single book" to put in all chapters, including desserts. Avis was absolutely convinced of the uniqueness of the book, though she confided to a mutual friend that she had serious reservations about Julia's writing ability. The talent she had nurtured after Smith had withered under the demands of government forms and recipe details.

ℒA CUISINE CHILD VS. CUISINE ''GUNK''

Julia and Paul developed a style of entertaining that endeared them to Washington circles, a style in keeping with a truly modern kitchen and dining space (which opened onto the garden) and the demanding work her cookbook needed. She and Simca returned to Washington from Boston to devise a new strategy for the book and their work. Any entertaining Julia did during 1958 and 1959 would be connected to their book. She never chose a menu because it was her best work; she was constantly experimenting and testing. If a dish went wrong, she said nothing. This was one of her maxims: no excuses, no explanations. She informed Simca, "I am not doing any elaborate entertaining at all until I get this MS out of the way. What we do is to have 4 people in on Sundays."

Guests long remembered the informal warmth of her kitchen here and later in Cambridge, where they continued their ritual. Lee and Gisele Fairley, both of whom worked with Paul in Bonn and were now stationed in Washington, remember many visits to the Childs' "dollhouse": "Julia was ensconced in her gleaming professionally equipped kitchen [and] we would sit around the kitchen table (a huge butcher's block of wood) sipping Paul's dry martinis . . . and watch Julia prepare the dish(es) of the day. After eating, there was a postmortem discussion, though mostly between Paul and Julia."

Lyne Few and his wife, whom they met in Düsseldorf, were also frequent guests after being posted to Washington. Few remembers:

> Julia's impressive kitchen with beautiful pots and pans hanging everywhere, and a large rough-hewn table in the center. The guests would sit on comfortable benches and consume delicious cocktails which were Paul's specialty. Julia would chat with us as she bustled around concocting fabulous dishes. Paul explained that she was working on a cookbook and hoped we would excuse her for using us as guinea pigs. Never were there more willing victims.

Paul usually made what they called "Ivan's apéritif" or what Julia later called the "Upside-Down Martini": in a red-wine glass, filled with ice, they poured both dry and sweet vermouth (they preferred Noilly Prat vermouth), then floated a little gin on the top, decorating with a twist of orange or lemon rind. "Hold it by the stem so it will ring," suggested Julia as they touched glasses.

Rosalind and Stuart Rockwell—he was director of the Office of Near Eastern Affairs for the Department of State—lived next door and were frequent guests, along with another neighbor, Bob Duemling, who walked to work with Paul. Because Duemling was single (he had dated Rachel Child for several years), he was frequently a guest. The Rockwells remember the chicken dishes (with one portion removed by Julia for tasting) that Julia would bring over for dinner—Paul had had his fill of them. Rosalind would never forget Julia's generosity to the mother of an active young son. "When Stuart took me to the hospital for the birth of our second child, Julia offered to take care of our son Steve. When I asked that she keep him out of the kitchen, she immediately moved all of the long knives."

The following January, to celebrate five birthdays around January 15— Paul and Charlie, Freddie Child, Paul Nitze, and Stuart Rockwell—Julia cooked a grand meal and Paul wrote a poem for the occasion they called "The Pentapolloi Party." Such care was typical of the Child hospitality, and Paul read his lengthy verse to:

> Splendid Nitze, Rockwell Bold
> and Glamor-laden Freddie,
> Plus Charles and Paul, those brilliant men,
> intelligent and steady.
> Behold the dawn of greater days,
> of love rejuvenate. . . .

In its informality, *La Cuisine Child* matched what *House Beautiful* called "the Station Wagon Way of Life" in the 1950s. But in the quality of the food and the time spent in its preparation, there was no comparison. Americans were then eating canned vegetables with marshmallows melted on top, frozen chickens cooked in canned mushroom soup, frozen fish sticks, and dishes that could be served during commercials or cooked on the barbecue outdoors. They were shopping the center aisles of the supermarket, to use food editor (*Gourmet*) Zanne Early Stewart's analogy, not the outside aisles where the fresh produce was waiting.

Processed food products and junk food led to unwanted poundage, which in turn stirred up a wave of dieting and diet books (sprinkled with saccharin and white sodium cyclamate powder), swelling by the end of the century into a tidal wave. Avis decried to Julia the "gunk" in American kitchens and the increasing number of manuscripts for diet books she was receiving, which would henceforth outnumber cookbooks. She described as "gruesome" one she had just received:

> [There is] not a single honest recipe in the whole book—everything is bastardized and quite nasty. Tiny amounts of meat . . . are extended with gravies and sauces made with corn starch. . . . Desserts . . . [are] sweetened with saccharin and topped with imitation whipped cream. Fantastic! And I do believe a lot of people in this country eat just like that, stuffing themselves with faked materials in the fond belief that

by substituting a chemical for God's good food they can keep themselves slim while still eating hot breads and desserts and GUNK.

In 1959 chemists pushed the tidal wave with Metrecal, a powder to be added to milk to make a meal—an "adult version of baby formula," as Harvey Levenstein called the "glutinous drink." Within two years sales would total $350 million. These dieters and instant home cooks were also consuming women's magazines, whose food editors and lifestyle or entertainment editors were setting the tone for the country. They, not the home economists or master chefs, were telling American cooks what to prepare and how to serve it.

Julia was completely outside the small but growing food world of New York City. She was familiar with many names from the national magazines she read in Europe and knew that Dione Lucas had a school and television program and that James Beard wrote many cookbooks and endorsed a stream of products (living, his biographer said, by "trade-offs, favors, freebies, and consulting"). But Julia had never met them or the real power brokers who edited the magazines, such as Helen McCully at *McCall's,* the first food editor of a major magazine who was not a home economist, and certainly the most powerful food editor in the country. She was learning their names, but harbored a certain skepticism. She had yet to meet Craig Claiborne *(New York Times),* Ann Seranne *(Gourmet),* Poppy Cannon *(House Beautiful),* or Cecily Brownstone (Associated Press). But her time was coming.

Their Audience

When Julia and Simca put aside their weighty manuscript, began their streamlined version, and copyrighted the name L'Ecole des Trois Gourmandes, they did not change their purpose or what they called their "intended audience." Their purpose always remained to teach "the servantless American cook" authentic French techniques, not "adaptations," to achieve, as nearly as possible, French results. The audience, as Paul once said, is *"Everybody,* like birdshot from both barrels, from Brides to Guides and from Sophisticates to Wistful Mates." Julia told Avis in 1952 that they wanted a book "understandable to the novice, interesting for the practiced cook." She and Simca first agreed in 1954 that they were "writing for an audience that knows nothing about French cooking; that will follow every word that we utter . . . or be put off if we do not explain thoroughly." For this reason, she occasionally—as in the case of *velouté aux champignons*—rejected a recipe that was "too complicated for our audience." The following year it was "a literate audience that

LIKES TO COOK AND WANTS TO LEARN." Now, with her growing awareness of the shortcut cooking in the country, she suggested to Simca they include fewer *grande cuisine* and more *cuisine bourgeoise* dishes,

> . . . which is complicated enough for them. They are not used to taking the time and care we are used to taking in preparing things. . . . Nobody has a mortar, sieve, or pilon for pounding things . . . we shall have to emphasize in our introduction that LOVE is one of the big ingredients . . . and that the taste of food (not its looks, ease of preparation, etc.) is what you are striving for, and why some shortcuts won't work.

To keep in touch with their future audience, Julia occasionally taught cooking classes, the first one on April 27, 1957, for a group of women who met every Monday to cook lunch for their husbands. Later that year she responded to a request to teach a class of eight in Philadelphia, four hours away by car, which she did monthly through the spring of 1958. From ten until two, when the food was served, she hurriedly cooked the following menu: *oeufs pochés duxelles, sauce béarnaise* (which in their book would be called *oeufs en croustades à la béarnaise); poulet sauté portugais; epinards au jus* (the blanched spinach would also appear in their book); and *pommes à la sévillane.* Every detail was carefully typed up ahead of time and later narrated to Simca, who was giving cooking classes to a group of U.S. Air Force wives in Paris. During her visit to Washington, Simca was involved in a couple of the classes Julia was giving in 1958 at her own home, under the name L'Ecole des Trois Gourmandes. The first menu: *quiche aux fruits de mer, coq au vin,* and *tarte aux pommes.*

Not long after Paul told friends their "nest is feathered," he learned they were to be transferred to Oslo, Norway. This time he would not repeat his Germany experience of transferring before he learned the language, and so he negotiated a six-month delay—and then two more months—so he could learn the language and Julia could get further toward completing the book. Beginning in September 1958, Paul began what would amount to 116 hours of Norwegian study from the wife of the press attaché at the Norwegian Embassy, who offered to teach him (the U.S. State Department did not teach the language) without pay. By the next spring he and Julia were very chummy with the Norwegian ambassador and his wife.

Bob Duemling, who would leave for Rome in the spring of 1960, remembers the party that Paul and Julia gave for a dozen friends to honor the woman who had taught him Norwegian. "Paul made a delightful speech to thank her, then gave her a small box. She burst into tears." Later Duemling examined the gift Paul made: the wood was covered with gesso, painted as a replica of a famous Norwegian fresco of a saint which he had copied, then antiqued to look like a medieval icon. "It was an elegant and thoughtful gift that showed Paul's imagination and talent."

A PERMANENT HOME IN CAMBRIDGE

There was a storm in Cambridge in January 1959 when Avis DeVoto called to say a house was coming on the market at 103 Irving Street and they must come immediately to see it. They took a train in the freezing rain and literally bought the house out from under a family who were walking through the house at the same time. According to Avis, Paul tapped on the walls of the four floors (counting the full basement) and Julia looked longingly at the two pantries and large, well-organized kitchen with a restaurant stove.

A half year before, during the 1958 Fourth of July weekend with Avis, Julia and Paul had expressed an interest in eventually settling in Cambridge. But a walk about the town with an agent turned up nothing available. Now, with only three months left before leaving for Oslo, they bought the three-story house for $48,500 and asked the third and present owner, Mrs. Margot Smith, to remain on while she looked for another home. Julia explained their decision:

> Paul said he did not want to be in government any longer than sixty years of age. He wanted to devote himself to the creative arts. So we decided where we wanted to live. We looked in California, but that was too far away. Paul had grown up in Boston and loved the area, and we stayed with Avis DeVoto, who had a friend in the real estate business. Avis was wonderful to us. We looked at the house for twenty minutes and immediately took it, while the other people were talking it over among themselves.

Josiah Royce (1855–1916) and his wife were the first owners of the house from its construction in 1889 until 1944. Royce was the famed idealist philosopher during the "Golden Age of Philosophy" at Harvard, when he taught with George Santayana and William James (whose mother-in-law lived at No. 107). One of Royce's students was Gertrude Stein, who lived with her brother Leo at No. 123 when she attended the "Harvard Annex" (later Radcliffe) from 1893 to 1897. Poet e.e. cummings was born across the street at No. 104. This area, once part of the Norton Estate, was called the Shady Hill area (Paul had taught at the Shady Hill School in 1930–31) or the Divinity School area, between Beacon Street and Harvard Divinity School, north of Kirkland Street.

Julia and Paul had already met some of their neighbors three years before: the John Kenneth Galbraiths (Julia went to Smith with Mrs. Galbraith) and the younger Arthur Schlesingers were a part of the DeVoto group that Bernard celebrated in his famous little book *The Hour.* Buying here among all the university professors and writers was like buying a piece of Bloomsbury for a Londoner. More important than the heady environment was the fact that this was Paul's hometown, where he taught school one year, and later where his love Edith Kennedy lived and died; indeed, two of her sons, Robert (architect for the restoration of the DeVotos' house) and Fitzroy, still lived in Cambridge with their families. It seemed natural for a girl reared by a New England mother and sent to Smith College to choose New England. In 1957 Julia told Simca that New England "is the cradle of our country and has a very special character."

Julia had twenty-seven daffodils blooming in their Georgetown yard by the second week of April. Paul was feeling older than fifty-seven years, as he was slowly recovering from a tonsillectomy, when the shippers picked up their goods for Oslo. The painters prepared the Georgetown house for renting, while Julia sent her copy of the rejected manuscript to Avis. "I thought you might just hang on to it in case HM might need another copy," she wrote. "I have not been able to proofread it at all, but have confidence in . . . the proofreader and typist. She is a jewel, and it looks beautiful, I think." Avis would recall that "Julia left the book in my lap."

"Elegance of Cuisine Is on Wane in U.S.," Craig Claiborne announced four days later in his front-page article in the *New York Times.* The fault of the decline lay in the decline in its Frenchness, he asserted, and among those he interviewed was James Beard, who said, "This nation is more interested in preserving the whooping crane and the buffalo than in perpetuating classic cooking and table service. We live in an age that may some day . . . be referred to as the time of the decline and pall of the American palate." One food historian called this article "a news report of national crisis of some import, at least for the well-heeled readers of the *Times.*" Houghton Mifflin was not listening. Julia was preparing to walk out the door.

The routine was familiar: lunch with Jane McBain, cocktails with the Lippmanns, dinner with the Bissells, and the farewells went on for days and days, despite Paul's fatigue. From the deck of the SS *United States* on a beautiful sunny day in New York Harbor, they waved to Charlie and Freddie, Alice Lee Myers, and John and Phila McWilliams (who had recently visited them in Washington). Julia wept with sorrow to be leaving, though, always upbeat, she told Avis, "We are indeed awfully lucky to have this post . . . which I hope will be our last!" They knew that when they returned from this last station, they would have a new and bigger house. Now they began talking about the new world they were to conquer and the French and then Norwegian soil that lay ahead. After a day and a half of champagne, caviar, and truffled pork loin, Julia spent two days in bilious discomfort, recovering in time to meet Simca in Rouen to re-create that first *sole meunière* lunch that had changed her life.

The reunions with Max Bugnard, Hélène Baltrusaitis, and others were sweet. The USIA's special exhibit, "The Twenties: American Writers in Paris and Their Friends," which Hélène coordinated for the embassy, had concluded just five days before and she introduced Julia to the woman whose collection had been the basis of the exhibit: Sylvia Beach, the publisher of James Joyce's *Ulysses*. After dining at Lipp, La Grille, Closerie des Lilas, La Méditerranée, and other sentimental places of memory, Julia was down again with a fatigued liver. But she and Simca got in two days of hard work (their ham *en croûte* was "not a success") and a meeting with the Gourmettes before Paul and Julia drove away on a beautiful May day to Bonn. They lunched beside the Rhine and visited friends for three days. After dining with Erica and Hector Prud'homme in Amsterdam, they drove past the whitewashed stone houses of the flatlands of Denmark toward their ship to Norway.

Chapter 15

"*I* AM AT HEART A VIKING" (1959 – 1961)

". . . far from the extravagances of Place Pigalle."

PAUL CHILD

THE SHIP wove its long, winding way through the deep, island-strewn fjord toward Oslo. Julia and Paul awakened at five to take in the drama of this "land of the generous sea," and were not disappointed to discover that the steep forested cliffs, granite boulders, and smell of pine woods reminded them of Maine and the Washington State coast. Little wooden clapboard houses dotted the water's edge. The day began as slate-colored, the air cold and damp, and the experience strange, as any new land is to a visitor. But the smiling faces of Fisher and Debby Howe on the wharf warmed their 7 A.M. welcome. Debby had attended Bennington College with Julia's sister Dorothy. Howe, whom they first met in the OSS in India and last saw in Washington, had been in Oslo three years as Deputy Chief of Mission.

Marching bands and more than five thousand children holding red balloons and red Norwegian flags filled Karl Johan Street, making their way to the palace to greet the royal family for Norway's Constitution Day. May 17, 1959, was a new beginning for Julia and Paul, as well as the beginning of the planting season in Norway. "The color and noise of thousands of kiddies lifted my spirits—dashed by a terrible lunch," Julia noted, going through her usual "wish we were home" reaction, which always followed a bad meal in a new country.

The sun broke through to blinding brightness. They were picked up at their hotel by Eline and Bjorn Egge, whom they had met briefly at one of their farewell parties at the home of Mary Belin in Georgetown (Lieutenant Colonel Egge served at NATO headquarters in Paris with Captain Peter Belin). Their first Norwegian friends drove them up to Holmenkollen, where the Winter Olympics had been held seven years before. At 1,150 feet above sea level, they looked out like eagles over the city of Oslo. "I feel better about things," Julia wrote in her datebook.

"Julia and Paul [were] excellent representatives of their country in Norway," said Bjorn Egge, who would be elected president of the World Veterans Federation in 1995. "They liked people and the Norwegians were very fond of them. They were in fact the incarnation of American culture in Norway at a time we badly needed to have that aspect of the United States emphasized. From the very first moment they put a great deal into learning to know the very special brand of Norwegian outdoor culture."

For five long weeks, while Paul was at work in the embassy, Julia worked on the new cookbook—the one-volume edition—and explored the city. They lived consecutively in two different hotels, surrounded by unopened boxes. When Julia was not working she was roaming around the city with her usual energetic curiosity, often with Debby Howe, who showed her the commissary, the War Resistance Museum (the Norwegians had been under Nazi occupation for five years), and the statue of Ibsen (their greatest dramatist) outside the National Theater. The sightseeing was interspersed with house hunting.

The summer sun in this land of Vikings, herring, and the sea seemed never to set. Though everyone was off the streets by 9:30 at night, twilight did not arrive until 11:30 P.M. and dawn came at 4 A.M. The days seemed nightless in this northern land, a third of which was within the Arctic Circle. Sharing the Scandinavian peninsula with Sweden, Norway swept up the western half of the peninsula to take in the entire fractured coastline northward into the Arctic and over the tops of Sweden and Finland to the Russian border. A country of coastline, in places only four miles wide.

Fjords sliced deep into the mountain interiors for the most dramatic vistas, unions of the power and beauty of nature, where the sea pounded the rock walls. The land was stunning, the people close to nature, open and innocent ("lean and glowing with health," Julia wrote in the first postcard to her sister Dort). Later she said, "They look like New Englanders, with the healthy color of Californians [for] they live outdoors every minute they can."

As June approached, Julia noticed the hungry way the Norwegians drank in the brilliant sun and realized how long and cold the winters must be. Paul was amazed that "there are virtually no fat people at all!" He underlined that sentence in his letter, contrasting the people in the United States, "where baby-blubber bounces," and in Germany, "where pig-fat is almost a virtue." He was also impressed with how much time the fathers spent with their children, crediting the workday routine of quitting at about 3:30 for dinner and a nap, then family time. The Norwegians were the best-looking (especially the women), "clearest-eyed, healthiest, most vigorous and characterful we have ever seen." "We like the Weegians very much," Julia repeated in several letters.

PALAZZO LIVING OUTSIDE OSLO

Seagulls squawked above. The air, Paul informed Charlie, smelled of spruce, pine, moss, and apple blossoms. Spring burst out in tulips. By July there was a heat wave and drought—the clearest, hottest summer since 1903—that by mid-October had broken all records. Paul Child sweltered in his corner office in the new and controversial building designed by Eero Saarinen, a building in which no windows opened. By August he felt he was baking "like a *pâté en croûte.*"

Oslo, in southeastern Norway, was the capital and largest city, as well as the main port. The country's chief commercial center, Oslo got its produce from the mountains and the sea: forest products and processed food (chiefly fish). Night after night while they lived in hotels, Julia and Paul tried different restaurants, looking for a satisfying cuisine, but concluded that the food was the "worst" they had ever eaten anywhere. Julia's immediate and private reaction was that the cooking was "hideous," especially the fried foods. Publicly and privately, she would rave about the fish, especially the gravlax, "the best smoked salmon I ever ate."

> Gawd, the salmon are splendid! [she wrote her family]. There is a great fish store here with a stupendous window display of crossed salmon 3 feet long, surrounded by salmon trout, and interspersed with lobsters, mackerel, flounder, and halibut. Above them is a garland of little pink shrimp . . . They also have a "gravloch" [sic], which is salmon . . . served with *Stueder poteter* (diced in cream with mace), and a dill/cream sauce.

"[We seem] far from the extravagances of Place Pigalle," Paul observed concerning the upright Norwegians. The state church was Evangelical Lutheran, the citizens devoted to rectitude, fresh air, and early nights. As one wag said, the liveliest thing about a Norwegian is his sweater. Their puritanism showed in their food and drink. The beer was good, but all alcohol was heavily taxed. The breads were varied and honest, but the vegetables, salads, and meats were, in Paul's words, "lousy." These were friendly and hardy people who had been fishing the sea for many centuries. Pleasures were simple.

Thanks to the Howes, they found what Julia called a "peachy" and "nifty" house on a hill next door to the Howes and almost across the street from the University of Oslo. Erica Child came from Amsterdam for ten days to help her aunt and uncle move into their house. She went to the stores with Julia to help furnish an empty house.

> I went to department stores with Julia, who just bought towels and dishes, a sofa, can opener, beds and tables, and a gas stove with butane bottle. I had never seen anyone do that before. She had her Norwegian phrase book with her and she talked to everyone, gestured, lay down on the floor to illustrate that she wanted a bed. She took care of business. She is so disciplined, such an extrovert. The people gathered round, drawn to her. We had such a good time.

For two weeks after Erica left, Julia set aside her book while she unpacked her *batterie de cuisine* (Paul said he hung seventy-four items), put up curtains, and ordered a large sideboard, chairs, and a table seating sixteen made of maple and suitable eventually for their Cambridge house.

Paul wrote to Charlie about the "desperation [with which] one thrusts down one's roots in each new country," and surely Julia demonstrated this eagerness to be a part of the life of Oslo, where they expected to spend four years. She took the Trikk, Oslo's electric train, into the downtown area and opened herself up to meeting everyone and learning everything she could about the country. Professionally, her years in Norway opened her horizons to new ways with fish and gave her the time to complete her book and test her recipes.

On Sunday mornings the church bells chimed from every neighboring village, as they do, Paul noted, in Venice. "I would be happy to take this house and view with me everywhere," Julia told Dorothy and Ivan. From their bedroom window Julia could see across a field and then a forest of trees to the blue-green fjord below. According to the Howes, the house, which was some distance outside of Oslo, was owned by the biggest and wealthiest shipowner in the city. Paul discovered that he liked "palazzo living." They had a huge basement with laundry and Paul's 200-bottle wine cellar (replenished via Copenhagen), a large attic, many rooms, a terrace, lawn, fruit trees, and by July more strawberries, raspberries, currants, and *fraises des bois* than they could jam, liqueur, or eat.

For Julia's forty-seventh birthday they went to a restaurant with Fisher and Debby Howe. With the gift of a brass elephant from Muttra, Paul wrote to Julia about how much "we owe to Ceylon for providing the golden moment, the perfect environment, the necessary atmosphere, which revealed us to each other. I am happy, astonished and delighted that we met at all, that we had the good sense to marry each other, and that our life together is such a pleasure. Thank you for every concession, every restraint, every thoughtfulness, every cooperative act, every darling endeavor, that you contribute to our mutual life."

Rebuffed by Houghton Mifflin

"Thank god I got this book cookery done before we came here, as it would have been impossible otherwise," Julia said about the lack of produce such as chicken ("they have only stewing chicken and baby chicken"). The vegetables were good in season, but the season was short.

Julia devoted July and August to completing her reorganization, recipe narrowing, and typing for the cookbook. "Julie's working like a bastid [sic] on her book—always *has*," Paul wrote Charlie, "but now that she actually sees the leet [sic] on the other side of the forest and realizes that, after 8 years of slogging through the windfalls, swamps, and underbrush, she will actually *emerge* in a few weeks, the realization is sweeping her on like a windstorm." She sent off the manuscript for Simca's approval (the last pieces were mailed on September 1), and then to a typist friend in Washington, DC, who sent it on to Houghton Mifflin. She felt "rather lost" without her book.

Julia knew Houghton Mifflin would take months to accept or reject the book, now called *French Recipes for American Cooks,* so she joined a class at the university nearby to study Norwegian more seriously (she was working through the grammar book on her own and practicing on shopkeepers). As in Bonn, she would learn the language faster than her linguist husband because she dealt with shopkeepers, housekeepers, the gardener, and service men.

But it was not until she attended her first embassy luncheon and sampled the tasteless fare that Julia made plans to resume giving cooking lessons. When the canned shredded chicken in what Julia called a "droopy, soupy sauce" was passed to her, she looked across the room to Debby Howe, who gave her an apologetic, knowing look. Years later she would recall the phallic-shaped aspic filled with grapes and cut-up mushrooms: "It was sitting on a little piece of lettuce so you could not hide what you didn't eat. I didn't think anything like that still existed!" When the coconut frosted cake-mix cake, molded lime Jell-O salad, and artificial Key lime pie were served, Julia glanced wide-eyed at Debby. "I knew how bad the food was," Debby Howe said in 1994, "and I knew what Julia would feel about it." The entire meal was appalling, thought Julia; everything was sweet, and sickening.

Julia determined that no such embassy meal would ever be served to her again and made plans to offer cooking classes for those who wanted them. Few did, but her Norwegian friends were enthusiastic. She began two practices here in Norway that continued for several years: she would cook a meal in the kitchen of a family, showing them how to prepare the lunch, and she would offer small classes for six to eight women. Debby, who thought she "was a good sport, especially with diplomatic wives," cared nothing about learning to cook herself, for she had two young children and planned a number of the functions for the ambassador, a woman named Frances Willis, whom Julia admired. "Julia was appalled that I did not want to learn to cook," reported Debby Howe.

Their living pattern changed considerably now that Paul was Cultural Attaché. His work hours often included evenings and weekends (with only four on the USIA staff, everyone played a second role as entertainer and greeter of planes). He had always planned exhibits and run a photography library, but here he was in charge of all the cultural events: directing the Fulbright program and the library, mounting all exhibits, working with the director of the Institute of American Studies at the University of Oslo, meeting the planes of arriving celebrities, and entertaining the likes of Pearl Buck, Buckminster Fuller, and every Washington junketeer who had anything remotely to do with the arts and education. He entertained Leonard Bernstein and the New York Philharmonic (the King came to this performance) and hosted Thanksgiving dinner for all the American Fulbright scholars in the embassy cafeteria.

Paul's boss, the head of the USIA, was Marshall Swan, who with his wife, Connie, befriended the Childs. Swan had a Ph.D. and spoke Italian and Dutch, for he previously served as Public Affairs Officer (Paul's job) in Milan and The Hague. His outlets, much to Paul's delight, were writing, music, and literature. Together, he and Paul traveled to many cities for lectures, film showings, and conferences on behalf of the United States. As everywhere Paul served, he worked for the promotion of his country and consequently as a counterforce to Russian propaganda. A "running contest with the Russians" for friends, Paul called his work.

Julia sympathized with Paul's work demands, but, as Paul pointed out to Charlie, "Julia just *can't understand* bastardry, neurosis, hard luck, illness, suffering, sleeplessness, the quiver of fear, the sense of inadequacy, the frustration of having to do something fast and perfectly which you never did before, etc., etc." Julia clearly took the vicissitudes of life differently than Paul did.

After a letter from their Houghton Mifflin editor in September, which praised the manuscript, Julia received a letter from Paul Brooks, an executive at Houghton Mifflin, 2 Park Street, Boston, dated November 6, 1959. He commended the book as "a work of culinary science as much as of culinary art," but declared it too expensive for them to publish: "In a letter of March, 1958, you yourself spoke of the revised project as a 'short simple book directed to the housewife chauffeur.' The present book could never be called this," he explains. The cost of publishing such a large book was not a risk they would take; he suggested Doubleday, which had a large assortment of book clubs, and added that if they did not succeed in placing it with another publisher, HM would take a look at a possible "smaller, simpler version."

Julia and Paul, as well as Simca and Jean, were devastated. A letter from Avis five days later affirmed the economic basis of the publisher's decision: "the decision was based on a very cut and dried equation: probable costs against possible sales." She was sending the manuscript immediately to Bill Koshland at Knopf, where she once worked, because Koshland had already seen parts of the manuscript and tried some of the recipes with enthusiasm. Therefore, she added, "assuming authority I realize I have not got," she took decisive action: "I am sending this down to Bill. Do not despair. We have only begun to fight."

When Julia called Avis to ask if she should return the Houghton Mifflin advance they were given, Avis told her to keep the money. At this point, Avis already knew of William Koshland's interest: in a June 19, 1959, letter to Avis he asked her when he was going to have a look at the "big book." She knew that he would not just read, but cook from the book.

Paul cynically concluded their book was ten years too late because the cooks of America were already "conditioned to speed and as little work as possible, combined w/a belief in magic (the 'secret' of French cooking lies in a mysterious white powder that chefs shake on at the last minute. It has

GLYCODIN-32 in it! Only 89 cents!)." Charlie picked up on Avis's suggestion that Julia would do better with a publisher with more imagination. "I still think Joolie a natural for TV, with or without scribble-pub, but this [is] only one man's opinion." In a letter informing all her family, Julia calmly and sanguinely told them Knopf is looking at the manuscript:

> If nothing comes of this, I shall drop the whole thing until we get back to the States, and just continue on with my self training . . . I have loads to learn in patisserie, and many hundreds of types of regular cooking recipes which I have never gone into. I just feel sorry for poor old Simca who has been in this for years, with nothing yet to show for it. She just picked the wrong collaborator, and it is too bad. [And to Freddie:] I don't seem to be very much upset. I got it done, and now I have for myself a whole batch of fool-proof recipes.

Julia expressed the same practical attitude twenty-seven years later when asked if she regretted creating such a huge book when only a portion of it was published: "Oh, no, I have been drawing on those recipes ever since."

Nonetheless, she was, quite naturally, lost without the book, and disappointed that eight years of work would not be published. In the meantime, she kept on with cooking classes "to keep my hand in" and continued cooking for dinner parties in her home, for, as Paul declared, "one of the magical aspects of this household is its potentialities for gustatory pleasure." One such meal Paul declared "one of the Great Eatments of the century—an eatment that we would not be ashamed to share w/Curnonsky, Prince des gastronomes, were he still alive": *rognons de veau* (veal kidneys) sautéed whole in butter, sliced into a sauce of reduced wine, butter, and mustard; sautéed potatoes and snow peas; served with red burgundy Grands-Echézeaux '53 (given to them by Alice Lee Myers at the dock in New York City in May). They ended the meal on a regional note with creamy Danish blue cheese and *knekkebröd*. "Both food and wine were glorious, and it left us in the kind of esthetic transport that you can get from a wonderful symphony or a tremendous sunset."

"You have to know how to eat in Norway," Julia wrote, and in a letter to a complaining embassy employee a decade later, she suggested eating sea trout and legs of lamb (and contacting her friends the Egges and the Heyerdahls). She remembered "the big dinner parties we would have with a big leg of lamb or a big poached sea trout, just delicious, with butter and potatoes. I loved Norway."

Winter Travel and *Værsyk*

After months of beautiful hot weather and little moisture, the rain arrived at the beginning of November and snow the beginning of December. The sea turned pewter and the sky "woolen," but the Weegians were conditioned to respond, their inner nature in rhythm with the power of the elements. With the deep white snow, they donned rubber boots and brightly colored rubber raincoats—not just yellow sou'westers, but bright red and green and blue hooded jackets. The days grew shorter, ending at 3:30 in the afternoon.

Skiing was both a necessity and a religion in Oslo. Julia and Paul bought skis so they could maneuver in areas not plowed. Because Paul worried about broken bones and Julia about her weak knees, they did not do much downhill skiing. "We are being careful and middle-aged," she assured her father. But in fact, just as she always overbid her hand in card games, so she took on any challenging hill. "I've broken toes half a dozen times," she told Avis years later. "The first time I was rushed to the emergency section of the Oslo hospital, but they said toes heal by themselves."

"Julia and I skied just outside the door some mornings," said her neighbor Debby Howe. "We did a little cross-country skiing or went to a nearby hill. It was nice to have a friend then. We could say anything to each other and not have diplomatic worries. Neither of us was a tremendous skier, but Julia had skied in California. We had lunch at Julia's or a restaurant together—those times were precious. We would fix a simple lunch of quiche or omelet, salad, bread, and wine." On any sunny winter Sunday a fifth of the population navigated the mountain trails within the city. Every electric train carried skis along the outside bars. Julia loved the outdoors: "I am at heart a Viking."

Jan and Froydis Dietrichson became the second Norwegian couple to befriend them. According to them, the Childs "were very popular among the natives . . . and made friends here that Julia will keep till the end of her days." Paul studied the Norwegian language with Froydis. She and her husband, a lexicographer and linguist at the university, were "intensely intelligent," Paul concluded. He learned soon after arriving in Oslo that the dialect he studied in Washington, DC, was a Danish-based tongue and not one of the two main dialects. This discovery, together with his perfectionism and lack of daily opportunity to speak with shopkeepers, brought on considerable frustration.

According to one of Paul's colleagues, he "took everything so seriously, dear soul that he was." Once when someone sent a (now forgotten) complaint to the embassy, Paul wrote a long personal letter of three pages, handwritten, when a simple letter of two paragraphs would have served him better. "He overdid it," admits Fisher Howe. "We had a long go-around about how much I could mess with his prose." His perfectionism, along with his evening and weekend work, explains why Paul did not have time to put paint to canvas or touch his violin while in Norway.

While Paul focused on the artistic, cultural, and educational issues for the embassy, others, particularly Fisher Howe, concerned themselves with the economic issues, which usually dealt with navigation (Norway had the second-largest maritime fleet in the world). Behind all their work were two overriding issues: NATO and the Berlin shuttle, the rescue mission between West Berlin and West Germany. The Norwegians were staunch supporters of NATO, and the following year were caught in the glare of international attention when American Gary Powers's spy plane was shot down by the Russians as it was headed toward northern Norway.

For many of the events Paul planned or attended, Julia accompanied him: travels to interview Fulbright applicants in Trondheim, the former capital and still the gateway between northern and southern Norway; a conference for librarians in Bergen, a port reminding them of Marseilles; a conference for Scandinavian Teachers of English in Leangkollen, forty-five minutes away. When their niece Erica visited they took her to Lillehammer, later the site of the 1994 Winter Olympics. They also visited the Egges' cabin near the Swedish border and the Telemark region with the Dietrichsons. All Norwegians rushed, lemming-like, each weekend to their mountain huts. During an Easter week at a mountain hotel, Julia considerably improved her downhill skiing. According to Froydis Dietrichson, Paul never really learned to enjoy skiing in this country in which only about 5 percent of the land is flat enough to cultivate.

Paul and Julia returned to familiar ground for the Christmas and New Year's holiday. Erica and Hector joined them at Mari and Peter Bicknell's home for Christmas in Cambridge, England. Then after four days at the Pont Royal in Paris, Julia and Paul drove to Marseilles and on to Grasse to visit with Simca and Jean in their stone home they called Bramafam, on a Provençal hillside in the land where perfume had been made for centuries. On January 4, 1960, they drove to Rome, to see Lyne and Ellen Few (she had been stricken with polio in Düsseldorf). Lyne Few would always remember that Paul, with his "generous nature" and "athletic physique," gave Ellen her first pedestrian view of Rome, pushing her wheelchair all day over cobblestones, in and out of churches, up flights of stairs, and through museums. The Childs then flew to Copenhagen and took the ferry train home.

The almost dayless winter season brought on *værsyk,* or winter sickness, a kind of short-tempered depression bred by gray skies and short days. Julia and Paul had yet to acclimate to the winter sickness the Norwegians understood all too well. Paul was too busy to create a Valentine artwork for 1960, so they sent one of his verses. And Julia waited to hear if Knopf was interested in publishing the cookbook. "I've started a cooking school here in Oslo with 5 Norwegians, 1 Hungarian/English, 1 English, and 1 American . . . and will be putting you on the mailing list for recipes," she wrote her sister Dorothy. She gave three classes at three different homes this spring, with lessons on fish, veal, poultry, eggs in aspic, and omelets. Many of her students were drawn from a reading group, according to Margie Schodt, whose husband was an economic officer at the embassy. Schodt believed Julia was "an impressive figure" who performed a patriotic service with her classes, yet was modest about her cooking.

Among her cooking students was Mosse Heyerdahl, an attractive blond woman, who with her husband, Jens, a tall, slender lawyer in horn-rimmed glasses, befriended the Childs. The Heyerdahls were Francophiles who liked theatergoing. Julia golfed with Jens, taught Mosse techniques of French cooking, and visited their summer cottage on the Oslofjord. They took Julia and Paul to Norwegian theaters, translating "a bit," and afterward for a light meal and discussion of the play. Jens remembers that when they attended Stig Hegerman's *Skyggen av Mart (The Shadow of Mart),* Julia and Paul "insisted on going behind the stage to greet the actors, all very famous. This was not customary here, but they were received with enthusiasm. The great actor Toralf Maurstad even mentioned this event in his book about his life as an actor. He was flattered that the Cultural Attaché of the American Embassy came to pay him compliments."

SPRINGTIME WITH KNOPF

Spring and the annual Constitution Day celebration marked both the first anniversary of their arrival in Norway and the launching of Julia's career as author. While the Norwegians celebrated the end of Danish rule on May 17, 1960, Julia and Simca celebrated the end of almost a decade of work on their cooking masterpiece. The season of *værsyk* had passed, and with spring came a letter from Mrs. Judith Jones of Knopf saying she was "convinced that this book is revolutionary and we intend to prove it and to make it a classic." Senior editor William (Bill) Koshland and Jones were cooking their way through the book, Mrs. Jones explained in the May 6, 1960, letter. Koshland's first letter on June 30 credited "Avis's missionary work with me over the years."

Avis gave the manuscript to Koshland, a vice president of Knopf, who enjoyed cooking, and not to Alfred Knopf himself, because, as she said later, he and his wife, Blanche, would not have known what to do with themselves in the kitchen. She also knew that Blanche was enthusiastic about Knopf's *Classic French Cuisine* by Joseph Donon and would consider this new book competitive. Koshland said, "I immediately gave it to Judith, who was sold on it."

Because she was a young editor, Jones enlisted a reader's report from senior editor Angus Cameron to accompany her report for the editorial committee meeting. Cameron had worked on Rombauer's *The Joy of Cooking* and was both an excellent cook and an experienced editor. Jones's reader's report called the book "first-rate and unique" in its teaching of techniques: "I swear that I learned something from this manuscript every few pages." Cameron's reader's report called it "an astonishing achievement" and "the first really useable cookbook of fine French cookery I have seen." At the committee meeting (Jones was too low in rank to attend), Cameron argued that the book was a *working* French cookbook which would make books that were merely compilations of recipes more functional. The Knopfs apparently disagreed. Blanche, so the story goes, walked out. Alfred said, "Oh well, let Jones have a chance, why not?"

The terms of the contract, dated June 24, were that the manuscript be submitted in full by August 15 with publication slated for the fall of 1961. The advance of $1,500 seemed like a fortune compared with the $750 from Houghton Mifflin, but in reality it did not begin to cover the expenses that the authors incurred over these many years. The money was an advance against royalties of 17 percent on the first 10,000 copies, 20 percent to 20,000 copies, and 23 percent thereafter (computed, typically, after booksellers' discounts, thus equivalent to 1990s percentages). Julia asked that their lawyer (nephew Paul Sheeline) be sent the contract first for approval.

Knopf (as had Houghton Mifflin) demanded that their contract be with Julia Child only (she would have a separate contract with her partners). They also would use different line drawings (subject to her approval). John Moore sent all his drawings and Paul's photographs to Knopf without any request for reimbursement.

Mrs. Jones was a respected young editor of Knopf's cookbooks and also an accomplished cook who had spent three years in France with her husband, Evan, a distinguished food writer and historian. She loved French food. "I spent about two months" on the cookbook, she says, "and felt, 'This was the book I had been waiting for all my life.' I had only one old French cookbook, and I was always frustrated because they didn't tell you enough. There were so many secrets to French cooking and the only way I learned was by watching someone." This enthusiasm and thoroughness come through in their months of correspondence. She praised the organization and clarity of the manuscript, and Julia in turn praised her editor's professional eye.

Julia devoted the summer of 1960 to book details and typing lengthy correspondence to keep her co-authors apprised of every detail. She went through the manuscript several times, sending in her last line edits on August 31. The problems that emerged were twofold. The size of portions, which Jones and Cameron thought too small for American appetites ("2½ pounds of meat won't do for 6–8 people"), was resolved by Julia's decision to use a half pound of meat per serving.

The second issue involved Jones's request for old favorites such as cassoulet and more hearty peasant dishes, especially more meat dishes (the latter a request from a "male editor," probably Cameron). Julia sent a long list of dishes already included that were earthy peasant dishes. In all, Julia mailed four new recipes to Jones at the end of July: *carbonnade à la flamande* (beef and onions braised in beer), cassoulet (French baked beans with sausage and goose), *pièce de boeuf,* and *paupiettes de boeuf* (braised stuffed beef rolls).

Julia got embroiled with Simca in a quarrel about the inclusion of goose in the cassoulet: every time Julia typed up the recipe, Simca changed her mind ("I remember Julia saying to me, 'That old goat!'—she was just so tired of the book," declared Avis). To Jones, Julia wrote, "Ah, so French she is!" Simca declared that the white bean dish was not cassoulet without goose, with Julia maintaining that Americans had trouble finding goose. Julia prevailed with the recipe, but the "blah-blah" (their reference to the text) spoke of the "infinite dispute" about the ingredients of the dish, the authenticity of goose for anyone preparing it in the Toulouse manner, and included preserved goose in a variation of the dish (this resolution is typical of the book).

Increasing the number of French bourgeois dishes would still not have pleased implacable critics like Karen Hess, who told me in 1995, "Julia and her collaborators were cooking *haute cuisine* like the chefs, not like the French woman at home . . . who cooks in pots that can be stirred occasionally during the day. Julia's fussy cooking is what chefs with time and staff do. *Mastering* is restaurant cooking, not home cooking." Hess "missed the point," says Jones, who maintained that the book included peasant, *bourgeoise,* and *haute cuisine,* "practically everything French cuisine had to offer." Indeed, the volume offered domestic dishes such as *pot-au-feu* and several beef stews (*daube*) along with *haute cuisine* dishes such as *pâté de canard en croûte* and others using such expensive ingredients as lobster. Hovering between these two extremes—extremes that chef Jacques Pépin compares to a Thoroughbred horse and a plow horse—is *cuisine bourgeoise,* prepared in homes with hired cooks and in bistros. Julia and Simca's book, both Pépin and esteemed culinary historian Barbara Wheaton agree, is in "the tradition of *cuisine bourgeoise* with touches of *haute cuisine."*

Aside from the four additional recipes, Jones only "tinkered" with the details, she says. Some of the details included cutting down on the number of techniques for making an omelet, changing the phrase "main" recipes (with variations) to "master" recipes, and not using the "paper collar stuff" for soufflés that Dione Lucas used because "it is not done in France" and "why complicate things?" Julia wrote to Jones. They also agreed that the simple line drawings should be limited to kitchen equipment, to techniques in the making of omelets, soufflés, and pastry puffs, to cutting procedures for artichokes, beef, mushrooms, and to the making of several desserts.

Years before, Julia and Simca had worked out the format for the book, the two-column approach with the ingredients on the left and the directions on the right. They insisted on keeping this format, having a running guide at the top corner of each page, and using French accents—to which Jones heartily agreed. Judith more clearly matched the beginning of a new set of directions (in the right-hand column) with the beginning of the ingredients that went into the dish (to the left). Julia suggested that lines be drawn. The result made the directions even clearer.

The style and clarity of this first volume, now considered a genuine masterpiece in culinary history, were already present when Knopf bought the manuscript. The few additional recipes and the usual stylistic adjustments (for example, taking out some dashes) were made, but there were so few apparent changes that the full manuscript was never returned to Julia in Norway before the copy editors saw it. Adjustments were made by letter. Julia approved of the illustrations by Sidonie Coryn, Warren Chappell designed the book, Paul wrote the dedication ("To La Belle France whose peasants, fishermen, housewives, and princes—not to mention her chefs—through generations of inventive and loving concentration have created one of the world's great arts"), and Julia wrote a half page of acknowledgments thanking their teachers (Bugnard and Thillmont) and Avis DeVoto, among others.

Paul made plans for his early resignation from the government (they were determined to be settled in their Cambridge home in time for the publication of the book in October 1961) and settled on the details of their vacation in Paris and Grasse for the end of September 1960. Meanwhile, among their final visitors that summer was Richard Bissell, Paul's longtime friend and the self-assured chief of covert action under Allen Dulles of the CIA. They talked about the coming presidential elections but nothing about Bissell's recent briefing of Vice President Nixon on the psychological warfare against Cuba's Castro. (Not until the following April, three months after Kennedy's inauguration, would they learn that Dick had masterminded the abortive invasion of the Bay of Pigs in Cuba.) When Julia's father and Phila visited in September, Julia had to avoid any political talk, though she was fascinated to see tapes of the Nixon-Kennedy debates.

The book demanded her immediate attention, particularly the difficult decision concerning the choice of a title. Family, friends, and the staff of Knopf were volleying with names for the book, mostly bad, such as "A Map for the Territory of French Food." In a list Julia sent to Jones in mid-July were two titles closest to the final choice: "The Art of French Cooking" and "The Master French Cookbook." By mid-October, Jones was tinkering with "The Mastery of French Cooking" and a thirty-one-word subtitle. Julia returned a list of twenty-six, including "Mastery of French Cooking" and her preference, "La Bonne Cuisine Française," which Knopf immediately rejected. By mid-November, Judith submitted the title the Knopf staff had chosen—*Mastering the Art of French Cooking*—and on November 23, 1960, Julia said *oui!*

When a new book entitled *French Provincial Cooking,* by English culinary writer Elizabeth David, appeared at the end of 1960, Julia was initially worried about their competition ("this is our most serious competition so far, I think"). But they all clearly saw the difference between the volumes. Julia noted that David's book was not as easy to follow; nor was it classic French, though she admired David's knowledge and "masterful" writing, which was conversational and anecdotal. Judith Jones said the recipes were too casual for Americans. She summed up the pitch Knopf would make for the book when she wrote to Julia on May 10 that *Mastering* was the "best and only *working* French cookbook to date which will do for French cooking here in America what Rombauer's *The Joy of Cooking* did for standard [American] cooking."

A STORM OF SNOW AND GALLEYS

Paul sent in his resignation from the government on December 19, 1960, then a four-page letter to someone named "John" on December 23, 1960, mentioning the fact that in twelve years of service he received only one promotion. He wrote Charlie, "I do a great many things well, but the coercive structure of foreign service need and regulations makes no place for them." His official resignation took effect on May 19, 1961, with his annuity of about $3,000 beginning one month after his sixty-second birthday, January 15, 1964, at which time he would have served sixteen years, one month, and a few days. They prepared for what promised to be a strangely snowless Norwegian Christmas. Paul wrote "A Christmas Prayer," beginning "O, where art thou Snow?" and ending:

> Get going thou fluffy
> bastard, and pile up thine self on twigs
> and things. Art we in Florida or Norway,
> for God sakes? Amen.

The "prayer" worked and they celebrated a white Norwegian Christmas holiday with the Howes and Robert Duemling, the young man with whom Paul had walked to work in Washington, who was visiting from Rome. For Duemling's gift of wineglasses, Paul wrote more verse of gratitude, the last in a number of light verses this month, suggesting the relief and pleasure his decision to resign had brought. Duemling believed that if one of the Childs were to become famous, it would be Paul, with his array of talents and mental agility ("Paul was fascinating"). As he did for the birthday parties of Erica and Rachel in the 1940s, Paul made a spiderweb of string, filling the living room and directing the Howe children to their presents. After a feast of goose (which disappointed the children), they had dessert and coffee at the Howes' house.

When Frances Willis left as U.S. ambassador to Norway, Clifton and Leonie Wharton, their dear friends from Marseilles, arrived. Julia and Paul almost regretted their decision to leave early, but they were in an excellent position to prepare the embassy staff and the Norwegians for the arrival of the first Negro ambassador to rise through the U.S. Foreign Service. Even before Wharton presented his credentials to the King, Paul and Julia gave a party to introduce them to their Norwegian friends.

From the time of JFK's inauguration in January 1961 until May 18 when the galleys were returned to Knopf, Julia was overwhelmed every day with checking details, compiling lists, composing letters, and responding to the copy editing of their manuscript. Every logical and organizational skill she learned in the OSS was put to excellent use. "You are such an extraordinarily efficient worker," Mrs. Jones informed her.

For more than four months she did all the work required of the authors. About the only input that came from her co-authors was a request from Louisette to have her name changed (she had recently divorced), but it was too late. Also she wanted *Cooking* changed to *Cuisine* in the title, but Julia dismissed this as overused in recent titles and not simple enough. Simca requested a few changes in the introductory comments on wine (they dropped the reference to Grand Marnier because Simca's grandfather developed the formula for Bénédictine—they changed it to *soufflé à la liqueur*). "Ah, the French! I don't envy Kennedy having to try and persuade De Gaulle about anything!" Julia wrote to Judith Jones.

Simca lined up a series of articles to include their recipes in *Cuisine et Vins de France,* and Julia gave an interview and photographs for two illustrated articles in a Norwegian women's magazine. Judith Jones was delighted: "If we can wrestle up the same kind of publicity that you have been getting for yourself in Oslo, when you are here in New York we should really get this book off the ground." In a letter to Jones, Julia had revealed her understanding of the importance of promotion for the success of the book and her own career as teacher and journalist: "But [I] will not, under any circumstances, be a 'figure,' merely an authority, I hope. It is a tough racket to crack among the NY magazines, but I want to do it."

Week after week the snow fell, melted, and fell again. The mails from Oslo to New York City carried letter after letter and package after package with illustrations and galleys. Avis DeVoto's friend Benjamin Fairbank cooked the recipes and found several flaws in them, and a second copy editor found inconsistencies in the subdividing of the book, each with a different typography. These problems were all resolved to make this a book with clear directions and uncrowded pages. Julia was determined to complete the galleys in time to pack before the arrival of her family, which planned a last-minute holiday visit.

The Algerian crisis, and Julia and Paul's recognition that the book was their first priority, led them to cancel the family visit and a final trip to Paris. They would go straight to New York City and devote their time to reading the final proofs, which incorporated the galley corrections. Julia was also determined to do the index herself. She had nine days after sending in the final galleys to pack and to attend farewell parties. The Howes said, "There were lots of farewell parties for them. People were in total tears when Julia and Paul left Oslo." Bjorn Egge, who would soon go with the UN peacekeeping force to Zaire, expressed the sentiments of the Norwegians: "Julia and Paul [were] excellent representatives of their country in Norway. . . . We are also proud to underline the fact that Julia and Paul, after their return to the States, became the best ambassadors of Norwegian culture we could ever dream of."

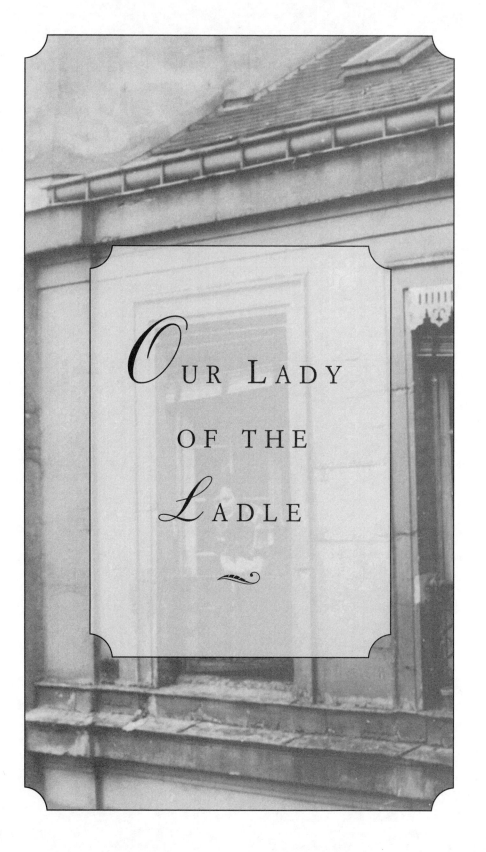

OUR LADY OF THE LADLE

Chapter 16

LAUNCHING THE BOOK
(1961 – 1962)

"Cook-books are fairy-tales for grown-ups."
The Times (London)

FOR HER FORTY-NINTH birthday and at the brink of a new career and a new home, Paul Child wrote his wife a birthday sonnet:

> O Julia, Julia, Cook and nifty wench,
> Whose unsurpassed quenelles and hot soufflés,
> Whose English, Norse and German, and whose French,
> Are all beyond my piteous powers to praise—
> Whose sweetly-rounded bottom and whose legs,
> Whose gracious face, whose nature temperate,
> Are only equaled by her scrambled eggs:
> Accept from me, your ever-loving mate,
> This acclamation shaped in fourteen lines
> Whose inner truth belies its outer sight;
> For never were there foods, nor were there wines,
> Whose flavor equals yours for sheer delight.
> > O luscious dish! O gustatory pleasure!
> > You satisfy my taste-buds beyond measure.

Staying in New York City and Lumberville after landing on June 5, 1961, Julia and Paul read proofs, then rushed to Lopaus Point for rejuvenation of body and soul, salt air, and the ministrations of many lobsters and fresh blueberries. They also corrected proofs for the index they had prepared before returning to Cambridge with George and Betty Kubler to show them their Irving Street house, recently vacated by the tenant. The day following Julia's birthday, the furniture stored in Washington, DC, arrived at Irving Street. Architect Bob Kennedy (Edith's eldest son) conferred with them on plans for renovating the kitchen and adding an elaborate entrance tower to the third-floor apartment, which they would rent out. While they were awaiting the shipment from Oslo, they joined Avis in Vermont, where she was working for the Bread Loaf Writers' Conference outside Middlebury. Paul's photographs of the poets and writers were called, by the assistant director of Bread Loaf, "some of the best" ever taken "on the mountain." Julia had little time to help Avis in the office because she was correcting the last page proofs. There was talk of Julia and Paul returning the following year.

ℒAUNCHING THE BOOK

Julia was sitting at her desk in Cambridge at the end of September, the furniture and boxes from Washington and Oslo unpacked but the noise of construction in the kitchen disrupting the peace and quiet. She held in her lap her first creation, *Mastering the Art of French Cooking,* after a ten-year gestation, fraught with hard work and future hopes. "It weighs a ton!" she said of the three-pound, 734-page book. After months of physical labor on the book and the move from Oslo, her joy was tempered by personal crisis. She consulted with several doctors, who informed her that she needed a hysterectomy. There was no time now. She would wait until January, after the promotion of the book. After making the decision, she wrote the letters to arrange a tour for the last months of the year. In her letters to family and friends asking for help in setting up private demonstration classes, Julia emphasized, "I do not care at all for the public end of this . . . but I love to teach."

Simca arrived in New York City for the launching of the book. They won the two biggest prizes just days before: a rave review in the *New York Times* and a coming spot on the *Today* show with John Chancellor. Craig Claiborne, the food editor of the *Times,* had called their recipes "glorious" in the first review, on October 18:

[T]he most comprehensive, laudable and monumental work on [French cuisine] was published this week . . . and it will probably remain as the definitive work for nonprofessionals. . . . This [book] is . . . for those who take fundamental delight in the pleasures of cuisine. . . . It is written in the simplest terms possible and without compromise or condescension. The recipes are glorious. . . .

Claiborne, one of the premier food critics in America, singled out their cassoulet recipe, noting that it covered nearly six pages, "but there is probably not a wasted syllable." His only criticism was their use of a garlic press and the absence of recipes for puff pastry and croissants.

In the middle years of her life and in the tradition of late bloomers, Julia McWilliams Child embarked on her public career. Her eight years in Europe, where she studied cooking techniques, her organizational skills developed in the OSS Registry and writing advertising copy for Sloane's, even her drama productions for the Junior League—every life experience was used to bring her to this moment.

Carrying omelet pan, whips, bowls, and three dozen eggs, Julia and Simca appeared at NBC at dawn to practice on a hot plate. With their usual thoroughness, they worked out a routine together the night before at the home of Rachel and Anthony Prud'homme, cracking dozens of eggs. Julia, out of the country for years and without a television, was unaware of the *Today* show's audience of four million. Until show time they practiced on this miserably inadequate hot plate, which was finally hot enough for the successful omelet demonstration. "We liked [John] Chancellor, who was so nice," Julia said thirty-five years later.

The next day they gave a cooking demonstration at Bloomingdale's, and Julia reported to her sister, "The old book seems, for some happy reason, to have caught on here in New York, and our publishers are beginning to think they have a modest best seller on their hands. . . . They have ordered a second printing of 10,000 copies, and are planning a third of the same amount." They visited Dione Lucas, the most visible figure on the 1950s food scene, at her combination of restaurant and cooking school called the Egg Basket, where they got some pointers on doing public cooking demonstrations. They also visited James Beard ("the living being performing in his lair," as Julia described his cooking school on Tenth Street). He responded to their book by saying, "I only wish that I had written it myself." According to his first biographer, "he made it his role to see that the fledgling American food establishment did what was necessary to put *Mastering the Art of French Cooking* on the map."

Lunch sponsored by *Vogue* at the Cosmopolitan Club was an elegant affair ("I'm no Voguey type, heaven knows," she told Dort) arranged by their longtime friend Helen Kirkpatrick (now Milbank). The following day, after appearing on Martha Dean's radio program, they met food editor José (pronounced Josie) Wilson to discuss articles they would write for *House & Garden* magazine ("All the fancy types like J. Beard and D. Lucas write for them," she told her sister).

After the launch in New York City, Julia, Paul, and Simca traveled by train to Detroit, where Simca had done cooking demonstrations years before. By the time they got to Detroit, Knopf had published a second edition with twenty corrections (Knopf had mistakenly said in the note about the authors that Beck and Bertholle also graduated from the Cordon Bleu). From Chicago, they went to San Francisco, where Julia visited her sister and the Katharine Branson School and dined with the French consul (a cousin of Simca's husband, Jean Fischbacher). They were traveling with pots, pans, whips, knives, and bowls, for Julia drummed up several private demonstration classes. In Los Angeles she met Beard's collaborator, Helen Evans Brown of Pasadena, and she and Simca gave benefit demonstrations for charity. In Washington, DC, on the way home, Rosie Manell had a big dinner party for them.

It was a trip planned by Julia, not Knopf, whose publicity director, Harding LeMay, wrote to Julia's sister, Dorothy Cousins, that his "wife" tells him the contents of the book "are every bit as extraordinary as the format." Julia paid for her own tour, taking advantage of her network of friends and family to contact the press and set up demonstration classes. Avis also helped by sending books to the leading social figures in Georgetown (wives of McGeorge Bundy, Arthur Schlesinger, Jr., George Ball, and Kenneth Galbraith, the latter in New Delhi). On this first book tour, Julia began to establish a network of food contacts.

In Chicago, they made the cake that would remain the favorite with readers for decades: Reine de Saba, the Queen of Sheba chocolate and almond cake on page 677. It was based on a more complicated and slightly different cake of the same name by Madame Saint-Ange. Julia and Simca carried their eight-inch pan, a blender to whip the egg whites separately, and pulverized almonds to blend with the butter, sugar, and melted chocolate. They assembled the following ingredients:

Reine de Saba
4 ounces or squares semi-sweet chocolate melted with
   2 Tb rum or coffee
¼ lb or 1 stick softened butter

²/₃ cup granulated sugar

3 egg yolks

3 egg whites (1 Tb granulated sugar at end
   of whipping process)

pinch of salt

¹/₃ cup pulverized almonds

¹/₄ tsp almond extract

¹/₂ cup cake flour

While the audience watched, Julia and Simca creamed together the butter and sugar first. Then, as they blended in the egg yolks, they explained that
the batter would become very stiff. Next they stirred in the melted chocolate
and coffee, then the salt, almonds, extract, and half the stiffly whipped egg
whites. Finally, they alternately folded in the remaining egg whites and the
sifted flour before turning the mixture into a buttered and floured cake pan.
While the cake baked 25 minutes at 350 degrees, they answered questions
about the recipe and their book. Because the cake needed more time to cool
before frosting, they served it warm without a butter chocolate frosting or
almond decoration. The audience fell in love with the warm cake with its
creamy center, and with Julia.

The last stop was culinary fireworks in New York City, where they had
dinner at the Four Seasons with James Beard, chef Albert Stöckli, and Joseph
Baum, president of Restaurant Associates. "I adore both women, and Paul
came to life [for me]," Beard informed Helen Evans Brown, after he listed the
menu: cheddar cheese soup, barbecued loin of pork, and coffee cup soufflés.
In what Judith Jones calls "an extraordinarily generous gesture"—for neither
she nor the Knopf staff then knew the food world—Beard planned a party at
Dione Lucas's restaurant, including its guest list.

Dione Lucas's party for Child and Beck followed on December 15 at the
Egg Basket, which was closed for the occasion. Julia and Simca soon realized
they would have to do most of the food preparations for the thirty people,
and, true to form, they pulled it off at the last minute. (Julia had sent out the
invitations from Pasadena.) Lucas, who once owned the London Cordon Bleu
with Patience Grey, made sole with white wine sauce, Julia and Simca a
braised shoulder of lamb, with Lucas preparing the final courses (*salade verte*
and *bavaroise aux fraises*). The thirty people included those most important to
the success of the book (though Claiborne and the Knopfs were absent):
Judith and Evan Jones, James Beard, Bill Koshland, Avis DeVoto, and several
of the press, including editor Poppy Cannon, the queen of molded Jell-O,
frozen food, and canned soup (*The Can Opener Cookbook*) of *House Beautiful*

and CBS's *Home* show fame. Avis declared it the "snazziest dinner" she had attended, but Beard pronounced Lucas's Bavarian cream "the worst." Simca flew home to Paris the next day, and Julia returned to Cambridge to face surgery and bed rest after the holidays.

Julia made certain that "my husband, Paul, our manager" was included in every event. Not only were they partners, he was indispensable in the planning of trips, managing the heavy bags of equipment and the mechanics of the presentations. Some people found him "off-putting" and cool until "you earned your way with him." According to Bill Koshland: "Paul was one of those people who knew his own worth, and he certainly knew what he regarded as Julia's worth, and I think he saw it his mission in life to see that everything worked for her."

"Paul was such a perfectionist," Jones told a journalist. "Julia struck me as more a big Smith College girl." Judith was a petite five-foot-five-inch New Englander with reserved old-school manners, and an intuitive businesswoman. She immediately formed a bond with Julia based upon their love of French cuisine and a mutual determination to make *Mastering the Art* the major success that would launch both their careers. Indeed, with the success of *Mastering,* she would become a powerful editor of cookery books, as well as fiction. In her opinion, "Julia has a highly analytical mind," and the book would not have happened without her. "It was completely Julia's contribution to analyze, to teach, to translate, to hold you by the hand because she had been that ignorant cook. [Simca] had not."

Judith introduced Julia to Alfred and Blanche Knopf, the "Jupiter and Juno" of the publishing world, according to one of their authors. But according to Avis, "it was *years* before Alfred would admit that he had a great book on his hands. And Blanche was quoted as saying, 'Oh, I don't give a damn about Julia Child.' Blanche was a very ill-tempered lady."

The reviews of the book over the first few months were not numerous, but the reviewers that mattered took a strong and enthusiastic stand. In December, the *House & Garden* editor José Wilson declared she "flipped when she saw the first copies": it was a "commonsense approach to French cuisine that dispenses with . . . the heady prose of so many recent books intent on building up a snob mystique of gourmet cooking. Wow!!" That same month the *Foreign Service Journal,* read by their OSS and USIA friends all over the world, ran a photograph of Julia and Paul and said the book was "sure to become a classic." The following March, Naomi Barry in the *International Herald Tribune* called it "one of the most satisfactory cookbooks . . . in years." And a year after publication, in *The Saturday Evening Post,* Claiborne, who privately told friends she was not born with a wooden spoon in her mouth, declared it "the most lucid volume on French cuisine since Gutenberg invented movable type. . . . This work is brilliant." According to Avis DeVoto, "the only person who was less than enthusiastic was Charlie Morton, then on *The Atlantic Monthly,*" but Avis worked on him until he came around privately.

By contrast, Sheila Hibben in *The New Yorker* criticized them for underestimating the American cook by allowing canned bouillon and canned salmon and for "lack[ing] a certain intuitive connection" with their food. Some reviewers more gently criticized the detail, but others praised that very attention to detail. Raymond Sokolov later wrote, "Child, Beck, and Bertholle [possess the same] certitude about the fundamentally immutable structure and principles of French cooking [as] . . . Auguste Escoffier, had." Evan Jones declared, "No previous U.S. culinary manual had been so detailed and yet so encouraging to those hesitant to try complicated procedures."

Few critics, except for the Hesses in 1977, criticized the adaptations to American tastes, such as their firmer soufflé. The French soufflé is "fast and runny," said André Soltner of Lutèce in 1996. "Julia adapted it to the American taste, yet even Escoffier said 'a real chef has to adapt to his time.' " Culinary historian Barbara Wheaton adds: "But of course they were adapting the techniques to her American generation." Using the language of 1996, Camille Paglia told a reporter, "What Julia Child did is deconstruct this French, classical, rule-based cooking tradition and make it accessible . . . as a source of pleasure."

Mastering the Art of French Cooking set a standard in three ways. The physical beauty and quality of the published book is superb. With large margins and print, it lies flat when opened. Thirty years later people stood in lines to have their food-stained copies autographed, only a few with the pages loosened from the cover. The presentation of the recipes set a standard for clarity and precision that changed cookbook writing and editing, heretofore chatty and sometimes sketchy in explanation. According to Beard's latest biographer, soon after the publication of the book Beard did what he called "a Julia Child job" on all the recipes of his cooking school, retyping them clearly and precisely. The pedagogical style of Beck and Child became widely imitated. According to cookbook editor Narcisse Chamberlain (daughter of Narcissa and Samuel), who at that time was editing her first book by Michael Field, *"Mastering* put good authors on notice that cookbooks had to be honest. As an editor I greatly admire that volume." Paula Wolfert, respected for her excellent books on Mediterranean cuisine, said in 1997, "Just as it's been said that all Russian literature has been taken from Gogol's overcoat, so all American food writing has been derived from Julia's apron."

Most important, *Mastering* became a landmark in food history. M. F. K. Fisher praised the volume, though on one occasion said its explanations were "so complicated." Food people as diverse as Gregory Usher, who until his death in 1994 headed the Ritz Escoffier Cooking School in Paris, Barbara Wheaton, and Mimi Sheraton, author and longtime ruling restaurant critic (after Claiborne retired) of the *New York Times,* say that this volume is among their favorite books and the best of Julia Child's work. Wheaton is on her second copy. Sheraton's book falls open to food-stained pages of *boeuf à la catalane* (page 321), *pouding alsacien* (page 626), and *pêches cardinal* (page 630).

Several other important food books were published the same year as *Mastering,* including Crown's English translation of *Larousse Gastronomique,* edited by Julia's Smith pal, Charlotte Snyder Turgeon. Craig Claiborne's *The New York Times Cook Book* appeared the same year he generously reviewed Julia and Simca's efforts. Unlike the effusive responses of Beard and Claiborne, Field's first words to his editor were: "Oh my, is this going to ruin the sales of my book?"

TELEVISION PILOT

On January 3, Paul drove Julia to Beth Israel Hospital for her operation, and laboratory tests determined that her tumor was benign. During her convalescence in Cambridge, Julia began testing recipes from Lady Bird Johnson, Jacqueline Kennedy, Mrs. Stewart Alsop, and others for José Wilson's series on Washington hostesses, which would run all year in *House & Garden.* At the end of February, Julia had an offer to be interviewed on educational television in Boston and, because there was little promotion for the book in the Boston area, she accepted. The opportunity began when they invited Beatrice Braude for dinner, a friend fired in 1953 from the USIA Paris office who had also been caught up in the McCarthy witch hunt. Bibi came to Boston to work as a writer and researcher for Henry Morgenthau, who was producing Eleanor Roosevelt's *Prospects of Mankind* for WGBH. She urged Julia to publicize her book by appearing on Professor Albert Duhamel's interview program entitled *I've Been Reading.* Though Duhamel had never interviewed the author of a book so "trivial," or practical, before, he yielded.

When Julia called the station to talk to Duhamel, Russell (Russ) Morash, a young producer in his twenties, answered the telephone. "I heard this strange voice which sounded like a smoker's pack-a-day-combined-with-asthma voice who asked if the station had a hot plate. I said I doubt it." He thought she was "very eccentric."

Julia and Paul appeared with copper bowl, whip, apron, and a dozen eggs for her interview. "It was my idea to bring on the whisk and bowl and hot plate. Educational television was just talking heads, and I did not know what we could talk about for that long, so I brought the eggs," said Julia. The interview and demonstration were not taped, as usual, because of the expense of tape ($220 to $300) and the difficulty of storing it. The response to the February interview was positive, and she received many requests for classes, briefly entertaining the idea of opening a cooking school in Boston. The station had other plans. Though several people have suggested that the station telephones "rang off the hook" and the station received "hundreds" of letters, they received twenty-seven letters, which they considered overwhelming support, says Morash. "A remarkable response," adds WGBH's president, Henry Becton, in 1996, "given that station management occasionally wondered if 27 viewers were tuned in to the modest program." Julia later told a Smith College interviewer, "Most of the letters didn't mention the book. They said, 'Get that woman back. We want to see some more cooking.' That gave them the idea." The station manager, Bob Larson, and program director, David Davis, decided that young Morash would put together three pilot programs of Mrs. Child cooking.

Amid their preparations, Julia was suddenly called back to Pasadena (she had spent a week there in March). Her father died on May 16 at eighty-two years of age. The public funeral included his business associates and members of the California Club, as well as friends such as Andy Devine, the actor. The three children discovered after the funeral that their father had kept the urns with ashes of their mother and grandparents in his study. A chapter of Julia's life, a chapter she walked away from years before, was finally closed. If there were any regrets, she would never acknowledge them. "Eh bien," she wrote Dort, "it is hard to believe that old Eagle Beak is no longer around. Thank heaven his last 15 years were so happy, and that the actual death was so quick." (Dorothy and Phila Cousins would remember in later years Julia's eyes tearing up when they spoke of Pop.) Now she needed a new will, converting her assets to a Living Trust, and she and Dorothy turned over the monthly management of the family estate to brother John.

It took nearly three months to find the sponsors, but by June WGBH was ready to tape the pilots with a minimum budget of only a few hundred dollars. Not enough money to pay for rehearsals, but enough to buy tape. Educational television was largely a volunteer effort, with Boston University students running the cameras. Paul's retirement and her $15,000-a-year family estate income allowed her to do her teaching on educational television, then as always a nonprofit venture.

"Russ, Ruthie, and I worked on the name," Julia says of their program. They considered and rejected "The Gourmet Kitchen," "French Cuisine at Home," "Cuisine Magic," "The Gourmet Arts," "The Chef at Home," "Cuisine Mastery," "Kitchen à la Française," and "Table d'Hôte." "We called it *The French Chef* because it had to be brief enough to fit into the newspaper's television guide." Ruth Lockwood, who was working on the Eleanor Roosevelt program, remembers acting as associate producer, and planning the three programs while sitting around the Norwegian-built table with Julia and Paul. Everything was written out ahead of time. Ruth, who had both a graduate degree in communications (with a concentration in television) and experience at the Fannie Farmer Cooking School in Boston, drew the layouts.

Because the station burned down in 1961 (the first copy of *Mastering* that Bibi gave to Ruth Lockwood burned with it), they filmed in the auditorium of the Boston Gas Company just off Park Square. Morash worked out of a huge Trailways bus ("with seven million miles on it") and long cables running from the generator into the building and across the terrazzo floor. Morash remembers that someone built a simple set and borrowed the appliances from architect Ben Thompson's firm, Design Research; Julia recalled that "Ruth dug around somewhere and came up with the anonymous but sprightly musical theme song." Lockwood remembers taking a red-checked tablecloth from her mother and cutting it up to make the curtains for the set and helping Julia with her makeup.

Julia and Paul arrived with all their pots and pans and eggs, piling them inside the lobby of the Boston Gas Company. While Paul parked the car, she waited for him and for a dolly to move the heavy equipment. "Hey, get that stuff out of this lobby!" said the uniformed elevator operator, as office staff and executives in business suits rushed by with disapproving looks. They finally found a janitor and got everything moved to the basement auditorium. When the crew arrived, Ruth was setting up the dining room for the final scene (she believed the "third act" should show the finished dish), Julia was arranging her detailed notes ("Simmering water in large alum. pan, upper R. burner") and to the side Paul was arranging his notes ("When J. starts buttering, remove stack molds"). Every detail was scripted, dialogue on the right, what was to be pictured on the left. "Let's shoot it!" called Russ.

We used 16 or 35 millimeter black-and-white film which ran continuously during the taping [says Morash]. There was no editing, no cutting in, and the only way to edit videotape was to literally cut the tape with a razor and tape it. We used two cameras, each the size of a coffee table, four only for the Boston Symphony, and when Julia moved from the stove to the refrigerator it was a very big deal that took careful planning.

The first pilot, "The French Omelet," was set up and filmed on June 18, 1962. The second two, "Coq au Vin" and "Onion Soup," were both filmed on June 25. The tapes were reused, as was the station's practice, and ultimately disappeared from history. But on the typed script it is clearly shown that at the last minute they added the two words that would become her signature sign-off: "This is Julia Child. Thank you, *bon appétit.*"

At 8:30 on July 28, after a big steak dinner, Paul pulled out the television they purchased and kept in an unused fireplace and watched the first program. Julia was shocked to see herself for the first time: "There was Mrs. C swooping about the work surface and panting heavily. I had put too much into the program. The second would be much better. Perhaps if I did twenty more," she told James Beard, "I'd get on to the technique a bit better." What the audience enjoyed in part was the *lack* of studied technique, the natural enthusiasm of Mrs. C.

I "careened around the stove, and WGBH-TV lurched into educational television's first cooking program," Julia wrote six years later. At the time, Morash says, "I did not think that this was going to be momentous. This was an extremely disposable medium, and I was doing important stuff like science and language. I was on data overload in those days." He would later produce *The Victory Garden* and *This Old House.* Yet the timing was significant, for the January before *Mastering the Art of French Cooking* was published, President John F. Kennedy and his Francophile wife, Jacqueline, had moved into the White House and in April hired a French chef named René Verdon. French cooking was trendy and chic but seemingly unattainable, its techniques mysterious, the words unpronounceable.

Television was a relatively new medium, with the station signing on at four in the afternoon. Julia's programs ran in what is now called prime time, precisely because it was educational and family-oriented. The introduction of French cooking attracted educational television's usual audience of university and privileged people. "These pilots would not have worked in Bayonne, New Jersey," says Morash. "It had to have happened in Boston. Julia was a child of academe, well connected to Harvard people."

*B*READ LOAF AND
THE CAMBRIDGE CIRCLE

For the second year, before the Child family holiday in Maine, Julia and Paul went to Bread Loaf, this time for the full term of the writers' conference, from August 14 through August 29 (the third in her pilot series aired while she was in Vermont). The day after her arrival they celebrated her fiftieth birthday. For the fun of being with Avis and sitting in on the lectures and readings, Julia worked as "assistant deputy typist" to Mary Moore Molony, managing editor of *The American Scholar* and secretary in the summers at Bread Loaf (it was she who typed the Houghton Mifflin draft of Julia and Simca's first, rejected version of the cookbook). Paul was official photographer, "the Photographic Consort," as assistant director Paul Cubeta called him, the man who captured Robert Frost against the clear Vermont sky. "Julia is an absolute dreamboat," he added in a letter that year. In recompense for their work they paid no room and board. Julia loved the classes: "I learn so much from the lectures, even the poets," she told James Beard without apparent irony.

The Bread Loaf environment was both intellectually heady and physically relaxing. The writers' conference, founded in 1926 and directed by John Farrar (then at Doubleday), was a summer camp for professors and writers, with the lure of drinking and fishing. Even the waiters were writers, unpublished but "highly promising." Isolated and peaceful on acres of tranquil green grass, Bread Loaf offered only intellectual stimulation, and that was dulled nightly by alcohol. In truth, it had the reputation for alcoholic and sexual stimulation, earning the name Bed Loaf among insiders. The summer literary colony was also, at that time, "exclusively New England," says Peter Davison. Julia and Paul became friends of poets Richard Yates, David McCord, John and Judith Ciardi, John Nims, Robert Frost, who lived just down the road, and Carlos Baker (Hemingway's future biographer). They all gathered in the soft evening air, laughter emanating through the bushes of Treman House, which Avis oversaw. Here was the scene of the late afternoon alcoholic socials, much like Bernard DeVoto's Sunday evening "hours" in Cambridge. Indeed, many of the people at Bread Loaf were connected to Cambridge circles.

Ciardi was the director, though Paul Cubeta made all the arrangements. The great poet was called "Big Daddy" behind his back, and his national reputation and hauteur kept him from being questioned about any decision. Frost, who was considered the unofficial poet laureate of the country, especially since his reading at the Kennedy inauguration the year before, was always the guiding light of the writers' conference. Katherine Anne Porter, Eudora Welty, Carson McCullers, and Louis Untermeyer attended in past

years, as did Wallace Stegner (Stegner and DeVoto had been boys together in
Utah). Bernard DeVoto taught at Bread Loaf for decades before his death,
after which Houghton Mifflin endowed a fellowship in his name. DeVoto
insisted on teaching fiction, though David H. Bain, whose history of Bread
Loaf is called *Whose Woods These Are,* claims rightly that DeVoto was a
terrible novelist but a brilliant historian. Avis continued to work after her
husband's death and was paid a modest salary to put some order in the Bread
Loaf house party.

"Treman House, a cream-colored cottage at the edge of the writers'
conference area, was dedicated to the generous drinking habits (Bloody Marys
before lunch, cocktails before dinner, other drinks or beer after the evening
lecture or reading). Treman was open to leaders, fellows, and visitors like me,"
says poet Peter Davison, but "it was off limits to ordinary students." There
was a large veranda under two of the upstairs rooms. Davison remembers that
the summer before, when the sun was setting on the downhill side of the
mountain at the cocktail hour, Avis introduced him to Fletcher Pratt, William
Sloane, and Julia ("a tall woman, robust, genial and smiling, with a remarkable
voice"). Julia reminisced:

> We went because of Avis, who was in charge of the bar. I went to a lot of
> the lectures and learned about writing and how vivid it should be. Our
> house had a lot of fun, and Treman was where everyone drank a lot,
> screaming and yelling. Once when I went back to our house, I could
> hear the screaming from there. Ran into my old friend Joe Sloane who
> had lived in Pasadena, and we made many longtime friends.

Though Julia and Paul lived in Maple House this and later summers,
they worked and hung out at Treman Cottage, which Avis ran "on a strict
system, like a military social club where, before equality came in, they welcomed only the anointed few," according to a later assistant director. Edward
(Sandy) Martin, professor of English at Middlebury, said, "It was a social
center of the colony and only the staff were welcome for drinks. They drank
until just before dinner and then walked into dinner almost late and all sat at
the 'high table,' a long table at the rear near the window where it was cooler.
Since they were not paid well, Ciardi felt they should have privileges."

"The social tides of Cambridge washed us up on the same beaches as the
Childs quite frequently," said Peter Davison, then a thirty-one-year-old editor
at the Atlantic Monthly Press. After meeting Julia and Paul the previous summer at Bread Loaf, he and his wife, Jane Truslow Davison (a distinguished
writer in her own right), dined with the Childs at the home of Theodore and

Kay Morrison—he taught at Harvard and was longtime director of Bread Loaf before Ciardi took over. At Avis's book party for Julia, the Childs met two other Atlantic Monthly Press colleagues, including Wendy Morison Beck and her husband, H. Brooks Beck of Hill & Barlow, who eventually became the Childs' first lawyer. Julia was partial to Jane Davison because she was witty and literate, a Smith sister (housemate and graduate with Sylvia Plath in 1955), and unafraid to invite the Childs for dinner. These were what Davison calls "the days of ambitious dinner parties given by underemployed literary housewives."

Through the late Davis Pratt, Paul's former student and prodigy at Avon Old Farms School and a curator of photography, they met Davis's twin brother, Herb, and his wife, Pat, lifelong residents of Cambridge. The Herb Pratts became very close to the Childs, traveling back to Europe in coming years, and Pat would become one of a host of volunteers on Julia's television shows.

If Boston, with all its educational institutions, was "an academic tribal reservation," as one of its journalists claimed, "the reservation was centered in Cambridge." In addition to their OSS colleague Cora DuBois at Harvard, Paul had a childhood friend, the distinguished composer Randall Thompson, head of the music department. Harvard was "a carbuncle of cabals and cliques," wrote novelist Wallace Stegner in his biography of Bernard DeVoto, but the Childs' faculty neighbors all became lifelong friends, especially those who were part of Bernard DeVoto's *The Hour* (his mock-heroic hymn to alcohol published anonymously in 1951) and whom Julia and Paul met in November 1959: Marion Schlesinger, then married to Arthur Schlesinger, Jr., and Kitty Galbraith, wife of John Kenneth. Both were off serving the Kennedy administration when Julia and Paul moved to Cambridge. Schlesinger, who like his father before him was a history professor at Harvard, was serving as special assistant to the President. Catherine (Kitty) Atwater, Julia's Smith classmate, was then living in India, where Galbraith was serving as U.S. ambassador. The Galbraiths would return in 1963 to Harvard and Francis Street, behind the Child house. Kitty told Julia she gave *Mastering the Art of French Cooking* as a wedding gift in India. Galbraith admired the intelligence Julia brought to her profession and her height: "We encountered each other as people whose heads were always above the crowd." The nearly seven-foot Galbraith believed that "if she had been a foot shorter, she would have had a much more difficult time. The only form of discrimination that is still allowed in the world is in favor of tall people and it's a very subtle matter." Marion Schlesinger called Galbraith and Child the "benign storks" of her neighborhood.

Literary Boston of the late 1950s would be portrayed by Peter Davison in *The Fading Smile*. The center of this literary world, and the subject of Davison's longest chapter, was Robert Lowell, whose "For the Union Dead" young Davison published in *The Atlantic Monthly,* where he was poetry editor. His literary memoir is a group portrait not only of Davison himself and Lowell but also of Robert Frost, Anne Sexton, Sylvia Plath, Richard Wilbur, W. S. Merwin, Donald Hall, Maxine Kumin, Adrienne Rich, and Stanley Kunitz. Julia and Paul moved to Cambridge just as Boston was beginning to lose its attraction as the central watering hole, to use Richard Eder's image, of American poetry in this century. None in this tweedy or seersucker (depending on the season) Boston knew that the voice that would become the most famous in their city (after Kennedy) had just moved into the Josiah Royce house on Irving Street.

These overlapping circles of WGBH, Harvard, Shady Hill, and the Atlantic Monthly Press groups washed together through the years. Many of their friends became regular habitués of Lopaus Point in Maine in the summers, where they all met Walter and Helen Lippmann over cocktails. Also on Mount Desert Island with the Charlie Childs was the summer home of the great Harvard historian Samuel Eliot Morison (Wendy Beck's father).

"We live in a lovely town because everyone is doing something," Julia was fond of saying. That they belonged in the intellectual circles of Cambridge and Boston was clear in the minds of their friends. Paul was a learned conversationalist whose interests and knowledge ranged widely. Julia had a New England dignity everyone respected and she remained clearly noncommercial, never endorsing a product. She could become a television personality without loss of stature because she was on educational television. "Julia was a scholar," said Morash, "because she eats and breathes her subject, researches every detail, can take a set of directions and understand what the result will be, is totally comfortable with her subject, and is a recognized authority."

As early as August 23, Julia informed Beard that there was a plan for a series of television cooking classes with guest chefs such as Stöckli of the Four Seasons and there was a good chance New York City's Channel 13 would buy the series. She saw the television classes as an extension of her teaching, not as a career in itself. In her world, television occupied no major space, and indeed it was suspect. They did turn it on to see Richard Nixon's farewell to the press ("I hope this is the last we shall see of him publicly," she said, having just read Teddy White's *The Making of the President).*

She went to New York City in October and November to teach classes at James Beard's cooking school, hoping to team up with Beard and Helen Evans Brown for joint lessons and demonstrations. Julia and James Beard were drawn to each other for many reasons. Both were Westerners (from California and Oregon), companionable, generous, and big. They loved the theater of the kitchen and hated pretension. Beard, who became her news line to the New York food world, was a jovial and natural man who folded his egg whites with his hands. They would be "brother and sister," wrote his first biographer, Evan Jones.

While Julia was in New York, Beard arranged for her to demonstrate the making of *pâte feuilletée* at the Four Seasons. ("Don't know why they want me to do them, when all those fancy types are in NY," she wrote to Dort.) She also took every opportunity to teach small groups in private homes in her neighborhood:

> As a way to earn money and get a class going I gave cooking lessons at a friend's house for her friends [she told food writer Barbara Sims-Bell]. I would give them a great lunch, such as poached egg on mushroom and leek salad, a little pastry thing with béarnaise sauce, and chocolate cake. I did not have to worry about buying the food or getting the friends; I only charged $50 dollars; sometimes I would buy the food and give them the bill. They provided the wine. Then I would leave them with the dishes. I would leave with $200. I would not have made money in my own home. For all that work, you should make some money.

The last months of 1962, before they left for Christmas in San Francisco with Dorothy, were devoted to preparations for the January filming of thirteen (of a projected twenty-six) half-hour programs of *The French Chef,* produced by Russ Morash. Associate producer Ruth Lockwood, Paul, and Julia planned and named each segment. Life would never be the same again.

Chapter 17

LET THEM EAT QUICHE: THE FRENCH CHEF (1963 – 1964)

"I'm a teacher and I'll stay with
the educators."

                      JULIA CHILD

AS THE CAMERA moved in toward the steaming pot, Julia leaned down with her kitchen pinchers and lifted the cheesecloth cover to peer inside, then looked up into the camera and said, "What do we have here? The big, bad artichoke. Some people are afraid of the big, bad artichoke!" The music swelled and the title *The French Chef* filled the screen. "Welcome to *The French Chef.* I'm Julia Child."

She stood behind the counter on another day, with a large knife held high over a row of naked chickens, each resting upright on its tail, or what was traditionally called (she would later point out to a few angry viewers) the "pope's nose." As she moved from her left to her right, the smallest chicken to the largest, she tapped each chicken as if knighting them and announced dramatically, "Miss Broiler, Miss Fryer, Miss Roaster . . ." The music announced *The French Chef* and Julia introduced herself last.

On another occasion, after making a potato pancake that did not properly brown on one side, she demonstrated how to flip it over in the pan. "You have to have the courage of your convictions," she said, giving the pan a short, fast jerk forward and back. She succeeded only partially and had to pick a piece of the potato mixture off the stovetop. "But you can always pick it up. If you are alone in the kitchen, whooooooo is going to see?" she sang with confidence.

At the end of each program, even one in which she was moist with stove heat and exhausted by chopping, she carried her dish to the demonstration "dining table," lighted the candles, poured the wine, and tasted the dish with obvious relish and triumph, almost with an air of surprise. Once again, "the forces of art and reason," as Lewis Lapham put it, had "triumphed over primeval chaos." *"Bon appétit!"* she called out, lifting her glass of wine. Brought to you by Hills Bros. Coffee and Polaroid.

Theater, as Aristotle pointed out two thousand years ago, is both spectacle and a well-turned plot with beginning, middle, and end. To Ruth Lockwood's credit, Julia's half-hour programs were mini-dramas beginning with the presentation of the characters (chorus line of chickens, steaming artichokes), then the plot (the challenge of creating a dish called *poulet en cocotte bonne femme),* the rising tension (deboning, stirring, mixing), the climax (cooked chicken drawn from the oven), and the resolution (nibbles from a beautifully presented dish). Each program had about it, one critic noted, "the uncertainty of a reckless adventure." Drama and resolution.

Julia's sense of timing and her dramatic skills were an integral ingredient in the success of *The French Chef.* The gangly girl who staged plays in her mother's attic with her brother John and the Hall children, who acted in plays for the Katharine Branson School, Smith College, and the Junior League, had long prepared herself for performing in front of an audience. Even when she and Simca were creating their book, she urged her partner to think in terms of an audience and "clean up" any bad habits.

Julia understood the value of the visual presentation, whether it was lining up naked chickens according to size or holding up two baguettes to the camera, watching one fall slowly and limply until it formed a circle, then tossing it over her shoulder with disdain, saying, "Terrible, terrible bread!" Or holding up two lobsters and explaining how to tell the boy lobster from the girl. Julia credits Lockwood and later Morash with some of her great openings and closings. Later she named a suckling pig John Barrymore because of his beautiful profile. "She is a natural clown," Paul pointed out to the numerous journalists who in the years to come would visit the tapings. Many reporters commented on the ease of her performance. One reporter mistakenly called it "an ad-libbed show," and a magazine termed her approach "muddleheaded nonchalance." The best dramatic talents make their work look "easy." As her friend Betty Kubler, a founder of the Longwharf Theater in New Haven, said of Julia's acting genius, "Well, she's got it! It is something you have or don't have . . . a presence, timing, instinct for what's funny, the ability to carry through with a gag or prop, it's instinct." Food writer Jeffrey Steingarten adds: "It is her personality. She didn't invent herself for the show."

MAKING *THE FRENCH CHEF*

Behind the scenes, as few in the audience would know, were many people, hours of preparation, four to six versions of the same dish at various stages of preparation, numerous notes and lists, and—as it is in legitimate theater—a lot of mess and fakery: though she appeared alone, there were several technicians and a hardworking husband behind the camera. The "wine" in the bottle was really Gravy Master (a darkening mixture) diluted with water. One false behind-the-scenes story that took on mythical proportions had assistants crouched under the table to take away dirty bowls. That scene was staged as a skit for a WGBH fund-raiser.

The first program of *The French Chef* was filmed on January 23, 1963. WGBH began with a series of thirteen episodes, then added thirteen more—never knowing there would eventually be 119 half-hour programs. Each program lasted 28 minutes and 52 seconds. Julia began with *boeuf bourguignon* and French onion soup, and ended with lobster *à l'américaine* and *crêpes suzette:* "Ruth, Paul, and I decided to start out with a few audience catchers, dishes that were famous [Russ called them her old chestnuts], like *boeuf bourguignon,* and then gradually work into the subject."

When the Boston Gas Company dismantled their original kitchen, Russ Morash found a demonstration kitchen which would accommodate his outdoor bus at the Cambridge Electric Company on Blackstone Street. It was on the second floor of "a warehousey-looking building behind the smokestacks that line the Charles River." Citizens paid their electric bills elsewhere in the building, but the kitchen, used for home economics demonstrations, "was a real *Leave It to Beaver* kind of kitchen with chintz curtains looking out on a fake background with sink and countertop, refrigerator, and built-in oven. We built an island for the stove and the cutting and chopping area." Design Research again sent over the dining-room set to be used in the final scene of each program.

Paul, who arrived early and shoveled the snow off the fire escape steps above the parking lot, was porter and unpacker, even dishwasher. "Paul was the entire physical part of it," said Ruth Lockwood. "He was there from the planning to the wash-up." Julia and Ruth arranged the equipment Paul brought up the fire escape and, while Ruth called out each item on a long list, Julia said "check." Julia arranged simple idiot cards ("put butter here," "turn on burner #3"), and Ruth held a loose-leaf notebook and stopwatch as well as cards that said "stop gasping" and "wipe face." Marian Morash, married to Julia's producer, Russ, describes Julia as "an incredibly organized person who would come to the location with everything organized. I loved the no-nonsense care when working with food, and [her] spontaneous gaiety and sense of humor that surrounded the business at hand." They began doing four programs a week, then cut back to three, eventually two, and at the end of two years finally one. Russ Morash believes that as the idiot cards got more detailed and numerous, the program became "less spontaneous" (though more professional). "The best programs were the first ones we made, which are no longer available." Avis also thought these were "the best of the lot" because they "had a sort of purity to them." In the introduction to her next book, Julia explained why they became more structured: she had no sense of whether one or five minutes had passed, and making onion soup one day she thought she had too many techniques to demonstrate—cutting, softening, browning the onions, *croûton*-making, gratinéing:

> I rushed through that program like a madwoman but I got everything in, only to find that when I carried the onion soup to the dining room I had gone so fast we still had 8 minutes left. Agony. I had to sit there and talk for all that time. Russ erased the tape back to about the 15-minute point, but after it happened again, Ruth devised the plan of breaking up the recipe into blocks of time. I could go as fast or slow as I wanted in the allotted time block, but I could not go into the next step until I got the signal.

For the first series Julia spent the weekend planning and writing the program, spent Monday shopping with Paul, preparing the food and rehearsing at home. On Tuesday, they moved everything over to the studio and taped the program. On Wednesday, Julia began the process again while Morash filmed *The Science Reporter,* and on Thursday they set up and taped another one or two programs. For the next series they taped on Wednesdays and Fridays, putting the program together live, meaning they taped without stopping the film. Julia had to come prepared with a raw goose, a partially cooked goose, the cooked goose, and a spare.

The purpose of the programs, as in all her teaching, was to present French techniques, such as wielding a knife, boning a carcass, cleaning a leek, whipping or folding egg whites. "The idea was to take the bugaboo out of French cooking, to demonstrate that it is not merely good cooking but that it follows definite rules. The simplicity of a velouté sauce, for instance, is butter, flour, and seasoned liquid, but the rule is that the flour is cooked in the butter before the liquid is added. If you don't cook [in this sequence] your sauce will have the horrid pasty taste of uncooked flour." Julia the teacher spent nineteen hours preparing for *each half hour* of teaching: a fraction of the time taken for a recipe in their book, yet a disproportionately long amount of time for "classroom" preparation; but her ephemeral art was being made permanent on film and her audience was a thousand times greater than an average demonstration class. "Mrs. Child," said Lewis Lapham, "thinks of herself as a missionary instructing a noble but savage race in a civilized art." When the news went around that "commercial networks are begging her to come aboard," she informed one paper that "I'm a teacher and I'll stay with the educators."

Russ operated on a shoestring, and he believes that his ability to keep down expenses was "one reason for the lengthy success" of the program. He called it "guerrilla television," for operating with huge machinery under an urgent sense of time was like going to war. At first the studio paid $50 per episode to Julia and Paul, who did all the shopping. By 1966 she received $200 plus expenses per program.

Educational television (now called public television) began in Boston as an outgrowth of lectures at the Lowell Institute. It got its money from government grants and industry donations but did not operate for a profit, and was especially blessed in Boston, which granted it a low number (Channel 2). Because lower frequencies are easier to tune in, most big cities gave their lower numbers to commercial stations such as ABC, NBC, and CBS (a commercial exploitation that held back educational television a generation, says Morash). The efforts of Boston banker Ralph Lowell and the power of the city's educational and cultural institutions—WGBH is licensed by the FCC to MIT, Boston University, Harvard, the Boston Symphony, the Boston Museum, and Boston College, among others—resulted in getting the lowest number for their educational channel. But, as Morash points out, "we did not have the money to buy a transmitter big enough to get the signal up to New Hampshire then. It was like putting the signal out with a fifty-watt bulb and a guy pedaling." Nevertheless, Julia was there at the beginning; indeed, she helped to build what would be one of the most influential educational stations in the country.

When the taping was over, the crew usually ate the edible food, though sometimes they refused to eat produce such as asparagus, which was unfamiliar. Slowly, they became more adventuresome and ate asparagus, mushrooms, and chicken livers. "The best free lunch in town," said one grip. Julia sent the raw or partially cooked version home with Russ, with detailed instructions for its cooking. Marian, his wife, prepared the dish as if she were taking at-home classes with Julia. Her burgeoning talent for cooking eventually won out over her shyness and she came onto the set of a 1970s series as a regular assistant to Julia.

They set an incredible pace the first year of taping by working twelve-hour days and finishing thirty-four shows during the first half of the year. "I like working with men," Julia often said. "Russ," who was not yet thirty, "was the boss!" In 1994 he said, "By today's standards the schedule was heroic." "It's the hardest work I've ever done," Julia informed Helen Evans Brown, who wrote from Pasadena that she heard Julia's programs "are terrific. . . . It takes a certain very definite personality to come over the air and you have it. Poor Jim [Beard] doesn't, which is a pity as he is 7/8th ham!" (By October the Pasadena station was airing *The French Chef.*) Beard, with whom Julia hoped to collaborate, invited her down whenever there was a break in her filming to teach several classes at his cooking school. Her letters reveal that Julia intended to present other cooks, both professional and talented amateurs, on her television program, but while she was waiting until the program was professionalized enough to invite Beard to appear, she became the only performer the audience expected and wanted to see each week.

In addition to this back-aching schedule, Julia managed to correct the page proofs of the British edition of *Mastering,* tape promotion ads for WGBH fund-raisers, teach classes for Beard, give special demonstrations at the Women's City Club, the Boston Club, and Newburyport's Smith Club, as well as sit for interviews with the press in Boston and New York City. That summer she and Paul missed Bread Loaf, but took two and a half months in the fall to visit Norway (sailing on the *Oslofjord* for Oslo on August 22), France, and England. Julia saw for the first time France's only television cook, Raymond Oliver, who appeared every two weeks and "took five minutes to peel the peppers," she wrote Avis DeVoto. But the most important result of these weeks in the south of France was to plan with Simca for a second volume of *Mastering.* They also discussed the possibility of building a small house for Julia and Paul on Jean Fischbacher's family land in Provence.

Julia also met Elizabeth David, England's doyenne of cookery writing. Their meeting was preceded by several important moves: advance buildup by DeVoto and Beard, a mailing of *Mastering* to David (who responded on May 10, 1963, that it was "marvelous" and "meticulous"), and the publication of the British edition of *Mastering* by Cassell, for which David wrote a review. Formerly an actress, David now shunned the public spotlight and wrote enduring culinary literature *(French Provincial Cooking,* her penultimate book, was published in 1960); indeed, her first books did not even list ingredients. "Her recipes were the reverse of Julia's," says Alice Waters, her most ardent American disciple, "she begins at the market and then makes the recipe." Julia, overlooking her anti-American reputation, found her "nice, quiet, shy," and when she read David's review ("the first one from a real pro") she was ecstatic: David drew a lengthy and exalted comparison of Julia with her "predecessors" Eliza Acton and Madame Saint-Ange—all three had "quiet persistence . . . style . . . and heart." As happy as Julia was with the review, she shuddered at the "translation" into English by someone who was not a cook.

Julia returned to Boston for immediate resumption of filming *The French Chef* in the first week of December 1963. One-third of the recipes for the program came from *Mastering the Art of French Cooking,* but most were slightly revised because time constraints necessitated cutting a few steps. She learned to bring in one prechopped onion and one on which she would demonstrate the chopping technique before showing the viewer what the fully chopped onion was to look like. Some of the recipes would be used later in *Mastering II.* "How am I going to squeeze in another book?" she wondered. "That is the big question."

One of the most imaginative aspects of the programs concerned the invention of titles. Ruth Lockwood remembers laughing uproariously at the Childs' kitchen table as they created the titles for later programs: "Waiting for Gigot," "Introducing Charlotte Malakoff," "Lest We Forget Broccoli," and "A French Cape." "We were so proud of our titles, but no one paid attention to the titles," said Mrs. Lockwood ruefully.

In 1964 she taped thirty-one more programs, filming every Wednesday and Friday for six weeks, then resuming after a month off and repeating the process in the spring (in November and December they made one program a week). They also initiated formal rehearsal time and used more unpaid assistants to help in preparation and washing up. Rosemary Manell came up from Washington, DC, to work for the spring shoot as Julia's unpaid assistant and food arranger. They had cooked together in Marseilles, Georgetown, and Brussels (when the Childs were in Bonn). Rehearsal time and other factors increased the cost of the production.

Julia continued to teach at Beard's cooking school and sat for an important interview with Craig Claiborne. His article featured her kitchen and *batterie de cuisine* on half a page of the March 5 issue of the *New York Times.* Except for sold-out demonstrations at Wellesley for the Smith alumnae scholarship fund (she raised more than $2,000), Julia had to turn down most requests for her time. She avoided public speaking, but would ad-lib through a cooking demonstration. Her first public speech (on cookbooks) was in a small library in Massachusetts and was a chore, even with Paul's assistance. When the second shooting of the TV series was finished in the late spring, she spent a week in Lumberville for the publication of Charlie's book on the building of their Maine cabin, *Roots in the Rock,* edited for the Atlantic Monthly Press and Little, Brown by Peter Davison, who spent repeated summers on Mount Desert Island and knew it well.

THE BOSTON GLOBE AUDIENCE

Julia was eager to add the written word to her television teaching. Before the first television program was shown on Monday, February 11, 1963, at 8 P.M. (and rebroadcast, as always, on Wednesday at 3 P.M.), Julia wrote an article about her first program for the *Boston Globe.* On Sunday, February 10, she was on the cover of *Boston Globe TV Week,* a pullout section of the Sunday magazine, sitting behind a large wooden bowl of almonds and holding a two-handled rocker knife. "Mrs. Child does actual cooking on camera in a delightful, easy and informal manner," the paper announced. During 1963 and 1964, Julia offered forty-five short essays and recipes to the newspaper free of charge, with the stipulation that they not be bound. "40 Cloves of Garlic May Not Be Enough" was an essay about a visit from James Beard in which they cooked together, making *poulet aux quarante gousses d'ail.* From Grasse she submitted "Caves Age Roquefort Cheese to Perfection," an essay with no recipes, but suggestions for using the cheese in dishes such as *omelette au Roquefort.* In another essay, she described her visit with Elizabeth David.

This fifty-year-old housewife—the profession she then listed on her passport—became a local celebrity. "Dear Skinny" letters came from her former Smith classmates still living in New England. She received 200 cards and letters during the first twenty days of the television program. (Ruth Lockwood served as her business manager and personal producer when they were in Europe that first fall.) Her renown grew as her program was aired elsewhere. By the fall of 1964, when *The French Chef* was added by seventeen more stations, from New York City to Los Angeles, Julia would be sending recipes and photographs all over the country. Her face and voice were reviewed almost on a weekly basis. That fall she was invited to address the Newspaper Food Editors Conference at the Waldorf-Astoria in New York City. As usual, she donated her $500 fee to WGBH. "As long as I can get clothes, and have a decent car, I'm not really interested in the money end of it," she said to *The Nation's Business.*

Even her butcher on Kirkland Street became a celebrity. Jack Savenor and his wife, Betty, became close friends and their picture appeared in the paper dining with Julia and Paul. Twenty years later, the man who would say, "Hello, Julia, baby," when she answered his telephone calls—"Hello, Big Jack," she always replied—testified that she taught him much about the food business. She later established a strong bond with her fishmonger, George Berkowitz of Legal Sea Foods. But it was Savenor's friendship with Julia that was the longest and strongest, and is typical of the respect she earned among her purveyors and associates in greater Boston.

A careful study of the press coverage of these first few years reveals that Julia's audience was broad, including both high and low culture, "from professors to policemen," according to *TV Guide*. A group of avant-garde painters and musicians in Greenwich Village gathered every week to view her, believing initially that she was doing a parody of the traditional cooking program, but staying on as faithful watchers after learning otherwise. They especially enjoyed repeating the opening lines of the artichoke program. The *San Francisco News Call Bulletin* said in 1965 that she drew "more men than women viewers" to their Channel 9. The great American fear of being outré and gauche was diminished by this patrician lady who was not afraid of mistakes and did not talk down to her audience. With the Kennedys in the White House boosting the snob appeal of French dining and associating it with ruffles and truffles, Julia was making it accessible to everyone. Some, of course, would try to acquire culture merely by cooking a French dish, skipping the travel and study and suffering.

In later years when she was asked about her audience, Julia denied that she was talking to what people thought of as "the stupid housewife." "My audience is not *la ménagère,* but anyone interested in cooking, no matter the sex or age or profession. I want to show that there ain't no mystery. Those who mystify are aggrandizing themselves."

In a profile in *The Saturday Evening Post* (with the Beatles on the cover), Lewis Lapham admired the fact that she "possesses none of the pretentious mannerisms so often associated with practitioners of *haute cuisine."* Terrence O'Flaherty, in his *San Francisco Chronicle* column, called her "television's most reliable female discovery since Lassie." The *Globe* said, "She's like a fairy godmother . . . she makes me a child again." She "looks like someone's older sister—the one who teaches high school gym class." Such warm and fuzzy familiarity was not contradicted by the numerous references to her strength (implied in the gym teacher allusion). Even her assistant producer thought "she looked like the kind of person who should be out showing dogs or racing horses, not doing French cooking." Another reviewer said she looked like she was off to play eighteen holes of golf because of that towel tucked into her belt. And the verbs used to describe her movements were strong ones, such as "crunch" and "bash."

Publicity doubled, tripled, and quadrupled as new stations aired the program around the country. *Newsweek* (July 15, 1963) said her program was helping "to turn Boston, the home of the bean and the cod, into the home of the *Brie* and the *Coq* as well." She had to compose form letters to answer frequently repeated questions or comments. Most of the letters she received were full of praise, though some were filed in the "Julia Is Dirty" folder. The latter included complaints about her failure to wash her hands and her habit of touching food ("I just can't stand those oversanitary people," she responded). "You are quite a revolting chef the way you snap bones and play with raw meats," one viewer wrote. Another: "I have turned off your program before today, when you seem bent on wine drinking, but this is the last time."

The most serious criticism emerged later when a French cooking teacher moved to Massachusetts and openly remarked that the star of *The French Chef* was neither French nor a chef. Even before this, Julia realized there was a problem with the title, but those who defended Julia pointed out that even if she was not a French chef, she was a damn fine home cook who knew French and French cooking techniques. Apart from the title of the program, Julia only referred to herself as a home cook. Never, even for playful skits or posing with French chefs, would she ever agree to don the traditional tall white toque.

By August, less than a year since publication, *Mastering the Art of French Cooking* had sold 100,000 copies at $10 each and was in its fifth printing. Growing royalty checks, together with her third of her father's $300,000 invested estate (probated in March 1964), allowed her to remain faithful to the world of public education. "Fortunately," Paul wrote Charlie, "we are in a position where we don't *have* to snap at the bait [of commercial temptations]." Now she was receiving 400 letters a week and hired temporary secretarial help to answer her mail. Ruth Lockwood took care of the requests for appearances and interviews when Julia and Paul left for two weeks in Maine and then five days at Bread Loaf in Vermont.

But not before Julia attended her thirtieth reunion in Northampton. The celebration of the Class of '34 provided the atmosphere for which all longtime graduates long: recognition and nostalgia. Mary Chase and many of her Hubbard Hall girlfriends were there, and everyone had read or seen Julia. She presented an improvised skit at the last minute with Charlotte Snyder Turgeon, daughter of a leading meat distributor in Boston, cookbook author, editor of the English translation of *Larousse Gastronomique,* and wife of King Turgeon, chairman of the French department at Amherst College. Charlotte and Julia stirred a big pot into which they threw various objects, including an old tennis shoe, and kept up a running commentary that made everyone laugh until they cried.

TELEVISION'S ALL-STAR COOKS

Julia was not the first to demonstrate her techniques on the little screen. James Beard had made his debut August 30, 1946, on network television: "Elsie presents James Beard in *I Love to Eat!*" announced Elsie the Cow, Borden's promotional puppet. It was a fifteen-minute spot, expanded to thirty minutes, and canceled by his new sponsor, Birds Eye, the following spring. Beard may have begun in the theater, but he was ill at ease and awkward in front of the camera. Nevertheless, he appeared again on CBS's *In the Kitchen* that fall, in *At Home with Jinx and Tex,* sponsored by Swift & Co. on May 11, 1947, and, after an interim of fifteen years, in *The James Beard Show,* a chatty, uninformative, and dated women's talk show filmed in 1965–66 in Canada.

But Beard was not the first television cook. In the early years of commercial television, local home economics teachers would come on in white uniforms and white shoes to illustrate the four basic food groups, most sponsored and influenced by food companies. Commercial television stations had built-in kitchen studios because advertisers were usually food related and the stations produced the commercials. Educational television stations, including WGBH, did not have kitchens.

The first real food-centered teaching was done by Dione (pronounced Dee-o-nee) Lucas, who cooked on local commercial channels from 1948 to 1953. Lucas was in many ways the mother of French cooking in New York City. Born in 1909 in England, she came to New York City in 1942 and ran the Egg Basket, her combination restaurant and cooking school, which failed by the mid-sixties. Her first television cooking classes still stand up with integrity nearly fifty years later. Lucas was a crisp and neurotic woman whose apprentices thought her bossy. Others alleged that she was a veritable soap opera of eccentricities, dramatics, and migraine, exacerbated by drugs and alcohol; but she was generous and kind to Julia and Simca. After seeing one of her live demonstrations for the first time in November 1964, Julia wrote to Helen Evans Brown that "she is wonderfully expert." Paul concluded she was "marvelously deft manually" despite the confusion of having three helpers on the stage, and he left "feeling bloody good about" their own program.

Poppy Cannon, the can-opener queen, occasionally appeared nationally on CBS's *Home* show, demonstrating, for example, how to make vichyssoise with frozen mashed potatoes, one sautéed leek, and a can of Campbell's cream of chicken soup. The name of the soup and the only fresh produce in the recipe—that one leek!—seemed exotic enough for the American viewing public, most of whom had never seen a whisk before Julia Child made her televised omelet.

"Child's predecessors in the medium were less Dione Lucas or Poppy Cannon than Steve Allen and Ernie Kovacs," said Robert Clark, Beard's most recent biographer. Though the comparison diminishes her expert knowledge and teaching techniques—which are on a par with those of Dione Lucas—it does accurately note that she was a natural comedian belonging neither to the stern and serious Lucas approach nor to the glamour girl school demeanor of Betty Furness and Bess Myerson. She "was a droll six-footer with a Seven Sisters tone whose hearty and unself-conscious aplomb was the perfect foil to the pretensions of both fancy food and television," Clark adds. She "transformed cooking into entertainment," proclaimed Jane and Michael Stern in their *Encyclopedia of Pop Culture* (1987).

Two other factors, apart from her humor, that distinguish her from other cooks on television then and even now—though there has been a legion of imitators since—are her voice and her mistakes. The *Boston Globe* published the following query:

> Q—Every time I see Julia Child, television's "French Chef," she seems to be out of breath. Does she suffer from asthma or emphysema?
> —H.B., Everett, Mass.

> A—Miss Child's response is that her lungs are healthy. The art of cooking is a labor of love and involves a lot of manual labor. Try whipping a soufflé sometime.

Her shallow breathing was reflected also in the high pitch of her voice (which got more pronounced with age), which would unexpectedly drop down, slide up, gasp, and pitch forward with a whoop—covering a full octave in the course of one recipe. Luckily, she found an audience before the television image-makers could discover that she was "all wrong" for television. Certainly today she would probably not have a chance at breaking into television. Despite the warbles, gasps, and breathlessness, she could keep talking—a considerable talent for a live demonstration—and speak in full sentences, interspersing narratives and effective references to France and to food.

Reviewers could never place her accent. The first cover story in the *Boston Globe Magazine* (there would be many) described her "charming

French accent," but others described it as follows: "a flutey schoolmarm tone," "a voice that bellowed its New England regionalism," "not all that different from standard Californian," and "that preposterous Boston Brahmin accent." Many have tried to capture her unique vocal tone: "plummy," "like a great horned owl," "trills in that unmistakable falsetto with its profusion of italics," and "a voice that could make an aspic shimmy." Others used comparisons: "a combination of Andy Devine and Marjorie Main," and "two parts Broderick Crawford to one part Elizabeth II." Molly O'Neill says she "sounds like a dowager doing a burlesque routine," and Clark Wolf says "it's the voice of an English cookery lady." Collectively, the impression was that hers was a voice as recognizable as those of Eric Sevareid, Walter Cronkite, and William F. Buckley, Jr. Her husband wrote a poem to her "mouth so sweet, so made for honeyed words."

The language Julia used was also a part of her unique character. Her choice of words and phrases reflected in part her age and the period in which she lived (she called her menstrual period "the curse" and homosexuals "fairies"). In conversations she could swear and speak frankly about private matters to the point that one of her lawyers would blush. On television she spoke of the icebox, not the refrigerator (though in her letters she called it the "frigo"), and the "chest," not the breast, of the duck, and said "eek," "wang," or "bang" when she lowered her rolling pin or butcher knife with a thud to the table. She got a permanent every few months, wore falsies, and always wanted to be called "Mrs. Child," yet she loved gossip, talking dirty, and a good belly laugh. Her favorite dismissive word—for abstract art, as an example—was "balls."

Among her friends, her expressions are legendary. Paul called it "Julie's sleight of tongue," naming double stainless-steel sinks "stinkless stains." Or saying "blend the bladder" instead of "blend the batter" (or was it bladder blending instead of batter blending?). Of a minor mishap, she would say, "I did not have my glasses on when I was thinking." In several restaurants she was heard to say, "The wine here flows like glue." Leaving a noisy restaurant, she said, "It was so noisy I could not hear myself eat." *Gourmet* magazine's reviews were "a lot of mushmouthery!" She emphasized the last syllable of "shallot," probably from the French *é-cha-LOTE,* and told Simca that she was "trying to get back into the grindstone." When her work was interrupted, she exclaimed *"Fistre, alors!"* misspelling *fichtre* (screw it!) in dozens of letters to Simca. Bad news was punctuated by "Woe!" When she tapped the floured cake pan and flour fell to the floor, she quipped, "I have a self-cleaning floor." There were many letters after that incident.

She was known for delightful mistakes on her program, which became a frequent motif in news articles. The *Boston Herald* claimed she was blending olives when the top of the blender flew off, then the whole machine broke down: "Oh, well, who needs the mechanical age anyway?" she said. At first Morash could not correct minor problems because they had to keep the film running and did not have time to refilm an episode. He remembers stopping the film on only six occasions, including when the soufflé fell and when the kidney flambé failed to catch fire. Soon Julia realized that her recovery from near-catastrophe was an effective teaching tool and explained this fact to inquisitive reporters. She also explained to Helen Evans Brown that "people enjoy spilled wine bottles, dropped glasses, and potato plopped onto the stove—makes it so homey, they say." Apocryphal stories have grown up around her accidents, including a story that she dropped a fish on the floor, picked it up, and continued. The only food that ever fell to the floor, according to Ruth Lockwood, was a piece of turkey wrapped in cheesecloth that rolled out from beneath a board. But the story of dropping a chicken (or fish) on the floor was continually embellished until the *Washington Post* in 1992 had her dropping an entire side of lamb.

Her ability at improvisation helped turn uncarveable suckling pig, flaming pot holders, and a melting dessert into human and humorous moments. One example of her improvisation that both Lockwood and Morash remember is the ringing of the freight elevator bell. Though they left a note downstairs saying they were taping, a loud ring sounded in the middle of a program and, without skipping a beat, Julia said, "Oh, that must be the gas man. But I am too busy and cannot answer it." (Morash remembers her saying, "That must be the plumber, about time he got here. He knows where to go.") Whatever the line, it was a great save. The melting dessert was *charlotte aux pommes,* made with bread and apples, rum and apricot preserves. Because she had used Gravensteins or McIntosh instead of the firmest apples, when she lifted the mold, the cake gave a sigh and slowly began to collapse. "Oh well, I don't like these things too rigid," Ruth Lockwood remembers Julia saying, picking it up and taking it to the dining table. It "began to sag," as Julia described the incident a decade later, "and the whole dessert deflated like an old barn in a windstorm."

The other factors distinguishing Julia Child as a television cooking teacher are interrelated: she was noncommercial and she was located in Boston. Julia refused to become commercial, especially when what Paul called "the Madison Avenue hounds" began calling in 1964. Olivetti offered her $2,500 to be photographed with their typewriters, but she declined. She represented public television: she believed she could never endorse a product or accept money to represent a profit-making institution. This stand lent credibility both to WGBH and to her own opinions. She could not be bought. In later years, her lawyer would stop anyone who tried to borrow the Child name for promotion purposes.

Her choice of Boston as her home base kept her out of the food wars and competition of New York City, though Barbara Kafka believes that "the competitive atmosphere in New York was not that bad then." New York City thought of itself as the center of food and cooking and television. Boston was a smaller town with a greater reverence for history and tradition, if not a sense of intellectual superiority. Boston "suits her to a T," adds Kafka. Most significantly, it was the home of WGBH: "New York City could not have afforded to bring her in," Kafka remarks. "Her proximity to WGBH was critical to her career."

Boston was also the home of Fannie Farmer, the maiden aunt of home economics and "scientific cookery," as well as *The Boston Cooking School Cook Book* in the late nineteenth century. Julia Child brought a new aesthetic to food, one based on the centrality of pleasure and taste. Though Boston named some of the streets in its older neighborhoods Fish Lane, Bean Court, Corn Court, Grouse, Quail, Milk, Water, Fruit, Berry, Millet, and Russet, the food tastes of its natives were as simple as the street names suggest. Privately, Julia complained that Boston was "a gastronomic wasteland." Yet the city took its new celebrity to its heart, and in the decade to come, like Boston Pops director Arthur Fiedler, she would become a beloved institution along with Faneuil Hall, Durgin-Park, and the Red Sox.

LIGHTENING UP THE DARK AGES

"We did not have freshly ground pepper or leeks, copper bowls or whisks, fresh garlic or herbs other than parsley. And our wine had screw tops," says Russ Morash. "Except for a few gourmet shops in New York City, we lived in the Dark Ages." Culinary historian Barbara Wheaton says that when she returned to the United States from Europe in 1961, she could find leeks only at a farm stand near Concord. For those with gardens, the produce was excellent, the preparation simple. Salt cod and baked beans were the dishes most revered in Boston, and fish was eaten every Friday, no matter how it was cooked or what your religion was. Across America, consumers were being urged to buy canned and frozen TV dinners, and their TV tables stood in the corner of most living rooms or family rooms. Though there were regional specialties, such as Boston's beans and cod, there was no American cuisine. Such was the cooking world that Julia was trying to change.

Disinterest, ignorance, even fear of food were endemic in suburbia. Every new health warning *(Poisons in Your Food)* reinforced America's puritanical relationship to food and wine. Food was either sinful or a bothersome necessity. The most popular food books in the early 1960s were *Calories Don't Count* and the *I Hate to Cook Book,* though every bride received the red-and-white-checkered *Better Homes and Gardens Cookbook.* Peg Bracken was the author of the *I Hate to Cook Book,* which, like Poppy Cannon's *Can Opener Cookbook,* came with attitude, saucy and satiric, and an attack on both home economists and gourmets. Surprisingly, when Peg Bracken, who sold three million copies of her book, reviewed Lyndon Baines Johnson's barbecue recipes in 1965 she made the following suggestion: "Elect Julia Child—if we want a cook for President, let's get a good one."

The first challenge to Julia's efforts to teach French cooking to Americans arose just before she left Oslo when she read a "horrible" article in *Time* about cholesterol and wrote her editor that she "hoped it blows over before September . . . I don't believe a word of it." She might momentarily stem the "hate to cook" tide, but thereafter would always have to fight the cholesterol battle. In her favor she had Americans' increasing travel abroad, the wider prosperity and habit of eating out, and the growing interest in both ethnic produce and French chic. "For all Julia has been attacked by nutritionists," said Barbara Wheaton in 1994, "she has done more to make nutritious food palatable than an army of nutritionists armed with no-calorie oil. More people eat fruit and vegetables because of her. She is living proof that moderation is the key."

Julia made vegetables and basic dishes familiar to many. One interviewer in 1964 had to explain to his readers that quiche is "a cheese pie," something that would never occur to a journalist today, thanks in part to Julia's efforts. Perhaps the eggs Benedict and quiche craze of the late 1960s and early 1970s was introduced by Helen and Philip Brown in their *Breakfast and Brunches for Every Occasion* (1961), but it was Julia who showed more Americans, from Saugus to Sacramento, how to make the dishes.

The commercial impact of *The French Chef* was considerable. *Time* magazine (March 20, 1964) said, "She provokes a rating more accurate than Nielsen ever measured." When she cooked broccoli, *Time* noted, the vegetable was sold out within two hundred miles of the broadcast station. When she made an omelet, every omelet pan was sold out of the few specialty stores stocking them. The *San Francisco Chronicle* reported that Williams-Sonoma had "many requests for special cooking utensils [that were] received the day following the telecasts." Charles Williams, who met Julia in 1961 when she was in San Francisco promoting her book with Simca, opened his kitchen equipment store in 1956 and moved to the city on the bay two years later. He carried all sizes of quiche pans, omelet pans, charlotte molds, soufflé dishes, sauté pans, and porcelain ovenware made in France. "Much of the baking equipment was unknown then," said Williams in 1995, "but Julia helped to change all that, and her shows clearly impacted what people bought, even the very next morning."

Her social impact was already evident in May 1965 when the first public parody of *The French Chef* appeared at a charity event in San Francisco. In "Varieties of 1965," a man named Charles Huse donned a toque (which Julia would never have worn) and stuffed a turkey with everything but the bottle of wine that he was chugalugging. "Cooking While Gassed," he called his show, and it brought down the house, according to the *San Francisco Examiner* on May 13.

Julia began several important trends during the 1960s: home entertaining, television cooking (cooking *became* entertainment), a greater precision in teaching cooking, and the phenomenon of the cook as star. She was the first major television-created personality in the cooking world. Changing Americans' attitudes toward food would take decades, but the impact is undeniable: she celebrated her appetite, the joy of the kitchen, and the pleasure of food, a pleasure conveyed in the way she patted the bread dough and caressed the chicken.

Julia finished taping shows on brioches and veal Prince Orloff, in time for the WGBH 1964 holiday party and for Christmas at Lumberville with Charlie and Freddie. They were filming that fall in a kitchen with a movable set in WGBH's new building. Julia thought it was "beautifully decorated in the French Provincial style. It looks airy, dignified, chic, and I would like to bring the whole thing home with me." She and Paul were worried about the escalating costs of building their house in Provence and preparing to tape a new series of programs in January before they sailed on the *Queen Elizabeth* for France.

The following year, in 1965, they filmed another twenty-two programs, taking a break between July and September for family and visitors, for Bloody Marys and the spirit of Robert Frost at Bread Loaf, and for chowder and croquet in Maine. Before completing her fall taping and entertaining an enlarged family of twenty-one for Thanksgiving dinner, Julia held a September 17 taping for the press. She announced that the following year they would open up the programs for audiences of 100 for a fee benefiting WGBH. *The French Chef* was now syndicated on sixty-six stations; it would grow to ninety-six by the end of the year. In addition, sales of *Mastering the Art of French Cooking* were picking up speed; 200,000 copies had now been sold!

Chapter 18

PROVENÇAL WINTERS
(1965 – 1967)

"We are, after all, partly European,
and just must return."

JULIA CHILD *to* Elizabeth David,
April 14, 1964

AFTER TWISTING and turning along French roads built during medieval times, Julia and Paul drove the last sweep down a steep hill beneath Plascassier, passing La Ferme de le Brague and turning right onto a dirt road. They crossed a small brook and drove between two stone pillars to a fork in the road. Instead of taking the road to the left for Simca and Jean's three-story, rectangular stone house, they turned right and climbed the hill where they first encountered their new peach-colored stucco house with green shutters. They called it La Pitchoune, "The Little One."

They were in the hills above Cannes, the Riviera community made famous by the French film festival and Hollywood, just off the road that leads into Grasse, the perfume capital of France. Olive trees and bushes dotted the hillsides, alternating with flower-growing fields of roses and jasmine, local crops for the perfume factories. Grape vines and olive trees signaled more earthly physical nourishment in this Alpes-Maritimes province. Their address was Plascassier, later attached to the town of Châteauneuf de Grasse.

Of all their previous homes, this one resembled most those in Julia's native Southern California, with its warm climate, stucco houses, and red-tiled roofs. In this fertile pocket, flowers bloomed year-round and the mimosa and violets perfumed the air. They had thought of building in Maine or California, but Provence was in sunny France, she was the French Chef, and Simca was next door. This vacation house was Julia's reward for years of hard labor as a writer, teacher, and cook, a reward for doing what she most loved.

> Essence of long-held dream was in the air
> When, on a slope with olive trees above,
>   Foundation stone took root. . . .
>   *Paul Child (1967)*

𝒯HE HOUSE BUILT BY A BOOK

The first formal plans were agreed upon by mail back in November 1963, the week John Kennedy was assassinated. Julia wept openly at the President's death, Paul reported in his letters to Simca and Jean. When they decided on a single-level dwelling, Paul opened a line of credit for Jean and Simca to use for the building. Paul had originally struggled with the builder, who wanted to create a palazzo. But Paul and Julia wanted a more modest home requiring little maintenance, one built from book royalties, where they could live a simple life. "I finally got what we wanted," Paul said. "I'm tough and I speak perfect French." Despite Paul's public frugality, Julia's January 1966 royalty payment of $19,000 paid for half the house (the previous midyear royalty total had been $26,000).

That December, they walked through the front door facing the hill town. Before them was the long living and dining area with a fireplace on the left wall, all in white stucco. The floors were tiled. Down the hall to the right were the kitchen on the left, guest room to the right, and at the end of the hall, Julia's room on the left, with her built-in desk shelf along the window facing south, and to the right Paul's room with a little fireplace and door opening out to the front stone terrace. His room contained the double bed, where Julia, a prodigious snorer, could cuddle with her insomniac husband every morning. "The house is a jewel, even in its unfinished state," she wrote Avis. Julia told the Smith College alumnae newsletter that they planned to "smell the mimosas all winter, curing our own olives and cooking entirely with garlic and wild herbs." She wrote Helen Evans Brown (a month before Helen's death): "We live on an olive-strewn land, and we hope to hobble about the vineyards there when we are 80 and 90—the Lord willing."

This first five-month stay, from early December 1965 through March 1966, would set the pattern—from three to six months a year in La Pitchoune—that was to continue through the 1970s, when Paul's declining health necessitated shorter visits. While Julia wintered in Provence, her television programs continued running, now in nearly a hundred cities. Her audience always felt her presence in their homeland, if not their own homes, and Avis mailed weekly analyses of each program to Julia in France.

"All the essentials are here," Julia wrote to James Beard at the beginning of the new year. "Paul [with Charlie's help] has 'hung' the kitchen, so we feel we are in business. In fact, we are so happy I doubt if we shall go to Paris at all. The weather has been sunny, rainy, warm, cold, and the garden is growing. Simca and Jean have been so thoughtful of every detail, we are quite overwhelmed."

With the new year coming to a close, Julia settled in to preparing her recipes for what would be the final shooting of *The French Chef.* The hope by 1966 was to suspend making new tapes until they finished *Mastering the Art of French Cooking II.* Paul turned sixty-four in mid-January with a sense of peace, listening to the wind sighing in the cypresses and what he called "my favorite woodpecker . . . tap-tap-tapping away on TV recipes."

This first lengthy stay in La Pitchoune was devoted to cooking, writing, and typing recipes for the tapings, a preparation made easier without the constant telephone calls and appearances. She was talking to WGBH, Beard, and Michael Field about having a weekly half-hour cooking program featuring a variety of chefs. She confided to Avis that if WGBH would get Michael Field (who had a New York cooking school) and others on the Educational Television Network, it "would let me off the hook, and would give others a chance, and be refreshing to have a change." Such sentiments express her generosity as much as they do her possible naiveté about the growing competitiveness of the market.

Among their favorite guests was Sybille Bedford, the English novelist (best known for *A Legacy,* 1956), who rented nearby with her mate Eda Lord (a former classmate of M. F. K. Fisher and, according to Paul's description, "[Bedford's] Alice B. Toklas"). When Julia was particularly busy, Simca's maid and sometime cook, Jeanne (Jeanette) Villar, an illiterate but much adored domestic who lived on the property, would prepare the roast lamb for their dinners together. They liked Sybille (a Cora DuBois type, Paul thought), bearlike and direct, colorful and outspoken, who poked into every drawer and cupboard on her first visit. They admired her eccentricity, intellect, and passion for wine and food (Paul took her advice on wine purchases). They pumped her with questions about her coverage (for *Life*) of the Jack Ruby trial in Dallas.

Other favorite guests, whose visits were "cozy and relaxed," were Robert Penn Warren and Eleanor Clark, who lived nearby in 1967. It was only when "Red" received the Bollingen Prize that Julia discovered he wrote poetry as well. On a return visit to the Warren house, they dined with Max Ernst (and, according to Paul, his "loud-mouth" American wife). Other visitors in 1967 included Bob and Mary Kennedy of Boston, Bill Koshland of Knopf, Hélène Baltrusaitis (without "old Yogourt," her husband) from Paris, and Peter and Mari Bicknell from Cambridge, England, who would stay on during April after the Charlie Childs and Kennedys drove back to Paris and headed home (with a trunk full of French cookware for the WGBH auction). "No hidin' place . . . ," Paul informed Charlie. It was as if old friends and gastronomes would arrive in Cannes or Nice and follow the smell of mimosas. "It's aston-ishing how many of our friends and family have reached this semi-demi-mini hermitage since we first touched down," he wrote to Charlie on April 7, 1967. And each year the numbers grew.

Julia was also caught up in the local community, nursing Jeanne Villar when she was ill, getting involved in the lives of all the local shopkeepers, including the illnesses and deaths of their neighbors. She seemed to know them all by name, according to her letters.

Julia and Simca were in the talking stages on their second volume of *Mastering the Art of French Cooking*. Julia constructed the outline in 1966 (by then their first volume had sold a quarter of a million copies); they were choosing and testing the recipes in 1966 and 1967. Recipes went back and forth in their weekly letters (when they were not together). *Mastering II* would include some of the recipes, particularly the baked foods, they had not put in the first volume. Simca continued to teach her class in Paris during the winter months. Julia would visit occasionally on her way to or from La Pitchoune, with a detour to see her own chef, Max Bugnard, now eighty-two and crippled with arthritis.

"Simca was outspoken and a lot like my mother," said one of Simca's students, Ailene Martin. "Everything was black and white, there was no mid-dle ground." This French dogmatism did not always endear her to Paul. Simca had a ferocious concentration that some called driven or obsessive, and her laughter could be harsh. One journalist described her as having hints of Mar-garet Leighton and Marlene Dietrich in her manner. She was vivacious, stub-born, and opinionated, and sometimes Julia and Simca had major disagree-ments. Each called the other, behind her back, *une force de la nature*. Betty

Kubler confirms the willfulness of Simca: "Julia had an instinct about when to go along and when to hold back . . . it was the same instinct she had on the stage; it was sheer drama working with Simca."

When Julia walked out onto her stone terrace with coffee cup in hand early in the morning, she looked over the rolling layers of hills and listened to the silence. She particularly admired the 150-year-old olive tree in front of their house where the workman had carefully lowered it for replanting. In the spring, when the almond trees were flowering, she "would hear the frogs croaking in the little river at the bottom of our hill," she wrote Avis. One or the other of the cats, Minouche or her mother, Mimimère, rubbed against her leg in greeting. Later, when the warm sun would bake the floral smells, and mimosas scented every breath, she would take the fieldstone and grass path to the side kitchen door of Simca's kitchen, where they planned their day and discussed the problem of a particular recipe.

Proximity spurred their creativity. Julia made a deboned chicken breast stuffed with mushrooms for Simca and experimented with croissants. Simca created a frozen mousse with caramelized walnuts and kirsch in cookie cups. These experiments, dated February and March 1966, appeared radically transformed in the second volume of *Mastering the Art of French Cooking*. In July they were corresponding about chocolate cakes and finding the best method of melting chocolate. By 1967, they were testing soup and *pâté en croûte*, then moving in on their perfect chocolate cake (Julia brought American chocolate with her). The only cooking Julia disliked was deep-fat frying and the making of "little" hors d'oeuvres or canapés.

Two or three times a week, Julia would go to one of the surrounding towns and walk through the shops or markets, filling her blue-and-green-plaid cloth baskets. Her kitchen quickly filled up, for, as Paul described it, "Julia is a compulsive gadget, cooking-vessel, and tool buyer." They would buy wine at Clenchard's in Cannes, check out the new *supermarché* in Cannes to compare it with the Giant in Washington, DC, visit the Fondation Maeght gallery in St.-Paul-de-Vence, and sometimes take brief trips to meet friends in Montreux, Gstaad, Lausanne, and Paris. Julia always visited Elizabeth Arden on Thursdays in Cannes for her hair trim and set (Paul called it getting "Ardenized," and later approved of her purchase in Cambridge of a wig for "unexpected" public appearances—"slightly more chestnutty than her own hair color"). When they ate out it was at the Auberge du Coin in Biot or the two-star L'Oasis at La Napoule, just outside Cannes. After one such dinner, Julia and Simca re-created *loup en croûte* (French bass), which Paul photographed.

The coming of the *supermarché* was not the only change the Childs observed through the years. As early at 1967 Paul declared, "We are in a Los

Angeles 1915 situation," referring to the mushrooming of new houses around Cannes. He bemoaned the "progress." Julia was disheartened by the trend of French women to be "assembler cooks," like American women who put together canned or frozen things with a bit of fresh stuff and flavoring before baking it. With prosperity, more conveniences, and hired help, French women soon would not be able to cook, Julia lamented. Simca agreed.

The influence of Provençal cooking was evident in the Childs' Valentine's Day card of 1966: A chef wearing a toque is carrying a large spoonful of red hearts over his shoulder, the other hand is dragging a chain of garlics. ("Jeanne Villar taught Julia and Simca everything about Provençal cooking," declared Ailene Martin.) In 1967 they just sent a photograph of La Pitchoune, for the mailing list was growing to more than 300 names and they were ready to end this tradition.

Over the years, James Beard, M. F. K. Fisher, Michael Field, and other culinary luminaries were drawn to the shrine of good eating at the Beck/Child compound. In 1966, James Beard rented La Pitchoune for June; and Michael (and Frances) Field in July and August. In 1967, Poppy Cannon, now the food editor at *The Ladies' Home Journal,* came by for a visit in March—Julia did not like the name of the journal (Ezra Pound once called it *The Ladies' Home Urinal)* but invited her to lunch and later in the year gave an interview and recipes for a Christmas-in-Cambridge piece. Beard spent several summers renting La Pitchoune (May through July), working on his *American Cookery* there. Jeanne, who adored him, called him her *"gros."* Perhaps all these food writers were unknowingly inspired by the ghost of Auguste Escoffier, who was born nearby in Villeneuve-Loubet.

Each winter for nearly twenty years, Julia and Paul took the train (or flew) down from Paris, rented a car from Hertz, and spent the winter and early spring months at "La Peetch." They adhered to their habit of early rising, marketing (Julia's favorite was in the rue Meynadier in Cannes), and painting for Paul; and, after work, a cocktail hour on the terrace in warm weather. They walked every path and hill in the region, visited a restaurant every week (usually with disappointing results), kept up with events through letters, the *International Herald Tribune,* and *L'Express.* Paul resumed both his diary-letter to Charlie, in his best pen-and-ink script, and his painting in a renovated *cabanon* (a Provençal shepherd's hut of two rooms, one atop the other) just yards from their home. The entire estate had been inherited by Simca's two sisters-in-law and was called Bramafam (in local dialect, "cry for hunger").

AWARDS AND HONORS

If La Pitchoune was the major material reward for her labors, the honorary public awards began that April 1965 at the Hotel Pierre in New York, when Julia was given the Peabody Award. She told Simca that their program was "receiving an award of some sort" in New York, not apparently impressed that the George Foster Peabody Award was the top award for broadcasting. Yet Paul was "all swollen up with vicarious pride."

The next month, she and Paul went to the Americana Hotel in New York for the East Coast ceremony for television's Emmy (named for "Immy," an engineering term for the camera tube). The ceremony was to be hosted by Bill Cosby, then a co-star of *I Spy*. The West Coast participants were gathered at the Palladium in Hollywood, where the show was hosted by Danny Kaye. Both audiences were being hurried through their dinner when a man came to the table and handed Julia her award: *The French Chef* won for the best program on educational television. Her producer, Ruth Lockwood, was sitting beside her and heard Julia, who rarely watched television, ask Cosby, "Would you mind telling me what your name is?" "Certainly," Cosby replied, "Sidney Poitier." When the ceremony began, all the Educational Television Network people at their table realized there would be no airtime for the presentation of their award. Commercial television had its prerogatives; Julia lodged a strong complaint, less for herself than for the snub of public broadcasting.

Julia was the first educational television personality to win an Emmy.

With the increased publicity and business, she hired a full-time secretary, Gladys Christopherson, who would work for her for the next ten years. When Julia was on the road or abroad, Gladys opened and forwarded mail. Ruth Lockwood always handled the business and appearances, saying no to some very important interview requests (such as *The Times* of London) so that the program taping could be finished and the book could progress.

In August, while they were in Maine (where Julia baked dozens of experimental batches of brioches and they roasted a suckling pig), Joan Barthel's lengthy feature story on Julia in *The New York Times Magazine* appeared, calling her "educational TV's answer to underground movie and pop-op cults—the program that can be campier than 'Batman,' farther-out than 'Lost in Space' and more penetrating than 'Meet the Press' as it probes the question: Can a Society be Great if its bread tastes like Kleenex?" Her "simultaneously gravelly and trilling" voice emphasized the "comic vein running through the program": the "chatty asides," and occasional acrobatics (such as demonstrating on her own body the various cuts of meat). Barthel also reported that Ruth Lockwood had to talk Julia out of washing and toweling the suckling pig ("Please don't call it 'him' "). Instead, Julia mentioned on the air in passing that she brushed the teeth and cleaned the ears.

A very different take on the appeal of her programs comes from MIT's Douwe Yntema, who reports that a group of physicists and applied engineers at the Lincoln Laboratory gathered weekly to watch Julia. The men, according to Yntema, were interested in her technique, her attention to detail and rules. Here was a woman on television who was not sexy and was not selling something; she was demonstrating technique, and they were fascinated. Over 350 letters a week came into WGBH alone. Among the 104 stations, New York City's WNDT sometimes received 1,000 requests for a particular recipe. Many letters could be answered by the stations, which had copies of the recipes, but Julia's correspondence was always burdensome.

She and Paul topped off their Maine vacation that year with a stay at Bread Loaf in Vermont, where Julia attended every lecture ("I learn so much! . . . But can't say much for the institutional food") and met with their old friend poet John Nims. After six years, Bread Loaf's "spirit of Robert Frost and Bloody Mary" had not faded for Julia and Paul. She was one of many writers there, though she would not have considered herself one. The fame did not seem to affect her except for the influx of letters, which by September numbered more than her secretary and she could handle, even with the growing use of form letters.

In the third week of October 1966, *Life* published an article featuring Julia "hamming it up in the *haute cuisine*" and three of Paul's photographs. The article praised her "wizardry," guessed that "a sizable portion of her following are people who wouldn't know a truffle from a toadstool," and asserted that her program "has immeasurable effect on the commodity market." Julia confided to Simca that she was getting used to the publicity: "I find I am shamelessly avid for sales of the book. I can't say I would do anything at all, of course, but I will certainly expose myself (or you!) to any number of things which would have appalled me some years ago, when good breeding meant never having one's name in print!" Her next-door neighbor, Ithiel deSola Pool (MIT professor in communications and public opinion), often remarked to his wife, "You know, Julia is revolutionizing what women can do in this country. She may not know it, but she is doing it."

Then, on November 25, *Time* put her on the cover of the magazine in a feature article on American food, "Everyone's in the Kitchen." The article documented the increasing availability of American produce, the growing number of cookbooks (of the 206 "last year alone," their five-year-old *Mastering* was still the best seller), and the history of American cooks (picturing

Fannie Farmer, Dione Lucas, Craig Claiborne, and James Beard). Julia declared in 1984 that the *Time* cover story was the fifth most important event in her career, after meeting Paul, attending the Cordon Bleu and meeting Simca, the book, and television.

The food community also considered the *Time* cover story something of a "watershed" event, conferring "genuine legitimacy on gastronomy and cooking after years of mockery and condescension," according to one food writer, who went on to mistakenly claim that "the cult of Julia drew its initiates almost entirely from the most affluent strata of society and the inhabitants of Georgetown, Cambridge, Beverly Hills, the north shore of Chicago, and the Upper East Side of New York."

Here she was, "our lady of the ladle," gazing benevolently from the cover of *Time* at her vast American following. She was now a reassuring and familiar icon, a national treasure, cherished for her pervasive presence on television. The large spoon she waved on the pages and covers of magazines was never threatening: like the baton of the conductor, it was calling her countrymen to a celebration of good food and wine, a magic wand offering entry to the secrets and joys of cooking. Every class of people loved her, as her mail and the greetings of workmen and tradespeople affirmed. If at first it was chiefly the affluent class of New England that cooked with her, her appeal reached out to the great middle class. "French cooking now rose from the ashes in middle-class America," says historian Harvey Levenstein, and it was Julia, he says, who gave it "an energetic push."

While the feature stories and awards heralded her influence on the way Americans were learning to cook, the preponderance of citizens still tossed together casseroles of ground beef and canned soup and were enthusiastic about Tang, Cool Whip, and salads with bacon bits sprinkled on top. In the university communities they played folk music and ate paella, the most recent fad. And McDonald's was, in one food historian's view, "the nation's greatest cooked food retailer." While American tastes were still largely pedestrian, they were slowly evolving from green Jell-O and mock apple pie made with Ritz crackers to *quiche lorraine* and *boeuf bourguignon*. "The same working mother who repairs to McDonald's three times a week," claims one economist, "may settle down on the weekend for a bout of gourmet cooking."

Consequently, food writing and food consulting grew fast. According to food writer Robert Clark, "the stakes in food writing and consulting were rising exponentially . . . [and] it still seemed for most people in the food business as though there were too few opportunities and too many rivals." Oblivious to rivalry, Julia urged Beard and others to come to Boston and "cook exactly the way you want." The pay was only $200 plus food costs for each program, but she wanted them to teach on her local station. The benefits from television lay in book sales, she assured Beard.

In return for the boost in her book sales, Julia gave much back to WGBH, including the earnings from her demonstrations, for which she received about $500 for a two-hour performance. She also participated in fundraisings and auctions, helping them take in $126,000 in May 1967. Julia kept all her own financial books and did her own agenting until, at one of their Harvard/Atlantic Monthly group cocktail parties, Brooks Beck expressed horror that Julia was not involved in estate planning, establishing a revocable trust, and making provisions to protect her name from "invasion of the right of privacy." Julia and Paul made plans to hire him.

The *Time* cover and the resulting increase in book sales, which tripled in December (the months following the magazine's appearance) and quadrupled in January, was most important financially to Simca and Louisette. Simca's husband, Jean Fischbacher, was just beginning a struggling pharmaceutical company called Sederma, and Julia said, "I don't know how they would have gotten along at all otherwise." Louisette also needed money, though her share was only 18 percent (Julia and Simca each had 41 percent). One weekend in early 1967, when Louisette visited her two former partners with the man she was soon to marry, Count Henri de Nalèche (titled but poor), Julia realized that Louisette's modest royalty check of nearly $3,000 meant a lot to them financially. More than a year before, Julia wrote Simca: "Well, who would have thought we'd ever get so much money out of that book, great as it is, I never thought we'd do much more than make expenses."

In 1967 she would receive more accolades. *Harper's Bazaar*'s hundredth anniversary issue named her one of the "100 Women of Accomplishment" in America.

$\mathcal{T}$HE FINAL TELEVISION PROGRAMS

The previous May in Boston, they had frantically taped twenty-two more programs to complete what would be the first series, before Julia would quit to complete her second book with Simca, and Ruth Lockwood could go on to produce Joyce Chen's Chinese cooking shows. Before each program Julia pinned on her blouse the round insignia created by Paul for L'Ecole des Trois Gourmandes, the cooking school they started fourteen years earlier in Paris (one letter asked if the insignia was a De Gaulle button). She complained to

Simca about the demanding television work, adding: "It certainly has sold that old book!" She laughed when Beard wrote her that Clementine Paddleford announced at a Dione Lucas dinner that "cookbooks don't make any money."

Typically, Julia and Paul arose before dawn to pack their car with food and heavy equipment. "If it weren't for Paul," Julia said at the time, "I wouldn't do the television." She always wrote to Simca about the success and failures of each program, including the unmolding of a potato mold that "just quietly collapsed. So we had to shoot that final bit again. . . . Did learn something though, that you have to have them well browned down the side of the mold, indicating they are done and will hold."

The audiences, now invited for the final tapings, turned out in droves. "WGBH has to turn away hundreds of people weekly, each willing to pay $5 to the WGBH Building Fund for the privilege of watching the show backstage on tiny monitor screens," said *Boston* magazine. It fell to Paul to warm up the audience by talking about Julia and warning them, "Whatever you do, please don't laugh." Keeping silent was a challenge, whether Julia was stuffing a pipe between the teeth of a big white fish or carrying a collapsing soufflé from the oven to the table. At one point, when the blender kept spitting out food particles until it groaned and sputtered, Julia feigned concern and said to the machine, "Now, are you all right?" As Alyne Model, a local journalist, noted:

> Not since the late Gracie Allen has television seen such a Mrs. Malaprop hold court. Hers is a kind of cameo theatre of the absurd ("what a wonderful little im*pren*sion, I mean in*ven*tion, the garlic press is") that is all the more endearing because unlike the Burns and Allen Show, *these* minor *bon mots* are totally unrehearsed. "I don't think we *could* rehearse them if we wanted to," confides one station executive.

Julia believed that her audience was among the middle class who shopped at the local A&P, where she herself shopped. Though Safeway, Sperry & Hutchinson, and Hills Bros. Coffee subsidized *The French Chef,* Julia made no endorsements and frankly criticized any product she found wanting. The audience trusted her and wrote her with questions and corrections, which she took seriously. Some were shocked at her "wine drinking," but embraced her as America's cook nonetheless. "Julia Child is the Chuck Berry of *haute cuisine,*" said one rock music promoter, "the One Who Started It All, She Who Cooked with Gas." The mountain of letters was so overwhelming she sought help from volunteers. Until 1981 she kept typed lists of corrections for each book, often changing a word that confused a reader.

In part to answer the requests of the watchers, she planned to publish a paperback book of recipes from the television series. She conceived the idea after talking to Beard in 1965, thinking (she informed Simca) that she could "just . . . send [Bill Koshland] the mimeo'd recipes (I hope)." By July of the next year she concluded that they were "pretty bad" one-page recipes that needed to be two pages. The 1967 contract was for an advance of $25,000 on a book entitled *The French Chef Cookbook* (1968), which would include recipes from her 119 black-and-white programs. The first fourteen, which no longer existed, had been redone in the series. She dedicated the book to WGBH and her crew of twenty-four and signed over 2.5 percent of the royalties to the station and to Ruth Lockwood. Half the recipes were taken, but slightly altered (usually simplified for television), from *Mastering the Art of French Cooking*. Her Reine de Saba chocolate cake (#100), for example, added a pinch of cream of tartar and another tablespoon of sugar. According to her editor, there were no complaints about the duplications.

During 1967 and 1968 her programs were rerun, though she confided to Simca that she feared their large royalty checks might grow smaller. However, the appearance of the paperback edition of the recipes, together with the reruns on television, kept up the interest in their *Mastering* book. Julia turned to their new volume and to eight years of magazines with recipes yet to be clipped. She maintained her files in order to trace the origins of recipes as well as to get ideas and test alternative ingredients.

The Julia cult, people within the industry called it. The ingredients that brought her to national prominence included the rise of educational television (to 54 million households), her unpretentious personality, her natural comic timing, her encyclopedic knowledge, and very hard work, to say nothing of Paul's organizational skills. She was outdrawing William F. Buckley, Jr.'s political forum, and *bon appétit,* her signature sign-off, was now a familiar salute in restaurants and homes across the country.

NOT A PRINCE CONSORT: "WE ARE A TEAM"

" 'Julia Child' . . . is actually a husband and wife team," wrote Paul Levy, who visited them in Provence. Numerous friends agree: "He was her manager on the road. They were true partners" (Debby and Fisher Howe). "He was a man one would instinctively trust" (Lyne Few). "He was always there . . . supportive and not obtrusive" (John Moore). "There was an atmosphere of reason, good sense, and endless affection between them" (Sally Bicknell Miall). Peter Davison admired their partnership and the manner in which they "treat life with a healthy irreverence." Paul made a strong impression on her professional world. One news reporter said, "He sounds like [the actor] George Sanders, but claims his accent is Boston." He said of himself, "I'm part of the iceberg that doesn't show."

Accompanying the recipes and brief essays sent to food editors at newspapers around the country were photographs of the dish or of Julia herself preparing the dish for the week's program. Paul spent decades serving as her official photographer. In addition he had an exhibition of his own work during the summer of 1966 in Wiscasset, Maine, as he had in Bonn and New Haven, and as he would later in Boston, much to Julia's proud delight. His photographs would also appear in *Yale Alumni Magazine, Middlebury College Bulletin, Vogue, Foreign Service Journal,* and *Holiday.*

His artistic skills were silently visible in many places, such as in the final (sixth) decorated cold salmon that was brought to the table at the end of one of Julia's television programs. He set the table and coordinated the color scheme for every important dinner, including decorating the suckling pig in Maine, surrounding the platter with boughs and putting daisies in the eyes. "There would be no French Chef without him, that's for sure," she informed Simca.

He also put his USIS exhibit skills to use when Julia went on the road to present demonstrations. The first major effort had been for the San Francisco Museum of Art benefit in March 1965 (the second was in Providence in May). Paul designed the set in the Ghirardelli chocolate factory, where Julia cooked for a week. The plans were as elaborate as for a military invasion, with floor plans, equipment and produce, training assistants, and timelines. Ruth Lockwood did the setups. Rosie Manell (who now lived near San Francisco) did some of the preparation, such as peeling the asparagus. When she had trouble flambéing, a local restaurant maître d'hôtel showed her his flamer filled with alcohol paste. ("Learn something new just about every day, as old Bugnard used to say!" Julia informed Simca.) Julia preceded the events with press conferences and small society lunches in various homes, and Paul was in charge of all their travel arrangements.

Wendy Morison Beck, echoing most of their friends, suggested that "he was the temperamental one in that relationship." But "I liked the no-nonsense way that she handled him," Beck said in 1996. A few of Julia's acquaintances called him "rude" or "in the way" or "harsh" in his criticism of Julia, but they were few and probably the feeling was mutual. Paul did not pander to those he did not like, and he could be strident. But for Julia he would do anything helpful—he called it "keeping the Julia-banner flapping." He shelled peas for a later appearance on *Good Morning America.* During a women's club demonstration in a Pasadena theater, when there was no water and they had to have clean dishes for a second demonstration, Paul took the dishes into the women's rest room backstage and, using the little soaps on the side of the sink, washed every dish and pan. "I don't care what it is," he said, "I will do it."

He was her manager and photographer. They always shopped together. She cooked, he designed their kitchen and worked out schedules (with the precision he had used for Lord Mountbatten and General Wedemeyer), arranged the table for guests, and kept his eye on the clock during her programs. Occasionally he answered the fan mail (in verse). Together they planned the titles for her cooking programs and he helped her index the first volume of *Mastering.* "We did everything together until the end," said Julia. "I was at my desk and he was in his studio. That is why you get married, as far as I am concerned. The main thing about Paul and me is that we were always together so that he could carry on his work and I could carry on mine. We got along very well. And except for a few incidents, we liked the same people." They "moved as a unit, never more than a floor away from each other," adds Phila Cousins.

"Each time that I talked to Paul," said Martha Culbertson of the Fallbrook Winery in 1995, "somewhere in the conversation he would make a fist with each hand, put the knuckles of his two hands together so that they fit perfectly and would say, 'When I met Julia, that's when everything started to happen.' It was as if his life didn't really begin until he met her."

Paul also organized and carried what her colleagues called her "magic bag" or "Julia's black bag." She went everywhere with it. It contained an apron, an overblouse, pocketknives, heavy pans, plates, straining spoons, serving spoons, a plate to offer the host a taste of the food, and every other necessity for performing on the road.

However, it was not for carrying Julia's black bag that Paul underwent a double hernia operation in the fall of 1966 soon after they celebrated their twentieth wedding anniversary. Contrary to George Meredith's dictum: "Kissing don't last, cookery do!" Julia and Paul's love affair thrived. Theirs was a thoroughly modern marriage of passion and professional partnership. When they were apart, which was seldom, he wrote, "The whole house creaks and echoes with loneliness" and "Life is like unsalted food" without her.

Paul's ambition to publish his lengthy letter-diary, an ambition stirred by the publication of Charlie's Maine memoir, *Roots in the Rock,* was discouraged by Peter Davison, Charlie's editor at the Atlantic Monthly Press. Julia's secretary typed the letters, but he feared he had given Wendy Beck too much to read. She wanted more about Julia. The plan was dropped. Davison says, "In these years Paul was increasingly becoming Julia's amanuensis, publicist, adviser, and alter ego. She in her turn nurtured his own creative juices and impulses. They were a wonderfully interactive couple, but they were able to speak briskly to one another when so inclined."

In 1967 and 1968, while Julia concentrated on working with Simca on their second volume of *Mastering the Art of French Cooking,* Paul's role was to photograph her completed dishes as well as her techniques. He also helped with the interviews with the press, which ate up days of their lives. And, perhaps unknown to most people other than Simca, he also began baking French bread while Julia was experimenting with bread recipes. He loved the scientific aspect of the testing, and he told his brother that making bread was as natural and joyful as making babies.

M. F. K. FISHER, MICHAEL FIELD, AND TIME-LIFE

Among the growing group of cookbook writers, television cooks, and cooking teachers there was some emerging rivalry, though the letters between Julia and James Beard and Mary Frances Fisher do not reveal any attitude of competitiveness. Michael Field, by contrast, probably typifies the awareness of what Clark called "too many rivals."

A former concert pianist, Michael Field ran a cooking school in New York City and was publishing articles in periodicals. He was ambitious and involved (for $25,000 a year and over his head) in editing a book on French provincial cooking for a new (lavishly photographed) series of Time-Life books, "Foods of the World." He rented La Pitchoune in order to research his volume on country cooking (*The Cooking of Provincial France,* the first of his eighteen books). Julia was being paid for "consulting"—though she remembered that he never took any advice—and M. F. K. Fisher (Mary Frances) was being paid for writing an introduction (she was billed as author). Julia counseled Field not to call the book "Provincial" cooking but "French Cuisine Bourgeoise," a piece of advice that would have saved him some criticism down the road.

Mary Frances Fisher, four years older than Julia, was a writer, poet, and memoirist of great style and literary merit (John Updike called her "a poet of the appetites"). Once called "the American Colette," she was credited with carrying on "the tradition of Brillat-Savarin by documenting tales of feasts ancient and modern." She translated his *Physiology of Taste* and did as much for eating as Julia did for cooking. Mary Frances was a prolific writer, though her books sell better today than when she was trying to support herself and her two daughters (she was thrice married). She took the job with Time-Life in good faith.

Thus it was that Mary Frances met Julia and, as their letters of 1966 reveal, became what Mary Frances called "so suddenly and firmly a friend." (Julia at first thought her too "self-absorbed," she told Field, and "didn't warm to her," she told Simca.) It was not until Frances began writing to Julia while staying with the Fields at La Pitchoune that Julia warmed to her and invited her to come by Cambridge on her way home so they could drive to her daughter's home in Kennebunkport, Maine, when they took their vacation at the Childs' cabin. In Cambridge before the drive, Fisher immediately responded to Paul's photographs of Provence: his camera "saw what I have seen, as none ever has." In 1967 she asked him to collaborate with her on a book about Provence, with her words and his photographs (nothing came of the plan). Letters between the two women express Fisher's admiration for Julia's "use [of] other senses than merely looking and tasting [in her writing] . . . you often mention the *Sound* of good cooking." She believed *Mastering* achieved "classic importance."

Fisher remembered (in an unpublished letter of September 9, 1982, to Julia) flying back from France to Logan Airport in Boston to meet Julia for the first time in 1966: "And there you were, standing at the bleak airport gate like a familiar warm beacon . . . old tennis shoes, a soft cotton shirtmaker . . . tall boarding-school teenager from Pasadena! We'd met before, not in this life but *somewhere*. I went happily along with you, and felt home again. And I still do . . . Plascassier, Nice, Glen Ellen, Marseilles."

They shared childhood California living (though Fisher was born in Michigan, her family moved to Whittier the year Julia was born), an enchantment with France, a love of cats, and hunger. "Like most other humans, I am hungry," she wrote in *The Gastronomical Me* (1943). Both had interests beyond food, though Fisher's ran toward the philosophical; when she wrote about security, pleasure, appetite, decay, and memory, she always got around to food, gently folding recipes into her narrative. She shared Julia's wit and flirtatiousness, but Fisher was more vain in what Molly O'Neill called her "penciled Betty Grable brows" and glamorous dust-jacket photographs. Mimi Sheraton, who admired her, called her wily, "a tough cookie"; Barbara Kafka saw in her "a great beauty," who, "like Julia, had a complete career." Both were intellectuals ("our two intellectuals," says Anne Willan), and their difference is implied in motivations behind their differing answers to a food journalist's question, "What is your favorite junk food?": Julia answered, "Pepperidge Farm's fish crackers"; Mary Frances, "Iranian caviar."

Fisher wrote to Julia: "I saw you once on TV and thought you were *exactly* right . . . a quiet but exciting breeze clearing the kitchen murk." It was a program about potatoes Anna, she remembered. Later: "People are starved for the synthesis in you of breeding, maturity, youthfulness, charm, education, subtlety, honesty . . . and you know that I don't speak here of naive young housewives, but of mean cynical old English professors, and (last Saturday) a group of about eight teenagers near Napa who breed their own horses, work their way through school, dance and drive wildly, and watch Julia Child without fail every Thursday night."

When James Beard suggested to Fisher that they meet the following Easter in New York and include Julia and Paul, thus making it "The Big Four!" Mary Frances informed Julia modestly, "He was being polite about me, for I am not *in any way* in your class, except perhaps now and then with a snippet of Deathless Prose . . ." (February 24, 1967). Beard did not include Craig Claiborne, who, Julia believed, was "really in the 'business' of food." When she dined with Claiborne in July 1966, he told her that "he turns all his material over to an editor to put his books together and he doesn't even proofread anything or make an index." Julia relayed all this to Simca in amazement and evident disapproval. Her feelings about Claiborne, whom "we do not warm up to very much," she shared only privately with Simca, for he had given them their first great review. Publicly and privately she defended him and gave him credit for being responsible for making restaurant reviewing professional.

Slowly and discreetly Julia and Mary Frances shared their belief that Field, whom they liked, was not the man to edit the book on French cooking in the provinces. Fisher reported he was a high-strung man isolated in the countryside with no knowledge of the language, had a "cooking block," "snacked" from a virtually empty refrigerator, and dined out daily. "Michael is the glamour boy around New York at the moment," said Julia, "a dabbler, a charmer, a word-monger, a butterfly, and ambitious." She and Fisher both preferred the dedication, calm, and knowledge of Beard (they "are not in the same class," Fisher concurred). Though Fisher did not meet Beard until April 1967, Julia pointed out that he was "dear and generous" and "has allowed himself to be used" by a greedy agent of commercial interests. As she would do with any dear friend, Julia explained Beard's weaknesses (his commercialism) as someone else's fault.

She and Mary Frances had strong reservations about the entire Time-Life series, from which Fisher tried to resign when they began rewriting her words. Though Julia did not like her friend's halfhearted introduction either, she referred to the project in letters to Mary Frances as "this venture about which I cannot but have misgiving tremors." She told Simca she (regretfully) got involved because she thought she "should do something to be more in the swim." But finally, less for the money (this gravy train was rich) than for "poor Michael," they stayed aboard. Later she referred to him as a "front man"—a "Darling, I'm so busy" man. Julia limited her reading and consultation on photographs in New York to ten days and agreed to adapt two cake recipes from Madame Saint-Ange for his book. The best thing that came out of their misadventures with Time-Life, Julia and Mary Frances agreed, was meeting each other.

Julia saw the first Time-Life recipes in November 1966 and thought them "AWFUL . . . a hodge-podge of copying," incompetent and incomprehensible, she told Simca. Many of the recipes were poorly written copies from *Mastering the Art of French Cooking.* (But they were "stuck with" the theft because she agreed to be a consultant.) By February 1967 they were correcting early proofs, Mary Frances in Glen Ellen, California, and Julia in La Pitchoune, both seriously worried about the errors, of which Paul declared there were "an inordinate number." (Julia liked her friend's introduction—"she writes beautifully and sensually about food"—but it romanticized a France that once was.) Field, she told Simca, "is a real *fumiste,* but he certainly is a fine talker!" Buried in a letter to Avis is Julia's motive for getting involved: "Takes a lot of time, and has to be done carefully, but I am so grateful for that *Time* article it is the least I can do." A month later she conjectured to her sister-in-law Freddie that she wondered if she would have been given the cover of *Time* had she not agreed to help Field.

The fears about Michael and his book on provincial French cooking were realized when the Time-Life book appeared later. Craig Claiborne attacked the many fake French recipes and called Michael Field "a former concert pianist who might be excused perhaps on the grounds that he never played in the provinces." Time-Life imprudently planned a translation into French, asking Robert J. Courtine, who had just edited the 1967 French edition of *Nouveau Larousse Gastronomique,* to write the introduction. (Several years later, when it appeared, Courtine mocked the mistakes in the book, and the reputations of Julia and Mary Frances—and Elizabeth David, who contributed some research—were besmirched by their association with the book.) Several typed recipes for Michael's book, recently found in Simca's Bramafam attic, contain comments in Julia's handwriting ("but not French, alas," she writes beside the mention of soy sauce in a chicken recipe). These documents and Julia's correspondence with Mary Frances and Simca reveal their early suspicions about the volume. Indeed, when what she called Claiborne's "blast" appeared in the *New York Times* (on the very day of Field's book-launching party), Julia wrote to Simca, "I think he's right!"

Julia learned another important lesson when she refused to write an introduction to an American "adaptation" of Pellaprat's classic *L'Art Culinaire Moderne* without seeing the galleys first. Field accepted the job, and Julia later judged the adaptation a "travesty." It is "a good lesson to learn," she told Simca, "he got $1,000 for it, but at what cost!" Thereafter, with a couple of rare exceptions, she gave no book endorsements.

While the leaders of the American food world worshipped at the Child-Beck culinary shrine in Provence in the summer months, Julia and Paul chose to live there in the winter. For the next three winters, she and Simca tested and compiled their second volume. Julia wanted to be the best teacher and writer she could be, yet her respect for technique and productivity was always in the service of congeniality.

The tricolor French flag flew from the front door in Cambridge when thirty guests arrived for a Bastille Day dinner on July 14, 1966. The hot weather cooled down enough for the guests to linger over drinks in the garden, then to admire the food arranged in the dining room. Julia cooked several salmon in a large wash boiler so they appeared "lively," curved in the Chinese manner as if swimming upstream. Paul decorated the cold salmon with green mayonnaise. Julia kept it simple with a large salad of crudités, a cucumber salad with fresh dill and watercress, and, for dessert, fresh fruits around pineapple ice, and almond madeleines. Jane Howard and photographer Lee Lockwood (Ruth's son) of *Life* magazine were there to record the festivities for an article they were writing. Julia wrote Simca with a detailed analysis of the food and cost ($6.50 per person, including the serving women, bartender, and cleaning woman). "No wonder restaurants are so expensive!"

Christmas dinner in Provence began at ten in the evening with velouté of onions, mushrooms, and red pepper, followed by goose stuffed with chestnuts and pork sausage, chestnut purée, cheese and fruit, and Moulin à Vent. Paul opened champagne for the *bûche de Noël*. The Childs, the Fischbachers, and Avis DeVoto touched glasses for *le carillon de l'amitié,* the bell of friendship, holding them by the stem both for clarity of sound and to keep the wine from heating.

The cast for New Year's Eve *(le réveillon)* at La Pitchoune included not only Avis DeVoto, Simca and Jean, but also Smithie Helen Kirkpatrick Milbank and her husband. Helen peeled chestnuts with Avis; Paul and Robbins Milbank opened Belons and Bouzigue oysters; Julia prepared two foie gras marinated with fresh truffles in port and cognac (one in *périgourdine* style, the other packed in a pig's caul, *à l'alsacienne).* Pouilly-Fumé washed down the oysters. While sipping the 1872 Madeira and a Meursault with their foie gras, they discussed their preferences in the cooking methods for foie gras.

Dessert: *charlotte aux poires* with *marrons glacés,* a hot strawberry sauce laced with kirsch, accompanied by Pommery Brut champagne.

During the previous days of foie gras preparation, Avis took careful notes, concluding that watching Julia and Simca work together was inspiring: "This is certainly one of the great collaborations in history. They are absolutely necessary to each other and it is a happy miracle that they met. . . . It is the *combination* which makes their work so revolutionary, and for my money they are benefactors of the human race." Words that could have applied as well to the "team" of Paul and Julia Child.

Chapter 19

THE MEDIA ARE THE MESSAGE

(1967 – 1968)

"The dining-room is a theater . . .
the table is the stage."

CHATALLON-PLESSIS

⤳

PAUL ROLLED UP ten copies of the *Boston Globe* and wound sticky masking tape around the bundle while Julia grabbed a bowl and dumped in the contents of an entire can of Crisco. The photographers were waiting as Paul sawed off on the slant both ends of his newspaper roll. Julia had already added some powdered sugar and cocoa to her mix when she took the *Globe* roll from her husband's hands. With a spatula she slathered the brown lard all over the paper roll and decorated her "Yule log" or *bûche de Noël,* running her knife in irregular lines along the lardy mass to simulate the bark of a tree. The only thing edible on the "cake" was the fake mushrooms, which were made from meringue.

PHOTO FAKERY AND THE COMMERCIAL FOOD WORLD

Inside the oven, the temperature was a cool 57 degrees; outside the August sun was baking their seventy-eight-year-old Cambridge house. The photographer and designer from *House & Garden* were intent on creating "Christmas with the Childs" for their eager holiday readers several months hence. "But we don't even spend Christmas in Massachusetts anymore," she told José Wilson, food editor of *House & Garden,* when asked for this interview. "We spend every winter in our little house in Provence." No matter.

"And I do not have time to prepare a Christmas meal," she added, glancing at Paul, who was helping her test a bread recipe for the second volume of her *Mastering the Art of French Cooking.* But José hurriedly explained that they would provide everything and stay only long enough to arrange and photograph the dishes and the table. The recipes printed in the magazine, of course, would be Julia's carefully tested television recipes.

True to her word, the professional decorator arrived and swiftly arranged a little tree covered with cookies. They put together a mixture of buttermilk, canned tomato paste, and egg yolks to represent lobster bisque. "That would probably keep a starving Bengali alive for three days," Paul muttered as the crew arranged the table. His eyes lit up when he saw them open a 450-gram box of foie gras. They would keep that for themselves.

Each time the photographer moved his tripod, he swiftly made four separate exposures, saving hours of preparation time. Click, click, click, click, dishes, furniture, food, holly . . . and lard. "The world of photo fakery," Paul called it in a letter to his brother, "unlike our TV show where everything is superbly edible." Fakery, like the "hoked-up dinner" *The Ladies' Home Journal* had staged just a month before.

When Julia was approached by the *Journal* that winter, her first reaction was negative; she did not equate serious cookery only with "ladies," nor was she impressed with the reputation of its food editor, Poppy Cannon, author of *The Can Opener Cookbook.* She seemed to represent everything Julia stood against. But the circulation was six million, she explained to Simca, and "as long as there is no new book, and no new TV shows, it would be useful to keep the name in the public eye." It still sounded "ghastly."

The sophisticated and well-dressed New York "designer" arrived at one o'clock to choose the plates, napkins, glasses, silverware, and serving dishes for the *Journal*'s feature piece, which they were tentatively calling "Julia Gives a Dinner Party." When Julia protested that her long hours of recipe testing and typing for the new volume did not allow time for more than half a day, Poppy Cannon said, "No problem." The *Journal* would furnish the food, the flowers—*and* the guests.

The designer returned with masses of exotic blooms and greenery to match their color scheme. At two-thirty a tough-looking "manager" wearing a bold stare and white fishnet stockings appeared. At three o'clock the two New York home economists arrived carrying the dinner, which they had prepared in the studio kitchen of the Cambridge Electric Company, where Julia's early television programs were shot in 1962. The dinner was to be cooked according to Julia's menu and television recipes: soup, veal Prince Orloff, braised endive, molded pineapple sorbet with orange. And five bottles of Médoc wine.

Soon a tall, unshaven man in dark glasses named Levy entered, followed by a Japanese man named Matsuoka and a black man named Pinder sporting bush jacket and shades, all carrying suitcases. The photographers had arrived. Lights, cables, and cameras were almost set up when the "guests" showed up: four young women wearing miniskirts and false eyelashes, accompanied by their husbands, each couple obviously recruited from Beacon Hill or Harvard Yard.

All this time Julia was upstairs trying to ignore the ringing doorbell. She was leaning her six-foot-two-inch frame over her desk, furiously typing letters and recipes she mailed sometimes every day to Simca in France. Having completed the soup chapter for the new book, they were struggling with a perfect recipe for Americans to make French bread.

When Paul came up to report on the events in his colorful narrative style, Julia fumed. She muttered something about being "put upon by a bunch of hard-boiled New Yorkers with a flock of cheap models, spilling cigarette ashes all over the house, and telling us what to do in our own kitchen." She refused to get dressed and come down until her morning's work was completed.

Paul reasoned with her and she eventually put on the many-colored dress that Paul had chosen for her that spring in Cannes. She composed her smile as she descended the stairway and was soon charmed by the young guests, all in their twenties. Beatles music played in the background to enliven the atmosphere. The cat was shut up in the large basement.

The meal appeared good enough, though it was evidently undercooked to look better for the cameras. They took 432 pictures; Paul counted. When Julia offered a chilled bottle of Château d'Yquem to go with the dessert, she and Paul were amazed to discover that Julia's *glace à l'ananas aux oranges glacées* was made of Crisco and powdered sugar. Fake food, a fake dinner, and fake "Julia's guests." Later she would learn other tricks, such as rubbing a turkey with bitters, olive oil, and soy sauce and cooking it briefly just enough for the oil to stay on the skin for a tight, glossy photogenic bird.

When the October issue of the *Journal* appeared, subscribers read that the four men "guests" had written to Julia to thank her for teaching their wives how to cook. To express their gratitude—and allow the magazine to illustrate the convenience of freezing ahead—the men made "a raid on the four couples' freezers" and put together "a complete Julia Child meal [for their] date with their wives' teacher." The article was ironically entitled "The Julia Child Way to Plan Your Own Ready-Ahead Dinner."

America's "scholar cook" met Madison Avenue full in the face that summer. These slick magazine spreads—and there would be others this year and next—and the reruns of the *French Chef* television program would keep the sales of *Mastering the Art of French Cooking* alive while Julia and her partner spent three years preparing their second volume. The care Julia took with the recipes, cross-testing every variable, baking thousands of brioches, croissants, and loaves of bread, would always set their books apart from other cookbooks. Hadn't Mary Frances (M. F. K. Fisher) just written her that their first volume was now a "classic"?

Though she was swept into the commercial food world of New York, her head was not turned by the national attention she received following the *Time* cover six months before. She was fifty-four when fame hit, a California girl who was natural and forthright, the daughter of a practical New England mother. Food writer Paul Levy remarked pungently, and with admiration, that she could call a fart a fart when talking about cassoulet.

By and large, she followed her own steady dictates, aware that she was different. When in September she was asked to attend the *Harper's Bazaar* luncheon ("100 Women of Accomplishment"), her letter to Simca revealed her sense of remaining outside the glamorous world of New York City: "I hesitated about going, but then thought it would be great fun to look at all the fancy ladies, and I do know a handful from among them. This sort of thing is rather rich for our blood and I shall never have the right costume to wear, however there will be other simple souls like myself who are not dressed and coiffed by the great salons!"

THE IRVING STREET BAKERY AND *MASTERING II*

When they prepared their detailed outline in early February 1966, Julia and Simca believed the second volume would be completed in two years. It would take twice that long. Julia had to conclude her final work for the Time-Life people and *The French Chef Cookbook,* and she had a difficult time saying no to the many demands. But the major complication came when Judith Jones, their Knopf editor, asked them to include a recipe for "French" bread and prevailed with the argument that because Americans cannot buy this bread in their own country, they might want to try making it. Julia agreed, as long as they could come up with a recipe and technique to produce a bread that was both different from what Americans made in their own homes and close to the color, taste, and texture of the French. The book now changed from one that resembled the first volume to a book that would include a large chapter, following the first one on soups, on baking.

They originally agreed the volume would be a "continuation" of the first volume. In this way, the publishers were assured the second volume did not diminish the value or relevance of the first. Eventually they would integrate recipes for both volumes in the complete index, distinguished by red and black ink. Their audience would be, in Julia's words "as before, those who like to cook and/or want to learn, as well as those who are experienced cooks, including professionals. So we have to keep dumb debutantes in mind, as well as those who know a lot, and who are thoroughly familiar with the classic French cookbooks." She wrote these words to Simca two days after giving a large family luncheon for nephew Jonathan Child's graduation from Harvard.

In 1967 alone, Julia and Paul used hundreds of pounds of white flour experimenting to find the best techniques for making brioche, croissants, *pain de mie* (sandwich bread, which did not interest Julia), a variety of pastry doughs, and—the most significant and challenging—French bread in all its various shapes (baguette, *bâtard, champignon, boulot,* etc.). The ingredients never changed: yeast, water, flour, and salt. (American recipes, including Fannie Farmer's, always used sugar.) Why the difficulty? Paul soon learned, when he decided to experiment alongside Julia, that there were "ten thousand variables" involved in the yeast, the rising, the shaping, the moisture, the timing, and the oven. Consequently, they had to cook batches of bread, making only one variation each time. Though a few critics would fault her for using American grocery store flour, that was precisely the point: Julia maintained that Americans must be able to use the ingredients they can buy.

She and Paul experimented with fresh and dried yeast, various flour mixtures (Wondra, Gold Medal A&P, unbleached), rising times, and how to get moisture into the oven to simulate a French baker's oven and to give the bread the color and crispness of French bread. Soon Paul—"M. Paul Beck, Boulanger," she called her new partner—was baking his own batches with Julia in their Cambridge kitchen in the summer and fall of 1967. He hung the molded baguette dough, after its second rising, in a large dish towel hooked in a closed drawer; Julia would lay hers in the folds of a flowered canvas. Paul got steam on the top of the baking bread by squirting water from a rubber nasal decongestant sprayer every ten minutes; Julia used a washed and wet whisk broom. Finally, they settled on getting steam into the oven by dropping a red-hot stone or brick into a pan of water in the hot oven.

It was the dueling bread makers who, each time they thought they had a perfect process, found out that it was not as good the second time they followed the same procedure. Mary Frances wrote back one day that she had a dream that Paul, the size of a cat, was slid on a long flat paddle into a hot oven, holding his nasal sprayer. They all had a good laugh. By July their bread was better than anything they could buy in Cambridge, but it was not yet "French" bread. They came to two conclusions: the bread must rise slowly and it must cook with frequent steam infusion.

Their neighbors on both sides, the deSola Pools and the Browns, remember that summer when many loaves of warm bread were passed over the fence to them. Even old friends ("They fit us like a pair of old shoes," Paul would say) whom the Childs would visit—the Pratts in their summer home and the Mowrers in New Hampshire—remember the bread baking at their houses. One host discovered a rising loaf hanging from one of the guest room's drawers. The Child nieces recall the summer bread baking at Lopaus Point (where Julia also visited a factory to learn about professional cracking of crabs). These family and friends, incidentally, were not intimidated by inviting Julia to a meal; she reassured them, "Nonsense, it is only I who am expected to prepare a perfect meal."

In 1968, when they spent months in France making croissants every day—feeding every visitor, guest, and family member croissants until they settled every nuance of preparation and procedure—young Jean-François Thibault, Simca's nephew, thought, "They must be terrible bakers because they have to keep making these croissants."

WORKING WITH SIMCA

Writing Volume II was similar in many ways to writing the first. Julia was in charge of writing all the copy (both the blah-blah and the recipe directions), which she would send to Simca, who read and tested the recipes. Julia was the authority on how American produce and ingredients worked with French techniques and recipes. "I hope you will accept my findings," she wrote Simca, "I am the one here in the USA who gets blamed if our recipes don't work." In turn, after Simca tested each recipe, she reported her findings and had the final say on all the French names and terminology.

Simca was the major supplier of recipes. In fact she could not stop sending recipes, even after they constructed their final outline. "Simca is a great improvisationalist," wrote her student and assistant Michael James. Peter Kump claimed her recipes, like her stories, "changed slightly every time." Julia told Mary Frances in both admiration and complaint, "She is a fountain of ideas." She wrote Avis, who insisted upon being a part of the second volume: "I cannot trust Simca's recipes at all, except as great idea fountains, so every single one will have to go through the chocolate-cake type of testing. I'm just not going to have anything in this book that doesn't work well—we have 3 in Vol. I which are far too tricky, and which gall me every time I think of them. Vol. II has to be *better* than Vol. I, and I ain't going to be rushed over it." Finally Julia placated Simca with a line about saving a particular recipe for Volume III (though she never seriously considered a third). Back and forth, Julia in English, Simca in French, they would comment in detail on each experiment and on the other's comments on every experiment. Today the thousands of onionskin pages are brown with food stains and age. As before, Julia reminded Simca they had to keep their recipes and discoveries secret from both colleagues and students.

The initial differences in writing this new book were several and went far beyond the fact that they no longer sent a carbon of their work to Louisette. Julia, who always did all the typing, had Gladys, her secretary, who could type up the final double-spaced recipes in the form already worked out in the first volume. They also had a book to work against; even basic techniques were already explained in the first volume. Now, however, there was the bread recipe and more desserts, which were Simca's specialty.

Julia was frustrated earlier in Plascassier when she was not satisfied with the chocolate cake recipe Simca chose. Julia had brought the chocolate from the States, but Simca did not test it fully, she believed. In Cambridge, Julia invited a chemist from Nestlé to come for lunch and talk about the chemical composition, cocoa butter content, and melting methods of their chocolate. Americans made the mistake of melting chocolate in a pan with boiling (not simmering) water under it. She worked and reworked the directions herself. She also hated the pound cake (*le quatre quarts*), "a heavy horrid cake and not my idea of good French cooking."

The temperamental and philosophical differences between Julia and Simca both aided their joint work and created frequent friction. Julia's approach was evident in a letter she wrote to Simca: "I shall also take notes on every method of *pâté-en-croûte* making that I run into—I am sure this drives you crazy, but it is the only way I can work—I want to know everything, and why, and what's no good and why, so then when our master recipe is done there are no unsolved questions." Simca, Paul told Charlie, "seldom subjects anything to operational proof [and] lives in a totally verbal world." Earlier he wrote that she "roars through life like a hurricane, smashing her way toward her goals." Of course, he added, that is the quality that got her house renovated, her trees planted, her cooking school up and running. In a contrasting view, Jane Owen Molard, who worked with Simca in the 1980s, says, "Julia and Simca were much alike. They both had busy exteriors but calm centers."

In the lengthy report Avis DeVoto wrote to William Koshland the previous Christmas season in Provence, she made the following observations about the culinary "sisters": "Simca is a creative genius . . . [but] also inaccurate, illogical, hard to pin down, and stubborn as a mule. Julia is also very creative and is becoming more so. But the two women think differently. Julia is deeply logical, orderly, accurate, painstaking, patient, determined to get all this knowledge clearly on paper. And she can be just as stubborn as Simca is, and will plug away trying to convince Simca until suddenly Simca changes her position, and from then on she will talk as if it were her own idea all along."

Paul did not like Simca's bossy, know-it-all attitude; it "drives me up the wall," he confided to Charlie. But Julia would not countenance anyone criticizing Simca. Angry one day, Paul wrote the following indictment: "Simca pays no attention to anything Julia tells her about all the researches she's done, the findings of the U.S. Dept. of Agriculture, or the careful scientific comparison she's made between the various commercial starches based on corn, rice, potatoes, etc. She drives me nuts." At Julia's insistence, he added at the bottom of the letter: "An impurely personal opinion, resented by Julia, who asked me to change it. I can't; but she has *tremendous* value, is a *real half* of the combination which I may not have made clear."

If Paul and Simca sometimes got along just for the sake of Julia, probably the same could be said of Paul and Jean. The hearty French chemist would immediately put on his blue work coveralls and boots when he came to Bramafam and putter around the property, in sharp contrast to the well-dressed Paul, who was preoccupied by his painting and photography. The Fischbachers and Thibaults thought Paul could be moody and distant. He in turn thought they sometimes treated foreigners disdainfully.

Julia and Simca were loyal to each other out of respect and love. Like sisters, they argued and made up. Julia believed Simca distrusted the scientific approach, in part because she lacked formal higher education and was ruled by her emotions and instinct. When Julia was testing for the perfect crust for their *pâté en croûte,* she informed Avis she did not think Simca was the least interested in her research. "I don't think she believes in it." Paul said she was "a mountain of unscientific instinctiveness." He had even harsher words in other letters to Charlie. In several of Julia's letters to Simca it is clear that Julia is urging her to experiment, to visit local bakers. Many years later, Julia would be more frank about the dogmatism of Simca, imitating Simca's loud *"non, non, non"* at the top of her voice.

When Simca reported that in a brief visit to the master bread maker

Calvel he let his dough rise only once, Julia wrote back that in his book he specifies twice. All her experiments proved that the dough must rise twice: "Kneading by the usual system forces the gluten molecules to stick together so that the starch and yeast molecules will be dispersed intimately among them, and then the yeast forms little pockets of gas which push up the gluten network; a pushing down and second rise disperses the yeast into new starch pockets, and these in turn make the gluten network more fine." And so on. Simca was probably asleep by that point.

THE LOUISETTE PURCHASE

Originally Julia and Simca assumed that Louisette's name would be on Volume II. Though she was not involved at any point in the book, she was still a part of L'Ecole des Trois Gourmandes, though she did little teaching at the Paris school with Simca anymore. She and her new husband, Henri, were now settling permanently in Vouzeron, in the center of France. Beyond initiating the first book, she did next to nothing; including her name on the second would have been giving credit and money where it was not due. Moreover, she no longer got along with Simca.

Julia and Paul decided earlier they needed to create a will protecting their growing assets from television and publishing and to set up a system by which Julia herself would not have to send the royalty checks to her partners. Julia also realized, after talking with Bill Koshland at Knopf and the lawyers of WGBH, that she had to determine the ownership of recipes, which were mixed up between television, newspapers, and books. She was facing the complications of two new contracts. Typically, Julia and Paul wanted "absolute order" in their financial affairs. They hired Brooks Beck the same week Paul boasted he made his twenty-first batch of bread.

Beck, of the Hill & Barlow law firm in Boston, was no Wall Street lawyer type, but a handsome man of great culture and humor, a real character with a bit of an acid tongue. Not incidentally, he was a member of their Cambridge circle of respected associates. They had met, after all, at a DeVoto party, and his wife, Wendy, was an editor at the Atlantic Monthly Press. Julia was particularly impressed that Beck represented two of their neighbors, Arthur Schlesinger, Jr., and John Kenneth Galbraith.

Beck's first response was that he thought the two women should buy out Louisette Bertholle (an offer of even $25,000 would be a lot of money for someone who was doing nothing), and that Julia should no longer act as comptroller. He warned about the tax consequences in both countries, but untangling the issues would take months. Their next royalty payment was held up until this issue could be resolved, and in the interim Simca and Louisette eventually got their own lawyers. Julia warned her partners about the tax implications and was relieved when she learned Simca was declaring something to the French authorities.

When Julia casually mentioned to Louisette the idea of buying out her share of the partnership (the book was copyrighted, but they were never able to copyright the cooking school), Louisette sounded interested. But no official offer was made because they believed she would demand too much money (she mentioned to Julia she was thinking of about $45,000). She had already earned $33,000 in royalties for *Mastering I,* and any buyout of her 18 percent would come out of the advance for the second volume. Thus, they held up signing any contract with Knopf for their second volume until the question of Louisette could be resolved. Brooks Beck suggested they hold up making any offer to Louisette, who by December informed Simca she would sell all rights for $30,000.

Neither Jean Fischbacher nor Paul Child wanted to damage the trust between Simca and Julia, so they let their lawyers handle everything. Julia and Paul were anxious to settle their estate, which was to be left to their nieces and nephews. The only matter remaining to be cleared up—and this involved Louisette—was the issue of copyright to the book and partnership. By February 1968 the papers were signed.

In the matter of royalties for Julia's book of television recipes, *The French Chef Cookbook,* she initially spoke about sharing the royalties, but her lawyer must have thought otherwise. Simca agreed (though her lawyer initially held out) that Julia should have the copyright and all royalties on that book because, though some recipes were taken (and changed) from their first book, Julia's television and promotion made an appreciable difference in the sales of *Mastering I,* which doubled, then tripled, after the television program began, and leapt after the *Time* cover. On the television work she perhaps broke even; thus her only compensation for seven-day workweeks came from book sales. (The first and only time Julia mentioned this issue to Simca was in a letter dated October 18, 1967.) There was no question that the difference between the 1,000 books they sold the first month and the 3,000 books they were selling every month now, was Julia Child.

Finally, by the spring of 1968 the contract between the lawyers for Simca and Julia was settled and signed. Two complications were involved. Julia wanted her payments from Knopf to be set at a low enough figure to make her tax bracket more reasonable, and Julia and Simca had to work out the complications of their disproportionate expenditures of time and money (Julia did all

the typing, proofreading, arrangements for drawings, and appearances). Finally, Julia bought sole rights to the first volume from Simca, and they shared
the second volume, with Julia as the agent who kept track of expenses. By
March 1969, *Mastering* had sold 600,000 copies, with Simca and Julia already
making back half of what Julia called their "Louisette Purchase."

The pressure of time involved in Julia's numerous appearances led to
Paul's decision to take to the air. He had always broken into cold sweats and
relived memories of treacherous flying in China when faced with the idea of
plane flight, but he determinedly conquered his vertigo by applying the practical sense and the logic he always lived by. No more transatlantic voyages on
the *Queen Mary*.

ᗪINING AND DIPLOMACY:
FILMING AT THE WHITE HOUSE

Just before flying down to film a documentary on the White House kitchens
for WGBH, Julia opened her door to the French consul general, who came to
pin the green ribbon and bronze star of France's Médaille de Mérite Agricole
on her dress and kiss her on both cheeks. "We don't know whether to laugh,
or be proud, at this backhanded gesture from the government for which she
has done so much," Paul wrote to Charlie. Nevertheless, half a dozen friends
celebrated with champagne, *Time* magazine reported. The *Smith Alumnae
Quarterly* proudly announced that the green ribbon now rested beside the
cordon bleu. What Julia did not know was that a Smith College committee
turned down an effort by several alumnae to award her an honorary degree
that year.

"Dinner and Diplomacy" (the initial title) was conceived when a plan by
WGBH for a documentary on the French Chef in Paris (featuring Les Halles,
which were closing down) fell through due to a lack of funding. In August
1967 they proposed making a color documentary of how the White House
kitchens operate, what equipment they use, the staff, marketing, even menu
planning. Ruth Lockwood, with contacts through her journalist son, did all the
preliminary work with Liz Carpenter and her assistant, Mrs. Poulain. There
would be several trips to Washington as the arrangements were made and the
date moved several times. Julia and Paul flew down in August, September, and
October; first it was going to be a dinner for the King and Queen of Nepal,
then one for the Japanese Prime Minister.

President and Mrs. Lyndon B. Johnson honored her with an invitation to
be a part of the state dinner on November 14, 1967, for the Prime Minister of

Japan. Originally, the program for educational television was to be a study of the kitchen and behind-the-scenes of a state dinner, but now Julia and Paul were honored guests and the film crew would be allowed in the dining room (with releases from everyone).

Julia thought the meal exquisite: vol-au-vent of seafood, noisettes of lamb, artichoke choron, white asparagus polonais, a garden salad, cheeses, and strawberry Yamaguchi (a tart). Three wines were poured: Wente Pinot Chardonnay, Beaulieu Cabernet Sauvignon, and Almadén Blanc de Blanc (with no vintages given on the menu, Paul noted with amazement).

Julia and Paul were sitting next to Vice President and Mrs. Hubert Humphrey, and Julia found him delightful ("I've always liked him, but didn't realize how thoroughly warm and attractive he is," she informed Avis). Paul was pleased to get reacquainted with Professor S. I. Hayakawa, whom he had met in Germany and with whom he had spent a week studying just two years before. Because the Japanese guest (His Excellency Eisaku Sato) was crazy about baseball, the commissioner of baseball was there, as were a pitcher from the St. Louis Cardinals and George Steinbrenner. Maxwell Taylor, John D. Rockefeller IV, cabinet ministers, and other dignitaries rounded out the 190-guest list.

Julia had a wonderful time meeting the President and the other distinguished guests, but she was just as excited to meet Swiss chef Haller and his pastry chef, Ferdinand Louvat, a Frenchman ("Loved the two chefs, and being able to talk shop in French with them was a great help to us," Julia wrote Simca). And she talked at length to Mary Kaltman, the food coordinator and housekeeping director. These professionals were people she respected enormously. Originally the program was going to be called "Behind the Scenes at the White House Banquet."

She was also excited to work with her old crew from *The French Chef.* Russ Morash was the director, Peter the Dutchman operated the one handheld camera, and Willie was the sound engineer. The script, written by a professional but lacking in dignity, they believed, was rewritten around the Child kitchen table by Ruth, Paul, and Julia. This program would not be live, but edited by a professional (with assistance from Ruth and Russ) and shown on American educational television, now called the Public Broadcasting Company, the following April (Julia would have to come back from La Pitchoune to do the voice-overs).

"The White House Red Carpet," its final title, began with the doors of the White House opening and visitors streaming in. The camera panned down the line of guests to pick up Julia Child, the narrator, who informed the audience that 40,000 people a week enter the White House. Later, in the video's flashbacks, the Prime Minister of Japan deplaned and Julia interviewed James Symington, the protocol officer, and chef Henri Haller in the kitchens of the White House.

Ruth Lockwood told Bill Koshland that it "was a nerve-wracking experience, but as usual Julia was relaxed and lovely." Indeed, her only worry was what dress and shoes to wear. She was used to being on television with her sneakers on. Ruth helped her choose the shoes and dress—Paul called it rainbow-colored. She wore the wig. Lady Bird Johnson wore a gold draped chiffon gown by Adele Simpson, and Tony Bennett entertained with songs after the banquet.

This was Julia's first White House experience ("splendid," she said, "neither of us shall ever forget it"). During this first visit she thought briefly about what it would have been like with the Kennedys, but concluded, "The food could not have been any better." This White House dinner would remain her most memorable, not because she was "a Roosevelt Democrat at home, an Acheson Democrat abroad" (as one journalist observed), but because of the food. She admired Henri Haller and thought that the service and organization of the evening was elegant. The servers were professional staff, black men who had worked in the White House for years and served with quiet flair, "like clockwork." Thirty years later, after visiting during two other administrations, she would tell a Boston University audience that "the food was great" at the Johnson dinner. Otherwise the "culinary reputation [of the White House] is dreary indeed." Gerald Ford's people were uneasy about the pomp and show—fearful of spending the taxpayers' money—so the state dinner Julia attended was cheap, the food undistinguished, the service sloppy. The Reagan White House served chipped beef, cream cheese, green mayonnaise, veal madeleine in dough, and a platter of purple sorbet with canned peaches.

Julia was also quick to point out that WGBH's tribute was to the White House, not to the Johnson administration. "We were there . . . at the height of anti-Johnsonism and the attitudes in Cambridge Mass were quite frightening—making me realize that academics are too seldom intellectuals!" she wrote to Ellie and Basil Summers the following spring, when the video was played. She and Paul could not drive through Harvard Square without seeing the Students for a Democratic Society (SDS) carrying pickets reading: "Napalm—Johnson's Baby Powder," for the atmosphere at the university was "chaotic" and "somber." She and Paul were also opposed to the war in Vietnam, but she thought the protest "has really pulled the country to pieces." She mentioned "pride in the White House" on the video, and, fortunately, the political landscape would change before the spring to make their film more acceptable.

The morning after the state dinner, they taped more interviews for their documentary before flying to New York to catch the night plane to Nice, via Paris. Soon they were lounging on the terrace beside the purple bougainvillea and smelling the jasmine. Watching Jeanne pick olives to take to the local press, they thought only of the five months in France ahead of them and the completion of the book.

Page proofs for Michael Field and M. F. K. Fisher's Time-Life book had been delivered to the plane as they left, and proofs of her own *The French Chef Cookbook* arrived in December. She corrected "plenty" of errors in both manuscripts. "America is beginning to fade," she wrote Avis after just a week in La Pitchoune.

Julia and Simca flew up to Paris the first week of December for a morning session with Professor Calvel, head of the Ecole Professionelle de la Boulangerie, a world expert on bread making. After talking and observing, Julia concluded their bread dough was too firm (his was soft and sticky and rose slowly to twice its size). Amid the market din and smell of Les Halles, Julia bought three fresh foie gras and truffles for the coming holiday feasts. "God, it was great! Ten thousand smells, sounds, and faces! I kept thinking what a movie we could have made if that plan of ours hadn't fallen through," she wrote Avis.

They were happy and clearly feeling financially well-off, for they had their trunks air-expressed to their door and bought a "miniature television machine" (to see De Gaulle's press conference) and a large Kelvinator refrigerator with separate freezer space. They knew that in a month they would have to return briefly for Julia to read the voice-overs for the documentary, but for now they were away from all the daily business of life. For the last six months, amid the bread baking and recipes testing, the occasional interview, and preparations for the White House filming, they were overwhelmed with guests and dear friends from every part of their rich past.

"This is really the first time either of us has been able to work without interruptions in months," Julia wrote Avis. She finished twenty-seven pages of blah-blah introducing French bread and sent copies of it to Simca, Avis, and her editor (Avis was horrified at its length and said it should not go into the book) before moving on to pork. She and Paul visited the Alvaro pig farm to watch a crew of four slaughter a 300-pound pig in a ceremony as old as the Middle Ages. She was calm, unflinching, and curious to learn everything she could about it, for Paul was going to photograph her preparation of their Christmas suckling pig.

Louisette and Henri visited one weekend, and an occasional American or English reporter would find her, including one from *Newsweek*. But most of their days were uninterrupted. Simca and Jean were in Paris. Only Sybille and Eda were invited for Paul's birthday feast, which included a flaming mountain of ice-cream cake. It was Le Kilimanjaro, the chocolate and almond ice cream dessert, which would appear in the second volume of *Mastering* (page 420). She added a touch that is not in the book: on the top of the dessert "mountain," she placed an empty half eggshell, filled it with liquor, and lighted it before taking the flaming volcano to the table.

Here in La Pitchoune they were at peace. Paul would listen to the banging of his "Mad Woman of La Pitchoune" in the kitchen and write to his brother: "Well—I'm . . . smelling all these breads, chickens, pâtés, dorades, cooking, and hearing my tender little wifelet crashing around in the kitchen, scolding the pussy for meowing, whacking something metallic with something else metallic, like a Peking street vendor. A very jolly house." Just two weeks before, he told his brother, "How fortunate we are at this moment in our lives! Each doing what he most wants, in a marvelously adapted place, close to each other, superbly fed and housed, with excellent health, and few interruptions."

A PERSONAL TRAGEDY

"Left breast off" is all she wrote in her datebook for February 28, 1968. They had flown back to Boston on the first day of February to do the voice-over for the White House documentary, thinking that they would be gone no more than two weeks. Julia had scheduled an appointment to see her gynecologist during their stay, having felt a small lump several busy months ago. Dr. Arnold Segal wanted to do a biopsy but could not schedule an operating room in Beth Israel Hospital until the twenty-eighth. It would only be an overnight affair, she assured Simca in her frustration at not being able to return to La Pitchoune. "It is a very simple matter to take care of," she added. It was routine. Two days before she entered the hospital, she wrote to Simca that she took the ten days to cut down the introduction to bread (it would be nineteen published pages), and she would be out of the hospital in two or three days and back to France.

As it turned out, it was not "a simple matter," as it might have been twenty years later. At the time they did the biopsy, they removed her breast and the lymph nodes in her left arm as a precaution against spreading cancer, a practice typical of that time. Today the surgery would be considered too radical, for on March 4, in the middle of her ten days in the hospital, she was told the small tumor had been neatly removed. "All analysis OK & negative," she wrote in her datebook. She would have to wear a rubber sleeve and exercise that arm for months to remove the fluid and restore its use. "After seeing a photo of a naughty woman who refused to wear her rubber sleeve and what happened to her arm, I really hardly dare take mine off!" she told Simca. When she returned to Avis's house, where they were staying because they had rented their own house, she sat in the bathtub and privately wept.

With the same practicality she expressed when she told the doctor to perform the operation and get it over with, she told herself to get on with her work and not complain. "No radium, no chemotherapy, no caterwauling," she said in 1996. Thank God it was my left side and not my right, she wrote to Simca in a letter full of details about their manuscript and plans to get on with the recipes for tripe, calves' feet, and calves' heads. Each week when she returned to the doctor she asked when she could get back to France. They spent a weekend on Martha's Vineyard with Bob and Mary Kennedy, the weekend that LBJ said he would not run again for the presidency. World events would soon put her own pain into perspective: the next Thursday, Martin Luther King was assassinated in Memphis.

Paul was devastated by Julia's experience. He suffered when she merely had a bad cold. His friends say he had a terrible time, fearing he would lose her. "He was good and loving about both [the operations]," Julia wrote Simca. "I bless him and feel very fortunate." This man who wrote nearly every day of his life apparently did not write a word for weeks. Charlie and Freddie came to visit, as did John and Jo McWilliams, then Dort and her Phila, who decided to apply to Radcliffe for her college education and to live near her Aunt Julia.

At noon on April 11, Julia and Paul attended the press preview of "The White House Red Carpet" at WGBH. She tossed her last cigarette out the car window when it made her nauseous. That afternoon she saw Dr. Segal once more, and the following evening the Childs flew out of Boston for two months of recuperation. When the documentary ran nationally on April 17, Julia and Paul were entertaining Simca and Jean at La Pitchoune.

In June, Avis visited the Childs there, and she confided to Bill Koshland that she was "a bit taken aback" by Julia's appearance. He agreed that when he had seen her in mid-May she was just beginning to come out of it. No one ever talked openly about mastectomies until Mrs. Nelson Rockefeller and Mrs. Gerald Ford were publicly candid several years later.

Julia's decision to stop smoking was reinforced in the spring of 1969 when Bob Kennedy was operated on for lung cancer and continued to smoke.

A damned fool, Paul called him. He had the same opinion of Cora DuBois, who kept smoking after a diagnosis of emphysema. Three of their friends, all heavy smokers, died in 1969.

That year, Julia retreated even further to work on recipes for their second volume, which she and Simca constructed and tested for three years. The following year in Cambridge she wrote most of the book by retreating to the stove and typewriter. The deadline was moved again and again, but finally met in March 1970.

Chapter 20

Celebrity and Solitude
(1968 – 1970)

"There is really no such thing as an original
recipe. . . . But cooks must feed their egos as well
as their customers."
M. F. K. FISHER *to Julia Child, October 4, 1968*

AT THE INTERMISSION of the Boston Symphony, after Beethoven's Symphony No. 1 and Debussy's Rhapsody for saxophone and orchestra, Julia and Paul walked up one flight to see the little art exhibit (Paul called it "the usual second-rate painting exhibit") and were once more reminded, as they were in their walks about Cambridge, of her growing fame. Julia Watchers, as Paul called them. Would she just sign their music program? You have changed my life! They sent her gifts (and would for decades), and she would give most of them to friends or charity. In a letter to Charlie, Paul quoted one reviewer of her *The French Chef Cookbook* speaking for her fans: "We will march with Julia, our banner an impeccably clean towel, and *'Bon Appétit!'* our cry, as our soufflés rise higher and higher. We will conquer new Malakoffs and let our apple charlottes fall where they may."

Mary Frances wrote to tell Julia that her own fan mail often told her she had "a lot to learn, mostly from JC. You are mostly called 'Julia' . . . their husbands can't keep their eyes off you for one thing and . . . there seems to be no overt jealousy . . . just a general amazement!" Even in her own Boston, Julia received honor. She was fast becoming an eccentric and lovable icon who, without pretension, brought honor to their city. The man who refinished her copper pots would not allow her to pay. And she was sought out socially by Stan Calderwood (a neighbor and vice president of Polaroid), Frank Morgan *(Newsweek* bureau chief), Tom Winship (editor-in-chief of the *Boston Globe),* and Louis Kronenberger (theater critic) when he retired to Brookline in 1970.

*T*HE PUBLIC JULIA

Julia could not help but be aware of her public persona when she was stopped at the A&P, at the intermission of the symphony, or on the streets of Boston, or (by American tourists) in Paris. She was aware of it when the national journalists and photographers came for interviews and pictures. But the articles often came out when she was working with Simca in France; during the six months after her *Time* cover, she was out of the country and again in the months after her operation. She guarded her private life and did not need to stay around for the early edition displaying her face for the public. "She's very reserved," says restaurant consultant Clark Wolf. "If her physicality matched her voice, she'd be Soupy Sales."

"She had become a mover and shaker like her father," her sister said. "He would have been proud!" Even when she was in France, she remained in the public eye. Television reruns and journal articles fed the public image, while the private Julia was testing recipes with Simca or typing long letters about their recipes in her office.

When she was back in Cambridge, Julia was at ease with the press and, though she preferred cooking demonstrations, gave an occasional public speech. She was becoming a better speaker, Paul noticed. During an interview with Frank Morgan of *Newsweek,* Paul told Charlie, he became aware of a quality in Julia after she had several vodkas (only gin or vodka had this effect) that reminded him of the description of Tallulah Bankhead, who died that week, as "a personality as much as a star. Her vibrant energy, explosive speech and impetuous behavior seemed at times a phenomenon better suited for study by physicists than by the journalists who chronicled her antics. I simply do not know her," Paul added, "no blurring of speech . . . [but] up go the decibels and the big swooping gestures. Interruptions-by-the-yard. The law is laid down, decorated by cuss-words, jokes, stream-of-consciousness . . ." In other words, Paul did not get a word in edgewise.

Her name appeared in several *Newsweek* articles in 1968 as well as in

McCall's, New York magazine, *TV Guide.* ("The only national television female of real authority is Julia Child . . . because her opinions are confined to the natural and universal passion, Food. Nobody can knock a woman Doing Her Thing in the Kitchen. And nobody cares if she doesn't look like Raquel Welch or have her hair done by Kenneth. In fact, quite properly, they care for her more because she is, simply, herself," wrote Marya Mannes.) In dozens of articles about other food professionals, Julia is always the one with whom they are compared or contrasted.

Vogue came to interview her in Plascassier, where she and Paul spent the 1968 holidays with Bob and Mary Kennedy. The *Vogue* interviewer was one of Judith Jones's authors, as were several of the chefs chosen for Julia's later cooking-with-Julia books in the 1990s. A more welcome guest was Beard, whose visit led to two grand meals, at least in terms of cost, at L'Oasis and the Casino in Monte Carlo. Together they watched (via satellite from Houston to Madrid) the astronauts return to earth on Apollo 8. In 1969 it was journalists from *McCall's* and *House & Garden* who came to Pitchoune for interviews to be published in 1970.

Julia and Paul were always interested in national and international arts and politics. He was going to vote for Humphrey, but she, despite Kennedy's "kiddie spawning," was voting for Bobby Kennedy. She was devastated by his assassination, which they heard on their tiny transistor as the church bell was tolling in Plascassier in June 1968. She felt personally let down when Jacqueline Kennedy married Onassis, and was disturbed by the violence at the Democratic convention that summer.

American produce was a political issue as well. Julia took on fish as a cause when she was back in Boston that fall. She privately blamed in part the Catholics for the reluctant consumption of fish by the rest of the country (their traditional obligatory Friday fish regimen made many equate fish with penance and privation). With James Beard she planned a cooking demonstration for thirty newspaper food editors, asserting the need for government support for better boats and docks. Their efforts, she informed Simca, were "a public service involving our educational station, the fishing industry, the government and the press." As important as the issue itself was what she learned about fish from the demonstration (she informed Simca that "individually peeled and flash-frozen shrimp are tough, but nonpeeled, block-frozen shrimp are better").

Nixon was a "very dull man, self-righteous, ambitious, solemn, [with] no interest in food, no cultivated tastes," said Julia: a litany of qualities she most disliked in people. She repeated her opinions—and the same fish recipe—for the Chamberlains, who came to lunch on election day, and for the Brooks

Becks the following night. She may have been perfecting her recipe, but she really wanted to talk about the dangerous "swing to the right" with the election of her fellow Californian, the man her father had helped enter national politics.

She and Paul were swept up in the political unrest that defined Harvard student life and the streets of Cambridge that fall ("hippy-cum-Panther-cum-drug" scene, Paul called it). There were riots in Harvard Yard, numerous break-ins in the neighborhood, and at the deSola Pools' next door (he was head of MIT's Center for International Studies) two bricks flew through the front window with a note attached: "Down with all Fascist Imperialists!" Paul had his own idea of fascists ("God alone can't get rid of J. Edgar Hoover," he lamented). In February 1970, Paul put in unbreakable plastic windows on the ground-floor windows and installed an elaborate alarm system, informing Charlie that their house was now "an illuminated monument to fear and to greater safety." (For aesthetic balance, he had a new wine cellar built, just for red wines.) In April the antiwar violence became familial when a second cousin of Julia's named Diana Oughton blew herself up accidentally (while making bombs) at a Weatherman house on Eleventh Street in Greenwich Village. "We are all swole up w/pride. Ho! Ho! Ho Chi Minh," Paul wrote cynically to Charlie.

Their letters reveal the Childs as classic liberals. "If you eat right, you vote right," she told a journalist in Northampton. Their old friends were now part of the establishment—Abe Manell was an assistant to the President, former Washington neighbor Stuart Rockwell an ambassador—but they themselves were sometimes antiestablishment. Each position was nuanced. They opposed the violence at Harvard, yet were in favor of abortion rights and the peaceful opposition to Nixon and the Vietnam War. She believed many students were in college "to grow up," much like her own academic career at Smith ("Somebody like me should not have been accepted at a serious institution").

With the pressure on to complete Volume II, Julia resented every interruption and longed for solitude. If she had to travel she continued her experiments with friends and family. She worked on puff pastry (*pâte feuilletée*) in Maine in August; pâtés and terrines on Martha's Vineyard while visiting Bob Kennedy; beef and fowl in Dublin, New Hampshire, with Helen Kirkpatrick Milbank for two Thanksgivings; and cakes on Long Pond beyond Plymouth at the Howes' summer home. One tradition was always honored: once a week she and Paul went across the Charles River to have Julia's hair washed and set and to dine together at the Ritz Grill (where women had to be accompanied by men). Another ritual was always to shop for groceries together, as much for companionship as the need for two people to transport their voluminous purchases.

Every dinner guest was a guinea pig for the book, whether it was Sybille Bedford when she came to Cambridge to research her biography of Aldous Huxley; Gay Bradley or Rosemary Manell from California; or Alfred Knopf himself, to whom she fed her *mousse de poisson.* She never wasted time on a meal preparation that did not relate to her research. If the recipe was less than perfect, she said nothing. Their guests ate informally but well around the large Norwegian table in the kitchen.

COMPLETING *MASTERING II*

"Rushing from stove to typewriter like a mad hen," she described herself midway through their final three-year push to complete the second volume of *Mastering the Art of French Cooking.* She worked seven-day weeks during the first five months of 1969, went to France to cook with Simca—though Simca was there only part of the time—then returned for the final eight months (until nearly April 1970) for more seven-day workweeks. She even worked that Christmas, bemoaning only that they were missing for the first time the winter foie gras and truffle season in France.

"I think we are the English-language Saint-Ange," Julia confided to Simca. This book must be "better and different," they agreed, for the competition is now greater, and "people expect to get the absolute word of the lord from us." Because they had a great responsibility to live up to, Julia tested some recipes fifteen or twenty times if necessary. She was disappointed to learn that her beloved James Beard used his assistant to test his recipes and that there were errors in his *Theory and Practice* (1969). He is "doing too much else," she confided to Simca. Then she heard that Michael Field signed on for twelve 150-page booklets, one to be published each month. By contrast, when Simca suggested they include couscous in their volume, Julia spent a full month researching the origins and ingredients and testing recipes until she finally rejected it.

If a name or recipe was not French, they made note of the fact, as in *filet de boeuf en croûte:* "Whether the English, the Irish, or the French baked the first filet of beef in a crust we shall probably never know, but [it] is certain that the French would not have named it after Wellington," she wrote on page 182. Also, in a passing reference to sour dough, Julia wrote (on page 57), "Sour dough is an American invention, not French, and you adapt your sour dough recipe to the method described here for plain French bread." Later,

food writer Karen Hess, who believed that the beef Wellington should not
have even been included, disagreed with Julia about the origins of sour dough.

Julia checked every recipe with the French classics. "We cannot use
tomato in bisque," she said, "because neither Carême or Escoffier or others
give tomatoes in their bisques, therefore to protect ourselves from criticism by
knowing types" she said no. They also remade some classic dishes too briefly
described in the older texts and occasionally found inspiration when they ate
out. After eating a delicious *loup de mer en croûte* at L'Oasis, Julia and Simca
tried to copy it, revising and refining it several times over two months. Because
she had all the French classic texts and subscribed to current French (*Cuisine
et Vins de France* and *La France à Table*) and English-language food periodicals, she checked their recipes carefully for originality. "It cannot be copied—
if close it must be improved," she told Simca. And if it was improved, they
must acknowledge its origins. While making *pain d'épices,* Julia discovered it
was an adaptation of one in Ali-Bab that had too much liquid. "We cannot
copy an Ali-Bab classic," she said, and did not use it. When Simca suggested
adding orange marmalade to *pain d'épices,* Julia said she did not want to add
ingredients that echoed "ladies' magazines and English additions."

Again, their recipes fell between the *haute cuisine* of the three-star chef
and the bourgeois cooking one would see at a wedding feast. Julia, who wrote
all the script, applied the techniques of the chefs to dishes from middle-class
and farm regions. "Is it French in technique?" she would ask, or declare,
"Don't add milk, it is not in the French tradition." When she labeled the cuts
of meat or questioned American produce, Julia wrote to national and government sources, always asking questions. "She was good because she was curious," notes Russ Morash.

Finally, of course, they had their same publisher, illustrator, and editor.
Judith Jones was an editor made for these volumes and for working with Julia.
Julia respected her knowledge of cooking, Paul her "New Englandy" restraint.
She kept a "loose rein" on Julia, but paid a couple of encouraging visits to
Cambridge when Julia needed them (William Koshland was leading the com-
pany since Knopf's retirement). After one weekend of work with Judith until
one in the morning, Paul informed Charlie that Judith Jones "could be a Fairy
Queen who has chosen to take on human form. She is also perceptive, kind,
shy, skillful at her job and (curiously) tough. It's a great pleasure to work with
her."

One of the major differences in Volume II was that Julia was now closer
to home and American produce, as she frequently pointed out to Simca.
("Things are different here . . . our sole fillets are thicker . . . [and] you
have to be here to know what is available, and what things taste like.") Also,

they included several recipes and food groups not appearing in Volume I: *choucroute,* bisques (with illustrations of cutting up lobster and crab), broccoli, courgettes, and, of course, the French bread she and Paul tested and tested.

Julia discovered that the gluten content differed between French (9 percent) and U.S. (11.5 percent) flours. They also came up with a new puff pastry recipe that was superior to all they tasted, using 1⅓ cups of A&P flour and ⅓ cup of cake flour (or ¾ to ¼). Much better results than using regular flour, she discovered. Julia picked up the idea from the pastry chef at the White House. The puff pastry section soon swelled to a comprehensive thirty-two pages.

The tension mounted as the months passed and more people at Knopf tasted their recipes. They feared their French bread and puff pastry recipes would be stolen. They trusted only their secret testers, including Freddie Child, Avis DeVoto, and neighbor Pat Pratt. But when Time-Life asked to publish their bread recipe, Julia was surprised that they even knew it was in the works. She refused, and they soon came out with a supplement claiming to give "an American version of French bread." Julia wrote to Simca: "I am happy to report that theirs has no relation whatsoever to the way French bread is made in France—thank heaven. I was so afraid they would get hold of Calvel, too! Michael Field, I am quite sure, knows nothing at all about yeast." Calvel gave them (after months of their own experimenting) private lessons in Paris using American flour they took to him. When a man in Japan wrote about the Calvel techniques of bread making, Julia worried needlessly. No one else paid any attention.

In the second, as in the first, volume Julia focused on time-saving devices, such as what portion of a recipe could be made in advance, while staying away from what she called cuisine express, which was growing in France. She was now concerned with fat content because of the increased attention to cholesterol in the United States. She wrote Simca:

> Do you think we shall have to think a little about cholesterol and not too much butter and cream in Vol. II? I am afraid we may have to, and will ask Judith what she thinks. A most disturbing report has come out of the American National Heart Association, saying there should even be a law, to save people's lives, etc. I am asking a girl from a big butter company what they are doing to combat this horrible situation.

She told Simca that her *boudin* recipe had too much fat in it. On the other hand, she rarely cut down on the number of eggs or amount of cream called for in a traditional recipe, though they were not afraid to improve on a traditional recipe.

"Food is not static," French chef Jacques Pépin recently observed. "It shows a lack of intelligence to criticize someone who is changing a recipe. Food progresses like language progresses. When it becomes static, it dies. Food has to move forward. Escoffier would be the first one if he were alive today to make changes and learn. If he were alive today, he would be the first one to use the food processor." Indeed, Julia insisted that, when possible, they should use the new machines on the market. ("We have to keep up with new household inventions, Simca!")

Some of the differences between the two major books of Julia's career are accounted for by the changes occurring in the decade of the 1960s. Indeed, even the mail between Julia and Simca took half the time to arrive. Xeroxing now saved much time. Wondra flour was invented, as were new machines such as the Cuisinart. Cake mixes were better and thus challenged them to make their cake recipes more outstanding. Even frozen and canned food improved, and Julia encouraged Simca to visit and learn about these changes, though Simca never did.

Most importantly, recipes were now more sophisticated and detailed, thanks in part to the influence of Julia and Simca. There were more and better-quality cooks. Many of the present recipe writers were Simca's former students in Paris. The world was growing smaller.

By 1970, Julia's letters revealed a subtle change in her estimation of the audience for this volume. She informed Simca that public food is on the whole worse (because of the lack of trained chefs and the cost of hand labor), but "home food, among those who cook and there is a growing number, is far better." (She contrasted these serious home cooks with "the assemblers," as she called those who assembled frozen and canned foods.) These improved home cooks and the growing number of professional cooks who read Julia's books brought about a change in her perception of their audience, explaining the relatively increased difficulty of Volume II. "The chefs and men are interested in our book," she told Simca, and "it does very much interest the serious and intellectual types, of which there are a lot in this country."

An ironic change Julia noted during her frequent movement back and forth between the two countries was that France was becoming more like America every day, and not just in the increased number of its supermarkets. The French were using more canned milk, she pointed out to Simca, but we cannot do it because it is not traditionally French, "because that is very American and would shock those romantic people (which means most of the Americans) who still think French cooking is very special and that they do not use such canned things. Little do they know how the two countries are coming ever closer together." Perhaps this was a pivotal reason to preserve the classic dishes of France.

By the summer and fall of 1969, months before she was finished with the book, Knopf was starting to print up three-chapter sections and Avis DeVoto was brought in for copy editing and proofreading; a three-part interview and prepublication of recipes was being prepared for *McCall's* magazine; and Ruth Lockwood was organizing a new series for *The French Chef* to be shot in color and to appear at the time of the publication of the book. The pace was hectic; the stress and testing added pounds. Julia and Paul were on a protein diet (Paul gave her five-pound dumbbells for her fifty-seventh birthday), and she and Ruth were half seriously talking about finding a plastic surgeon for a face lift.

Though Julia believed the manuscript could easily take five more years, she had only five months. She and Judith cut the eleven chapters down to seven, leaving out enough recipes to fill another volume. Frustrated by the many months locked away with her typewriter, Julia was actually looking forward to her television teaching schedule. She took the minimum amount of time for two family weddings and a ceremony at Smith College, where she received one of five medals (three of the five alumnae were honored for their volunteer work).

Two crises saddened her private life and interrupted her work. The first was the sudden death in August 1969 of Brooks Beck, her friend and lawyer. He died of a pulmonary embolism after difficult hip surgery at the age of only fifty-one, leaving three children with his widow, Wendy. The second crisis occurred while she was racing for a deadline in February 1970 and her gynecologist informed her that there was a small mass on her right breast. This time she had only a biopsy, which showed the lump was benign. The news left them feeling released from "bondage" and Paul, with what he called his "capacity for self-torture," in "a state of nerve-wracked joy." Their friends Herb and Pat Pratt celebrated this, as well as the seventh birthday of *The French Chef,* with a bottle of Griotte-Chambertin '62.

No More Collaboration

What became increasingly clear to Julia during the last two years of work was that she no longer wanted to write books and that she could no longer collaborate with Simca. Writing Volume II demanded she do nothing else but work on the book. It was "too confining." As early as August 1968 she told

Simca that it was "too damned much work and no let-up at all. *Fistre [fichtre,* meaning 'screw it'].*" By the following February she said, "I have no desire to get into another big book like Volume II for a long time to come, if ever. Too much work. I am anxious to get back into TV teaching, and out of this little room with the typewriter!" Nineteen months later, her resolve was even firmer.

The second reason was the growing intractability of Simca and an equally stubborn drive in Julia to make her own independent decisions. The contrast between Simca's temperament and that of Julia had always been there, but the more intense working conditions made their differences more acute. Julia was more than annoyed when Simca left to return to Paris to vote for Pompidou just when an important journalist flew in for a joint interview. But the sharpest criticism of Simca would be found in the letters of Paul, who implied that Simca was neurotic and undependable (as usual, Julia added a disclaimer in the margin of his letter). Julia's "exhaustive research goes for nothing," Paul wrote Charlie on June 21, 1969. "Simca will NOT listen to anything Julia says. . . . NO MORE COLLABORATION has become the watchword."

Though she would not allow open criticism of Simca to go unchallenged, she did confide in M. F. K. Fisher, sharing with her a French article she also sent to Simca. In the copy to Mary Frances, mailed on September 1, 1969, Julia highlighted the line "Every Frenchman is convinced he is a connoisseur who has nothing to learn from the experts." It had taken her fifteen years, she added, to learn this truth, which was "exactly what has been bugging me in my collaboration, and why I can't take any more of it. I don't know why I have been so dumb, but it is something one can hear, but not feel viscerally because how can anyone (but the French) have such arrogant nonsense as to live by that conception."

No evidence suggests that Julia tried to drop Simca from the team. Indeed, all the letters suggest that she kept her partner fully informed and asked her repeatedly for more research. "I think that the trouble with our collaboration is that the recipes do not come out as Simca, but as Julia—which is natural because I have to be *le responsable.* There is no reason at all why you should be wedded to me in English!" Julia insisted, sending her the names of editors at *Gourmet* and at England's *Wine & Food.* She talked to Beard and others about publishing articles by Simca. "The more Julia tried to include her, the more Simca resented Julia's skyrocketing success," says Phila Cousins. Simca pulled away from her partner and concentrated on her cooking class with small groups of devoted American students. In the end, it was to be the fame of the French Chef that drew their careers apart.

On the personal level, they remained sisters devoted to each other and presided, often together, at what many called the Bramafam/La Pitchoune culinary salon, even after Julia found out that Simca had never even tried Julia's French bread recipe.

AMONG THE FOODIES

Although it was growing, the cookbook world at that time was still small. Small enough so that they all knew each other, as evidenced by Julia's comings and goings in the 1960s and early 1970s. Julia went back and forth to their cooking schools and celebratory dinners in New York. She attended a big foodie dinner hosted by José Wilson at her summer home in Rockport (only Pierre Franey, former chef at Le Pavillon, and Craig Claiborne could not make it). When James Beard and then Franey and Claiborne came up to the Beverly Music Circus to give cooking demonstrations, she was in the audience, keenly aware that none of them were trained performers. Each year there were more books and more cooking shows on television.

The rising stakes in the food world were first signaled by Claiborne's properly devastating review of Michael Field's book for Time-Life (readers should "mourn in the name of Georges Auguste Escoffier, Carême, Vatel, and Ali-Bab"). M. F. K. Fisher called the review, repeating a rumor, "a personal vendetta." (Claiborne, ironically, ended up doing the *haute cuisine* volume for the Time-Life series.) Field retorted in *McCall's* with an attack against Claiborne's favorite New York City restaurants.

The food world seemed to be ushering in the "ME decade" of the 1970s, with its mood rings and mood swings. The narcissism of the Manhattan food world echoed what food writer Robert Clark called the "gay camp culture: set pieces of bitchery, betrayal, and revenge dramatized by drag clichés [such as] Callas-like opera divas."

The flak the foodies were catching was from outside the tent. Lit by the Vietnam War and rioting, the food world looked mighty self-indulgent and trivial. The swelling egos and endorsements brought out several blasts from writers. When a Nora Ephron article satirizing the "food establishment" appeared in *New York* magazine the previous September, Julia felt "fortunate to be living quietly in Cambridge rather than getting all involved with that to-do." Mary Frances told her the article was "delicious" and Ephron a "bright girl," then asked if she didn't think the caricature of Claiborne looked like Vice President Humphrey.

Julia was in Cambridge and Mary Frances in the Napa Valley, but they were indeed still a part of the food world. Julia was in deep with the Time-Life project, thoroughly enjoying wining and dining with editor-in-chief Dick Williams and his wife, Mary. She enjoyed their company, but did not need a job with Time-Life. More important, Julia's natural instincts still served her well: her immediate reaction was always to be frank and honest. She never developed a hard edge, like those whose "backgrounds geared them to competitiveness and Big Time urban living," as she put it. "In a world of megalomaniacs," says Russ Morash, "it is refreshing that Julia Child is always so self-critical." The self-criticism came, her neighbor Jean deSola Pool claimed, because "Julia has self-esteem and extraordinary intelligence." She is "a focused and centered lady," adds cooking colleague Lynne Rossetto Kasper, "one who knows who she is, her desired place in the world, and is fulfilled by it."

In 1968–69, a spate of articles exposed the close business connections among publishers, food writers, and the manufacturers of food and cooking equipment. Pointing out that there were twice as many cookbooks published in 1969 as in the year before, writers charged the food authors with a cynical approach to the intelligence of their audience. Too many recipes were untested, stolen from others, or taken verbatim from recipes developed by food manufacturers. There were no standards or certification procedures in this "profession."

"It's a world of self-generating hysteria," Nika Hazelton told Nora Ephron, whose article began with Time-Life's book-launching party being disrupted by Claiborne's review that morning. Ephron chronicled the sellouts: "French's mustard people turned to Beard. The can-opener people turned to Poppy Cannon. Pan American Airways turned to Myra Waldo. The Potato Council turned to Helen McCully. . . ." Then she described the "mortal combat" between the home economists and writers concerned with the "needs of the average housewife" and the "purists or traditionalists" who tout primarily French *haute cuisine,* lumping Julia among the "Big Four" of this latter group. "Julia Child has managed thus far to remain above the internecine struggles of the food world" less because of her "charming personality" than because she lives in Cambridge. Ephron's last volley was against the food fakery and "the influence of color photography on food." It all made for delicious gossip.

Julia may have seen herself as a moderating factor among her bickering colleagues, because when Simca told her about French rivalries and backstabbing, Julia suggested she act the role of James Beard and bring the French cooks together. "All he has done in the USA is to bring food types together— that's what you might be able to do in Paris." Part of Beard's generosity flowed from his eagerness to recruit acolytes. A difference between James and

Julia, said their mutual friend Clark Wolf, was that "Julia was more attracted to accomplished success, she likes more complete people, whereas James likes people unformed; James had protégés, Julia never did."

Julia clearly favored James Beard and Samuel and Narcissa (Bisquit) Chamberlain, the latter now retired in Marblehead (his *Clémentine in the Kitchen* was published first pseudonymously in 1943). She thoroughly enjoyed their company. Beard called himself the "biggest whore" in the food business, but Julia believed in his generosity. The names of Julia and Jim, who frequently cooked together in Julia's kitchen or onstage, were almost pronounced together by their friends, sounding like "GiGi." "Julia is essentially a con-able woman," Paul told a reporter. "She's naive in the *nicest* possible way. She just can't believe people have bad motives, when it's a palpable fact."

Dione Lucas, wracked by a double mastectomy and a collapsed lung, was fading slowly from her influential place in the cooking world. Stepping from the wings in 1969 was a young man from Australia named Graham Kerr, who called himself "The Galloping Gourmet." Ruth Lockwood told Julia to watch his noontime program, and her New York friends (including Beard and Field) telephoned to say they "hate it." Julia disliked both his cute and funny way of making semisexual remarks and his apparent lack of seriousness about his cooking. They were horrified by his behavior and his cooking techniques, as he himself would be two decades later when, after burning himself out, he soberly transformed himself and his cooking. Unrefined though his first programs were, he had then what only Julia had, a warmth and rapport with the television audience.

Julia tried to keep out of the backbiting and bitchery that occasionally marred the cookbook scene, a world characterized by what Paul called "snatch-grabbing." Michael Field had taken Simca and Julia's recipes and reworded them for his Time-Life book on France, and *Gourmet* pirated their garlic mashed potatoes. But when the subject came up in correspondence with Mary Frances, she said there was "no such thing as an original recipe," shrugging at the common practice of lifting from others' work.

Though Karen and John Hess's food criticism was directed at most of the food world, including Julia, there was one voice that singled her out for particular vituperation: Madeleine Kamman, a French woman (married to an American) who had worked in her aunt's restaurant in France and studied briefly with Simca. Julia met Kamman during the busy final months of preparing her *Mastering II* manuscript, but invited her into her home and was in turn invited to a dinner at the Kammans'. The Childs found her cooking "outstanding" and her intentions "ambitious," according to Paul.

Kamman opened a cooking school and then a restaurant nearby in New-

ton and published *The Making of a Cook* in 1971. One of her students wrote a
signed letter telling Julia to beware: Kamman demanded her students destroy
their copies of *Mastering the Art of French Cooking* and not watch *The French
Chef* because it was not "authentic." (Yet Kamman's résumé boasted of her
L'Ecole des Trois Gourmandes certificate.) "Mrs. Child was neither French
nor a chef," she informed everyone who would listen. Mrs. Kamman's unhap-
piness and anger would alienate many beginning students, but she eventually
did become a fine teacher of advanced cooks. Though she will no longer speak
on the record about Julia Child, the quotes from her newspaper interviews
and her letters to Julia tell the story. Kamman, the letters reveal, began by
seeking out a relationship with Julia and then moved to condescending innu-
endo and veiled attacks, referring to Julia's surgeries and to her not being a
mother.

One of Julia's letters to Simca, dated November 10, 1969, suggested the
"feud" was a one-sided affair:

> Madeleine Kamman and her husband came to dinner several weeks ago.
> . . . She is, obviously, very ambitious, and someone said that she in-
> tended to push us off the map! How long did she have lessons with you?
> Well, good for her, is all I can say, and I hope she is as good as she thinks
> she is, as we do need more professionally trained people in the business.

A year later Julia wrote a letter asking the food editor of the *Boston
Globe* to take favorable note of Kamman's cooking school. Julia's seeming
aplomb in handling what would eventually become twenty years of personal
antagonism on the part of Kamman, reveals an aspect of her character that
Ithiel and Jean deSola Pool, her professorial neighbors, have best articulated:
"Julia has a strong ego and knows who she is and likes herself," declares Mrs.
deSola Pool.

Julia only once gave away her hurt and anger, as well as her humor,
when she answered a question from Harvard's Institute for Learning in Retirement in 1985: "How do you feel about criticism?" After a reasoned discussion
of the question and an example of the criticism of "one woman" in her life,
whose "put-downs and belittlements . . . I remember them all" had accumulated over the years, she adds, with a wink, that if the woman comes close, "I
shall grab her by the short hairs (wearing gloves, of course), and I will grind
her alive, piece by piece, in my food processor."

There was also little time to fret about the feuds while celebrating the
many positive reinforcements, including new young cooks who needed encouragement and help. Indeed, for Julia the conviviality and warm friendships

far outweighed the petty words and thievery. A greater challenge came with the rising food consciousness first triggered in 1962 by Rachel Carson's *The Silent Spring* (warning about DDT and malathion), then by nutritionists Adelle Davis and Euell Gibbons, which led to the brown rice, bean sprouts, and tofu wave of healthy eating as well as to what Harvey Levenstein called (and so well documented) "nutritional terrorism."

Julia and Paul flew through a snowstorm to attend a dinner for 1,800 in New York honoring the French President in the Waldorf-Astoria's biggest ballroom. She left the final chapter of her manuscript (eight months before publication date) to attend this state dinner with Presidents Pompidou and Nixon. The bejeweled and beribboned sat at tables for twelve, filling balconies and boxes and corridors, with the decibel level wiping out every note the musicians offered. Julia sat at one of the two tables for people in the food world, a table sponsored by Foods From France, a French government organization that would help with the WGBH filming in France, scheduled for later in the year. Beard sat at their table, which held magnums of Meursault, Beaune, and champagne. Julia loved the social whirl and glamour, and Paul (despite being distressed by the presence of Nixon) thought his wife was "smashing" in an *aou dai* of Siamese silk, wine-dark, sea-blue pants with a long, flowing turquoise overshift—"made in Bangkok, though inspired in Vietnam."

Color and noise served as prelude to a new stage in her very public professional life.

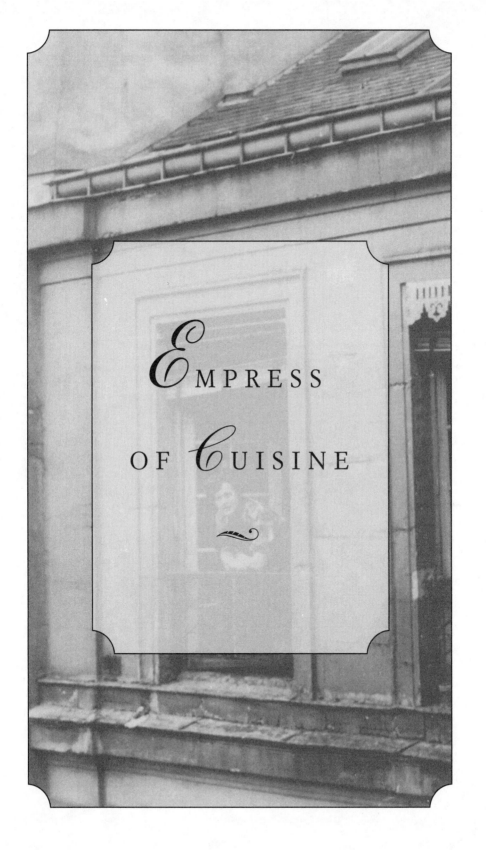

EMPRESS

OF CUISINE

Chapter 21

RIDING THE SECOND WAVE
(1970 – 1974)

"We must come in with a bang and not
go out with the Hoover."

RUTH LOCKWOOD

AS EDUCATIONAL television executives watched the black-and-white demonstration tape on the monitors at WGBH, they saw the camera focus on the
French tart Julia was preparing, then zoom in on the strawberries. Suddenly
the picture burst into color: the strawberries were red! "Everyone stood up
and applauded," remembers Ruth Lockwood. It was the first time they had
seen color and the contrast between the strawberry and the white *crème
pâtissière* was breathtaking." Paul remarked, "Christ may be risen, but I am
nearly flattened."

Five years later, those hopes for a color television in every home and a
French Chef in living color were realized. Now the technology was available at
WGBH (the 1965 demonstration had taken a dozen technicians from New
York City to arrange) and Julia had completed the second *Mastering* volume.
Next, on October 6, 1970, the New England press and media reporters were
given a demonstration of the first program, on bouillabaisse, to air the next
day.

THE FRENCH CHEF IN COLOR

In the spring of 1970, WGBH had began filming with a grant from Polaroid. Producer Ruth Lockwood had no trouble getting a large block of money from the company because *The French Chef,* even after four years of black-and-white reruns, still had Nielsen ratings equal to its highest. The money covered filming both the typical demonstration programs as well as scenes taped in France. Three technicians in direction, filming, sound, and lighting, with handheld cameras, would accompany Julia and Paul on a film tour of France. The budget also included a makeup specialist, 35 millimeter movie footage and equipment, payment to Paul for still photography, and travel and hotels for the group in France. Even the theme music was to change, to what Paul called a "bouncing cancan" tune.

While Harvard students and townies rioted in Harvard Square against Nixon's Cambodian incursion, Julia and her crew filmed for several days in early spring in the markets of Boston's North End in order to work out the color implications and teamwork. After a full dress rehearsal (a "walk-through" with real food), the team filmed two programs a week for three weeks in the studio. Finally technicians spliced scene footage into the demos: Julia's buying capers and garlic at the North End street market was edited into the niçoise salad show. By the end of April, Julia and Paul were in France awaiting the arrival of the crew and correcting the proofs for her *Mastering II.*

The French Chef and her crew filmed olive pressing in Opio (near Plascassier), the fish market in Marseilles (eighteen years after her posting there), baking fish at Les Oliviers (outside St.-Paul-de-Vence), cheese at Chez Androuet in Paris, kitchen equipment at Dehillerin, the preparation of frog's legs at Prunier's, and duck pressing in Rouen (they shot between midnight and 5 A.M. at La Couronne, where Julia had eaten her first French meal in 1948). On a hot day, in a tiny basement in the rue du Cherche-Midi in Paris, they filmed Lionel Poilane making bread. Calvel, who had taught Julia the final secrets of bread making, was also filmed in his school. Julia stressed in several letters to friends that they were collecting historical, rare footage of artisanal skills rapidly disappearing in France. They also filmed a modern French supermarket, thanks to Jacques Delécluse, husband of Paul's former embassy assistant.

Back in Boston, they spent July editing and preparing voice-overs, and September and November filming new programs (including two on breads). In a studio of her own for the first time, at 125 Western Avenue, Julia and the *French Chef* crew filmed twice a week, each day preceded by a rehearsal day. The stakes were higher than during those first years when the black-and-white film had to be kept running. Now 134 stations nationwide would carry the show. As Ruth Lockwood frequently said: "We must come in with a bang and not go out with the Hoover."

Julia was excited about the new series. Because she had not filmed during the four years she spent completing the book, she forgot (in her eagerness to get out of her isolated writing closet) how grueling and all-consuming filming was. It ate up twelve to sixteen hours in a day, especially when bread rose too fast or chocolate melted under the sixty-five floodlights. The procedure, in Ruth Lockwood's words, was now "very sophisticated." It was "a Persian Circus," said Russ Morash, no longer on the series. "The committee got larger and larger."

The thirty-five-person Boston crew included eight volunteer "associate cooks" (Julia honored people by giving them titles) who both watched the monitors for proper cooking angles and washed dishes. Paul took rolls of black-and-white photographs for newspaper publicity. The days she was not filming, Julia was writing, buying food, testing and preparing food, or rehearsing (to say nothing of the inevitable press interviews and her own correspondence). She and Paul chose this concentrated, exhausting film schedule to allow themselves blocks of time during the next two years to live in France. She prepared thirty-nine programs so she could have a regular slot on any station's season program.

Jan Dietrichson sat in the audience "hypnotized—like a rabbit under the gaze of a cobra," according to Paul. Dietrichson, their dear friend from the University of Oslo, was spending the winter semester at Harvard and staying in the Childs' house. He was amazed by the daily crisis and chaos of shooting. Laughter was Julia's release, and Paul remained her "balancing wheel," noted Dietrichson.

The first week of October, WGBH used Julia's *French Chef* set to host eighty press and media reporters from the area reached by WGBH. They were fed a catered lunch of recipes from *Mastering II,* then previewed the first show, "Bouillabaisse à la Marseillaise." The *Boston Globe* reporter called the "lusty, peasant concoction" a fitting debut for Julia.

ℒAUNCHING *MASTERING II*

Almost the same week that radicals bombed the MIT offices of their next-door neighbor, Ithiel deSola Pool, Julia's new book and new series appeared. The political turmoil almost encircled them as they launched this second wave of her culinary career. *Mastering the Art of French Cooking II* was published by

Knopf on October 22, 1970, nine years after the release of the first volume. It had a first printing of 100,000 copies (matching the advance).

Twelve days after the official publication date, the new series of her weekly *French Chef* began on PBS with "Bouillabaisse" on October 8 and "Napoleon's Chicken" on the twelfth. The cooking series launched the book. According to Julia's introduction, the second volume was a "continuation" of the first and would "bring the reader to a higher level of master[y]" and "add to the repertoire." Its principal feature was French bread: "the first authentic, successful recipe ever devised for making real French bread—the long, crunchy, yeasty, golden loaf that is like no other bread in texture and flavor—with American all-purpose flour, in an American home oven." She gave proper credit to Professor Calvel as well as to Paul, who added a large tile of asbestos cement, pan of water, and red-hot brick to the oven-baking process. According to letters to Julia, many people (at least half of them men) took the nineteen-page recipe (with its thirty-four drawings) through to its conclusion.

The book was dedicated to Alfred Knopf and included in its 555 pages were seven sections: soup (much enlarged), baking, meats, chicken, charcuterie (new), vegetables, and desserts. She identified her culinary context as *la cuisine bourgeoise* ("meaning expert French home-style cooking"). Certainly the charcuterie may have been French, but no French home cook made bread every day or flamed baked Alaska. The recipes in the vegetable chapter, for example, were both traditional *(pommes Anna)* and original. Her audience, as suggested by the wording of her introduction ("part of your training," "stepping out of the kindergarten," "start you off in a whirl of success") and the detail of her recipes, was the relative amateur; but the difficulty of many of the recipes, including the one for bread, assumed a more sophisticated or advanced cook.

The number and quality of the illustrations also enhanced this volume. They included thirty-eight pages on the modern equipment made available since the first volume had appeared. Admitting to a "rather holy and Victorian feeling about the virtues of sweat and elbow grease" in their first volume, which "reflects France in the 1950's," they now "step into contemporary life" and "[take] full advantage of modern mechanical aids." Only in the second edition, more than a decade later, were they to add the food processor for dough making. These illustrations, and a wealth of drawings on the recipes (twelve drawings for *pâté en croûte),* were carefully integrated with the text. The most respected American cookbooks thereafter would be influenced by these 458 careful illustrations.

On September 27, 1970, in the Crystal Ballroom of the Plaza Hotel, PBS helped Knopf launch the volume, with Hartford Gunn, the president of PBS, as host. Two days later a press conference was held in the Royal Ballroom of the Americana Hotel, and on October 22, the official date of publication, the Ford Foundation (one of PBS's sponsors) gave a party in its garden for Julia and Simca. The party naturally focused primarily on Julia, much to Julia's distress; Paul assured her that this was inevitable because Mr. Ford "never heard of Mrs. Beck." Such fanfare signaled the distance Julia had traveled since the first collaborative book when their own feeble promotion was all they had.

Gael Greene in *Life* magazine said that in her set of highly competitive New York City foodies, everyone was testing Julia's bread. Noting as well the three-page bisque recipe and the thirty-eight pages of basic accessories for the kitchen cook, she added that if "Volume I was mud-pie stuff," Volume II "is no longer Child's play." Greene's nod to the bisque recipe was confirmed by Mimi Sheraton, in whose copy the pages on shrimp bisque were still stuck together with food stains some twenty-five years later.

There were two negative responses to the book. In the *New York Times,* Nika Hazelton said the volume was "heralded like the second coming," praised the "elegance and accuracy" of the book, then snipped about its excessive detail, saying an ideal reader needed to have the kind of mind "that people [do] who learn to drive a car by having the workings of the internal combustion engine explained to them in full detail." She suggested rewriting a recipe before using it. For example, the three-page roast suckling pig in *The French Chef Cookbook* had swollen to five and a half pages in this new book. A second criticism came later, when Karen Hess said that Mrs. Child included too many dishes *en croûte.* Indeed, the *French Chef*'s "Operation Chicken" recipe became transformed into *poularde en croûte,* and joined *filet de boeuf en croûte, gigot farci en croûte,* and *jambon farci en croûte.* Not surprising, considering how many years they had been caught up in making bread, brioches, puff pastry, and the like.

In 1970 the level of cookbook criticism was still amateurish and the food world small enough so that few were qualified to analyze new books with any depth or candor. Julia's stature loomed large in this world: at fifty-eight, she was a beloved television personality with her first volume already a classic, its techniques and recipes "adopted" in numerous magazines and cookbooks. An exception to the amateur's level of reviewing was Sokolov's review in *Newsweek,* which declared it a "daunting book. It leaves Volume I behind in a shower of spun sugar and makes that honorable world of the trout mousse and cassoulet seem in retrospect as naive as Spam. . . . It is hard to conceive of a cookbook to follow this one. It is without rival, the finest gourmet cookbook for the non-chef in the history of American stomachs."

For her French bread recipe, Julia was honored by the Confrérie de Cérès in France. Public response was vigorous and sustained. Julia was delighted by the number of men who were cooking. When readers complained about a problem that was clearly of their own making, Julia was privately critical; when their difficulties were based on her own error or lack of clarity, she wrote back in detail and took steps to make minor changes. She answered all questions. As with the voluminous television mail, she created form letters for common queries concerning her published work.

Knopf's promotion was better planned than any promotion to date. The media blitz began a year before the publication: *Vogue* did a June 1969 feature on Julia's Provençal kitchen (*Esquire* would later do a full inventory of her Cambridge kitchen); *House Beautiful* presented the kitchens of five "master chefs," including Julia (first), Beard, Lucas, Field, and Claiborne. Just before publication, she was on the cover of *Publishers Weekly.* The most effective stroke was *McCall's* cover and three-part profile of Julia and the "Making of a Masterpiece" (October, November, and December 1970). During the filming in La Pitchoune, Simca was awkward and stiff before the camera, and *McCall's* slighted Simca (which angered Julia and hurt Simca). The *New York Times* made amends with a profile.

Knopf gave them a real author's tour, despite the insistence of WGBH that she stay home and continue her taping. With Jane Friedman, then a twenty-two-year-old Knopf publicist (who later became a vice president), Julia, Simca, and Paul traveled to Minneapolis, Cleveland, Columbus, Cincinnati, Chicago, Philadelphia, Washington, DC, and Boston. "We had a ball," says Friedman, who booked them into hotel suites for entertaining the press:

> There was not then such a thing as an "author's tour," but I figured that with the keen interest of local public television stations and the book departments of department stores (such as Marshall Field in Chicago) . . . we could have a good tour. We flew into a city, did all the media, and had a big party co-sponsored by the public television station and the department store that was sponsoring the demonstration the next day (and always took out a full-page ad). In Minneapolis I saw nearly a thousand people on the street at 7 A.M. waiting to go into Dayton's department store for the demonstration in Sky's Restaurant to make mayonnaise (that is all Julia did!) and then she would sign books.

At the second stop, at Halle's department store in Cleveland, she dropped an egg in a blender with the lid off and the chocolate mousse mixture shot a splat on her face. "Now you see why I always have a towel stuck in my apron!" But the funniest moment, according to two attendees, was her disapproval of the pots and pans arranged behind her. "How wonderful of Halle's to put these up here so I can tell you Never, Never, buy a pot this thin," she said, flinging one after the other over her shoulder onto the stage behind her. "All of us chuckled," said a man in attendance, "thinking about how the poor Halle's buyer must be twisting in agony at the review of his/her choices." The Bunsen burner representative singed her eyebrows and beehive hairdo at another stop. These stories became legend.

They appeared on the *Today* show (Simca took an immediate dislike to Barbara Walters), were given a luncheon by the editor of *McCall's,* Shana Alexander (a "lovely creature," thought Paul), and Julia was interviewed by David Frost. Simca continued touring while Julia resumed taping the television series so they could get back to France for Christmas. By November 1, her butcher, Jack Savenor, and George Berkowitz of Legal Sea Foods, her fish dealer, displayed the volume for sale on their counters. Their loyalty through the decades was reciprocated by Julia. When Savenor was caught in a scandal about possibly short-weighing his customers the following year, Julia remained fiercely loyal, blinded (according to Paul) by his charm. When asked, she informed a reporter she disbelieved the charges.

$\mathscr{P}$ROVENCE, JAMES BEARD, AND RICHARD OLNEY

The plane from Paris to Nice, flying over the Rhone River, descended from the mountains and canyons of coastal Provence, banking left over the Mediterranean and gliding low along the rocky coast, past Cannes, St.-Tropez, and Cap d'Antibes. Lower and lower it moved over the water, until finally, and to the relief of Paul, sand appeared beneath them and the plane touched down at the Nice–Côte d'Azur airport at water's edge. Julia was always exhilarated by the flight and by the sun and palm trees. For Paul it was deliverance mixed with some pride in his having overcome his fear of flying. When they were not rushed, they took the train from Paris or drove a rented car on a slow gastronomic journey south. Marc Meneau, before he earned any of his three Michelin stars at L'Espérance in Vézelay, remembers Julia stopping to taste and encourage his cooking.

With thirty-nine programs in the can and the book launched for the Christmas 1970 season, Julia and Paul, nearly caramelized from exhaustion, had only five weeks in France. The pattern of their busy lives was illustrated in the activities of the coming months. They returned to Cambridge before Feb-

ruary to tape thirteen more programs and to begin renovation on Julia's office,
the guest room, and the bathrooms as well as to install a new security system
(by 1973 crime in Cambridge increased by 38 percent). On May 5, the morning after she narrated Tubby the Tuba at the Boston Symphony, the Childs left
for three months in France, during which they took a tour of Norway with the
Pratts. By August they were back in Cambridge to film twenty-six more programs, then back to France with plans for another book based on this color
series. The book would use the television recipes, which she now typed out
before each show and mailed to the newspapers. They rarely missed a Christmas at La Pitchoune until 1973, when Julia began writing monthly recipes for
a magazine and finishing a new book.

At La Pitchoune, they sipped Chinese tea in the morning on the olive
terrace (the mulberry terrace at the side of the house was for shaded afternoon
cocktails or barbecues). Under the mulberry tree, Julia drank "reverse [or
Ivan] martinis," dry vermouth flavored with lemon and a dash of gin. They
looked out to the Estérel Mountains and on a clear day to the distant sea,
listening to the sounds of frogs and nightingales. Only at night would the quiet
be occasionally disrupted by the noise of rock music and motorcycles as local
youth gathered at the "ranch" down the hill. Julia and Paul were rather more
disturbed by the building boom in the region, which threatened to turn the
Riviera into a French Miami Beach. Even Simca and Jean were now building
another house just below them, to be called La Campanette, perhaps anticipating (sister-in-law) France (Fischbacher) Thibault's desire to reclaim the old
house, which Simca named Le Mas Vieux.

Upon arriving at La Pitchoune, Julia's first efforts were always to warm
the house, restock the kitchen with produce from the market and household
products from the Casino *supermarché.* She wanted some frozen puff pastry in
the freezer for an ever-growing number of visitors. Initially, there were quiet
days for reading newspapers and magazines and keeping up with what Paul
called their "weekly dose of Watergate medicine," which left him with a bad
taste in his mouth but feeling good. Avis's witty reports—especially by 1974
when "Nixon [was] melting like a Popsicle in the sun"—kept them amused.
Paul's rantings against Nixon, he admitted, reminded him of Julia's late father's ranting about the liberals. They also read contemporary biographies,
such as Nancy Milford's *Zelda* and Eric F. Goldman's *The Tragedy of Lyndon
Johnson.*

Julia always had her eye out for her own or a neighboring cat who would
come for a daily feeding and eventually stay. As Paul told his brother: "A
cat—*any* cat—is necessary to Julia's life." When she was in Cambridge, she
kept in touch with Simca concerning the lives of all the cats and dogs of the

compound. Indeed, as late as the mid-1990s, the Thibault family was still caring for one of "Julia's cats."

In Plascassier she was "Madame Shield," the tall American who smiled and chatted with each shopkeeper and market seller, especially with the wine merchant in Grasse whose son ran Le Cygne, one of the Childs' favorite New York City restaurants. When they went to Grasse to shop, they carried a large Styrofoam box with plastic bags of ice cubes to keep their market produce from wilting while they enjoyed lunch at Restaurant des Oliviers.

Because Boston in 1971 was "still a gastronomical wasteland when it comes to restaurants," Julia and Paul loved the great simple country restaurants of Provence with their garlicky odors emanating from kitchens and their sunny terraces shaded by heavy grape arbors. Julia detailed the restaurant food in letters to Beard and Fisher. Paul's letters described Julia's cooking. During their summers in Provence, Paul depicted the olive and jasmine world for Charlie, who was describing for Paul his spruce and granite Maine.

Paul painted in the small *cabanon* across the driveway while Julia cooked, tested, and wrote programs for future taping, composed her monthly recipes for *McCall's,* which would eventually constitute her second *French Chef* cookbook in 1974. She was moving far beyond the recipes of Simca to her own creations. When Simca and Jean came down from Paris, they shared meals and recipes with each other. One day Julia served them her new creation, named after a recent and scandalous film (*La Grande Bouffe*) shown at Cannes, *La Grande Bouffe aux écailles et au chocolat* (the scales were sliced almonds covering the outside). Julia read and made a few corrections on the manuscript of *Simca's Cuisine,* the first American book by Simca herself, and one that Knopf would publish in 1972. Julia and Judith had talked Simca into doing the book, though the woman who worked on translating the manuscript into English had difficulty working with the irascible author.

Julia was occasionally caught between Paul's continued dislike of Simca and her own devotion to her colleague, whom she got along with much better now that they were "just friends" and not collaborators. She agreed with Paul that Simca was stubborn, opinionated, proud, and an "eccentric whirlwind," but Julia was still faithful. Paul had little in common with Simca, who he thought had a voice that could "be heard in Montevideo" and an interest level focusing solely on clothes, gossip, manners, and bridge. And he was not crazy about the "feeble fops" who crowded her parties.

The guests they most enjoyed were Sybille Bedford (now working on the second volume of her biography of Aldous Huxley), her companion Eda Lord, and Jim Beard. These three friends were gay, but Paul, who used the term often, would never have called them "fairies," a distinction based on class as well as the absence of precious behavior. When Beard visited, he and Julia spent all day in the kitchen together, though they also enjoyed testing the best restaurants in the area. Their mutual friend Peter Kump believed Beard and Child shared an upbeat attitude toward life and a joy of cooking. When they prepared a meal together, Paul called it *la cuisine de l'enfant barbu* (bearded child).

After Simca, Julia probably most enjoyed cooking with Beard. Her letters to him are full of food talk and gossip, news of restaurant meals and new inventions. She kept him informed about France, he kept her up on the New York gossip. ("He loved the skullduggery and the bitchiness in the food world," Barbara Kafka told me recently, "and he was not a bit player himself.") When Julia learned in France from a student of Gaston Lenôtre the secret of using a blowtorch to brown crème brûlée and other dishes, she immediately wrote to tell James about it (and to say she was buying one). Always fascinated with gadgets, she would use the blowtorch to brown food and unmold aspic at La Pitchoune, where she had no broiler.

When Beard came to visit, they drove him to visit Richard Olney, an American cook and painter now settled permanently against a rocky hill in Solliès-Toucas, just east of Toulon on the coast. Olney and his brother James, a professor of English, dined at La Pitchoune on several occasions. Though Julia considered Olney creative and eccentric, she thought that he should do more to build a career. She wrote to Mary Frances that she could not find his books in bookstores in the United States because "he won't do anything to make himself known."

Olney was an instinctive cook who eschewed rules and formal education in cooking. He published recipes in *Cuisine et Vins de France* in the 1960s and published *The French Menu* in 1970, which is when Julia went to meet him. (When his masterpiece, *Simple French Food,* was published in late 1974, he stayed with the Childs in Cambridge and she reported to Simca and Mary Frances that she liked the book—"it is entirely honest, entirely Richard"—that his reviews were marvelous, and that "he is a natural on TV.") He also demonstrated cooking at Lubéron Collège in Avignon. One summer Madeleine Kamman, visiting from her cooking school in Newton, Massachusetts, came to Olney's class and was overheard saying of Julia that she was "going to Boston to teach that bag to cook."

The professional tension—one need not call it a battle, except perhaps in Kamman's mind—between her and Julia escalated in the 1970s, as their correspondence in the Schlesinger Library attests. Kamman told one newspaper she had "learned nothing" from the Cordon Bleu or L'Ecole des Trois Gourmandes (with Simca, who had refused to write an introduction to her first book) and indeed it was she (Kamman) who "taught them something!" Yet her publicity continued to list among her credits the school created by Child, Beck, and Bertolle. At first Julia did nothing, then wrote to ask the publisher never to mention her name in publicity about Kamman (they stopped). Then Julia repeated to a reporter the rumor that Kamman dominated Olney's class, perhaps an impression she received from Olney himself, who had become very nervous when he discovered Kamman in his class. The following year (1974), when an article in the *Washington Post* claimed Kamman was an "enemy" of Simca and Julia, Kamman wrote a letter accusing Julia of gratuitously twisting the facts to harm another woman and claiming that she had been helping Olney by offering to teach a beginning class in Avignon so he could teach the advanced class. She also reprimanded Julia for saying that men are better cooks than women and accused her of making the Kamman family suffer. Julia did not respond, nor did she publicly talk anymore about the issue. She simply sent copies of all of Kamman's letters through the years to her lawyers.

Julia lent La Pitchoune to family, including Dorothy and Ivan Cousins and their family, and she rented to friends from the OSS and their diplomatic world, including Janou and Charles Walcutt. Others in the food world, such as Gael Greene and Peter Kump, visited or rented La Pitchoune. Kump, a native of California and student of Simca, who remembers the Childs attending Simca's weekly cocktail parties, would open a professional cooking school in New York City under his own name in 1974. Kump in 1994 told me that four people changed American cooking: "Beard, Henri Soulé [Le Pavillon], and Claiborne created this big bonfire and Julia came along with the match."

The Walcutts, in turn, lent Julia and Paul their Paris apartment for April 1972. At 81, rue de Longchamps, in Neuilly, Julia lived again in her beloved Paris and tested restaurants, including Drouant, Chez Les Anges, Prunier-Duphot, Chez Garin, La Truite, and Tour d'Argent. She wrote detailed reports of her dining to Beard and to Waverley Root (*The Food of France,* 1958), whom she invited to dinner so they could meet. He had stayed two nights at La Pitchoune when Michael Field was renting it and wrote to inform Julia that he "admired" her kitchen. But he was suffering from a slipped disk and their meeting did not occur until February 1973.

Her month in Paris studying restaurant cooking coincided with the emergence of what Henry Gault and Christian Millau (in their *Nouveau Guide)* would later call "nouvelle cuisine," a term first used in 1742 but which now referred to a group of young chef-entrepreneurs who owned their own restaurants and valued originality, simplicity, and lighter sauces. Paul Bocuse, the Troisgros brothers, Michel Guérard, Alain Chapel, and Roger Vergé were the stars, and all of them were influenced by Fernand Point (as well as by

André Pic and Alexandre Dumaine). Nouvelle cuisine was characterized by the aesthetic presentation of the dish, or, as Julia quipped about American nouvelle cuisine (in a phrase that would be repeated for twenty years), "the food is so beautifully arranged on the plate—you know someone's fingers have been all over it."

Julia described for James Beard their collapse at La Pitchoune with post-work fatigue and colds, followed by a revival of holiday celebration. Olney came for Christmas dinner. On New Year's Eve the Childs and Kublers dined with chef Roger Vergé at Le Moulin de Mougins, then joined a crowded party at Simca's home. Paul detested Simca's parties and described this one in detail to Charlie—the blaring television and record player turned to high, the crowd of giggling people, the forced conviviality. An artificial note in their harmonious natural world. He also described their reluctance to leave Provence: "I walk around, look at the olive trees, smell the lavender, bend my ear to the nightingales, taste the dorade, the loup, the pastis, but in a few days, after the tidal wave of Boston-Cambridge has rolled over me, these living vital impressions will be glimmering, evanescent, dream-like, vanishing."

They returned from Europe after each visit with written programs ready for the intense filming schedule of more *French Chef* programs in color. For a few months it appeared they would not be able to continue the series when Polaroid, assuming another company would pick up *The French Chef*, moved on to support another program. They had been underwriting her program since 1965. No company stepped in to assume sponsorship, undoubtedly because PBS did not allow commercials. When news got out, the public response inundated Polaroid, who quickly resumed their $80,000 grants.

Julia was both happy to be renewed and reluctant to continue the demanding work of filming. When she received a letter from Madeleine Kamman about rumors of her retirement, she hastened to inform her she intended never to retire. *The French Chef,* which now featured themes such as "Open House" and "Sudden Company," moved to 9 P.M. on Sundays, with a rebroadcast at 5 P.M. the following Saturday. Because the letters and press inquiries never let up, Avis DeVoto was hired to write Julia-replies to letters that came into WGBH.

The tapings continued despite various anniversaries, including their silver wedding anniversary on September 1, 1971, and Paul's seventieth birthday the following January. They had to wait to celebrate the birthday of Paul and Charlie until August 1972, when the Child family also celebrated Julia's sixtieth birthday in Maine. She would later tell *The New Yorker,* "One of the good things about getting to be sixty is that you make up your mind not to drink any more rotgut wine." For her birthday, Paul penned another poem to his "birthday queen" and to the "Recognition that the years don't count" because her "leaves are ever green."

> Salute, O Queen! We never thought to eat
> So well before your reign. *"Bone appetite!"*

By December of that year, they taped the final program of *The French Chef* and headed back to Provence. Julia believed she had presented all the important recipes she wanted to teach.

THE PRESS AND THE BBC

Again the press invaded the Childs' privacy at La Pitchoune. Reporters from *Vogue, McCall's,* the *New York Times,* and others came for interviews, photographs, and tapings. Suzanne Patterson, an American in Paris writing articles for *Réalités,* came down to interview Julia and met Simca, with whom she would later cooperate on a memoir. But none betrayed Julia's precise location in print until a former Paris colleague of Paul's gave step-by-step, turn-by-turn, directions to La Pitchoune in an article entitled "On the Trail of Julia Child." On their next visit, a camper filled with Americans drove in to see The French Chef's house. Julia and Paul were gracious, but Paul reprimanded his former colleague.

There was hardly a newspaper or magazine in the country that did not cover Julia. Terrence O'Flaherty of the *San Francisco Chronicle* proclaimed: "A Big Child Shall Lead Us." He found her "more convincing than Walter Cronkite." "Even the lowliest thaw-and-serve sloth has felt the vibrations of Julia's cult," declared Gael Greene in *Life,* "the lady unleashed our gastronomic repressions." That year *Newsweek* called her the "Queen of Chefs"—though she never called herself a chef, and Craig Claiborne, in an essay entitled "Changes in the Sixties," called her a major phenomenon of that decade.

Reviewers continued to mention her awkwardness, but always with a loving tone: "Julia breathes hard and loves food. She is human. She is plump. She can be messy, a bit clumsy . . . she can drop a duck on her foot without coming apart at the seams." One newspaper columnist described her "glid[ing] around her oversized studio kitchen like a herniated ostrich, tossing off one-liners." Another reviewer perceptively noted the dramatic action and violence of her manner, saying he hated to miss her program as much as he did Monday night football: "Perhaps for the same reason—all that programmed and controlled violence is a vicarious purging of the juices."

Money magazine picked up on a little-mentioned aspect of Julia's professional success: Paul was her full partner. *Money* featured her inclusion of Paul in her career ("our books" and "our show") in an article about successful women and their business careers. She and Helen Gurley Brown were "extreme exceptions" in their financial success and partnership with their husbands. Indeed, Paul at seventy was keeping up an occasionally grueling pace of television and press. Julia still did the taxes and handled the finances (as did Freddie Child for Charlie), but Paul was her business partner in planning the career and working alongside her. His refrain in letters to his brother—"to keep Julie before the public as a vivid and viable personality"—explains the new series and books as well as the public appearances and press interviews. Though she was pulled into his diplomatic current during the first decade of their marriage, he told his brother in a September 19, 1973, letter, "I am still, in a sense, an accessory-after-the-fact of Julie's rhythms," part of that unseen iceberg.

Julia Child was a household name, as exhibited in the avenues of popular culture. The cartoon strip "Beetle Bailey," distributed in seventy-three countries through the *International Herald Tribune,* carried a strip showing Beetle's General, sitting under a picture of George Washington, explaining that he was inspired by the portrait of George Washington over his military desk: "I try to live as he did." In the final scene, Beetle is shown sitting under the photograph of a woman in a chef's toque, and to a private's question about who it is, responding with a satisfied "Julia Child." In 1970 her name appeared in the *New York Times* crossword puzzle under "noted cook, 34 across" in April and again as "Chef for the French [sic], 10 across" in August.

Time magazine planned a cover story on McDonald's (the nation's largest dispenser of meals) and wanted a quote from Julia. She insisted she had never been to the golden arches and was not interested. They persisted (Paul described it as begging on bended knees), and Julia's curiosity worked in their favor. After they promised that her opinion would not constitute an endorsement (and informed her that other food critics such as Beard and Claiborne gave their judgment), she and Paul went to Davis Square in Somerville and ordered one of everything. She delivered her opinion: "nothing but calories," not a balanced meal, bread soft and too much of it, cheap—"But the French fries are surprisingly good." Seven years later, John and Karen Hess in their *Taste of America* would claim she tried very hard "to find something positive to say without losing the gourmet franchise." In truth, she did like the fries. They had taste because they were fried in lard, she later learned when they switched to vegetable oil. Julia was judging taste alone; a nutritionist at Harvard, however, documented that "McDonald's is good fare nutritionally, but could be improved by tossing in some coleslaw and the fruit of the season."

Scores of newspaper features on Julia during the first half of the 1970s appeared in papers around the country, repeating the outlines of her life in repetitive detail. Many quoted her themes during this period: her insistence that anyone can eat well if they are willing to learn to cook, that American meats are better than the meats in France, and that fast food and airline food are terrible (she and Paul carried their own food on their flights).

Coverage during the early 1970s emphasized her media role (CBS did a half hour on the making of *The French Chef,* and the *Christian Science Monitor* covered the film tour of France), her private life (Barbara Walters interviewed her on *Not For Women Only),* and her artistic contribution (in August 1973 she was guest of honor at a party on Long Island that included Max Lerner, Jerome Robbins, Willem de Kooning, and many other artists). Her honors included a press award (the only one given to PBS) by *TV Guide.*

Julia and Paul went to London from Provence in February 1973 to tape promotions for the trial run of five of her programs for the British Broadcasting Corporation and to see the first show broadcast. Watching with Elizabeth David, England's favorite cookery writer, Julia was appalled when she realized they had cut off her introduction (in which she said she was a home cook and not a chef, an American and not French) and began with her laughingly brushing her blouse in a disoriented way after having lifted the two lids of the chicken pans, not realizing there was steam on the lids as she touched the lids together like cymbals. She was demonstrating two chicken dishes ("Coq au Vin vs. Chicken Fricassée, Sisters Under the Sauce"). Because she was cooking with wine, the British press suggested that she was drinking—or that she was slapdash, untidy, and unprofessional—and the show fizzled. It also suffered from the time slot at 3:40 in the afternoon and was twice preempted. Julia privately complained that the programs were "ill-used, if not demeaned," but publicly she said, "Too bad it laid an egg" and "The English are used to stiff aprons." Her British supporters, notably Sally Miall and Anne Willan, blamed in part an anti-American attitude and a sense of British superiority.

American-born "British" food writer Paul Levy declared twelve years later, "Deprived by this rejection of the best television cookery series ever made, the British now have an appallingly low standard—our television 'cooks' would not be tolerated by the more sophisticated American audience."

IN PERSON: TOURING AND DEMONSTRATING

Because "teaching is a very good way to learn," as she phrased it, and because she wanted to sell books and raise money for public television, Julia offered public demonstrations. She received hundreds of requests through the years, turned every commercial one down, but usually responded to work for a charity. "I like public service," John McWilliams's daughter often said. They paid her expenses, paid a fee to WGBH, and she profited only by the sale of her books.

She embarked on her first whirlwind tour to meet her fans in 1971 to promote her Bantam paperback boxed edition of the two volumes of *Mastering the Art of French Cooking*. Knopf sold the paperback rights to Bantam, with Julia's one-third share ($115,000) paid to her over several years—a smart tax decision on the part of her lawyer. She called it "a really hard sell, at last!" campaign, beginning in a suite of the Dorset Hotel in New York City by fielding serial interviews with the press. Then she went on the road to sign books and hold clusters of demonstrations at leading department stores such as Bloomingdale's.

From Hackensack to Houston, from Stanford to Seattle, she made fast omelets on talk shows around the country and responded to the same old questions as if she were hearing them for the first time. The formal demonstrations for large audiences were planned and diagrammed in minute detail. They were warmly welcomed in San Francisco, where Dorothy lived, and nearby at M. F. K. Fisher's house at Bouverie Ranch in Glen Ellen. When Dinah Shore interviewed Julia on her television program, Paul remarked that they had an "immediate rapport" because Dinah was "as warm and as charming, as sensuous and as beautiful as Julia."

With the assistance of Rosemary Manell, who flew in from San Francisco, and Elizabeth Bishop, an "associate cook" from the TV series, helping her on all of her demonstration trips, Julia's routine was more professional and her teaching more advanced. Julia learned, she said, that "I need my own persons—Rosie Manell and Elizabeth Bishop—to travel around with me; you need somebody who knows your style." According to Paul: "The team of Rosie, Liz, Julia and Paul works marvelously well together." Yet with her performance skills, familiar assistants, and Paul's talents (he was no longer washing dishes in rest-room sinks), her planning and schedules were still grueling experiences, as his detailed letters to his brother reveal, even with limousines and good hotels.

Now that she was broadcast in color, she seemed closer to her audience, who crowded her every appearance to touch her and have her autograph her book. Paul described the hourlong lines as "waves of love." Frequently he was included in local television interviews. "She always had him sit beside her," says Jane Friedman. "Paulski, as she called him, was always most important for her. It was charming to see them hold hands and kiss, to talk playfully of food and sex."

Paul called fans "JW's" or "Julie-watchers with cameras" when they traveled and were approached by American tourists in Oslo, Provence, or Paris. The Dehillerin brothers found that when they hung her picture on the wall of their French kitchen equipment store, the customers would exclaim, "Oh, Jooooolia!" The Boston JW's spotted her at the market or movies, the symphony or a Red Sox game (Julia loved sports, but Paul thought the game "more interesting anthropologically than sportively"). Her neighbors often noticed her car: a large tin spoon was attached to the antenna.

To raise money for public television and keep her image before the public, Julia undertook another demonstration tour of the country in March and April 1973, just after her BBC failure. This time she also took along Ruth Lockwood. For these appearances, they sent ahead a detailed list of the equipment illustrated in *Mastering II*. Nevertheless, Julia transported eight pieces of luggage, including a two-burner stove. At each stop she would, as in Boston, write and record local pitches for public stations. Some stops were for book signings and media appearances only. Demonstration stops were for a particular charity (Chicago was for Smith College alumnae) and a fee was paid to WGBH. She was emotionally, intellectually, and financially tied to public television.

Paul believed that one was "a kind of Public Property in this epoch's culture, if one's name and face are well known." In Brooklyn the police helped keep the book-hugging mob in a neat line, but in Chicago there was nearly a riot. Paul felt Julia had "created a speaking style and method that is first class." (When she gave a lecture at the Harvard Law School, they had "the biggest audience [they] had ever had!" Even when the fuses blew, she kept on talking.) Her audiences responded immediately to her relaxed manner and spontaneous humor. She often began by reading some of the letters of complaint, and the audience roared. Her demonstration skills transferred from her television appearances and vice versa. She always wanted as many people as possible to see the demos, yet talked as if no one could see: "cut it on the shoulder, where the upper arm joins," she said instead of "cut it here." She pretended a blind person was in the audience.

Julia and Paul chose to keep up their heavy schedule. We "love it," Paul told Charlie, it keeps "our juices flowing," and "we are not wondering what to do in our retirement." Michael Field died in May 1971 because he drove himself to overwork, Julia believed, but she did not feel she was overworking. She chose her focus—a book or a television series—and then gave it her total commitment. She told Elizabeth David about her television work: "We've brought this rush on ourselves, since we'd rather get it all done in a series of 2 lumps than let it drag all year." Though Paul suffered from occasional serious insomnia and was beginning to be aged by the schedule, Julia seemed to thrive on activity and the contact with people.

Phila Cousins, then completing her education at Radcliffe and graduating magna cum laude in social psychology, was an important ingredient in Julia's life during this time. Paul initially acted as a father-mentor figure, correcting and educating her ("first class mind but sloppy thinker," he pronounced). "We McWilliams women had to be molded Pygmalion style," Phila said. When she met and set up housekeeping with Bart Alexander, Paul believed she was in good hands and relaxed and enjoyed her growth and beauty. The two young people were frequently at the Childs' or entertaining them at their apartment. When they married on July 14, 1974, in Sausalito, Julia and Paul were tied up completing a book in Provence; but they planned to celebrate Christmas at La Pitchoune while the young people spent a year of study in London.

Both Julia and Paul deliberately cultivated youth, both to keep themselves young and to avoid becoming fixed in their views and habits. Living near Harvard helped, for they had Phila and the numerous children of their friends and acquaintances, among them the children of David Brinkley and of Wendy Beck, whom they invited to a large party for young people in December 1973. "It was quite charming for me as a young person," said Jane Friedman, "watching these older people who really liked each other. They liked my youth." Julia also went to Pittsburgh to fulfill a promise to Mister Rogers, who had a long-running children's program on television. For his vast audience of three- to six-year-olds, she demonstrated the making of spaghetti to be eaten with chopsticks. Unknown to the television world, children were avid watchers of "Julia."

But Julia was most at home with her WGBH staff and her neighbors. In 1973, she was thrilled to be free of "our television maelstrom," as she put it (Paul said, "Julie is going crazy from her new freedom, combined with a sudden release of her long-backed-up desire for social life"). They joined in the neighborhood traditions, according to Jean deSola Pool, their next-door neighbor, which were Christmas caroling in the neighborhood ("We were Jews and Moynihans are Catholic, and Julia and Paul were anti-religious, as were the people whose home we went to after the caroling," Mrs. Pool says) and the John Kenneth Galbraiths' June commencement party ("Oh, everyone went. They are still doing it"). Paul always called him "moose-tall" Galbraith and liked to talk economics and the oil crisis with him.

SOLIDARITY FOR THE FOOD WORLD

Julia's career and personal life were inexorably connected to the food world of chefs, cookbook writers, and cooking teachers. She believed in showing what she called "solidarity for our friends in the food world." She attended their book signings and lectures (Paul thought that Claiborne's lecture at Boston University was formless and embarrassing), wrote letters of support (to White House chef Henri Haller, whom Claiborne publicly criticized), bought equipment from Elizabeth David's cookware store in London, and visited new restaurants. For their twenty-seventh wedding anniversary, after going to see the French film comedy *Le Sex Shop,* Julia and Paul dined at Maison Robert, an excellent new restaurant in the old Boston city hall building. She took an interest in the young chef Lydia Shire, transferring her loyalty to The Harvest and then to Shire's own Biba, overlooking Boston Common.

Julia particularly enjoyed Chinese restaurants in Boston, or the upscale La Grenouille and Le Cygne in New York City, but she wrote Simca, "Food is getting too much publicity, and is becoming too much of a status symbol and 'in' business, and the fancy restaurant types are getting too commercial—all with their own wines for sale everywhere." Later, after hearing for the third time that an American food person played tennis with the Troisgros brothers in France, she told Anne Willan (then at the *Washington Star,* one of the few non-"home economist" food editors), "I find I'm getting tired of all this foodie one-upmanship."

When President Ford made dismaying comments on his food preferences in 1974, Julia wrote to chef Henri Haller with her regrets and sympathy. They could share private criticism about various Presidents' bad taste in food: Nixon's preference for catsup on cottage cheese and Ford's remarks about eating being a "waste of time" and his preference for instant coffee, instant tea, and instant oatmeal ("I happen to be the nation's first instant Vice President").

After Beard met Graham Kerr, who had just moved to the United States, he called Julia for a long conversation about his seriousness. Julia suggested that he not leave his television program, *The Galloping Gourmet,* as he planned, because he had "a good TV personality." What he needed, she told Beard, was "the right kind of program, and not a silly one," because he could be "good and useful for the good cause of *la bonne cuisine.*"

Julia supported the development of several cooking schools, particularly La Varenne. When it looked like Madame Brassart was going to retire and sell her Cordon Bleu, Julia and several friends decided to see if they could influence the sale to ensure a strong school for teaching French cooking to English speakers in Paris. Several were involved in the summer of 1972, including Odette Kahn, editor-in-chief of *Vins de France* and *Cuisine et Vins de France,* Marie Blanche (Princesse de Broglie), and Anne Willan with her husband, Mark Cherniavsky, whom Julia had met in Cambridge earlier that year. The Cherniavskys (Mark was at the World Bank) wished to move to Europe, where he had earlier lived for twenty years with his cellist father. Because Anne, who was a British food journalist and author, had studied at the Cordon Bleu in Paris and taught at the Cordon Bleu in London, they wished to own a cooking school, either by buying the Cordon Bleu (which turned out to be too expensive) or by founding their own. Julia and Paul saw their own partnership echoed in the marriage of this "civilized and charming" couple and kept involved over the years in the planning for their school (La Varenne). "Julia was very much responsible for the germ of the idea and for keeping us on track," says Anne Willan.

On January 2, 1974, Paul and Jim Beard accompanied Julia past klieg lights and cameras to a celebrated dinner at the Four Seasons restaurant in New York, but the men stayed at the bar and drank wine, waiting for morsels of the meal to be brought to them. This was a dinner for women only, indeed for twelve leading women, a meal cooked by notorious male chauvinist Paul Bocuse and his fellow Frenchmen Jean Troisgros and Gaston Lenôtre "in response to criticism that no women had been invited to [an earlier] Bocuse dinner." Gael Greene of *New York* magazine planned the promotion for these three French chefs and the press was crawling about hoping to taste samples along with Paul and Jim. Julia did not think the food was exceptionally good, and she seemed to resent the fact that the men tried to bring *all* the ingredients with them (some, including the foie gras, were confiscated at immigration). But she was excited to meet the other guests, who included Lillian Hellman, Pauline Trigère, Bess Myerson, Naomi Barry, Sally Quinn, and Louise Nevelson. Nevelson told a friend she attended just so she could meet Julia Child. Kay Graham, publisher of the *Washington Post,* had to back out at the last minute. Lillian Hellman, Julia told Simca (who had had *le lifting),* had a "wonderfully raddled face (no *saquépage!).*" Julia thought it was soon boring without men and, she told Simca, these women had "nothing whatsoever to do with serious gastronomy." She "wouldn't have missed it for the world," however. Paul concluded that this "Dinner of the Century" was a "vulgar affair," but an amusing "publicity stunt."

In the spring, the "magnificent quadrumvir," as Paul called "Rosie and Lizzie" and themselves, gave thirteen demonstrations for local charities in Seattle, San Francisco, and Honolulu, netting an additional $10,000 for WGBH. At the Kabuki Theater in San Francisco, Julia's trouble with a caramel cage to cover a dessert was one she would talk about for years. "It was during the Patty Hearst kidnapping in San Francisco and everyone was nervous and thinking about killers walking the streets. I was doing a dessert in a caramel cage in which I had to get the caramel just right and dribble it over a bowl to harden. I buttered the stainless-steel bowl, but the cage broke. It broke again during the evening demonstration. It was not pretty. Why am I doing this? I thought." She later figured out that the caramel was too hot, thus melting the butter and sticking to the pan. "We learn so much through mistakes!"

Calvin Tomkins had joined them in San Francisco to write a profile of Julia for *The New Yorker,* which was published at the end of the year. He described her "unique blend of . . . earthy humor and European sophistication" and quoted Beard ("She has the kind of bigness that all great artists have. Singers especially . . . she just sweeps everyone up and carries them away") and Merce Cunningham ("She moves like a dancer. Everything is direct and clear"). Another journalist remarked on her "sense of control, a feeling that everything has been organized."

Two weeks later they flew to Provence (for the first time, her passport read "television and writer") to spend as many months as they needed to complete the manuscript for her book based on the color version of *The French Chef.* Julia set her deadline for September 1. This second book on her own, again to be published by Knopf, was handled by her lawyer, Bob Johnson, who took over her account in 1969 after the death of Brooks Beck and suggested that Knopf was taking Julia's books for granted.

A tough but dapper man of only thirty years who escorted various grand ladies to the Childs' house and to official functions, Bob Johnson was gay but chose to keep his sexual preferences to himself. Because he came from a humble background and worked at a Brahmin firm, he had what one colleague called a "grandiosity and manner that could be [mis]interpreted as arrogant." He was soon caught up in Julia's business and celebrity.

The Bantam paperback paid her handsomely (it had a printing of four million) and their sales promotion was better than Knopf's. Johnson threatened to take her next book elsewhere, giving Judith Jones the impression that

Knopf was cheap and ungrateful for not offering a higher advance. Relations with Judith and Knopf became strained in the late summer of 1971. Eventually Knopf countered an offer from Little, Brown and Julia remained with Knopf. Julia would call it "my one little fling" of unfaithfulness to Knopf.

Before they settled in to complete the manuscript for *Julia Child's Kitchen,* they took a trip to Italy with Herb and Pat Pratt. In Venice, Paul suffered what Julia called a "dreadful case of shell-fish poisoning." His letters to his brother detailed a number of small physical problems; Julia says he is "cross and touchy" and he does "not know why! Must hold on to self." Back at La Pitchoune he was particularly irritated by Jean and Simca's bossy ways, and by the parties for nine (including Beard and Olney) and the foodies' visits to three-star restaurants such as L'Oasis ("pretentious . . . too rich food").

Julia, Paul, and James Beard were sitting on the terrace enjoying their last cup of morning tea, Jim sitting under the olive tree in what Julia called "his big blue Chinese kimono." Whenever Jim was around, Julia's letters were full of more foodie news and Paul was amused by his wit. Paul was working to prepare more illustrations for Julia's new book and correcting the first proofs of his own book of verses a friend was printing. He did not tell Julia he was suffering from chest pains. He soon stopped writing in his diary, explaining to Julia that the Empirin he was taking gave him a rash.

When she was not interrupted, Julia worked from 9 A.M. to 7 P.M. on the manuscript. In a philosophical letter to Charlie and Freddie in May, she declared, "Paul and I shall certainly go on about our work well into our 90s and 100s . . . we are fortunate to be so tough and healthy." Still, she was worried about signs of aging in Paul, though the doctor had pronounced him in perfect health before they left Cambridge. She completed her manuscript by August 31, and they stopped off at the Willan/Cherniavsky home in Paris to celebrate. Anne and Mark remember that Paul was irritable, distracted, and probably not feeling well when they were dining at L'Ami Louis.

Finished with *The French Chef* and the two books based on it, and freed of her collaboration with Simca, Julia was looking forward to a new challenge. A year before, she told Simca that if she ever did another television program, she wanted "all kinds of chefs and cooks." But by January she told Simca she wanted to do "only demonstrations." Whatever the next phase of her professional life, she would "work for the good cause of *la bonne cuisine* by finding good young people to carry on." Instead, this next stage of her career would be inaugurated by personal crisis. It was in Paris that Paul finally revealed to Julia the severe chest pain that signaled a possible heart attack.

Chapter 22

A TIME OF LOSS
(1974 – 1977)

"I am making no future plans."
JULIA CHILD, *March 20, 1975*

ON SEPTEMBER 27, 1974, immediately upon their return, Dr. Julian Snyder put Paul in Beth Israel Hospital in Boston. For two weeks they administered angiography, anticoagulant treatment, and medication to slow his heart, trying to determine the extent of his infarction and artery blockage. His heart attack had "crept up on tiny, padded feet, like a field mouse," he later informed Charlie. Five years before, he had had mild pain, which he attributed to gas and which stopped if he rested. Since 1970 the pains recurred almost daily, relieved temporarily by Empirin. Yet at every semiannual examination, doctors told him he had the "heart of an athlete of thirty." On August 4 at La Pitchoune, Paul had a series of nosebleeds in the night, perhaps a result of the amount of blood-thinning aspirin he was taking. When he finally told Julia the extent of his pain, she insisted they see the doctor. Now she informed Louisette (who was working on a new cookbook) and others that he was hospitalized "with a slight heart condition." For Paul, the long hospitalization was traumatic and unsettling:

> There's a phrase in Nabokov's new book *Look at the Harlequins* [he wrote Charlie]. It goes like this: "As she opened the door of the hospital

room I emitted a bellow of joy, and Reality entered." This describes exactly my sense of pleasure (and nightmares passing) when Julia comes into my room at Beth Israel.

When the doctor asked if they wanted to test a new surgical procedure, Paul and Julia said yes, anything to save his life. Only 5,000 heart bypasses had been done since the first one in 1967, and only 64 patients, or 1.3 percent, had died. The odds looked good. The surgery was scheduled for October 18, 1974.

"LUCKY TO BE ALIVE"

During the surgery, while veins were taken from his left leg to graft three bypasses around clogged arteries to his heart and clean out other entrances and exits, Paul had several small strokes. They would only learn this months later, so at the time Julia's spirits were high as she told everyone that "the surgery is a miracle. He is lucky to be alive. If he had not had this operation, he would have been dead."

As the weeks went by and he remained "weak and groggy"—or, as she admitted later, "in a vegetable state"—she kept thinking it was just a slow recovery. She canceled a heavy schedule of fall and winter demonstrations, which also allowed her the time to complete the manuscript for *From Julia Child's Kitchen*. When Paul came home on November 24, he was clearly frustrated by his inability to process information. Surprisingly, the doctor gave him no dietary restrictions or any prescribed therapy, saying (according to Julia), "You don't have cholesterol blockages, you obviously diet sensibly." There was no known cause for coronary arteriosclerosis, the doctor informed them. The presence of Abe and Rosie Manell for Thanksgiving cheered them both. But by Christmas, Paul still could not read, and when he tried to write, the words came out scrambled. Neither food nor wine tasted good. And his French was gone.

At the suggestion of her sister Dort, Julia began taking Paul to a speech clinic in February. She described his aphasia to M. F. K. Fisher as comparable to dyslexia. But it was more than reversing letters or words: he was having trouble processing what he heard. For the first time in her letters she mentioned arteriosclerosis and the strokes that caused brain damage during the surgery. He has "scrambled brain trouble," she told her closest friends.

Ever the activist, Julia took charge, installing a costly elevator on the back side of the house to allow Paul to move easily between the bedroom and office floor, the first-floor kitchen, and the basement, where his carpentry tools

and wine cellar were located. In May she took him for a week of sun in
Bermuda. By April he was able to write a coherent letter to Charlie, but only
after several drafts and several hours. At Paul's request, Charlie and Freddie
had waited five months to come for their first visit. Paul's pride was hurt (by
the devastating results of his strokes), his masculinity and perfectionism frustrated ("I am only half a man," he said). But his willpower was strong and he
struggled on, applying those powers of deduction he had assiduously honed all
his life. The recovery was slow, and never full. His spark was gone, Julia
confided to a few friends.

During all the months of his illness and recovery, Julia worked full days
completing her manuscript, which grew beyond the inclusion of her seventy-
two recipes from the new *French Chef* television series. From June 1974 until
February 1975, she added reminiscences and cooking tips accumulated over
twenty-five years. Narrative sections spoke about her neighborhood shops, her
French cooking teacher, chef Max Bugnard, her neighbor "Jean [deSola
Pool]" and her English friends "Peter and Mari [Bicknell]." She also hired
Judith Jones to help her with editing above and beyond her usual editorial
duties. During the summer of 1975, Julia redid the index after receiving the
version done by someone who was not a cook. Because Paul could not work
his camera or construct any more drawings, she and Judith conferred on using
what was already on hand and hiring a photographer to complete a few more.

Coincidentally, during this first year of Paul's recuperation, Julia revealed to the world she had had a mastectomy six years before. In a serious
article about the frequency of this cancer in women, Julia, Betty Ford (the
President's wife), Happy Rockefeller (the Vice President's wife), and Shirley
Temple Black (the movie star turned diplomat), among others, testified that
they were still alive and wished other women would carefully examine themselves. Julia's desire to save "even one life" and her natural frankness over-
came her Yankee sense of privacy. For the same reason, in October 1977, she
would appear in a National Cancer Society fashion show in New York City.

She could not easily retreat from the public arena as Paul would have
preferred ("It is very important for Julia," Paul said about the presence of
other people). Though she kept the groups small for Paul's sake, the entertaining of friends and reporters continued. Rosemary Manell came to cook, "with
her unfailing good humor"; Olney visited on his book tour for *Simple French
Food* (Rosie helped him with his television appearances). Julia remained matter-of-fact about Paul's illness, neither apologetic nor embarrassed. Jim Beard
visited with young Carl Jerome (Julia called him James's "acolyte" and was
grateful that someone was looking after her dear overweight friend). Beard
was as inquisitive and restless as Julia, though Paul had described his arrival at

Cannes that previous summer as "ponderous, sweating, panting, walking in short steps on those swollen legs."

For the national bicentennial year, Julia and Jim made a pilot television program together in February on American food of the Revolutionary War period, which they hoped would include other cooks in its thirteen segments (they were never able to sell the series). Julia also was deeply involved in the Paris cooking school plans of Anne Willan and her husband, Mark Cherniavsky; upon the advice of their lawyer, Julia and Paul privately agreed to invest $10,000 in their friends' new school, the future La Varenne. Jim and Simca soon followed with $5,000 each.

The frenzied cooking world rushed on around them, with Julia staying close to Paul and planning their book tour. Simca was teaching for two weeks in Rutherford, California; James Beard gave Simca a party in his Greenwich Village home; Julia saw Simca cooking on NBC; Simca's student Peter Kump opened his own cooking school in New York City; Poppy Cannon jumped to her death from her twenty-third-floor apartment in New York City (in 1980, the chronically depressed José Wilson would jump to her death into a deep quarry); and Paul's beloved friend Samuel Chamberlain died in Marblehead. Julia kept in touch with triumphs and tragedies by telephone with Jim and by letter to Simca, who since the completion of La Campanette had moved herself and her school from Paris to Bramafam. Julia got caught up momentarily in investigating the issue of nitrates in swordfish and considered teaching with Simca and Anne Willan the following year at the Gritti Palace Hotel in Venice. Plans for the release of her book in the fall continued. It would be a year after Paul's surgery, and he was able to face the inevitable book tour if it had built-in rest and free days. Julia would not consider leaving him to travel alone. He had always expressed disdain for what he called the "geriatric-living syndrome." First she took him for a holiday at the Child cabin in Maine, driving in tandem with the Kublers.

During this period of post-television calm, Julia wrote several articles, including a piece about her Cambridge home for *Architectural Digest* and a review of the new *Joy of Cooking,* which she placed first on her list of indispensable cookbooks in English. She informed *Architectural Digest,* a Los Angeles-based "slick, clubby *ne plus ultra* monthly" (in *Newsweek*'s words), that her Cambridge place "was not grand, just a comfortable working place." *Architectural Digest* added the Irving Street home to the celebrity series that included the homes of Truman Capote, Robert Redford, and Richard Nixon. Doug Dutton of Dutton's Brentwood Bookstore, a noted bookseller and music professor, observed that the Childs' bookcases were only one of two homes shown with a "not bought by the foot" library.

From Julia Child's Kitchen

To launch both the publication of *From Julia Child's Kitchen* and the founding of Anne Willan's La Varenne cooking school in Paris, she and Paul spent ten days at the Dorset Hotel in New York City. At her own expense, Julia had Rosie Manell and Liz Bishop with her at five demonstrations at regional Bloomingdale's stores and one at Altman. After appearing on *A.M. America* and the *Tomorrow* show, they attended a dinner party at Beard's house for Julia and Paul, Jacques Pépin and his mentor Helen McCully, and Mark and Anne Cherniavsky. Finally, she and Jim hosted (and La Varenne paid for) the American launch party for La Varenne at the Four Seasons "to introduce Anne to the Foodie types, and the travel people as well" (she told Simca). La Varenne would open a month later (November 10) in Paris, and Claiborne would be there to cover it for the *New York Times:* he had made the winning bid on American Express's French meal in any restaurant, money-no-object contest (he and Pierre Franey dined at Chez Denis for $4,000 at American Express's expense).

Published on October 6, 1975, *From Julia Child's Kitchen* was a beautifully designed book, full of Paul's black-and-white photographs. Filling the title page is his photograph of Julia in the window of their first Marseilles apartment, the harbor and boats behind her. The title page of each chapter contained a photograph of Marseilles, Provence, or Paris, and most sections began with a memory. The book was dedicated to Ruth Lockwood, her producer, "always steady, even-tempered, able, astute—she has been my everloving friend." Ruth was moved to tears. "I went over to Julia's house and stood eye to eye on the stairs and told her what it meant to me."

Instead of the seventy-two *French Chef* recipes being presented in chronological order, as was done in *The French Chef Cookbook,* they were organized by category, from soup to cakes (the latter included her *Grande Bouffe* cake with almonds). She put in her French bread recipe, two recipes for madeleines, and the essential sauces and primary dishes from her other three books. Of course, most of the recipes were French—"because that is my training"—but there were also American favorites such as coleslaw, pizza, chicken Kiev, pumpkin soup, and hamburgers. Because 55 percent of the 714-page volume was made up of WGBH material, she gave WGBH 20 percent of the advance ("They put me on the map," she reminded one reporter).

Reviewer Bill Rice said she "departed from the professorial tone of earlier works." Her voice is indeed less pedantic, but the text is still thorough, offering full teaching charts on measurements and terminology. She included the use of the Cuisinart for the first time. Part of the informality of the book came from the inclusion of reproduced cartoons by the *New Yorker*'s George Price ("Any word as to the nature of the soupe du jour?" asks one man to another in a charity soup line). She also broke her rule about naming dishes and included *pommes Rosemary, les tartelettes Bugnard,* and her own Mrs. Child's famous sticky fruitcake. This was her most personal book. She told Mary Frances seven years later that she found it "difficult to be personal" in her writing, but this was "my own favorite book, which is entirely my own, written the way I wanted to do it."

Judith Jones encouraged her to establish her personal voice and include stories such as her encounter with Colette in France. In this volume the voice of Julia clearly speaks to "my fellow cook." This is your own "private cooking school" she told her readers in the introduction, and even the most knowledgeable learned something. "She finally explained the background and theories," says cooking teacher Betty Rosbottom, who adds, "I learned for the first time, for example, the formula for stewing fruits on pages 510 and 511." Julia told Mary Frances, "This is the summation of my 25 years in the kitchen. I have little more to say about anything. I'm writ out, dry," she added. "NO MORE BOOKS!"

She took Paul with her on the tour, for he was uneasy away from her, his mind still scrambled. She had moved from heartbreak to a sense of loss, from an acceptance of the inevitable to a determination to get on with life, no matter what people thought. Those who met Paul for the first time in Minneapolis, Chicago, Cleveland, or Pittsburgh knew only that he was withdrawn and grumpy. The food coordinator at Lipman's department store in Portland, Oregon, remembers Paul sitting in the front row during her demonstrations. Sometimes he sat in on the interviews, though his answers did not always match the question (Julia did not think it mattered).

Her reception in New York City was positive, from appearances on Barbara Walters's *Not For Women Only* to Beverly Sills's *Lifestyles* and the New York Wine and Food Society's "A Gentle Roasting" of Child and Beard at the Hotel Pierre. In *New York* magazine, Mimi Sheraton (who would soon become the chief restaurant reviewer for the *New York Times)* selected fourteen out of the one hundred cookbooks published that year and named *From Julia Child's Kitchen* the best of the fourteen, a list that included Jacques Pépin's splendid *The French Chef Cooks at Home.* She praised Julia's "personal [and] no less precise and enticing" book, preferring her new listing of ingredients first. Another reviewer said that Julia was "as elegant as *médaillons de porc sautés à la crème,* and as unpretentious as good *ragoût.*" *People* magazine gave her the cover for the first week of December, featuring the thirty-

The Cordon Bleu cooking school, Paris, 1949 or 1950. Julia's mentor, chef Max Bugnard, is the second from the left. Julia, the only woman, attended a class for future professionals studying under the GI Bill.

Cooking in her Paris apartment kitchen, built out from the maid's quarters under the roof and reached by a narrow, steep stair. The ovens are to her right. (PAUL CHILD)

*M*atron of honor Julia Child and best man Lt. Jack Kelly witness the marriage of Jack Hemingway and Puck Whitlock at the American Church in Paris, June 25, 1949.

(COURTESY JACK HEMINGWAY)

*T*he McWilliams sisters in Paris. Dorothy, left, lived with Julia and Paul from April 8, 1949, until she got her own apartment nearly a year later, after falling in love with Ivan Cousins, a former U.S. Navy man living in Paris.

(PAUL CHILD)

A photograph of one of Paul Child's paintings of the Paris rooftops. Painted in the summer of 1952, it shows the view from the balcony of the apartment of Rosemary and Abe Manell on the Ile St.-Louis.

*W*edding reception of Dorothy McWilliams and Ivan Cousins, June 23, 1951, in New York City. From the left: Paul Child, sister-in-law Josephine McWilliams, Julia, Ivan beside his mother (Pearl Marie Cousins), Dorothy (standing behind Ivan), John McWilliams III, stepmother Phila, and father John McWilliams, Jr. In the front row are John and Jo's first two children, John IV (Jay) and Carol.

Julia and Simca visiting Chinon for the weekend, April 2, 1952. They were personal and professional "sisters," both animal lovers with boundless energy. (PAUL CHILD)

L'Ecole des Trois Gourmandes in 1953: Louisette Bertholle, Simone (Simca) Beck, and Julia Child. In the Childs' kitchen at 81, rue de l'Université, where they taught American students. They were also hard at work on their book *Mastering the Art of French Cooking*, published eight years later. (PAUL CHILD)

Julia in 1953 in the window of the Childs' apartment in Marseilles, where they lived in the Old Port. Julia loved the sea, experimented with bouillabaisse, and typed thousands of pages of recipes and letters to send back to Paris. (PAUL CHILD)

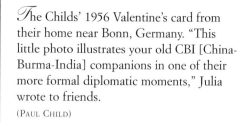

The Childs' 1956 Valentine's card from their home near Bonn, Germany. "This little photo illustrates your old CBI [China-Burma-India] companions in one of their more formal diplomatic moments," Julia wrote to friends.
(PAUL CHILD)

Avis DeVoto, "the godmother" of *Mastering the Art of French Cooking*, here with Paul Child.
(COURTESY MARK DEVOTO)

Just back from two years in Oslo, Norway, Julia and Paul correct proofs on the index of *Mastering the Art of French Cooking* (published October 1961) at Lopaus Point, Mount Desert Island, Maine.

Avis DeVoto and Julia Child at Charnel House Court, Rouen, France, May 1956.
(PAUL CHILD)

*J*ulia and James Beard in the back garden of Beard's house at 119 West Tenth Street, Greenwich Village, May 21, 1964. Julia periodically flew down from Boston to teach in his cooking school.
(PAUL CHILD)

*Th*e French Chef in front of the camera at WGBH for a filming, "Sweetbreads and Brains," show #123, December 9, 1965. She wears the insignia designed by Paul for L'Ecole des Trois Gourmandes.
(PAUL CHILD)

*R*uth Lockwood, her second WGBH producer, ties Julia's apron before the taping of *The French Chef*, which ran in black and white from 1963 to 1966, in color from 1970 to 1973.
(PAUL CHILD)

"YOU MAY BE AN ESCARGOT TO JULIA CHILD…
BUT YOU'RE JUST A SNAIL TO ME!"

The old house at Bramafam in Provence. Julia is working at Simca's outdoor table about 1960, before her own house was built beyond the trees behind her.

Julia's kitchen in the Childs' Cambridge home, 1969. The table was bought in Oslo, the mortar and pestle on the left in Paris, the six-burner Garland gas range on the right in Washington, DC. The house was built for the eminent philosopher Josiah Royce in 1889, the counters raised when the Childs moved in in 1961. Her last two PBS series were filmed in this kitchen.

(Reprinted with special permission of King Features Syndicate)

Founders of the American Institute of Wine and Food: Richard Graff (Chalone Vineyard), Julia, Robert Huttenback (chancellor of the University of California at Santa Barbara), and Robert Mondavi, March 17, 1984, at a lunch honoring Graff at the Mondavi vineyard in the Napa Valley.

Judith Jones, her editor at Knopf beginning in 1960, and Julia, at work on *Cooking with Master Chefs*, 1993.

(BARRY MICHLIN PHOTOGRAPHER)

year partnership between Paul and his "wonderfully sensuous" Julia. The *Washington Star* gave her a front-page Q&A (she touted La Varenne), and, closer to home, her butcher sold 400 copies of her book along with his meat.

$\mathcal{N}$OUVELLE CUISINE

The tone for the tour of *From Julia Child's Kitchen* was set before the plane tickets were purchased when John Kifner of the *New York Times* asked her about the undercooked vegetables of "nouvelle cuisine" now sweeping upscale U.S. restaurant kitchens. Julia pooh-poohed nouvelle cuisine as "just that Paris PR game." The controversy made for good conversation and copy. She could rise to the quotable occasion: "A plate should look like food, not a Japanese dinner." And "This food looks fingered. It doesn't look foody to me." When journalists asked about heavy French cooking with sauces, she said they must be talking about French tourist food cooked in starred restaurants. She knew, as did most food people, that nouvelle cuisine was, in one food historian's words, "the apparent culinary equivalent of the sixties miniskirt revolution . . . [and] the old food journalism trick of proclaiming their own current project the latest news." The expression "nouvelle cuisine" had been used two hundred years before. In 1975 it meant innovative cooking, lighter sauces, fish and vegetables, decoratively presented smaller portions.

If there was a conflict, it was conducted largely in the press. After all, Julia knew most of the chefs, and when Bill Rice, the respected food editor of the *Washington Post,* gathered a group of them together for a dialogue in a French restaurant in Washington, DC, on November 8, Julia was glad to participate. She was on the penultimate stop in her tour, and she met four three-star French chefs (Paul Bocuse, François Bise, Alain Chapel, and Louis Outhier) as well as the French and U.S. press. They discussed in French the trends in American and French cooking. Paul recorded that the French chefs "treated Julia with deference." She later wrote to Helen McCully that "we all agreed on everything."

The French chefs denied reports they were "down on Escoffier" (famous himself for lighter if saucy cooking) and concluded that nouvelle cuisine meant freedom to create and to improvise on the fundamentals. No longer would every restaurant in France have on its menu the same dishes with the same names. Reading menus has been a challenge for diners ever since, and Jacques Pépin asserts that "nouvelle cuisine has destroyed the repertoire and nomenclature of French cooking."

In Julia's opinion, the most innovative chef among those in the nouvelle group was the modest Michel Guérard, creator of *cuisine minceur,* France's first calorie-counting *haute cuisine.* Narcisse Chamberlain, who edited Guérard's book for Morrow the next year, brought him and his wife, Christine, to the Childs' for dinner. According to Chamberlain, "Michel and Christine were thunderstruck by Julia," her voice and height and informality. The master of *cuisine minceur* (at Eugénie-les-Bains) soon rolled up his sleeves and began cooking with Julia. "It was a howl and they had a fabulous time. The Guérards continued their exhausting book tour as far as California, but nothing matched the Cambridge meal."

It was the American press and Gault-Millau's *Nouveau Guide de la France* who polarized the issue of nouvelle cuisine. (Gault-Millau, according to Julia, "browbeat" nonconforming restaurants by awarding red toques to nouvelle chefs and black toques to the old-fashioned traditional holdouts.) The American press's obsession with the "news" of nouvelle cuisine initiated a trend that would persist in culinary journalism: "trend handicapping," Robert Clark called it. As in the fashion world, journalists looked for the latest direction in food preparation and featured its leaders in personality profiles. (The real news story, noted Clark, was the public concern with health, which would emerge in the coming decade.)

Troisgros, Guérard, and Frédy Girardet (near Lausanne) were the true innovators, Julia believed. Others have said the late Fernand Point (La Pyramide in Vienne) was the presumed spiritual father (because many of the young chefs had worked for him). Though she credited Bocuse (near Lyons) for elevating the professional profile of the French chef, she said when his book was translated that it was "hardly anything but classical cuisine" (indeed, two years later she learned Bocuse had put his own introduction on a dead man's book). Troisgros's book was just "a list of recipes," and only Guérard's book was a good, serious "personal book." The extremes of nouvelle cuisine (Bocuse called them "a big piece of merde" at their Washington, DC, meeting, Julia reported to Helen McCully) have been called "kiwi-zine"; Julia said they all steamed things in seaweed. If the converts of nouvelle cuisine ever looked back, wrote Laura Shapiro, "they might see Fannie Farmer, whose passion for novelty led her to marshmallows and candied fruit rather than warm liver salad and lemon-flavored fettucini, but whose impact on a generation was no less powerful for that."

Julia made her definitive statement on nouvelle cuisine in *New York* magazine the following year (July 4, 1977), and by explaining its history and the French rating guides, she demonstrated her extensive dining experience in the great restaurants of France. She had scoffed at journalists' descriptions of Bocuse's truffle and foie gras "Dinner of the Century" several years before as being new ("Obviously somebody was pulling somebody's leg"). She had high praise for Guérard and even admitted she loved the experimental new cooking—as she believed Escoffier would. She did not like blood-rare game and undercooked vegetables, which failed to bring out their flavor. And she warned against throwing out "the comfortable old glories" of traditional French dishes.

*F*EMINISM

If nouvelle cuisine was the major food topic of the 1970s, a larger controversy long haunting Julia now clearly emerged: feminism. "Women's liberation" had frequently come up in a decade of her interviews with the press, though she never brought up the issue herself. With *From Julia Child's Kitchen* it surfaced again because she made it clear in her book and interviews that "I *never* have anything to do with housewives." She repeated this caveat again for the *New York Times* reporter. Some readers saw this as "anti-woman," deprecating the word "housewives." It was the word Julia disliked, but then so did most feminists. "I have nothing to do with housewives," she said on several occasions. "We never talk about women cooking. It is PEOPLE who like to cook, and we don't care who they are—race, color, sex, animals, ANYBODY," she told a reporter for *Dial.*

In interviews she denied feeling discriminated against in what then was primarily a man's field, though she admitted that had she "gone into restaurant work," she would have "encountered French male chauvinism." "You know," she told one reporter, "it wasn't until I began thinking about it that I realized my field is closed to women! It's very unfair. It's absolutely *restricted!* You can't [teach in] the Culinary Institute of America in New York! The big hotels, the fancy New York restaurants, don't want women chefs."

Camille Paglia would later call Julia Child a prewar feminist like Eleanor Roosevelt. She refused the mantle of "feminist," assuming, as did many women of her generation, that it meant anti-men. And Julia adored men! She always noticed a handsome man and loved to flirt. She was sometimes critical of women, disdaining whining women who were afraid to take risks. One reviewer, misunderstanding feminism, said Julia was "no feminist" because she "unabashedly [gave] her husband credit for her achievement." When she pointed out that there were few women in professional kitchens, she was again characterized as antifeminist. She believed she was merely stating a lamentable fact. She rejoiced in the success of Lydia Shire, a Boston chef, and told Simca: "So it shows that women chefs can go places, which is nice to know."

When asked directly in 1985 if she was a feminist, she declined the label (her sister Dort proudly wore it): "No. I'm from a different generation." Yet, as one journalist noted, Julia was the embodiment of feminist achievement and independence. Her friend Charlotte Snyder Turgeon says, "She has always been a nonfeminist, even though she epitomizes them." Helen Civelli Brown said that Julia "is a symbol of women's liberation. Through her own intelligence, wit, and hard work, she rose to the forefront in a field traditionally dominated by men." What Julia seemed to object to was the domination of any group by women, men, or homosexuals: "Others will not want to go into it," she observed. "I think Julia opened cooking for women," said Gregory Usher. Corinne Poole, who owns the Giraffe restaurant in British Columbia, says that "Julia inspired me and other young women to open restaurants."

Had Julia cared, she would have openly challenged the so-called women's liberation movement for attacking the women who chose to cook. Women (and men) took up cooking with "a real passion" in the early 1970s, says John Mariani, but then "the Women's Liberation Movement shamed their sisters out of the kitchen and into the workforce." It was not just the feminists, of course, for as one anthropologist asserts, "Western philosophers have persistently ignored—or marginalized—one of the most common and pervasive sources of value in human experience—our relations with food."

When the *San Francisco Examiner* put the question directly to a dozen famous women in 1975, Julia admitted, "I guess I am liberated," pointing out that she was of her own free choice doing what she wanted and loved. "You'd call ours a liberated marriage," she added, and "my hat is off to the movement."

California beckoned for the last two weeks of her book tour in the fall of 1975: visiting the Gateses as well as niece Rachel and her husband, Anthony Prud'homme, in Pasadena, staying with Dort and Ivan in San Francisco, driving to M. F. K.'s house for lunch, and signing books at Williams-Sonoma before flying to Portland for more of the same. Pamela Henstell, on her first job with Knopf publicity for the West Coast, remembers Paul's "big stopwatch" and him sitting "in the very front row . . . startling the people around him" by calling out the time. Henstell testifies that Julia "is the least egocentric author I have ever dealt with."

Two years after Paul's surgery and strokes, Julia accepted with resignation that Paul would not recover from his mental confusion and would always need to rest and avoid large groups. One neurologist told her to "keep on living a normal life," and she knew she needed to keep promoting her books to keep the income flowing (a fact she always mentioned to Simca). But she had lost her vital and independent partner, her confidant and guide. The

resulting loneliness, which would eventually push her toward a frenetic professional pace, initially led to a retreat. Because she wanted a break for herself as
well, she took Paul in mid-December 1975 to Paris and Provence for three
months. Indeed, she would have him away from Cambridge for most of 1976.
She called it her sabbatical ("We have been on deadline for fifteen years!!").
She was not planning a book or a television series, and she gave up (only
temporarily, as it turned out) writing features for *McCall's*.

EUROPEAN SABBATICAL

The five days in Paris in the middle of December 1975 meant dining at
Archestrate and Prunier-Duphot, attending a Gourmettes luncheon, and,
most important, checking on her personal and financial investment in La
Varenne ("so unlike the nastiness of the Cordon Bleu," she wrote to several
friends). She saw the school, which she said was "warm and earthy and professional," as a place for weekly gatherings of foodies in the Paris world, and she
freely gave her advice. During several interviews in the year since the school
had opened, she gave it repeated positive mention and endorsement. But in all
the years she dropped in, she only met informally with the students; she never
gave demonstrations.

La Varenne used a variety of French chefs, most connected with Sofitel
(a French hotel chain), and printed its recipes for the students. Gregory
Usher, who had become director of La Varenne, believed Julia's name as an
adviser added integrity to the school, which was 95 percent American. Steven
Raichlen, who had just graduated in French literature from Reed College,
where he survived on Julia's French onion soup (the only dish he could afford
to make, he says), was one of the many students who were delighted by Julia's
active interest in La Varenne. Raichlen worked there for the next six summers
and remembers how they scrubbed every pot and pan before Julia's visits.
Another student, Zanne Early, who had left *Gourmet* (but would return as
food editor), was impressed by Julia's example: "She does not live in the
shadows, she lives in color."

The Train Bleu took the Childs to Cannes for a La Pitchoune Christmas,
but Paul's bad case of bronchitis and consequent medication seemed to disori-
ent him more than ever. His "severe communication problems" meant it took
him one and a half hours to write a page to Charlie, saying, "Aphasia is
shocking—because it's YOU doing it. And you don't know when or why . . .
I simply don't understand most of what people say." Earlier he wrote, "I can't
adjust to my present incapacities, as though some evil witch has waved a wand

over my head and The Prince finds himself all at once a hedgehog, like the Grimms' tale."

While staying at La Pitchoune, Julia learned that for her efforts on behalf of French cuisine, she would receive the Ordre de Mérite National from the French government, an award which Jean Fischbacher and Simca instigated. She was the most visible representative in the United States for French food, had feted many French chefs in Cambridge and New York, and demonstrated French techniques (with Simca and Anne) that summer for Natale Rusconi at the Gritti Palace Hotel in Venice. Though she did not intend to return to the Gritti (the work actually cost her money, the publicity was nonexistent, she reached too few students for her efforts, and she doubted that any of the profits promised to the "Save Venice" fund found their way there), she made important friends in Marcella and Victor Hazan, who had a cooking school in Bologna, and Faith Heller Willinger, who had sought Julia's advice in 1972 and consequently apprenticed herself to Italian chefs. Willinger, from Cleveland, married an Italian man and eventually coordinated the Cipriani cooking school (after Rusconi left the Gritti).

Julia and Paul returned to Boston in time for the presidential political conventions, staying up until 4:30 A.M. to watch and celebrate Jimmy Carter's win. She often gave her time for patriotic efforts, participating in a film, *The Chemicals of Life,* for the Smithsonian National Air and Space Museum, which they dubbed "Julia Child's Primordial Soup." And she encouraged young cooks, many of whom dialed Julia's *listed* telephone number for help in preparing a recipe or menu.

CONFLICTS OVER "AMERICAN" CUISINE

Despite all her French dining and concern with French cuisine, whether classical, nouvelle, or *minceur,* Julia was chiefly interested in how *Americans* cooked and ate. Via books and television, she was primarily a teacher of home cooking. The aborted plan with Beard for a bicentennial cooking show—featuring turkey, pumpkin, succotash, Indian pudding, and the like—was part of her larger plan to improve American cooking and eating. She had urged Sam Chamberlain before he died to give his papers to the Schlesinger Library in Cambridge (Radcliffe), where there was a growing collection of valuable books on cookery. She also supported the Culinary Institute of America by attending its commencement in Hyde Park, New York, in 1976.

Never parochial, she tried all cuisines, preferring fresh Chinese when there wasn't a good French restaurant in town. She knew all the great French chefs and supported the growing number of teachers (the ever-hostile Madeleine Kamman, who had just opened a restaurant in Newton, being a noted exception). Anne Willan and Mark Cherniavsky came for the 1976 Thanksgiving weekend of cooking together. Anne and Julia discussed the early growing pains of La Varenne and, specifically, the visit of Queen Elizabeth to the Ford White House earlier that year, a state dinner that Julia had attended. She was still in the throes of writing an article about it for *The New York Times Magazine.*

Julia had attended the White House dinner with WGBH, filming in the cramped kitchen before dinner and nibbling the food. Ruth Lockwood had encouraged the *New York Times* to do a feature on the event, but Mimi Sheraton ended up criticizing chef Henri Haller (who was Swiss) for serving French food (the lobsters were in aspic). Where was the American food? Sheraton and others asked. Julia was caught in the middle of what she labeled "public caterwauling." She believed in French techniques and American ingredients (lobster certainly qualified), but always wanted the best food whatever its provenance. (The Fords had insisted on only American wine.) When *W* magazine published an article of advice for the new Carter administration, including "Pamela Harriman's Peanut Pâté," Julia was quoted as saying that the "tiresome" chauvinists "should be knocked in the head." The only criteria for food and wine should be that it be the best and can be served to a large group.

The "culinary reputation" of the White House "is dreary indeed," Julia concluded in her essay—in the form of a "letter" to the First Lady—published in *The New York Times Magazine* in January 1977. She defended the chef, Henri Haller, and challenged the new First Lady, Rosalyn Carter, to be practical in her "packaging and public relations." Though "we most certainly must act to preserve our culinary heritages," she urged a menu that was appropriate for large, sit-down dinners and changing the names of the dishes from international French to national American. Thus *quiche aux crevettes* became "open-faced tart of Louisiana shrimp," *homard en belle vue* became "cold boiled lobster from the coast of northern Maine, in fancy dress," and *selle de veau farcie et braisée* became "stuffed boned saddle of New Hampshire veal," and *glace aux pêches, sauce aux framboises* became "fresh Georgia peach ice cream with Rose Garden raspberry sauce." Practical American advice.

The old contest between American and French produce and cooking was one Julia largely ignored except when she was dragged into the White House debates and dunned for an occasional reference to the superior American beef. Paul initially preferred French wines, though they were surprised by the results of a contest set up in Paris by Englishman Steven Spurrier, a thirty-four-year-old wine purveyor who owned a wine shop, the Caves de la Made-leine, and a wine school, the Académie du Vin, near the Place de la Madeleine in Paris. It was a blind tasting and among the judges were several friends of Julia, including Odette Kahn, editor of the *Cuisine et Vins de France,* and Raymond Oliver of Le Grand Véfour. Much to everyone's shock, the Americans won.

Soon a salvo from the other extreme added a different note to the culinary celebration of the American bicentennial. "It was hot stuff then," Peter Kump says of *The Taste of America,* which food writers Karen and John Hess published in February 1977. "No one had ever dared to blast Julia and Jim before. Karen was angry and wrote the explosive chapters, though I don't think she had the credentials." Beard's biographer called it "a vituperative and angry critique of American gastronomy." Julia told Beard, "The less said about them the better."

The Hesses (he was briefly the food writer for the *New York Times)* essentially said there was no taste in American food. Some of the criticisms had validity: they alleged that American "gourmet" cooking was largely second-rate Escoffier; corporate agriculture rendered the American diet tasteless and unhealthy; the food press and the food industry were indeed incestuous; reviewers were afraid to be honestly critical; American food products and cooking had declined; there was a "gourmet plague" in America. Yet the Hesses were sensational and extreme, blaming it all chiefly on Child, Beard, and Claiborne—the easiest targets. With rare exceptions, they attacked almost all of the food writers and cooks in the country.

The Hesses admired the purists and held to the idealism of the Jeffersonian agrarian tradition. And to their American tradition of dissent. Claiborne was a plagiarist, Beard a sellout. They admittedly struggled to find anyone to praise. Their book was a sensational read, at least in New York City. But it was self-defeating with its tone of snide cynicism and bitchery which gave the impression that it was settling scores against everyone. The controversy was healthy for an essentially closed food world, but its impact was weakened by the angry tone.

Julia took more than her share of lumps—for liking McDonald's French fries, for using too many *en croûte* dishes in her cookbooks, and for aiming her *Mastering* books too much toward *haute cuisine.* Yet Julia frequently said, "It is a teaching cookbook, not a chef's notebook." A mutual friend (praised in the Hess book) countered that Julia's way of handling her recipes made it look like a chef's cookbook, "but I see no other way to do it for people who do not have the background." Indeed, "Julia includes quenelles, but she also has daubes (stews), pâtés, boeuf bourgogne, coq au vin, and soups of the bourgeois." Peter Kump also countered, "Loving Simca and exposing Julia is dead wrong—they were one." If Julia was vulnerable to some charges, she was clearly wronged by their statement that she did not enjoy cooking.

The Hesses were certainly right about Julia's mention of canned consommé and frozen pastry, but some of their other criticisms indicate they may not have read the introductions to Julia's books, where she clearly says that the French do not make their own French bread (*Mastering II,* page 53) and that she is including more than French dishes (*Kitchen,* page ix). Does one refuse to make bouillabaisse if one cannot get rascasse? Does one ignore the fact that most of Julia's readers can only buy their produce in a supermarket? Again, her pragmatic compromises were turned against her. Ironically, in a 1974 article, Karen Hess had said, "French cuisine in America must be something of a compromise."

Julia, the embodiment of common sense and practicality, walked the moderate road between the extremes of French classical and nouvelle cuisine and between the elitism of the Hesses and the catsup-on-cottage-cheese served at the White House. However slow she was to question the heavy floured cream sauces of classical French cuisine, she did modify her own French recipes. She shared the ideals for French cooking that the Hesses articulated, but she eschewed their ivory tower snobbery, believing Americans had to use the produce they had on hand—and most people did not have fresh produce markets. She did indeed like the taste of fat in McDonald's fries ("I'd rather eat them than airline food"), but demanded that only the best cooking be offered in the White House.

A final, hurtful blow came from the Hesses in October 1977, when, on the basis of their reading of one sloppy newspaper article about Julia, they declared that "after a crash course for amateurs she became a teacher, and ultimately a television 'chef' virtually overnight." Finally, frustrated that no one had answered the Hesses' "pretentious drivel . . . and their latest attack on available windmills," George Lang, owner of the Café des Artistes in New York City, wrote a rebuttal for the same magazine, *Politicks.* "Their interest is not to evaluate, but to hurt," and by attacking "the biggest" and "most famous," they gain "instant notoriety."

Julia's practicality was both innate and kept steady by her contact with the American people (the Hesses rarely left the Upper West Side of Manhattan, one critic noted). When in the winter of 1976 Knopf sent her on the final tour for *From Julia Child's Kitchen,* this time to Rochester, New York City, Atlanta (for the Food Editors Convention), Detroit, Richmond, St. Louis, and Houston, she met people from every walk of life. She also had the good fortune, when she was in New York City, to meet Simca, who was still promoting *Simca's Cuisine* and doing demonstrations with her co-writer, Michael James. Paul, now more than two years after his surgery, seemed to enjoy a certain amount of activity and stimulation.

During the two years since Paul's strokes, Julia had resumed her Q&A columns for *McCall's,* sat for numerous interviews, visited France, England, and Italy. She would now spend several months of 1977 in Provence "translating" *From Julia Child's Kitchen* into British English (which meant, for one thing, testing the bread recipe with English flour). The U.S. edition of *Kitchen* had passed the 100,000 sales mark. She was also writing more book reviews, of the new French translation of Ali-Bab, books on French cooking by Jacques Pépin and Louis Saulnier, and three books on wine. Little wonder, with this activity and the reruns of *The French Chef,* that her books continued to sell briskly.

TRANSITIONS

For each of the three winters after Paul's strokes, they spent a few weeks in California. During the obligatory visit to Pasadena and her stepmother, Julia mulled over her career options with an infirm husband who once carried half the burden of travel and project preparation. As they moved slowly up the coast, the Childs reveled in the isolated beauty of Santa Barbara, especially the San Ysidro Ranch. Proceeding north, they took Simca to meet Mary Frances on her ranch. Also, they met Dick Graff, who with his brother Peter owned the Chalone Winery in Northern California. Shirley Sarvis, a food writer for *Sunset* magazine and a friend of both Julia and Richard, set up the meal, pairing the wine and food, and the Childs were "so tremendously impressed with [Dick's] wines." Julia told a journalist that "the older we get the more American we get."

Paul Child, the poet and semanticist, now struggled for lost words, so it was particularly poignant that his book of poems, many of them addressed to his beloved Julia, was finally published. *Bubbles from the Spring* was privately printed in 1976, and *The New York Times Magazine* printed four of the poems on its endpaper on May 16. First was his birthday poem of 1961, opening "O Julia, Julia, Cook and nifty wench," and concluding "O luscious dish! O gustatory pleasure! / You satisfy my taste-buds beyond measure." The fourth poem was "The disgraced orifice" and referred to Julia's mouth, "made for other lips to press, for love," which made such weird noises when confronted with food: "squawks . . . twittering coos . . . groaning."

Many factors contributed to the Childs' final transition back to the

United States, foremost being Paul's disability, which slowed down her pace of work. They struggled with the decision for months before Julia had a sense of turning a corner. Hiring Elizabeth Bishop to bring order to her Cambridge office seemed to signal a new level of acceptance of Paul's condition. Soon they were housecleaning and discarding clothes (including many of Julia's size 12A shoes—bought simply because they were the right size): most significantly, they boxed up books and letters—all her correspondence with Simca, Mary Frances, and others—and sent them to the Schlesinger Library, where Julia hoped to add to the best collection of culinary historical books and documents. She kept the books she needed for reference. She also bought a Dictaphone (insisting Simca do the same) and hired a new secretary to alternate days with Gladys.

Adding to her discomfort was the fact that Julia was between books and television programs. Just a year earlier she told a journalist she did not want to do any more television. "It's gotten much more expensive to do, and it involves a 12-hour day and a 7-day week, and we've had it." Yet by the spring of 1977, persuaded by the promise of a slower pace and a new format, Julia had agreed to do a new series. Russ Morash would come back as her producer, Ruth Lockwood (recently widowed) would be her personal manager, they would shoot one episode a week on a permanent stage, and she would move out of what she called "the straitjacket of French cuisine."

"May we go out like rockets, rather than delayed fuses!" she had written Simca three years before. Thus, she planned her reentry by taking Paul to Europe to enjoy La Pitchoune, plan menus for the new series, undertake a diet, and have what Paul called a little facial "touch-up." The plastic surgery, suggested by her producer, occurred amid worries about Freddie Child's health. Erica had called from Maine on June 10 with news that her mother had a heart attack but was rallying. Because Paul had had dental work and Julia's face was still a little swollen by mid-July, they delayed their flight home one more week. They had just walked in the door of their Cambridge home on Saturday, July 23, when the call came from Maine: a second heart attack had proved fatal. They took the plane to Bangor that night for private weeping and six quiet days with the family. On Thursday they offered Freddie's ashes to the rocks and waves off Lopaus Point.

After fifty years of marriage, Charlie Child was devastated. So were Paul and Julia, who also worried about what would happen to Charlie, who was losing his sight. (After Freddie's memorial service three months later in Pennsylvania, Charlie threw away his paints and stopped writing letters.) Freddie's death would bring Julia closer to Rachel and Erica. But she handled this death as she had the loss of her grandparents and parents (and a dozen relatives during her youth), by an emotional outpouring and then determinedly getting on with the life ahead. Julia had lost a beloved sister-in-law; all the more reason, she knew, to keep working. On October 25, after returning from Lopaus Point, she walked into her studio kitchen to begin rehearsals for *Julia Child & Company*.

Chapter 23

THE COMPANY SHE KEEPS (1977 – 1980)

"As soon as you're off television, in a few months nobody will know who you are . . ."

JULIA CHILD, *January 1980*

THE MECHANICAL pea sheller was attached to a portable mixer. When Julia turned it on, the shiny machine began shooting the fresh peas out one side and the discarded pea pods out the other. Pop, pop, pop. It was hilarious, yet no more efficient than shelling the peas by hand. As Julia knew, however, it was a great visual for the television camera, and she loved gadgets. "We have to have fun on this show sometimes!" she told Mary Frances Fisher. Julia had a flair for anticipation and, as one journalist would say, gave the impression of "a child who can hardly wait."

GOING AMERICAN WITH THE PERSIAN CIRCUS

Julia Child & Company was filmed in 1977–78, and *Julia Child & More Company* in 1979–80. After five years away from a television series, Julia was "getting back in harness again," as she described it to several friends. She made both series as much fun as she could, both behind and in front of the camera. But the giggles provoked by the mechanical pea sheller (for the show "Chafing Dish Dinner") belied the complicated hard work behind the scenes.

Julia upped the ante on these two series, in terms of concept and of cost. According to Russ Morash, producer of both shows: "She insisted on rehearsal days in the studio (the economics of it should not be overlooked, for every minute was costly). To give her what she needed, we went to a warehouse so the set would not have to be taken down. We built a studio kitchen at 495 Western Avenue [across from where the Star Market is today]." The kitchen was blue, green, and white—the colors of her own kitchen. They also built a ready room with a preparatory kitchen. Julia and her crew could walk in any day and begin cooking, saving the two hours for setup and the two hours for dismantling. Initially the new studio and the new equipment were leased for only thirteen shows, eight filmed at the end of 1977 and five the following year, and they would film only one program a week, not the two or four episodes they were accustomed to shooting in previous series. Three of these thirteen, in shorter version, went into her monthly column for *McCall's*.

Robert J. Lurtsema, a friend of Paul and the measured, orotund voice of classical music on public radio, wrote the theme music for the series. It was "all bassoons, which sounds like an elephant walking," according to Julia.

Julia remade her persona from the French Chef into the Elegant Hostess. This series focused on the dining room and a full menu, unlike any series or book she had done before, but similar in one regard to *Simca's Cuisine* ("An Alsatian Supper"). In the "Chafing Dish" menu, for example, the first course was sliced fresh artichoke bottoms and raw marinated scallops with fresh tomato fondue; the main dish was steak Diane (with those bouncing peas); and dessert was a chocolate mousse cake consisting of a pound of chocolate, six eggs, a half cup of sugar, and one cup of whipped cream. She informed Mary Frances that the cake was *gâteau Victoire au chocolat, mousseline,* but for her viewers it was a flat chocolate cake decorated with whipped cream.

In this series, the titles of dishes were in English and she would have, she informed Simca, "a lot of plain old American cooking—like corned beef hash, corn timbale, coleslaw, roast beef, Boston baked beans, and New England fish chowder." She was "out of the French straitjacket," but putting her French techniques to use in making creative variations on American dishes. Of course, the foundation recipes (such as the sauces) did not change, and there were some French dishes, such as chocolate truffles and *coulibiac* (sole in *choux* pastry).

The ambitious concept of presenting an entire meal for guests on a special occasion—"Buffet for 19," "New England Potluck Supper," "Dinner for the Boss"—was matched by money and a large crew of volunteers. Co-producer Ruth Lockwood was her "collaborator and colleague," performing all the duties she always did for Julia personally as producer, but, she said, "without the ultimate responsibility, which is what I did not want." Rosemary Manell came from the San Francisco area and moved in with Julia and Paul. She was, in Julia's words, "a marvel of cookery, workery, good humor, and everyone warms to her and loves her." Elizabeth Bishop headed a group of six to eight volunteers who "did prep," preparing food and washing dishes. In addition, there were Julia's elderly secretary, Gladys, a makeup artist, and two office managers, including Avis DeVoto.

Julia personally hired Rosie and Liz, who were her best buddies, both of whom had uncontrollable wit and appetites—Rosie for food and Liz for drink. Julia, who had put on weight after Paul's operation, had taken off fifteen pounds in Provence. She hoped to stay on her diet along with Rosie, who had arrived thirty pounds lighter (with that many more to go). "[Rosie has] a terrible duel with appetite and she is, as you say, a compulsive eater, as am I," Julia confided to Mary Frances in September. "If there is anything in sight anywhere I'll eat it unless I most sternly and with supreme willpower and reasoning turn from it."

The second series (More Company) included the same crew, with the addition of two young women: Marian Morash, the wife of Russ, and Sara Moulton, chef at a Boston catering company. (Neither woman knew the other was hired until they both showed up on the set.) Sara looked like a small teenager. After graduating second in a class of 450 from the Culinary Institute of America, she worked for several years in restaurants and wanted to leave catering. Both women, along with Rosie, were hired by Julia to help her with creative menu ideas. Marian worked three days, Sara two (the other five at a restaurant nearby). With the six or eight volunteers and everyone jealous for Julia's attention, it was soon evident Julia had to decide the pecking order. Characteristically, she gave everyone an executive position. Elizabeth Bishop was Executive Associate, Marian Morash Executive Chef, Sara Moulton Associate Executive Chef, and Rosemary Manell Food Stylist. Patricia (Pat) Pratt was in charge of buying and arranging the flowers for the dining-room table and the set (which Russ always thought was "too flowery").

Elizabeth played the "bad guy." A few of them found her difficult to work with, jealous and competitive. One described her always walking around with what looked like a water glass in her hand. Yet another noted, "Julia and Liz together were like Abbott and Costello." Paul always liked her naughty tongue, according to Judith Jones. Now she played the role that Paul had had in moving everything along and allowing Julia to be the "good guy." Liz, the women believed, could make anything happen. Surrounded by women with a serious purpose, Julia was again the center of the pack, the Head Girl, as she had been in Pasadena and Northampton.

"It was a Persian Circus," according to Morash. The women called themselves "Harmony Inc. Complete Food Production." In the introduction to the second volume of the books based on the two television series, Julia called them "our team," and later "a family of intimates." Rosemary said the "camaraderie was like the old sewing bees, like a party." Sara, who would marry a man in the music business, probably had the best tag: "Julia's Posse . . . rappers always have their posse":

> What is both so frustrating and so great about Julia is that she treated us all like equals [said Sara Moulton, chef of *Gourmet*'s kitchen in 1994]. She did not behave like a big, important teacher, like she was, or an expert. She really valued our opinions. There were times when I wished she had, because I wanted to sit at her feet and learn everything from her. She made us feel good. It was really an exciting experience.

Behind the elaborate plans for a series in which Julia and Paul would not have to work late hours was their lawyer, Bob Johnson. Johnson believed Julia was a national treasure who should be treated as such. Polaroid agreed and underwrote the series. He had spent several days the previous June at La Pitchoune planning the circumstances that would be best for Julia (and Paul): no work in their home, no shopping, no dismantling of the set, and plenty of assistants. According to one of Julia's colleagues in the food business, "Johnson was a very good lawyer, who negotiated good contracts for Julia."

The week began on Friday morning at the studio when at least ten people gathered—all but the film crew—for "talk-through" from 7:30 A.M. until they had lunch together. Final decisions were made on what dishes and procedures would be demonstrated and what food was to be purchased (Rosie went shopping). Monday was "cook-through," in which the same crew tried out the meal, and Tuesday was "dress rehearsal": Pat bought and arranged the flowers, Ruthie constructed the cue cards, Rosie chose the colors of plates and everything on the table, and the food crew prepared food for the next day's shoot (they made the chocolate cake thirteen times before getting it right).

The taping with fifteen people was done on Wednesday, with Russ Morash outside in an enormous bus full of television monitors and lights. Lines and cables connected him to the floor manager, who took his directions. Electricians and cameramen all had headphones and Julia was wired down the back of her blouse (she told Simca she would continue to wear the L'Ecole des

Trois Gourmandes insignia on her blouse). Although they had several versions of each of the three dishes at different stages of preparation, they took a break in filming between each section. At that time, Julia's silent partner Rosemary brought out the dish she had cooked in the prep kitchen and the still photographer went to work. They taped four hours in the morning, sat down to lunch with wine at a long table, then worked until late.

Paul was able to be in charge of keeping the knives sharpened and taking black-and-white photos for distribution from their home. He was always "amazed," he wrote Charlie, "that all these moving parts work so well together on each show." James D. (Jim) Scherer, a young professional still photographer, launched his career by taking all the color photographs for WGBH and for the books based on the two series.

Julia took direction well from strong men, her assistants noticed. In turn, Morash admired her because she was "curious, professional, and scholarly about her art . . . these are the three keys to Julia," he adds. "She was never casual. She does not sit around and worry, she trusts professionals. She trusted me! That was a responsibility. I wanted to do the best for her. She asked, 'Is that enough or should we do it again?' She always delivers."

After filming a couple of programs, Julia realized she could not both write the book and film the series. She needed a professional writer to draft the text for the program. At Peter Davison's suggestion, Julia hired Esther S. (Peggy) Yntema, a longtime editorial colleague of Davison's at the Atlantic Monthly Press. Peggy Yntema attended all the remaining talk-throughs, dress rehearsals, and tapings, even helping out on the set. With her excellent memory, she went home and typed up crucial points. She wrote the frontispiece material and introductions to the dinners, then got recipes from Julia and smoothed out the inconsistencies (asking Judith Jones for model recipe forms). Soon she was completing a chapter with each show. An examination of the drafts of the two books reveals that Peggy was the writer, Julia the rewriter. Julia wrote all over the "esy" (Yntema) drafts, taking out wording, such as a literary allusion to Henry V, saying, "It's not my style at all." Occasionally Peggy returned some phrasing to the text and Julia left it in on the second read ("It was completely unpredictable what she wanted in or out"). Remarkably, she captured Julia's voice well, and she had the book ready in time for the appearance of the series.

Chris Pullman did the layout, following Julia's desire to break up the visuals with lots of white space, headings, and subtitles ("We want it to look very magaziney"). Focusing on segments ("You do not want to read every single section every time you make the dish") reflected Julia's organized mind as well as the growing influence of slick food magazines in the 1970s (*Gourmet* was followed by *Bon Appétit, Food & Wine, The Cook's Magazine).* The photographs were lavish. Peggy made a major contribution by adding the shopping lists, suggestions on what to do with leftovers, alternatives to the menu, and variations at the end of each menu, looking back through Julia's other books so as not to be repetitive. Julia also wanted a postscript to each chapter, and they added menu alternatives and "cooking to bring" (when invited to dinner) to fill out the slim book. (In the second volume, they added a gazetteer and dropped the menu alternatives.) When the first volume was in galleys, Julia—in a further easing up on control—allowed others to proofread and took Paul to Provence for four months.

When the first book appeared in 1978, Knopf printed 190,000 copies, and it was an alternative selection of the Book-of-the-Month Club. Peggy was surprised: "I read the proof and saw my name on the title page ["In collaboration with E. S. Yntema"]. It would have been terribly ungracious to say no, thank you, but I would have preferred not to have my name used." Indeed, the copyright page rightly lists her as "joint author." After anonymously serving as midwife to a number of noteworthy books at the Atlantic Monthly Press, including a famous novel of the decade, she preferred anonymity. She was also surprised by a large royalty check (Julia had added a share of the royalties to Peggy's contractual flat fee) and gave $2,000 to the Schlesinger Library in Julia Child's name.

Peggy Yntema, who preferred the first volume ("fresher and less strained") to the second, said of Julia's organizational skills: "She could have been a general." Of her character: "There is absolutely no falsehood to Julia at all; she cannot gild the lily; perfectionism is very important; she will make any number of tries to get it just right." Of her style: "Her conversational style was born before she met Paul; her conversational style is so much like her books." A good example of the style ("Julia wrote this section herself") is found in the recipe for cassoulet, where she discusses what in private she would call farting: "Intestinal motility is polite gobbledygook for flatulence, which in turn means gas," then quotes the scientists at the USDA on beans and their digestive qualities.

WGBH made a one-time payment to Julia for each program (most of which was used to pay her extra assistants) and no residuals, though the programs ran for twenty years. Julia did not make money on any series, but she did on the books based on the series. At this point she had combined sales of more than a million books. As she told food writer Barbara Sims-Bell, "I don't think that I made fifty dollars a television show; there is no money on public television. Caterers probably make more money." She told the *New York Times* the same thing, adding, "I don't do anything commercial except selling books of mine." In 1991, Wings Books (distributed by Knopf) combined the two books—hurriedly, it would seem, from the number of typographical errors—in a big slick book entitled *Julia Child's Menu Cookbook*.

THE RESEARCHER AND THE CRITICS

Jack Shelton in San Francisco, whom Clark Wolf calls the first food writer (pre-Claiborne) to call himself a "restaurant critic," was Julia's most devoted reviewer. He praised two qualities in her: "Julia knows how to listen" and she possesses an "unslakable thirst for greater knowledge." The women who worked with her all recall her intense curiosity and her investigation of food-related issues, contacting national scientific groups such as the Bureau of Weights and Measures when she went on a losing crusade to promote the metric system. She told an exhausted Marian Morash, who was going home to her family, that Marian should "work on a fish terrine a certain way" and Julia would try another way and they would compare notes in the morning. Julia herself remembers trying to get a certain recipe from "a nasty French pastry woman who had a world-famous flourless cake." When the woman refused, Julia spent years of experimenting until she made her own *gâteau Victoire au chocolat* with whipped cream in time for *Julia Child & Company*.

A passage in a letter to Louisette at the end of 1978 reveals another reason for Julia's persistent research: "There are now so many people in this country, teaching and writing, who have had wonderful training such as working in restaurants in France, taking courses at Lenôtre, etc. I can't pretend to keep up with them. It is amazing what a revolution in cooking has taken place in this country—I wonder if young people in France are that much interested? Or as expert? It has perhaps not yet happened there as it has here."

"I learn something new every day," she told one reporter. "It's endless. You're never going to live long enough. I would very much like to go over to Paris to go to the Lenôtre pastry and catering school." She also wanted to study charcuterie. Again she told a Chicago reporter, "I'd like to get some more training. . . . Maybe I could work as an interpreter at La Varenne."

When Marian Morash suggested Julia come to Nantucket, where she was chef for three years at the (summer-only) Straight Wharf restaurant, Julia spent a weekend in mid-August cooking on-line with the crew, serving 80 to 90 customers for lunch and 125 for dinner. With delight, she reported to Simca that she had done "actual on-line cooking" for the first time, detailing the dishes she helped to prepare. She reveled in the adventure, the learning, and the camaraderie.

Hard work does not immunize one to criticism; indeed, and publicity attracts it. The first reviews in October 1978 brought a new attack by Madeleine Kamman, who sent Julia a copy of a letter to a Boston periodical in which she said Julia opened her oysters with "a can opener," but "I will continue clicking an oyster open every fifteen seconds with an oyster knife." Julia did not reply, as usual, but noted at the bottom of Kamman's missive that fifteen seconds was slow. Through the years Julia did not write or utter Kamman's name, yet never failed to report to Simca every appearance in the media of "your French pupil from Newton." The following year Kamman informed Julia by letter that she was professionally dying in the small town of Boston, where Julia's celebrity made her the only person to know. Soon afterward Kamman made the front page with news that she was returning to her native France to "battle the sexism of the French cooking establishment"—because the people of Boston did not appreciate her restaurant. The *Philadelphia Inquirer* reported that she was going back to France to open a restaurant run entirely by women. When asked if anyone cooked better than she, she replied perhaps Frédy Girardet—maybe not better, but as well as she. (Many considered Girardet, in Crissier outside Lausanne, the best chef in the world.) Julia, in reporting this to Simca, added that "life will lose much of its savor without her, that's for sure."

Privately to Simca or Ruth Lockwood, Julia could refer to Simca's former pupil with some favorite epithet, but she also acknowledged Kamman's talent and teaching skills. Chez la Mère Madeleine at the Modern Gourmet cooking school in Newton Center, which was opened in 1974, was sold to several of Kamman's cooking school pupils in 1980 (at which point Julia and Paul visited, but were disappointed). One magazine called Kamman a "Woman with a Vision" and pictured her in Annecy, but the *Boston Globe* called her "the Cast-Iron Lady." By 1983 she had opened a school in New Hampshire as well as Annecy and several years later settled in the Napa Valley to teach chefs. Eventually, her resentment against Julia abated somewhat as her reputation as a teacher of teachers became secure.

Julia Child & Company, which focused on occasions, sold very well and won the 1978 Tastemaker Award (voted on by a nationwide panel of book and periodical editors) as well as the American Book Award ("the only cookbook to win a major literary prize," Jane Davison noted). Marcella Hazan's *More Classic Italian Cooking* and the Troisgros brothers' *The Nouvelle Cuisine of Jean and Pierre Troisgros* were runners-up. *Julia Child & More Company,* which focused on specific dishes, was not bought by New York public television and sales of the book were poor until she began a cross-country tour. Nevertheless, she was named Woman of the Year in 1979 by the New England chapter of the National Academy of Television Arts and Sciences. The following year, the Katharine Branson School, at its sixtieth anniversary celebration, bestowed on her one of its Distinguished Alumnae Awards.

Reviewers of her books praised the variety of her dishes and the clarity of her recipes. In the *New York Times Book Review,* Mimi Sheraton praised Julia's streamlined (from four- to one-hour) puff pastry recipe ("alone worth the price of the book"), but mentioned "some unnecessarily gimmicky recipes (skewered vegetable salad) that smack of ladies' magazine cookery." Because Julia had said it was silly to fawn over the French, she was accused of a "patronizing view of the French."

Another criticism of the first book by reviewers was of its use of older recipes to fill out a menu (though only new recipes were demonstrated on the tapes). Between the two series and their books, Peggy Yntema composed a detailed assessment of the recipes, at which time Julia hired more assistants. A careful look at the dishes that were repeated in these volumes, however, reveals that Julia's recipes evolved and improved. They were "recast into the prevailing food style," one food writer noted, giving as an example the bouillabaisse made with chicken as the centerpiece of a low-calorie dinner. Julia did not just copy recipes. The most striking example, other than the new puff pastry, is her cassoulet, which she says on page 72 of the second volume is her fourth version, each "lighter and leaner."

Ratings for the television series were modest (the time slot was not prime) and the book reviews were sparse, but rarely negative. The *Chicago Tribune* said her meals were "syncopated like jazz." All reviewers noted the emphasis on shopping, preparing a full meal, and serving the meal, with most preferring the highly personal approach; another reviewer, however, thought the books were "too chummy." Most newspaper writers focused on Julia herself, for her honest directness always gave the reporters a good quote. For example, Jeannette Ferrary featured the reasons why America found Julia Child so interesting—everything from her eccentricity to her feeling comfortable with being a woman. Ferrary adds: "She gives us a Magic Show every week, with slapstick (she's a little like *I Love Lucy),"* and always seems to be having a good time. Of course, the last line in Julia's very first book was "Above all have a good time." Julia wrote in the introduction to *More Company,* "It's more fun cooking *for* company *in* company."

Often reviews indulged culinary metaphors, but few as cleverly as Stephen Wadsworth, who was once editor of *Opera News:* "She's a serenely gawky six feet one [sic] inch, a ripe roast of *gourmande* stuffed with fresh chortle, chesty guffaws, and twenty cloves of humor. She's wrapped in a no-nonsense dress and poured into two one-quart sensible shoes, and she serves herself with quantities of élan." Ferrary and Wadsworth were exceptions to the journalists who for decades covered Julia using the same profiles and clichés. Julia never made a meal of her past, yet was asked by reporters for the same basic menu over and over.

If journalists were soft, her colleagues were not. One friend called the second volume "not up to her standards." Yet, M. F. K. Fisher, who did not like the first volume, praised the language of the second: "1,000% better *in every way* . . . more pure class . . . more true spirit of Julia's own spirit." The innovative use of ginger in butternut squash, the inclusion of a vegetarian dinner and a low-calorie dinner, and Julia's reinterpretations of classic dishes such as chicken melon and vegetarian gâteau are all praised twenty years later by Betty Rosbottom, food writer and cooking school owner. Rosbottom particularly commends Julia's wit, illustrated by her *poulet de Charente à la melonaise* in the first volume and, in the second, "Una furtiva lagrima," a postscript on ways to peel an onion (echoing the opera *L'Elisir d'Amore*).

$\mathcal{T}$AKING THE POSSE ON THE ROAD

Julia, Sara, and Marian stood behind a long table on the stage in a contest to see who could make the fastest and best spun caramel cage. They were giving a benefit for the Schlesinger Library of Radcliffe College in 1979, and Julia knew how to put on a good show. Recalled Marian: "She used a glass bowl, I used one covered with Saran Wrap, and Sara used something else. The audience of five hundred went crazy. The suspense was breathless as Julia said 'okay,' and we dribbled the warm caramel. Mine came off first and people screamed with joy, but Julia did not care that hers was not perfect; it was a performance. She did not have to have the perfect dish, as other cooks would have insisted upon."

When the familiar seasonal rhythm called for her Provençal interlude, she and Paul were eager "to sit under our olive tree and breathe in the air of Provence." Julia brought all their Christmas cards unopened for five months and had them answered by mid-June. She took time out for a week in Spain and a week in England, where she made brief television spots for the release of the English version of *From Julia Child's Kitchen* ("Nobody will take me for a home economist!" she told Elizabeth David). Her sense of the contrast between the two countries (she had never been in Spain before) says much about her: she loved the people (if not the food) of Spain, a country reminding her in its broad plains and scattered great oak trees of Southern California, whereas in cold, damp England, there was a "lack of openly expressed gutsy sensuality," she informed Mary Frances. "Things just don't work very well there in old Blighty, but we adore our English friends." After a dinner with Mark and Anne in Paris, Julia and Paul took the Concorde home because Bob Johnson told them to spend more money.

Though Julia was not one to rush back for reunions, she returned for the hundred-year celebration of Hubbard House at Smith, where she and room-mate Mary Warner reminisced about Julia's trip to the speakeasy in her con-vertible. When she told a local reporter she would "rather eat a tablespoon of Charlotte Malakoff than three bowls of Jell-O," she was revealing how far the young, jelly-donut-eating coed had come.

"She is a tomorrow person, not a yesterday person," said Russ Morash. "I frankly love that about her." Julia's present and her future would be as a public person, the representative of good cooking and eating and a major television personality. Her public appearances included a nomination at the Emmy Awards in Los Angeles in 1978 and speaking at the graduation cere-mony of the Culinary Institute of America in 1979. She also judged the na-tional Beef Cook-Off in Omaha, Nebraska, in 1979 and in Scottsdale, Arizona, in 1980 ("I need my beef," she was fond of saying, much to the dismay of a growing number of vegetarians in America). She taught with Rosemary at a weekend school called Cooking at the Cove, on the Sonoma peninsula in California. For the *Boston Herald American,* she judged the food at Boston Red Sox's Fenway Park (the hot dog was "thin and pale," but she liked the beer and popcorn). If she could join 30,000 fans to taste their food and watch the Red Sox, perhaps they would watch her in their homes. Indeed, most did, even if they had no intention of preparing one of her recipes.

Paul still went along to every appearance and performance, even after he was diagnosed with "prostate malignancy" in July 1979 and began a series of radium treatments. Julia told Simca earlier that his "understanding of the spoken word was getting more difficult." As one representative of Knopf noticed: "Paul would drift in and out of paying attention, but she was incredi-bly sweet about making him a part of it all: he sat at the table and signed the books with her. She is a tough old broad, but she is kind, and having him sign was a way to keep him a part of things." Occasionally he would add a pithy remark to an interview ("She only liked food and men").

Every member of her troupe reported the same enjoyment ("She likes to have fun"), weight gain, and exhaustion upon traveling with her: "I was a wet rag left in her wake," said one of her publicity directors half her age. "When I needed a nap, she would say, 'Let's go to the tall gals shop (The Forgotten Woman, Lane Bryant, or Big and Tall)!'" Another observed pointedly: "Even when the line was two blocks long, she was gracious. People do not stand in line for shits. She was as pleasant to the first person as to the last one, four hours later. She stays to the bitter end."

In 1979 Julia assisted both Simca and Louisette with their respective newly published books. When Julia was busy filming *More Company* in April 1979, Doubleday asked if she would read the galleys of the English translation of Louisette's *French Cuisine for All* and write an endorsement, a request she could not turn down. But when Doubleday asked the next month if she would write her own memoirs, she called it "an impossible enterprise." Julia arranged with the Schlesinger Library at Radcliffe to give a reception for Simca when she toured the country in late 1979 and early 1980.

ℛELUCTANT TOUR

At the beginning of taping the *More Company* series, Julia (almost sixty-seven) said to Simca, "We all had *so much fun* cooking together . . . however this *is the end—no more.*" While correcting proofs for the book four months later, just after Paul's hospitalization, she added: "But this is THE END, Finito. No more TV, no more anything of that sort, and I am even hoping I won't have to go out and promote it this time. I'm really saying [no to] anything, and hope that will do the trick." Then she added: "I'm really getting tired of all the cuisine brouhaha, jockeying for place and prestige."

Because she stayed home in 1979 to work personally on the proofs of *More Company,* publication was delayed until November, too late for a tour before Christmas. Therefore, after a two-week trip to the usual spots in California, Julia and Paul left for Provence just before Christmas of 1979. It was cold and damp, Paul got influenza, and their pussy cat died. Judith Jones, who called Julia in the hopes of setting up a book tour, found Julia enjoying herself despite the weather, illness, and her cat's death. She had eleven people for Christmas dinner, including a writer and photographer from *Bon Appétit* magazine. But Paul was unhappy and chilly and told her he did not want to return again in the winter. Though she did not want to leave, Julia knew, as she told one journalist in January 1980: "As soon as you're off television, in a few months nobody will know who you are, which is fine. That makes fame quite bearable." Bearable because one can always quit, though she was not ready to do that.

Upon their return, Julia embarked on a thirteen-city tour in three weeks. Initially the schedule was geared for plenty of rest for Paul, but opportunities for appearances were added as the tour went along. *McCall's,* where several recipes were previously published in shorter form (exactly three per volume), took out full-page advertisements. (She had been writing her monthly column since 1977.) Knopf had a new publicity director named Janice Goldklang, who arranged promotions with Macy's and Bloomingdale's. These stores sent invitations to their credit-card customers, "who would pour in," according to Goldklang:

> A thousand people would show up, for her celebrity was a big deal. . . . You should see the cookbooks people brought to have her sign. You could eat them, they were so covered with food; and the pages were torn and covers fallen off. They would say, "This is my most beloved book."
> . . . Whatever city they visited, the Wednesday papers would have huge features; sales were worth the expense for the department store. It doesn't happen this way anymore.

Knopf, who scheduled Julia on every show from Dick Cavett to Johnny Carson, paid for Julia, Paul, Liz Bishop (and Rosie or Marian to do prep work). Julia had to fly first-class because of her height. She needed the same leg room in cars, so she preferred sitting up in the front with the limo driver, adds Goldklang, who arranged for hairdresser, makeup person, and limousine.

"We were awfully lucky," Julia said to reporter Nao Hauser, who was catching an interview on the way to O'Hare Airport after the Chicago appearance. Just as Julia was recalling her romance with Paul in 1946 and "going to Paris with my loved one," she noticed Paul stumbling up ahead, then turning back toward her. To the reporter, out of earshot of Paul, Julia said, "Oh, it's rotten getting old," and hurried to guide him to the limousine, hand him his cap and briefcase, and assure him that she was there. She was now the anchor, haven, and direction for her once wise and worldly guide.

She began the tour reluctantly, for Paul's infirmities complicated the logistics. She did not intend to leave him behind nor would she allow her career to languish. She loved the action, and she was their major financial support. As her career moved away from cookbook writing, she had to continue tours, demonstrations, and television.

"It's my job," she would say. But the contact with people energized her. She did, in fact, enjoy her career and could not imagine the adventure coming to an end. Her only problem was her knees. "[My] cartilage is worn out from standing around too much," she wrote Mary Frances on September 30, 1980. "It will gradually get worse and when [I] can't walk, [I] will get an operation (new joint). This is the first real evidence of the machine wearing out (except for the glasses) that I've had so far."

They concluded their tour on the West Coast with Dorothy and Ivan in

San Francisco, and then Los Angeles, where Charlie was now living with his daughter Rachel. Julia appeared on all the major talk shows, including one day on both *The Mike Douglas Show* at 1:15 P.M. and Johnny Carson's *Tonight* show at 5 P.M.

*T*HE SINCEREST FORM OF FLATTERY:
PASTICHE AND PARODY

The most famous talk show incident occurred on the *Tomorrow* show, hosted by Tom Snyder, when Julia appeared with Jacques Pépin, who had been on the show five or six times before. "Julia brought enough food to feed a hundred people, and I was late," said Pépin, who always carried his knife with him. Before they began their hour and a half of cooking, she cut her hand with his knife. According to Pamela Henstell (Knopf's West Coast representative), Julia wrapped a towel around her hand and went to the hospital afterward: "To Julia it was nothing, but it was a very big cut," adds Henstell. Julia says she went to the first-aid station on the Burbank lot. Pépin recalls that they got the studio infirmary to bandage the wound, then went out to eat afterward at L'Ermitage restaurant ("after she had stitches and a tetanus shot"). Julia also claims that Jacques said something very macho, such as "She's probably not used to sharp knives." She was not amused. Though the stories differ, they all agree on the cut and that Tom Snyder brought up the topic on the program. News traveled fast at NBC. The story lives on through repeated showings of Dan Aykroyd's "reenactment" on *The Best of Saturday Night Live.*

Comedian Dan Aykroyd, dressed in full Julia drag, stood with a large knife in one hand and a naked chicken in the other. Adopting her high swinging vibrato and gay anticipation, he announced the making of a *poularde demidésossée* and began talking about the uses of the giblets and liver. The *Saturday Night Live* audience recognized the parody and was convulsed in laughter. "You can't do nothin' without a sharp knife," he said as he ran the knife along the spine of the chicken, "toward the pope's nose," he said, presumably slicing off his thumb. The bleeding began. Mimicking her unflappability in crisis, her desire to turn any adversity into a teaching experience, he kept right on talking as the blood spurted profusely, filling the pan holding the chicken. "Chicken livers are a natural coagulant!" he said, applying one to his spurting hand. Chattering calmly on about every home needing the 911 number programmed into its phone, he reached for the phone: "It's a prop phone. What a shame . . . ," he said, dropping it to the counter. "Why are you all spinning?" he asked the audience as the blood shot over the table and floor. Voice fading, he began slumping toward the table. Weakened by the loss of blood, he called *"Bon appétit!"* and hit the Formica (to great applause), then raised his head once to gasp, "Save the liver!"

It may have been one of Aykroyd's (and *Saturday Night Live*'s) finest hours, but it was not the first or the last Julia Child parody.

This parody, and the apocryphal stories of her dropping chickens and ducks on the floor and swigging wine (the latter she resented strongly), were part of the lore of a beloved television figure. The accidental cutting off of Aykroyd's thumb at least had a semblance of basis in fact. Paul's letters record her tripping on the way to the table and spilling the salad for six people all over the tiles in La Pitchoune. At least three times she broke her toe. Several times she cut her hands and had to see a doctor. When Simca was coming to dinner, Julia cut her hand while trimming butternut squash and had to go to the hospital while Sara Moulton finished the meal for eleven. Julia was back in time to eat with everyone. Stories of her car accidents, particularly backing out of her driveway, are repeated by colleagues and employees. In the summer of 1978, after "a little episode," they had to get another rental car and stick to the larger roads in Provence. Another friend evokes Julia's joie de vivre in a story of Julia driving her car toward a crowded intersection in Provence and shouting out one of her favorite expressions: "Lurch!"

Fannie Flagg also did a takeoff on Julia earlier in her career. M. F. K. Fisher wrote to ask Julia if she saw the spoof of her by Fannie Flagg: "I did think it was quite funny, and hope you do too." Carol Burnett did a takeoff on Julia for her 1968 variety show, Englishman John Cleese gave a convincing imitation, and "Sister Julia, Child of God" cooks the poisonous stew in *Nunsense,* a musical comedy by Dan Goggin. Julia learned to take them all in stride and was known to play the Aykroyd tape that NBC sent her.

The dozens of cartoons that appeared over forty years assumed that every reader knew Julia Child: two thin men staring enviously at three fat men in a television studio ("They're the crew for the Julia Child show"); Macbeth's three witches peering into their cauldron and holding a copy of a cookbook with Julia Child's name on it; "The Cat Who Tasted Cinnamon" refused food until its owner studied Julia Child. More references appeared in the beloved "Beetle Bailey" cartoon strip than in any others.

From *The Muppets* to *Saturday Night Live,* she understood the humor and the compliment. It was only when manufacturers crossed the line, calling their products "Julia Chives" or "Julia Chicken," that she saw their intentions for what they were and had her lawyer take action. Any "use of her name for advertising purposes" was a "con game" and "hucksterism." Ocean Spray Cranberries was threatened and withdrew its cartoon character named "Julia

Chicken"; the Sheraton Hotel in Boston promptly withdrew an advertisement that suggested her endorsement when the lawsuit was drawn up; one company paid $5,000, another $40,000. All proceeds went to public television. Such integrity allowed her to praise a blender by name onstage or comment on the tasteless mealiness of an apple by name (even if the apple grower was sponsoring the event).

Her lawyer seriously considered an offer by a ceramics company for a line of Julia Child ware in 1979. He allowed the talk to move to six figures, discussing with Julia scholarships for study at La Varenne, until the correspondence suddenly stopped. She nixed the idea. Occasionally she would allow a company to use the cover of a book, but not her name or photograph. She did allow her name to be used in a French textbook, but that was in keeping with her career as teacher and her association with educational television.

GOOD MORNING AMERICA

In 1980 she finally became associated with commercial television, telling Mary Frances she was "now through with public television." She had appeared on many commercial television stations before, but never on a regular basis. Now she began cooking on ABC's *Good Morning America,* a sort of variety show interspersed with news. Julia performed two-and-a-half-minute cooking spots produced by Sonya Selby-Wright, from whom she willingly took orders as she did from her editor, Judith Jones. Julia earned $605 per appearance plus expenses for herself and an assistant. She took the job less for the money than because public television was not using her. And she was able, she told Mary Frances, to "do six spots in just a few hours." Nevertheless, "Julia's segments were a bigger production than the others," says Jane Bollinger, who would become her second producer.

Julia explained to John Wadsworth, an interviewer for PBS-TV, New York: "We just KILLED ourselves [on *Julia Child & More Company].* We had the best team we've ever had. But PBS—I don't know whether they forgot we taped it or what, but it never got on in New York, and if you're not on in New York, you ain't nowhere." Just beginning to warm up to her subject, she went on:

> Knopf . . . gave the advance for the book, and [the series] never got off the ground, and I just thought to hell with that. It's a twelve-hour day and a seven-day week, and I'm not going to go into that kind of thing and have it just lay an egg. That's a damn good book, and they were

damn good shows and very original recipes. A lot of places didn't get it because they never announced that it was going out there and everybody made their fall schedules without it. So I'm through, frankly. It was so good, that's what annoys me.

Wadsworth published what sounded like her farewell to PBS in *Dial* and added: "Julia is a gentlewoman and a scholar, a cook in the classical tradition who is just as preoccupied with *la nature des choses*—the essential flavor of things—as any of the people she calls the nouvelle boys."

After she taped the first group of spots for *Good Morning America,* she hired another person to help her when ABC took her on permanently and planned to shoot on a variety of locations, whether on a shrimp boat or wherever Julia happened to be. Nancy Verde Barr was a perky five-foot-two-inch cooking school owner—Paul soon named her "Sparkle Plenty"—who was in charge of the "food stuff" for the demonstrations. Julia was impressed by her efficiency and invited her to lunch in Boston to meet Sara and Liz. Incidentally, Nancy had studied with Madeleine Kamman, now in Europe, but left when she got pregnant before completing her practice cooking experience. "I loved working for Julia. Her mind is so incredible. Something is always happening in her life," says Nancy. "She is nurturing but not motherly. She takes people under her wing, but she is very businesslike and nonjudgmental. When she hired me, she did not hold it against me that I had studied with Kamman." By 1981 Nancy was an integral part of the team; and Julia's spot ran every Tuesday morning at 8:40, during the last half hour of *Good Morning America.*

Julia's two latest books, still selling well as the 1980s began, reflected the changes in America's growing obsession with food. "There was a big wave of home cooking through the late seventies," says Mimi Sheraton. Certainly Julia—as well as the Cuisinart, the pasta machine, and television cooking—ignited the trend, she adds. Claiborne long encouraged home cooking in his *Times* articles, which gave real (not home economist's) recipes. If you were a good person, you made your own ice cream, notes Sheraton, it was almost a moral imperative. If you were a serious cook, you bought a Garland range. Perhaps because they were tired of the Vietnam War and Watergate, Americans focused their interest on home cooking. Tired too of the classical or codified approach to anything, cooks turned to American regional food and to ethnic food, as evidenced by the broad array of new cookbooks: Diana Kennedy, *The Cuisines of Mexico;* Madhur Jaffrey, *An Invitation to Indian Cooking;* Marcella Hazan, *The Classic Italian Cook Book;* Paula Wolfert, *Couscous and Other Good Food from Morocco.*

America was also waking up to problems in food. The health food counterculture, begun as early as the 1890s, surged in the 1960s and, with each new scientific study, grew steadily through the 1970s. Julia eagerly read and investigated all the reports, beginning with Rachel Carson's *Silent Spring* (1962) and the first studies on cholesterol in 1969. She was also aware of a young woman who opened a small restaurant in California in 1971 called Chez Panisse, where only organic foods and garden produce were served: Alice Waters would become the mother of what was then an intellectual and bohemian approach to food, eventually labeled California cuisine. "I'm [also] interested in the freshness and goodness of produce," Julia told reporter Susan Rogers, but then pointed out that there are not enough horses for the manure to feed 200 million people organically. "Several hundred people per day are dying of hunger in Pakistan; there's a need for scientific agriculture," she insisted.

Underlying all her answers to each food crisis was her sense of the practical and her trust in the essential good nature of people. Because the first decade of her culinary education was in Europe and because of her good health, hearty pioneer stock, joie de vivre, and casual approach to life's worries, she resisted joining any crusades or food-fear causes. She was more worried about overpopulation, hence her commitment to Planned Parenthood. The fear of mercury in swordfish in 1972 led to a remark about how much of the fish would have to be eaten in order to endanger one's life. Moderation is what she preached. Moderation and a balanced diet. She was a teacher and a promoter of pleasure in eating.

Chapter 24

PACIFIC OVERTURES
(1981 – 1984)

"I am, as you know, a Californian,
and still have that feeling in my bones . . ."

JULIA CHILD to Louisette Bertholle,
January 20, 1981

~

IN SANTA BARBARA, where steep green mountains meet the blue Pacific,
Julia and Paul found a home amid what she called "towering eucalyptus trees
that smelled sweet and spicy." Great twisted oaks, heavily perfumed camellia
bushes, and the sounds of birds and pounding waves made Montecito Shores
a paradise. Of course, the costs were high, since there were no high-rise buildings permitted under the city's strict building code, and after weeks of renting
and looking at condominiums, they became accustomed to the prices. When
Bob Johnson assured them the money they had in bonds was making less for
them than real estate would, they made the leap, buying a top-floor apartment
in a three-story, secured community across the street from what used to be
called Montecito Park when Julia was a child.

On a hill twenty miles away at Hope Ranch, Julia's parents had courted
in the early spring of 1905, when Caro Weston brought her sister Dorothy
Dean to the desert climate for her health, where they found Easterners sunning themselves, playing tennis, golf, and bridge. Young Johnnie McWilliams
came courting to take the two Weston girls horseback riding in the hills.

Seventy-six years later, in 1981, Easterners still migrated to Santa Barbara, including Caro and John McWilliams's eldest daughter, Julia, who preferred a beach near the city. "Montecito is indeed a bit of heaven," Julia wrote Mary Frances Fisher.

$\mathscr{S}$ANTA BARBARA BEACH

Julia settled in at Seaview Drive in Montecito Shores, just yards from her summer playing field. For years the McWilliams family had rented a large gray shingled house on the grounds of what became the Biltmore Hotel, with its Spanish red tiles and bougainvillea, white stucco arches and vast green lawn sweeping to the sea. Her brother John was born in this town in 1914 when Julia was two years old. Now many of her Pasadena childhood friends returned to their summer town of Santa Barbara to retire. "Our gerontology group," she called them, especially when they engaged in memory recitals and lists of all those who had "slipped off the raft." What an expression, she exclaimed, and would be busy when they next called. Unfortunately, Charlie Child was no longer in Southern California. Recovered from his two-year depression after the death of Freddie, he left daughter Rachel's Pasadena home and was now living in a senior citizen home near his old house in Lumberville, Pennsylvania.

The warm sea breezes through their third-floor windows, the walks along the beach each day, and the warm swimming pool nearby offered daily succor for the seventy-nine-year-old and infirm Paul. Julia even enjoyed the domestic convenience of a nearby trash chute and the elevator beside her front door that whisked them belowground to their car. Both saved her aching knee, now almost stripped of cartilage. But she had no plans to be caught up in a swirl of retirement parties and litanies of death. No retirement in the near future for her!

The year 1981 was a watershed in her life and in the larger culinary world: the purchase of a third home, where they intended to spend their winters and eventually settle; a greater involvement in furthering the cooking profession—a heavy schedule of live teaching in cooking schools and, most significantly, the founding of the American Institute of Wine and Food. Also during this time she made two promises that ensured full activities for years to come: to become food editor of *Parade* magazine in 1982 and to make a new television series, this time in Santa Barbara, in 1983. It was as if the warm Pacific breezes gave her a second or third wind, as it would the new President of the United States (just a few months older than Julia), who lived here when winter weather threatened the District of Columbia. Ronald and Nancy Reagan owned Rancho del Cielo high in the hills above the Childs. Nancy was also a Smith graduate, Julia pointed out to Avis DeVoto, who was in snowbound Cambridge when she issued a needless warning: "Don't turn into one of those California Republicans!"

"Because the continental shelf drops down so fast here, the fish selection is now immense," Julia wrote Simca, Avis, and Louisette. The Dungeness crab, fresh shrimp, spiny lobsters, and sea bass excited her, as did the "wonderful fresh vegetables" from nearby Oxnard. The restaurants were nothing to get excited about, but she would soon have an impact on the local food scene. She turned the dining room next to her kitchen into a study, Paul hung pots and pans in the kitchen, and Julia enjoyed cooking with all the fresh local produce at home. Not unlike others who move to California, she was on a diet, having slowly put on weight through the years. She had heard about the new diet sweeping the country when she went to her Cambridge hairdresser and complimented his slimmed-down waist. She walked straight to a local bookstore after the shampoo and set to buy Herman Tarnower's *The Complete Scarsdale Medical Diet.*

By 1980, as Robert Clark points out in his biography of Beard, the American public had become schizophrenic about its food: encouraged to eat deep-fat-fried potato skins, McDonald's hamburgers, and goat cheese with their bitter green salads on the one hand, and on the other to monitor fat, cholesterol, sugar, and salt and take up jogging. Media images conveyed the full range from hearty-eating gourmets (James Beard was extreme at 260 pounds) to Twiggy-thin commercial models.

Throughout Beard's life, Clark notes, he "could effectively lose weight only as a captive in hospitals and clinics, a Ulysses of appetite lashed to the mast." Julia's weight never varied widely because she did not have an eating disorder. At age forty-two (after purchasing her first pair of reading glasses) she put on eight pounds in ten days of pasta eating in Italy, pounds which she quickly lost. Upon quitting smoking after her mastectomy in 1968, she gained ten pounds in three months. This time, after taking the ten pounds off, she slowly put back twenty. When she decided to lose weight in 1974 on a 1,200-calorie diet, she lost ten and put back twenty—typical of dieting patterns. By 1981 she realized she would have to change her eating patterns permanently and found a jump start with the high-protein, low-carbohydrate Scarsdale plan. The daily discipline appealed to her very nature, and the weight came off. When she was filming a series of spots for *Good Morning America* that fall, food writer Betty Fussell made a note on her taped interview about Julia's "slender hips" and the "length of torso from waist down. [We] don't see this on [the] TV frame, but she has an elegance that is not the bosomy matron projected from the waist up."

Julia turned her weight-loss and change-of-eating routine into a lengthy article with recipes for one of her monthly *McCall's* articles. In this, one of her last features, she vowed, "I do solemnly swear that I shall never be fat again." She kept her word. After all, she was nearly seventy, not able to exercise as much because her knees bothered her, and constantly surrounded by food. At home she cooked lighter, as illustrated in the fat-free tomato sauce she featured in the *McCall's* article—a sauce that could be used in stews, a squid dish, chicken bouillabaisse, and any pasta dish. The recipe included ripe tomatoes (chopped and drained), canned Italian plum tomatoes or tomato paste, and small green tomatoes, but the flavor came from the onion, garlic, half cup of wine, a few drops of hot-pepper sauce, pinch of saffron, and basil (or thyme or oregano). She simmered the mixture, cooled it, then kept it in her refrigerator in a covered jar. When she dined out, she learned to leave food on her plate. She could take just two bites of a rich dessert. But she never gave up quality products such as "rich creamery butter" (the three words always went together in her vocabulary). Everything, but in moderation.

Except for two months in the spring and two months in the fall in Cambridge, Paul and Julia spent the first year in Santa Barbara. They even canceled their trip to France (for the first time in nearly twenty years), to have two porches enclosed for extra space in their condominium. They left only to tape *Good Morning America* in New York City and to fulfill commitments to conventions and professional organizations.

"Only Moses disrupting the Red Sea caused more commotion than Julia Child's hike down the housewares-jammed aisles of McCormick Place in Chicago." She fingered, squeezed, patted, bent, and lifted the new appliances, skillets, and microwaves at the National Housewares Manufacturers Association's semiannual exhibition. Yes, she would try anything in her kitchen if she could send it back. "I am not a prisoner of any manufacturer," she informed a reporter. The next year they invited her back as the principal speaker.

"THE LIGHTBULB DINNER"

Gertrude Stein was correct when she said the French love to talk about talking about food. But conversation among foodies is not always about the food eaten yesterday, today, and tomorrow. During a Santa Barbara dinner on February 9, 1981, at the home of a woman named Flora Courtois, the talk turned to doing something significant about the way Americans cook and eat. The dinner was initiated by Richard Graff, whom Julia had met earlier in Provence and then at his (and his brother's) Chalone Winery in Sonoma County. He invited Julia and Paul to dinner, again enlisting his friend Shirley Sarvis. Also at the dinner was Robert Huttenback, then chancellor of the University of California in Santa Barbara.

They would dub this evening "The Lightbulb Dinner." It began when Julia expressed frustration about there being no educational center for culinary arts and sciences, which she believed was not acknowledged as a very serious subject for study in the United States. She seemed ready to take on American academia the way she had tackled French cooking thirty years before.

"It is a shame that the program they have at Antioch is not more of a success," Julia remarked, comparing gastronomy to architecture—"you have the history, theory, and the hands-on as well."

"Well, why don't we do it out here at the University of California?" Bob Huttenback remarked. "There is a piece of land with a house out on the west campus [by the ocean] that is not being used."

Such was the beginning of what would ultimately be called the American Institute of Wine and Food, but the talk that day had less to do with an "institute" than with an academic center like that tried by Professor John Ronsheim of Antioch College in Ohio. Ronsheim was a brilliant eccentric who championed academic degrees in food studies. ("He was nuts and full of wonderful, crazy ideas," says Alice Waters.) Julia was keen for education; Huttenback (a historian) was interested in an independent research center and clearinghouse outside the traditional academic disciplines. Anticipating the faculty response, he said it was too early for an academic program. He was a creative chancellor at the Santa Barbara campus for three years, raised millions for the university, and was determined to turn what was called "Surfer Tech" into a world center of academic excellence.

The group met a second time in July, this time at Julia's Seaview condominium, with Rosemary helping her prepare the lunch of stuffed quail. The group now included Robert Mondavi and his wife, Margrit Biever, Kate Firestone, Alice Waters, and British-born Jeremiah Tower, former chef at Waters's Chez Panisse, now owner of the Balboa Café (and later Stars). Marion Cunningham, who (with Jeri Laber) had rescued the old *Boston Cooking School Cook Book* by revising it in 1979 as *The Fannie Farmer Cookbook,* was also there. "This was a brainstorming session," says Graff, and they discussed the purpose of the center and its location on the west campus. Graff took notes.

Waters strongly argued for a garden and a computer center to help in the research for better food. Consequently, Huttenback says, he "offered more land for the herb garden."

> Julia and I had a difference of opinion on what was a priority [says Alice Waters]. Julia thought people should get a degree in the culinary arts. I was intent on an experimental garden and felt that the practical information that would be gotten from the garden should be put on computers and available to people all around the country. I wanted people to be taped who were involved in all these processes of food in Europe and America. Jeremiah Tower was interested in this also.

They all discussed naming their organization (the phrase "enology and gastronomy" was used repeatedly), opening "a place where chefs and wine-makers could meet and discuss common problems," and beginning a journal.

After the initial meeting, Julia heard that her Cambridge neighbor David Segal, an economics professor and bibliophile, had purchased for $120,000 the André Simon and Eleanor Lowenstein collections of historical cookery books from Lowenstein (whose Corner Book Store Julia patronized in New York City). Simon, the founder of the London Wine and Food Society and a great bibliophile, had collected books covering the sixteenth through the nineteenth century. When Julia heard that Segal had to sell the collection (except for cutlery books, which he wanted himself), she realized it was just what the new organization needed and suggested that Segal call Graff, who immediately went into action to find a buyer for the books. They would then have a tangible foundation ["real substance," says Huttenback] for the research center. This "most important assemblage of French, English, and American books on gastronomy" would be, according to Graff, "a perfect beginning." Tower found a guardian angel in Lila Jaeger of the Freemark Abbey and Rutherford Hill wineries in the Napa Valley, who offered to pay the $65,000 (Graff estimates) in trust until the group could reimburse her.

In order to give Lila Jaeger a promissory note, the group needed to have a legal basis. Thus, on September 23, the American Institute of Wine and Food was founded, and purchased the Simon-Lowenstein collection. "Lila actually bought the collection herself with the understanding that she would hold it until we could pay her off," says Graff. Because they needed bylaws, Graff's lawyer handed him the Sierra Club's bylaws as Graff was running out of the office. Segal catalogued the approximately 850 books and sent them to John Howells Books on Post Street in San Francisco to be stored.

Julia was in Cambridge at the time of the "founding," and Graff wrote

(October 9) to tell her they had chosen the name Wine and Food as "more accurate and straightforward" (Huttenback also thought that "Wine" had more cachet). Julia had provided the inspiration, but it was Graff who carried the ball. He wrote to leading members of the food and wine worlds in October, saying, "Together with Julia Child and Jeremiah Tower, I am writing to you to announce the formation of the American Institute of Wine and Food and to invite you to become a Founding Member . . . [and] to be on our Board of Advisors." The location of the AIWF would be the Santa Barbara campus. Paul Levy, the American food writer in London, was upset that the organization would not have "International" in the title. Dick countered that the name London Institute of Tropical Medicines merely denotes the location of the organization. (Fifteen years later, the Paris chapter unsuccessfully revived the same Levy argument.)

As the university students walked by with their surfboards, the third meeting of the group was "hanging ten on their own indubitable wave—the unprecedented surge of interest in food and wine in this country, especially . . . in California," wrote Charles Perry, a foodie friend of Waters and Tower from Berkeley. He called it "a gastronomic think tank . . . the first meeting of an organization without parallel in the world." They could feel the crest that sunny December 2, and were full of hope, grand plans, and a lunch of cold Pacific lobster and salads prepared by Julia and Jeremiah in the Cliff House on the rustic west campus of UCSB. The group now included those who responded to Graff's invitation, vintners, restaurateurs, and food writers. Already on the Board of Advisors were Julia Child, Robert Mondavi, James Beard, M. F. K. Fisher, Danny Kaye, and Michael McCarty (of Michael's restaurant in Santa Monica), as well as Paul Levy and Alan Davidson of London and the Oxford Symposium on Food. The following January the UCSB administration approved the location of the site.

Alice Waters's commitment to videotaping (and selling) food-making processes before they passed away was still on the agenda, as were a scholarly journal, a library of original books and reprints, and research fellowships. The group formally agreed to establish "a center for the advanced study of enology and gastronomy, a repository of knowledge, and a source of information for its members as well as for the public." Their fund-raising goal was $3 to $5 million in the first year. Huttenback expected his faculty to vote approval of the use of the building and land, but he was already hearing dissension from some, including his good friend Professor Henry Dorra, a Frenchman upon whom he had assumed he could count. As John Ronsheim discovered at Antioch, traditional academic departments did not recognize gastronomy as an academic or worthy study.

"The person who really grabbed it and ran was Dick Graff," says Huttenback. During the coming year, Graff worked diligently to raise funds for the center and for the purchase of the books, sometimes taking Julia and Paul with him to visit major donors, notably a group hosted by Martha Culbertson of the Fallbrook Winery near San Diego. They eventually enlisted most of the big-name vintners of California: Graff, Mondavi, Sanford, Phelps, Sebastiani, Sterling, Culbertson, Martini, Mirassou, and Du Pont "SilverStone." They also had Fritz Maytag, the washing machine heir, better known as founder of Anchor Steam beer and Maytag Blue cheese. Graff's office, at 655 Sutter Street in San Francisco, was the provisional headquarters of AIWF. "Dick is an extraordinary man, a Renaissance man. He travels extensively and has many interests and is a great winegrower. He is responsible for most things in writing from the AIWF," said future chair of the board of the AIWF Dorothy Cann Hamilton.

By November of that year he began publishing a monthly newsletter, a folded paper of four pages, written by Jackie Mallorca (collaborator for Beard's columns). In the first issue he announced that $50,000 in seed money had been raised by the ten founding members: Child, Graff, Mondavi, McCarty, Tower, Fritz Maytag, Joseph Phelps, D. Crosby Ross, Richard and Thekla Sanford, Audrey and Barry Sterling.

A group of the founding members dined together with Julia on January 15, 1983, planning for a giant fund-raising dinner in San Francisco for May of that year. Julia said she would be in the middle of filming a new television series for Russ Morash at that time, but she would be there without fail. It was imperative they have a home and pay for the book collection.

Santa Barbara organized the first local chapter of the organization and asked Mary Dorra, the wife of Professor Henry Dorra and a good cook and writer, to be on its board. The Childs and Dorras shared Francophilia and occasionally Thanksgivings in the 1980s, says Mary Dorra. "Because my husband is French and prefers the formal style," cooking with Julia "helped loosen things up for me as a hostess. She taught me to relax." One night after Julia experimented with a new way to cook lamb that left it quite raw, the four of them were silently pushing the lamb around on their plates when Paul said, "I fail to see why with all the cooking that goes on around here we have to eat raw meat!" Julia replied, "Well, that's the way it is sometimes."

Though UCSB would not become the culinary research center they envisioned in the early years of the 1980s, Julia's presence had an impact on the town. "Food before she moved here tended toward fancied-up meat and potatoes," said one local resident. "However, Julia Child occasionally showed up at these places. Overnight, somehow, they learned to cook—at least to cook better." "She's a landmark at Von's market," said a neighbor. There were other international figures who moved to town. In 1984, Page Rense, the editor of *Bon Appétit, Architectural Digest,* and *Geo,* bought a house, and Julia was invited to the unveiling of Opus One, the joint venture of Robert Mondavi and Baron Philippe de Rothschild, a frequent visitor to Santa Barbara. But it was chiefly Julia who "revolutionized restaurant eating in Santa Barbara," the neighbor maintains.

Tower, Waters, and Perry were part of a growing food cult in the San Francisco Bay area. Perry, who would become a distinguished food writer at the *Los Angeles Times,* remembers it started with a group of architecture students from Cambridge, Massachusetts, who had cooked their way through Julia's *Mastering* books and were now in San Francisco growing their own vegetables and holding bimonthly potlucks. "Two of the best cooks in the group were an architect named Jerry [Tower] and his friend Alice [Waters]." Twenty-five years after Alice opened her Chez Panisse in 1971, Laura Ochoa of the *Los Angeles Times* would call her "the earth mother of California cuisine," and S. Irene Virbila could name "an entire generation of chefs" who trained with her. Though she was devoted to Elizabeth David's books, and especially to Richard Olney's recipes, she used Julia's books as reference and her life as a model: "She paved the way for Chez Panisse because she was an unpretentious Francophile who taught the generation who became my customers to value good food."

San Francisco's many wealthy families and the vintners of Napa Valley also added to what one food writer called the "social ether" of San Francisco. For Julia, San Francisco was the home of Dorothy and Ivan, Rosie Manell and Gay Bradley Wright, as well as the Stanford Court, run by James Nassikas, where James Beard held cooking classes in the 1970s assisted by Marion Cunningham, his former student. San Francisco was also the location of a serious cooking school, founded in 1977, offering a sixteen-month diploma for professionals: the California Culinary Academy. In his *The Official Foodie Handbook* in 1985, Paul Levy named it one of only two seriously "foodie-approved" schools in the United States, meaning not for home cooking or catering.

Los Angeles was also fertile ground for the AIWF, where co-founder Michael McCarty had his restaurant in Santa Monica. "In the early 1980s, Los Angeles was the most exciting place to eat in America," Ruth Reichl declared in the *New York Times* in 1997. Because of her close proximity to Los Angeles, Julia was familiar with the many French-trained chefs at Ma Maison, a restaurant founded by Patrick Terrail, nephew of the owner of Paris's Tour d'Argent. Julia first noticed what she called the "Swiss-German Mafia" among the French chefs in Los Angeles, probably referring to Wolfgang Puck, who left Ma Maison on July 4, 1981 ("my independence day," he calls it). Julia soon visited his Spago restaurant as well as St.-Germain, where the chef was Patrick Healy, grandson of her friend Harriet (who had studied at their Trois Gourmandes school in Paris). Healy had lived at La Pitchoune when he was apprenticing with Roger Vergé, and would later open Champagne, which he lost in a divorce from his French-born wife.

JULIA THE TEACHER

"We at last have time to give some live cooking classes, which are fun to do again," Julia informed Louisette when she moved West. That August, on her sixty-ninth birthday, when her knees were hurting her, she informed Simca that "we survive because we stay active!" Indeed, her work with the AIWF, her support of a growing number of professional food organizations and schools, her charity demonstrations, and her live teaching at cooking schools would characterize this decade of her professional life. She was about the same age as chef Max Bugnard when she had studied with him at the Cordon Bleu.

For a woman with bad knees, Julia stood for too many hours behind the table and stove of many home cooking schools during 1981 and 1982. For each series of classes she prepared, sometimes using recipes she could adapt for national magazines or for *Good Morning America,* she worked in her Santa Barbara kitchen or typed in her office, looking out over the green meadow to the sea. She taught four-day weekend classes at the Stillwater Cove Ranch on the Sonoma coast in 1981, at Ma Maison in Los Angeles that December, and the following year in Phoenix and Longview, Texas.

Her most elegant experience was teaching for three years in the week-long "Great Chefs" series for the Mondavi vineyards. It was "the total gastro Rolls-Royce treatment," she wrote to Mary Frances. Designer Billy Cross and chef Michael James (Simca's student) conceived of the series, whose expense Mondavi now assumed, and everything about the week was first-class. In addition to fifteen Mondavi assistants, Julia had Rosemary Manell, whose pizzas were always the sensation of the Sunday lunch. A friend was visiting to assist Julia at Ma Maison, and Maggie Mah, a friend of Rosemary Manell and of Marion Cunningham in San Francisco, helped her in Northern California appearances. Julia loved the personal aspect of teaching classes and the absence of the time pressure she had on television.

She was a natural teacher. When the sauce curdled while she was talking to the students, she washed off the chicken, put the sauce in the blender and it was fine. "We always have to be ready to wing it. Know what you are doing so you don't get flapped," she declared. Martha Culbertson, who was in the class the first time with Julia, remembers Paul having trouble photographing Julia's work. "Julia stopped her demonstration, went to his side, and helped him solve the problem. It made a statement about love and loyalty."

Julia and the Mondavis became fast friends during these weeks in Oakville as a result of the series and their joint effort for AIWF. Julia admired couples who were partners in their work and confided to Simca that the "Mondavis seem happy together." She expressed genuine fondness for Margrit Biever (Mondavi), who was in charge of all cultural events. Biever, in turn, admired Julia's common sense and earthiness: "I can see her planting both feet on the floor in front of the class, her hands on the kitchen table, and speaking with total honesty to the students. 'Hello,' she would say, 'I hear some of you don't like butter!' " The fair, diminutive Swiss wife of Robert Mondavi saw her tall California friend as both strong and feminine: "She is not maternal, but she could have managed ten children. . . . Men react to her and she truly interacts with men."

Julia also put her teaching skills to work doing charity demonstrations until the end of 1982. She spent two days in New Haven for a large fund-raising event for Betty Kubler's Longwharf Theater (and would do it twice again in the 1990s), and cooked with her sister Dorothy for one of her and Ivan's annual food fairs for charity in San Rafael (a picture of the two tall sisters in matching aprons was published in *People* magazine). But her favorite charity, for which she made three appearances in 1982, was Planned Parenthood. At a dinner for Planned Parenthood husbands at Ma Maison in Los Angeles on February 28, 1982, she sat next to chef Ken Frank (La Toque), who was babysitting his newborn, asleep in a baby harness on his chest. Though two generations separated Ken and Julia, they shared the experience of being born and reared in Pasadena and attending the Polytechnic School. Julia cooed over the Frank baby, wishing that all babies would be loved. Her next contribution was at a three-day fund-raising cooking class for the Planned Parenthood in Memphis, where she was confronted by demonstrators who picketed her every day. Upset, Julia wrote to syndicated columnist Dear Abby, who promptly published Julia's letter, part of which says: "What are your plans [she asked the picketers] for these children once they are born? Are you going to help provide, for instance, for the child of a retarded 13-year-old daughter of a syphilitic prostitute? . . . If you insist on their birth, you must also assume responsibility for their lives."

By the time she completed a three-day cooking demonstration to benefit St. Mark's Cathedral in Seattle, she declared she would do no more charity demonstrations. She had no time, because the filming Russ Morash was planning to begin in 1983 was rapidly approaching. Morash, who had filmed *This Old House* and *Victory Garden* series since his last *French Chef* series, was making grand preparations for an entirely new series for Julia.

Julia left *McCall's* for *Parade* magazine in 1982 because she could reach a larger audience with her teaching skills. She was also paid a great deal more. She had contributed a monthly column to *McCall's* for five years and was ready for a change and a promotion. *Parade,* distributed in Sunday newspapers to millions of readers, named her food editor. She was required to prepare one article each month, entitled "From Julia Child's Kitchen," with recipes for a full meal. And she could keep the photography rights for any future book. She could plan, test, and write these installments in Cambridge or Santa Barbara, with the dishes photographed on either coast. A friend came West in December 1982 to help her prepare the food for the photographs in the first issue. Later Julia hired Barbara Sims-Bell, owner of the Santa Barbara Cooking School, to help her cook for *Parade.* In a couple of years Julia would refer to their "Beverly Wilshire [Hotel] home" because of the frequent filming for *Parade* or taping for *Good Morning America* in the Burbank studios.

"How to Cook for 40,000,000 by Julia Child," the full-page advertisements shouted. Standing in front of her wall-mounted pans, a big smile on her face and her hand holding a green-and-red pepper for color, America's favorite home cook appeared on the cover of her first issue, February 28, 1982. *Parade* editor Walter Anderson said he had a phenomenal response to her appearance, especially from men. This issue also presented her personal side with an article about her marriage to Paul. Each issue had several sections, each broken up with bold headings and illustrated by color photographs: how to cut up a chicken, sauté a chicken, make three variations on sautéed chicken (with potatoes and onions, with cream and mushrooms, with peppers, onions, and garlic), make a good pot of coffee, and "the greatest apple tart." Finally, there appeared a small box telling a personal tale about cleaning an "evil-smelling refrigerator." Mary Frances was one of the forty million: "I always find something very good and very *Julia,*" she wrote her D*E*A*R*F*R*I*E*N*D (as she always addressed her letters).

She managed her obligations to both *Good Morning America* and *Parade* as well as the numerous other endeavors through teamwork. Whether Pat Pratt or Marian Morash was visiting, or cooking friends were over for Thanksgiving, or she and Rosemary were demonstrating together, she was talking over ideas for recipes. "One gets so many ideas working as a team," she declared. By 1985, she was filming four segments of her *Good Morning America* spots in one day. She also found that she could plan four issues of *Parade* at once and later film them together. Every four-month cycle taught her something that she passed on to Simca. During their cooking and filming two years later, Julia discovered that new flour with potassium bromate strengthened the gluten and made better bread than she ever made before. And when she noticed that Jacques Pépin would recycle a new recipe three times (in teaching, in a magazine, and in demonstrations), she decided she did not need entirely new recipes every time she prepared her *Parade* articles.

When Julia returned to France from late June through late September 1982, she had already planned, tested, and written eleven shows for *Good Morning America* and completed a list (with Rosemary) of the upcoming *Parade* issues. As this was their first trip to France in two years, they stopped at the Pont Royal Hotel in Paris, where Julia wrote a nostalgic letter to Dort about the St.-Germain-des-Prés area. In Beaune they enjoyed a weekend of Burgundy wine and grand dining. Accompanying them from Cambridge in June and again in September were the Pratts. Pat worked well with Julia in testing recipes at La Pitchoune. Julia also discovered the fiction of Edith Wharton, she wrote Jim Beard. While reading R. W. B. Lewis's new biography of Wharton, Julia connected with Wharton's descriptions of Paris and Wharton's years in Lenox, Massachusetts, near her mother's hometowns of Pittsfield and Dalton.

After Sara Moulton had to leave La Pitchoune, Susy Davidson came to visit. Susy worked for Trois Gourmandes Productions as Associate Chef on *Good Morning America* and at other demonstrations in 1981 and 1982. She was a tall, twenty-nine-year-old Oregon native with lovely dark hair and a first diploma from La Varenne. She had worked a year and a half with Simca to earn her final diploma, and both Julia and Simca thought she was "a dear girl." Susy says, "Julia sets the pace. As far as I'm concerned, she is the professional by whom all other professionals are judged." Also visiting briefly to show off his future bride was Steven Raichlen, who had finished his degree from La Varenne and would become its representative in the United States. It was during that summer that Susy and Julia discussed the number of homosexuals who seemed to dominate the food organizations, a discussion Julia put into writing to Anne Willan, which would come back to haunt her in years to come. Julia would always maintain that the comments were not personal; her only concern was that the culinary profession have more heterosexual men in its ranks.

Julia, who enjoyed saying, "I love being bicoastal," was really tricoastal. When she and Paul left the Provençal coast, they drove to Joigny (where Willan and Cherniavsky had bought a château nearby in Villecien), then to Paris and the flight to Boston. After a late McWilliams family celebration of her seventieth birthday (August 15, 1982) in New Hampshire, Julia was honored by a birthday dinner offered her in New York by Peter Kump (all her cooking friends sent letters). She then embarked on a final burst of cooking school demonstrations before preparing for a new television show to be co-produced by WGBH and her renamed corporation, Julia Child Productions, from which she drew a "salary" (for tax purposes).

DINNER AT JULIA'S

On the twentieth anniversary of their first work together, Russ Morash planned to film a video magazine series for Julia, beginning the filming in Santa Barbara. Julia had often told reporters after each series that she wanted to go on the road to where food was grown. Now American Express agreed to pay for the flights. As executive producer, Morash raised nearly a million dollars from Polaroid for a limited series of thirteen shows featuring segments of Julia gathering food, cooking, and then hosting a dinner party in Santa Barbara. Each program would have an accomplished chef prepare one dish in a three-minute appearance. Most significantly for Julia, they would take a week to film each program, there would be no book to accompany the series (though she would have the dishes and techniques photographed for a later book project), and she had a full-time makeup and wardrobe person.

After a brief trip north to visit Alice Waters at Chez Panisse and meet with the Mondavis about the AIWF, Julia devoted the first five months of 1983 to filming at the rented mansion at Hope Ranch, the twenty-five-acre ranch on the California coast thirty minutes from her Seaview home. The Morash family lived in the Hope Ranch home where work, filming, and dinners were held. Marian and Rosemary served as Julia's Executive Chefs.

They began by flying to Seattle to tape segments for four shows, showing Julia salmon fishing on Puget Sound, sampling rich chocolate at the Filettante, visiting the Port Chatham smoking-salmon works in Ballard, and going on a crab boat trip at dawn. Sitting impatiently in the rented van outside Seattle, Julia waited for Debbie Wait to apply a thin coat of makeup before it was time to board the *Destiny,* a forty-six-foot Kodiak salmon boat. Puget Sound was windy and cold, and Julia was wrapped in a bright yellow waterproof jacket and pants. The waters were gray and choppy as Ken Thibert, the skipper, who had never seen Julia on television, guided the boat toward the crab pots. She was excited by the action and climbed up and down the boat's ladders, bombarding the experts with questions: "How was the crab season this year?" ("Lousy.") "What kind of bait will we use?" ("Geoduck stomachs.") She was still going strong when Morash had the tape he needed and the boat headed back. Later that day, Julia made another appearance, followed by a wine reception before returning to film the next morning in Santa Barbara.

Because the series emphasized fresh American regional produce, she would also visit (with Paul) an artichoke field, a chicken farm, a date farm in Indio, and the Firestone Vineyard in Los Olivos. When there were too few chanterelles in the mountains above Santa Barbara, they "planted" them. Like a modern-day Dr. Livingstone, says one reporter, Julia approached in pith helmet, stout stick, wet weather gear, and New Balance shoes, "slogging through viscous mud that bogged down her party's four-wheel-drive Bronco" (noted a visiting *Time* reporter), to gather a basketful of the yellow precious (and planted) chanterelles.

Visiting wine experts talked about the vintage to be served with each course (the marriage of wine and food) and a guest chef prepared a dish: René Verdon of San Francisco's Le Trianon (White House soufflé with zucchini), Louis Evans of New Orleans's Pontchartrain Hotel (crayfish bisque), Jean-Pierre Goyenvalle from Washington, DC, and Wolfgang Puck from West Hollywood's Spago. Puck remembers arriving at the mansion early one morning slightly hungover after a late-night party. "Julia greeted me on the step and gave me a big hug, which planted my face somewhere in her chest region." Austrian-born Puck came to make Santa Barbara shrimp in mustard/butter sauce.

The main dishes were prepared by Julia and her crew, though only a part of the actual preparation was shown because this was not a how-to program. The main courses included a chicken dish called Winged Victory (a version of which she later used in *Parade),* Santa Barbara bouillabaisse, whole salmon steamed in white wine, roast deviled rabbit, and braised sweetbreads in puff shells. Morash filmed Julia and these dishes with a single handheld camera, and also filmed small segments featuring techniques, both for the program and for later use in a video series he was pitching called *The Way to Cook.* (She also told reporters she would be doing a book by this title.) He did not have Julia's words fully scripted, except for opening and closing lines, for he believed she did best with spontaneity (indeed, even on the *Good Morning America* segments, after a couple of practice beginnings, she was best with partially improvised narrative). After all these segments were shot and the food ready, the show ended with a cocktail party and dinner for ten people, including hosts Julia and Paul. Sometimes when friends or journalists were bumped for more important guests, they joined the cocktail party scene and ate dinner off-camera. Her sister Dorothy can be seen at the table in her first segment, "The Salmon Dinner," and her editor Judith Jones attended "The Turkey Dinner." One of her honored guests was James Beard, who had to remain seated. She was worried about her "Dear Jim," who, in and out of hospitals, did not look well.

On February 8, 1983, just when the film crew of *Parade* magazine left and Morash was beginning the shoot another *Dinner at Julia's* segments, Julia and Paul received the news that Charlie Child died suddenly at Pennswood, his retirement home. He and Paul had recently celebrated their birthdays: "He and I had eighty-one years of understanding, of fun, of mutual learning, of creativity together, and admiration, not to mention, especially, letters from each other when we were apart during the war years. I find that I am still, unconsciously, storing up in my mind things to write [to him] about. . . . We were truly parts of each other," Paul wrote their longtime friend Fanny Brennan.

Julia and Paul shared their grief in quiet private moments amid the frenetic activity of dozens of people filming; Paul, the introspective twin, was especially grieved: "I suffer because of Chas' death," he wrote in his datebook. Julia, typically matter-of-fact about death, threw herself into immediate tasks and looked ahead. For the Child children and grandchildren, Julia and Paul were all that remained of that generation. Charlie's body was cremated and waited until the family gathered that August at Lopaus Point, Maine, where during a week together to memorialize him, they sprinkled his ashes along the coastal walks he loved so well and described in his memoir *Roots in the Rock*.

The glamorous *Dinner at Julia's* began airing on PBS on October 14 of that year (it was rerun the last three months of 1984 as well). In the first program, when the limousines pulled up to the mansion and Julia appeared in heavy makeup and dark curly hair (one reporter called it an "Afro"), some of her friends were dismayed. Ruth Lockwood was sorry about the change of Julia's image, feeling almost "betrayed." Most food colleagues and longtime friends enjoyed the segments of fishing, mushroom picking, and date harvesting, but thought the series was "too elite, very non-Julia to be driving up in a Mercedes or Rolls-Royce." A family member blamed Bob Johnson for pushing her into a "publicity stunt" series.

Reviewers were more positive, emphasizing the celebration of regional produce ("the French Chef has come home"), the slick new format, and the variety of segments crammed into each thirty-minute program. The variety drew some criticism for fragmenting the program, but most reviews were puff pieces, such as *United* magazine's "Shows her at her bubbly, chirrupy best." *Time*'s only swipe was at the wardrobe person who dressed her "in a wardrobe worthy of Auntie Mame." The *New York Times*'s John J. O'Connor wrote that the attempt to "convey a sense of elegance" resulted "too often" in a "silly and distracting" program which appeared to display a "cavalier attitude toward cost." (The *Washington Post* detailed the expenses, noting that the food alone "cost $1,000 a week.") O'Connor liked Julia's enthusiasm and the final barbecue segment, but not the full bottle of vermouth on the whole salmon and the Rolls-Royce pulling up to the door with a piano rendition of "These Foolish Things" playing in the background.

Despite the negative notes, Julia enjoyed the communal experience in the mansion, with everyone working on the project, including students from Santa Barbara City College Hotel and Restaurant School who assisted in the preparation of the food. The final segment was a barbecue with mariachi band and Julia in Western garb, while overhead the helicopters churned—not for her filming or a nearby forest fire, but for President Reagan's arrival to and departure from Rancho del Cielo.

Julia toured for the new series to Washington, DC, and elsewhere, always working to organize chapters of the AIWF wherever she went. She and Paul, who continued to be depressed about losing his brother, returned to Santa Barbara to spend the first five months of 1984 by the sea.

"AMERICAN CELEBRATION"

Fresh oysters from Puget Sound, Tomales Bay, and Vancouver Island opened the eleven-course feast at the Stanford Court in San Francisco on May 4, 1983. Many predicted that the eleven chefs would not be able to work in the same kitchen to prepare the eleven specialties for the meal, but Michael McCarty of Michael's in Santa Monica, who arranged the dinner, and Mark Peel, a chef at Spago, disagreed. The chefs had a ball.

The "American Celebration" feast fed 372 patrons, most of whom paid $250. It was called "the dawning of a new age for American cuisine," by one well-fed journalist. Julia, who was in the kitchen until moments before the dinner began, called it "an amazing event." One newspaper announced: "A Summit of U.S. Cuisine." Another: "extravaganza." The "American Celebration" was a fund-raiser for the American Institute of Wine and Food. (Three months later 700 people showed up—300 had to be turned away—at an AIWF fund-raising garden party on the grounds of the Hope Ranch.) But it was the San Francisco "Celebration" that both inaugurated an era of high living for the AIWF and was emblematic of a new decade in American cuisine: American chefs were emphasizing ingredients over technical skills.

When Jimmy Schmidt (Detroit) was preparing his stuffing of wild root vegetables, fiddlehead fern, and hazelnuts from Michigan, Larry Forgione (River Café in Brooklyn) and Bradley Ogden (Kansas City) rolled up their sleeves and helped him chop and slice. When Paul Prudhomme's blackened redfish was ready to be prepared, Jonathan Waxman (Michael's in Santa Monica), Wolfgang Puck, and Mark Miller joined in the last-minute cooking. When Jeremiah Tower was ready to put the chocolate and sabayon sauce on his pecan pastry, Alice Waters and Barbara Kafka (New York City) joined the assembly line. Each course was accompanied by a different wine, with Mondavi's 1974 Private Reserve Cabernet Sauvignon served with the American cheese selection (California chèvre, Iowa Maytag Blue, and a New York Camembert). By midnight, everyone joined the "After Hours Party" for the final courses: Mark Peel's "Spago's pizza" (served with Domaine Chandon Blanc de Noir) and Barbara Kafka's tripe gumbo (served with Christian Brothers Private Reserve Centennial Sherry). All the wines were Californian. And all the chefs were known for his or her quest for a distinctive American cuisine. Several had cooked at Chez Panisse or Ma Maison, and all, Alice Waters admitted to a reporter, were "from the controversial end" of the American spectrum. Indeed, only Puck and Ogden were guests on *Dinner at Julia's* (being filmed at that time), suggesting the traditional nature of *her* guest chef list.

Upscale restaurant dining would boom in the Reagan years of the 1980s, and the chef became a new hero during that so-called decadent decade. In a panel discussion during this three-day event in San Francisco, William Rice, the editor of American Express's *Food & Wine* (and a sponsor), said restaurants will play "an important part" in American culture and "chefs are taking their natural role as leaders." Significantly, at the "American Celebration" there were no live speeches, just four giant television sets showing the preparations in the kitchen. "Chefs are on a par with artists and musicians," Julia confided to a journalist at her table.

Mimi Sheraton (who ate at home only five times the previous year) later called the 1980s a period of affluence, generous news coverage of restaurants, celebrity chefs, and dining out. "Julia criticized me directly and obliquely for being a bad influence on restaurants," says Sheraton, "because I terrified chefs by having such negative reviews." Yet it was the reviewers who stirred the pot. And, as the press and panel discussions noted, diners were getting more discriminating. "The revolution in food began in 1963," the food authorities agreed, "when Julia Child went on television and alerted Americans to the pleasures of gastronomy."

If chefs are known for cooperation—as illustrated in the San Francisco "Celebration"—the food writers were territorial and competitive, as evidenced in a scandal that rocked the food world in 1983. The story, which broke on December 7, Robert Clark calls "a kind of Pearl Harbor for the food community." In February, Richard Olney sued Richard Nelson (*Richard Nelson's American Cooking*) for copyright infringement and punitive damages, asking $1,050,000. Nelson was a past president of the International Association of Cooking Schools, based in Washington, DC, and strongly supported at its founding by Julia Child; he was also on the advisory board of AIWF (and a cooking school founder and food columnist for the *Portland Oregonian*). Because a recipe is a formula, Julia always believed they could not be copyrighted, though she tried to give credit for any original recipe inspiring her own variation. According to Ann Barr and Paul Levy: "Julia Child is . . . generous [about her recipes], and was the first to telephone Nelson to give him her support." She told Simca a decade before that she felt "the recipe business is about hopeless." Through the years they both recognized their own work in *Gourmet* and other places: "I agree with someone who said that the recipe is only the score (for the music), and that each virtuoso interprets it as he sees fit, and according to his own personality. . . . After all, at the Cordon Bleu there were no recipes provided at all, which made it easier."

Nelson allegedly "stole" at least fifty-six recipes, some from Julia, without creative variation in ingredients or language. He took thirty-nine recipes from Olney's *Simple French Food* (1974), including every turn of phrase and personal narrative introduction. The fault, Olney soon learned, was that the recipes he sent to Beard, who was going to write the introduction to Olney's book, were xeroxed and circulated in cooking classes Beard and Nelson taught in Portland. "Nelson thought he was stealing from Beard," Olney concluded. Nelson did not give any indication that he understood what the fuss was about, but he paid out of court an undisclosed amount that August. Beard, who had perhaps misjudged Olney's originality, felt betrayed by Nelson and humiliated. Olney never spoke to Beard again.

The AIWF board searched for an executive director for more than two years until Dick Graff finally found the man to lead the organization. Julia agreed with Graff's selection of George Trescher, who, she said, "made a great hit with everyone." Though born in California, Trescher had made his career on the East Coast, working for Time-Life and fund-raising for the New York Public Library and the Museum of Science. He had just the right "East Coast credentials," Julia explained to Simca, because "the East Coast knows nothing at all about us out here . . . it is like starting something in Lyons—how do you get the Parisians to take it seriously? We like Trescher very much indeed—think he will finally get the Institute on its feet and going." Trescher, later called "Party Chairman . . . one of the people who make New York tick," moved to San Francisco for a reported income of six figures. Julia, Mondavi, and the millionaire founders believed that to get the organization on its feet, they had to buy the best talent. Child and Mondavi, who co-sponsored the fund-raising feast in San Francisco the year before, emerged as titular leaders of the AIWF (Graff preferred to stay out of the limelight). Under Trescher, the AIWF was characterized by its rapid growth and grand national conventions, beginning with the first, in Santa Barbara in 1985. When they announced a goal of raising $2 million in nine months, Paul Levy responded from London: "Two million dollars! That cake certainly rose."

Julia was invited by the Reagans to attend the state dinner for French President François Mitterrand in the spring of 1984. She hated the food, right down to the purple sorbet with canned peaches. When she sent her thank-you note to the Reagans on April 14, she talked about the progress of the gastronomic arts in the country and the goals of the AIWF, and added: "A number of us in the cooking profession have wondered [given the existence of an advisory committee on the decoration of the White House] if it might also be possible to have a panel on food served at official dinners." Though her family and friends knew her dislike for the Reagans' politics, this appeal to improve state dinners was a long-standing concern without a political basis. Indeed, earlier that year the *Washington Post* declared, "Julia Child is about the only hero left. She . . . as far as we know has never had a political thought."

At the peak of her career, Julia was never so aware of her own mortality. Even while she kept up a professional pace commensurate with her energy (taping *Parade* segments in Cambridge, attending the Association of Cooking Schools conference in Paris), she was reminded of her age. Paul was still haunted by the loss of Charlie. Her seventy-year-old brother had been hit by a car and was slowly recovering. Brother-in-law Ivan Cousins had a prostate operation and radiation. Most distressing was the gradual decline of Paul, who fell asleep at meals, even after she gave him a poke. Then what she had been fearing for several years happened: James Beard was taken to the hospital with only one functioning kidney and a very weak heart. He died early in the morning of January 21, 1985, and his ashes were eventually scattered along the coastline of his native Oregon.

$\mathcal{S}$EASONED WITH LOVE
(1985 – 1989)

"Boutez en avant!"
JULIA CHILD
~

THE PRESS, the food world, even Hollywood (represented by Danny Kaye) turned out for what was billed as the First Annual Conference on Gastronomy of the American Institute of Wine and Food on January 25–27, 1985. Trescher hired Gregory Drescher as Program Director to help him plan the Santa Barbara conference. "Dining in America—Inside or Outside the Home" was the vague and all-encompassing title under which leading American culinary figures from the United States and France spoke on a variety of issues. Trescher remembers the conference as "magic." When Alice Waters spoke too evangelically about organic food, Julia turned to her and said she was bringing the whole spirit of the thing down with this endless talk of pollutants and toxins. The founder of Chez Panisse was stung and embarrassed. Julia herself downplayed pesticides because it reinforced the country's ingrained fear of pleasure and she believed that Alice's "romantic beliefs" would not help feed two hundred million people. Later that year, for example, she told *U.S. News & World Report,* which was doing a cover story on America's "Diet Wars," that "too many experts are trying to scare people" and her best advice for a healthy life was to eat a great variety of fresh food. With the death of Beard just days before and worries about funding the renovation of Cliff House on the campus of the University of California at Santa Barbara, Julia wanted to keep the mood of everyone upbeat. For her, it was always *"Boutez en avant!"* (full steam ahead), as she loved to shout.

THE WAY TO COOK BY CASSETTE

Julia was optimistic after the conference as she drove on Channel Drive, along the coast in front of the Biltmore Hotel and by the Bird Refuge, to 40 Los Patos Lane, to see the kitchen built for the new filming project. She (Julia Child Productions) signed a contract with Knopf's new VideoBooks for a series of six one-hour cassettes called *The Way to Cook* and a future book. The cassettes were at the cutting edge of technology, they all believed, and would mean enormous sales, perhaps as many as if not more than the book. Not for television this time, but for direct sale, with an accompanying pamphlet of recipes. Knopf had a contract with WGBH to make the cassettes and share the profits. Knopf's VideoBooks handled distribution and sales. WGBH was financially responsible for building the kitchen in a studio rented from Michael Hutchings's Waterside Inn, which occupied an antique house next door. D. Crosby Ross, a founder of the AIWF and of a culinary emporium in Santa Barbara, did the design and furnishing (as he had for *Dinner at Julia's).* The studio and kitchen were spacious. More important, most of the old gang was arriving from Boston for the preparation.

Since a planning meeting the previous November, when Russ showed the demo they filmed during *Dinner at Julia's,* there had been a tug-of-war between Morash and her lawyer Bob Johnson over who was in charge of the production. Johnson wanted to be the producer. He was enamored of the media food world, of Julia and her fame (the food was secondary). Morash, who "insisted upon complete control," would not stand for someone who did not understand television making decisions for him. Marian intervened with Julia, who was able to resolve the conflict by interrupting her *Parade* shooting in California that fall to return to Cambridge for what she called a "long friendly session with Russ." Her resolution, typically, was to hand both a title: Morash was producer/director; her lawyer was executive producer of Julia Child Productions, meaning, among other things, that he hired someone to do her hair and clothes. She informed Mary Frances later that Russ is "wonderful at this, the Alfred Hitchcock of how-to . . . a real boss, and someone with lots of imagination and visual style." What Julia and others did not know was that Johnson was ill with AIDS and in later weeks would be acting more erratically. Also behind the conflict was Julia's desire to have an editor to ensure a more polished result than they had on *Dinner at Julia's*. Stung by the criticism of that series, she focused her blame on Morash's editor, who was not a cook. "I need a writer who could take care of continuity, sparkling and meaningful dialogue where necessary . . . and a more professional series," she informed Judith.

Tension now diffused, they began in early February a rhythm of one week's discussion and planning for two programs at the house (Russ and Marian rented an apartment in Montecito Shores near Julia), followed by two weeks of filming in the studio—a one-hour cassette each week, shot in fifteen-minute segments. Russ was creating six one-hour teaching videos, conceived as a cooking school on cassette for the home cook. Marian Morash (Executive Chef) and Rosemary Manell (Food Designer) were Julia's left and right hands, and they hired four others to assist in the preparation work. Occasionally someone had to run to the back door of the Waterside Inn to borrow some food. They scripted the opening and closing lines, but Morash filmed, as always, without a script. For the "First Courses and Desserts" tape, Julia made Reine de Saba: "Here's my *all*-time favorite chocolate cake!" This fourth version of the cake ("new and improved") used two kinds of chocolate and five eggs. The final cassette was shot the first week of April.

Julia had been given her biggest contract yet from Knopf for the series and book *The Way to Cook*. She received $100,000, or a fourth of her advance, but worried that she would not be able to deliver the manuscript within Knopf's deadline. She had written to Judith Jones that she would return the "mazuma" if she missed deadlines, "because I am only interested in doing another book in my own way by myself." Her own way meant waiting until the taping was over (the writing would take her several years to complete). Judith was on the set every day where she worked on Julia's recipes, watched the filming, and prepared the inserts for the videos, using cross-references for ease of shopping and meal planning.

During planning sessions and taping, Julia attended the Association of Cooking Schools conference in Seattle, where a memorial luncheon for James Beard was held. Madeleine Kamman was scheduled to give a talk, "A Philosophy of Teaching," but first ten people were to memorialize the pioneering work of Beard. When it was Julia's turn, she whipped away the funereal tone with a call for action. She heard from Peter Kump that Reed College (where Beard was kicked out as a student), which inherited the Beard house, was going to sell it and that some of his belongings were already auctioned off. In her typically practical and authoritative manner, she announced that something had to be done immediately to preserve his memory and the home that meant so much to their profession. Some heard her suggest they buy his house as a memorial; others heard her say they needed a place to drop in for culinary fellowship and a spot of sherry. Whatever the clarion call, it fell most heavily on the ears and shoulders of Peter Kump and Kathleen Perry, a food professional from Longwood, Florida (the Perrys gave a three-month loan of $100,000, not repaid until 1995). Kump began raising funds with dinners in honor of Beard around the country.

Julia got back to Cambridge in time for the arrival of the cassettes and a trip to Northampton to receive an honorary doctorate from Smith College. President Mary Maples Dunn called her "one of our national treasures" as she presented her with a Doctor of Humane Letters. Julia had to bend very low for the short president to place the colors over her head. The menus for the inaugural weekend of President Dunn were planned by Julia, including an original dish, *crêpes Maples Dunn en flammes,* for the inaugural garden party. The New England ingredients, to be prepared as a filling for her crêpe recipe in *Mastering II,* included Granny Smith apples, raisins, maple syrup, walnuts, and spices, and the recipe was published in the *Smith Alumnae Quarterly* that fall. She had turned down previous honorary degrees, including one from Middlebury College in 1983 when she was busy filming in California, but Julia was moved by this tribute from her alma mater.

"Knopf is going all out to promote [the cassettes] because this is the first venture into video for them," Julia told Mary Frances. After a ten-city promotional tour for *The Way to Cook* VideoBooks, Julia returned to Cambridge and asked Rosemary and Nancy to take over the photo sessions of the *Parade* series so she could care for Paul and complete her book. In 1986 she resigned her role as food editor and turned the job over to young Julee Rosso and Sheila Lukins, of the Silver Palette cookbooks fame. They promptly inaugurated their term with recipes using goat cheese, arugula, and pesto. Gone were Julia's traditional puff pastry, savory lamb, and braised ham menus. It was certainly a generational shift, she thought while writing to Elizabeth David, who had sent Julia her latest book: "We miss Jim Beard a great deal. I did lots of telephoning and talking and gossiping with him and I seem to miss him more now when I realize that he is just not there."

During their six weeks in France that summer, Julia and Paul received word that Robert H. Johnson, their lawyer for sixteen years, had died of AIDS at the age of forty-five. "It was a big shock to her when he died of AIDS," says Marian Morash. "I know she was surprised," added Jane Friedman. Even some of his colleagues did not know he was homosexual, nor did they know what AIDS was. Paul had written a poem to Johnson years before, celebrating his long line of lady friends, whom Johnson was careful to bring to social occasions. His occasional grandiosity offended many, including Judith Jones

and Russ Morash, but he was a tough negotiator for Julia until he was incapac-
itated. She was grateful for his work and deeply grieved at his death. Though
her passport still read that in case of emergency Johnson was to be notified,
Julia had already been visited by William Auchincloss Truslow, a colleague of
Johnson's at Hill & Barlow, who informed her that he would assume her
representation. She willingly concurred, for Bill Truslow was a friend of two
decades' standing.

Truslow, a graduate of Yale and Harvard Law, had represented John
Kenneth Galbraith since the death of Brooks Beck, Julia's first lawyer. Truslow
left Wall Street to work with Beck and to enjoy the human exchange: "Trusts
and Estates is people," he points out. His sister Jane was married to longtime
friend Peter Davison. Truslow admired Julia's generosity. Five years before,
when his sister Jane was diagnosed with breast cancer, Julia had been one of
the first to call, and when Jane's cancer returned the next year, Julia lent her
Santa Barbara apartment to Jane and Peter for a holiday just before Jane's
death. Truslow also admired Julia's frankness (though she could make this
New England lawyer blush) and her honesty ("She does not waste psychic
energy on deception . . . her personal persona and her public persona are
the very same"). In turn, Julia adored this personable gentleman and scholar
who had a well-bred politeness and was so comfortable with wit and laughter.

If her occasional frank talk could make him blush, her gusto for exotic
foods sometimes frightened his palate. One day when he was visiting Santa
Barbara and a man dropped off a bucket of sea urchins at Julia's door, he
watched in amazement as she opened the sea urchins, still alive, and spooned
out the orange/pink reproductive organs and tasted them, murmuring with
pleasure. She picked up the second, scooped it out, and passed it over to him.
After swift mental calculations, he opened his mouth and swallowed, gagging
it down. When she reached for another, he mumbled something about having
to call his wife and dashed into the other room.

The second AIWF Conference on Gastronomy was held at the Weston/
Copley Plaza in Boston on October 23–26, 1985. There were now nine regional chapters, and the Boston chapter, as host, was determined to impress
the national body. The head of the Boston chapter was K. Dun Gifford, whom
Julia first met in the early 1970s. "Julia was quite taken with the tall and
elegant Dun," says Robert Huttenback. According to Gifford, he had watched
The French Chef (which came on the television immediately before *The Man
from U.N.C.L.E.)* all during law school, then worked for the Kennedys until
after Chappaquiddick. Gifford's brother John (Jock) owned the Straight
Wharf restaurant in Nantucket, where Julia had worked line crew with chef
Marian Morash. It had been Julia who said the year before to Dun, with whom

she loved talking politics, "Why don't you be the president" of the new Boston chapter.

Paul, who continued to travel with her, was increasingly forgetful and occasionally could not grasp what was said to him. "The only thing that really upset him," according to Anne Willan, "was when she was not there." Julia encouraged him to keep active at La Pitchoune, but he did not want to go for walks. He would lift his weights, but walking activated the arthritis in his back. Though she continued to write to distant friends for another year or two that he was happily painting away, he, in fact, no longer painted. During this visit he started a crude outline of several links in a chain he once photographed. The painting is disturbing, just black suggestions of chain links on a white canvas, and remains unfinished.

Despite the ten-city tour earlier that summer and more traveling in the fall to promote the Knopf cassettes, sales were disappointing. It was not that Julia failed to carefully demonstrate the cooking techniques of poultry, meat, soups, vegetables, eggs, and fish. Morash insists, "They are very valuable . . . ahead of their time. Someday they will be shown as a series and sold because they are Julia at her best. It is classic stuff." Four reasons account for the weak sales. There was poor distribution for cassettes in the 1980s; few people had television or videos in their kitchen; these videotapes were expensive at $39 each. Also, poor sales may indicate that people watched Julia Child on television because they loved to watch a master in action and they enjoyed her personality, not because they wanted to make the dish she was cooking. They would show up during her tour because they wanted to see her, not necessarily to use her cassette.

While on the road promoting her cassettes, Julia met with persons interested in beginning a chapter of AIWF. When she spoke at the Smithsonian in the fall of 1985, for example, she met with the Washington, DC, chapter. In San Francisco, Jim Wood, who had covered her activities and books for the *San Francisco Examiner* took her to eat at Tu Lan, his favorite Chinese restaurant, located near the newspaper's office but in the scuzziest part of town. Long before he became food editor, Wood had learned to cook from *Mastering the Art of French Cooking*. Now, after twenty interviews with her, he was in awe of her physical stamina and the breadth of her fame. When Julia emerged from the Knopf limousine, one of the street drunks announced, à la Ed McMahon on the Johnny Carson show: "It's Joooooolia!" Wood noticed over lunch that as she was talking about her cassettes, "the cooking school of the future," she and Paul were handling their chopsticks like experts and eating with relish. Soon the talk turned to their OSS work in China and their admiration for Barbara Tuchman's biography of General Joseph Stilwell. As the limo pulled away from the curb, and before Wood headed back to his office, another drunk walked into the middle of the street, lifted his cap in a large bowing circle to Julia, and called out, *"Bon appétit!"*

The first six months of 1986 were spent in Santa Barbara, where, Julia told Avis, "the mimosa are in bloom, the avocados ripening, flowering bushes, fresh broccoli and spinach in bunches" at the local farmers' market. When she wrote to "Red and Eleanor" Warren to congratulate him on his appointment as Poet Laureate, she described their "condo overlooking the green meadow and blue Pacific"—the colors of her many kitchens and book covers. Paul was briefly hospitalized with shingles, which was treated successfully. They were able to attend the Third Annual AIWF Conference in San Diego, a charity cooking demonstration at the Stanford Court Hotel to benefit the San Francisco Museum of Modern Art, and a weekend in the Napa Valley, but increasingly she was limping around with an aching knee. She told the Walcutts the bum knee was "the result of an old ski injury and forty years behind the stove." Finally she had what she called "a total knee replacement" the first week of February. She took her physical training regime seriously, she wrote, and was on the knee-flexing machine soon after surgery, in a walker the next day, home in eight days, and "in three months I can start ballet."

She had to get back to her book and, more important, she felt, keep being involved with people and the professional world. In March the Childs attended the First Annual AIWF Founders Banquet and the Monterey Wine Festival, as well as the Association of Cooking Schools (later renamed the International Association of Culinary Professionals) conference in Washington, D.C. Peter Kump, the next president, planned a dinner honoring Simca, with a reading of letters from her friends and colleagues, including Julia, who wrote about "our lasting and loving culinary sisterhood." Simca remained in France to work on her memoirs with Jane Owen Molard ("I thoroughly empathized with what Julia must have gone through when writing the first *Mastering,*" she says today). But a greater reason for staying in France was her husband, Jean, who was ill (and would die that summer). The next month Paul had his second prostate operation as well as a number of other physical ailments. The year 1986 was not a good or healthy one, though some letters Julia wrote painted a jolly picture of "Paul . . . busy and happy, painting and photographing." In truth, she was cooped up with her book and a disoriented husband. Nevertheless, she pressed on this spring with a visit to the Sebastiani estate, another week of classes at the Mondavi vineyard (with Maggie Mah and Rosemary assisting her), a gala at the Mark Hopkins Hotel in San Francisco, and attendance at the San Francisco Food Writers dinner—always accompanied by Paul.

By summer she was beginning to doubt she would ever complete *The Way to Cook*. In a letter to the Walcutts, after discussing her worries about the conservative Supreme Court, the new laws against sodomy, and the abortion question, she added: "I am engulfed in my mammoth new cookbook and doubt, at this point, if I shall ever get it finished. There is so much to do, and I have to *think*, which takes so much time. The IBM-PC is marvelous, and I bless it every day." She completed the poultry and vegetable chapters and left Santa Barbara erroneously thinking a secretary that fall could put various recipes from *Parade, Dinner at Julia's,* and *The Way to Cook* tapes onto her computer disk.

Leaving the manuscript behind, Julia took Paul, just after their fortieth wedding anniversary, back to France while she could. It would turn out to be his last Provençal journey. As usual, according to the Pratts, who accompanied them, she had the itinerary to Alsace, Switzerland, Italy, and Provence carefully typed out and planned. She always told people she returned to Europe "to see what they are up to." That is why she visited Patricia Wells, whom she met at a cooking school meeting in the fall of 1984 in Paris (after having written her a fan letter that spring when *A Food Lover's Guide to Paris* was published). "They came to my fortieth birthday party that fall," Wells told me in 1995. "I had never watched her on television, but I knew her from her books. There was no other way to learn to cook, and there never will be another like her." She was impressed with Julia's generosity, curiosity, and breadth of knowledge ("though she does not wear her knowledge overtly"). It little mattered that Wells and Julia would not always agree on their assessment of French restaurants they visited together over the next decade. Julia could be stubborn once she made up her mind, and "she hates trendiness . . . and frozen food."

"My God, it's Beverly Hills in the south of France," said Clark Wolf when he first visited coastal Provence. Wolf, a quick-witted food retailer, later a restaurant consultant, and active member of the New York chapter of AIWF, was visiting Bramafam for Simca's annual cocktail party, which included the Childs and Susy Davidson. Wolf could be just as outspoken as Julia and they liked each other. "When you get to Julia's base, it's about very sophisticated, very simple life . . . she is deeply intuitive. She just loves men and she makes men feel special, though she is enormously supportive of women. Her thinking is liberal but her approach is conservative because she likes structure and discipline. She's very American, very grounded."

The trip to France was a disaster for Paul, according to one friend they visited. "He would eat everything during very rich meals and developed a digestive tract blockage. He could suddenly become fractious. But whatever embarrassment Julia may have felt, she never showed it." As they were leaving France, Julia herself told friends that he would drop off to sleep during meals.

They stopped in New York for her appearance on *Good Morning America*. Julia and her crew were waiting for the cameras to roll, one key assistant missing because her husband had deserted her. "She forgot the three F's," Julia whispered to Sara Moulton: "Feed 'em, fuck 'em, and flatter 'em." Seven minutes later, on-camera, she pronounced her *Bon appétit*. Charlie Gibson, who began working with her when he joined the cast as host in 1987, adored Julia and her outspoken matter-of-factness:

> Julia is game to do anything; she is marvelous to work with and asks no quarter because of her age. She is an incorrigible flirt and she loves to talk politics, especially about Congress, which I used to cover. Once as I left after dining with them, I said to Paul, "It is a very impertinent thing for a young man to say, but I have always been in love with your wife." Paul answered immediately, "That's okay, I have been in love with her too."

$\mathscr{A}$ GREAT GATSBY ERA

Even before D. Crosby Ross and Dun Gifford took over the American Institute of Wine and Food in late 1987, Julia was having trouble with the organization she envisioned—or rather the organization that was *not* what she envisioned. The more money they worked to raise, the more money they seemed to need. She enjoyed the first-class conferences that brought together the best thinkers and practitioners in the country, but she was getting tired of the constant dunning for dollars. George Trescher, who was hired for $100,000— a huge sum for a small organization with no endowment (and a library debt)— returned to New York City after fourteen months as president, he says, in order to run his business there. For one more year he remained on retainer, spending ten days a month in San Francisco.

The Fourth Annual AIWF Conference on Gastronomy, in Texas, on November 6–9, 1986, was the most extravagant to date and was sponsored by the Campbell Soup Company, Food and Wines From France, and Rosewood Hotels (the program insert listed seventy corporations and vineyards as "contributors"). The institute flew in medical doctors, academicians, national journalists, food producers, editors, chefs, and winemakers. From France they flew in chefs Jean-Pierre Billoux, Jacques Cagna, and Gérard Besson, as well as Patricia Wells, Anne Willan, Rudolph Chelminski, and Richard Olney. It was a star-studded gathering with first-class accommodations, intellectual stimulation, sumptuous meals, and a variety of wines, champagne, and stretch limousines.

The champagne and caviar conferences, planned by Trescher and Program Director Greg Drescher, may have reinforced the image of a "wine and cheese" society that the students and faculty at UCSB had complained about. Indeed, the conferences were worthy of F. Scott Fitzgerald's Jay Gatsby and in part a reflection of the frenzied trend-making and the conspicuous consumption of the 1980s. They drew civilian food and wine lovers, many of them wealthy, for the admission was expensive. These conferences were heavily underwritten and costly, but they dispensed enough mental and gustatory stimulation to sate any palate. Those who made frequent presentations at the conferences included England-based wine expert Hugh Johnson, the *New York Times*'s R. W. Apple, Jr., anthropologist Lionel Tiger, *Esquire*'s John Mariani, food historian William Woys Weaver, and Albert Sonnenfeld, a professor of French and comparative literature.

The same tone of splendor, but without the corporate underwriting, existed at national headquarters. Hiring of staff and travel expenses were unrestrained, given the cost for administration and publications. The seeds of the problem lay at the founding: Child, Mondavi, and Graff (who in their own businesses always had business managers) hired Trescher, who was an outstanding fund-raiser and conference planner, but not strong on managing and budgeting an office. D. Crosby Ross, whom one founder called "the most profligate with his champagne and limousines," was now earning $125,000. Under Ross, who served as president in San Francisco, the debt reached $285,000. Under Dun Gifford, chair of the board of directors, the debt soared to $635,000. "They were all great at spending money," according to Richard Graff, "but no one could touch Dun Gifford for that. He had great ideas but tripled the deficit."

The *Journal of Gastronomy* was published quarterly at enormous cost. Dedicated to the theory and history of cuisine and initially edited by David Thomson, the journal was the most scholarly element of the organization. First published in the summer of 1984 and running about 125 pages each, its early issues featured essays by such nationally and internationally recognized scholars and artists as Roland Barthes, Alan Davidson (founder of the Oxford Symposia on Food History), M. F. K. Fisher, Jan Langone, Barbara Ketcham Wheaton, Raymond Sokolov, Joyce Carol Oates, and Harvey Levenstein. Topics ranged from "On the Esculent Fungi," "Paradise Lost: The Decline of the Apple and the American Agrarian Ideal," "Food in France After the Revolution," to "The Cooks of Concord." Artwork (René Magritte's *L'Invention*

Collective opened the first volume) as well as photographs of the covers of antique culinary books were included. As Paul Levy wrote from London: "The rates of pay are . . . appetizing. Foodie writers passed the word around that for a long piece, *Gastronomy* pays the equivalent of 40 four-toque dinners."

The *Newsletter,* which Dick Graff had published as a four-page report to all the members, became an eight-page, and then early in 1987 a twelve-page AIWF monthly newsletter redesigned and edited by Robert Clark (who would author Beard's biography five years later). The February issue included articles by Ruth Reichl, then food editor of the *Los Angeles Times* and later of the *New York Times,* as well as pieces by Julia Child and culinary scholars Barbara Wheaton, Philip Hyman, and Mary Hyman. By 1988 it took on more news of the business of the organization.

After reading the May 1987 issue of the monthly newsletter, Julia wrote a letter to the editor (published in July) commenting on two articles that made it evident the AIWF was risking a fall into what she called "The We Happy Few Syndrome: Nothing produced for the mass market is worth considering by the cognoscenti, be it coffee, bread, vegetables, wine, or whatever." They must, she insisted, be just as concerned about the quality of canned and frozen produce as they are about truffles and foie gras. Coffee magnate Tim Castle, who wrote one of the articles, responded immediately to insist he was being grossly misinterpreted, his career hurt, and asking for an emendation. There is no indication that she responded.

Politics reared its ugly head when Bob Huttenback was charged with "embezzlement, insurance fraud, and tax evasion" at the university in the spring of 1987. Julia was as shocked and saddened as she was sure he was innocent and would be released. An ambitious district attorney, the *New York Times*'s purchase of the local paper, and a faculty that was out to get him were the explanations bandied about by his friends. In addition to his own political naiveté (he did not even have a lawyer), his support of the AIWF center may have been involved. When the charge of using university money to renovate his private home (he failed to have the renovation written into his contract, as the last chancellor had) was published, much was made of a presumed $104,000 cost of his new kitchen (apparently a particular sore spot for the students). By July, he was indicted and forced to resign (he was convicted and sentenced to community service). Without him, the center seemed doomed.

The next month, in Larry Wilson's "Julia Child's Crusade" in the *Los Angeles Times Magazine,* she is quoted staunchly defending Huttenback as the victim of a witch hunt. Her dream was still to have the AIWF center in Santa Barbara and to recruit 20,000 more members to the organization. The article also talks about her thoughts on another television series, in which she would visit the sources of food production (a frequent theme only partially fulfilled in the *Dinner at Julia's* series), and AIWF plans to videotape great chefs in action for posterity (they taped Beard before his death). The most interesting revelations in the well-researched article deal with the real problems of the building plans of the AIWF: the Huttenback scandal; the resistance of students and faculty; Vice-Chancellor Michaelsen's statement that the university would probably "need that land in the future"; and an East Coast–West Coast schism in the leadership of the AIWF. An Easterner called it a "sleepy, backwater California institute, filled with deadwood and supported by rich ladies from Santa Barbara." Nancy Harmon Jenkins, the new editor of the *Journal* and a Boston area resident, was quoted as saying she would resist the attempts of Drescher to trim the financial fat by asking her to do more than her job description, which was to edit the *Journal*. It was not a pretty picture, and was discouraging for Julia, who had invested her image and money for five years.

In November 1985 the *Newsletter* listed Julia as offering a $100,000 matching grant for the building fund and placed her name in the $100,000 donor category. She wrote Ross that it was time they straightened out her financial situation and removed her name from the list of donors in that category. "We do not have a formal pledge," only a charitable trust with money reserved for the building fund if the association "ever manages to get itself on a sound financial basis." In the meantime the money was accruing interest, but she "had no intention of releasing" the funds into operating expenses for the national office. She would not rise to their bait. "I don't want that cash to go down the faceless maw of general expenses," she wrote on February 23, 1988. Ross sent a copy of her letter to Graff, along with a yearly listing of her donations. Graff, who poured a great deal of his own money into the AIWF as well, saw the figures that showed that her giving already exceeded that amount, if they counted her founders' fee, her quarterly gift of a thousand dollars, her special underwriting for a new director, then the journal, and finally the corporate fees she diverted to them. She was generous, tolerant, even lenient in allowing professionals to do their job, but when she straightened her back on an issue, she could be brutally frank and stubborn. When she told a couple of friends she was tired of "being used" by the AIWF, the word got back rapidly to headquarters.

Julia was extremely busy trying to complete her book, which was long past deadline, to tape her regular *Good Morning America* spots, and to care for Paul, who in early 1987 slipped from her grasp and fell down a flight of wooden stairs, injuring his ribs and wrist. He was growing weaker and she more concerned for him. Those who met him for the first time in the 1980s believed him to be sullen, distracted, or acerbic. Except for those trips to New York City for ABC, she isolated herself most of that year in Santa Barbara with her computer, missing her cooking gang. She was only halfway through the third chapter early in 1987, she told Mary Frances. By the next spring she was midway through the meat: "I never feel I know enough, and have to keep going out looking at chops, cooking them, etc. A book is so final, even though I keep saying 'in my experience,' to show that I am not stating eternal truths as I see them." The "quite presumptuous title" intimidated her, but Mary Frances encouraged her to write "pure Julia" and not be cut down "into corporate wastebaskets." Julia may have been counting on Judith to cut and edit, but, from the receding deadlines, it was clear to Julia and Mary Frances that Julia was indeed writing her magnum opus.

PROFESSIONAL COMMITMENTS

"Julia was always the first one to put on her badge at a convention," many of her friends point out. Patricia Wells noticed that she always wore her badge throughout a conference. It was a signal of her camaraderie with the professional circle and an instinctive democratic impulse. It echoed her opening of every television program: "Hello, I'm Julia Child."

Though her primary professional commitment was to the AIWF, she was a very active member of what would eventually be called the International Association of Culinary Professionals (IACP). In particular she worked with the organization to construct standards and certification procedures. When they established an examination (Certified Culinary Professional: CCP), she insisted on taking it herself. Whereas the IACP was practical, the AIWF was supposedly more scholarly.

Julia encouraged women culinary professionals within a sorority of good cooking schools, such as Anne Willan's La Varenne. She spoke out also in support of Dorothy Cann's excellent French Culinary Institute in lower Manhattan. (Both Willan and Cann taught French cuisine, not coincidentally, but Julia welcomed dozens of other home cooking schools around the country.) She both visited schools and encouraged individuals. When they had met at La Varenne, Julia informed Susy Davidson: "You know, you are in the right place at the right time for a woman." (Susy would henceforth follow her anywhere.) Another woman, the first female graduate of the Ritz-Escoffier cooking school, wrote to complain to Julia about the terrible way she was treated and the insistence of the director (Gregory Usher) and chefs that there are no good women cooks. Julia always lent a sympathetic ear and words of encouragement to the women and the schools, filing all the letters for later recommendations.

She helped to found the Women's Culinary Guild of New England, attended its meetings as well as those of the Les Dames d'Escoffier, Culinary Historians of Boston, and the IACP. She continued to support the Beard House by allowing them to use her name as a founder. Her donations went to the AIWF, but "her name was magic," declares Kathleen Perry. Julia did not cotton to competition among these groups, only joint efforts toward the goals in which she believed. She loved the lectures, sessions, and camaraderie of every culinary conference. She waited in line with everyone else, Patricia Wells remembers, except once when there was a huge line for Dungeness crab, which Julia adores, and she went directly to the head of the line in a rare moment of pulling rank.

During this decade Julia had several broad commitments: professionalizing the craft, educating the public about food, and the practical improvement of food, specifically the quality of mass-produced food. As she said in her "We Happy Few" letter: "With 250 million mouths to feed, we have to mass-produce." She refused to have her name on any board on which she was not active, and turned down several honorary degrees. She chose her charities carefully (refusing a request for a large donation to her Katharine Branson alma mater in the spring of 1980, for example). As a favor to AIWF executive board member and old friend George Gruenwald, Julia was his guest star at the annual PBS board meeting in San Diego in 1989. Bob Johnson had once encouraged her to cut back on giveaways, believing that every time she did a demonstration for Planned Parenthood, she was chipping away at her image. She disagreed, and wrote a lengthy appeal to the new First Lady, Barbara Bush, on November 28, 1988, asking her, as a Smith sister, to plead the cause for having only wanted babies. She feared for Planned Parenthood under the Reagan Supreme Court.

Two institutions of higher education in the Boston area would become major projects occupying her devotion and time during the coming decade: Radcliffe's Schlesinger Library and Boston University. When she and Paul returned to Cambridge for four months toward the end of 1988, she was feted on two occasions by the Arthur and Elizabeth Schlesinger Library on the History of Women in America (named for the parents of Julia's neighbor, the famous Kennedy historian). To their large collection of women's history, Julia added most of her own cookbooks and her papers, including her correspondence with Elizabeth David, M. F. K. Fisher, and Simone Beck. That fall she was elected an honorary member of Phi Beta Kappa, and in December she was there for the dedication of and the party for the renovated Julia Child Research Area, housing 5,000 cookbooks and study carrels. She did not miss an opportunity to talk to Barbara Wheaton, honorary curator, and Barbara Haber, curator of printed books, about her desire to see an academic program in the history and writing of gastronomy. Haber and the library were featured that fall in a *Newsweek* article celebrating "a classic women's library," mentioning Julia's papers and Louise Nevelson's sculpture.

Two days after the dedication ceremony at the Schlesinger, Julia was in front of a packed audience at Boston University teaching a seminar in the culinary arts. For years, Julia and Jacques Pépin (who had a graduate degree in literature from Columbia University) had advocated a Department of Gastronomy, but were as yet unsuccessful. A year before, the acting president refused a direct written appeal by Julia. But the university had a four-month certificate in Liberal Arts and, under its Seminars in the Arts, included seminars in the culinary arts. Julia gave her first one on December 3, 1988. Paul was in the front row and Elizabeth Bishop was assisting. As Julia was preparing steam-roasted goose, she noticed the extremely large back cavity of the bird and tried to disguise it with parsley, then discarded the idea with a caveat about pubic hair. It was a lively seminar.

Though she would devote nearly five years to writing her last book, leaving her with the feeling she did nothing else seven days a week, she did in fact do a great deal to develop the profession. Anne Willan and Mark Cherniavsky, who see the AIWF "as a kind of albatross" for her, best describe Julia's relations with all these professional organizations: "She will give any help within reason that she can give, but she does not want to run things for other people."

THE LAST BOOK

From 1985 through 1988, Julia focused on two tasks: caring for Paul and completing her final book. The food world rose and the professional organizations boiled and coagulated around her, but she was often too preoccupied to turn on the blender and smooth out the sauce.

Projected deadlines came and went as she kept to the course she believed in, a thorough compendium of teaching techniques. She kept Mary Frances up-to-date on her progress. As early as 1987 she was telling people she was no longer tricoastal and would not be getting over to France, a decision based on the failing strength and awareness of Paul. She took Paul to the conferences and to the taping of *Good Morning America,* but one of her gang of young women assistants sat next to him to act as babysitter.

As Julia was finishing her meat chapter, she received a letter from Ruth J. Robinson, whose former husband had worked with Nathan Pritikin at his Longevity Centers. The issue of fats and cholesterol was already a long-standing issue which Julia addressed in her form letters sent out by WGBH over her signature. Copies of Mrs. Robinson's letter, accusing Julia of gross promotion of obesity and heart disease, went to Polaroid and Trader Joe's (her television sponsors). The accuser, a resident of Santa Barbara, said she saw Julia at the farmers' market on Saturdays and friends saw her eating large salads at the Biltmore Hotel, so why could she not advocate healthy foods? Before his death Pritikin had been disturbed by Julia's promotion of wine and fat. Julia sent her answer immediately, including an AIWF brochure and her recipe for a healthy and happy life:

> Moderation in all things—
> A great variety of food—
> Exercise and weight watching—
>> And, most important of all,
>> PICK YOUR GRANDPARENTS.

"I must say," she added, "after learning something about the severity of his diet and knowing not only of Pritikin's long illness but of his relatively early death, I have often wondered if a good meal once in a while might have kept him going a little longer." No response came except from one of her sponsors, who said he would add a bottle of wine to that "good meal." "We are proud and happy to sponsor you," he ended. In her cover letter to the sponsors, she tucked in a postscript: "Letters like this are fun! Remember the Pope's Nose?"

When the *National Enquirer* called because they got wind of the Pritikin letter exchange, Bill Truslow informed them there was "no story." Julia, used to frankness, said no more at his suggestion. The American public agreed with her, for its consumption of fat per capita went from 52.9 pounds in 1970 to 62.7 pounds in 1990. Had he still been living, Pritikin would have noted, however, that deaths by "heart attacks" dropped from 226 to 104 for every 100,000 Americans between 1950 and 1992. An AIWF *Newsletter* at the end of that year quoted Julia: "What we have is panic at the table. We're afraid of fat, meat, pesticides. Going to the dinner table has become more a pitfall than a pleasure." The following year Molly O'Neill quoted her in the *International*

Herald Tribune: "[America has] a fanatical fear of food. . . . I still insist that an unhappy stomach is going to curdle your nutrition." After a speech by Julia on this theme at a Santa Barbara AIWF Taste and Health Conference, her friend Marshall Ackerman followed her as panel chairman and introduced himself: "I am Marshall Ackerman, former publisher of *Prevention* magazine—we *created* the fear of food."

"It's like taking care of your car," she liked to say to reporters. "If you don't give it enough oil, it breaks down." Her stand on "rich creamery butter" (waiters were told to remove margarine from her table) was vindicated in 1994 when studies were released showing the dangers of margarine (because of the hydrogenated oils) and that the price and calories were the same as for butter. Scientists were also saying, "There are 120 flavor components in butter, and the taste is impossible to duplicate," the *New York Times* reported.

However, when a local food writer in Boston several years later tried to set up a meeting, at Julia's request, between her and Tufts president Jean Mayer, "the affable French war hero and nutritionist wanted no part of her," because her rich desserts had undone what he was working to change in American diets. In 1996 the go-between revealed the incident: *"Hélas!* Jean Mayer, who could never say no to another pat of butter, is now dead of a heart attack . . . and Julia . . . is the thriving and still disciplined mistress of small portions."

Julia fell over her computer cord in Santa Barbara that spring and broke her hip ("I was plunging around, and I caught my foot in it and lost my balance"). Governor Dukakis's letter of sympathy arrived at the Santa Barbara Cottage Hospital. His great supporter, ever a Democrat, Julia replied it was like a "shot in the hip" to hear from him. In fact, she was furious at what she had done and the time lost, and immediately got busy on therapy through the summer. Rosemary came down to help during her recovery. The injury made Julia realize that Paul could not manage on his own and she must consider future organized care for him. She told one journalist who was interviewing her for a *McCall's* feature on their "recipe for love" that their only regret was not having children. "I would have been a complete mother," she said. "I would have liked to have had grown children and grandchildren. But we do have wonderful nieces and nephews, and we're close to them."

Discouraged about the setback from her broken hip and questioning whether people wanted to do any more real cooking, she decided at the end of May to cut down *The Way to Cook* in order to meet her July deadline. She wrote to Mary Frances in late May that she was "about to start on what I think is the last chapter of my book! I have decided to omit EGGS AND SOUF-

FLÉS, since I have nothing new to say about them, and MAIN COURSE MISC.—to hell with that. There will be slogging through to tighten up the early chapters, but I shall make that deadline in July—perhaps not July 1st, but it will be done before we leave here July 22nd." However, she could not exclude eggs, and her deadline unfortunately moved back again.

She had said for several years that her own cooking changed, as she had, but she included several recipes (with small changes) that remained successful and beloved to her readers, such as her "famous Queen of Sheba cake" (she used now both sweetened and unsweetened chocolate and less sugar). With variations through the years, this Reine de Saba cake had appeared in the first *Mastering* and in *The French Chef.* This final volume, after all, was her magnum opus, an oversized book that would number 511 pages and have eleven traditional chapters, from soups to cakes and cookies. There would be 650 photographs (given her by *Parade),* for she believed one learned best by seeing. Julia emphasized her debt to her cooking gang, naming in the introduction those who worked with her on *Parade, Good Morning America,* and the *Dinner at Julia's* television series, including "our friendly ayatollah" Russ Morash. The collective effort also shows up in the narration of the recipes. She includes "Rosemary's classic pizza dough," a fillet of salmon braised with a mousseline of scallops, which she and Marian Morash created when Julia was working on-line at the Straight Wharf restaurant, Maggie Mah's grandmother's applesauce fruitcake, and the grated potato galette Sara Moulton made when she was sous-chef at La Tulipe in New York City.

The Childs returned to Cambridge in September 1988, not only for the Schlesinger and Boston University appearances, but to complete the final work on her book and confer with Judith Jones on the layout. There would be three columns per page, thus six columns with the book opened. Julia agreed to lower her royalties to 7 percent on the first printing of 60,000 in order to keep the price down. Knopf would ultimately earn back far more than their nearly half-million-dollar advance with future printings and serial sales. It seemed as though she had done "nothing else for the last five years at least," she wrote Simca. "This is certainly my last book—too confining." And, in a familiar refrain, she told Anne Willan, "Never again."

In an article in the December issue of the *Radcliffe Quarterly,* under the title she would have preferred for her book, "Cooking My Way," Julia expressed doubts about writing to an audience in the 1980s: "Are they interested in real cooking anymore, or is it all pasta salads? I personally love the pure mechanics of the art, including the chopping, the shredding, the sautéing, the butchering, even the cleanup. And I am fascinated by the basic principles, and what you can do with them once mastered." In a letter to Simca praising Anne

Willan's new illustrated encyclopedia of cookery, Julia said, "Our *Masterings* still sell, but classic French cuisine is 'out' because of health and cholesterol fads."

$\mathscr{I}$N THE END IS THE BEGINNING

Because Paul was unhappy in the Cambridge winter, waiting around while Julia corrected proofs, she took him back to Santa Barbara in February 1989. For the next six months he could walk on the beach in balmy weather. This was a turning point in Julia's life, the end of her last, long book and looking ahead to months of promotion in the fall and winter. Again bowing to the necessities of modern television and photographs, the suggestion of professionals, and her own practicality ("If you look old and gray, you feel old and gray"), she had more facial surgery. The result was wonderful, her friends believed and photographs confirmed. If any friends were disappointed in her, they said nothing. She was largely recovered when Jean Stapleton first performed Lee Hoiby's *Bon Appétit,* a musical theatrical rendition of Julia's chocolate cake recipe *(gâteau Victoire au chocolat, mousseline,* from *Julia Child & Company).* It was first performed in Washington, DC, then at California State University, Long Beach, and finally Santa Fe. They sent her tickets and she went to see it on opening night with the Gateses, but says, "I did not think of it as being me."

By 1989, the AIWF's debt was over half a million dollars and both D. Crosby Ross and Dun Gifford resigned. First (during 1987 and 1988) came the revolt of the AIWF chapters, which had been gaining power for several years, especially the New York, Los Angeles, and San Francisco chapters; second was what some saw as betrayal by Dun Gifford, who quietly organized his own competing company, Oldways, an educational group focusing on diet and culture. When Child, Graff, Mondavi, and Michael McCarty confronted Gifford at the Four Seasons Hotel in Chicago with his conflict of interest, he resigned from the board. He also took the backing of the Olive Oil Council with him and the AIWF remained "very bitter" toward him. Julia was hurt and incredulous, but rarely talked against him (one of her best friends said, "Julia did not want to hear about it. She is loyal to the end"). He was gone only months when he hired away Gregory Drescher (Program Director) and Nancy Harmon Jenkins (editor of the *Journal).*

David Strada had already been hired as AIWF executive director ("I was appointed to clean up and turn around"), with a salary commensurate with the income of the organization, and now Graff talked Dorothy Cann, who was

AIWF board secretary and managed her own French Culinary Institute, in to being chair of the board of directors. Though disappointed by the betrayal by Gifford, Julia would remain his friend and neighbor. Soon she would give more time to helping the revolutionaries reinvent the AIWF and pay its debts.

Julia lost two dear friends in early 1989. Ivan Cousins, the husband of her sister, Dort, finally succumbed to prostate cancer in San Francisco on January 2. They had known for more than a year that he would die and she had grieved with her sister. Then on March 8 her beloved friend Avis DeVoto died of pancreatic cancer at the age of eighty-four. The obituaries mentioned her marriage to the well-known historian and columnist, her office management at Bread Loaf for decades, and her job as a secretary at Harvard's Lowell House and then at the office of the Dean of Students at Radcliffe. But as far as Julia was concerned, Avis's greatest claim to fame would be her championing of *Mastering the Art of French Cooking* and taking the manuscript to Knopf. Julia grieved the passing of her proofreader and editor, lively correspondent (and clipping service), loyal friend, and pinch hitter.

Confronted with the most difficult decision of her life, one that would change her life irrevocably, Julia told Simca in the summer of 1989 that she believed Paul's "days are numbered." Since his heart bypass and strokes in 1974 and the slow return of only part of his memory, Paul had had two prostate operations and carried a slow-growing tumor. Unable to care for himself, he was confused and incontinent. When he was hospitalized in June, she called her lawyer and friend Bill Truslow and then met with the doctors for "a big medical pow-wow" on the twenty-third. She would listen to the experts, as she always did. They advised putting him in a medical care facility in Santa Barbara, and on good days Julia would bring him home or take him out for a short time. She assured one friend in mid-September, "He has had a good and interesting life." His family believed she kept him out of long-term care far longer than she needed to or should have. Friends like Margrit Biever (Mondavi) admired Julia's commitment to Paul: "They stood by their commitment to each other; there was a point of honor there. It was love, but beyond love."

On August 6 she took him to see an exhibit of some of his paintings at a "Salute to Paul Child," planned by the Southern California Culinary Guild and hosted by the Santa Barbara Winery. According to Karen Berk and Mitzie Cutler, who led the organization, Julia brought him in before the crowd arrived and walked him slowly around to see these paintings capturing the Venice, Provence, and China scenes they had shared. She took him back to the nursing home and returned herself before the crowd arrived. The *Los Angeles Times* did a feature in its food section on the party for Paul, but few knew how much she had already lost of Paul or of the second decision she made to take him out of the Santa Barbara facility, which she decided she did not like, and back to Cambridge.

As her friend Maggie Mah said: "Julia doesn't twist herself inside out or waste time agonizing when making a decision; she just does it. She is a deeply compassionate and generous person with the ability to balance her own needs with the needs of others. She has a certain moral toughness that is very well illustrated by her competence and devotion in taking care of Paul." The best description of Julia's own feelings was expressed nearly eight years before in a letter she wrote to Fanny Brennan. Julia observed Alice Lee Myers, Fanny's mother, who had dementia and was living with them. She wrote to tell Fanny she had to put her mother into a home: "You must get her into a senior citizen place . . . so that she can be taken care of, and so that you can be at peace and lead some kind of normal life. I am sure she herself would be horrified if she knew [your suffering]. . . . You will feel guilty, as everyone does, but you have, Fanny, been a generous, loving and caring daughter." Then she added a few words about "the agony of being tough about it."

Bill Truslow walked across the street from Julia's Santa Barbara condominium to sit in the garden and read the latest copy of *The Atlantic Monthly*. He turned a page and saw a full-page drawing of a thistle and a poem written by his brother-in-law Peter Davison about the death of his wife, Jane. Truslow sat silently, swept by the old grief at his sister's death. Eventually he walked back to the Child apartment and found that Julia's galleys of *The Way to Cook* had arrived. When he saw the dedication to Bob Johnson, he told her about running into Peter's poem. They talked quietly about Bob and Jane, as they did about Paul, and then fell silent, both grieving. "I suddenly felt I knew why I was so at home with Julia. Yankees do not indulge themselves. No keening or verbal analysis. Yes, Julia can weep, but she will not beat her breast. She is open, but she never spills."

To avoid the traffic in Los Angeles, they got Paul from the nursing home and left at 4:30 in the morning. As they flew to Boston, Paul asked where they were going, and Julia reminded him of what the doctors told them in Santa Barbara. When they drove to the nursing home in Lexington, Paul asked the same thing. He wanted to go home. Julia never lied to him. The tears were streaming down her cheeks as they left the Fairlawn Nursing Home. It was the most painful thing she ever did.

$\mathcal{N}$OTRE DAME DE LA CUISINE
(1989 – 1993)

"She's the nation's energy queen."

  JIM WOOD, San Francisco Examiner, *1991*
  ∽

"SIGN YOUR OLD name and address," Mary Fran Russell said, opening her copy of *The Way to Cook* and giving Julia a hug. "Julia McWilliams, 1207 South Pasadena Street," her former classmate wrote on the first page of her five-pound book. Vroman's bookstore in Pasadena was jammed with admirers. Standing patiently in the snaking line that ran out the door were several of her now gray-haired friends from the Polytechnic School and the neighborhood. "Oh, Bill, are you still alive!?" Julia called out as he leaned down to kiss her on the cheek. They all remembered her old address and reminded her of childhood events they had shared. Julia was home, and her buddies were there to celebrate her great success.

$\mathcal{P}$ROMOTING *THE WAY TO COOK*

She began the late-1989 press tour for *The Way to Cook* in San Francisco two days after the October earthquake and never considered not going. Knopf's West Coast publicist, Pamela Henstell, was pregnant and not certain she wanted to be there, especially when they felt a strong aftershock. Nothing deterred the seventy-seven-year-old author from her demanding two-month promotion tour and the moving line of book buyers greeting her at every stop. Too many years and solitary hours had been spent writing the book, and she also felt the responsibility of an enormous advance. Pre-Christmas sales should be remarkably strong. For the first time a cookbook was given the coveted position of main selection of the Book-of-the-Month Club. The editors there were not intimidated by the $50 price.

Her talent was an offshoot of her vigor. She and her team traveled the country, sometimes taking five meetings or interviews a day with press, radio and television. She made crêpes for David Letterman, who tossed them to the audience. She signed books at the November AIWF Conference on Gastronomy in Chicago. She signed 300 books at a Boston bookstore, attended a reception at the Schlesinger Library for French women chefs, participated in a champagne tasting at the Meridien Hotel, then fed eight people for dinner that night because old friends Sally [Bicknell] and Leonard Miall were visiting from London. Her only bow to time was the dessert, store-bought ice cream over which she poured bourbon and sprinkled ground coffee beans. One journalist observed that she "maintains a schedule that might exhaust a teenager." Another called her "the nation's energy queen."

She had a particularly crazy travel schedule because she insisted on going home at least once a week to see Paul, whom she phoned every day. When she first put him in Fairlawn, she visited him three and four times a day, especially if he called her to come. With his short-term memory gone, he was not certain when he last saw her. Hanging up the telephone, she never knew if he recognized her loving voice.

"This was her last big tour," said Janice Goldklang, Knopf's publicity director for the tour, "Crowds and sales were incredible." It was her magnum opus, and everyone came out. "Such a show and outpouring of love. Local publicity people are not prepared for the crowds and that is why we travel with her. We can get a line going and organize it, insisting on signatures only, nothing personal." Henstell, who accompanied her in the West, reported that people would stand in line an hour and then demand a personal message ("To my favorite cook" was one). "Somebody else has to play the bad guy, and I would step in and say that there is not enough time." There was a limit to how long one person could sit and sign, she said, but "Julia always continued to the last person." In addition to the Knopf staff, Susy Davidson occasionally accompanied her in the South, Sara Moulton (with the most professional experience) helped out in New York City, and Liz Bishop in Boston. "I don't know how she does it," says Davidson, remembering a spiraling line of hundreds in a hotel in Dallas. "It's my job," she would tell those exhausted women trying to keep up with her. She was, as John Updike said of one of his characters, "an athlete of the clock."

The press either wrote profiles of her or reviewed the book with several other books by heavy hitters that fall and winter of 1989–90. At the annual Beard Awards in May 1990, her book came in third after Anne Willan's *La Varenne Pratique* (the winner) and the Silver Palette's *New Basics Cookbook* (officially she tied for second). She reported to Simca the inside results (only the winner was ever announced at the Beard Awards), adding her usual *Tant pis pour moi!* The IACP also awarded Willan first place, with Julia tying for second place. Classic techniques with contemporary style was her approach. She informed the press that her book was written for "someone who wants to learn to cook but already knows the basics . . . a lot like learning backhand in tennis." Which explains why Mimi Sheraton said five years later, "She taught the basic techniques best in *The Way to Cook*, which, with her first *Mastering*, is her best. I have given *The Way to Cook* as a gift more than any other book because I subscribe to the philosophy that you learn to cook the basic techniques and then you adapt them."

Before she began the tour Julia entertained journalists who flocked in for profiles to run upon the release of the book. As she was driving Molly O'Neill to the train after one interview, she backed her car across the street and into the neighbors' station wagon. "Oh, dear. I've really done it this time," she said, and O'Neill closed her *New York Times* profile with this incident. The accident was carried around the world when the piece was picked up by the *International Herald Tribune.* "At seventy-seven, she's so Julia!" O'Neill exclaimed.

If she had not been Julia Child, her book would have been lost in the crowd of giant primers or reference books that appeared between 1988 and 1990: new editions of *Larousse Gastronomique, Better Homes & Gardens New Cook Book,* and *The Fannie Farmer Cookbook,* as well as the books by Rosso and Lukins, Willan, Pépin *(The Art of Cooking),* Craig Claiborne, and others. Christopher Lehmann-Haupt called it "a magnificent distillation of a lifetime of cooking." Florence Fabricant, reporting on all these books for the *New York Times,* said they indicated that "after years of takeout, many are returning home [to learn the basics]."

When the tour was over Julia hired a secretary named Stephanie Hersh from the Katharine Gibbs School (she was the only one in her class with a culinary background). Julia hired her on a part-time basis only, fearing she was just trying to get into her kitchen, as Stephanie had a college degree as well as a two-year degree from the Culinary Institute of America (1985) and had worked as a banquet manager and a private family chef. The only thing Stephanie faked was her computer skills. She had word-processing training at the business school, but had never seen a computer mouse. She typed Julia's letters on a typewriter, took the computer book home for the weekend, and came back to master the machine. It was that quick intelligence and bravura that Julia needed. "I have office gridlock," Julia confessed. But Stephanie realized when a forgotten Canadian Public Television crew showed up that first day to film "A Day in the Life of Julia Child" that more than computer skills were needed in the Cambridge office.

Someone needed to see the entire picture for Julia: "She had kitchen people, book people, television people, a part-time typing woman, a cleaning lady . . . [but] no one seemed to have the full picture of Julia's needs," Stephanie remembers. Within days she urged Julia to replace her longtime assistant (who had a drinking problem and worked only when Julia was around), took the schedule book and coordinated publishing and AIWF demands (Julia did not need to go to Chicago twice in one month), requested first-class flight arrangements and pickup, saw to it that she got frequent-flier miles, and drove her to local events. When she told Julia she was a bad driver, Julia responded, "Okay, then, I will get a Volvo," and purchased a fire-engine-red Volvo, which she also backed into the neighbor's car across the street. When Julia was out of town Stephanie visited Paul and took him for walks until it was no longer possible for him to leave Fairlawn. Some friends and family would resent her organization of Julia's life, but Julia was soon pleased with the humor and organizational skills of her young office manager. They were both at a local AIWF event at Locke-Ober's restaurant, unaware they were standing almost back to back. Stephanie heard someone ask Julia if her new secretary was on an apprenticeship. When Julia answered, "No, we are together until death do us part," Stephanie leaned her head back and asked impertinently, "Whose?" Julia laughed and said, "Time will tell."

THE BULLY PULPIT

Julia Child was a formidable preacher. With her national stature as a television personality, the unquestioned trust people had in her integrity (Anne Willan called her "the voice of reason"), and her physical height and stage presence, everyone took notice and listened. She knew how to sound-bite (newsman Jim Wood called her "always quotable"). She became, in *Newsweek*'s words, "our leading national symbol of gustatory pleasure." Her message was her philosophy of life: life is to be joyous, and joy comes from sensory pleasures shared with others. The Gospel According to Julia: Good food and wine are central to health and pleasure. The table she shared with others was her altar. *"Le carillon de l'amitié,"* Paul had called out when wineglasses rang together. "I don't think pleasure is decadent," she said in a 1992 article entitled "Julia Child, the Pleasure Shark": "It's part of life, it's the juice of life, it's the reason for living, for *everything* we do."

She "reopened the American kitchen as an arena of Old World sensuality and pleasure," one food writer asserted. She could have preached the importance of sexual pleasure—as Paul did in a 1975 cover story of their marriage in *People* when he spoke of "eating, drinking, and love-making"—but she was New England and of a certain generation. Privately she had a bawdy frankness. It was not just that food was her profession; it was central to health, nourishment, and happiness. "I want to be healthy and well fed up to the end. What will prolong my life is eating well and enjoying it," she asserted.

She seemed at times to be proclaiming the message of variety, balance, and good taste to a dark and puritanical country, which feared ecstatic tastes ("sinful" and "to die for" were common adjectives) and good wine. Years earlier, she had lifted her glass at the end of her first program in 1963 in front of families who (except for those in ethnic neighborhoods) had no wine bottles on their shelves. Thirty years later, more families were drinking wine with their meals, but as wine critic Frank Prial asserted, America is a country that will never become wine drinkers. Beer and hard liquor, but not (as Julia believed) the basic food group (wine) that should be enjoyed with meals.

The least well-attended Conference on Gastronomy was held in February 1991 in Los Angeles: "Wine in American Life," with workshops full of medical doctors, professors, and wine specialists from around the country. The conference was elegant and groundbreaking, but it took AIWF a year to pay the Biltmore and American Express bills (staff members had their personal cards revoked by AmEx) because the cash-poor national office used most of the $100,000 conference income to pay office expenses. The educational influence of such conferences is difficult to measure (nonmember registration cost $590). The next year Julia appeared before a congressional hearing to have wine regulation taken out of the Bureau of Alcohol, Tobacco, and Firearms and placed in the hands of the U.S. Department of Agriculture.

If suspicion of the pleasures of the table undermined the furthering of good cooking, certainly the pace of contemporary life also undermined the goals of Julia Child. (Burger King was selling two million Whopper hamburgers per day.) Food writer Paul Levy called Julia a "scholar-cook . . . like Elizabeth David, Alan Davidson, and Jane Grigson," who "has taken on the unenviable task of civilizing the cooking and eating habits of the Junk Food continent." Julia cautioned one journalist, "I think snacking is a terrible, terrible habit," adding that Americans snack because they do not have balanced diets. Filling up on one-calorie sodas, "Healthy Choice nutritious frozen en-trées," and "rubbery fat-free cheese" inevitably leads to a binge at Häagen-Dazs, says Michelle Stacey in *Consumed: Why Americans Love, Hate, and Fear Food* (1994). Numerous columnists joined her. Erma Bombeck: "I'm with Julia Child; we're sick of 'lite.' Frankly I'm bored to death with lite, non-fat . . . no flavor, taste-like-the-bottom-of-a-clogged-drain food. . . . Neither Julia nor I is saying good nutrition is not a good thing. We're saying, just eat less of the real stuff."

If the 1970s had been marked by a craze for home cooking, with the Cuisinart and the proliferation of cooking schools, and the boom of the 1980s brought people out to restaurants, especially those with celebrity chefs, the 1990s featured takeout food. "Time and money dictated," says Mimi Shera-ton, who gave up restaurant reviewing. Worried by recession and violence, perhaps even sated by restaurants, people cocooned. They cooked a few dishes, but brought prepared food home from supermarkets and takeout from some of the finest restaurants. Julia predicted in an article in the *Boston Globe* that "home cooking is slowly making a come-back." If she had her way, the basic food groups would no longer be take-in, eat-out, frozen, and canned.

Julia used the bully pulpit of her beloved status to preach the pleasures of home cooking. The message was reinforced in the films of the mid-1990s, which celebrated the connection between home cooking and its sensuous and communal associations: *Like Water for Chocolate* (1993), *Eat, Drink, Man, Woman* (1994) and *Big Night* (1996)—all art films drawing wide interest and attendance.

As Julia had rejected her ancestors' corpse-cold Presbyterianism as life-denying and judgmental, so she fought the food puritanism so ingrained in America: the embarrassment with too much talk about food, expressions about "wasting" too much time preparing and eating food, and the fear of food impurities by those who grew up in the 1960s. Ideas of hell and damna-tion found secular expression in bad cholesterol, high blood pressure, and fat. Julia was one of the first to champion fish inspection in Boston, but she believed crusaders injected fear into the heart of already inhibited eaters. Food Nazis came in many forms by the 1990s, and the large number of competing periodicals led to both food faddism and headline scare tactics: pesticides, Alar sprayed on apples (Meryl Streep testified before Congress, in fear for her children's lives), cruelty to calves—in her words, "animal-rights people, screwy nutritionists and dietitians, neo-prohibitionists" and "the health po-lice." She restated her opinions frequently: about pesticides ("in moderation, we have to feed millions"); about cholesterol ("If we do not eat at least two [the number varied] tablespoons of oil each day our hair will begin to fall out: it is a basic food group"; "Chimpanzees fed less cholesterol are meaner and more violent than others"). She preferred one bite of a great dessert to a box of Entenmann's fat-free tasteless sugar concoctions. Entenmann's fat-free line ("This is chemistry, not cuisine," declared Laura Shapiro) was introduced in 1989.

Two years later a longevity study, reported by television's *20/20,* revealed that people who live to be ninety or a hundred do not do so by eating a high-fiber diet of self-denial. A "sense of humor and an active life" were actually the factors that made for a healthy life. While the country was yo-yoed from fear to reassurance by the press, Julia kept the middle ground of moderation.

Scare tactics, intolerance, and headline fads only fed the American fear of good food, good wine, and good times. Fearful reports only comforted the lazy cooks (66 million boxes of Hamburger Helper were sold the year Julia published *The Way to Cook)* and those who viewed food as just a necessity of physical survival (food as intravenous drip), not as essential to the spiritual, aesthetic, and social life. "Cooking is not a chore, it is a joy. Dining is not a fuel stop, it is recreation," she exhorted. Her book sold 300,000 copies that first year, but she believed that no book would change the country's eating habits. She was enough like her father—John McWilliams served on school and hospital boards for decades in Pasadena—to approach the problem through education. She continued to lobby for advanced programs in gastronomy, but she also envisioned the American Institute of Wine and Food as playing a key role in educating the public. She had been busy completing her book and promoting it during the "Gatsby years" that led to the "revolution" (Dorothy Cann Hamilton's terms) among the ranks of the organization. Julia was now ready to spend a year traveling and reviving the enterprise that she, Mondavi, Graff, and Huttenback founded.

With a bottle of rare Chenin Blanc from his Chalone Vineyard, Dick Graff talked forty-year-old Dorothy Cann into taking over as chair of the board of AIWF because "she was a good businesswoman." Cann was fair-haired, sophisticated, and literate, owner of the French Culinary Institute, and of Slavic heritage. She, George Faison, and Clark Wolf, along with the revolution of key local chapters, forced the AIWF to face its deficit and reassess its mission. In three years, while she was chair of the board and David Strada was executive director, they would reduce by half the bank debt and all the current, payable debt by cutting administrative salaries and staff, eliminating the *Newsletter* and the *Journal of Gastronomy* ("I was called a philistine," says Cann Hamilton, "but we were bleeding financially"), cutting back on office space, and sending Julia on the road to organize or revitalize chapters during

1990. "She saved it," said Clark Wolf of Cann. The concept of an educational center had been replaced by a chapter-centered organization, and the Simon-Lowenstein books were finally divided between the University of California at San Diego and the Schlesinger Library of Radcliffe College. Henceforth, the synergy of the institute would lie with its local chapters.

"Julia supported the revolution," says Cann Hamilton. "She came down firmly on reducing the debt and insisting that we were not dilettantes." Several on the board of directors, including Julia, Dick Graff, Robert Mondavi, and Dorothy Cann, guaranteed the $650,000 bank loans (there was also a debt of $300,000 in payables): "No one wanted this to fail." That first year they paid down $300,000 of the debt as well as meeting office expenses and articulating a new manifesto.

Initially, Julia and the AIWF planned an eight-city tour from March through July 1990, beginning in New York City and ending at the Fetzer Vineyard in California. With her "indefatigable" and "unflappable" spirit, Julia continued through the following year as well, from Cincinnati to Carmel, from South Beach to Seattle. When she was in Phoenix, Barbara Fenzl, the local organizer and chapter president, arranged with the chef at Main Chance (vulgarly known as a fat farm) to have her stay in their luxurious surroundings, where the Founders Banquet would be held. As Barbara walked her to a four-room house usually housing a President's wife or a Vanderbilt, they passed numerous women dressed in fluffy pink bathrobes. Julia politely said nothing and soon dismissed the four servants who were unpacking her bag, ironing her pink towels, and offering a manicure and beauty treatments. She had to leave for meetings in town. The next evening when the chef asked how she was enjoying Main Chance, she blurted out, "What do those women DO all day?!" Not a surprising question from a woman whose good friend Pat Pratt says, "I've never seen her do nothing." She told Simca that Main Chance was "interesting, but not my type of place at all—very ladylike, pastel pink, and subdued."

Wherever she went, membership bloomed. In 1989 there were 5,500 members; at the end of 1991 there were 6,900. Julia even wrote in her alumnae quarterly that the AIWF offered "great fun and serious seminars." She swayed many, but when the time came for renewal of their membership she was not there, and too many dropped out. It would take a year or two for the national headquarters in San Francisco to figure out why there was such a high attrition rate (52 percent in 1992). Nevertheless, after expenses, the profit from the 1990 Julia tour came to $170,435. In part through her efforts in 1991, twelve new chapters were opened, almost doubling the number. She called herself "window dressing" for the chapters.

Julia championed education for herself as well as others. There was never time enough in life to learn everything, but she attended the annual IACP conferences and in September flew to London with Nancy Barr to the Oxford Symposium on Gastronomy, a scholarly conference she tried never to miss. She sought out producers, scientists, and conferences, eager to learn, especially about the raising of veal. Mary Risley, who learned to cook using the two *Mastering* books and now owned the Tante Marie Cooking School in San Francisco, remembers how amazed she was during a Food Writers workshop in her city in 1992 when Julia enrolled in a class to study writing techniques with those less than half her age.

Julia allowed a short piece from one of her television shows to be used in the background of a Nike commercial and sent the money to the AIWF. "I wear New Balance," Air Julia informed them frankly. "This is not an endorsement of Nike." But the largest block of money for the AIWF was promised from the Norwegian salmon industry, which gave $100,000 to sponsor "A Taste of Norway with Julia Child," an hour-long tape made for WGBH and produced and directed by Russ Morash. With additional backing from SAS airlines, they left in mid-July 1991 for a nearly two-week shoot in Oslo, visiting all her favorite places, including the home where she and Paul had lived. The American Embassy gave a big party in her honor, and she dined with the Egges and the Heyerdahls (the latter sent gravlax to Paul). One journalist reported that Julia called Paul three times a day, at the hours she usually called, regardless of her schedule or the time difference. "The Norway video nearly killed us," says Morash. "The crew started at 7 A.M. and we worked until 10 P.M. with intense filming. Julia had the most energy and would call at night saying, 'Let's step out and get a bit to eat.' " The film, which would be edited by Morash and shown the following year during her birthday celebrations, shows her fly-fishing for salmon, knee-deep in icy water, hopping a helicopter, looking out over Oslo from the Olympic ski run, and declaring, "I am at heart a Viking!"

Almost immediately after returning home from Oslo, she took a trip to Prince Edward Island and Halifax. While she was gone, Elizabeth Bishop, who was vacationing on a boat with her husband in waters not far from Julia, lay down with a headache and died in her sleep of a brain aneurysm. Julia lost a good friend and manager in Bishop. The posse still had Susy Davidson and Nancy Barr. As a former member of the posse noted: "Julia likes to have a lot of girls around."

Whether she was attending a dinner honoring René Vernon (the former White House chef), or the Aspen Food and Wine Classic every June (she drew audiences of 2,500), or doing a benefit for the San Francisco Public Library, she was a guiding spirit, revving up the celebration and speaking out. Even when she spent a week in France in November 1990—where she had not been in four years—she sat for an interview with Simca and Susy Davidson. Simca reinforced every point that Julia made about good eating habits. The only place she did not give interviews was during the family gatherings in Maine each August.

Julia tasted the cooking of the best chefs in America as she traveled. In an interview in 1990 she commended Stephan Pyles in Dallas, Rick Bayless in Chicago, Alice Waters in Berkeley, and in Los Angeles, Herbert Keller, Joachim Splichal, and Patrick Healy. The best restaurants in New York were French: Boulud, Bouley, Côte Basque, L'Espinasse, and Le Cirque. She criticized the fussiness of contemporary chefs, but in fact her dining experience sometimes differed from that of other diners: when she walked in the door each chef sent his or her best and most elaborate dishes. By the mid-1990s the food on plates was being stood on its side to create vertical, architectural structures. "Food should have a natural look . . . I would rather cut my own quail, not have it fanned out for me." Her philosophy of "balance, moderation, variety" was sorely tested by these travels, especially moderation.

Controversy about what Julia said sometimes heated up into the news. "Julia Child, Boiling, Answers Her Critics," read the story about the Aspen Food and Wine Classic in the *New York Times,* which noted that she had been called the Cholesterol Queen. Her outspoken support of Planned Parenthood continued to bring controversy, but her commitment was unwavering. She and Ella Brennan (the mother of New Orleans's restaurants) would vote for "Hillary's husband." When they were watching the Clintons defending him against charges of philandering, Julia was overheard saying, "At least we know he's a man." Responding to *Vanity Fair*'s "Proust Questionnaire" in 1996, Julia answered that the woman she admired most was Hillary Clinton. It was an anointing as if from the great Eleanor Roosevelt herself.

Much to Julia's delight, almost thirty years to the October day she published her first book with her partner, Simca's last book, *Food and Friends,* was published in America. "My Chérie: Memories . . . !" she wrote Simca, enclosing several photographs Paul took of them presenting their Reine de Saba cake to a group of women at the *Chicago Tribune.* Suzanne Patterson had done the writing on Simca's book and Peter Kump's group tested the recipes. A European journal criticized the "Americanized colloquial style," but it won a prize at the Beard Awards the next year. At eighty-seven, Simca was not able to come to the States to promote her book. Thirty-four years before, Julia had written her tightly wired partner that she should take care of her blood pressure the way Julia's mother had: "always take a half-hour nap" or lie down with a book. They "both must live past eighty years old," she had insisted as early as 1957. Julia promised her dear "sister" Simca she would return again this winter of 1991 for a visit.

In the meantime, plans were thwarted when Julia went into the hospital to have her knee operated on—her fourth or fifth knee surgery. She had taken anti-inflammatory medicine for six years until her legs were numb, then stopped taking the medicine and tried living with the pain. At the moment Julia was making plans to enter the hospital in Boston, Simca fell in her room on the top floor at Bramafam and was not found for two hours. She came down with pneumonia and died on December 20. I have lost a "fond and generous sister," Julia mourned. Mary Frances died the following June. Part of her association with France died with them, but after the tears she would typically not allow herself to dwell on what was lost of the past.

"MERCI, JULIA":
STILL COOKING AT EIGHTY

Julia stayed busy and surrounded by young people. Her eightieth birthday almost took her by surprise. Never one to look back or bow to her years, she would have preferred to ignore the ugly fact of age. Indeed, she did not think of herself as old. For example, when she had flown to France more than a year before with Susy Davidson and arrived at Orly airport to take a cab to the Gare de Lyon, they looked in vain for a porter to carry their bags to the train bound for Provence. Ever one to *bouter en avant* (barrel on through), she seized her bags and dragged them up and down stairs until they were in the train. Once settled, Julia exclaimed how terrible it was that there was no one to assist them. "What do old people do?!" she wondered. When Nancy Barr ordered an electric cart at another airport, she settled beside Julia, each holding their portable computers, and remarked how she had always wanted to ride "one of these." Julia announced, "I've always wanted to *drive* one of these!"

Julia returned to La Pitchoune in 1992 to pack her pots and pans and vacate the house, which was to go back to the Fischbacher/Thibault families. She was filled with the memories of Paul and Simca at every noise and aroma. Her niece Phila, Bob Moran, and their little son Nicholas were there to help. By the end of June she was packed to leave for good, saddened only by the loss that initiated her leaving Provence. "Without Paul and without Simca much of the heart has gone out of it," she wrote Peter Kump. Much had also gone out of the country: Plascassier no longer had little shops, and the narrow roads were crowded with cars. Paul predicted in the 1960s that the place would someday look like Southern California, but it was worse. "It is 1920 France with an undigested appliqué of the year 2000," she told Bill Truslow. "I left France this time with no regrets whatsoever." *Boutez en avant!*

She came home to a steady stream of press running through her house with television cables and steno pads, all covering the birthday story. For some time now, her home had been a public place, with no sense of privacy; everything from the coffeepot to the toilet had notes stuck up with instructions for visitors. Julia would spend the actual day of her eightieth birthday celebrating with the McWilliams family at her brother's home in Vermont, and later that month celebrating with the Child family in Maine. She also agreed to participate in a series of birthday dinners as a financial benefit for the AIWF. When she agreed she did not know she would have more than 300 appearances over the coming year. Her only regret about the coming plans for birthday parties all over the country was the realization that ninety-year-old Paul could not share it with her. He no longer knew where he was or recognized most of his family. She went to see him one to three times every day, and a nurse's aide fed, walked, bathed, and put him to bed from four until eight. When Julia was not there, longtime friends, including their butcher Jack Savenor, visited him. The body that had sailed the seas on freighters and hauled logs with Charlie to build the family's summer home in Maine, kept on living after the memory was gone, eventually even the memory of the voice now soothing him with loving endearments.

When asked by the president of the Unitarian Universalist Association about the difficulty of Paul's deterioration, she answered, "Well, it's part of life. . . . As it is [with Paul in a nursing home], now when I go to see him, I go full of love and help and everything else." When asked if they had living wills she replied affirmatively. "We also belong to the Neptune Society. Our funerals are paid for—$600 each—and when we're gone, you just call them up and they pick you up and cremate you."

As she arrived at the Hay-Adams Hotel in Washington, DC, at the end of July, nearly two and a half weeks before her birthday, a crowd of protesters was gathered outside. "Animals, beware! Julia is Hungry" read some of the placards. Inside, chef Jean-Louis Palladin and other prominent chefs in the area were preparing a feast with a finale of three cakes that took the pâtissiers three months to prepare. Atop the first cake were likenesses of her five books, the second the seal of L'Ecole des Trois Gourmandes and a wire whisk, and the third a sugary painting of her Cambridge house.

Despite the fact that fifty free-range chickens from Iowa were missing from the kitchen, lost by the airlines and found rotten three days later, the party went on smoothly. The loss of the chickens, had the protesters outside known, would have punctuated their outcries about cruelty to animals. Julia, one magazine said, "made hash of the protesters" by announcing, "I am a card-carrying carnivore. I've got to keep my strength up." Her objection was as much to their methods (trying to force their beliefs on her) as to their philosophy. In her experience, particularly in French gastronomy, there was never a consideration of the issues articulated by the protesters.

At times the carnivores and vegetarians were intolerant of each other, including Julia, who apologized in 1987 for a flip remark she made about "hating vegetarians." For decades she received letters about her cruelty to oysters, to lobsters, to rabbits, pigs, and calves ("You shrill-voiced shrew—you would skin your grandmother and eat her if you could get her into your mouth," one anonymous letter said). Paul Prudhomme called it the "Bambi Syndrome." Peter Kump called protesters outside the Washington party "vicious vegetarians" and said they reminded him of the right-to-lifers. Julia's paternal grandparents would have read Romans 14:3: "Let not him that eateth despise him that eateth not; and let not him which eateth not judge him that eateth: for God hath received him."

When Julia left the Washington, DC, gala, and was walking past the protesters, a journalist asked her how she kept up the pace of her travels and she replied, "Well, you know, dear, I eat well." She was "having [her] *génoise* and eating it too," another reported, adding she had no immediate plans to retire, but would "move permanently to California when she turns 86 [in 1998]."

She wanted David Letterman to emcee her Boston birthday party, but he was busy. This second memorable birthday celebration, at the Copley Plaza Hotel on November 2, 1992, was given by her hometown and WGBH, which filmed the event for PBS. Her neighbor John Kenneth Galbraith sat at her table and gave a tribute. Dun Gifford sat at her right hand. Robert Hastings came from Los Angeles to remind her of their good-times gang in Pasadena before the war. Her office staff and television cooks paid tribute. Because gastronomy reconciles all the arts—painting, religion, theater, and music—it was fitting that at her local eightieth birthday party the Boston Pops played music on pots, pans, and whisks. Arthur Fiedler would have been delighted by "Fanfare with Pots and Pans." When Diana Rigg read Paul's poem to his "Cook and nifty wench," the camera caught Julia wiping a tear from her cheek.

Fourteen chefs cooked New York City's dinner for Julia in the Rainbow Room on January 24, 1993. The three hundred guests (sixty more were on the waiting list) paid $200 and more to hear Jean Stapleton read a poem and Joe Baum deliver a tribute, to see clips of Julia and those who best imitate her, and to feast with Julia on a menu that began with sweetbreads and ended with baked Alaska topped with sparklers. The room overlooking Manhattan was filled with votive candles and lavish floral arrangements topped by eighteen-inch whisks with a single red rose inside each wire cage. When Julia was given a four-foot whisk festooned with flowers and dripping with pearls, she placed it on her shoulder and marched around the room.

If New York's birthday party was the most elegant, Los Angeles gave the largest and, at $350 a ticket, the most expensive. Five hundred people dined at the Ritz-Carlton Hotel in Marina del Rey on February 7. Michel Richard of Citrus organized "Merci, Julia" with nine great chefs from France who had never cooked together before. They were thanking "La Dame du Siècle" for introducing French cooking to the middle-class American home. "After so many years of Julia Child, Americans have improved their taste," said Jacques Cagna, owner/chef of the restaurant that bears his name. In addition to Cagna, with his two stars in the *Michelin,* were Roger Vergé, Paul Bocuse, Marc Meneau, Alain Ducasse, and Michel Rostang, among others. A favorite pastime of the evening was counting the number of *Guide Michelin* stars on what was billed as the "Dream Team." Moët's Jean Berchon said, "Even in France if we wanted to gather so many chefs, we couldn't [do so]."

Sixty hors d'oeuvres preceded the sit-down meal, said Merrill Shindler. "This was not a feed for amateurs, the faint of heart, or those watching cholesterol. It was an exercise in excess, in the midst of an era of lowered expectations." Assisting the dream team were forty-four of the best French chefs from Los Angeles (Ken Frank, Michel Richard, Patrick Healy, Joachim Splichal), New York City (David Bouley, Jean-Georges Vongerichten, Alain Sailhac, André Soltner), and Washington, DC (Jean-Louis Palladin). Jacques Pépin, Anne Willan, Drew Nieporent, and others assisted, as did about twenty sous-chefs brought by the big-name chefs (Bocuse sat in his tuxedo next to Julia). The French sponsors were prominent: Air France, Moët et Chandon (who put up $100,000), and Nestlé. The only sour note was the paucity of women chefs, a few invited at the last minute. "Thanks, Julia, but Where are the Women?" asked the *Los Angeles Times Book Review.* When the women's anger at their exclusion escalated, Julia called the feminists "tiresome." Madeleine Kamman declared that all these men chefs were "going to . . . cross their arms on their chests and put perfectly disgusting food on the table." However, Ruth Reichl said afterward, "Dinner took five hours—and it was terrific." When Kamman said, "Good old Julia is going to be with all these male chauvinists.

The mere fact that I haven't been invited is absolutely grotesque," Marian Burros of the *New York Times* wondered "why Mrs. Kamman, who has been saying unkind words about Mrs. Child for years, would want to be invited."

"Merci, Julia" was really a celebration of the French chefs in America— an effort she gladly assisted. French restaurants were in trouble, and Julia could help them. More than a year before, *Newsweek* writer Laura Shapiro had announced that formal French restaurants were "almost extinct" in America. "Our love affair with French food is over, done in by new passion for our own chefs and ingredients." Those that have survived and thrived, she noted, were the French chefs who had evolved "California French" cooking, such as Los Angeles's Joachim Splichel (Patina) and New York's Vongerichten (Jo-Jo). Pépin agrees that the best French restaurants surviving were "French with a twist," those that adapted according to the produce of the region. "The temples of haute cuisine are an anachronism," said Marian Burros, and Faith Willinger (an Italian chef) called it "Americans' sweet revenge" for being treated as unworthy. Michel Richard frankly admitted before the "Merci, Julia" event, "We want to be loved again." The evening was their way of saying, "I'm all right, Jacques!"

Because Julia's fame went beyond her French Chef persona, she did not seem to be affected by the waning influence of French cuisine and the rise of Italian cookbooks and restaurants. Chef Roger Fessaguet (Pavillon) said she "created a generation who understood and appreciated French cooking. She did more than any of us." George Faison, co-founder of D'Artagnan, importer of foie gras and other specialty foods, says, "She sparked a transformation of American gastronomy, . . . articulated the flavor, smell and texture of exotic ingredients. . . . Because of Julia, everything changed." She was the grande dame of all cuisine, the name synonymous with cooking in this country, as trustworthy as Walter Cronkite, as beloved as George Burns, as recognizable as the Pope.

ℬONFIRE OF THE VAINGLORIOUS

In February 1992, before the official birthday parties began and in between the AIWF conference in New Orleans and the IACP conference in Miami (at which Julia was the keynote speaker), the AIWF executive committee was interviewing potential candidates when the following headline appeared in the *Los Angeles Times*: "Julia Child 'Rabidly Homophobic,' Lawsuit Alleges."

Daniel Coulter had filed a three-million-dollar lawsuit against Julia Child, the AIWF, and its directors for denying him the job as executive director of the AIWF because he was gay. The *Boston Globe* the next day carried more details of his charges: that his friend Richard Graff had suggested he apply, and that Dorothy Cann (chair of the board) told him their founder was "rabidly homophobic" and would undermine his effectiveness if he won the job. Speaking for the executive committee, Graff said that Coulter was not hired because he did not have fund-raising qualifications. Cann made no statement. Julia publicly (and accurately) said she "had nothing to do with the selection. . . . I haven't heard of Coulter or any of the applicants, so I don't have any comments at all." In the *New York Times*'s coverage, she was quoted as saying "I don't care who he or she is as long as they have the qualifications." In the spring issue of *The Advocate,* a reporter for this gay journal said Julia was "incredulous that 'someone named Daniel Coulter' is blaming his own homosexuality—or rather her homophobia—for having been passed over." This line was the only negative comment in an otherwise positive article about her. Privately, Julia called the lawsuit "silly" and observed that there was "very little backlash." Her chief concern was that the AIWF was going to have to spend money on lawyers just when it was almost in the black. Dorothy Cann privately denied the charges ("No, I do *not* believe that Julia is homophobic. I believe she is a product of her age") and was disappointed that she never received a personal word of support from Julia.

Neither Child nor Cann was ever deposed, for Coulter's flimsy suit was settled immediately after his own deposition when he agreed to a small settlement from the AIWF. He had left them a $195 room service charge on the hotel bill when he was in town for his interview, according to two members of the executive committee. One of the men on the executive committee, who himself was gay, said, "Julia was the target because she had money. It was green mail, extortion, and it was slimy. It had nothing to do with Julia as a person because he had never known her. But the lawyer told us not to respond."

Julia's place in the food world seemed to be unaffected for several reasons: her almost untouchable stature with the public, the fact that she had close working relations with gay men, and because people knew that there were gays on the AIWF board, among the founding members, and working in the national office (including the man who did get the job). What Julia may have paid in bad public relations is difficult to assess.

The response from some in the gay community was dismay. One man gave away all of his beloved cookbooks when he mistakenly heard she had "fired someone on her staff for being gay." Another shrugged and said, "Like any other fag sophisticate, I've always been rather a fan." A few contacted her directly:

My God! Julia—

You've been the goddess of the gays for 20 years!!! I've got a shelf full of your books! You are mentioned at every gay dinner party (with great affection). How could you get this reputation as a homophobe!!?

[signed] Martin

Her response was not ringing. She spoke of unjustified claims. Whatever prejudice she shared with her generation and possibly with Paul—who occasionally expressed antihomosexual views, according to his family and friends—she would never have acted upon it. The evidence of her private attitude is mixed. On the one side is her close friendship with many gays, including Cora DuBois, Sybille Bedford, James Beard, and the children of some of her closest friends, as well as several passages in letters (one encouraging a friend for being "out of the closet at last! Makes things easier all around"). She did, nevertheless, pick up the slang expressions for male homosexuals and in writing once (a decade earlier) expressed (to a close friend) her displeasure that gays seemed to dominate the food business, particularly the cooking schools, thus discouraging women and heterosexual men. However, the letter can be read as an argument for inclusion of others rather than exclusion of gays.

"It's a world of self-generating hysteria," Nora Ephron quoted Nika Hazelton as saying about the food establishment more than twenty years before. Ephron, who was then reporting on the Michael Field versus Craig Claiborne feud when Field's first Time-Life book was published, added that it was a "bitchy, gossipy and devious" world. Olney's plagiarism suit in 1984 may have exposed the corruption of recipe stealing, but nine years later, when Christopher Hitchens reported Martha Stewart's lifting of a Julia Child recipe for chaudfroid sauce, he almost passed it off with the quip: "To be a culinary plagiarist is to be no more than an omnivore." Hitchens called the "foodie world . . . a bitter and competitive one, roiled by great, passionate gusts which it is given to few to understand." When Evan Jones's new biography of James Beard stirred up a veritable cat fight among the New York Beardians who were "fighting over [his] remains," *Newsday* described it as a "bonfire of the foodies."

One potential scandal that never reached the press, perhaps because it is so pervasive in the food world (as it is in the academic world), is the use of work done by one's assistants. James Beard is probably a prime example, for he leaned heavily on the work of assistants. Few have written about the hardworking second tier of writers and editors who actually wrote the books for the stars, pinch-hit prepping and washing their dishes, chauffeuring them and carrying their suitcases. They did all this out of love or learning or both. For her later books, Julia Child used assistants for writing, food design, and demonstrations. But unlike some, she acknowledged her assistants by name in each book and paid their expenses and salaries. The public at large, however, never fully knew the indispensable role that Rosemary Manell played in designing the dishes for every photograph, helping to develop recipes, and proofreading.

Julia was no longer hurt by the criticism of others, specifically the Hesses and Madeleine Kamman. And she seemed almost oblivious to the private embittered attacks by Richard Olney, who was stung by Julia's recommendation years before that he was not qualified to edit the Time-Life series (she was echoing Beard's judgment). His letters to Simca and Julia were friendly, however. After the death of Simca, who had many photographs of him on her wall, Olney asserted that the two authors of the *Mastering* books were just after money and fame, did not like to eat or to cook, and could not do the latter.

Julia was fortunate that she was in her eighties and a national treasure when the full impact of others' money and vainglorious ambitions were at their peak. She occasionally got enmeshed in the tensions among the national food organizations and in what has been called the food world's "log-rolling" and "mutual back-scratching" (the flip side of its feuding)—because her first instinct was not to suspect the motives of people ("She sometimes is not the best judge of character," several of her friends insist). The conflicts within the AIWF and her own staff and entourage reveal something of Julia's management style and means of dealing or failing to deal with conflict. The "head girl" never wanted to play the "headmistress," preferring to avoid controversy and bitterness. According to her family and closest friends, "she had learned to deal with Paul's occasionally disagreeable nature" by creating a pleasant atmosphere "as a form of control to keep the negative away." If pushed to do so, she might write a letter, but she always backed away from confrontation. If she scheduled two friends into one of her vacation homes, she asked them to resolve the conflict. One day Stephanie Hersh was left on the porch with her suitcase when another assistant accompanied Julia on tour. It was sometimes difficult for Julia to set limits. She could not ask a slothful boarder to leave or fire anyone. "She has trouble confronting relationship problems. Paul always took care of this," notes one friend. "She wants to be loved," adds a family member. Another associate believes she played people off against one another to promote her own autonomy.

Others, particularly her men friends, saw her management style as a wise executive skill. By virtue of the confidences each group gave her, she could watch the infighting of employees and assistants, food groups and academic institutions, while maintaining power and interest as she evaluated her own opinion and position on the issues. Dun Gifford compared her executive style with others he had worked with, especially the Kennedys. She tested her position by listening to the warring sides, maintained chaos control by being the only person who knew the entire story, and kept the social interaction intellectually stimulating for herself. Gifford also compares her to Ronald Reagan in her willful resilience that does "not forget to smile."

Another woman executive cynically analyzes this interpretation of the Child administrative style as one of a "Teflon leader . . . who stays above the fray." It is "her and Bob's [Mondavi] institute, but they get none of the blame for its fiscal irresponsibility":

> It is cunning: she listens to every side, but does not take sides. Here she is in the cattiest, back-bitingest industry and she has risen above it; nobody is mad at her. Her personal generosity is second only to the Pope's, yet she is a guarded, complex woman under the guise of a simple one. She has all this warmth, yet I do not know her after years of working with her. . . . I have a hard time talking to her. She knows just what she wants and come hell or high water, she is going to get it. She has played all her cards right, yet the simplicity and bumbling make her no threat to anyone.

She was an executive who had direct control or influence over millions of dollars. In December 1989 *The Nation's Business* featured her in the "Lessons of Leadership" series. She told Anne Willan if they had gone into business they would have made millions. She sought out professional expertise in her personal and professional life and played good cop to her assistant Stephanie Hersh's bad cop. Because she had the assistance of Stephanie, plus an accountant, lawyer, editor, and publisher's public relations staff, she could keep to a demanding personal schedule and serve on the board of directors of several of her favorite causes—like any successful CEO. The woman who once told Smith College's personnel bureau that she was looking for a position "being someone's general and all-purpose assistant" became her own general, directing a group of assistants.

COOKING WITH JULIA

Geoffrey Drummond, who made *New York Master Chefs* in the mid-1980s and was working in France, approached Julia through Jacques Pépin and Rebecca Alssid (head of the Boston University culinary program, where Julia occasionally demonstrated). Drummond was a producer, director, or executive producer for *A Prairie Home Companion* and *Going Home*. Now he wanted to do a series on master chefs for Maryland PBS to be hosted by Julia, who had not made any new series with Morash and WGBH since 1984 and whose work at *Good Morning America* was now only occasional. His original intention was to film the chefs in action, as he had for his *New York Master Chef* series, but this time he would send her the tapes and she could provide the opening commentary in her own kitchen. "There was no way she was going to let me go off and work with the chefs and not be there. She wanted to be involved. . . . Ultimately she became my collaborator and partner." Drummond, a young and personable producer, serious but sensitive to others' needs, was a collaborative director (though compulsive about his work) and perhaps suited to her experience, as Russ Morash was to Julia's inexperience. This time, it was Julia who was pushing to be part of the action, a real partner in the venture, working with her laptop from 6:30 in the morning until 11:30 at night.

Drummond packed his cameras and crew, Julia her suitcase, and on March 12, 1993, they began flying from city to city, taping sixteen prominent chefs for a new series entitled *Cooking with Master Chefs*. She had talked to Drummond, co-owner of A La Carte Communications, and Maryland Public Television for two years about hosting a sixteen-part series featuring American master chefs. Though this was a new stage in her career, it was an old idea for her. From the very beginning, after every series she talked to the press about having guest chefs on her program. From her list of sixty names and a list from Drummond, they consulted and chose sixteen chefs who were available and represented variety (location, race, gender, food type, age). Now she proudly announced she was going to play the role of Mrs. Alistair Cooke or Alistair Cookie, an allusion to the august host of PBS's *Masterpiece Theatre*.

When they finally had the money for sixteen shows and a book contract from Knopf, they traveled to New York (André Soltner), Washington, DC (Jean-Louis Palladin), New Orleans (Emeril Lagasse), Houston (Robert Del Grande), San Francisco (Jeremiah Tower), Los Angeles (Michel Richard), and Hawaii (Amy Ferguson-Ota) to film these chefs and others in their own kitchens. She also visited Jacques Pépin, a Connecticut neighbor of Drummond. It was not difficult to stand in the role of the viewer, for Julia took great delight in learning from each chef. She loved their "nifty knife work" and was fascinated to learn from Alice Waters, who turned a fork, tines down, and rubbed a naked garlic clove over the tines for a quick puree. After filming with Lidia Bastianich of New York's Felidia, Julia declared she "finally understands" risotto. She was especially proud that ten of the sixteen chefs were American, and of that ten, half were women. They returned to Cambridge and filmed Julia's introductions to each segment at her kitchen table, the produce from the recipes of each chef displayed in front of her.

There were two major difficulties with the first series: traveling to each location, where a local film crew joined the core film crew plus the simultaneous filming and book writing for joint release. She had to record exactly what each chef did, relate it to their list of ingredients, and have the recipe tested again. During the second half of the production, Julia's computer crashed and she realized that she needed help with the writing. She called Nancy Barr, who sat with her laptop during each filming, taking down what each chef said and later helping with their biographical profiles, the reediting, and proofing. Most chefs presented a full menu. For example, Charles Palmer of New York's Aureole prepared venison steaks, large herb potato chips, timbales of butternut squash, and chocolate tarragon mousse cupcakes. Susan Feniger and Mary Sue Milliken, owners and chefs of the Border Grill in Santa Monica, on the other hand, prepared dal (a spicy lentil dish), curry popcorn, a curry of spinach and eggplant, pickled tomatoes, and ginger-lemon tea.

Although each chef cooked his or her recipes in their home kitchens, they were professional chefs working in restaurants—a shift from Julia's emphasis on home cooking, though a teaching program nevertheless. "It's not a show for fluffies," she explained at each stop, but for serious cooks. Another shift that disappointed some of her fans was the minor presence of Julia on the program. These two factors and the shortness of the series may account for the weak sales of the book. The video series, however, was nominated for an Emmy, the only food show to be nominated for a national prime-time category, Drummond says proudly.

Julia promoted the book with vigor, especially in the city where each chef lived. According to Janice Goldklang, her Knopf publicist: "She was very insistent that it not be just her show, that it was a collaborative effort." Frequently the chef cooked a high-priced dinner to benefit the local PBS channel. In San Francisco, for example, Jeremiah Tower and Alice Waters cooked for KQED. When Knopf scheduled in rest stops after a flight, she asked for more book signings. She tried to arrive early because people were always lined up, a line that often took two hours to thin out. "I may not be a spring chicken anymore, but I'm a tough old bird." Despite her promotional efforts, the book was not nominated for a book prize.

Reviews were complimentary but brief. She appeared on *Good Morning America* and had the usual profiles in *People, Modern Maturity,* and other magazines. Her early cohorts in the television world thought the book was "thin" on teaching. Charlotte Snyder Turgeon says it was "just showing off what great chefs can do, not extolling home cooking." Ruth Lockwood called her to suggest she stand up straight on-camera. ("I can't," Julia replied. "When I try to do it, it hurts.") Narcisse Chamberlain says the series was excellent, particularly the episode with Alice Waters "because the two of them work together and get along beautifully." The Waters' tape was an exception in having Julia so directly involved, because Drummond, believing the shy Waters would need support, suggested they appear together. Julia sat beside her so the Chez Panisse owner could talk directly to her. The program with Nancy Silverton, who was "the most nervous about the taping and just froze in front of the camera" (according to Drummond, who had her do it over and over again), sold ten times as many tapes as any of the others. She made the famous bread—showing how to begin a fermented bread starter using crushed grapes—that she sold at her La Brea Bakery in Los Angeles.

Accompanied by the Pratts, Julia took a week in Venice in October to teach a course at the Cipriani. According to Natale Rusconi, the managing director of the hotel and the founder of the cooking classes there, Julia brought in the largest classes they offered. By her request, she actively demonstrated after that first year. She wanted to be an active participant, not merely an icon who served as a magnet for money or sales.

"We did the second series because people wanted more of Julia," says Drummond. There would be no grueling road trips and people would see more of Julia on each program. Drummond would film *In Julia's Kitchen with Master Chefs* in Julia's Cambridge house. Because sales of the first volume were disappointing, they doubled the number of chefs to publish a more substantial book and ensure a regular slot on PBS. Taking a clue from the popularity of the Alice Waters program, in which the two women talked through the cooking steps, they moved Julia from being an "Alistair Cookie" to being an active observer. In the new book she would add a variety of tips and explanations in sidebars to accompany the chefs' recipes.

Geoffrey removed her kitchen table and built a stage island with a stove in its place, mounting overhead lights in the ceiling. They had to pull a big truck into the street, according to neighbors, to house the generator for the power needed. The control room was in the dining room, the preparation kitchen in the basement. They hired a prep cook, flew in the chefs, who stayed at the Charles Hotel, while Nancy Barr continued as assistant writer and Kathleen Ankino served as recipe tester. It was a complete disruption of the house, but easier on Julia, who did not have to travel and could retire for a short nap when she had eight minutes.

At the private center of that crowded public world were two important men. Her nephew David McWilliams lived in her upstairs apartment while he completed his business degree at Boston University (commuting back to his wife and children in Vermont on weekends). Julia relished his company every evening she was home until his graduation in May 1995. The second was John McJennett, who with his wife (now deceased) had socialized with the Childs decades ago in Washington, DC. McJennett had survived Iwo Jima and carried himself with the bearing of a general, standing straight, taller even than Julia. "It's nice to have a chap around," she liked to say. They made a handsome pair, though after a trip to the Aspen Food and Wine Classic in June 1994 his health began to fail.

Harvard's "Veritas"

It had been thirty-two years since Julia and Paul settled into their Cambridge home to become citizens of greater Boston—Beantown as the natives fondly referred to it. They lived in the bright shadow of Fair Harvard for these decades, socialized with its faculty, watched in dismay and disbelief when "crimson blood defiled the Harvard Yard" (as Paul described it) during the Vietnam War, entertained students in their kitchen, and talked to numerous campus groups in this institution whose motto was "Truth" or "Veritas." Though many faculty did not watch much television, Galbraith claims, they were well aware of their friend's impact on the wider world and ready to acknowledge that truth.

On June 10, 1993, Harvard honored her with an honorary doctorate in a ceremony that was the ultimate moment validating Julia's life as scholar-cook and teacher, as pioneer of educational television, an intellectual who spoke for no company. There was no controversy concerning her degree that sunny day. The only controversy that day involved the degree conferred on Colin Powell, who had recently spoke out against President Clinton's "Don't Ask, Don't Tell" policy on gays in the military. Pink balloons supporting gay rights in the military dotted the blue sky when thousands filled Harvard Square and Harvard Yard. Someone handed Phila Cousins, the only family member accompanying Julia, a pink balloon; she carried it with conviction.

When the two-hour ceremony marking Harvard's 342nd commencement began, Julia sat in a blouse and skirt next to General Powell in the front row. Her flowered long-sleeved blouse with underblouse and belt looked too informal among all the black robes. She looked out over the sea of faces, pink balloons, and signs that read: "Lift the Ban" (against homosexuals in the military). The audience even cheered the invocation that made an oblique reference to barriers to "ways of discerning and expressing love." When Powell's degree was presented at the end of the program, many students stood with their backs to Powell.

Twice during President Neil Rudenstine's description of Julia, an eloquent speech mixed with allusions to food, he was stopped by applause. He ended with *"Bon appétit"* to thunderous applause. She was a wildly popular choice for the students and alumni. Julia stood by her chair and smiled broadly when they handed her the citation, honoring her stellar career as an educator. It read: "A Harvard friend and neighbor who has filled the air with common sense and uncommon scents. Long may her soufflés rise. *Bon appétit."*

Chapter 27

$\mathcal{D}$O NOT GO GENTLE
(1994 – 1997)

"It's a shame to be caught up in something that doesn't
absolutely make you tremble with joy!"

JULIA CHILD, 1991

~

IN JULIA'S KITCHEN, they had just finished filming George Germon and
Johanne Killeen, husband and wife chef/owners of Al Forno in Providence,
Rhode Island, for *In Julia's Kitchen with Master Chefs*. The crew had packed
up, loaded the van, and left, for the production was taking a month's hiatus to
accommodate Julia's schedule. "Mr. and Mrs. Al Forno" (as they were called),
producer Geoffrey Drummond, and Julia went for a late dinner, joined by
Julia's friend John McJennett and her nephew David McWilliams, who was
just ten days away from completing his business degree. They went to Jasper's
at the Boston waterfront, for Julia loved his pan-roasted lobster.

GOODBYE

Stephanie Hersh received the call from the Fairlawn Nursing Home soon after
9:40 that night, Thursday, May 12, 1994. She called Bill Truslow to find out
how she should tell Julia. (Earlier in the week, Truslow had come by the house
and Julia told him Paul was fading.) He said to wait until she had finished her

meal. When the telephone rang at the restaurant, Geoffrey was called to the phone by the maître d', knowing what it meant.

When he returned to the table, Geoffrey put his arm behind Julia's shoulder, and told her as gently as he could. "She immediately stood up; it was a visceral response. Her whole expression changed," says Geoffrey. "David looked over and realized what had happened. The timing was fortuitous because there was family there." She headed out within minutes, but encouraged Geoff to continue production because all the crew were there. David McWilliams drove her to Fairlawn to see Paul's body before the Neptune society took him for cremation. David had been a companion at meals and quiet times for several years now, and she leaned on him during her grief. According to David, who says, "I discovered not a famous aunt but a friend while living there," Julia was "pretty self-supporting" when Paul died. The cause of death was listed as "coronary artery disease." "Even though it was totally expected, there is still that shock of realization," Drummond said, privately relieved that Paul's death had not occurred in the middle of the taping, when Julia "would have felt she had to finish," despite her pain.

> As for death itself: I fear and loathe it—as I always have [Paul wrote to Charlie on November 7, 1972]. It sits there, waiting, on my back, like the Devil in that Norse saying: "Når man har djevelen på ryggen må man baere ham frem! [Once the Devil gets fastened on one's back, one will have to bear him there henceforth!]. I do *not* wish "to be returned to the common microbial and atomic pool" as you say so loftily, and I do *not* feel like either a microbe or an atom. I am *P. Child,* painter, photographer, lover boy, poet, judo-man, wine-guzzler, and Old Sour Ball, and it's taken me 70 mortal years to sculpt this masterpiece, and I do not relish the inevitable *Chute de la Maison Shield.*

The wisteria he had planted around the front yard and could never get to bloom sprouted blossoms for the first time three days after Paul's death. Julia began quietly weeping and could not stop. She suggested the office staff might want to leave early. Paul's ashes awaited the family gathering that was to take place in Maine in August. The daily routine changed little for Julia, except for the succession of trips to Fairlawn, but her sense of loneliness grew deeper. After long tearful telephone calls to her immediate family, she did what she always did in grief, find those who could relate to her emotionally and fill her days with activity. She moved on.

Soon after Lesley Truslow Davison, daughter of Peter and Jane, moved into Julia's upstairs apartment, Julia and Kitty Galbraith drove to Northampton for a brief trip to the past. It was the sixtieth reunion of the Class of 1934, and they dined with President Mary Maples Dunn and heard that a third of the women board members of Fortune 500 businesses were graduates of women's colleges. But for Julia, the sight of all the gray-headed grandmothers was depressing; then and there she decided she would not go back for another reunion. She went to New York City for an investment in the future.

The new television network devoted to food and cooking (TVFN) had premiered the year before (November 1993). Reese Schoenfeld and Joseph Langdon had come to Cambridge with Sue Huffman, whom Julia knew through the International Association of Culinary Professionals, to seek her approval and involvement. Julia paved the way for her WGBH tapes, as well as those of James Beard and Dione Lucas, to be licensed for showing on the television network. In April 1994 she sat for a series of brief interviews with news anchors David Rosengarten and Donna Hanover, who asked her questions on such topics as French food, restaurant smoking, and "food Nazis." By June of that year, in Aspen, Julia was taping segments with herself as interviewer called "Dishing with Julia." "She is a good interviewer because of her natural curiosity," says Huffman. By the following year she was appearing only briefly, answering "Julia's E-mail" on *In Food Today*. She, along with alternate columnists Marcella Hazan and Jacques Pépin, also began writing columns for *Food & Wine* magazine, founded in October 1992. Her first article was on lobster tails, the second on chicken breasts. Both the Food Channel and *Food & Wine,* the best magazine for new recipes, would become her new commitments.

The return of the *Master Chef* film crew chased quiet and loneliness from the house. All around her the air was charged with frenzy as the twelve young staff members worked that summer to complete the filming delayed by Paul's death. She walked a little unsteadily over the black quilts that covered the electrical cables running from the brightly illuminated kitchen, through the pantries, and into the control room (formerly her dining room). Giant Mylar tubes snaked along the edge of each room, carrying air conditioning. Her nonchalance was grounded in experience and in her love of intense group work.

"Her kitchen has some sort of magic," noted Geoffrey Drummond, who was delighted to be filming all twenty-six chefs in this room so rich with memories and the patina of age. The chefs felt that magic too. They were more relaxed than the sixteen who had worked in their own kitchens for the first series. Three sous-chefs helped Charlie Trotter of Chicago sear scallops with wild mushrooms, Jean-Georges Vongerichten prepared crab spring rolls, and Jasper White his famous pan-roasted lobster and corn fritters. Alfred Portale of the Gotham Bar and Grill in New York City prepared foie gras ravioli and duck breast with Chinese peas, and Gordon Hamersley made his garlic roast chicken.

On her eighty-second birthday, she and Geoffrey finished filming the last program of *In Julia's Kitchen with Master Chefs*. Joachim Splichal of the Patina restaurant and the Pinot bistro in Los Angeles made potato-chanterelle lasagna and lamb shanks. Splichal was West German-born, Swiss-trained, and considered by many to be the finest chef in Los Angeles. Julia's sister Dort flew in that day and attended the wrap party for the series, hosted by Hamersley at his bistro in Boston. The next day, Julia and Dort drove to Woodstock to see their brother John, but the pain in Julia's knee soon took her back to Boston to see her doctor, who prescribed pain pills. She would put off any further surgery.

Ashes to the Sea

The family gathered that August amid the craggy grandeur of Mount Desert Island, where the salty air was heavy with their collective memories of decades of tree clearing, cabin building, lobster traps, and family feasts. This was their third memorial service. Rachel, Erica, and Jon came with their children and grandchildren, remembering their parents, Charlie and Freddie, whose ashes had been sprinkled on the paths and into the sea. Paul's nephew Paul Sheeline and his wife, Sandra, were there, as were two other children of Meeda Child. Julia's sister Dort and her son Sam, his wife, Susan, and son Max came, as did the extended "family": the Kublers, the Bissells, and the Truslows.

> One *must* do something ceremonial at the passing-out-of-life of a person who has lived a long time [Paul wrote to Charlie on March 21, 1954]. It needs punctuation marks of a special sort to set it off from the endless script of life. The friends need it, want it. It's like [John] Donne's "piece of the maine" breaking off: We are all involved. We will all go through the same door—the bell tolls. . . . Death and life may be meaningless: they often seem so . . . but we can imbue a death with meaning, for us, by *declaring* it to be meaningful. . . . let this funeral equal the importance of the loss of a valued [person].

On Saturday, August 27, forty-two people who loved Paul the most gathered in a circle and spoke of his life. Jon Child stood on the hearth and began by talking about how his Uncle Paul loved process, emphasizing the concrete and tangible by tying a knot the way Paul taught him and placing the rope on the floor; Rachel remembered her first visit to Paris and the confidence Paul instilled in her; Erica read from his letters and a poem. Julia, who had worried that the ceremony would go on too long, said only a few words, emphasizing that this gathering was also for Charlie and Freddie.

After all the guests had left, the family walked to the rocky cliffs to scatter Paul's ashes to the sea. Jon had transferred the ashes into a colorful clay pot. Here, on the land where forty-six years ago Julia first met his family and she and Paul decided to marry, they took turns sprinkling a few ashes— the younger people from the rocks below where the tide was coming in, the older from the grassy cliff above. Betty Kubler took several photographs, thinking how much better Paul's photographs would have been.

"So long, old boy," Julia said as the wind caught the ashes and blew them toward the sea. Her nephew Sam heard her say "Goodbye, Sweetie."

A thousand letters and calls poured in, including one from "the gentleman who always brings you three roses at your book signings at the [Harvard] Coop," who reminded her that the Dear Lord "must have a greater job for Paul in Heaven." But, like Paul, Julia did not believe in the afterlife. "There are no mooring hawsers in the sea of time," Paul had concluded in his poem "Everything Is Go." Julia's dislike of her father's "cold, unforgiving religion" was reinforced by Paul's strong hatred of organized religion, instilled in him by his harsh treatment at St. Joseph's Academy near Wellesley. His mother had come from Methodist stock but was a Theosophist who sent them to Quaker meetings to learn about the Bible. To the president of the Unitarian Universalist Association ("That's a fun religion, isn't it? Not like those 'evil' Presbyterians!") two years before, Julia had said: "If I wanted a religion, I'd be either a Jew or a Catholic. . . . But I think if you have a good personal philosophy, you don't need them." Yet, on the "Proust Questionnaire" in *Vanity Fair*'s March 1996 issue, she gave as her life motto "Love the lord your god with all your heart, and soul, and mind—and thy neighbor as thyself."

When it is her turn to die, she says, "I do not care at all what happens [to my body]."

ℐHE FOOD CIRCUIT

At the end of September 1994, Julia flew to Europe with Pat and Herb Pratt, as they had for so many years. This time, with no worry about being suddenly called back to be with Paul, they flew first-class. And as usual, they visited Anne Willan and Mark Cherniavsky near Joigny. After a full week of rest in

Fiesole, in the Tuscan hills above Florence, they drove to Venice for Julia's classes at the Cipriani Hotel. Wherever she went she felt a profound sense of loss; though she had missed her husband's companionship for years, no longer being able to call Fairlawn dramatized her irrevocable loss. But giving in to that melancholy was beyond Julia. She would go on with the responsibilities of her career.

The fall of 1994 was filled with appearances on *Good Morning America,* articles for *Food & Wine* magazine, demonstrations (often with Jacques Pépin) at Boston University, cooking classes at the Mondavi vineyards, and numerous appearances for the AIWF at board meetings, chapter meetings, the annual wine auction, and the annual Conference on Gastronomy. In May 1995 Julia accompanied Joan Lunden and Charles Gibson on *Good Morning America*'s "Passport to Europe: Burgundy" filming in France. The annual pattern always included the Greenbrier Food Writers' Conference in March, the IACP conference in March or April, the Aspen Food and Wine Classic in June, the Cipriani Hotel in October, and the AIWF conference in October or November.

La Varenne's Greenbrier cooking classes, demonstrations, and writers' conferences were a regular extension of Julia's long involvement in the work of Anne Willan and Mark Cherniavsky. Willan remembers complaining about how sticky her shoes became when she and Julia were cooking together in the Greenbrier kitchen. Take them off, Julia said, and then proceeded to clean the bottom of Anne's shoes.

In 1994 at the Greenbrier, Julia awakened in the night, tripped over a chair, and landed on her face, cutting her mouth so severely that she had to have stitches in her lip and cancel her plans to attend the annual AIWF conference in Monterey. As the doctor was stitching her up, he asked, "Other than this, how has your stay at the Greenbrier been?" The food was "terrible," she said animatedly, forgetting her pain. Just days later, Walter Scheib, the head chef at the Greenbrier, was appointed by Hillary Clinton to head the cooking staff of the White House.

Although unable to be as fully involved with the AIWF as she was in 1990 and 1991, Julia annually attended five chapter events chosen by the executive director, Roberta Klugman. (Julia maintained her primary involvement in the Boston chapter, often hosting cocktail parties at her house.) She continued to attend national board meetings, an annual conference, and a glittering wine auction as well as special events honoring the eightieth birthdays of Robert Mondavi in 1994 and Chuck Williams of Williams-Sonoma in 1995. In a gesture of great generosity, Mondavi liquidated the debt (of nearly $200,000) of the AIWF in 1994. Of the Mondavi money, $40,000 was assigned to provide AIWF support for the Mondavi Center in Napa, then in the planning stages. A year later, with an additional grant of $250,000, he revitalized the *Journal of Gastronomy*, which was to be linked to promotion for the Mondavi Center. The journal was transformed into a large and beautifully illustrated book, retitled *Wine, Food & the Arts* (edited by Betty Fussell), and published in 1996 and 1997. In exchange for the grant, the AIWF reaffirmed its commitment to move its headquarters to the Mondavi Center in Napa when the conference center and wine museum were constructed. The $40,000 from his 1994 grant was used to print additional copies of the journal.

The AIWF continued its original focus on education. "It has come back toward my idea of the Institute with the school lunch program and nutrition for children," says Alice Waters. Those who were not happy with the change wanted the wining and dining atmosphere back, feared the "domination by nutritionists and dietitians," and pointed to what they called the politically correct Monterey Conference on "Children's Education: Feeding Our Future." Others criticized the growing bureaucracy and lack of vision. Yet the working relations with the Dairy Council, School Lunch Programs, and the Olive Oil Council, begun under Wolf and Cann Hamilton, were restored. The power base of the AIWF shifted from New York City to San Francisco with the appointment of Roberta Klugman as executive director in 1992 and the election of Maggie Mah as chair of the board (the second woman chair) in 1995. Sandra McCauley succeeded Mah in 1997.

Julia coordinated her board meetings, conferences, and charity work with the promotion of the television series and book *In Julia's Kitchen with Master Chefs* in the spring of 1995. Whether she was demonstrating at her last Long Wharf Theater benefit for Betty Kubler, attending a Planned Parenthood benefit, doing a PBS, Boston University, Smithsonian, Radcliffe, or Smith College benefit, receiving the Blue Ribbon from the Cordon Bleu in Paris, or doing a fund-raiser for the Boston Public Library or the Boston Art Institute, her publisher provided discounted books for sale. "She works hard when she has a book come out," says Goldklang. Her one truly commercial appearance was a windfall: on QVC, the television shopping network, she sold 10,000 copies in just moments, and was as delighted with the new technology for selling books as she was with the numbers. The following year she won the daytime Emmy Award for Outstanding Service Host at the National Academy of Television Arts and Sciences ceremony in New York City. Her producers, Drummond's A La Carte Communications and Maryland Public Television, received an Outstanding Service Show award as well.

When Julia arrived in Seattle to promote *In Julia's Kitchen with Master*

Chefs, her hotel room had a large fruit basket with cheese, but she was *hungry.* Ordering a juicy hamburger from a nearby hamburger joint, she began signing books. This was one of those three-day multiple events, including a meeting with Microsoft and an AIWF founders dinner. At Sur La Table, a Seattle cookware store where she had signed 600 copies of *The Way to Cook* in 1989, people began lining up at 6:30 A.M. to be one of the 250 persons promised a meeting and signing with Julia. The first woman in line had flown in for the occasion from West Palm Beach, Florida, but there were a thousand more who wanted her signature. The Pacific Northwest AIWF held a Taste & Health workshop, Julia spoke to a full house at the Washington Athletic Club, and Sur La Table held a $1,000-a-plate dinner for sixteen. The weekend netted $25,000 for the AIWF. One news reporter compared her arrival in Seattle to a papal visit.

MARTHA STEWART AND THE ELECTRONIC FUTURE

"Every age gets the house-hold goddess it deserves," wrote Margaret Talbot in a *New Republic* cover story on Martha Stewart: "The Tyrant of Taste." Half the first page was devoted to Julia Child, our first "house-hold goddess": "sophisticated . . . as permissive as Dr. Spock . . . anti-snob . . . [with] an air of Cambridge eccentricity—faintly bohemian and a little tatty." The contrast was easy. Julia was "something of a sensualist, a celebrant of appetite as much as a pedant of cooking"; Martha was the "corporate overachiever turned domestic superachiever . . . in earth-toned Armani . . . [who] generates some $200 million in profits a year."

Stewart, who started on Wall Street, then became a caterer, was rapidly building an empire that included cooking, home decoration, and gardening. She sold taste and beauty, or what was called "lifestyle," and published her own very successful magazine, *Martha Stewart Living* (circulation 1.5 million). She was a resident of Westport, Connecticut, and her energy rivaled Julia's— indeed, she was called "a bullet in flight."

The difference, of course, was style. When Julia left Seattle for a two-week stay in Santa Barbara, she had signed 1,400 books; the press called it a "marathon" signing. She never left anyone at Sur La Table with an unsigned book. In contrast, that December in Buffalo, New York, Martha Stewart was at a fund-raising luncheon for the Lupus Foundation of America and had to leave before signing all the 1,000 books purchased by her fans. When she was criticized by some outraged fans and the *Buffalo News,* she wrote a letter that was published: "I promise I'll think long and hard before I accept another invitation to your chilly and downright unfriendly city again."

Julia did agree, after some vacillation, to appear on Martha Stewart's pre-Christmas special. Other guests included Miss Piggy and Hillary Clinton. Strange bedfellows. In one segment, with Julia at her side, Martha put the finishing touches on a gingerbread house that looked remarkably like Martha's home. As she created delicate and glittering spun sugar icicles, Julia offered comments and asked questions. When the complicated creation was finished and they both marveled at her creation, Julia exclaimed, "Aren't we terrific?!" More than a few in the audience collapsed in laughter.

Their energy and administrative talents were indeed similar, and perhaps Julia professionalized home cooking the way Martha professionalized house-keeping. Thus one Boston journalist asked Julia, "Did you create Martha Stewart?" Julia answered, "I'm not driven. . . . I'm enjoying what I do and I don't have any great ambitions. I feel I'm lucky to be in this profession that I adore and meeting all the people I like. I'm just very fortunate." But Talbot calls Stewart "the anti-Julia" (though she does not fully carry through the contrast). Julia, who came from money and New England stock, cared little for the show of wealth (though she enjoyed the comfort it provided). Stewart, with humble bloodlines, made her own money and sold class-consciousness. Julia appealed to all classes and could talk to Presidents and governors as well as a poor student she had invited to dinner or a Sudbury man who raised dozens of varieties of potatoes in his backyard and invited her to the annual neighborhood blind tasting of his harvest. James Beard had a different persona for each class of people he associated with, says biographer Robert Clark, but Julia was always herself. Any adventure that would bring her a new experience was irresistible.

Julia made her special appeal to the middle class who shopped the su-permarkets, even when food professionals criticized her compromises. She was the first to marry California and France, which in part explains her cross-class appeal. She had aristocratic manners and connections, but talked to the mid-dle class, trying to change its attitudes toward food and cooking. She would never criticize Stewart, though she would muse about whether "Martha would ever be happy."

More important than the contrast between the two women (who admire each other) is what this contrast says about the changes in America. Julia emphasizes the priority of taste and pleasure; for Martha Stewart pleasure takes on "the qualities of work"—not unlike the use of a sex-advice manual, says Talbot, quoting from Christopher Lasch's *The Culture of Narcissism.*

Martha's didacticism and implied "moral up-lift of a well-ordered home" makes her a throwback to the nineteenth-century home economics movement, with its "commitment to painstakingly elegant presentation, [its] concern with the look of food even more than its taste," and its zealous home ec curriculum. American puritanism lives, and "Americans have lost confidence in their own judgment." If Martha Stewart's appeal is "saturated with nostalgia," Julia is moving as fast as she can toward the twenty-first century. "Julia is so hip. Julia is tomorrow," exclaimed Russ Morash.

THE MASTER TEACHER

Julia's view of herself as primarily an educator is documented by her numerous commencement addresses at culinary institutes (Johnson and Wales University and the Culinary Institute of America) and in her support of the Schlesinger Library at Radcliffe, Boston University, and Smith College (she attended the inauguration of the new president, Ruth Simmons, in the fall of 1995). Shortly before she received her honorary degree from Harvard, Julia became actively involved in demonstrations and fund-raising for Boston University's two-year graduate program as a Master of Liberal Arts degree with a Concentration in Gastronomy. At last her dream of a degree in gastronomy was realized, and much to her delight it was in her hometown of Boston. In 1996 she would see a full four-year academic degree with a focus in gastronomy inaugurated in the Napa Valley at the California branch of the Culinary Institute of America (a two-year program in Hyde Park).

During her promotion for *In Julia's Kitchen,* the CD-ROM for *Cooking with Master Chefs* was released by Microsoft. The compact disk was called *Julia Child: Home Cooking with Master Chefs,* and retailed for $39.95. She had been the first on her block to be computer literate and was eager to take on the latest media tools. The compact disk for computer, which contained all sixteen segments of her first *Master Chefs* book as well as a tour of her kitchen, wine cellar and pantry, was underwritten by Microsoft. It had the same disadvantage as the video series of *Dinner at Julia's,* more than a decade before, in that few kitchens have computers (they once did not have televisions). But the compact disk had a distinct advantage because it was interactive, meaning it could be stopped and the user could move around to any part, find all the recipes using carrots (for example), recalculate the proportions of a recipe, hot-link an ingredient to an illustrated dictionary, or print off the ingredients for a shopping list. The cursor turned to an oven mitt when it hit a hot spot.

Microsoft for Windows was fairly new technology and sales grew slowly, but the disk was included in new computer sales packages. Meantime, Julia and her book were all over the Internet on dozens of home pages and on-line food chats, including the Cooking Club. A pioneer in the fight against bad food and cooking since the early 1960s, she continued the crusade on this medium of the twenty-first century. Her ideas and recipes were on thousands of computers, but so were those of lesser lights, with recipes using Velveeta, Jello-O, Tang, Cool Whip, and Shake 'n Bake chicken nuggets. Just as they had corrupted the printed pages of home magazines eighty years before, now Kellogg, Campbell Soup, Kraft (owned by Philip Morris), and other packaged food companies established their interactive sites on the World Wide Web. Instead of Ed Herlihy's mellifluous phrasing of "Kraft Jet-Puffed Miniature Marshmallow," now clicks, beeps, and whistles filled American homes.

COOKING IN CONCERT

If her favorite public cooking partner of the 1960s was Jim Beard, in the 1990s it was Jacques Pépin. "It is easier not to rehearse with Julia," says Pépin. "It is much better to just go with it. She is natural. There is no fakery or pretense." Growing out of her involvement at Boston University, where Julia and Jacques both taught, came a plan for Geoffrey to tape the cooking duo for a PBS special. The crew worked three days building a set and preparing the machinery and cameras. When Julia arrived on the day of taping, she placed her wooden cutout of a cat somewhere in the backdrop of pans, fruit, and flowers as she had done since the beginning of her career. She was too practical to call it a lucky charm, but she never forgot it. The first taping was called "Julia Child and Jacques Pépin: Cooking in Concert," filmed on March 28, 1994, and first aired in its two-hour edited version that August.

On their first televised concert, if not before, they established their shtick. "Jacques and Julia sizzle," wrote one journalist. They casually set up dramatic tensions for their Boston University and PBS audiences: he wanted to add more garlic, she wanted to add more liqueur or butter. When she turned her back, he slyly added extra lemon; when he turned his back she added vanilla. Together they prepared a four-course meal with the audience applauding Julia's one-liners and Jacques's virtuoso knife techniques ("You can certainly tell who is the professional chef and who is the home cook," she noted).

During preparations for the second filming, two years later on Boston's Patriots' Day (also the day of the Boston Marathon), Julia wanted plain glass bowls, not white ones, for her English pudding. A staff member navigated police blockades and closed stores to find her what she wanted. Instead of putting her boiled potatoes in a Cuisinart, she pressed them through the enormous German potato ricer she had bought in Bonn in the 1950s. While Jacques, who had published *Simple & Healthy Cooking* the year before, prepared the veal, his eyes widened as she added more and more butter to the potatoes. She seemed to delight in quoting Alice B. Toklas: "We don't want nutrition, we want taste." When there were friendly disagreements of style, he usually deferred to her or did it his way when her back was turned, much to the delight of the audience. When he suggested putting garlic in the fourth dish, a sauce for the salmon, she tapped her head in despair and exclaimed, "You're a real garlic freak, aren't you!" It was delightful theater.

This second show, "More Cooking in Concert," aired in August and December 1996. Their two "In Concert" shows are the most popular tapes played for PBS fund-raisers around the country.

They also packed the venue for every public appearance together, whether at the Smithsonian "Gala Celebration" in June 1995 or Sotheby's "Conversation" the next December. At the Smithsonian, which holds sixteen lectures a month, they drew the largest audience on record. At Sotheby's, two hundred applicants were turned away for a conversation that included Jacques's Connecticut neighbor Morley Safer of *60 Minutes.* Julia and Jacques were comfortably linked because they both represented education, not commerce, a respect for French culinary techniques, and a distrust of faddishness in cooking. Jacques, with his graduate studies in French literature from Columbia University, was a dean at the French Culinary Institute in New York and the major luminary in the master's degree program at Boston University. Because teaching was their talent and French cuisine their passion, they teamed up for education and for demonstrations. They were also both professionals in front of an audience and had a familiar repartee and rapport. When a member of one audience asked Julia what her cholesterol level was, she replied, "Medium." Jacques, after a moment's pause, added, "Medium rare."

Julia appeared to some of her associates to have an ambivalent relationship with Jacques, flirting one moment and on another offended by a seeming male condescending remark. One assistant says, "Julia likes to be the event. Neither one likes to share the spotlight. They bicker sometimes before a concert, though they admire each other. But he is a Frenchman and grew up in a French kitchen. Men bang the knife three times on the table to get the noise going before they cut. Women don't do that. Hut one! Chop, chop, chop." To a viewer it is clear that when they work together, he takes charge of the preparation, in part because she is not as fast and accurate as she once was. During the taping of "More Cooking in Concert," she seemed to lean on the demonstration table during the entire performance (she had been on her feet for hours during the preparations). But if he carried the physical labor, she carried the spirit and humor of the evening.

Julia also began appearing with Graham Kerr in 1994, because they played leading roles in the IACP and always announced the winners of the cookbook awards each year. He had never before cooked onstage with anyone. They were a pair of Scots: Graham Kerr in his green plaid kilts and Julia "McWilliams" in her bright jewel-colored dresses. At the 1995 IACP convention in San Antonio, their first filmed "Master Class" was an unfortunate disaster because it was interminable. After six hours, a staff member was reduced to tears, and after all that work Geoffrey was not able to sell the tape to CBS. The second Child-Kerr public cooking took place at a December 1995 PBS fund-raiser in Seattle, where Kerr is based. Sue Huffman of TVFN believes that only Kerr comes close to Julia in connecting directly with a television audience.

For their third teaching appearance ("Birds of a Feather") at the 1996 IACP national convention in Philadelphia, Julia cooked pheasant *en croûte,* and he roast ostrich tenderloin. She slathered on the butter while he sprayed olive oil and boiled up his aromatic fruits and herbs for sauces. During the banter about butter and the Dr. Dean Ornish no-fat diet, it was Kerr who came across as the tolerant and open-minded cook. When he tasted her heavy sauce at one of their demonstrations, he swallowed hard and said, "I think that as an Englishman I have just been violated." She turned around immediately and answered, "Really, darling, I did not think it would be that easy!"

When Julia first saw "The Galloping Gourmet" on television early in 1969, she told Simca he was "cute and funny," but he would be better without a live audience and if he took his cooking more seriously. She and Simca tried one of his suggestions (to add a teaspoon of water to egg white before beating them) and discovered the height of their whipped egg whites was improved. After a serious accident and a religious conversion, Kerr had transformed himself into a sort of dietary disciplinarian in the 1970s. When his wife, Treena, suffered a stroke and then a heart attack in the mid-1980s, he stopped evangelizing and began cooking for her, making his low-fat, low-salt recipes as flavorful and pleasurable as he could. He was editor-at-large for *Cooking Light,* with a 5.7 million circulation, and his books sold 14 million. The "gallop" and alcohol were gone, but Julia found his gray-bearded charm irresistible.

The contrast between Pépin and Kerr is dramatic and may in part explain why the first taping with Kerr was unsuccessful. Whereas Pépin takes charge and pushes the program along, Kerr defers to Julia. Kerr, once the boisterous Englishman (via Australia), is deferential and empathic. One can almost see in his concentration on her that he mouths the words she speaks. "Graham is nonalcoholic and ten percent or less fat, which is absolutely what I am NOT," says Julia, "so we are each going to do our separate things. He is just charming." But there does not seem to be an edge to their contrasting philosophies, though the contrast allows some dramatic tension when they cook.

Pépin, Kerr, and the master chefs were happily cooking with Julia, but some questioned whether the country was cooking with her. Despite a plethora of cooking books and cuisines, the ascendancy of pasta and risotto, Julia insisted on the primacy of French cooking techniques. At the Aspen Food and Wine Classic and on the pages of *Food & Wine,* she exclaimed, "Bring Back the Quiche!" The influence of French cooking, according to both Julia and Jacques, was as strong as ever. At the French Culinary Institute, on a recent panel entitled "French Cooking Is Dead, Long Live French Cooking," they agreed that what was dead was the idea of French cooking, the image of its being heavy cream, which had been dead even longer in France than it had been in the United States. "Classic cuisine died in 1950 with Escoffier," says Pépin. "We have had the thesis (Escoffier), the antithesis (nouvelle cuisine), and now the synthesis," he adds.

Perhaps more important is the question whether the American people at the end of the century were eating better than they did in 1961, when *Mastering the Art of French Cooking* was first published. Certainly those who wanted to eat well had far greater access to the best variety of fresh produce; indeed many were eating better than they did in their parents' home. In 1960 most shops carried only iceberg lettuce and button mushrooms. "It used to be Rice-A-Roni and noodles," says Zanne Stewart of *Gourmet,* "now there is risotto, couscous, and dozens of other products." Pépin insists, "The rate at which we have moved forward in produce and cooking in the last decades is faster than in the last hundred years in Europe . . . and if we keep it up we will have the best in the world."

But the eating habits of far too many are worse than they have ever been, in part because of the proliferation of fast food (McDonald's spends nearly $800 million a year on advertising). Julia often pointed out during her appearances that there are more and more books on cooking and a greater variety of produce, but kids are fed at school by pizza franchises. On September 4, 1996, Jane E. Brody reported in the *New York Times* that the American diet improved over the last three decades, but that only 25 percent of the people were eating healthy diets. The diets of wealthy whites were improved, the diets of poor blacks deteriorated, "a discrepancy the researchers attributed to the difference in ability to afford substantial amounts of meat and other foods high in saturated fat." The study measured "improvement" on the basis of saturated fat and consumption of grains, fruits, and vegetables (not on taste or artistry).

The junk food versus good cooking battle will always be fought, and people on both extremes will choose their statistics to argue which side is "winning." There are paradoxes aplenty. Brody points out that more skim milk is now consumed, but more burgers and fries as well. Four and a half million Americans watch *The French Chef* on TVFN, but in 1996 the Pillsbury Bake-Off winner (the first man in its forty-seven-year history) won a million dollars for inventing a recipe made of packaged devil's food cake mix, canned sliced pears, sweetened condensed milk, eggs, chocolate chips, macadamia nuts, and butterscotch-caramel fudge topping (for a whopping 460 calories a serving). Only the eggs were fresh (one hopes).

When news of what is called the French paradox reached the growing army of American food writers via CBS's *60 Minutes,* Julia Child and the French chefs in America seemed at least momentarily vindicated. "Why aren't the French dropping like flies?" asked Jeffrey Steingarten, *Vogue*'s food editor (and one of the many men at Harvard Law School who used to regularly watch *The French Chef).* The paradox is that the French, who eat fat goose liver (foie gras) and drink red wine, have lower cholesterol, lower obesity, and fewer heart attacks and other cardiovascular diseases. At this news, Americans nearly emptied the shelves of the cholesterol-lowering red wine—but for the usual puritan reasons (self-improvement).

The paradoxes are evident in restaurants as well as in homes. Restaurant diners are experimenting with all kinds of ethnic cuisines, displaying a more sophisticated American palate. But the "fusion" of these cuisines (Thai barbecue pizza) threatens to blur the native cuisines. On the other hand, one of the most popular books of 1996 was Rozanne Gold's *Recipes 1-2-3,* using recipes with no more than three ingredients. Doomsayers point to the number of major French restaurant closings, citing Ma Maison, La Toque, L'Escoffier, and L'Ermitage—yet Le Cirque remains. France was suffering even more, it seemed: Alexandre Lazareff told a conference at the French Culinary Institute in 1996 that twenty years ago in France one could count from fifty to a hundred great restaurants that were prospering; now, after years of recession, he can name only twelve.

Competition in both television and publishing grew with the interest in food during the last decade of the century. Approximately 700 cookbooks were published in 1995 alone, racking up more than $50 million in sales. *Stand Facing the Stove,* a dual biography of Irma Rombauer and her daughter Marion Becker, who had edited *The Joy of Cooking* until 1975, was published late in 1996. A "reissue" of *Joy,* Julia's first cookbook when she became Mrs. Child, was being rewritten by committee, "a parade of superstars," Laura Shapiro called them. When Shapiro asked the woman hiring and firing this "Keystone Kops in the Kitchen" why so many writers were needed for a book once written by Mrs. Rombauer, the editor declared that cooking had grown so complex no one cook could know both cakes and meats.

BAKING WITH JULIA

In her eighty-fourth year, Julia played her final "Alistair Cookie" role in *Baking with Julia,* a television series with master bakers ("Baking is anything that has flour in it," she explained); no one had yet done a baking series for television. Moreover, the most popular segment of their *Cooking with Master Chefs* was with Nancy Silverton baking her La Brea bread, and two of the most successful programs on *In Julia's Kitchen with Master Chefs* were with Carol Field of San Francisco baking Italian bread and Jim Dodge of Montpelier, Vermont, making chocolate fudge cake and apple pie. For this series, Julia agreed to write the introduction to a book based on the series, but this time she refused to write the book.

The controversy over the accompanying book began in 1995 when, after Julia insisted she would not write another book and Geoffrey hired Dorie Greenspan to author the book itself, he mailed multiple submissions of his (A La Carte Communications') proposal to several publishers for bidding because he needed a large advance to finance the filming. Judith Jones was surprised and angered by the multiple submissions, and Knopf did not make a bid, knowing that a bidding war would drive up the price of the book. Ink spilled in *Publishers Weekly* and the *New York Times,* leaving the impression first that Knopf was dropping its longtime author and second that Knopf refused to relinquish electronic rights (though it had relinquished them for the first two books of the series). Misleadingly, the issue looked like it was part of the larger battle of the 1990s for writers to control their own electronic rights. A La Carte's lawyer, Carl DeSantis, told *Publishers Weekly* it was over "control of electronic rights." Yet both Judith Jones and Jane Friedman at Knopf/Random House insist that "it had nothing to do with electronic rights."

Morrow made the winning bid with A La Carte Communications to publish the book, including payment for all photographs. Whether Knopf would have matched the bid no one will know, but it is doubtful. A La Carte received far more money than expected, and misleading reports that Julia always kept her electronic rights became big news. Writers from around the country called her for advice on retaining their electronic rights, just as they did when the *New York Times* decided to claim copyright on all articles written for the paper (Pépin announced he would no longer write for the *Times*). These two issues would define writers' battles for claims to their work during this decade, and many turned to one of the oldest members of their profession for advice and leadership.

Drummond's budget for his master chefs and bakers series (about $35,000 per episode) compares with the cost of a half hour of Martha Stewart ($90,000), but contrasts dramatically with the millions spent for each episode of a weekly drama like *E.R.* or *Law & Order.* These relative costs explain the growth of (inexpensive) cooking shows on television. Yet the search for sponsors was never easy because PBS policy limits all advertising to a preliminary half minute. Part of Julia's contractual agreements on the last few series involved help and support (though not endorsement) for their major sponsors, including Land O Lakes (they used 753 pounds of butter for the baking series) and Farberware. PBS contributed part of the funding and benefited most from the programs. A La Carte Communications and Julia, partners, benefited from book sales, which is why Julia was the chief promoter of what she honestly called "Dorie's book." This gracious honesty on celebrity-drive QVC "killed the book," said one publicist, and they sold one fifth the books she had on her previous appearance.

Drummond used three cameras for the baking series and made thirty-nine shows with twenty-six bakers, thus ensuring a regular slot in the season repertoire of local PBS stations. According to several of the crew, the major problem in making the series was in team morale when the ever-loyal Julia insisted Nancy Verde Barr be appointed associate producer. Baking was more complicated to dramatize in the filming, according to Drummond, because the magic occurs inside the oven. Thus, at one point they had seventeen bread machines working: "If we lost a bread in the middle of a second rise, we would need a second bread and a third bread." When Julia watched Mary Bergin caramelize the sugar on the crème brûléed chocolate bundt cake with a blowtorch, Julia remarked, "I think every woman should have a blowtorch."

Baking with Julia was shown thirteen shows per season in 1996 and 1997, featuring bakers like Michel Richard, who began his career with the famous French pastry chef Gaston Lenôtre; Lora Brody, who founded the Women's Culinary Guild and made the bread machine a common household appliance; Martha Stewart, who made "One Glorious Wedding Cake"; and Craig Kominiak, the tall and handsome baker of the Ecce Panis Bakery in New York City. "A real man," Julia purred upon seeing the tall, burly baker.

Fame came to Julia when she was mature, and she handled it with what

Fred Ferretti in *Gourmet* called "an innate ease" and grace, occasionally even being surprised by it. She had lived now so long that she was famous for being well known (no doubt the definition of an American celebrity). She became what one writer called "a familiar object next to which people might pose for photographs." But unlike Woody Allen, Charlie Chaplin, and Martha Stewart, the public has never turned on her. She never suffered the "perils of persona."

"Fame is a fickle food upon a shifting plate," the poet Emily Dickinson wrote in the nineteenth century. Julia seemed aware of this New England wisdom, and with the help of Bill Truslow's eye on "quality control" she kept her integrity, nurturing the national hunger for the famous, so that she could keep doing what she loved to do and avoid loneliness and boredom. She was observed by a local journalist greeting guests at a garden party in Woodstock, Vermont, in the summer of 1996. She appeared to be like the queen mother, the observer thought: "If her public demeanor is one of bemused acceptance of the attention showered on her, her private aspect is of an elderly and omniscient bird who keeps her own counsel and is rather less reverential than the treatment accorded her." Both R. W. Apple, Jr., and Dun Gifford, on separate occasions, compared her to Michael Jordan: at the pinnacle of her career, she remains an American icon who transcends a single task or definition.

The changes in her private life came as a result of her aging. After her friend John McJennett's health began to fade, he was put into a nursing home, where he died of bone cancer in February 1996. "All my California friends are dropping like flies," she reported just after the deaths of Robert Hastings and Jack Wright. Then George Kubler and Mary Ripley died. "Woe," she often said. When his health weakened, her brother John and his wife moved into a retirement home. She wanted her family close to her, and she talked to Dorothy regularly. She found her renewal in other people ("My greatest happiness is a good meal with friends") and in short catnaps. She never joked about her age and denied ever having jet lag or fatigue. She possessed what Margaret Mead had said were the prerequisites for any American woman to succeed: superhuman energy and an ability to outwit the culture's plans for her.

She always kept her private life private, even from her closest professional friends. In 1995 Jacques Pépin thought that she had children, and Dorothy Cann Hamilton said she did not think she really knew Julia. Her personal assistant Stephanie Hersh was never an intimate. A friend with whom she traveled for years said, "I do not really know Julia." She was a social and physical animal, not a philosophical one. She remained, in her eighties, the girl who adored peanut butter and raw dough, who cried at movies and loved cats. She had a huge collection of rubber stamps, many of them images of cats, which she would imprint on the bottom of notes. She laughed at dirty jokes and planned parties, did not take herself seriously in private, but steeled herself publicly. She was generous, tough, and stubborn.

Her friend M. F. K. Fisher said of herself that age meant she could "get away with more. Say more of what I want to say and less of what people want to hear." Julia also got past what Fisher called the "protective covering of the middle years" and became more incautious and obstinate. All her traits became exaggerated, said Anne Willan. A former school friend said she had "grown more caustic than she used to be," taking on some of Paul's attitudes. "She could be magisterial and imperious," said yet another. She had the stubbornness of Greta Garbo, the independence of Katharine Hepburn.

In January 1997 in Santa Barbara, she put the Seaview condominium up for sale and moved her furniture into storage and bought a private dwelling in a retirement village that she and Paul had chosen years before. She would not burden loved ones with any future infirmities (she thought); she was alone (she felt). She would keep the Cambridge house and office a few years longer before giving it to Smith College. She continued to teach and sell books, but perhaps her greatest triumphs came through television. Betty Fussell called her "a major woman television comic second only to Carol Burnett and Lucille Ball." Yet her true impact on television was changing the country's views on the importance of good food and good dining—while giving them a good show.

The passion for cooking that had gripped Julia in 1949 in Paris was finally legitimized in her own country. By 1997, the Bureau of Labor Statistics reported that the food service industry was the "fourth fastest-growing" in the country, a figure echoed by the National Restaurant Association's estimates that by 2005 there will be "1.5 million new restaurant jobs" available. The nearly 300 chef schools could expect "an average of six to seven job possibilities for every chef and baker they graduate."

The television audience Julia began gathering in 1963 had burgeoned by 1997. One third of the programs of PBS, which now reached 98 percent of all homes, were cooking shows. When they were joined by TVFN, which claimed 17 million cable subscribers, and the cooking programs on the Discovery Channel and the Learning Channel, one executive was prompted to claim, "Food is the live entertainment of the future."

M. F. K. Fisher and A. J. Liebling (*Between Meals*) may have first made it acceptable to love food and talk about it, but Julia spread that gospel to the middle class. She is most proud of bringing men into the American kitchen. Yet Christopher Lydon, in one of the best profiles of Julia in 1996, believes her impact was greatest on women: "Queen Julia has done more than [Betty]

Friedan, Gloria Steinem and Co. to show American women a model of power in public and expressive self-discovery at home."

Her career, and the example of John McWilliams and Paul Child, had turned a happy-go-lucky, aimless tennis player into a world-class educator and inspiration, what some called a workaholic (she herself would reject the word). "She fears death," says one of her family members. "I think that she fears if she stops she will die." At least she dreads professional death, for she loves what she does; if she stops she might be forgotten and not be able to continue.

HER LAST SUPPER

The meal would begin with foie gras, oysters, and "a little caviar." For thirty-five years she was repeatedly asked for the menu of her last meal. For one who loved a simple, well-cooked piece of meat and a ripe pear for dessert, she always named the most extravagant and rarest foods for her last repast:

First, caviar with Russian vodka (Duburovna) and oysters with Pouilly-Fuissé. And some foie gras, of course. Second, she wanted to eat pan-roasted duck—the duck never varied—accompanied by little onions and chanterelle mushrooms, her main dish. Sometimes she mentioned *pommes Anna,* "that lovely cake of sliced potatoes baked in butter to a crisp brown crust." Sometimes she wanted fresh asparagus with the duck. She would drink a 1962 Romanée-Conti, which she had had only once, for it cost $700 a bottle. When she was in a frugal mood, she chose a delicate red Bordeaux, a St.-Emilion or Château Palmer. Sometimes, Château Lafite-Rothschild. Third, good French bread with Roquefort and Brie would be eaten with a great Burgundy, such as Grands-Echézeaux.

Finally, dessert was a movable feast on which she changed her mind over the years. It varied from pungent sorbet with walnut cake to a simple ripe pear and green tea. She was never strong on desserts, but as she got older she decided she could eat a gooey chocolate dessert or a charlotte Malakoff. When she dreamed big, her dessert was the crème brûlée from Le Cirque with Château d'Yquem 1975 or 1976 at $450 a bottle.

"And I would die happy."

When she was asked for her "favorite comfort food," she responded firmly, "Red meat and gin!" A pioneer of pleasure in a puritan country. A sturdy "pre-war feminist," as Camille Paglia, the author of *Sexual Personae,* describes women like Julia Child, Amelia Earhart, and Katharine Hepburn. Paglia, once called a "motormouth gender contrarian," calls Julia Child "a major American woman" who has been neglected by the academic feminist establishment ("the anorexia- and bulimia-obsessed victimology of academic studies!") because Julia is the "opposite of today's victim psychology": "This country was a waste-land of Philistinism in terms of food until ('food-affirming') Julia Child came on the scene. . . . [S]he is one of those figures in history who totally transformed American culture."

In her old age, Julia joined that noble species, the Grand Old Gal—a common apotheosis for brilliant women. She may stand with her head tipped a little down and sideward, as Eleanor Roosevelt did when her back became stooped, but she is still the queen. Despite bum knees weakening her gait, and the occasional need to lean against the stove (or on the table), she worked at a barely diminished pace. After all, as she loved to point out, "Escoffier lived to be ninety-three and my old chef Max Bugnard lived to be ninety-six."

Her appetite for life will never be sated. "Retired people are boring," she claims. "In this line of work, you never have to retire. You keep right on until you're through."

Appendices

Ancestors of
Julia Carolyn McWilliams

James McWilliams
b: 1802 in Scotch Ridge, OH
d: July 31, 1883
married
   August 9, 1824,
   in Scotch Ridge, OH
Margaret Latimer
b: 1800 in Scotch Ridge, OH
d: December 28, 1939,
   in Griggsville, IL

John McWilliams
b: January 15, 1832,
   in Scotch Ridge, OH
d: November 12, 1924,
   in Pasadena, CA

John McWilliams, Jr.
b: October 26, 1880,
   in Livingston, IL
d: May16, 1962,
   in Pasadena, CA
married
   January 21, 1911,
   in Colorado
   Springs, CO

William Granville Dana
b: 1811 in Vermont
married
Hanna Elizabeth Carpenter
b: c.1824

Clara Maria Dana
b: March 22, 1846,
   in Sharon, VT

**Julia Carolyn
McWilliams**
b: August 15, 1912,
   in Pasadena,CA
married
   September 1, 1946,
   in Stockton, NJ

Isaiah Weston
b: 1804
d: 1835
married
Carolyn Curtis

Byron Curtis Weston
b: April 9, 1832
d: November 8, 1898,
   in Dalton, MA
married 1865

Julia Carolyn Weston
b: July 25, 1877,
   in Dalton, MA
d: July 21, 1937,
   in La Jolla, CA

Clark Mitchell
married
Ellen Shaw Clark

Julia Clark Mitchell
b: August 24, 1844,
   in Cummington, MA
d: September 4, 1902,
   in Dalton, MA

DESCENDANTS OF
JOHN McWILLIAMS, JR.

John McWilliams, Jr.
1880-1962
married
Julia Carolyn Weston
1877-1937

married
Philadelphia Miller O'Melvany
1896-1984

Julia Carolyn McWilliams
1912-
married
Paul Cushing Child
1902-1994

John McWilliams III
1914-
married
Josephine Gay Smith
1919-

Dorothy Dean McWilliams
1917-
married
Ivan Roper Cousins
1918-1983

John McWilliams IV
1941-

Carol McWilliams
1945-

David H. McWilliams
1949-

Patricia McWilliams
1952-

Philadelphia Cousins
1952-

Samuel Cousins
1954-

DESCENDANTS OF
JOHN RUSSELL CUSHING

John Russell Cushing
1838-?
married
Mary Hebard
1840-?

Bertha May Cushing
1871-1933
married
Charles T. Child
1867-1902

Mary Franklin Child
1900-1940
married
Paul Daniel Sheeline
1898-1979

Paul Cushing Sheeline
1921-

married
Jacques Aubert

married
Henry H. Munro

Fiona Munro
c. 1926-

David Munro
c. 1927-

Paul Cushing Child
1902-1994
married
Julia Carolyn McWilliams
1912-

Charles Jesse Child
1902-1983
married
Fredericka Boyles
1904-1977

Erica Child
1932-

Rachel Child
1934-

Jonathan Child
1942-

TELEVISION SERIES

	TITLE	NUMBER	YEAR(S) FILMED
1.	*The French Chef* (black and white)	119	1963–66
2.	*The French Chef* (color)	90	1970–73
3.	*Julia Child & Company*	13	1978
4.	*Julia Child & More Company*	13	1979
5.	*Dinner at Julia's*	13	1983
6.	*Cooking with Master Chefs*	16	1993
7.	*In Julia's Kitchen with Master Chefs*	26	1994
8.	*Baking with Julia*	39	1996

Acknowledgments

and Sources

JULIA CHILD'S friendly generosity and cheerful responsiveness to my many queries have not only made my five years of research a personal pleasure, they have immeasurably enriched this biography. Never has she asked to read or approve my work, a calculated wisdom that reveals trust and respect for the biographical process, bemused resignation based on decades of being misquoted, self-confidence, and an honest openness to life and to others. I could not have written her biography without the total access to her collected and uncollected papers she accorded me. She opened every file and datebook, offered the names of those (very few) who might give me negative opinions ("good quotes," she promised), and prepared meals for me when I visited. She has left me with the burden of responsibility for interpretations and (mis)judgments.

One's friends, they say, are a reflection of one's self, and in the case of Julia Child the cast is joyful, multitudinous, and multinational. They reflect her generosity and support and made my work a delight. Her sister, Dorothy Cousins, offered me family letters, photographs, her mother's diary, and a vast clipping file of Julia's career; her brother, John McWilliams, gave me photographs and a copy of their grandfather's memoirs; her nieces, nephews, and cousins shared letters and hours of their memories and insights.

Special thanks to culinary historians Phil and Mary Hyman, who, during one of their delicious dinners in Paris, first suggested to me they had the perfect subject for my next biography. They were most convincing that I should emphasize the French-American connection. Bert Sonnenfeld gave a hearty second to the Hyman's motion and has offered support, expertise, and, as always, the final read-through. I am particularly grateful to Stephanie Hersh, assistant to Julia Child, for her delightful wit and professional assistance; Kristine Dahl, my agent at International Creative Management, for her belief in the importance of this biography; and Elizabeth Lerner, my editor at Doubleday, for her perceptive editing and encouragement.

For research assistance, I wish to thank Michael Hargraves of the Getty Museum, who offered his M. F. K. Fisher archive, his www expertise, and unfailing research skills; Betty Rosbottom, whose energy is matched only by her mentor's, for insightful recipe and cookbook analysis; Kathleen O'Neill for hours of computerized genealogy assistance; Roberta Klugman, executive director of the American Institute of Wine and Food (AIWF), for answering all my questions; Peter Petraitis for rare books; Karen Walker for additional Paris research; and George Gruenwald, Barbara Hull, and Gwyn Erwin for research assistance. My gratitude to the family and friends of Julia Child who read portions of this manuscript that pertained to their experience.

Several people offered both hospitality and research sources, for which I remain in their debt: E. S. (Peggy) Yntema (Cambridge), Elisabeth Hill and Martha Starr (Washington, DC), Jeanine and Roland Plottel (NYC), Ronald and Betty Rosbottom (Amherst, MA), Anne Willan & Mark Cherniavsky (Burgundy, France); France Thibault (Châteauneuf de Grasse, France, where I spent two visits in Simca's room).

FOR SHARING their memories and meals, for giving me access to letters and photographs, insights and support, I wish to thank the following: Marshall Ackerman, Kathie Alex, Rebecca Alssid, R. W. Apple, Jr., David Haward Bain, Hélène Baltrusaitis, Elisabeth Brassart, Nancy Verde Barr, Michael and Ariane Batterberry, Mary Zook Beales, Emily M. (Wendy) Beck, Henry Becton, Jr., Mary Cootes Belin, Karen Berk, Fern Berman, Ailene (Martin) and Jean Berrard, Louisette Bertholle (Madame la Comtesse de Nalèche), Peter and Mari Bicknell, Margrit Biever (Mondavi), James Bishop, Tom and Frances Bissell, Corinne M. Black, Paul Bohannan, Jane Bollinger, Alison Boteler, Francis Myer Brennan, Joan Brewster, Benjamin H. Brown, Philip S. Brown, Barbara Ord Bryant, Marian Burros, Mary Ford Cairns, Lou and Mary Cannon, Thomas P. Carhartt, Page Carter, Narcisse Chamberlain, Brien and Rudolph Chelminski, Jonathan Child, Rachel Child, Robert Clark, Pat Brown

Clopper, André J. Cointreau, Eleanor Roberts Colt, Joseph R. Coolidge, Constance Thayer Cory, Dorothy Cousins, Philadelphia Cousins and Bob Moran, Samuel Cousins, Howard B. Crotinger, Martha Culbertson, Carol and B. J. Cutler, Marion Cunningham, Susy Davidson, Peter Davison, Elton Davies, Sylvie and Jacques Delécluse, Martha G. Dennis, Carl DeSantis, Mark DeVoto, Froydis and Jan W. Dietrichson, Mary Tonetti Dorra, Harriet Doerr, John P. Downing, Geoffrey Drummond, Robert W. Duemling, Madame F. du Couëdic, William Echikson, Bjorn and Eline Egge, Colin Eisler, E. Lee Fairley, George Faison, Barbara Pool Fenzl, Priscilla Parkhurst Ferguson, John Ferrone, Lyne S. Few, Carol Field, Lisbeth Fisher, Janet Fletcher, Ted and Linda Fondulas, Terry Ford, Pierre Franey, Ken Frank, Jane Friedman, Jean Friendly, James Fullerton, Betty Fussell, Catherine Atwater Galbraith, John Kenneth Galbraith, Katy and Freeman Gates, Catherine Gewertz, Charles Gibson, K. Dun Gifford, Janice Goldklang, Richard Graff, Agnes Green, Dorie Greenspan, Paul Grimes, George Gruenwald, Barbara Haber, Charles Hall, Orian Hall Hallor, Dorothy Cann Hamilton, Viola Tuckerman Hansen, Nancy Kirby Harris, Anne Hastings, Robert P. Hastings, Nancy Gregg Hatch, Harriet P. Healy, Patrick Healy, Louis J. Hector, Nancy White Hector, Susan Heller, Jack Hemingway, Pamela Henstell, Harriet Thacher Herrick, Stephanie Hersh, Karen Hess, Jens P. and Mosse Heyerdahl, Fritz Hier, Jim Hill, Alice C. Hiscock, Anita Hinckley Hovey, Fisher and Debby Howe, Sue Barton Huffman, Robert A. Huttenback, Philip and Mary Hyman, David O. Ives, J. Roland Jacobs, Susan Jacobson, Nancy Harmon Jenkins, Pamela Sheldon Johns, Anne Winton Johnston, Jeffrey Jones, Judith Jones, Barbara Kafka, Elizabeth Parker Kase, Lynne Rossetto Kasper, Edmond Kennedy, Graham Kerr, Mannie and Willette Klausner, Roberta Klugman, Susan Donnell Konkel, William A. Koshland, Harriet Kostic, Elizabeth and George A. Kubler, Christopher Kump, Peter Kump, Alexandre Lazaroff, Paul Levy, Lorance W. Lisle, Ruth Lockwood, James Londe, Jan Longone, James M. McDonald, Elizabeth McIntosh, John McJennett, J. Alexander McWilliams, Jr., David McWilliams, Josephine and John McWilliams III, Patricia G. McWilliams, Saba McWilliams, Maggie Mah, Rosemary Manell, Carolyn Margolis, Byron S. Martin, Dudley Martin, Edward A. Martin, I. Guy Martin, Michael McCarty, Marc Meneau, Sally Bicknell Miall, Barry Michlin, Juliana Middleton, Helen Kirkpatrick Milbank, Amy Bess Miller, Jane C. Owen Molard, Robert Mondavi, John L. Moore, Russell and Marian Morash, Sara Moulton, Richard S. Mowrer, Carrita Nelson, Kyle Nelson, Lizabeth Nicol, Eleanor (Ollie) Noall, Clara Rideout Noyses, Richard Olney, Deborah Olson, Carolyn O'Neil, Dana Gans Parker, Suzanne Patterson, Jacques Pépin, Kathleen Perry, Corinne M. Poole, Jean MacKenzie deSola Pool, Herbert and Patricia R. Pratt,

Erica Child Prud'homme, Wolfgang Puck, Edwin J. Putzell, Steven and Barbara Raichlen, Joan Reardon, Kenneth O. Rhodes, Mary Livingston Ripley, Mary S. Risley, Stuart W. and Rosalind Rockwell, Susan M. Rogers, Betty Rosbottom, Natale Rusconi, Mary Francis Snow Russell, Thibaut de Saint Phalle, Henny and Berge Santo, Marian C. Schlesinger, Margie Schodt, Laura Shapiro, Paul C. and Sandra Sheeline, Virginia Durand Shelden, Mimi Sheraton, James Sherer, Nancy Silverton, Roxane Ruhl Simmons, Barbara Sims-Bell, Joseph C. Sloane, Catharine Carton Smith, Charmaine Solomon, Carl G. Sontheimer, Darthea Speyer, Zanne Early Stewart, Perry and Moune Stieglitz, David Strada, Steven Sullivan, Eleanor Thiry Summers, Jeffrey Steingarten, Madame France Thibault, Jean-François Thibault, Grant P. and Sharon Thompson, Lionel Tiger, Elizabeth Cathcart Tisdal, George Trescher, Clay Triplette, William A. Truslow, Charlotte Snyder Turgeon, Gregory Usher, Margaret Clark VanderVeer, Louise Vincent, Freifrau Dorothea von Stetten, Janou Walcutt, Susan Walter, Mary Case Warner, Marjory Ellen Lacy Warren, Alice Waters, Nach Waxman, Jan Weimer, Patricia Wells, Andrea B. Werbel, Donald M. Weston, Jr., Mary Weston, Barbara Ketcham Wheaton, Aileen Johnson Whitaker, Jasper White, Frances Proctor Wilkinson, Anne Willan and Mark Cherniavsky, Charles E. Williams, Faith Heller Willinger, Craig Alan Wilson, Clark Wolf, Paula Wolfert, Jim Wood, Gay Bradley Wright, Douwe Yntema, E. S. (Peggy) Yntema. And thanks to more than 150 others who answered my *New York Times* query, including numerous journalists who had interviewed Julia Child, and others who answered brief telephone queries.

THE JOHN McWILLIAMS family records were burned in a fire in 1901. What remains are the personal *Recollections* of grandfather John McWilliams, who dictated them to his secretary during the later years of his life, a genealogy of the Weston family (1065–1951), and the letters and photographs which are part of the private collection of the McWilliams and Child families (Julia McWilliams Child, Dorothy McWilliams Cousins, John and Josephine McWilliams III, Phila Cousins, Rachel Child, Erica Prud'homme, Jonathan Child, Saba McWilliams, J. Alexander McWilliams, Jr., and Dana Gans Parker).

In addition to the family papers above, I am deeply indebted to the following persons (or their heirs) who shared with me their private and unpublished personal diaries and memoirs: Eleanor Thiry Summers, Joseph R. Coolidge, Elizabeth Parker Kase, Julia McWilliams Child, Paul Cushing Child, Jeanne Taylor, and Avis DeVoto. For direct access to additional letters of Julia

Child, I thank Barbara Pool Fenzl, Harriet Healy, Jens & Mosse Heyerdahl, Peter Kump, John L. Moore, Richard Mowrer, Kyle Nelson, Corinne Poole, Basil and Eleanor Summers, Anne Willan and Mark Cherniavsky, and others.

Many organizations provided access to special collections of documents, materials, and facilities. I wish to acknowledge the individuals who were especially helpful to me. In particular, I am indebted to the warm encouragement and sometimes special intervention of Barbara Haber, Curator of Printed Books, and Barbara Wheaton, honorary curator, of the Schlesinger Library at Radcliffe, where the papers of Julia Child, Simone Beck, Avis DeVoto, and M. F. K. Fisher are housed. The following libraries and institutions offered vital resources for the research for this book:

American Heritage Center. James Beard Collection, University of Wyoming. Laramie, WY. JB/JC Correspondence, 1953–73.

Avon Old Farms School. Elizabeth A. Coburn, Baxter Library, and Gordon Clark Ramsey, University of Hartford, Historian of Old Farms Schools.

Beard House. New York. Diane Harris, Mitchell Davis, and Clay Triplette.

Beinecke Rare Book and MSS Library. Yale University Library. Richard and Alice Lee Myers Papers and Robert Penn Warren and Eleanor Clark Papers.

Boston University. Rebecca Alssid, Director of Special Programs, Metropolitan College.

Branson School. Harriet Kostic, Alumni Director. Ross, CA.

British Library. Reading Room, London.

Central Intelligence Agency. Washington, DC. John H. Wright, Information and Privacy Coordinator.

Doheny Library. University of Southern California, Los Angeles, CA. Dace Taube, Regional History Center, Department of Special Collections.

Library of Congress. Washington, DC. Reading Room.

Middlebury College. Abernathy Collections, Starr Library, Vermont. Bread Loaf Archives and Correspondence of Julia and Paul Child, Avis DeVoto, and Paul Cubeta.

National Archives and Records Administration, College Park, MD.

Pasadena Historical Museum. Pasadena, CA. Tania Rizzo, Archivist.

Pasadena Polytechnic School. Pasadena, CA. Alumni Office.

Pittsfield Public Library. Pittsfield, MA.

The Arthur and Elizabeth *Schlesinger Library* on the History of Women in America, Radcliffe College, Harvard University, Cambridge, MA. Eva E. Moseley, Curator of Manuscripts; Janes Knowles, Archivist; Barbara Haber, Curator of Printed Books.

Smith College: Library and Alumnae Archives. Northampton, MA. Margery N. Sly, Archivist.

University of Texas: Harry Ransom Hall of Humanities (HRHRC), Austin, TX. Knopf Archives.

TVFN. The Food Network. Sue Huffman, Senior Vice President, Programming.

United States Department of Justice. Federal Bureau of Investigation, Washington, DC. J. Kevin O'Brien, Chief, FOI, Information Resource Division.

United States Information Agency. Lola L. Secora, FOIA/Privacy Act Officer, Office of the General Counsel. USIA Alumni Association, Dorothy Robins-Mowry, Director.

Veterans of the OSS. Jeffrey Jones, President, Rockefeller Plaza, NYC.

WGBH, Boston. *The French Chef* and other tapes, 1963+. Henry Becton, Jr., President; Mary A. Ide, Archivist.

NOTES

UNLESS OTHERWISE noted, all Julia Child quotations are based upon her numerous interviews with the author. Dates of Paul Child's letter-diary to his brother, which numbers in the thousands of pages, are given only if they fall outside the time period of each chapter.

ABBREVIATIONS USED IN THE NOTES

AD	Avis DeVoto
AIWF	American Institute of Wine and Food
CC	Charles Triplett Child (brother-in-law)
DC	Dorothy McWilliams Cousins (sister)
FC	Fredericka Child (sister-in-law)
IACP	International Association of Culinary Professionals
JC	Julia McWilliams Child
LB	Louisette Bertholle
MFKF	Mary Frances Kennedy Fisher
NRF	Noël Riley Fitch (author)
OSS	Office of Strategic Services
PC	Paul Cushing Child (husband)
SB	Simone (Simca) Beck [Fischbacher] (partner)
USIA	United States Information Agency/Service

CHAPTER 1
BEGINNINGS (1945, 1848–1912)

Unpublished Sources

Interviews: Basic to every chapter is the information drawn from numerous interviews with JC. Unless otherwise indicated, all JC quotations are based on these interviews. Family members: DC 3/30/93, 12/20/94, and 2/2/96, John McWilliams III 8/13/93, Dana Parker 6/6/95, Saba McWilliams 5/30/95, Philadelphia Cousins 3/31/95.
Correspondence: H. Alexander Smith to JC, 2/25/65 (Smith claims he introduced the Weston girls to McWilliams and Hemmings); J. Alexander McWilliams to NRF, 6/3/95; John McWilliams III to NRF, 1/2/95; Carolyn McWilliams to DC, 10/1/33.
Archives: Family archival materials generously provided by JC, DC, and John McWilliams III include: "Carolyn Weston Diary 1900–1905"; "Julia Mitchell Weston 1865–1897" diary. *Smith College. Berkshire Athenaeum,* Pittsfield, MA. *Princeton University:* alumni office records. *Schlesinger:* PC letter-diary to CC, 1945; JC to AD, 3/3/53. *Pasadena Public Library. Pasadena Historical Society.*

Published Sources

p. 3   "How like autumn's": PC, "Birthday, 1945," *Bubbles from the Spring* (n.p.: Antique Press, 1974): [39].

p. 4   "There were a lot of women": William F. Schulz, "Lunch Together," *The World* [National Unitarian Magazine] (Nov./Dec. 1992): 32.

p. 5   "Without Julia": Donna Lee, "The Man Behind JC," *Boston Herald American Magazine* (May 10, 1981): 10.

p. 5   "earliest restaurant": Peter Farb and George Armelagos, *Consuming Passions: The Anthropology of Eating* (Boston: Houghton Mifflin, 1980): 194. Hon-Lo, the first cookbook, was compiled by Emperor Sheunung: 244.

p. 5   "It wasn't like lightning": Edith Efron, "Dinner with JC," *TV Guide* (Dec. 5, 1970): 46.

p. 6   "going fever": John McWilliams, *Recollections of John McWilliams: His Youth, Experiences in California, and the Civil War* (Princeton: Princeton Univ. Press, [1919?]): 47.

p. 7   "Weston Field": Thomas Weston, Jr., and Donald M. Weston, Jr., eds. *Weston: 1065–1951* (Pittsfield, MA: Sun Printing, 1951): 27.

CHAPTER 2
A PLACE IN THE SUN (1912–1921)

Unpublished Sources

Interviews: This chapter relies heavily on a number of interviews with JC and DC as well as: John McWilliams III 8/13/93, Philadelphia Cousins 3/31/95, Orian (Babe) Hall [Hallor] 2/19/94, Charles Hall 2/9/94, Elizabeth Parker [Kase] 2/19/94, Elton Davies 2/22/93, Gay Bradley [Wright], 2/5/96, Eleanor Roberts [Phillips Colt] 9/11/94, and

Freeman Gates 4/24/93. Group interview with Pasadena Polytechnic School classmates Mary Frances Snow Russell, James Bishop, William (Bill) Lisle, Kenneth O. Rhodes 1/31/94.

Correspondence: Byron S. Martin to NRF, 1/26/95; Marjory Ellen Lacey [Warren] to NRF, 10/14/93; Lora B. Bragin to JC, 2/27/95; Mary Stuart Batson to JC, 9/27/67; JC to Mary Stuart Batson, n.d.; Dana Parker to NRF, 4/5/95; Charles Hall to Mary Francis Russell, 1/15/94.

Archives: *Family archives:* Caro McWilliams letters to DC, "Carolyn Weston Diary 1900–1905," JC diary written in the 1930s. *Private:* Babe Hall/Julia McWilliams childhood correspondence; Elizabeth Kase, "Betty Parker memoir," 1986. *Pasadena Historical Society. Pasadena Public Library:* records, city telephone books, histories, *Pasadena Evening Star, Pasadena Star-News. Pasadena Polytechnic School:* records. *Schlesinger:* JC to AD, 3/3/53.

Published Sources

p. 14   "First we'd do": Susan Goodman, "Penthouse Potluck," *Modern Maturity* (Nov./Dec. 1996): 35.

p. 15   "I started doing": Curtis Hartman and Steven Raichlen, "JC: The Boston Magazine Interview," *Boston* (April 1981): 78.

p. 16   "Our house": Anne Bryn, "JC Aims to Keep Fun in Food," *Atlanta Journal & Constitution* (April 12, 1990): W8.

p. 20   "dismal place": Lewis H. Lapham, "Everyone's in the Kitchen with JC," *The Saturday Evening Post* (Aug. 8–15, 1964): 20.

p. 20   "Fletcherizing": Donald Dale Jackson, "The Art of Wishful Shrinking," *Smithsonian* (Nov. 1994): 147–48.

p. 20   "Don't eat fried food": in "Plain Talk on Food," *Pasadena Daily News* (Nov. 6, 1912): 6.

p. 20   "whose theology": Gerald Carson, "The Yankee Kitchen," in *The American Heritage Cookbook: An Illustrated History* (NY: American Heritage, 1964): 82.

p. 20   "All my mother knew": Roberta Wallace Coffey, "Their Recipe for Love," *McCall's* 116 (Nov. 1988): 97.

p. 21   "such an utter loss": Ogden Nash, *Food* (NY: Stewart, Tabori & Chang, 1989): 31. In an essay on Boston food written with E. S. Yntema ("JC's Boston Birthday Buffet," *Boston Globe Magazine,* May 11, 1980, page 27), JC adds a small onion, 4 peppercorns, a bay leaf, specifies 2 cups of mashed potatoes, and calls it "Priscilla Weston's Duxbury Codfish Balls with Egg Sauce."

p. 22   "Jell-O was distributing": Robert Clark, *James Beard: A Biography* (NY: HarperCollins, 1993): 36.

p. 22   "cut down your food supply": J. C. Elliot and Arthur Taylor in *Pasadena Star-News* (March 7, 1916): 12.

p. 26   "extrovert": C. G. Jung, *Collected Works of C. G. Jung,* vol. 6, 2nd ed. (Princeton, 1971): 157–58.

p. 27   "When we went out": JC, "What Is Your Favorite Place in California?" *Westways* (July 1995): 11.

p. 29   "frontier legacy": "Pioneer Californian Is Called," *Pasadena Star-News* (Nov. 13, 1924): 1.

CHAPTER 3

EDUCATION OF AN EXTROVERT (1921–1930)

Unpublished Sources

Interviews: For *Polytechnic School:* JC, Charles Hall 2/9/94, John McWilliams III 8/13/93, Orian (Babe) Hall [Hallor] 2/29/94, DC 3/9/94 and 5/10/95, Mary Ford [Cairns] 9/14/94, Elizabeth Parker [Kase] 2/19/94; Eleanor Roberts [Phillip Colt] 9/11/94; Robert Hastings 2/9/95, Gay Bradley [Wright] 2/5/96; group interview with Mary Frances Snow [Russell], William (Bill) Lisle, Kenneth O. Rhodes, James Bishop 1/31/94. For *Katharine Branson School:* JC, Dana Parker 6/6/95, Aileen Johnson [Whitaker] 3/21/94, Mary Zook [Beales] 3/11/94, Marjory Ellen Lacey [Warren] 10/14/93, Dorothy McWilliams [Cousins] ('35) 3/9/94, Clara Rideout [Noyses] ('33) 3/19/89, Harriet Kostic 3/11/94.

Correspondence: For *Poly:* Charles Hall to Mary Frances Snow [Russell], 1/15/94; Joseph C. Sloane to NRF, 7/19/95. For *KBS:* Viola Tuckerman [Hansen] to NRF, 2/15/94; Barbara Ord [Bryant] (through her daughter, Babs Bryant Pomilia) to NRF, 3/16/94; Mary Zook [Beales] to NRF, 2/16/94; Roxane Ruhl [Simmons] to NRF, 3/10/94 and 4/15/94; Dana Parker to NRF, 4/5/95.

Archives: *Poly:* Polytechnic School, Georgia McClay, archivist, 1030 E. California Blvd.; the school was founded when Troop Polytechnique Institute (founded in 1891) dropped its lower grades to form California Polytechnique University in 1907. Private: Julia McWilliams to Babe Hall, childhood letters [n.d.]; Elizabeth (Betty) Parker [Kase] memoir, 1986; JC fragmentary diary "Oh So *Private*," 1935–42. *KBS:* Special thanks to Harriet Kostic, Alumni Director of Branson School, for opening the confidential records (with JC's permission), history of KBS, *KBS Scrapbook: 1920–1970,* the *Blue Print* literary journal, Oral History Projects.

Published Sources

p. 32   "I was always": Molly O'Neill, "What's Cooking in America?" *New York Times* (Oct. 12, 1989): 16.

p. 35   "New Women success story": Maureen Honey, ed., *Breaking the Ties That Bind: Popular Stories of the New Woman, 1915–1930* (Norman: Univ. of Oklahoma, 1995): 56.

p. 36   "One of my earliest": JC, *From JC's Kitchen* (NY: Knopf, 1975): 431.

p. 40   "courtesy, Christianity, and college": Mark Baur, "A World of Its Own: The Katharine Branson School, 1917–1945," typed transcript of thesis, n.d.: 40.

p. 40   "the nut of Christianity": JC to CC, 7/24/53 (from Matthew 22:37–38). She gave the same philosophy, in summary form, to "Proust Questionnaire," *Vanity Fair* (March 1996): 212.

p. 40   "enclosed, sprayed": Bauer, "A World of Its Own," 40.

p. 41   "Father Love": "Rites Close Father-Love Death Drama," *Pasadena Evening Post* (Dec. 10, 1927): 1. Extensive coverage of the Stevens murders in *Pasadena Evening Star* and *Pasadena Star-News,* Dec. 8–10, 1927.

p. 43   "love of jelly donuts," Gayle Murphy, *Ross Valley Reporter* (March 19, 1980): 5.

pp.   "The peculiar nature": Jung, *Collected Works of C. G. Jung,* vol. 6, 2nd ed.
44–45   (Princeton, 1971): 427, 332–33, 159.

CHAPTER 4

SMITH COLLEGE (1930–1934)

Unpublished Sources

Interviews: Classmates: JC, Charlotte Snyder [Turgeon] 8/14/93 and 5/23/94, Catharine
(Kitty) Atwater [Galbraith] 8/9/93, Elizabeth (Betty) Bushnell [Kubler] 9/26/94, Mary
Case [Warner] 11/3/93, Mary Coots [Belin] 11/93, Margaret (Peggy) Clark [VanderVeer]
2/13/94, Mary Ford [Cairns] 2/14/94, Anita Hinckley [Hovey] 5/25/94, Constance
Thayer [Cory] 5/15/94, Gay Bradley [Wright] 2/5/96. Other interviews: DC and Sam
Cousins 12/20/94, John McWilliams III 8/13/93, Mary Weston 5/19/94, Dana Parker
6/6/95, Orian (Babe) Hall [Hallor] 2/19/94, Charles Hall 2/9/94.
Correspondence: JC to Anne Dodge, 6/20/66; JC to Philadelphia Cousins, 7/8/79; Maida
Goodwin to NRF, 9/23/93 and 3/4/94; JC to Carolyn McWilliams, 1932–34; Carolyn
McWilliams to DC, 1933–34. *Classmates:* Catharine Carton [Smith] to NRF, 3/12/94;
Anne Winton [Johnston] to NRF, 4/20/95; Frances Proctor '37 [Wilkinson] to NRF,
7/96; Constance Thayer [Cory] to NRF, 5/23/94; Roxane Ruhl [Simmons] to NRF,
3/10/94 and 4/15/94.
Archives: *Smith College:* Sophia Smith Collection, Neilson Library, Smith Centennial
Study Oral History, JC & PC, Oct. 10, 1972, transcript for *College. A Smith Mosaic;
Sophian; Smith Alumnae Quarterly;* historical records of the college and JC. *Private: Smith
College Year Book,* 1933 and 1934 (courtesy Mary Case Warren). *Schlesinger:* JC to
MFKF, 5/29/86.

Published Sources

p. 50   "It slipped": Margo Greep, "JC Adds Spice to Banquet," Smith College *Sophian*
           (April 13, 1978): 1.

p. 54   "representing more than half": Jules Tygiet, *The Great Los Angeles Swindle: Oil,
           Stocks, and Scandal During the Roaring Twenties* (NY: Oxford, 1994): 310.

p. 55   "five percent": *Historical Statistics of the U.S.,* Part 1 (Wash. DC: U.S. Dept. of
           Commerce, Bureau of Census, 1995): 380.

p. 57   "model food of the twentieth century": Laura Shapiro, *Perfection Salad: Women
           and Cooking at the Turn of the Century* (NY: Farrar, Straus & Giroux, 1986):
           214.

p. 60   "Inspired": Nao Hauser, "JC: Her Life, Her Great Love, and Her Future,"
           Chicago Tribune (March 3, 1980): 4.

p. 64   "She will return here": "Pasadena Girl Achieves High Honors in East," *Pasa-
           dena Star-News* (clipping).

CHAPTER 5

CAREER SEARCH (1934–1943)

Unpublished Sources

Interviews: JC, DC, John and Josephine McWilliams III 8/13/93, Orian (Babe) Hall [Hallor] 2/19/94, Charles Hall 2/9/94, Peggy Clark [VanderVeer] 2/13/94, Mary Ford [Cairns] 2/14/94, Connie Thayer [Cory] 5/15/94, Charlotte Snyder [Turgeon] 8/14/93, Robert P. Hastings 2/9/95, Anita Hinckley [Hovey] (5/25/94), Katy and Freeman (Tule) Gates 4/24/93, Mary Frances Snow [Russell] 1/31/94, Gay Bradley [Wright] 2/5/96, John (Jack) L. Moore 5/20/94, Elizabeth (Betty) MacDonald [McIntosh] 11/3/93. Lawrence Deitz, a biographer of the Chandler family, on Harrison Gray Otis Chandler 1903–86. Transcript of Foreign Service Spouse Oral History, 11/7/91.

Correspondence: Carolyn McWilliams to DC, 1934–37; Harold J. Coolidge to NRF, 3/22/94 and 7/8/96; Catharine Carton [Smith] to NRF, 3/12/94; Edwin J. (Ned) Putzell, Jr., to NRF, 1/14/94 and 1/31/95; Alice Carson [Hiscock] to NRF, 2/6/95 and 2/23/95; Elizabeth Cathcart Tisdel to NRF, 3/4/97.

Archives: *Private:* JC (sporadic) diary 1935–42; JC unpublished writings, including essays and correspondence for W. & J. Sloane, *Coast* magazine, and plays for Junior League; "An Evening with JC: At the Valley Hunt Club," tape 11/7/90; JC's U.S. government documents; Richard C. Hiscock, "Development of Exposure Suits" (5-page report), n.d. (courtesy Alice Carson Hiscock). *Smith College:* alumni records; JC to Marjorie P. Nield (alumni office), 12/6/35; JC oral history transcription for *College. A Mosaic,* 10/10/72; *Smith Alumnae Quarterly. Schlesinger:* JC to AD, 2/12/53; JC to AD, 2/25/53; PC to CC, 10/25/71.

Published Sources

p. 65   "Middle-class women": Polly Frost, "Wild Child," *Interview,* xix (Fall 1989): 63.

p. 67   "I used to go to Grand Central": Susan Goodman, "Penthouse Potluck," *Modern Maturity* (Nov./Dec. 1996): 36.

p. 72   "climate is a scandal": John Steinbeck, "The Making of a New Yorker," *New York Times Magazine* (Feb. 1, 1953): 27. See also Susan Edmiston and Linda D. Cirono, *Literary New York: A History and Guide* (Boston: Houghton Mifflin, 1976): 235.

p. 76   "The Intelligent": JC, "The Intelligent Woman Voter," *Pasadena Junior League News* (Oct. 19, 1939): 13.

p. 77   "Oh why do you walk": a slightly misquoted passage from Frances Cornford's "To a Fat Lady Seen from the Train." My gratitude to E. S. Yntema for identifying this verse.

p. 80   "increase his needs": Dorothy Thompson, "On the Record: The W.P.A.," *New York Herald Tribune* (Oct. 21 [1942]), clipping.

p. 83   "a bunch of college professors": R. Harris Smith, *OSS: The Secret History of America's First Central Intelligence Agency* (Berkeley: Univ. of CA, 1972): 13.

p. 84   "potential postwar clients": Stanley P. Lovell, *Of Spies & Stratagems* (NY: Pocket Books, 1963): 194.

p. 84   "largely unvouchered": Smith, *OSS,* 3, 5.
p. 85   "helter-skelter but brilliant": Smith, *OSS,* 1–2.

CHAPTER 6

INDIA INTRIGUE (1944–1945)

Unpublished Sources
Interviews: JC, John L. (Jack) Moore 5/20/94, Elizabeth (Betty) MacDonald [McIntosh] 11/3/93, I. Guy Martin 9/30/94, Mary Livingston (Mrs. Dillon Ripley) 9/27/94, Fisher Howe 9/28/94, Thibaut de Saint Phalle 12/5/94.
Correspondence: OSS colleagues: Alice C. Carson [Hiscock] to NRF, 2/6/95 and 2/23/95; Louis J. Hector to NRF, 11/96; Eleanor (Ellie) Thiry [Summers] to NRF, 9/7/94; Virginia (Peachy) Durand [Shelden] to NRF 2/3/95; Edwin J. (Ned) Putzell, Jr., to NRF, 1/14/94; Thibaut de Saint Phalle to NRF, 12/5/94; Catharine (Kitty) Carton [Swett] to NRF, 1/31/95 and 1/4/97; Byron S. Martin to NRF, 1/11/95 and 1/26/95; Elizabeth (Betty) MacDonald [McIntosh] to NRF, 11/27/96, Geoffrey M. T. Jones, Pres. Veterans of OSS, to NRF, 5/19/94. JC to Sue Van Voches *(Encyclopedia of American Women),* 10/20/72; Peggy Wheeler to JC, 7/18/44.
Archives: *Private:* diaries of JC ("Oh So Private"), Eleanor (Ellie) Thiry [Summers] ("excerpts from letters home"), and Joseph R. Coolidge; PC to CC letters, courtesy John Moore and Rachel Child; JC and PC private records. *Schlesinger:* copies of PC letter-diary to CC, 1943–45. *Smith College:* JC and PC oral history transcript for *College. A Smith Mosaic,* 10/10/72. *National Archives:* files #9300811 and #9300812, 1993–95. *CIA:* file #F93-0455 (obtained with JC permission under the FOIA, 5/95).

Published Sources
p. 90   "had a veritable genius": Jane Foster, *An UnAmerican Lady* (London: Sidgwick & Jackson, 1980): 134.
p. 93   "Kandy is probably": Philip Ziegler, *Mountbatten* (NY: Harper & Row, 1985): 279.
p. 93   "direction [to] the sea" and "the future of Asia": Barbara Tuchman, *Stilwell and the American Experience in China, 1911–45* (NY: Macmillan, 1970): 446, 455.
p. 94   "a highly developed security": Elizabeth P. MacDonald [McIntosh]. *Undercover Girl* (NY: Macmillan, 1947): 26.
p. 97   "one hero in my life": Donna Lee, "The Man Behind JC," *Boston Herald American Magazine* (May 10, 1981): 9.
p. 99   "Morale in her section": Elizabeth P. McIntosh, *The Role of Women in Intelligence,* Intelligence Profession Series No. 5 (McLean, VA: Association of Former Intelligence Officers, 1989): 35.
p. 99   "held her ground": Colonel Heppner remembered that it was Mary Livingston Eddy [Ripley], Julia's colleague, who had the hole cut in the floor.
p. 100 "OSS brain bank": MacDonald, *Undercover Girl,* 26.
p. 100 "Ceylon was an Elysium": Jane Foster quoted in MacDonald, *Undercover Girl,* 132.

CHAPTER 7

TO CHINA WITH LOVE (1945)

Unpublished Sources

Interviews: JC, John (Jack) Moore 5/20/94, Elizabeth (Betty) MacDonald [Heppner] [McIntosh] 11/3/93, I. Guy Martin 9/30/94, Mary Livingston Eddy [Ripley] 3/31/94 and 7/94, George and Elizabeth (Betty) Kubler 9/26/94.

Correspondence: Elizabeth (Betty) MacDonald [Heppner] [McIntosh] to NRF, 11/27/96; Byron S. Martin to NRF, 1/11/95 and 1/26/95; Louis J. Hector to NRF, 10/16/96; Edwin J. (Ned) Putzell, Jr., to NRF, 1/31/95; Virginia (Peachy) Durand [Shelden] to NRF, 2/3/95; Eleanor (Ellie) Thiry [Summers] to NRF, 9/7/94; PC to "My darling Joan," 4/17/45.

Archives: *Private:* copies JC and PC U.S. government records, family letters; diaries of Julia McWilliams, Eleanor (Ellie) Thiry [Summers], Virginia (Peachy) Durand, and Joseph R. Coolidge; unpublished stories by Jeanne Taylor. *Schlesinger:* PC letter-diary to CC, 1943, 1945, and 8/2/53; JC to AD, 3/18/53. *National Archives:* Ref. #9300811 and #9300812, 1993–95. *CIA:* file #F93-0455 (obtained with JC permission under the FOIA, 5/95).

Published Sources

p. 106   "aluminum trail": Barbara Tuchman, *Stilwell and the American Experience in China, 1911–45* (NY: Macmillan, 1970): 302.

p. 106   "the C-54": Elizabeth MacDonald, *Undercover Girl* (NY: Macmillan, 1947): 150.

p. 107   "forced [and] unhappy alliance": R. Harris Smith, *OSS: The Secret History of America's First Central Intelligence Agency* (Berkeley: Univ. of CA, 1972): 251.

p. 108   "medieval cesspool": Theodore H. White and Annalee Jacoby. *Thunder Out of China* (London: Victor Gollancz, 1947): 154.

p. 110   "the atmosphere of a frontier town": Robert Hayden Alcorn, *No Bugles for Spies: Tales of the OSS* (London: White Lion, 1977): 63.

p. 111   "Old Testament Christian": *Theodore White at Large: The Best of His Magazine Writing 1939–1986,* ed. Edward T. Thompson (NY: Pantheon, 1992): 43. Originally published in *Life,* March 2, 1942.

p. 111   "corrupt political clique": White and Jacoby, *White at Large,* 104. Originally published in *Life,* May 1, 1944.

p. 111   "this rotten regime": Tuchman, *Stilwell,* 378.

p. 112   "bulged with reports": Smith, *OSS,* 269.

p. 113   "one of the most alert" and "Sub Rosy": MacDonald, *Undercover Girl,* 108, 210.

p. 115   "the terrible Army food": JC, "How I Learned to Love Cooking," *Parade* (Nov. 13, 1994): 13.

p. 115   "a knowledge of food and drink": Peter Farb and George Armelagos, *Consuming Passions: The Anthropology of Eating* (Boston: Houghton Mifflin, 198): 192.

p. 120   "There will be no more wars": Theodore H. White, *In Search of History: A Personal Adventure* (London: Cope, 1979): 224.

p. 120   "melt[ing]" his "frozen earth": PC, *Bubbles from the Spring* (n.p.: Antique Press, 1974): [37]. The published poem differs slightly from the PC letter to CC, Aug. 16, 1945.

p. 121   "model of ambiguity": Smith, *OSS,* 280.

p. 121   "greatest revolution": White and Jacoby, *Thunder Out of China,* 9.

p. 121   "We always talked": JC, *Parade,* 13.

p. 123   "a sudden vacuum": MacDonald, *Undercover Girl,* 227.

p. 125   "marginal part": Bradley F. Smith, *The Shadow Warriors: OSS and the Origins of the CIA* (London: Deutsch, 1983): 310.

p. 125   "amassed an incredible amount of information": Stanley Lovell, *Of Spies & Stratagems* (NY: Pocket Books, 1963): 219.

CHAPTER 8

EASTWARD HO (1945–1946)

Unpublished Sources

Interviews: JC, DC 4/30/93 and 2/16/94, Freeman and Katy Gates 4/24/93 and 2/16/95, John L. Moore 5/20/94, John and Josephine McWilliams 8/13/93, Philadelphia Cousins 3/31/95, Samuel Cousins 2/16/95, Rachel Child 2/24/94 and 11/8/96, Erica Prud'homme 9/22/94, Robert P. Hastings 2/9/95, William A. Truslow 4/20/95, Gay Bradley Wright 2/5/96, Thibaut de Saint Phalle 12/5/94, Francis Myer Brennan 9/23/94, Paul Sheeline 2/26/94, Edmond Kennedy 9/27/94, Eleanor (Ollie) Noall 2/25/94. Group interview with Child siblings, Rachel Child, Erica Prud'homme, Jonathan Child 8/17/93.
Correspondence: Katy Gates to JC, 9/14/82; Nancy Gregg Hatch to NRF, 8/29/96 and 9/3/96; Erica Prud'homme to JC, 5/26/94; PC to Erica Prud'homme, 6/9/86; John L. Moore to NRF, 9/14/94.
Archives: *Private:* JC & PC love letters (12/45–5/46), business files; James S. Cushing, *The Genealogy of the Cushing Family* (1905, 1979); Ellie Thiry's diary (on leaving China). *Avon Old Farms School:* Gordon Clark Ramsey, "Aspiration & Perseverance: The History of Avon Old Farms School," n.d. *Schlesinger:* PC letter-diary to CC, 1943, 1946, 11/22/52 and 11/25/68.

Published Sources

p. 127   "Ivy League clientele": Michael Lomonaco with Donna Farsman, "21: The Speakeasy That Became a Restaurant That Became a Legend," *Gourmet* (Nov. 1995): 208.

p. 130   "Mrs. Hill had never seen": quoted in NRF, "The Crisco Kid," *Los Angeles* (July 1996): 84.

p. 136   "My father was very difficult": Roberta Wallace Coffey, "Julia and Paul Child: Their Recipe for Love," *McCall's* (Nov. 1988): 98.

p. 137   "had to decline": *Recollections of John McWilliams: His Youth, Experiences in California, and the Civil War* (Princeton: Princeton Univ. Press, [1919?]): 67.

p. 139   "tall willowy": CC, *Roots in the Rock* (Boston: Little, Brown, 1964): 123.

CHAPTER 9

FLAVORS OF MARRIAGE (1946–1948)

Unpublished Sources

Interviews: JC, DC 2/2/96, John L. (Jack) Moore 5/20/94, Francis Myer Brennan 10/7/93, Fisher and Debby Howe 9/28/94, Elizabeth (Betty) and George Kubler 9/26/94, Colin Eisler 12/2/95 and 1/12/97, Sally Bicknell [Miall] 3/25/94, Peter and Mari Bicknell 3/21/94, Edmond Kennedy 9/27/94, Mary Case Warner 11/3/93, Philadelphia Cousins 3/31/95, Guy Martin 9/30/94, Paul Sheeline 2/26/94, Mary Tonetti Dorra 5/6/94. Group interview with Rachel Child, Erica Prud'homme, Jonathan Child 8/17/93.

Correspondence: Peter and Mari Bicknell to NRF, 3/94; Joan Brewster to NRF, 3/14/95; Elizabeth Bicknell to NRF, 1/20/94.

Archives: *State of New Jersey:* wedding certificate. *Dept. of State:* PC's government records. *Private:* PC private diary 1/48. *Schlesinger:* PC to CC, 10/29/48, 10/31/48, 11/24/49, 12/21/68 (no letter-diary exists for this period because both Child families were living in the same city); PC to George and Betty Kubler, 2/9/47, 3/6/47, 9/21/48, and 10/29/48.

Published Sources

p. 148   "wholly compliant femininity": Laura Shapiro, *Perfection Salad: Women and Cooking at the Turn of the Century* (NY: Farrar, Straus & Giroux, 1986): 227.

pp.   "toward flavor": Robert Clark, *James Beard: A Biography* (NY: HarperCollins,
148–49   1993): 93.

p. 149   "charming, civilized": Anne Mendelson, *Stand Facing the Stove: The Story of the Women Who Gave America The Joy of Cooking* (NY: Henry Holt, 1996): 144.

p. 149   "the real thing": James Beard quoted by John L. Hess and Karen Hess, *The Taste of America* (NY: Grossman, 1977): 65.

CHAPTER 10

À PARIS (1948–1949)

Unpublished Sources

Interviews: JC, DC 3/9/94, Hélène Baltrusaitis 7/28/93, Madame du Couëdic 7/95, Sylvie (Pouly) and Jacques Delécuse 7/95, Helen Kirkpatrick [Milbank] 9/19/95, Elizabeth (Betty) MacDonald Heppner [McIntosh] 11/3/93, John L. Moore 5/24/94, Philadelphia Cousins 3/31/95, Anne Hastings (granddaughter of Madame Ebrard Saint-Ange) 9/30/94, George and Elizabeth (Betty) Kubler 9/26/94, Francis (Fanny) Myer Brennan

10/7/93 and 9/23/94, Mari and Peter Bicknell 3/21/94, Sally [Bicknell] Miall 3/25/94, Janou Walcutt 2/3/95, Rosemary Manell 5/30/93, Paul Sheeline 2/26/94. Karen Walker interview with Darthea Speyer 1/31/97. Group interview with Rachel Child, Erica Prud'homme, Jonathan Child 8/17/93.

Correspondence: JC to Jeffrey Meyers, 10/4/84; Richard S. Mowrer to NRF, 2/21/95; Janou Walcutt to NRF, 2/3/95; Mari and Peter Bicknell to NRF, 3/94; Sally [Bicknell] Miall to NRF, 4/4/94; Mrs. Alfred (Jean) Friendly to NRF, 7/11/96; JC to Albert Sonnenfeld, 10/12/91.

Archives: *Private:* JC and PC datebooks, 1948, 1949; Mowrer/Child correspondence (courtesy Richard Scott Mowrer). *Schlesinger:* PC letter-diary to CC/FC (the major source for this chapter), 1948, 1949; correspondence JC, George and Betty Kubler, LB, MFKF, CC and FC; MFKF to JC, 9/24/67. *Beinecke:* PC/Myers/Brennan correspondence. *Smith College: Smith Alumni Quarterly,* oral history transcript for *College. A Smith Mosaic,* 10/10/72.

Published Sources

p. 155   "golden Normandy butter": JC, *From JC's Kitchen,* 117. All versions of her first meal in France—including the lengthy JC, "That Lunch in Rouen," *New York Times* (Oct. 10, 1993): 12—differ somewhat from the authoritative version, PC to CC Nov. 30, 1948, written that evening.

p. 156   "finest group of American civilians": Theodore White, *In Search of History: A Personal Adventure* (London: Cape, 1979): 284.

p. 161   "grimier": Herbert Lottman, *The Left Bank: Writers, Artists, and Politics from the Popular Front to the Cold War* (Boston: Houghton Mifflin, 1982): 238.

p. 162   "the heart of Paris in 1948": Lionel Abel, *The Intellectual Follies: A Memoir of the Literary Venture in New York and Paris* (NY: Norton, 1984): 162, 169.

p. 162   "Everyone came to Paris": Art Buchwald, *I'll Always Have Paris: A Memoir* (NY: Putnam's Sons, 1996): 105.

p. 162   "JC was the only one": Jack Thomas, "JC: Still Cooking," *Boston Globe* (March 6, 1997): E4.

p. 163   "holiday cooking disaster": Susan Goodman, "Penthouse Potluck," *Modern Maturity* (Nov./Dec., 1996): 34.

p. 163   "an adventure in the exercise": White, *In Search of History,* 204, 274.

p. 163   "We arrived at the Golden Age": Art Buchwald, "To Be Young and in Love in Paris," *New York Times* (Aug. 25, 1996): 25.

p. 164   "wedding party": White, *In Search of History,* 264.

p. 164   "The USIS was kind of a stepchild": Foreign Service Spouse Oral History, "An Interview with JC" (Nov. 7, 1991): 16.

p. 165   "to restore": Peter Farb and George Armelagos, *Consuming Passions: The Anthropology of Eating* (Boston: Houghton Mifflin, 1980): 244.

p. 166   "The artistic integrity of the French": Edith Wharton, *French Ways and Their Meaning* (NY: D. Appleton, 1919): 235.

p. 166   "subtlety of thought and manner": Farb and Armelagos, *Consuming Passions,* 3–4.

p. 169   "I would have been": Roberta Wallace Coffey, "Their Recipe for Love," *McCall's* 116 (Nov. 1988): 98. In her datebook, JC lists among her medicines a contraceptive jelly.

p. 170   "the national pastime": NRF, *Literary Cafés of Paris* (Wash. DC: Starrhill, 1989): 16.

p. 171   "When the two of them": Jack Hemingway, *Misadventures of a Fly Fisherman: My Life With and Without Papa* (NY: McGraw-Hill, 1986): 247–48. Photograph of wedding party, including JC, page 150.

CHAPTER 11
CORDON BLEU (1949–1952)

Unpublished Sources

Interviews: JC, DC 4/30/93, 3/9/94, 2/2/96, and 1/10/97, LB 7/12/92, Helen Kirkpatrick [Milbank] 9/19/95, Francis Myer Brennan 10/7/93 and 9/23/94, Janou Walcutt 2/3/95, Hélène Baltrusaitis 7/28/93, Rosemary Manell 4/30/93, Debby and Fisher Howe 9/28/94, Louise Vincent 7/18/95, Ailene Martin Berrard 5/8/94, Susy Davidson 2/25/94, Harriet Healy 4/5/94, Gay Bradley Wright 2/5/96, Elizabeth Heppner [McIntosh] 11/3/93, Elizabeth (Betty) Kubler 9/26/94, Anne Hastings (granddaughter of Madame Saint-Ange) 9/30/94, Lizabeth Nicol 8/3/94. Philadelphia Cousins 3/31/95, Suzanne Patterson 5/24/93, Mark DeVoto 12/14/94. Karen Walker interview with Elisabeth Brassart 2/9/95 and Darthea Speyer 1/31/97.
Correspondence: Shakurra Amatulla to NRF, 7/7/96; JC to editor of *Life International,* 12/18/51 (on poor administration of Cordon Bleu); LB to JC, 10/3/82 (courtesy Peter Kump); Joseph C. Sloane to NRF, 1/13/95 and 7/19/95; Catharine (Kitty) Carton Smith to NRF, 1/31/95; JC to Jeffrey Meyers, 10/4/84; Helen Milbank to JC, 10/4/82 (courtesy Peter Kump).
Archives: *Schlesinger:* PC letter-diary to CC, 1950–53; correspondence JC, SB, LB, AD, FC, Madame Brassart (3/28/51), Max Bugnard, Betty and George Kubler; JC, "L'Histoire de la Chef Française" (2-page typescript MS); typescript menus of "French cooking school"; copies *Embassy News;* "History of Our Relations with Ives Washburn," 12/30/52; Beck and Bertholle manuscripts; transcript of Foreign Service Spouse Oral History, 11/7/91. *Cordon Bleu, Paris:* records and publications *(Le Cordon Bleu Revue Illustrée de Cuisine Pratique et des Arts Ménagers,* vols. 16, 26, 37). *Private:* datebooks of JC and PC, 1948–53; JC/PC vacation correspondence; AD, "Memoir About Julia," 10/16/88 (courtesy Mark DeVoto); Peter Kump video of Bramafam and Simone Beck. *Beinecke:* correspondence PC and Richard E. Myers.

Published Sources

p. 179   "a horrifying chore": JC, *From JC's Kitchen,* 153. The first account of the fish pounding for mousse, which she mailed to "Bien Maître" Bugnard: JC, "It Took 11 GIs, Girl to Make Fish Cakes," *Boston Globe* (Feb. 13, 1964): clipping.

p. 179   "you would have to pass": JC, "Cooking with Julia: A Soulful Chicken Soup," *Food & Wine* (Jan. 1995): 30.

p. 179   "delicately known as": Frances Levison, "First, Peel an Eel," *Life International* (Dec. 13, 1964): 83.

p. 180   "first-class feasting": Catharine Reynolds, "Paris Journal: One Hundred Years of Le Cordon Bleu," *Gourmet* (Jan. 1995): 53.

p. 184   "One of the reasons I married her": Grey Stevens, "Ivan and Dorothy," *San Francisco Sunday Examiner & Chronicle* (Oct. 11, 1981): 32.

p. 188   "one of the great encounters": Michael James, "Simca Beck—Master of The Art of French Cooking; An Affectionate Portrait," *Food & Wine* (June 1987): 108.

p. 188   "a tall blonde": JC, "Introduction" to SB with Suzanne Patterson, *Food & Friends: Recipes and Memories from Simca's Cuisine* (NY: Viking, 1991).

p. 191   "instant chef": John L. Hess and Karen Hess, *The Taste of America* (NY: Grossman, 1977): 191.

p. 194   "I had there": Julian Street, *Where Paris Dines* (NY: Doubleday, 1929): 51.

CHAPTER 12

MARSEILLES (1953–1954)

Unpublished Sources

Interviews: JC, Rosemary Manell 4/30/93, John L. Moore 5/20/94, Robert W. Duemling 1/11/95, Fisher and Debby Howe 9/28/94, Mark DeVoto 12/14/95, Paul Sheeline 2/26/94, Elizabeth (Betty) Kubler 9/26/94, Philip and Mary Hyman 6/18/95.

Correspondence: Nancy [White] Hector to NRF, 11/5/96; J. Roland Jacobs to NRF, 4/3/95; Howard B. Crotinger to NRF, 2/14/95 and 3/14/95; E. Lee Fairley to NRF, 5/11/93 and 6/5/95; Joseph C. Sloane to NRF, 11/13/95; JC to Paulette Chaix, 4/67; JC to Eleanor and Basil Summers, 2/14/54; AD to JC, 9/25/82 (courtesy Peter Kump); Nancy [White] Hector to NRF, 11/5/96.

Archives: *Private:* JC and PC datebooks and address books, 1953, 1954, 1955; AD, "Memoir About Julia," 10/16/88 (courtesy Mark DeVoto); JC to DC correspondence (courtesy DC); 1950s *Michelin Guides* (courtesy Philip and Mary Hyman). *Schlesinger:* PC letter-diary to CC, 1953–55; correspondence JC, DC, SB, LB, MFKF, Katy Gates, and Paul Sheeline; Houghton Mifflin contracts and correspondence.

Published Sources

p. 202   "moved through Europe": Theodore H. White, *In Search of History: A Personal Adventure* (London: Cape, 1979): 356.

p. 203   "Most people were scared": Foreign Service Spouse Oral History, "An Interview with JC" (Nov. 7, 1991): 8.

p. 209   "all copy from one another": JC was using Escoffier's 4th (1948) edition, Simca his 1900. For an English edition, see Auguste Escoffier, *The Escoffier Cookbook* (NY: Crown, 1969).

p. 209   "an imperial look in her eye": JC, *From JC's Kitchen* (NY: Knopf, 1975): 20.

p. 213   "To choose bouillabaisse": Raymond Oliver, *Gastronomy of France,* trans. Claude Durrell (Cleveland: World Publishing, 1967): 163.

p. 216   "Populist . . . an honorable word": Arthur M. Schlesinger, Jr., "The Citizen,"
Four Portraits and One Subject: Bernard DeVoto (Boston: Houghton Mifflin,
1963): 41.

CHAPTER 13

A LITTLE TOWN IN GERMANY (1954–1956)

Unpublished Sources

Interviews: JC, LB 7/12/92, Rosemary Manell 4/30/93, John L. Moore 5/20/94, Mark
DeVoto 12/14/94.
Correspondence: Lyne S. Few to NRF, 4/20/95; E. Lee Fairley to NRF, 5/11/95 and
6/5/95; Freifrau Dorothea von Stetten to NRF, 7/28/96 and 9/5/96; Fitz Hier to NRF,
8/7/96; Martha Culbertson to NRF, 3/18/95; James M. McDonald to NRF, 5/10/96 and
6/10/96.
Archives: CIA, U.S. Depts. of State and Justice (latter still pending), and USIA ("file
routinely destroyed in January 1986," letter to NRF, 6/7/93). *Schlesinger:* PC letter-diary
to CC (their only surviving correspondence of the Bonn years is the period from 6/56
through 10/56); correspondence JC, AD, SB, LB, Jane Foster (10/15/55), Hadley
Mowrer. *Private:* JC and PC 1954–56 datebooks, PC to JC correspondence April 1955;
AD, "Memoir About Julia," 10/16/88 (courtesy Mark DeVoto). *Smith College:* JC, transcript of Smith Oral History (10/16/72): 25–27. *Beinecke:* correspondence PC and Richard Myers.

Published Sources

p. 220   "snuggled along the curve": *Theodore H. White at Large: The Best of His Maga-
zine Writing 1939–1986,* ed. Edward T. Thompson (NY: Pantheon, 1992): 188.
White's comparison between Bonn and Cambridge, MA: *In Search of History: A
Personal Adventure* (London: Cape, 1979): 314.

p. 220   "a wrinkled mummy": *White at Large,* 318.

p. 227   "secret war": R. Harris Smith, OSS: *The Secret History of America's First Central
Intelligence Agency* (Berkeley: Univ. of California, 1972): 366. The "hysteria,"
says David Caute, led to 10 dismissals and 273 resignations between May 1953
and June 1955: *The Great Fear: Anti-Communist Purge Under Truman and Eisenhower* (NY: Simon & Schuster, 1978): 246, 307, 315.

p. 228   "ignorance . . . existed largely": Robert McNamara, with Brian VanDeMark,
In Retrospect: The Tragedy and Lessons of Vietnam (NY: Random House, 1995):
32–33.

p. 232   "the golden age of food processing": Harvey Levenstein, *Paradox of Plenty: A
Social History of Eating in Modern America* (NY: Oxford, 1993): 101.

CHAPTER 14
BACK HOME (AND COOKING)
ON THE RANGE (1956–1958)

Unpublished Sources

Interviews: JC, DC 3/9/94, Francis Myer Brennan 10/7/93, John L. Moore 5/20/94, Helen Kirkpatrick Milbank 9/19/95, Robert M. Duemling 1/11/95, Stuart and Rosalind Rockwell 9/30/94, Fisher and Debby Howe 9/28/94, I. Guy Martin 9/30/94, Zanne Early Stewart 11/15/96. Group interview with Erica Prud'homme, Rachel Child, Jonathan Child 9/17/93.

Correspondence: Lyne S. Few to NRF, 4/28/95; John L. Moore to NRF, 9/14/94; E. Lee Fairley to NRF, 5/11/95.

Archives: *Private:* JC datebooks 1956, 1957, 1958; copies of PC's government records, 8/57; Charles F. Whiting, "Development of the Communities of Francis Avenue and the Norton Estate," Cambridge, MA, 3/66; AD, "Memoir About Julia," 10/16/88 (courtesy Mark DeVoto). *Schlesinger:* correspondence of JC, AD, JC, SB, and William Koshland; Houghton Mifflin contractual matters; mss. of JC's cooking classes; PC to CC, 11/56–4/59. *USIA:* #93-2375 (1993).

Published Sources

p. 237   "despised": David C. Acheson, *Acheson Country: A Memoir* (NY: Norton, 1983): 201.

p. 239   "precooked frozen gourmet glop": John L. Hess and Karen Hess, *Taste in America* (NY: Grossman, 1977): 62–63.

p. 243   "Splendid Nitze": PC, *Bubbles from the Spring* (n.p.: Antique Press, 1974): [28]. When published the poem was entitled "A Chime to Be Pealed Upon a Pentapolloi Carillon."

p. 243   "Station Wagon Way of Life": Harvey Levenstein, *Paradox of Plenty* (NY: Oxford, 1993): 101, 137.

p. 243   "gruesome": AD's 1957 letter to JC (about diet books) is quoted at length in Levenstein, *Paradox of Plenty,* 136.

p. 244   "adult version of baby formula": Levenstein, *Paradox of Plenty,* 137.

p. 244   "trade-offs, favors": Robert Clark, *James Beard: A Biography* (NY: HarperCollins, 1993): 143.

p. 247   "Elegance of Cuisine": Craig Claiborne, "Elegance Is on Wane in U.S.," *New York Times* (April 13, 1959): 1.

p. 247   "This nation is more interested": quoted by Claiborne (above) and in Clark, *Beard,* 188.

CHAPTER 15
"I AM AT HEART A VIKING" (1959–1961)

Unpublished Sources

Interviews: JC, Fisher and Debra Howe 9/28/94, Erica Prud'homme 9/22/94, Rachel Child 2/24/94, Anita Hinckley Hovey 5/25/94, Mari and Peter Bicknell 3/21/94, Gay Bradley Wright 2/5/96, William Koshland 10/8/93, Judith Jones 10/7/83, Mark DeVoto 12/14/94, John L. Moore 5/20/94, Robert M. Duemling 1/11/95, Karen Hess 12/1/95, Jacques Pépin 12/5/95, Barbara Ketcham Wheaton 11/17/93.

Correspondence: Bjorn and Eline Egge to NRF, 3/3 95 and 5/30/95; Jens P. Heyerdahl to NRF, 3/1/95; Lyne S. Few to NRF, 4/20/95; Froydis Dietrichson to NRF, 5/23/95 and 6/7/95; Mrs. Edward (Margie) Schodt to NRF, 2/6/95 and 2/25/95; Judith Jones to NRF, 12/3/96.

Archives: *Private:* JC's datebooks for 1959, 1960, 1961 (largely abandoned, only a few weeks with notations); McWilliams letters DC, JC, and "Pop and Phila" (courtesy DC); AD, "Memoir About Julia," 10/16/88 (courtesy Mark DeVoto). *Schlesinger:* correspondence JC, SB, AD, Judith Jones, CC/FC, Houghton Mifflin, William Koshland; PC letter-diary to CC is voluminous during 1959–61. Knopf business is housed both with the JC Papers, Schlesinger, and in the Knopf Archives, Univ. of Texas. *WGBH:* "A Taste of Norway" (video), 1992.

Published Sources

p. 256 "you have to know": JC, "That Lunch in Rouen," *New York Times* (May 16, 1993): 16.

p. 257 "woolen": Eduard J. Linehan, "Norway: Land of the Generous Sea," *National Geographic* (July 1971): 1.

p. 257 "I am at heart": "A Taste of Norway," Morash Productions (video), 1992.

p. 262 "To La Belle": JC, SB, LB, *Mastering the Art of French Cooking* (NY: Knopf, 1961): v. Paul had begun the dedication "Vive La Belle France," but Jones changed it to "To."

CHAPTER 16
LAUNCHING THE BOOK (1961–1962)

Unpublished Sources

Interviews: JC, William Koshland 10/8/93, Judith Jones 10/7/93, Narcisse Chamberlain 9/7/94, Gregory Usher 7/2/93, Erica Prud'homme 9/22/94, Barbara Ketcham Wheaton 11/17/93, Paul Sheeline 2/26/94, Mimi Sheraton 12/3/95; Ruth Lockwood 5/7/93, 12/18/94, and 1/30/97, Russell and Marian Morash 12/14/94, David H. Bain 8/10/93, Patricia and Herbert Pratt 5/24/94 and 12/12/94, Edward Martin 8/11/93, Robert Buckeye 8/11/93, Catherine and John Kenneth Galbraith 8/9/93, Emily (Wendy) Beck 4/12/96, André Soltner 11/2/96 (French Culinary Institute Escoffier conference), Betty

Rosbottom 1/18/97, Paula Wolfert 1/25/97, David O. Ives 1/29/97. Joan Reardon interview with JC, fall 1987. Barbara Sims-Bell interview with JC, 7/1/89.

Correspondence: Rachel [Prud'homme] Child to Peter Kump, 10/4/82; Russell Morash to JC, 10/5/82; Narcisse Chamberlain to JC, 10/2/82 (courtesy Peter Kump); James Beard to Knopf, 10/12/61; Peter Davison to NRF, 1/15/96; Joan Brewster to NRF, 3/14/95; Henry Becton (WGBH) to Linda Koch Lorimer, 10/9/96; Marian C. Schlesinger to NRF, 3/7/97; E. S. Yntema to NRF, 2/1/97; Judith Jones to NRF, 3/5/97.

Archives: *Schlesinger:* correspondence JC, DC, SB, James Beard, LB, Judith Jones, AD, William Koshland (Knopf), WGBH, Ruth Lockwood, James Beard, Helen Evans Brown; JC to SB 9/29/91 recalls the first time they made the Reine de Saba cake. *Private:* McWilliams family letters and memoirs, courtesy DC; AD, "Memoir About Julia," 10/16/88 (courtesy Mark DeVoto). *Middlebury College:* Bread Loaf files, correspondence PC, Paul Cubeta, and AD. *Smith College:* Smith Oral History.

Published Sources

p. 269 "O Julia, Julia": PC, *Bubbles from the Spring* (n.p.: Antique Press, 1974) [38].

p. 271 "[T]he most comprehensive,": Craig Claiborne, "Cookbook Review: Glorious Recipes," *New York Times* Oct. 18, 1961.

p. 271 "he made it his role": Evan Jones, *Epicurean Delight: The Life and Times of James Beard* (NY: Knopf, 1990): 258.

p. 272 "Reine de Saba": JC, *Mastering the Art of French Cooking* (NY: Knopf, 1961): 677–78.

p. 273 "I adore both women": James Beard, *Love and Kisses & a Halo of Truffles: Letters to Helen Evans Brown,* ed. John Ferrone (NY: Arcade, 1994): 299 [Dec. 16, 1961].

p. 274 "the worst": Beard, *Love and Kisses,* 300.

p. 274 "Paul was such a perfectionist": James Wood, "Greater Tuna Salad," *San Francisco Examiner* (Nov. 4, 1990): line-type 189–92.

p. 274 "flipped when she saw": José Wilson, "Christmas Bound," *House & Garden* (Dec. 1961): 21, 196.

p. 274 "one of the most satisfactory": Naomi Barry, *International Herald Tribune* (March 26, 1962): 8.

p. 275 "the most lucid volume": Craig Claiborne, "How to Cook by the Book" *Saturday Evening Post* (Dec. 22–29, 1962): 74.

p. 275 "lack[ing] a certain": Sheila Hibben, "Briefly Noted," *New Yorker* (Oct. 28, 1961): 207.

p. 275 "Child, Beck, and Bertholle": Raymond Sokolov, *Why We Eat: What We Eat* (NY: Summit, 1991): 94–95.

p. 275 "No previous": Evan Jones, *American Food: The Gastronomic Story* (Woodstock, NY: Overlook Press, 1991): 178.

p. 275 "What JC did": Camille Paglia quoted in Christopher Lydon, "Queen Julia," *The Improper Bostonian* (March 27–April 9, 1996): 12.

p. 275 "A JC job": Robert Clark, *James Beard: A Biography* (NY: HarperCollins, 1993): 205.

p. 276 "so complicated": MFKF, *Conversations with M. F. K. Fisher,* ed. David Lazar (Jackson: Univ. Press of Mississippi, 1992): 102.

p. 282   "academic tribal reservation": Robert Manning, *The Swamp Root Chronicle: Adventures in the World of Trade* (NY: Norton, 1992): 312.

p. 282   "a carbuncle of cabals": Wallace Stegner, *The Uneasy Chair: A Biography of Bernard DeVoto* (Garden City, NY: Doubleday, 1954): 214.

p. 284   "brother and sister": Jones, *Epicurean Delight,* 272.

CHAPTER 17

LET THEM EAT QUICHE (1963–1964)

Unpublished Sources

Interviews: JC, David O. Ives 1/29/97, Elizabeth (Betty) Kubler 9/26/94, Russell and Marian Morash 12/14/94, Ruth Lockwood 5/7/93 and 12/18/94, Charlotte Snyder Turgeon 5/23/94, Charles Williams 2/21/95, Barbara Kafka 9/22/94, Jeffrey Steingarten 10/29/96, Barbara Ketcham Wheaton 11/17/93, Mari and Peter Bicknell 3/21/94, Jean deSola Pool 4/19/96. Group interview with Barbara Ketcham Wheaton and Barbara Haber 12/94. Barbara Sims-Bell interview with JC 7/1/89.

Correspondence: Marian Morash to JC, 10/5/82; Lizbeth Fisher to NRF, 2/17/95; Peter Davison to NRF, 1/15/96; Jack Savenor to JC, 10/1/82 (courtesy Peter Kump).

Archives: *Schlesinger:* correspondence of JC, SB, LB, AD, James Beard, Helen Evans Brown, Elizabeth David, and Ruth Norman; PC letter-diary to CC, 1963–64; mss. of *The French Chef* programs, JC to WGBH 4/26/62 (initial proposal). *WGBH:* tapes of *The French Chef. TVFN* (Sue B. Huffman): tapes of James Beard, Dione Lucas, and JC TV shows. *Private:* JC and PC datebooks, 1963, 1964. AD, "Memoir About Julia," 10/16/88 (courtesy Mark DeVoto). *Smith College:* JC oral history transcript, 10/10/72.

Published Sources

p. 286   "the forces of art and reason": Lewis Lapham, "Everyone's in the Kitchen with Julia," *Saturday Evening Post* (Aug. 8–15, 1964): 20.

p. 288   "I rushed through that program": JC, *The French Chef Cookbook* (NY: Knopf, 1975): xii.

p. 289   "Mrs. Child . . . thinks": Lapham, *Saturday Evening Post,* 21.

p. 290   "The best free lunch": Alyne E. Model, "JC and Her Runaway Blender," *Boston* (May 1966): 31–34.

p. 291   "quiet persistence": Elizabeth David, "Capability's Child," *The Spectator* (Nov. 1, 1963): clipping.

p. 292   "As long as I can get": Michael Barrier, "Food for Thought," *Nation's Business* (Dec. 1989): 34.

p. 293   "from professors to policemen": *TV Guide* (Aug. 22–28, 1964): 9.

p. 293   "more men than women": Fred Storm, "Cook's Night In," *San Francisco News Call Bulletin* (Feb. 4, 1965): 32.

p. 293   "possesses none": Lapham, *Saturday Evening Post,* 21.

p. 293   "television's most reliable": Terrence O'Flaherty, "Miss Bavarian Cream," *San Francisco Chronicle* (Sept. 30, 1964): 43.

p. 293   "She's like a fairy godmother": Jane Harriman, "This Fairy Godmother Waves a Neat Spatula," *Boston Sunday Globe* (April 28, 1963): 26A.

p. 294   "to turn Boston": "Plain and Fancy," *Newsweek* (July 25, 1963): 77.

p. 296   "Child's predecessors" and "a droll six-footer": Robert Clark, *James Beard: A Biography* (NY: HarperCollins, 1993): 211, 212.

p. 298   "began to sag": JC, *From JC's Kitchen* (NY: Knopf, 1975): 192.

p. 300   "She provokes a rating": "How to Sell Broccoli, *Time* (March 20, 1964): 56.

p. 300   "many requests": Jane Benet, "Look at the French Chef," *San Francisco Chronicle* (Nov. 13, 1963): F7.

CHAPTER 18

PROVENÇAL WINTERS (1965–1967)

Unpublished Sources

Interviews: JC, DC, Mimi Sheraton 12/3/95, Barbara Kafka 9/22/94, Emily (Wendy) Beck 3/96, France Thibault 6/8/94, Jean-François Thibault 6/3–4/93, Kathie Alex 7/11/93, Elizabeth (Betty) Kubler 9/26/94, Philadelphia Cousins 3/31/95, Jean deSola Pool 4/19/96, Anne Willan 7/25/93, Ruth Lockwood 12/18/94, Judith Jones 10/7/93, Harriet Healy 5/5/96, Ailene Martin Berrard 6/8/94, Douwe Yntema 4/96, Fisher Howe 9/28/94, John L. Moore 5/20/94, Charlotte Snyder Turgeon 5/23/94, Charles Williams 2/21/95, Michael Hargraves 3/27/96, Joan Reardon 4/28/96, Peter Kump 9/22/94, Patricia and Herbert Pratt 5/24/94.

Correspondence: Lyne S. Few to NRF, 4/28/94 and 5/9/95; Martha Culbertson to NRF, 3/18/95; Peter Davison to NRF, 1/15/96; Peter and Mari Bicknell to NRF, 3/21/94; Sally Bicknell Miall to NRF, 4/4/94; Joseph C. Sloane to NRF, 11/13/95, Helen Kirkpatrick Milbank to JC, 10/4/82 (courtesy Peter Kump); MFKF to JC, 9/9/82 (courtesy Fisher estate).

Archives: *Schlesinger:* PC letter-diary to CC, 1956–67; correspondence JC, Ruth Norman, Judith Jones, AD, and MFKF; AD notes on her trip to Provence, 1/3/67; Knopf business. *Beinecke:* Robert Penn Warren and Eleanor Clark Papers. *Private:* datebooks of JC and PC, 1965, 1966, 1967; family scrapbooks (courtesy JC and DC); correspondence JC and Michael Field; Peter Kump video of Bramafam and SB, 8/24–25/90 (courtesy Christopher Kump); Michael Field ms. (courtesy Jean-François Thibault).

Published Sources

p. 303   "I'm tough and I speak": Quoted in Betty Fussell, *Masters of American Cookery* (NY: Times, 1983): 52.

p. 308   "educational TV's answer": Joan Barthel, "How to Avoid TV Dinners While Watching TV," *New York Times Magazine* (Aug. 7, 1996): 30.

p. 309   "hamming it up": Jane Howard, "Close-Up: JC, the Master Chef: Hamming It Up in the Haute Cuisine," *Life* (Oct. 21, 1966): 45.

p. 309   "last year alone" and "our lady of the ladle": "Everyone's in the Kitchen" (cover), *Time* (Nov. 25, 1966): 74.

p. 310   "watershed": Robert Clark, *James Beard: A Biography* (NY: HarperCollins, 1993): 226.

p. 310   "French cooking now rose": Harvey Levenstein, *Revolution at the Table* (NY: Oxford, 1988): 206.

p. 310   "the nation's greatest": Jeremy MacLancy, *Consuming Culture* (London: Chapmans, 1992): 188.

p. 310   "The same working mother": Walter Kiechel III, "Two-Income Families Will Reshape the Consumer Markets," *Fortune* (March 10, 1980): 119, cited in Levenstein, 210.

p. 310   "the stakes in food writing": Clark, *Beard,* 225.

p. 312   "If it weren't for Paul": Howard, *Life,* 52.

p. 312   "WGBH has to turn away": Alyne E. Model, "JC and Her Runaway Blender," *Boston* (May 1966): 32.

p. 312   "Not since the late Gracie Allen": Model, *Boston,* 31.

p. 312   "JC is the Chuck Berry": Tony Hendra, "The Heart and Soul of Toque 'n' Roll," *Vanity Fair* (June 1993): 88.

p. 313   "119 black-and-white programs": According to her records, 134 shows were taped. The first 13 were never saved, but 12 of the recipes were redone. One tape was "wiped" ("Bringing in the New Year") and several were repeated (e.g., "Bûche de Noël").

p. 313   " 'JC' . . . is actually": Paul Levy, *Out to Lunch* (NY: Harper & Row, 1986): 205.

p. 314   "I'm part of the iceberg": Mary Daniels, "A Supercook and Her Superman," *Chicago Tribune* (Aug. 20, 1977): 3.

p. 316   "the tradition of Brillat-Savarin": Joan Reardon, *MFKF, JC, and Alice Waters: Celebrating the Pleasures of the Table* (NY: Harmony, 1994): xiii.

p. 317   "Like most other humans": MFKF, "Foreword," *The Gastronomical Me* (1943), in *The Art of Eating* (NY: World, 1954): 353.

p. 317   "penciled Betty Grable brows": Molly O'Neill, "Wishes and Reminiscences from a Culinary Olympian," *New York Times* (Feb. 28, 1990): B1, 6.

CHAPTER 19

THE MEDIA ARE THE MESSAGE (1967–1968)

Unpublished Sources

Interviews: JC, Jean deSola Pool 4/19/96, Patricia and Herbert Pratt 5/24/94, Jean-François Thibault 6/3/93, France Thibault 6/8/94, Peter Kump 9/22/94, Kathie Alex 7/11/93, Ailene Martin Berrard 6/8/94, Emily (Wendy) Beck 4/96, William A. Truslow 4/20/95, William Koshland 10/8/93, Russell and Marian Morash 12/14/94, Ruth Lockwood 5/7/93, Philadelphia Cousins 3/31/95, Hélène Baltrusaitis 7/28/93.

Correspondence: Peggy Brown to JC, 10/5/82 (courtesy Peter Kump); Benjamin H. Brown to NRF, 4/10/96; Jane Owen Molard to NRF, 9/21/96; Judith Jones to NRF, 3/5/97.

Archives: *Schlesinger:* PC letter-diary to CC, 1967–68; correspondence of JC, SB, AD,

MFKF, William Koshland and Knopf Publishers; ms. for "The White House Red Carpet"; mss. and business for *The French Chef Cookbook*. *WGBH:* "The White House Red
Carpet." *Boston University:* Conversation with JC and Jacques Pépin," Boston University,
4/17/96. *Private:* JC and PC datebooks, 1967 and 1968.

Published Sources

p. 324   "a raid on": "The JC Way to Play Your Own Ready-Ahead Dinner," *Ladies'
         Home Journal* (Oct. 1967): 88.

p. 327   "Simca is a great improvisationalist": Michael James, *Slow Food: Flavors and
         Memories of American's Hometowns* (NY: Warner Books, 1992): 41.

p. 334   "a Roosevelt Democrat": Christopher Lydon, "Queen Julia," *The Improper Bos-
         tonian* (March 27–April 9, 1996): 14.

p. 334   "culinary reputation": JC, typescript for article on the White House for *New
         York Times* (Dec. 1, 1976): 1.

p. 334   "Napalm" and "chaotic": E. J. Kahn, Jr., *Harvard: Through Change and
         Through Storm* (NY: Norton, 1969): 78, 375.

CHAPTER 20

CELEBRITY AND SOLITUDE (1968–1970)

Unpublished Sources

Interviews: JC, DC, Jacques Pépin 12/5/95, Judith Jones 10/7/93, Jean deSola Pool
4/19/96, Peter Kump 9/22/94, Karen Hess 12/1/95, Barbara Kafka 9/22/94, Mimi Sheraton 12/3/95, Clark Wolf 4/23/96, Jeffrey Steingarten 10/29/96, Lynne Rossetto Kasper
4/27/95.
Correspondence: JC to John White, 11/30/85; Judith Jones to NRF, 3/5/97.
Archives: *Schlesinger:* correspondence JC, SB, MFKF, James Beard, Narcisse and Samuel
Chamberlain, Sybille Bedford, Madeleine Kamman (JC to Dorothy Crandall of the *Boston
Globe,* on behalf of Kamman, 9/6/70), Gladys Christopherson; PC letter-diary to CC,
1968–70. *Smith College:* Oral History of JC, 10/10/72. *Private:* uncatalogued carbon copies of correspondence and menus of JC and SB related to *Mastering II;* datebooks of JC
and PC, 1968, 1969, 1970.

Published Sources

p. 341   "The only national television female": Marya Mannes, *TV Guide* [1968] clip-
         ping.

p. 343   "sour dough": Hess *(The Taste of America,* 188) appears to equate sour dough
         with wild-yeast leavened bread. If there is any disagreement between Child and
         Hess, notes Steven Sullivan of the Acme Bread Company in Berkeley, it is both
         "semantic and substantive": no one "invented" acidic bread, but "the American
         taste for highly acidic breads is revolutionary."

p. 349   "gay camp culture": Robert Clark, *James Beard: A Biography* (NY: HarperCol-
         lins, 1993): 234.

p. 350   "It's a world of self-generating hysteria": Nika Hazelton quoted by Nora
           Ephron's September 1968 article in *New York* magazine, reprinted in her *Wall-
           flower at the Orgy* (NY: Viking, 1980): 4.

p. 350   "French's mustard people": Ephron, *Wallflower at the Orgy,* 5, 7–8.

p. 351   "Julia is essentially": PC quoted by Edith Efron, "Dinner with JC," *TV Guide*
           (Dec. 5, 1979): 48.

p. 353   "nutritional terrorism": Harvey Levenstein, *Paradox of Plenty* (NY: Oxford,
           1993): 160.

CHAPTER 21

RIDING THE SECOND WAVE (1970–1974)

Unpublished Sources

Interviews: JC, Jean deSola Pool 4/19/96, Karen Hess 12/1/95, Jacques Pépin 12/5/95,
Marc Meneau 5/94, Peter Kump 9/22/94, Richard Olney 6/26/95, Patricia and Herbert
Pratt 5/24/94, Carol and B. J. Cutler 7/94, Sally [Bicknell] Miall 3/25/94, Anne Willan
7/25/93, Jane Friedman 10/31/96, Judith Jones 10/7/93, William A. Truslow 4/20/95, Jan
Weimer 1/94, Philadelphia Cousins 3/31/95, Paul Levy 3/22/94, Sylvia and Jacques
Delécluse 7/95, Mimi Sheraton 12/3/95, Russell Morash 12/14/94, Ruth Lockwood
5/7/93, Rosemary Manell 4/30/93. Madeleine Kamman refused an interview, but the
written record of her correspondence with JC is housed at the Schlesinger. Barbara Sims-
Bell interview with JC, 7/1/89.

Correspondence: Sally Miall to NRF, 4/4/94; Susan Jacobson to NRF, 7/9/96; Richard S.
Mowrer to NRF, 2/21/95; Grant C. Thompson to NRF, 7/9/96; Sharon Thompson to
NRF, 9/24/96; Jan W. Dietrichson to NRF, 5/23/95; Carol Cutler to NRF, 4/13/95;
Susan M. Rogers to NRF, 8/14/96; Judith Jones to NRF, 3/5/97.

Archives: *Schlesinger:* PC letter-diary to CC, 1970–74; correspondence JC, SB, LB, Anne
Willan, Elizabeth David, Waverley Root, WGBH, Alfred A. Knopf Publishers, Elizabeth
David, Hill & Barlow, Craig Claiborne, and Madeleine Kamman. *Private:* correspondence
related to BBC-TV, 1970s. *American Heritage Center:* James Beard Correspondence.
Beinecke: Francis Brennan and Richard Myers Papers, Robert Penn Warren and Eleanor
Clark Papers.

Published Sources

p. 360   "continuation": JC, *Mastering the Art of French Cooking II* (NY: Knopf, 1970):
           viii.

p. 361   "Volume I was mud-pie stuff": Gael Greene, "Julia's Moon Walk with French
           Bread," *Life* (Oct. 70): 8.

p. 361   "heralded like the second coming": Nika Hazelton, "Genghis Khan's Sauer-
           kraut and Other Edibles," *New York Times Book Review* (Dec. 6, 1970): 96.

p. 361   "daunting book": Raymond A. Sokolov, *Newsweek* (Nov. 9, 1970): 94.

p. 366   "He loved the skullduggery": Quoted by Geraldine Baum, "Cooking in the
           Kitchen with Jim," *Los Angeles Times Magazine* (Nov. 1, 1996): A25.

p. 368 "One of the good things": Calvin Tomkins, "Profiles: Good Cooking," *New Yorker* (Dec. 23, 1974): 50.

p. 369 "birthday queen": PC, *Bubbles from the Spring* (n.p.: Antique Press, 1974): [41].

p. 369 "On the Trail": Bill Krauss, "On the Trail of JC," *International Herald Tribune* (March 1971): clipping. See PC to Bill Krauss, March 18, 1971 (Schlesinger): "Now, God damn it, you've blown our cover."

p. 369 "A Big Child": Terrence O'Flaherty, "The Perils of Julia," *San Francisco Chronicle* (Oct. 6, 1972): 44.

p. 369 "the lady unleashed" and "Julia breathes hard": Greene, *Life,* 8.

p. 369 "glid[ing] around her oversized studio kitchen": Philip Nobile, "JC: An Offbeat Chef," *Pasadena Star-News* (Nov. 13, 1972): 1.

p. 369 "Perhaps for the same reason": Don Stanley, "There was this woman splashing eggs about . . ." [1970]: clipping.

p. 370 "our books": *Money* (Oct. 1972): 58.

p. 370 "nothing but calories": JC quoted in "Ratings from the Gourmets" (cover), "The Burger That Conquered the Country," *Time* (Sept. 17, 1973): 86.

p. 371 "to find something positive": Karen Hess and John Hess, *The Taste of America* (NY: Grossman, 1977): 199.

p. 371 "McDonald's is good fare": Frederick J. Stare, MD, "Letter to the Editor," *Time* (Oct. 8, 1973): 10. Stare was chairman of Harvard's Department of Nutrition.

p. 371 "Deprived by this rejection": Paul Levy, *Out to Lunch* (NY: Harper & Row, 1986): 205.

p. 376 "in response to criticism": John Mariani with Alex von Bidder, *The Four Seasons: A History of America's Premier Restaurant* (NY: Crown, 1994): 120.

p. 377 "unique blend": Tomkins, *New Yorker,* 48, 50.

CHAPTER 22

A TIME OF LOSS (1974–1977)

Unpublished Sources

Interviews: JC, DC, Judith Jones 10/7/93, Betty Rosbottom 1/23/97, Rosemary Manell 4/30/93, Jacques Pépin 12/5/95, Ruth Lockwood 5/7/93, Pamela Henstell 5/10/93, Rachel Child 2/24/94, Charlotte Snyder Turgeon 5/23/94, Richard Graff 2/2/96, Narcisse Chamberlain 9/7/94, Anne Willan and Mark Cherniavsky 7/25/93, Steven Raichlen 12/18/95, Douglas Dutton 4/96, Natale Rusconi 5/31/94, Faith Heller Willinger 6/7/94, Mimi Sheraton 12/3/95, Karen Hess 12/1/95, Gregory Usher 7/2/93, Paul and Sandra Sheeline 2/26/94, Zanne Early Stewart 11/15/96, Peter Kump 9/22/94, Barbara Kafka 9/22/94, Susy Davidson 2/25/94, Jeffrey Steingarten 10/29/96.

Correspondence: Corinne Pool to NRF, 2/28/94; Pat Brown Clopper to NRF, 7/29/96; JC to Harriet Healy, 7/11/75, 6/12/75, 9/24/76, and 2/23/76; Craig Alan Wilson to NRF, 11/13/96; JC to Henri Gault and Christian Millau, 4/13/76; JC to Peter Kump, 6/11/77.

Archives: *Schlesinger:* correspondence, PC to CC (infrequent because of PC's aphasia), JC, SB, LB, Craig Claiborne, MFKF, AD, CC and FC, Elizabeth David, Helen McCully,

Anne Willan/Mark Cherniavsky, Robert H. Johnson, Alfred A. Knopf Publishers, Richard Graff, Shirley Sarvis, Narcisse Chamberlain; the Hess file; JC book and article manuscripts. *Beinecke:* Francis and Hank Brennan, Richard Myers Papers. *Private:* Family medical records, JC and PC datebooks, 1974–77; mss. of JC's *McCall's* reviews, itineraries, JC and DC correspondence (courtesy DC).

Published Sources

p. 383   "departed from the professorial": Bill Rice, "Julia and Simca: An Enduring Entente," *Washington Post* (Oct. 3, 1974): H1.

p. 384   "personal [and] no less precise": Mimi Sheraton, "The Best Cookbooks of 1975," *New York* (Nov. 24, 1975): 100.

p. 385   "wonderfully sensuous": Gail Jennes, "Couple" (cover), *People* (Dec. 1, 1975): 51.

p. 385   "just that Paris PR game,": John Kifner, "The New French Food Revolution? Julia Child Says 'Humph,' " *New York Times* (Sept. 5, 1975): L12.

p. 385   "This food looks fingered": Stephen Wadsworth, "Julia Sums Up," *Dial* (1980): 23.

p. 385   "the apparent culinary equivalent": Robert Clark, *James Beard: A Biography* (NY: HarperCollins, 1993): 290.

p. 386   "they might see Fannie Farmer": Laura Shapiro, *Perfection Salad: Women and Cooking at the Turn of the Century* (NY: Farrar, Straus & Giroux, 1986): 231.

p. 387   "Obviously somebody was pulling": JC, " 'La Nouvelle Cuisine': A Skeptic's View," *New York* (July 4, 1977): 32.

p. 387   "I *never* have anything to do with housewives": quoted in Walter Blum, "The Joy of Julia," *California Living* (April 28, 1974): 23.

p. 387   "We never talk about women": Quoted Wadsworth, *Dial,* 23.

p. 387   "gone into restaurant work": "Julia at 80: With Christopher Lydon" (1992), WGBH video.

p. 387   "it wasn't until": Interview, *TV Guide* (Dec. 5, 1970): 46. Repeated in video of Valley Hunt Club speech.

p. 387   "no feminist": Helen Civelli Brown, "Topic-hopping with JC," *San Francisco Examiner* (Dec. 4, 1975): 29.

p. 388   "No. I'm from a different generation": Curtis Hartman and Steven Raichlen, "JC: The Boston Magazine Interview," *Boston* (April 1981): 78.

p. 388   "is a symbol of women's liberation": Brown, *San Francisco Examiner,* 29.

p. 388   "the Women's Liberation Movement": John Mariani, *America Eats Out* (NY: Morrow, 1991): 217.

p. 388   "Western philosophers": Deane W. Curtin and Lisa M. Hendke, *Cooking, Eating, Thinking: Transformation Philosophies of Food* (Bloomington: Indiana Univ. Press, 1992): xiii.

p. 388   "I guess I am liberated": "Are Liberated Women Happier?" *San Francisco Examiner* (Sept. 4, 1975): 23.

p. 391   "public caterwauling" and "packaging": JC, "A White House Menu," *New York Times Magazine* (Jan. 16, 1977): 57.

p. 392   "a vituperative and angry critique": Clark, *Beard,* 291. Their book, says Clark, illustrates "the Hesses' own immersion in the bitchery and petty subculture they claimed to deplore," 272.

p. 392   "gourmet plague": John L. Hess and Karen Hess, *The Taste of America* (NY: Grossman, 1977): 152.

p. 393   "French cuisine in America": Karen Hess, "The Gourmet Plague," *Atlantic* (Aug. 1977): 62.

p. 393   "I'd rather eat them than airline food": Curtis and Raichlen, *Boston,* 83.

p. 393   "after a crash course": Hess and Hess, *The Taste of America,* 191. JC wrote to her friend Robert Manning, the editor of *Atlantic,* that "Mrs. Hess's brutal public flogging is too sadistic for enjoyment." George Lang responded on Jan. 3, 1978 (with a copy to JC), to the Hesses' "Palate, Politics and Puffery" in *Politicks & Other Human Interests* (Oct. 25, 1977): 26.

p. 394   "the older we get": Beverley Jackson, "Dinner with JC," *Santa Barbara News-Press* (Jan. 9, 1977): D4.

p. 395   "It's gotten much more expensive": Clifford A. Ridley, "La Cuisine? La Julia!" *National Observer* (May 1, 1976): 20.

CHAPTER 23

THE COMPANY SHE KEEPS (1977–1980)

Unpublished Sources

Interviews: JC, Russell and Marian Morash 12/14/94, Henry Becton, Jr., 1/21/97, Ruth Lockwood 5/7/93 and 12/18/94, E. S. (Peggy) Yntema 4/20/95, Betty Rosbottom 12/7/96, Anne Willan 7/25/93, Patricia and Herbert Pratt 5/24/94, Sara Moulton 9/23/94, Janice Goldklang 9/23/94, Jane Friedman 10/31/96, Pamela Henstell 5/10/93, Stephanie Hersh 11/29/94, Maggie Mah 2/4/96, Rosemary Manell 4/30/93, Richard Graff 2/2/96, Jacques Pépin 12/5/95 and 8/31/96, Nancy Verde Barr 12/13/95. Barbara Sims-Bell interview with JC 7/1/89.

Correspondence: Dorothea Freifrau von Stetten to NRF, 7/28/96; Catherine Gewertz to NRF, 7/9/96; Alison Boteler to NRF, 9/15/93; E. S. Yntema to NRF, 2/1/97.

Archives: *Schlesinger:* PC letter-diary to CC (intermittent), 1977–80; mss. and correspondence related to *& Company* books and TV programs; contracts with ABC; correspondence JC, MFKF, SB, AD, James Beard, E. S. (Peggy) Yntema (contract letter, 12/23/77), Madeleine Kamman, Elizabeth David, Rosemary Manell, Marian Morash, and Shirley Sarvis. *Private:* JC datebooks and records; correspondence JC and DC (courtesy DC). *Broadway Video:* NBC's *SNL,* 12/9/78 (courtesy Mike Bosey). *Alfred A. Knopf:* JC promotion itineraries (courtesy Pamela Henstell).

Published Sources

p. 397   "a child who": Jeannette Ferrary, "Julia—Child of Our Times" [review of *JC & Company*]: clipping.

p. 402   "I don't think": JC interview with Barbara Sims-Bell, July 1, 1989. By January 1978, the following numbers had sold: 803,455,000 copies of the two *Mastering* books (Vol. I accounted for 561,115); 259,870 *French Chef Cookbook;* 138,301 *Kitchen* (just pub.)—for a total of 1,201,626.

p. 402   "I don't do anything": G. S. Boudain, "JC Is Stirring Up More Treats," *New York Times* (Dec. 24, 1977): D27.

p. 403   "Julia knows how": Jack Shelton, "JC Knows How to Listen," *Focus,* San Francisco's KQED magazine (March 1980): 38.

p. 403   "I learn something new": Stephen Wadsworth, "Julia Sums Up," *Dial* (1981): 24.

p. 403   "I'd like to get some": Nao Hauser, "JC: Her Life, Her Great Love, and Her Future," *Chicago Tribune* (March 3, 1980): 4.

p. 405   "alone worth the price": Mimi Sheraton (review), *New York Times Book Review* (Dec. 3, 1978): 14.

p. 405   "syncopated like jazz": Hauser, *Chicago Tribune,* 4.

p. 405   "She gives us": Ferrary, clipping.

p. 405   "She's a serenely gawky": Wadsworth, *Dial,* 21.

p. 407   "rather eat a tablespoon": Cathy Von Klemperer, "JC Returns to Hubbard House," *Daily Hampshire Gazette* (April 11, 1978): clipping.

p. 407   "She only liked food and men": PC quoted by Hauser, *Chicago Tribune,* 4.

p. 408   "As soon as you're off television": quoted in Corby Kummer, "Turning Points: JC," *Quest* (1980): 104.

p. 409   "We were awfully lucky": Hauser, *Chicago Tribune,* 1.

p. 410   "You can't do nothin' ": Dan Aykroyd, *Saturday Night Live,* NBC, Dec. 9, 1978.

p. 411   "use of her name": "JC Sues Hotel on the Use of Her Name," *New York Times* (April 5, 1984): III, 11.

p. 412   "We just KILLED ourselves": Wadsworth, *Dial,* 23.

p. 414   "I'm [also] interested in the freshness": Susan Rogers, "Food for Thought from JC," *New York Post* (Feb. 18, 1972): 46.

CHAPTER 24

PACIFIC OVERTURES (1981–1984)

Unpublished Sources

Interviews: Interviews with JC, DC, Robert Huttenback 5/7/94, Richard Graff 2/2/96, Alice Waters 2/6/96, Dorothy Cann Hamilton 12/14/95, Mary Tonetti Dorra 5/6/94, Margrit Biever (Mondavi) 2/3/96, Maggie Mah 2/4/96, Rosemary Manell 4/30/93, Elizabeth (Betty) Kubler 9/26/94, Russell and Marian Morash 12/14/94, Ruth Lockwood 5/7/93, Charlotte Snyder Turgeon 5/23/94, Faith Heller Willinger 5/7/94, Nancy Verde Barr 12/13/95, Barbara Kafka 9/22/94, Mimi Sheraton 12/3/95, Dun Gifford 12/14/94, Roberta Klugman 5/7/94, Ken Frank 8/26/96, Wolfgang Puck 8/26/96, Barbara Sims-Bell, 9/6/96, George Trescher 10/29/96, Paul Levy 1/30/89, Marion Cunningham 2/9/96, Susy Davidson 2/25/94, Stephanie Hersh 11/29/94, Patricia Wells 9/4/95, Clark Wolf

4/23/96, Jane Bollinger 10/28/96, and Michael McCarty, 3/27/97. Betty Fussell interview with JC and PC 10/27/81. Barbara Sims-Bell interview with JC 10/27/81.

Correspondence: Paul Bohannan to NRF, 7/21/96; Jane Owen Molard to NRF, 9/21/96; Martha Culbertson to NRF, 3/18/95; Richard Graff to JC and others, 10/9/81; Barbara Pool Fenzl to NRF, 9/11/93.

Archives: *Schlesinger:* correspondence JC, SB, AD, LB, and James Beard; JC to SB, 11/6/76 (on recipes). *AIWF,* San Francisco: timeline, historical documents, charter, publications. *Private:* JC datebooks, 1981–84; JC to President and Mrs. Reagan, 4/14/84; JC files and records.

Published Sources

p. 417   "could effectively lose weight": Robert Clark, *James Beard: A Biography* (NY: HarperCollins, 1993): 175.

p. 417   "slender hips": Betty Fussell, typed notes of two-hour taping at ABC Studio, Oct. 27, 1981, for *Masters of American Cookery* (NY: Times, 1983).

p. 418   "I do solemnly swear": JC, "Recipes That Helped Me Lose 20 Pounds," *McCall's* (Oct. 1981): 54.

p. 418   "Only Moses disrupting the Red Sea": Judy Hevrdejs, "Julia at the Housewares Show," *Chicago Tribune* (Jan. 22, 1981): Sec. 7, 3.

p. 420   "most important assemblage": Richard H. Graff, "Launching the Institute," *Journal of Gastronomy* (Summer 1984): 112. Graff's account is a brief summary.

p. 421   "hanging ten on their own": Charles Perry, "Grade 'A' Gourmets," *California Magazine* (Feb. 1982): 27.

p. 423   "Two of the best cooks": Charles Perry, Laura Ochoa, and Irene Virbila's cover story of the 25th anniversary of Chez Panisse, *Los Angeles Times,* Food section (Aug. 22, 1996): A1, H1–2, 8, 10.

p. 423   "In the early 1980s": Ruth Reichl, "And for Dinner? How About Fun?" *New York Times* (March 26, 1997): B1.

p. 424   "We always have to be ready": Michael S. Lasky, "And a Child Shall Lead Them," *Focus* (Nov. 1982): 56–61.

p. 425   "What are your plans": the Dear Abby column ran in multiple cities, June 1982. JC requested that her lawyer, who collected all angry and threatening letters, send her all the Dear Abby/Planned Parenthood mail.

p. 429   "slogging through viscous mud": Michael Demarest, "Thoroughly American Julia," *Time* (April 18, 1983): 78–79.

p. 430   "Afro": Barbara Hensen, "JC Acquires Fresh Image for Her New TV Series," *Los Angeles Times* (June 9, 1983): VIII, 1.

p. 430   "Shows her at her bubbly" and "in a wardrobe": Michael Demarest, "Dinner at Julia's," *United* (Oct. 1983): 65, 66.

p. 430   "convey a sense": John J. O'Connor, "Dinner at Julia's," *New York Times* (Nov. 17, 1983): 27.

p. 431   "cost $1,000 a week": Phyllis C. Richman, "Making Dinner at Julia's," *Washington Post* (April 13, 1983): E1,16. Other chefs appearing on *Dinner at Julia's* were Brad Ogden (Kansas City), Leeslee Reiss (Chicago), Jean Claude (Dallas), and Yves Labbe (Miami).

p. 431   "the dawning of a new age": Harvey Steiman, "An Extravaganza of American Cuisine," *San Francisco Examiner* (May 11, 1983): E1.

p. 431   "A Summit of U.S. Cuisine": Margaret Mallory, "A Summit of U.S. Cuisine," *San Francisco Tribune* (May 11, 1983): clipping.

p. 432   "an important part . . . natural role as leaders": William Rice quoted by Steiman, *Examiner,* E2.

p. 432   "Chefs are on a par": JC quoted by Steiman, *Examiner,* E2.

p. 432   "the revolution in food": Maggie Crum, "A Festival of Food & Wine," *Contra Costa Times* (May 11, 1983): D2. Macy's (where Julia gave cooking demonstrations that week), American Express, and *Food & Wine* magazine (a publication of AmEx) sponsored the "American Celebration," May 3–5, 1983.

p. 432   "a kind of Pearl Harbor": Clark, *Beard,* 321–22.

p. 433   "JC is . . . generous": Ann Barr and Paul Levy, *The Official Foodie Handbook* (NY: Arbor House, 1984): 113.

p. 433   "Party Chairman": James Reginato, "Party Chairman," *W* (Nov. 1995): 150.

p. 434   "Two million dollars!": Barr and Levy, *Official Foodie Handbook,* 107.

CHAPTER 25

SEASONED WITH LOVE (1985–1989)

Unpublished Sources

Interviews: JC, Alice Waters 2/6/96, Russell and Marian Morash 12/14/94 and 9/5/96, Judith Jones 10/28/96, George Trescher 10/29/96, Pamela Henstell 5/10/93, Dun Gifford 12/14/94, William A. Truslow 4/20/95, Jim Wood 3/10/94, Patricia and Herbert Pratt 5/24/94, Patricia Wells 9/4/95, Faith Heller Willinger 6/7/94, Charles Gibson 11/12/96, Kathleen Perry 9/11/96, Roberta Klugman 5/7/94, Dorothy Cann Hamilton 12/14/95, Philadelphia Cousins 3/31/95, Dun Gifford 12/14/94, Richard Graff 2/9/96, Clark Wolf 4/23/96, Robert Huttenback 5/7/94, Karen Berk 9/4/96, Mitzie Cutler 9/4/96, Mary Tonetti Dorra 5/6/94, Nancy Kirby Harris 4/26/96, Anne Willan and Mark Cherniavsky, Susy Davidson 2/25/94, Peter Kump 9/22/94, Jacques Pépin 12/5/95, Janice Goldklang 9/23/94, Rachel Child 11/1/96, Maggie Mah 2/4/96, Jane Friedman 10/31/96, Jane Bollinger 10/28/96, Kathie Alex 7/11/93, David Strada 1/10/97, Betty Rosbottom 1/16/97, Michael McCarty, 3/27/97.

Correspondence: Peter Davison to NRF, 1/15/96; Nancy Verde Barr to NRF, 9/9/96; George Gruenwald to NRF, 2/10/95 and 8/29/96; Jane Owen Molard to NRF, 9/21/96; JC to Barbara Pool Fenzl, 7/28/87 and 9/12/89; Barbara Pool Fenzl to NRF, 9/11/93; Susy Davidson to NRF, 9/10/96; George Gruenwald to Simone Beck, 2/8/89; JC to Peter Kump 2/21/86 and 4/29/86; JC to CC and Janou Walcutt 3/1/86, 7/7/86, and 1/89; JC to Harriet Healy 5/17/87; JC to Eleanor and Basil Summers, 1/86; Judith Jones to NRF, 3/5/97.

Archives: *AIWF:* records and correspondence, *Newsletter, Journal of Gastronomy. Schlesinger:* correspondence JC, Alfred A. Knopf Publishers, Elizabeth David, SB, AD, MFKF, James Beard, Tim Castle, Robert Clark, WGBH, Pritikin-related (Ruth J. Robinson to JC 3/8/88; JC to RJR 3/12/88); ms. *The Way to Cook. Smith College:* interview with *Smith*

Alumnae Quarterly (Summer 1985, Fall 1985). *IACP:* conference program 1983. *Beinecke:* JC to Frances Brennan, 10/11/[80]. *Private:* JC datebooks 1985–89.

Published Sources

p. 435   *"Boutez en avant?":* "Charge ahead," a favorite expression of JC, dating from the 1970s. According to E. S. Yntema: "It is carved into a cornerstone at the old cavalry armory on Park Avenue in Manhattan."

p. 435   "too many experts": "Experts' Recipes for a Healthy Life," *U.S. News & World Report* (Jan. 20, 1986): 67.

p. 440   "the cooking school": Jim Wood, "Dining on Sixth with Julia," *San Francisco Examiner* (Nov. 17, 1985): S6.

p. 445   "The rates of pay": Ann Barr and Paul Levy, *The Official Foodie Handbook* (NY: Arbor House, 1984): 107.

p. 445   "The We Happy Few": JC (letter to the editor), *AIWF Newsletter* (July 1987): 2.

p. 446   "need that land" and "sleepy, backwater": Larry Wilson, "JC's Crusade," *Los Angeles Times Magazine* (Aug. 16, 1987): 9, 27.

p. 449   "a classic women's library": "The Scholar's Joy of Cooking," *Newsweek* (Oct. 24, 1988): 47C.

p. 450   "heart attacks": Dept. of Commerce, *Statistical Abstract of the U.S.,* 1995.

p. 451   "[America has] a fanatical fear": Molly O'Neill, "Savoring the World According to Julia," *New York Times* (Oct. 11, 1989): C6. Reprinted as "What's Cooking in America?" *International Herald Tribune* (Oct. 12, 1989): clipping.

p. 451   "There are 120 flavor components": Florence Fabricant, "Butter Bites Back," *New York Times* (March 22, 1995): B6.

p. 451   "the affable French war hero": Christopher Lydon, "Queen Julia," *The Improper Bostonian* (March 27–April 9, 1996): 11.

p. 451   "I would have been": Roberta Wallace Coffey, "Julia and Paul Child: Their Recipe for Love," *McCall's* (Oct. 1988): 3.

p. 452   "Cooking My Way": JC, "On Writing a Cookbook: 1988 versus 1960," *Radcliffe Quarterly* (Dec. 1988): 6.

CHAPTER 26
NOTRE DAME DE LA CUISINE (1989–1993)

Unpublished Sources

Interviews: JC, Pamela Henstell 5/10/93, Stephanie Hersh 4/27/95 and 12/19/96, Janice Goldklang 9/23/94, Susy Davidson 2/25/94, Nancy Verde Barr 12/13/95, Peter Kump 6/27/92, Sara Moulton 9/23/94, Mimi Sheraton 12/3/95, Richard Graff 2/1/96, Dorothy Cann Hamilton 12/14/95, Mary Risley 4/30/93, Roberta Klugman 5/7/94, Russell and Marian Morash 12/10/94, William A. Truslow 4/20/95, Suzanne Patterson 6/24/93, Dun Gifford 12/14/94, Clay Triplette 10/29/96, Jacques Pépin 12/5/95, Rebecca Alssid 4/15/96, Roger Fessaguet 11/2/96, Richard Olney 6/26/95, John McJennett 11/23/93, Geoffrey Drummond 9/26/94, Faith Heller Willinger 6/7/94, Natale Rusconi 5/31/94,

Philadelphia Cousins 3/31/95, Harriet Healy 5/5/94, Marian Burros 12/11/95, Harry Becton, Jr., 1/21/97.

Correspondence: Sally Miall to NRF, 4/4/94; Barbara Pool Fenzl to NRF, 9/11/93; Eline and Bjorn Egge 3/3/95; Mosse and Jens Heyerdahl to NRF, 3/1/95; George Faison to NRF, 11/26/96; JC to Barbara Pool Fenzl, 5/23/90 and 2/14/92; Dudley Martin to JC, 5/92; Dudley Martin to NRF, 9/23/96 and 1/2/97; Peter Kump to JC, 7/9/91, 5/13/92 and 7/29/92; JC to Peter Kump, 6/27/92; Anne Willan to JC, 10/18/89; JC to Harriet Healy, 7/20/90; Martha Willoughby to NRF, 9/19/96, James Londe to NRF, 7/7/96 and 9/20/96.

Archives: *Schlesinger:* correspondence JC, SB, DC, Anne Willan, MFKF, William A. Truslow, President and Mrs. Bill Clinton (12/30/92). *AIWF:* records, *Newsletter, Journal of Gastronomy. Beinecke:* JC to Fanny Brennan, 10/11/[?]. *IACP:* conference records. *Boston University:* records, history, articles. *Private:* JC's negative fan mail file.

Published Sources

p. 457   "maintains a schedule": Anne Byrn, "JC Aims to Keep Fun in Food," *Atlanta Journal & Constitution* (April 12, 1990): W1.

p. 457   "the nation's energy queen": Jim Wood, "JC's Full Menu," *San Francisco Examiner* (May 21, 1991): C17.

p. 458   "Oh, dear. I've really done it": Molly O'Neill, "Savoring the World According to Julia," *New York Times* (Oct. 11, 1989): C6, reprinted as "What's Cooking in America?" *International Herald Tribune* (Oct. 12, 1989): clipping.

p. 458   "a magnificent distillation": Christopher Lehmann-Haupt (review), *New York Times* (Nov. 27, 1989): III, 16.

p. 458   "after years of takeout": Florence Fabricant, "Hefty New Primers for Cooks Lacking Time and Practice," *New York Times* (Sept. 27, 1989): C6.

p. 459   "our leading national symbol": Laura Shapiro, "Eat, Drink and Be Sensible," *Newsweek* (May 27, 1991): 52.

p. 460   "It's part of life": Michel Roberts, "JC, the Pleasure Shark," *The Advocate* (May 19, 1992): 65. Moral philosopher Jeremy Iggers ("Innocence Lost," *Utne Reader,* Nov./Dec. 1993: 54) naively and romantically blames JC for ending Americans' innocence about food, mistakenly assuming there was a time when "food was simply something we ate." One has only to read Harvey Levenstein's *Revolution at the Table* to realize that food guilt has marked U.S. history.

p. 460   "reopened the American kitchen": Christopher Lydon, "Queen Julia," *The Improper Bostonian* (March 27–April 9, 1996): 11.

p. 460   "eating, drinking, and love-making": Gail Jennes, "Couples" (cover), *People* (Dec. 1, 1975): 51.

p. 460   "I want to be healthy": Shapiro, *Newsweek,* 52.

p. 460   "scholar-cook": Paul Levy, *Out of Lunch* (NY: Arbor House, 1984): 203, 206.

p. 460   "I think snacking": Lydon, *The Improper Bostonian,* 14.

p. 461   "Healthy Choice": Michelle F. Stacey. *Consumed: Why Americans Love, Hate, and Fear Food* (NY: Simon & Schuster, 1994): 58.

p. 461   "animal-rights people": Stephen G. Michaelides, "The Joys of Julia" (cover), *Restaurant Hospitality* (Jan. 1991): 95.

p. 462 "Chimpanzees fed less": Jim Wood, "Greater Tuna Salad," *San Francisco Examiner* (Nov. 4, 1990): proof lines 327–29.

p. 462 "This is chemistry": Laura Shapiro, "The Skinny on No-Fat Sweets," *Newsweek* (Nov. 15, 1992): 92.

p. 462 "Hamburger Helper": statistics quoted by Meryle Evans, "A Midwest State of Mind," *Food Arts* (Dec. 1989): 24.

p. 464 "I wear New Balance": "Air Julia," *Sports Illustrated* (Nov. 11, 1991): 68.

p. 465 "Food should have": Roberts, *The Advocate,* 65.

p. 465 "JC, Boiling": Carol Lawson, "Julia, Boiling, Answers Her Critics, *New York Times* (July 24, 1990): C8.

p. 465 "Americanized colloquial style": "Books Received," *Food & Wine* (Jan. 1992): 1.

p. 467 "Well, it's part of life" and "Neptune Society": William F. Schulz, "Lunch Together," *The World* (Nov.–Dec. 1992): 34.

p. 468 "made hash of the protesters": "Let Her Eat Cake," *People* (Aug. 10, 1992): 95. In 1981 she had expressed it more strongly: "I am a carnivore of the most enthusiastic persuasion. I feel much better when I have red meat—dripping with blood. I have to keep up my strength." Curtis Hartman and Steven Raichlen, "JC: The Boston Magazine Interview," *Boston* (April 1981): 84.

p. 468 "having [her] *génoise"*: Barbara Hansen, "Child at 80," *Los Angeles Times* (Oct. 15, 1992): H27.

p. 469 "Even in France": Betty Goodwin, "When French Food Is Child's Play," *Los Angeles Times* (Feb. 10, 1993): E7.

p. 469 "This was not a feed": Merrill Shindler, "Bistro Roulette," *Los Angeles Reader* (April 9, 1993): 21.

p. 469 "Thanks, Julia, but": Kathie Jenkins, "Thanks, Julia, But Where Are the Women?" *Los Angeles Times Book Review* (Jan. 3, 1993): 78.

p. 469 "Dinner took five hours": Ruth Reichl, "Julia Triumph," *Los Angeles Times* (Feb. 11, 1993): clipping.

p. 469 "Good old Julia": Madeleine Kamman quoted by Marian Burros, "For JC, an Intimate Dinner for 500 Guests," *New York Times* (Feb. 10, 1993): C6.

p. 470 "almost extinct": Laura Shapiro, "An American Revolution," *Newsweek* (Dec. 16, 1991): 57.

p. 470 "the temples of haute cuisine": Burros, *New York Times,* C6.

p. 470 "We want to be loved": Shindler, *Los Angeles Reader,* 21.

p. 470 "JC 'rabidly homophobic' ": *Los Angeles Times* (Feb. 9, 1992): A35.

p. 471 "rabidly homophobic" and "an old friend": Michael Blowen, "JC Is Under Fire," *Boston Globe* (Feb. 10, 1992): clipping.

p. 471 "had nothing to do with": "Wine Institute Is Accused of Anti-Gay Bias," *New York Times* (Feb. 11, 1992): A18.

p. 471 "incredulous": JC quoted by Roberts, *The Advocate,* 65.

p. 472 "To be a culinary plagiarist": Christopher Hitchens, "Martha, Inc.," *Vanity Fair* (Oct. 1993): 93.

p. 472 "bonfire of the foodies": Susan Brenna, "If You Can't Stand the Heat," *Newsday* (July 12, 1990): II, 1, 8–9.

CHAPTER 27
DO NOT GO GENTLE (1994–1997)

Unpublished Sources

Interviews: JC, Philadelphia Cousins 1/26/97, Stephanie Hersh 11/30/94, Geoffrey Drummond 9/26/94, 12/14/96, and 1/28/97, William A. Truslow 4/20/95, Sue Huffman 12/12/95, Elizabeth (Betty) Kubler 9/26/94, Erica Prud'homme 9/22/94, Anne Willan 7/25/93, Alice Waters 2/6/96, Jacques Pépin 12/5/95 and 4/17/96, Jean deSola Pool 4/19/96, Patricia and Herbert Pratt 12/12/94, Jeffrey Steingarten 10/29/96, Craig Kominiak 12/23/95, Nancy Verde Barr 12/13/95, Patricia Wells 8/4/95, R. W. Apple, Jr., 1/30/95, Zanne Early Stewart 11/15/96, Judith Jones 10/28/96, Jane Friedman 10/31/96, Dun Gifford 12/14/94, Alexandre Lazaroff 2/15/96, Janice Goldklang 9/23/94, Frances and Tom Bissell 10/95, Natale Rusconi 5/31/94, Barbara Ketcham Wheaton 11/17/93, Roberta Klugman 9/9/95, Terry Ford 2/3/96, Andrea B. Werbel 1/29/96, Graham Kerr 4/25/96, Dorie Greenspan 10/30/96, Paula Wolfert 1/25/97.

Correspondence: Susan M. Rogers to NRF, 8/14/96; Craig Alan Wilson to NRF, 11/13/96; Judith Jones to Geoffrey Drummond, 2/15/95; Carl DeSantis to NRF, 8/23/96; David McWilliams to NRF, 3/18/97.

Archives: *Lexington town records:* PC death certificate. *Schlesinger:* JC to SB, 2/4/69 and 2/13/69. *AIWF:* records, *Newsletter. Private:* JC datebooks 1993–95, file of condolence letters at PC's death.

Published Sources

p. 480   "It's a shame": JC quoted by Maryellen C. Costello and Ashok Nimgade, "Lunch with JC," *MIT Management* (Spring 1991): 23.

p. 484   "That's a fun religion": William F. Schulz, "Lunch Together," *The World* (Nov.–Dec. 1992): 34.

p. 487   "Every age gets": Margaret Talbot, "Les Très Riches Heures de Martha Stewart" (cover), *New Republic* (May 31, 1996): 30.

p. 488   "I promise I'll think long": Kim Willis, "Buffalo a Cold Place for Martha Stewart," *USA Today* (Dec. 2, 1995): clipping.

p. 488   "Did you create Martha": Christopher Lydon, "Queen Julia," *The Improper Bostonian* (March 27–April 9, 1996): 16.

p. 488   "the qualities of work" and "Americans have lost": Talbot, *New Republic,* 33, 35.

p. 489   "Julia is so hip": Russ Morash quoted by Lydon, *The Improper Bostonian,* 24.

p. 490   "Kraft Jet-Puffed": Glenn Collins, "Make Room in the Kitchen for Yet Another Appliance," *New York Times* (Sept. 16, 1969): C6.

p. 490   "Jacques and Julia": Jack Thomas, "Jacques and Julia Make Sizzling TV," *Boston Globe* (April 6, 1994): 73, 75.

p. 493   "a discrepancy": Jane E. Brody, "Study Finds a Three-Decade Gain in American Eating Habits," *New York Times* (Sept. 4, 1996): B9.

p. 494   "Why Aren't the French": Jeffrey Steingarten, "Food: Notable News," *Vogue* (Feb. 1991): 249. Steingarten was perhaps the first to disclose, though not to coin the expression, the French paradox. "It is only a paradox if you believe the nutritionists," he said in 1996.

p. 495   "a parade of superstars": Laura Shapiro, "Mother, Daughter and 'Joy,' " *Newsweek* (Nov. 11, 1996): 94.

p. 495   "control of electronic rights": Paul Nathan, "Rights: When as my Julia goes," *Publishers Weekly* (June 5, 1995): 18. Also: Mary B. W. Tabor, "Book Notes: JC Book Dropped," *New York Times* (May 3, 1995).

p. 496   "killed the book": Candy Sagon, "How to Sell 4,514 Cookbooks in 17 Minutes," *Washington Post* (March 5, 1997): E1.

p. 496   "If we lost a bread": Bill Daley, "The King of Cooking Shows," *Hartford Courant* (Aug. 1996): G2.

p. 496   "I think every woman": Quoted by Craig Wilson, "JC's 'Baking Brigade,' " *USA Today* (Oct. 15, 1996): 2D.

p. 497   "an innate ease": Fred Ferretti, "Julia: America's Favorite Cook," *Gourmet* (Feb. 1995): 70.

p. 497   "a familiar object": Robert Clark, *James Beard: A Biography* (NY: HarperCollins, 1993): 251.

p. 497   "If her public demeanor": Nicola Smith, Vermont/New Hampshire *Valley News* (July 31, 1996): C1.

p. 498   "get away with more": Bill Moyers, "M. F. K. Fisher: Essayist," *Bill Moyers: A World of Ideas II* (NY: Doubleday, 1990): 93.

p. 498   "fourth fastest-growing" and "1.5 million": Maria L. LaGanga, "At a Career Crossroads? Try the Kitchen," *Los Angeles Times* (March 2, 1997): A1, A24.

p. 498   "over 98 percent" and "Food is the live entertainment": Regina Schrambling, "TV or Not TV?" *Food Arts* (October 1966): 90, 92.

p. 498   "Queen Julia": Lydon, *The Improper Bostonian,* 12.

p. 499   "pre-war feminist": Camille Paglia quoted by Lydon, *The Improper Bostonian,* 12.

BIBLIOGRAPHY

UNPUBLISHED MANUSCRIPTS

Julia McWilliams Child Papers, Simone Beck Papers, Avis DeVoto Papers, and Mary Frances Kennedy Fisher Papers. The Arthur and Elizabeth Schlesinger Library, Radcliffe College, Cambridge, MA.

Julia Mitchell Weston. 1865–97 Diary. Excerpts transcribed by Katherine Weston Crane [granddaughter].

Paul Cushing Child to Charles T. Child. Correspondence. 1942–76. Largely collected in Julia McWilliams Child Papers, Schlesinger Library, Radcliffe College.

Unpublished/uncollected personal diaries/memoirs: Eleanor Thiry Summers, Joseph R. Coolidge, Elizabeth (Betty) Parker Kase, Julia McWilliams [Child], Avis DeVoto.

Private papers at the homes of JC, DC, John McWilliams III.

BOOKS BY JULIA CHILD

Mastering the Art of French Cooking (with Simone Beck and Louisette Bertholle). NY: Knopf, 1961.

The French Chef Cookbook. NY: Knopf, 1968.

Mastering the Art of French Cooking, Vol. II (with Simone Beck). NY: Knopf, 1970, 1983.

From Julia Child's Kitchen. NY: Knopf, 1975.

Julia Child & Company (in collaboration with E. S. Yntema). NY: Knopf, 1978.

Julia Child & More Company (in collaboration with E. S. Yntema). NY: Knopf, 1979.

The Way to Cook. NY: Knopf, 1989.

Julia Child's Menu Cookbook (one-vol. ed. of *JC & Co.* and *JC & More Co.*). NY: Wings (Random House), 1991.

Cooking with Master Chefs. NY: Knopf, 1993.

In Julia Child's Kitchen with Master Chefs (with Nancy Barr). NY: Knopf, 1995.

ARTICLES BY JULIA CHILD

Selected Individual Essays

"Architectural Digest Visits: Julia Child," *Architectural Digest,* Aug. 17, 1976: 52–55.

"Come Home to Cooking: Getting Off to a Fresh Start," *Boston Globe,* Jan. 15, 1992, Food Section: 65, 67.

"On Writing a Cookbook: 1988 Versus 1960," *Radcliffe Quarterly,* December 1988: 6–7.

"The Dinner Julia Cooked" and "The Kitchen Julia Built," *New York Times,* May 16, 1976: 74, 82–84; 76–81.

"Foreword" and "Introduction," in Dorie Greenspan, *Baking with Julia,* NY: Morrow, 1996.

"France, A Personal Affair," *Food & Wine,* May 1995: 58–63.

"How I Learned to Love Cooking," *Parade,* Nov. 13, 1994: 13.

"Julia Child Writes for *The Epicure* About the Pleasures of Cooking," *The Epicure,* Fall/Winter 1963: 19–24, 73–78.

"That Lunch in Rouen," *New York Times,* "Your Introduction to Europe" Travel Supplement, Oct. 10, 1993: 12, 14, 16.

"Mastering the Art of Choosing a French Cooking School," *Travel and Leisure,* Oct. 1973: 39, 74, 78.

"La 'Nouvelle Cuisine': A Skeptic's View," *New York,* July 4, 1977: 32–34.

"What Is Your Favorite Place in California?" *Westways,* July 1995: 11.

"What Am I Doing Here?" *McCall's,* March 1968: 120.

"A White House Menu," *New York Times Magazine,* Jan. 16, 1977: 56, 57, 60.

Series of Articles

Boston Globe TV Week (1963–67)

Food & Wine (1992–)

McCall's (1977–82)

Parade (1982–86)

PUBLIC TELEVISION, FILMS, VIDEOTAPES, AND CD-ROM BY JULIA CHILD

Series

The French Chef. WGBH (Boston), PBS 1963. Peabody, 1965; Emmy, 1966. Prod. Russ Morash.

Julia Child & Company. WGBH, PBS 1978. Prod. Russ Morash.

Julia Child & More Company. WGBH, PBS 1980. Prod. Russ Morash.

Dinner at Julia's. WGBH, PBS 1983. Prod. Russ Morash.

The Way to Cook. WGBH and JC Productions, 1984. Prod. Russ Morash (videotape series).

Cooking with Master Chefs. A La Carte Productions. MPT (Maryland), PBS 1993. Prod. Geoffrey Drummond.

In Julia's Kitchen with Master Chefs. A La Carte Productions. MPT, PBS 1995. Prod. Geoffrey Drummond. Emmy Awards and IACP Awards.
Baking with Julia. A La Carte Productions. MPT, PBS 1996. Prod. Geoffrey Drummond.
Julia Child & Jacques Pepin Cooking at Home. A La Carte, Drummond, 1999.

Regular Appearances
Good Morning America, ABC-TV
Food Channel, TVFN

Single Shows
"The White House Red Carpet." WGBH, 1968. Prod. Russ Morash.
"Julia's Homecoming: An Evening with Julia Child: At the Valley Hunt Club." Pasadena Valley Hunt Club, Nov. 7, 1990.
"Julia at 80: With Christopher Lydon." WGBH, 1992.
"A Taste of Norway." 1992. Prod. and Dir. Russ Morash.
"Julia Child and Jacques Pépin: Cooking in Concert." A La Carte Communications, 1995. Prod. Geoffrey Drummond. James Beard Award, Best Culinary Video of the Year.
"Julia Child and Graham Kerr, Cooking in Concert." A La Carte, 1995. Prod. Geoffrey Drummond.
"Julia Child and Jacques Pépin: More Cooking in Concert." A La Carte, 1996. Prod. Geoffrey Drummond.

CD-ROM
"Julia Child: Home Cooking with Master Chefs." A La Carte Productions. Microsoft, 1996. Prod. Geoffrey Drummond.

PERSONAL AWARDS
George Foster Peabody Award (1965), "distinguished achievement in television"
Emmy Award (1966), first ETV personality to win an Emmy
Ordre de Mérite Agricole (1967)
Ordre de Mérite National (1976)
Confrérie de Cérès (1972)
La Commanderie des Cordons Bleus de France (1980), first woman member
Honorary degrees from Harvard University, Boston University, Bates College, Rutgers University, Smith College

ORAL HISTORY TRANSCRIPTS
Jewell Fenzi. The Foreign Service Spouse Oral History. Interview with Julia Child. Nov. 7, 1991, Washington, DC, 22 pp.
Julia McWilliams Child '34 and Paul C. Child. Smith College Oral History recorded in Cambridge, MA, Oct. 10, 1972, 51 pp. (for *College. A Smith Mosaic.* Smith Centennial Study, 1971–73)

550   BIBLIOGRAPHY

PAUL CHILD PHOTOGRAPHS
Ackland Art Museum, University of North Carolina, Chapel Hill
Fogg Museum, Harvard University, Cambridge, MA

SELECTED SECONDARY WORKS

Ali-Bab (Henri Babinski). *Gastronomie Pratique.* 9th ed.; Paris: Flammarion, 1926 (orig. pub. 1906).

Bain, David Haward. *Whose Woods These Are: A History of the Bread Loaf Writers' Conference: 1926–1992.* Hopewell, NJ: Ecco, 1993.

Becker, René. "Julia: A Love Story," *Boston Magazine,* July 1992: 52–55, 121–23.

Barr, Ann, and Paul Levy. *The Official Foodie Handbook.* NY: Arbor House, 1984.

Beck, Simone, with Suzanne Patterson. *Food and Friends: Recipes and Memories from Simca's Cuisine.* NY: Viking, 1991.

Bertholle, Louisette, Simone Beck, and Helmut Ripperger. *What's Cooking in France.* NY: Ives Washburn, 1952.

Brockhurst, Paul. *Pasadena: A Heritage to Celebrate; 1886–1986.* Centennial Videotape, 1987.

Carpenter, Thomas D. *Pasadena: Resort Hotels and Paradise.* Azusa, CA: Marc Sheldon, 1984.

Chamberlain, Narcissa G. and Narcisse. *The Flavor of France in Recipes and Pictures.* Photos by Samuel Chamberlain. NY: Hastings House, 2 vols., 1960, 1964.

Chelminski, Rudolph. *The French at Table.* NY: Morrow, 1985.

Child, Charles. *Roots in the Rock.* Boston: Little, Brown, 1964.

Child, Paul. *Bubbles from the Spring.* Antique Press, 1974.

———. "Poems." Endpaper, *New York Times,* May 16, 1976: 103.

Clark, Robert. *James Beard: A Biography.* NY: HarperCollins, 1993.

Coffey, Roberta Wallace. "Their Recipe for Love," *McCall's,* Nov. 1988: 96–98.

Crocker, Donald. *Within the Vale of Annandale: A Picture History of South Western Pasadena and Vicinity.* Pasadena: Foothill Valley YWCA, 1960.

Cummings, Richard Osborn. *The American and His Food: A History of Food Habits in the U.S.* Chicago: University of Chicago Press, 1940.

Curnonsky (Maurice-Edmond Sailland). *Cuisine et Vins de France.* Ed. Robert J. Courtine. Paris: Librairie Larousse, 1974.

Curtin, Deane W., and Lisa M. Heldke, eds. *Cooking, Eating, Thinking: Transformative Philosophies of Food.* Bloomington: Indiana University Press, 1992.

Escoffier, Auguste. *The Escoffier Cookbook.* NY: Crown, 1969.

"Everyone's in the Kitchen" (cover story), *Time,* Nov. 25, 1966: 74–87.

Farb, Peter, and George Armelagos. *Consuming Passions: The Anthropology of Eating.* Boston: Houghton Mifflin, 1980.

Fenzi, Jewell, and Carl L. Nelson. "Bon Appétit: Julia Child: From Foreign Service Wife to French Chef," *Foreign Service Journal,* Nov. 1992: 40–43.

Ferretti, Fred. "A Gourmet at Large: Julia Child; America's Favorite Cook," *Gourmet,* Feb. 1995: 70–72, 99.

Fisher, M. F. K. *Among Friends.* NY: Knopf, 1970.

————. *The Art of Eating: The Collected Gastronomical Works of M. F. K. Fisher.* NY: World, 1954.

Fitch, Noel Riley. "The Crisco Kid," *Los Angeles Magazine,* Aug. 1996: 82–85.

————. "La Communion Gastronomique" ["Gertrude Stein and Alice B. Toklas—Food: The Sacrament of Their Devotion"], in *Lettre Internationale: Revue Européenne Trimestrielle,* 1989.

————. *Literary Cafés of Paris.* Wash., DC: Starrhill, 1989.

Flanner, Janet. *Paris Journal 1944–1965.* NY: Harcourt Brace Jovanovich, 1965.

Fussell, Betty. *Masters of American Cookery.* NY: Times, 1983.

Hartman, Curtis, and Steven Raichlen. "Julia Child: The Boston Magazine Interview," *Boston,* April 1981: 75–85.

Hess, John L., and Karen Hess. *The Taste of America.* NY: Grossman, 1977.

Honey, Maureen, ed. *Breaking the Ties That Bind: Popular Stories of the New Woman, 1915–1930.* Norman: University of Oklahoma Press, 1995.

Jennes, Gail. "Couples" (cover story), *People,* Dec. 1, 1975: 51–54.

Jones, Evan. *Epicurean Delight: The Life and Times of James Beard.* NY: Knopf, 1990.

Lazar, David, ed. *Conversation with M. F. K. Fisher.* Jackson: University Press of Mississippi, 1992.

Levenstein, Harvey. *Paradox of Plenty: A Social History of Eating in Modern America.* NY: Oxford University, 1993.

————. *Revolution at the Table: The Transformation of the American Diet.* NY: Oxford University Press, 1988.

Lovell, Stanley P. *Of Spies & Stratagems.* NY: Prentice-Hall, 1963.

Lydon, Christopher. "Queen Julia," *The Improper Bostonian.* March 27–April 9, 1996: 11–16.

MacDonald, Elizabeth P. *Undercover Girl.* NY: Macmillan, 1947.

McIntosh, Elizabeth P. [MacDonald]. *The Role of Women in Intelligence.* Intelligence Profession Series #5. McLean, VA: Association of Former Intelligence Officers, 1989.

McWilliams, John. *Recollections of John McWilliams: His Youth, Experiences in California, and the Civil War.* Princeton: Princeton University Press, n.d.

Mendelson, Anne. *Stand Facing the Stove: The Story of the Women Who Gave America The Joy of Cooking.* NY: Henry Holt, 1996.

Montagné, Prosper. *Larousse Gastronomique: The Encyclopedia of Food, Wine & Cookery.* Eds. Charlotte Turgeon and Nina Froud. NY: Crown, 1961.

Oliver, Raymond. *Gastronomy of France.* Trans. Claude Durrell. Cleveland: World, 1967.

Painter, Charlotte. *Gifts of Age: Portraits and Essays of 32 Remarkable Women.* San Francisco: Chronicle Books, 1985.

Pasadena City Library. *A Pasadena Chronology, 1769–1977,* 1976.

Pellaprat, Henri-Paul. *L'Art Culinaire Moderne: La Bonne Table Française et Etrangère.* Preface by Curnonsky. Paris: Comptoir Français du Livre, 1936 (reprinted 1948).

Reardon, Joan. *M. F. K. Fisher, Julia Child, and Alice Walker: Celebrating the Pleasures of the Table.* NY: Harmony Books, 1994.

Reynolds, Catharine. "Paris Journal: One Hundred Years of Le Cordon Bleu," *Gourmet,* Jan. 1995: 50–53, 58–59.

Rombauer, Irma S. *The Joy of Cooking: A Compilation of Reliable Recipes with a Casual Culinary Chat.* Indianapolis: Bobbs-Merrill, 1936; rev. ed. 1943 et seq. (After 1951: *The Joy of Cooking,* with Marion Rombauer Becker.)

Root, Waverley, and Richard de Rochemont. *Eating in America: A History.* NY: Morrow, 1976.

Saint-Ange, Madame E. *La Cuisine.* Grenoble: Editions Chaix, 1957.

Shapiro, Laura. *Perfection Salad: Women and Cooking at the Turn of the Century.* New York: Farrar, Straus & Giroux, 1986.

Smith, R. Harris. *OSS: The Secret History of America's First Central Intelligence Agency.* Berkeley: University of California Press, 1972.

Sokolov, Raymond. *Why We Eat What We Eat.* NY: Summit, 1991.

Stacey, Michelle. *Consumed: Why Americans Love, Hate, and Fear Food.* NY: Simon & Schuster, 1994.

Stegner, Wallace. *The Uneasy Chair: A Biography of Bernard DeVoto.* Garden City, NY: Doubleday, 1974 (Salt Lake City: Peregrine Smith, 1988).

Street, Julian. *Where Paris Dines.* NY: Doubleday, 1929.

Tomkins, Calvin. "Profiles: Good Cooking," *The New Yorker,* Dec. 23, 1974: 36–41, 44–52.

Van Voris, Jacqueline. Smith College Centennial Study. *College. A Smith Mosaic.* Oct. 10, 1972.

Visser, Margaret. *The Ritual of Dinner.* NY: Grove Weidenfeld, 1991.

Weeks, Edward. *The Lowells and Their Institute.* Boston: Little, Brown, 1966.

Weston, Donald M. *Weston: 1065–1951.* Pittsfield, MA: Sun Printing, 1951.

White, Theodore H. *In Search of History: A Personal Adventure.* London: Cape, 1979.

———. *Theodore H. White at Large: The Best of His Magazine Writing 1939–1986.* Ed. Edward T. Thompson. NY: Pantheon, 1992.

——— and Annalee Jacoby. *Thunder Out of China.* London: Gollancz, 1947.

Whiting, Charles F. "Development of the Communities of Francis Avenue and the Norton Estate." Cambridge, MA, March 1966.

Wittemore, Hank. "Julia and Paul" (cover story), *Parade,* Feb. 28, 1982.

York, Pat. "Julia Child," in *Going Strong.* Boston: Little, Brown, 1991: 66–69.

$\mathcal{I}$NDEX

Throughout this index the following abbreviations are used in subentries: JC for Julia Child, *Mastering* for *Mastering the Art of French Cooking,* and AIWF for the American Institute of Wine and Food.

$\mathcal{A}$

About the Author

NOËL RILEY FITCH is an internationally recognized biographer. Her critically acclaimed *Sylvia Beach and the Lost Generation: A History of Literary Paris in the Twenties and Thirties* (1983), now in its eleventh printing, and *Anaïs: The Erotic Life of Anaïs Nin* (1993) have been translated into French, German, Japanese, Spanish, and Portuguese. She has also authored books on Hemingway and on the literary cafés of Paris, as well as scholarly articles on the French-American connection. Fitch earned a Ph.D. in literature and is a lecturer at the American University of Paris and the University of Southern California.